D0891992

Financial Instruments and Institutions

Accounting and Disclosure Rules

Second Edition

STEPHEN G. RYAN

John Wiley & Sons, Inc.

For John and Arlene, my parents,
and Lisa and Jacob, my life

This book is printed on acid-free paper. ∞

Published by John Wiley & Sons, Inc., Hoboken, New Jersey
Published simultaneously in Canada.

Wiley Bicentennial Logo: Richard J. Pacifico

For general information on our other products and services, or technical support, please contact our Customer Care Department within the United States at 800-762-2974, outside the United States at 317-572-3993 or fax 317-572-4002.

Wiley also publishes its books in a variety of electronic formats. Some content that appears in print may not be available in electronic books.

Library of Congress Cataloging-in-Publication Data

Ryan, Stephen G.
Financial instruments and institutions : accounting and disclosure rules / Stephen G. Ryan. — 2nd ed.
p. cm.
Includes index.
ISBN 978-0-470-04037-9 (cloth)
1. Financial instruments—Accounting. 2. Financial institutions—Accounting. I. Title.
HF5681.F54R93 2007
657'.76—dc22 2006036780

Printed in the United States of America.

10 9 8 7 6 5 4 3 2 1

Contents

Preface

This book provides a comprehensive guide to the analysis of financial instruments and institutions using accounting information and disclosures that are publicly available in financial reports. It is primarily written for users of financial reports who must confront the complex, voluminous, and changing nature of financial reporting rules for financial instruments and institutions. My primary goal is to provide these users with the tools necessary to construct as coherent a story as possible about how financial institutions and also nonfinancial firms generate or destroy value using financial instruments. I show how financial reports provide clues to the construction of such a story through fair value accounting for financial instruments and accompanying estimation sensitivity and risk disclosures that users can, with focused effort, piece together and interpret in a consistent and conceptually sound fashion.

Most of the major accounting standards governing financial instruments and transactions are covered, including those for loans, investment securities, securitizations, the constituent elements of structured finance transactions, derivatives and hedging, leasing, insurance, and reinsurance. Those instruments and transactions for which the accounting is straightforward are excluded. The exposition of accounting standards reflects my belief that users of financial reports do not need to know all of the myriad details of each standard but rather only the critical features that make or break the representational faithfulness of financial reports. For example, in securitization accounting, these critical features pertain to the valuation and risk of retained interests; excess value assigned to risky retained interests has led to a sizable number of large losses by securitizers of risky assets, such as those experienced by subprime mortgage banks during the hedge fund crisis in the second half of 1998. This book hones in on these critical features.

My perspective is that fair value provides the simplest and most natural measurement basis for financial instruments, especially for financial institutions that hold many instruments with correlated values that hedge or accentuate risks at the portfolio level. However, I also emphasize that, aside from securities and other instruments that are publicly traded in liquid markets, fair value accounting for financial instruments inevitably involves some degree of subjectivity (and thus possibly intentional bias) and inadvertent error (i.e., random noise) in estimation. I discuss how financial report users can assess this subjectivity and error using required disclosures of estimation sensitivity, interest rate and other market risks, credit risk, and insurance claims risk. Most of the major required estimation sensitivity and risk disclosures are covered.

A distinctive aspect of this book is its integrated coverage of financial reporting for financial instruments and institutions. This coverage reflects my strong belief that financial reporting and analysis for financial instruments must reflect the economic context of the firms and transactions involved. I examine six types of financial institutions, which were chosen either because they reflect specific financial transactions in a clear fashion or because they have distinctive accounting or disclosure requirements: thrifts, mortgage banks, commercial banks, lessors, property-casualty insurers, and life insurers. These financial institutions constitute specific understandable contexts that are often unusually well described in financial reports because of risk and other disclosures mandated by industry regulators. These institutions also tend to have more extensive ranges or lengthier histories of specific financial transactions than nonfinancial firms. For these reasons, financial institutions provide the best available settings to learn disciplined analysis of financial instruments. Users of nonfinancial firms' financial reports will find learning such disciplined analysis useful in their settings.

WHY I WROTE THE BOOK

In teaching courses on financial instruments and institutions at the Stern School of Business of New York University over the past 12 years, I have found that the available treatments of the relevant financial reporting rules have three weaknesses from the perspective of users of financial reports. First, the available treatments usually target one of two audiences. Some are written for preparers of financial statements or practicing accountants, who naturally are concerned with how to account for specific complex transactions; these treatments tend to be poorly grounded in economic concepts and overly detailed with respect to implementation issues. Alternatively, some are written for the generalist student of financial analysis; these treatments provide little of the context necessary to understand financial transactions and institutions, discuss the relevant financial reporting rules inadequately if at all, and apply analytical schemas that invariably have been developed for nonfinancial transactions and firms. Either approach obscures the nature and usefulness of the financial report information about financial instruments and institutions from the perspective of users of financial reports. In contrast, while avoiding needless detail, I provide economically grounded descriptions of financial transactions and institutions, thorough treatments of the accounting standards and disclosure rules applying to financial instruments and financial institutions, and many cases drawn from the financial reports of actual financial institutions.

Second, most of the recently propounded and likely future financial reporting rules involve some form of fair value accounting for financial instruments. The available treatments do not provide sufficient discussion of the nature, strengths, and weaknesses of fair value accounting for financial report users to be able to evaluate the information provided by these rules. I provide a strong conceptual treatment of fair value accounting. I supplement this with numerous cases drawn from actual financial institutions' financial reports that illustrate when fair value accounting for financial instruments works well and when it is fragile. These cases span the various types of financial institutions covered in the book, which allows me to emphasize the common issues that apply across types of institutions. These common issues arise because financial transactions inherently have common features, but also because smart financial transaction designers quickly import innovations developed in other settings. Moreover, the distinctions among various types of financial institutions continue to blur over time, with the products they offer increasingly competing against each other. For example, I discuss how the retention of residual risk raises similar financial reporting and analysis issues in securitizations, leasing, and reinsurance. These features enable diligent readers to develop robust intuitions about fair value accounting for financial instruments. They also imply that readers interested in a subset of the topics will benefit considerably from reading the whole book.

Third, the available treatments give insufficient emphasis to the analysis of estimation sensitivity and risk disclosures. These disclosures are a critical complement to fair value accounting for financial instruments, since they indicate the sensitivity of the fair value of the firm's financial instruments to changes in risk factors and since assumptions about risk factors are required to estimate the fair values of financial instruments. Moreover, financial institutions are in large part and increasingly in the risk management business, and so risk disclosures are absolutely essential to the analysis of these institutions.

ENRON, SARBANES-OXLEY, AND CHANGES IN FINANCIAL REPORTING RULES FOR STRUCTURED FINANCE TRANSACTIONS

The importance and limitations of financial reporting for structured finance transactions was made apparent by the implosion of Enron, which engaged in a diverse and complex set of those transactions, many of which were accounted for properly but some significant examples of which were not. Enron illustrates how these transactions, even if accounted for properly, can place considerable stress on financial reporting, especially when they are used to exploit existing accounting rules to obtain desired outcomes such as off–balance sheet financing or income management. Enron along with other accounting scandals such as WorldCom created the political pressure necessary to pass the landmark Sarbanes-Oxley Act of 2002, which has led swiftly to many significant changes in financial reporting rules, many of them pertaining to structured finance transactions.

For example, since the passage of Sarbanes-Oxley, the Financial Accounting Standards Board (FASB) has issued significant accounting standards on derivatives and hedging, special-purpose/variable-interest entities, hybrid financial instruments, financial asset servicing rights, financial guarantees, and fair value measurements. The FASB's agenda includes significant projects on derivatives disclosures, transfers of financial instruments, liabilities and equity, leases, insurance risk transfer, and the fair value option. The Securities and Exchange Commission (SEC) has issued comprehensive disclosure requirements for off–balance sheet financing arrangements as well as a special report that describes its approach and recommendations regarding accounting-motivated structured finance transactions. The SEC, Department of Justice, Office of the New York State Attorney General, and other regulators have pursued their enforcement activities with unprecedented resources and zeal.

This book provides many insights about how structured finance transactions should be accounted for and analyzed using the information provided in financial reports. It describes the economic substance of and accounting for some of the most important types of structured finance transactions, including securitizations, (synthetic) leasing, and (finite) reinsurance as well as the constituent elements of those transactions including special-purpose entities, transactions related through netting agreements or by the intent of the counterparties, hybrid financial instruments, and financial guarantees. Structured finance transactions often partition the risk and value of underlying financial (and, in the case of leasing, nonfinancial) assets and liabilities nonproportionally; for example, securitizations frequently involve the value of the securitized financial assets being disproportionately but not fully transferred to asset-backed security purchasers while the risks of those assets are disproportionately but not fully retained by issuers. When this is the case, no single method of accounting for these transactions fully captures their nature, since accounting can describe either the value transfer or the risk transfer but not both. The critical questions for financial report users are how the accounting method chosen by the reporting firm does and does not describe the specific transactions the firm engages in, and, given the inevitable limitations of the accounting, how the estimation sensitivity and risk disclosures provided by the firm can be analyzed to address the limitations of the accounting.

In the preface to the first edition of this book, published in the immediate wake of Enron, I expressed concern that Enron might provoke overreactions from accounting standards setters and regulators that would have detrimental effects on financial reporting for financial instruments and structured finance transactions. Thankfully, this has not been the case. In particular, in most of its decisions the FASB has continued on a measured course toward broader fair value accounting for financial instruments. Although fair values are judgmental for some financial instruments and this judgment can be abused, fair value accounting is absolutely necessary to describe risky financial instruments and structured finance transactions, especially at the level of portfolios of instruments, which financial institutions by their nature hold. While not all financial instruments currently should be fair valued and errors in fair valuations will occur even for those that should, a desirable property of fair value accounting is that it corrects its mistakes over time, since financial instruments must be revalued each period based on current market conditions. In this regard, many of Enron's problems simply would have taken longer to uncover if its accounting were not based on fair value.

Moreover, in most of their decisions the FASB and SEC have recognized that the proper way to deal with the stress placed on financial reporting rules by structured finance transactions is not to jury-rig accounting standards in a futile attempt to dissuade abuse. Instead, they have worked diligently to develop conceptually sounder accounting standards, to require enhanced disclosures about the nature and purposes of these transactions, and to provide legal and regulatory (not accounting) disincentives to engage in transactions with no business purpose that impair the transparency of financial reports. For example, this approach is evident in the SEC's disclosure rule on off–balance sheet financing arrangements and its special report on structured finance transactions mentioned earlier.

Despite the progress made the FASB, SEC, and other accounting policymakers over the past five years, financial reporting rules for financial instruments and structured finance transactions remain highly limited in many key respects and so will continue to evolve rapidly over the coming years. Fair value accounting is required only for a small subset of financial instruments. Virtually all of the major accounting standards for financial instruments include bright-line, characteristic-based, or intent-based criteria that require very different accounting for substantively similar instruments, providing fertile ground for accounting-motivated structured finance transactions. Disclosures of financial instruments, while voluminous, are disjointed and often explained poorly or not at all by management. As a result of these limitations, users of financial reports must expend considerable effort and make significant assumptions in order to draw conclusions about the reporting firm. This book's conceptual approach will help financial report users understand and cope with this evolution in financial reporting rules.

TOPICAL COVERAGE AND STRUCTURE OF THE BOOK

The structure of this book reflects my belief that it is important for users of financial reports to recognize that the value and risk of financial instruments depends on the economic contexts in which they are embedded. I use the six types of financial institutions mentioned earlier as the source of context. The book is organized around these types of financial institutions, starting with relatively simple institutions and proceeding to related but more complicated ones. I describe the activities and risks of each type of financial institution in an economically grounded yet intuitive fashion. Financial reporting and analysis issues are discussed in the same chapter as or immediately subsequent to the chapter covering the most pertinent type of financial institution. This structure allows readers to progress naturally from relatively simple financial institutions and associated financial reporting and analysis issues to related but more complex institutions and issues. For readers interested in a specific topic, however, each chapter (or pair of related chapters) is written to be as self-contained as possible.

Chapter 1 overviews the financial reporting and analysis of financial instruments and institutions. Chapter 2 contains useful background material on the structure and regulation of the two main types of depository institution: thrifts and commercial banks. Chapter 3 describes the activities, risks, and financial reporting of thrifts, the simplest depository institution, which primarily take deposits and hold residential mortgage-related assets. Most of the material in this chapter also applies to commercial banks. Chapters 4 through 6 develop and illustrate the application of financial analyses based on the accounting for and mandated disclosures of interest rate risk, credit risk, and fair value of financial instruments, respectively. Chapter 7 describes the activities, risks, and financial reporting of mortgage banks, which write similar loans to thrifts, but which securitize or otherwise sell most of their loans. Chapter 8 explains the financial reporting rules for financial asset securitizations and develops and illustrates the application of financial analyses of prepayment risk and retained interests from securitizations. Chapter 9 discusses the accounting rules governing various important constituent elements of structured finance transactions, including special-purpose/variable-interest entities, transactions related through netting agreements or by the intent of the counterparties, hybrid financial instruments, and financial guarantees. Chapter 10 describes the financial reporting of commercial banks, which do everything that thrifts and mortgage banks do but are more involved with derivatives, hedging, and risk management activities. Chapter 11 explains the financial reporting rules for derivatives and hedging and develops a schema for the financial analysis of financial institutions' derivatives and hedging. Chapter 12 describes market risk disclosures and illustrates their critical importance in applying that schema. Chapter 13 describes the activities, risks, and distinct financial reporting of lessors, which compete with commercial banks for certain types of commercial lending. This chapter also develops and applies financial analyses of lessors. Chapter 14 describes activities, risks, and distinct financial reporting of property-casualty and life insurers, which provide different sorts of risk management services from commercial banks. This chapter also develops and applies financial analyses of these insurers. Chapter 15 describes property-casualty insurers' loss reserve disclosures and develops and illustrates financial analyses using those disclosures. Chapter 16 describes the accounting and disclosures by ceding insurers for reinsurance, focusing on retroactive and finite reinsurance.

SIGNIFICANT CHANGES FROM THE FIRST EDITION

The most significant changes from the first edition are the inclusion of new chapters on constituent elements of structured finance transactions (Chapter 9) and reinsurance (Chapter 16). Although these topics were covered briefly in the first edition, events occurring since the publication of the first edition made it clear that these topics demand fuller treatments. This is especially apparent in the case of finite reinsurance transactions currently receiving intense scrutiny from the SEC and other regulators. Both of these chapters contain comprehensive yet accessible treatments of their topics that are not available elsewhere.

All of the other chapters have been improved in their exposition and updated for the many significant changes in financial reporting rules, regulation, and economic conditions that have occurred since the publication of the first edition, only a portion of which have been mentioned. Although the conceptual approach taken is the same as in the first edition, readers of the first edition will find that the new edition serves as a decidedly superior reference guide.

Acknowledgments

When I began teaching a course on the analysis of financial institutions at the Stern School of Business in 1995, I was fortunate to inherit the materials and videotapes of the prior instructor, Gerald White, a gift that has influenced this book in many ways. Tom Linsmeier provided me with his materials on derivatives and hedging and wrote a valuable review of the first edition of this book, and he continues to provide insightful answers to obscure questions about the application of hedge accounting in practice.

I have been fortunate to have coauthors who have shared their understanding of financial institutions' financial reporting with me. My mentor Bill Beaver first involved me in research on banks' loss reserving in 1985. This led to a series of papers with Chi-Chun Liu and Jim Wahlen. Jim introduced me to Kathy Petroni, who taught me much of what I know about property-casualty insurers in our project together. I have learned about financial reporting in general and financial instruments in particular from my many interactions with the members and staff of the Financial Accounting Standards Board and my colleagues on the American Accounting Association's Financial Accounting Standards Committee and the Financial Accounting Standards Advisory Council, especially Jim Leisenring, Dennis Monson, Katherine Schipper, and Cathy Schrand. The book has also benefited from my interactions with many other accounting academics and practitioners, including Anne Beatty, Jeff Callen, Jack Ciesielski, Tom Frecka, Dov Fried, Dan Gode, Lisa Koonce, Doron Nissim, Mohan Venkatachalam, and Patricia Walters.

I am fortunate to have had hundreds of students at the Stern School with whom I shared my ideas as they developed, who have provided suggestions about or caught errors in my original draft chapters or in the first edition of this book, and who have alerted me to recent developments. Particularly notable contributions have been made by Andrew Henckler and Robert Young. I also appreciate the financial support of the Stern School, Dean Thomas Cooley, and Robert Stovall, who endowed my faculty fellowship.

I appreciate the capable editorial services of Sheck Cho, my executive editor, at John Wiley & Sons. Sheck kept me moving on the second edition of this book, which took longer than either he or I expected.

My parents believed strongly in the importance of education, and they sacrificed considerably to provide their six children with good ones. More important, they instilled in me the desire to learn a little more every day, and the many improvements in the second edition of this book reflect the gradual accumulation of knowledge over the five years since the publication of the first edition.

Day in and day out, I come home from work to find my dear and tenacious wife, Lisa, helping our one and only son, Jacob, with his schoolwork, which yields satisfactions and frustrations for both of them, while I get to read to Jacob before bed, a pure pleasure for both of us. I wish for Jacob the never-ending love of learning, in work and play, that my parents gave me, and for Lisa the knowledge that she carries on, nobly, a family tradition.

CHAPTER 1

Financial Instruments and Institutions

Financial reporting for financial instruments and institutions is undergoing a period of unprecedented change and salience for financial analysis. In the past decade, the Financial Accounting Standards Board (FASB), the primary accounting standards setter in the United States, has issued major standards on derivatives and hedging, transfers of financial instruments including securitizations, servicing of financial assets, consolidation of special-purpose/variable interest entities, hybrid financial instruments, financial guarantees, and fair value measurements. These standards reflect the FASB's attempts to address the limitations of prior accounting and disclosure rules that provided the settings for the huge losses recorded by firms that ineffectively hedged using derivatives during the interest rate run-up in 1994 or that held residual or subordinated interests from securitizations during the hedge fund crisis of 1998. They also reflect its attempts to improve the transparency of financial reporting for accounting-motivated structured finance transactions that provided much of the impetus for the Sarbanes-Oxley Act of 2002. During this period, the Securities and Exchange Commission (SEC) developed extensive disclosure requirements for market risk and off–balance sheet financing arrangements for much the same reasons.

This change will carry on for the foreseeable future, with the FASB's agenda including projects on the fair value option for financial instruments, transfers and servicing of financial instruments, liabilities and equity, leases, insurance risk transfer, and derivatives disclosures. All indications are that the FASB will continue to proceed on a measured course toward fair value accounting for almost all financial instruments as well as enhanced disclosures. This course should improve financial reporting both by providing more accurate, timely, and relevant information about individual financial instruments and by eliminating differences in the accounting for different types of financial instruments. While different accounting methods for different types of financial instruments may have been appropriate historically, such differences are increasingly arbitrary and yield noncomparability both across a given financial institution's financial statement line items and across different types of financial institutions' financial statements, thereby providing fertile ground for accounting-motivated transactions.

The development of financial reporting rules for financial instruments just described has provided users of financial reports with substantial new information about how firms generate or destroy value using these instruments. Considerable understanding and diligence are necessary for users of financial reports to identify and analyze this information fully, however, for several reasons. First, current accounting for financial instruments reflects a "mixed attribute" model, with some instruments recognized at fair value while others (most, in fact) are recognized at amortized cost. This model obscures the economics of natural hedges in which the two sides of the hedge are recognized using different valuation attributes, yielding excess volatility in owners' equity and net income. For example, commercial banks often hold investment securities recognized at fair value that are natural hedges of deposits or debt recognized at amortized cost. Although financial report users can address this problem using required footnote disclosures of the fair values of all financial instruments, these disclosures are invariably poorly integrated with the other information in the report, forcing users to perform this integration.

Second, fair value accounting, while preferable to amortized cost accounting, does not constitute a complete description of financial instruments. For financial instruments other than securities and other instruments that are publicly traded in liquid markets, estimated fair values typically include nontrivial subjectivity (and thus potential bias) and inadvertent error (i.e., random noise). Estimation subjectivity and error are of particular concern for financial instruments that are highly sensitive to valuation assumptions, such as residual or subordinated interests from securitizations and derivatives. Thus, the fair values of financial instruments need to be supplemented with information about their sensitivity to valuation assumptions. Relatedly, financial instruments can be risky and financial transactions often involve complex partitioning of risk among various parties. Thus, the fair values of financial instruments need to be analyzed jointly with information about their market and nonmarket risks. Although financial reports do contain some information in this regard, the quality, comparability across firms, and integration of this information are again poor, forcing users to rework and integrate this information.

Finally, current financial reporting for financial instruments and structured finance transactions is complex. Much of this complexity is unnecessary and should be reduced as the FASB develops a conceptually sound and coherent set of financial instruments standards, but some of it is an inevitable result of economically justified complexity in the instruments and transactions and the FASB's desire to describe that complexity through accounting. The only way for users to deal with this problem is to understand the economics of instruments and transactions and how accounting does and does not capture those economics in as complete and robust a fashion as possible.

The primary purpose of this book is to provide users with the tools to do this, in particular, to exploit fully the various sources of information about the fair values and risks of financial instruments provided in financial reports in order to construct the most coherent possible story about how firms generate or destroy value using financial instruments. In serving this purpose, the focus is on financial institutions, which provide the best available settings in which to learn disciplined analysis of financial instruments for two reasons:

1. The value and risk of the financial instruments held by a firm depend on the economic context of the firm and the correlations among the individual instruments. Financial institutions constitute specific understandable contexts that primarily involve financial instruments or transactions. Moreover, financial institutions frequently are required by industry regulators to provide extensive risk disclosures, which supply information about the correlations among the instruments.
2. Financial institutions generally have more extensive ranges and lengthier histories of specific financial transactions than nonfinancial firms, and so are more likely to have experienced the significant issues that apply to those transactions. For example, readers interested in securitizations of trade receivables by nonfinancial firms will find that the cases of mortgage banks' securitizations of residential mortgages discussed in Chapter 8 generalize to their concerns, since these cases clearly indicate the conditions under which securitization accounting works well and under which it is fragile.

The remainder of this chapter provides important perspectives and terminology regarding financial instruments and institutions. The first section explains the five main ingredients involved in using financial report information to construct the most coherent possible story about how firms generate or destroy value using financial instruments. As discussed, the two most important ingredients are fair value accounting for financial instruments and disclosures of the estimation sensitivity and risk of these instruments. The third ingredient pertains to financial transactions, such as securitizations, leasing, and reinsurance, in which the value and risk of underlying financial instruments are partitioned among various parties. Although the simplest and most flexible way to view these transactions is using a fair value partitioning (financial components) perspective, in cases of disproportionate risk retention by the firm under consideration, users need to temper this with a risk partitioning perspective. The fourth ingredient is the evaluation of individual financial instruments and portfolios of those instruments on both gross and net bases, because the market and credit risks of the instrument or portfolio may offset in part but not entirely, and because different risks may offset to different extents (e.g., market risks generally are easier to offset than credit risks). The final ingredient is that financial transactions are financial, even though in many cases, such as leasing and traditional insurance, these transactions are treated as operating under current financial reporting rules. These five ingredients are applied repeatedly in the various financial analyses described in this book.

The second section describes the various activities and risks of financial institutions. Financial report users need to recognize that historically distinct types of financial institutions increasingly perform the same or similar activities, and so it is most important to distinguish institutions based on the activities and risks in which they engage. In the last section, the valuation of financial institutions in practice is discussed.

MAIN INGREDIENTS OF THE ANALYSIS OF FINANCIAL INSTRUMENTS

Fair Value Accounting

This section explains why and how fair value accounting describes individual financial instruments and especially portfolios of those instruments—which constitute the primary rights and obligations of most financial institutions—better than amortized cost accounting. Definitions for financial instruments, fair value accounting, and amortized cost accounting that are used throughout the book are also provided.

The term "financial instruments" as defined by the FASB and as used in this book includes financial assets and liabilities but not the firm's own equity. The firm's own equity is a financial instrument, of course, just not one for which direct fair valuation generally is contemplated. Financial assets are contractual claims to receive cash or another financial instrument on favorable terms or ownership interests in another firm. Financial liabilities are contractual claims to pay cash or another financial instrument on unfavorable terms.

Fair value is the price that would be received to sell a financial asset or to transfer a financial liability in an orderly transaction between market participants at the measurement date, and so it reflects current expectations of the cash flows and priced risks of the financial instrument. Fair values can be estimated either by observing the market prices for the financial instrument or similar instruments or by using an accepted valuation model with observable market or unobservable firm-supplied inputs.

Full fair value accounting involves three aspects. On the balance sheet, it involves recognition of financial instruments at fair value. In the United States, this aspect of fair value accounting currently is required only for trading and available-for-sale securities, derivatives, hedged items in designated effective fair value hedges, and the financial inventory of broker-dealers. (Certain items, such as hybrid financial instruments and rights to service financial assets, may be accounted for using full fair value accounting under fair value options for those items. Certain other items, such as financial guarantees, must be recognized at fair value at inception but not subsequently.) On the income statement, full fair value accounting involves the recognition of unrealized gains and losses on financial instruments in net income in the period they occur, which often is prior to their realization through the sale or repurchase of the instruments. This aspect of fair value accounting currently is required in the United States only for trading securities, derivatives other than those involved in effective cash flow hedges, hedged items under fair value hedges, and the financial inventory of broker-dealers. In particular, this aspect is not required for available-for-sale securities or derivatives involved in effective cash flow hedges, despite the fact that they are recognized at fair value on the balance sheet. Also on the income statement, full fair value accounting involves calculating interest revenue or expense as the fair value of the financial instrument times the applicable current market interest rate during the period. This aspect of fair value accounting is not required for any financial instrument under current financial reporting rules in the United States. Interest usually is calculated on an amortized cost basis; when it is not, it is combined with gains and losses, and the total change in the value of the financial instrument is reported on a single line on the income statement, as is often the case for trading securities, derivatives, and the financial inventory of broker-dealers.

Fair value accounting for financial instruments is increasingly feasible for two reasons:

1. The markets for financial instruments have become much richer over time. For example, risky assets that previously were difficult to trade, such as commercial loans, now can be securitized.
2. Financial theory, such as options pricing, has developed and been applied successfully in many contexts by practitioners.

The fair value of most financial instruments now can be estimated with a reasonable degree of precision either through observation of the market prices of similar instruments or through the use of accepted valuation models. For financial instruments that currently cannot be fair valued with a reasonable degree of precision, the proper mind-set is not that amortized cost is unconditionally preferable to fair value accounting but rather that markets or valuation models simply need more time to develop sufficiently for those instruments to be fair valued.

Unlike nonfinancial firms, financial institutions typically hold sizable portfolios of financial instruments. These instruments often have correlated values—that is, they hedge or accentuate risks at the portfolio level. Full fair value accounting for all of the financial instruments in a portfolio is the simplest and most robust way to account for these correlations. In particular, gains and losses on effective hedges of one financial instrument by another will offset in net income. In contrast, gains and losses on ineffective hedges or speculative positions will not so offset.

The alternative to fair value accounting, amortized cost accounting, uses expectations of cash flows and priced risks determined at initiation to account for financial instruments throughout their life. Amortized cost accounting has three undesirable features compared to fair value accounting. First, amortized cost accounting uses old information and so provides untimely measures of the value of financial instruments on the balance sheet. This untimeliness resolves only as financial instruments amortize or when they are sold or repurchased.

Second, since financial institutions typically hold portfolios of financial instruments initiated at different times, amortized cost accounting provides measures of the values of these instruments that reflect expectations of cash flows and priced risks at different times. This yields noncomparability problems on both balance sheet and income statement. For example, net interest income for a commercial bank may include interest revenue that is based on older interest rates than those reflected in interest expense; if so, net interest income does not reflect the bank's interest rate spread at any point in time, and so it is likely to be a poor predictor of future net interest income. Admittedly, hedge accounting may mitigate these limitations of amortized cost accounting, but hedge accounting is more complex and less transparent than fair value accounting for all financial instruments. Moreover, hedge accounting applied to specific hedging relationships within a portfolio, as is required in most cases under current accounting rules, need not capture the effects of hedging at the portfolio level.

Third, amortized cost accounting provides firms with the ability to manipulate net income through realizing gains or losses on the sale of financial assets or repurchase of financial liabilities. This is particularly easy for financial institutions to do, since they usually hold numerous sets of matched positions, with one side of each matched position likely having appreciated and the other side likely having depreciated. For all three reasons, amortized cost provides a poor basis for accounting for financial instruments and institutions, especially given the existence of increasingly complex and sensitive financial instruments whose values are subject to rapidly changing information and market prices for risk.

Advocates of amortized cost accounting for financial instruments by financial institutions usually make two related arguments on its behalf:

1. The managers of financial institutions do not manage the fair values of financial instruments, since these values reflect changes in interest rates and other market prices that are outside their control. Instead they manage investment and financing decisions that yield income on financial assets that is expected to exceed the expense associated with financing those instruments over their whole lives.
2. These managers conceptualize financial institutions' risk not as the variability of their value over short periods but rather as the variability of their net income or cash flows over long periods.

Neither of these arguments makes much sense for most financial institutions. The current interest rates and other market prices embedded in the fair values of financial instruments are empirically better predictors of future market prices than are the differentially old market prices embedded in amortized costs. Thus, the managers of financial institutions who do not pay attention to the current fair values of their financial instruments are likely to find that they are unable to generate income or cash flow going forward. As discussed, most financial institutions hold portfolios of financial instruments, and these instruments usually trade in reasonably liquid markets. If financial institutions require liquidity, they usually can sell their financial assets. In this regard, fair value is the best available estimate of the sales price of assets and thus of financial institutions' liquidity. More generally, value variability, not income or cash flow variability, is clearly the right risk concept for all but the most illiquid financial institutions.

While preferable to amortized cost accounting, fair value accounting does not provide a full description of financial instruments. Three general threats to the economic descriptiveness of fair value accounting exist.

1. When estimates are required to calculate fair values, as usually is the case for financial instruments other than securities that are publicly traded in liquid markets, a degree of subjectivity and noise is inevitably involved. This degree varies substantially across types of financial instruments, and financial instruments do exist for which fair value accounting is more problematic than amortized cost accounting.
2. Fair value estimation errors are effectively leveraged in transactions such as risky asset securitizations in which a low-risk claim to underlying financial instruments is transferred to another party while a risky residual or subordinated claim is retained. The fair value assigned to the retained risky claim typically includes most or all of the estimation error in the fair value of the underlying financial instruments.
3. Even for financial institutions, it is unlikely that all their economic assets and liabilities are or will ever be fair valued, either because of estimation difficulties or because some of these assets and liabilities are real, intangible, or do not meet criteria for accounting recognition. If so, fair value accounting will not capture the value of all economic assets and liabilities of financial institutions, which will yield nondescriptive volatility in owners' equity and net income when these exposures hedge each other.

The first two limitations of fair value accounting are mitigated by its self-correcting nature, however, since fair values must be reestimated each period. This situation is in marked contrast to the predetermined nature of amortized cost values. The third limitation will be mitigated in the future by the expansion of fair value accounting to a broader set of financial instruments. All three limitations can be addressed through appropriate disclosures, as discussed in the next section.

Estimation Sensitivity and Risk Disclosures

Subjectivity and noise in estimating fair values, even when leveraged through the retention of risky residual claims, can be mitigated through clear disclosure of estimation assumptions and the sensitivity of fair values to those assumptions. For example, estimation sensitivity disclosures are required for retained interests in securitizations under Statement of Financial Accounting Standards (SFAS) No. 140, *Accounting for Transfers and Servicing of Financial Assets and Extinguishments of Liabilities* (2000).[1] Unfortunately, these disclosures tend to follow boilerplate presentations that do not clearly reflect the economics of retained interests. For example, the effects of changes in interest rate and prepayment assumptions on prepayment-sensitive residual interests typically are disclosed separately and independently, even though interest rate decreases drive prepayment increases.

Fair values are point estimates of the current value of financial instruments. Realized values can differ substantially from estimated values, especially for risky financial instruments such as residual or subordinated interests from securitizations and derivatives. Thus, fair values should be analyzed jointly with market, credit, and other risk disclosures. Risk disclosures are required under various FASB standards and SEC rules. In addition, for financial institutions, industry regulators often require additional risk disclosures.

A key aspect of this book is its emphasis on the importance of joint analysis of fair value accounting and estimation sensitivity and risk disclosures to construct the most coherent story possible about how firms generate or destroy value using financial instruments. This analysis invariably involves piecing together and consistently interpreting information from various places in the financial reports of financial institutions. Although burdensome, this analysis often provides a very different perspective on a financial institution's activities from what is conveyed in the financial statements or in management's discussion and analysis (MD&A). For example, it is not difficult to find financial institutions that properly apply hedge accounting to specific hedging relationships and that smooth their net income as a result but that are antihedging or substantially overhedging their aggregate exposures. Unfortunately, clear discussions of the effect of hedging on aggregate exposures in financial reports are infrequent for all but the simplest financial institutions.

Limitations arising from fair valuation of less than all assets and liabilities can be mitigated through separate presentation of unrealized gains and losses on the income statement and through management discussion of the existence of economic hedges of non–fair-valued exposures. In this respect, fair value accounting prods the managements of financial institutions to explain their economic exposures better than does amortized cost accounting.

Fair Value versus Risk Partitioning Perspectives on Financial Transactions

Many financial transactions, such as securitizations, leasing, and reinsurance, involve partitioning the fair value and risks of underlying financial instruments (or, in the case of leasing, real assets) among various parties. A financial components perspective, in which the claims to the underlying financial instruments are accounted for based on their (relative) fair values, is the simplest and most flexible way to describe these transactions. This perspective has two conceptually desirable features. First, this perspective is "history independent," meaning that the accounting at a given time is based on the rights and obligations held by each party at that time, not on the history of transactions that gave rise to those rights and obligations. History independence is critical to attaining comparable accounting for structured finance transactions, because these transactions can be structured in a literally infinite variety of ways that yield the same allocation of rights and obligations to the parties. Second, this perspective is also consistent with fair value accounting for financial instruments.

A financial components perspective is adopted in SFAS No. 140, which governs securitizations. It has not yet been applied broadly to financial transactions, although it may be applied more broadly in the future. For example, the FASB decided in July 2006 to comprehensively reconsider lease accounting, and it is likely to begin its reconsideration with the proposal of the G4+1 Group of Accounting Standards Setters (the standards setters of Australia, Canada, New Zealand, the United Kingdom, the United States, and, as an observer, the International Accounting Standards Committee) to apply a financial components perspective to leases in its special report *Leases: Implementation of a New Approach* (2000).[2] In its liabilities and equity and its risk transfer projects, the FASB is considering bifurcation of instruments with characteristics of liabilities and equity and (re)insurance contracts into components.

While a financial components perspective has desirable attributes, users of financial reports should be aware that it is not the only meaningful way to describe these types of transactions. A risk-partitioning perspective is also important in cases of disproportionate risk retention. It is possible to transfer most of the fair value of underlying financial instruments while retaining most of the risk. The breakdown of securitization accounting for subprime mortgage banks and other securitizers of risky financial assets during the hedge fund crisis in the second half of 1998 occurred in large part because these issuers sold most of the fair value of the underlying financial assets while retaining most of the risk.

Gross and Net Evaluation

Financial instruments exhibit both market (e.g., interest rate, exchange rate, and commodity price) and nonmarket (e.g., credit, performance, and insurance) risks. Individual financial instruments and portfolios of financial instruments may need to be evaluated on both gross and net bases, because the risks of the constituent elements of an instrument or portfolio may offset in part but not entirely and because offsetting is more likely to occur for market risks than for nonmarket risks. A gross evaluation considers the constituent elements of a financial instrument or portfolio separately, without taking into account any offsetting of the elements. Conversely, a net evaluation considers the instrument or portfolio after the effect of offsetting.

Specifically, the market risks of financial instruments usually are relatively easily offset across the instruments in a portfolio. For example, a bank can offset the interest rate risk of a fixed-rate loan asset by engaging in either a fixed-rate deposit liability or a receive floating-pay fixed interest rate swap. Because of this ability to offset market risks, for a portfolio of financial instruments these risks usually are best evaluated net.

In contrast, the nonmarket risks of financial instruments are relatively hard to offset across instruments. For example, a bank cannot offset the credit risk on a loan asset, which reflects the borrower's creditworthiness, with a deposit liability that reflects the bank's own creditworthiness. Although credit derivatives markets are developing to offset credit risks, these markets remain smaller and less liquid than the markets to offset market risk. Even when credit derivatives are available and used to offset credit risks, they rarely do so fully because of contractual features, such as the "cheapest to deliver" option. Because of this difficulty in offsetting, the nonmarket risks of a portfolio of financial instruments are often best evaluated gross. A number of exceptions to this rule exist, however; for example, the credit risk of a portfolio of financial instruments subject to a close-out or novation netting agreement is best evaluated net.

Structured finance transactions that include multiple legs raise the gross and net evaluation issue in a similar fashion as portfolios of financial instruments. The market risks of the various legs of the transaction are more likely to offset than are their nonmarket risks.

In contrast, individual derivative financial instruments raise the gross and net evaluation issue in mirror-image fashion to portfolios of financial instruments. Derivatives generally can be thought of as a long position in one financial instrument and a short position in another financial instrument, with the two positions settling net. For example, a receive floating-pay fixed interest rate swap is a floating-rate asset and a fixed-rate liability that settle net. Insofar as derivatives settle net, their credit risks are best evaluated at the net level of the derivative, not the gross level of the offsetting positions within the derivative. In contrast, the market risk of derivatives typically reflects only one of the gross positions within them. For example, the interest rate risk of a receive floating-pay fixed interest rate swap reflects only the fixed-rate liability. Hence, the market risks of derivatives are best evaluated at the gross level of the positions within the derivative.

Financial Transactions Are Financial

It is evident that financial transactions should be classified and measured as such in financial reports. Unfortunately, many financial transactions, such as operating leases and traditional insurance, are treated as operating under current accounting standards. Relatedly, by requiring different accounting based on bright-line criteria, characteristics of instruments, or the intent of management, the accounting standards governing financial instruments yield dramatic differences in the accounting for economically similar financial instruments. A nontrivial benefit of adopting fair value accounting for all financial instruments is that it would make transparent the common financial nature of these transactions and of the institutions that engage in them.

For example, lessors that primarily engage in operating leases appear to be capital asset management companies under current accounting rules, with rent revenue and depreciation expense dominating their income statements. This is despite the fact that these lessors often lease long-lived equipment or real estate under long-term contracts that are clearly primarily financing arrangements expected to generate an interest rate spread for the lessor. This financial nature would be far more apparent if the economic lease receivables arising in these transactions were recognized as such on the balance sheet, with the economic interest revenue on these receivables recognized as such on the income statement.

ACTIVITIES AND RISKS OF FINANCIAL INSTITUTIONS

Each of the financial institutions discussed in this book could be divided into subtypes that perform different activities. Moreover, due to deregulation, mergers and acquisitions, internal diversification, and new product development, many financial institutions have expanded the set of activities that they perform so that these activities overlap with those provided by other institutions. For example, some property-casualty (re)insurers now offer products that allow firms to hedge business and accounting risks in much the same way as the financial derivatives offered by securities firms and commercial banks. Thus, usually the best way to characterize and distinguish financial institutions is through descriptions of the sets of activities they perform and the risk-return trade-offs these activities involve, not through their historical distinct types.

This section describes nine nonmutually exclusive activities performed by financial institutions. The first four activities—funds aggregation, trading and investment, yield curve speculation, and risk management—apply to many types of financial institutions and are of broad economic importance. These activities are examined in detail, focusing on the risk-return trade-offs that they yield. The remaining five activities pertain to sources of fee income important for specific types of financial institutions, and so these activities are discussed more briefly. This set of activities, while fairly comprehensive, is by no means exhaustive. Moreover, some of these activities are complementary, while others are not.

Funds Aggregation

Many types of financial institutions raise funds from many relatively small depositors, investors, or other customers that they reinvest in larger chunks.

Examples of funds aggregators include thrifts and commercial banks with retail branch networks, life insurers offering annuities, and mutual funds. The funds raised may be very liquid, as is the case with most deposits, or less so, as is the case with most annuities. When the funds they raise are more liquid than their assets, funds aggregators are exposed to liquidity risk, for which they should earn an interest rate spread.

Funds aggregators exist to exploit some form of economy of scale in investing. Sources of economies of scale include transactions costs that fall in percentage terms with trade size, the sizable up-front costs of performing financial research, the expanded investment opportunity set available to larger investors, and the greater ability of larger investors to diversify investments. Some funds aggregators invest on their own accounts and provide a contractually specified return to their providers of funds (e.g., commercial banks), while others invest directly on behalf of their providers of funds (e.g., mutual funds). When they invest on their own account, funds aggregators attempt to generate income by earning more on their assets than the cost (including noninterest costs) of the funds they raise. When they invest directly on behalf of the providers of funds, funds aggregators earn fees that may be contingent on investment returns. These investment activities are described in more detail in the sections "Trading and Investment" and "Other Sources of Fee Income." Funds aggregators must maintain their stock of funds for their earnings to persist. This can be difficult because of the many investment opportunities available to providers of funds. For example, aside from the period of artificially low interest rates from 2001 to 2004 that has now ended, thrifts and commercial banks have found it increasingly difficult over time to raise core deposits, because of the increasing availability of liquid market-rate alternatives.

Funds aggregators that invest on their own account are strongly affected by their abilities to earn high returns on their assets and to attract low-cost funds. Since they transact with many small sources of funds, funds aggregators are usually also strongly affected by their ability to process transactions in a cost-efficient manner.

Trading and Investment

Financial institutions often trade or invest in financial assets on their own accounts. A financial institution usually holds a trading portfolio because it believes it has some advantage over its trading partners in valuing financial instruments that will yield trading gains. It also may hold a trading portfolio to facilitate or as a result of its other activities. For example, derivatives dealers hold trading portfolios of derivatives.

Financial institutions invest in financial assets to generate investment income. Financial institutions other than the yield curve speculators discussed in the next section usually try to match the timing of the cash flows of their financial assets and liabilities to mitigate interest rate risk. For example, insurers usually match the timing of payoffs of their financial assets to those on their claim liabilities. In the absence of perfect matching of financial assets and liabilities, trading and investment portfolios are subject to the same sort of interest rate risks as yield curve speculators.

The performance of financial institutions that invest is strongly affected by their ability to screen potential investments in order to accept credit risk only when it is desirable to do so.

Yield Curve Speculation

The values of fixed-rate (and imperfectly floating-rate) financial instruments are sensitive to changes in the appropriate interest rates. The value of a fixed-rate financial instrument varies inversely with interest rates, with the absolute magnitude of the value change rising with the financial instrument's duration, a measure of the weighted-average time to the cash flows or next repricing of the instrument. Increases in the appropriate interest rates yield losses on financial assets and gains on financial liabilities. Decreases in the appropriate interest rates yield gains on financial assets and losses on financial liabilities.

A yield curve is a function relating the yields to maturity (internal rates of return) on financial instruments with comparable noninterest rate risks and cash flow configurations to the maturities of the instruments. For example, Treasury notes and bonds are essentially credit riskless and pay coupons during their terms and face values at maturity; their yields can be plotted meaningfully against their maturities on a single yield curve. In stable economic times, interest rates tend to rise with maturity, so the yield curve tends to slope upward. The yield curve can move up or down and change slope or shape, however, subject to changes in current economic conditions and the market's expectations about future economic conditions. Financial institutions speculate on the yield curve when they invest in financial assets with durations different from those of their financial liabilities. There are various approaches to speculating on the yield curve that expose the financial institution to different types of interest rate risk.

The simplest and historically most common approach is to invest in long-term assets using funds provided by short-term liabilities. Since the yield curve tends to slope upward, this approach tends to yield a positive interest rate spread. In fact, prior to the mid-1970s, the yield curve sloped upward so reliably that virtually all thrifts and commercial banks as well as many other types of financial institutions employed this approach, which barely constituted speculation.

Changes in the level, slope, and shape of the yield curve strongly affect the value of financial institutions speculating on an upward-sloping yield curve by holding long-term financial assets and short-term financial liabilities. For example, these institutions benefit when the yield curve falls by a constant amount over its whole range (a parallel downward shift), because they gain more on their long-term assets than they lose on their short-term liabilities. The opposite is true for a parallel upward shift in the yield curve.

Financial institutions speculating on an upward-sloping yield curve bear more interest rate risk when the mismatch between the duration of their financial assets and liabilities is larger and when movements in the yield curve are more variable. In this regard, movements in the yield curve have been much more variable since the mid-1970s than they were before.

Upward-sloping yield curve speculators, especially thrifts, suffered large losses when the yield curve rose at various points in the mid-1970s, the late 1970s through early 1980s, and 1994. Reflecting this experience, upward-sloping yield curve speculators are now less common and, insofar as they remain, are typically less aggressive. They have been aided in this evolution by the rise of the loan syndication, securitization, and derivatives markets over the past few decades, which allow financial institutions to sell off long-term, fixed-rate assets and to hedge their remaining exposures more easily. Financial institutions that now speculate on an upward-sloping yield curve to a lesser extent now typically attempt to make up for the lost income by charging fees for performing services or processing transactions, or by generating gains on the sale or securitization of their assets. These activities are discussed in the section "Other Sources of Fee Income."

More elaborate approaches to speculating on the yield curve employed by some financial institutions are to exploit the existing shape of the yield curve or to bet on changes in the level, slope, or shape of the yield curve. These approaches are subject to interest rate risk in complex ways that are discussed in Chapter 4.

Risk Management

Risk managers adjust the risk exposures of their clients, usually—but by no means always—downward. They may do this by absorbing the risk themselves and diversifying across clients and time (e.g., insurers may hold the insurance they write) or by transferring the risk to a third party (e.g., a reinsurer or counterparty in a derivatives transaction). The primary examples of risk managers are insurers, but commercial banks and securities firms offer derivative securities and other products to manage risks, and virtually any financial instrument issued or purchased by a financial institution modifies its counterparty's risk exposure to some extent. For example, firms that securitize financial assets and hold residual or subordinated securities and lessors that hold the rights to the residual value of leased assets absorb these risks for the purchasers of senior asset-backed securities and lessees, respectively. Recently developed "alternative risk transfer" products, such as catastrophe bonds and credit derivatives that pay off on discrete events, increasingly blur the distinction between insurance and other financial instruments.

Risk managers attempt to generate income by charging a premium for absorbing risk. Assuming competitive markets, this risk premium should fall with the risk manager's ability to diversify the risk. For example, in life insurance, mortality risk is generally diversifiable, since it is uncorrelated across insured individuals in the absence of an epidemic or catastrophe that causes the death of a large number of people. In contrast, hurricane insurance in Florida is much harder to diversify, since a single hurricane results in many highly correlated claims, and climactic conditions yield no major hurricanes hitting Florida in most years, while several have hit in certain years. Hence, the risk premium should be considerably lower for life insurance than for hurricane insurance in Florida.

Risk managers also attempt to generate income by implicitly or explicitly charging fees. A portion of a property-casualty insurance premium is an implicit fee for setting up the policy and for expected future claim adjustment services. Securities firms and commercial banks selling derivative securities may charge either explicit fees or implicit fees tucked into the interest rates offered. This fact implies that the financial statement classification of fee income often depends on whether the fee is explicit or implicit.

As in any high-volume business like insurance, efficiency at obtaining business is important.

Other Sources of Fee Income

Syndication, Securitization, and Reinsurance. Syndication and securitization reverse the investment activities of financial institutions. Syndication involves splitting individually large financial assets and selling the pieces to other firms. Securitization involves pooling financial assets with similar features and selling asset-backed securities that convey rights to specified portions of the cash flows generated by the pool to investors. Similarly, reinsurance reverses the ceding insurer's risk management role, with the ceding insurer paying the reinsurer to assume the obligation to pay claims. Financial institutions that consistently syndicate or securitize their assets or that reinsure the insurance they write do so to generate fees for originating business and gains on sale without assuming the ongoing risks that business entails. Such financial institutions are cash flow–oriented businesses that require continuous origination to maintain their profitability and liquidity.

Market Making and Brokerage. Securities firms and large banks may make markets in or broker the trading of financial instruments. Market makers generate income either through a bid-ask spread or through the return on holding inventory in their trading portfolios. Brokers receive commissions. Spreads and commissions tend to be largest for new or unique products.

Deal Making. Securities firms and large banks may execute or advise on various financial deals (e.g., mergers and acquisitions and major security transactions) and receive commissions. They also may generate trading or investment income by holding a portion of the securities that are issued or by offering bridge financing up to the completion of the deal.

Asset Management and Investment Advice. Many financial institutions manage or provide advice regarding clients' investments for fees. For example, thrifts and commercial banks offer trust services. These fees can be fixed, a percentage of assets managed, based on the performance of the portfolio, or mixtures of these options.

Transactions Processing. The performance of any financial institution with a high transactions volume depends on its ability to process transactions efficiently in its "back office." For example, large thrifts, commercial banks, and securities firms may process millions of transactions in a given day. Some of these transactions result in explicit fee income. Some financial institutions specialize in performing these processing tasks for other firms for a fee. Financial institutions that process high volumes of transactions make substantial investments in information technology.

Fee income from different sources can have very different risk and persistence. For example, deals tend to be concentrated in bull markets. Sources of fee income may be correlated, however, since financial institutions aggressively "cross-sell" their services and so can gain or lose multiple sources of fee income when a major customer is added or dropped or when the firm becomes more or less competitive in a given market.

Exhibit 1.1 provides a useful matrix for organizing one's thinking about a specific financial institution. The matrix displays financial institutions' activities horizontally and risks vertically.

VALUATION OF FINANCIAL INSTITUTIONS IN PRACTICE

The value of financial institutions stems from two sources:

1. A portfolio of financial instruments that are or will be valued on the balance sheet at fair value. Most financial instruments are (or quickly become) commodities in which new investments have approximately zero net present value.
2. A set of future streams of noninterest income and expense with various degrees of risk and persistence. If the firm has market power in a given area, some of these sources of fee income could reflect positive present value prospects.

In general, the values of these future fee income streams are not recorded on the balance sheet.

Reflecting these two streams, most financial analysts adopt a two-pronged approach to valuing financial institutions. They value:

1. The institution's financial instruments using a balance sheet approach based on fair value
2. Its future income streams using a discounted cash flow or (residual) income approach

The relative importance of the two approaches in the valuation of a given financial institution depends on the types of activities it performs.

EXHIBIT 1.1 Financial Institutions' Activities and Sources of Risk and Return

	Main Activity				
Main Source of Risk and Return	**Funds Aggregation**	**Trading and Investment**	**Yield Curve Speculation**	**Risk Management**	**Fee Generation**
Liquidity risk					
Interest rate risk					
Cash flow risk					
Persistence of income					
Cost effectiveness					

This book does not attempt to prescribe how overall valuations for financial institutions should be performed, since history has shown that the market's approach to these valuations changes over time as financial institutions and the economy evolve. The specific analyses presented should remain useful for as long as financial institutions provide the types of services that they do today.

NOTES

1. All Financial Accounting Standards Board documents are self-published in Norwalk, CT.
2. Published by the Financial Accounting Standards Board.

CHAPTER 2

Nature and Regulation of Depository Institutions

Prior to the 1990s, depository institutions, which raise funds through deposits that they invest in loans or securities, were by far the most important type of financial institution in the United States. Depository institutions were the dominant mechanism for raising and distributing capital in the economy and so were the focal point of the government's regulation of the financial system and its conduct of monetary policy. Although some activities of depository institutions have been partly displaced by securities markets and other financial institutions, their regulation continues to have a strong influence on the structure and evolution of the financial system. Moreover, depository institutions remain very important players within that system.

This chapter provides background information about the nature and regulation of depository institutions in the United States. The first section describes the activities of the two main types of depository institutions, thrifts and commercial banks. When it is not necessary to distinguish thrifts and commercial banks, they are called "banks." The second section summarizes the history and current status of bank regulation. This section emphasizes capital regulation, which is the clearest embodiment of bank regulators' approach to the risk-concentration issues addressed in this book from the perspective of financial analysts and other users of financial reports. The third section defines important subtypes of banks. The final section discusses recent trends affecting banks.

ACTIVITIES OF DEPOSITORY INSTITUTIONS

Depository institutions are intermediaries between depositors, a specific type of lender of capital, and borrowers of capital. From the perspective of depositors, depository institutions provide uniquely liquid, convenient, and safe investments. Most deposits can be withdrawn effectively at will from many locations. Under the Federal Deposit Insurance Reform Act of 2005, the federal government currently insures individual accounts up to $100,000 and certain retirement accounts up to $250,000, amounts that may be indexed for inflation every five years beginning in 2010. These attributes allow depository institutions to pay relatively low interest rates on deposits.

From the perspective of borrowers, depository institutions provide an alternative to the public issuance of securities, which can be costly or cumbersome under certain conditions. The issuance of securities works well when borrowers are well-known entities that borrow sufficiently large amounts with long enough lead times and for long enough periods to justify the costs of such issuance. However, securities issuance is difficult for firms that do not have histories of financial information or that have relatively uninformative financial information (e.g., start-ups), because it would be difficult to price the securities based on public information. Depository institutions can obtain more detailed information from borrowers, monitor them better, and write more detailed debt contracts than can the holders of securities. These factors may justify a depository institution lending in circumstances in which securities issuance would either be infeasible or entail a higher cost of capital.

Depository institutions' role as intermediaries is summarized in the schematic balance sheets of borrowers, depository institutions, and depositors depicted in Exhibit 2.1. Depository institutions primarily obtain funds in the form of deposits. Subject to the reserve and capital requirements described in the "Bank Regulation" section, depository institutions use these funds to either make loans or purchase securities. The average size of individual loans or holdings of a type of security typically is considerably larger than the average size of individual deposits, so depository institutions perform the funds aggregation role described in Chapter 1, for which they earn an interest rate spread.

Until recently, depository institutions usually invested in financial assets with a substantially longer duration than their deposits, and so they also performed the yield curve speculation role described in Chapter 1, for which they earned an additional interest rate spread. However, this role subjected them to interest rate risk that led to large losses when interest rates rose at various points in the mid-1970s, the late 1970s through early 1980s, and 1994. As a result of these losses, most depository institutions currently perform this role to a much more limited extent, if at all.

EXHIBIT 2.1 Schematic Balance Sheets of Depository Institutions, Borrowers, and Depositors

Borrowers			Depository Institutions			Depositors	
Assets	Liabilities		Assets	Liabilities		Assets	Liabilities
	loans	←→	loans	deposits	←→	deposits	
	securities	←→	securities				

By making capital available for productive activity, depository institutions promote growth in the economy. The ability of depository institutions to do this depends on the willingness of lenders to hold deposits. In times of economic uncertainty or when other investments offer better returns, lenders may withdraw their deposits, forcing depository institutions to reduce their lending to remain liquid, a process referred to as disintermediation. During the Great Depression, disintermediation occurred when economic uncertainty led to runs on and restrained lending by depository institutions. Milton Friedman and other economists have argued that the Great Depression would have been much less severe if the Federal Reserve and other policymakers had intervened to a greater extent to stop disintermediation and the shrinkage of the money supply that it caused.

Disintermediation also occurred in a milder form during the mid-1970s and the late 1970s through early 1980s, when interest rates spiked but banks were constrained by Federal Reserve Regulation Q from raising the interest rates they offered on deposits. The possibility of disintermediation is less of a concern now, because the Federal Reserve focuses on maintaining liquidity in the economy, interest rate ceilings have been eliminated, and a variety of new lending institutions (e.g., finance companies) and market sources of financing (e.g., commercial paper and financial asset securitization) have arisen.

Thrifts include savings and loan associations, savings banks, and credit unions. Credit unions are not examined in this chapter, because they are nonprofit cooperatives, typically rather small, and regulated differently from other thrifts. Thrifts' major activities are to take deposits from households and to make residential mortgages. Savings banks typically engage in a broader variety of investment and borrowing activities than do savings and loans.

Thrifts are required by the qualified thrift lender (QTL) provision of the Financial Institutions Reform, Recovery, and Enforcement Act of 1989 (FIRREA) to hold at least 65% of their assets in qualified thrift investments (QTIs). Qualified thrift investments used to be defined only as residential mortgage-related assets, but the definition has been broadened over time to include educational loans, credit card loans, small business loans, and various other items. Certain additional assets are considered QTIs to the extent that they collectively constitute less than 20% of assets. One of these additional assets is thrifts' investments in service corporation subsidiaries, which are counted as QTIs as long as the subsidiary holds 80% of its assets in QTIs.

Commercial banks typically engage in a much wider set of investment and borrowing arrangements than do thrifts. In particular, they hold a much larger proportion of commercial and industrial loans, and they finance these loans through many sources other than household deposits. The capital acquired from these sources usually reflects market interest rates and is referred to as managed liabilities. Commercial banks also provide a broader variety of financial services than thrifts, such as financial advice, risk management, trading, market making, and securities underwriting.

Due to deregulation and increasing competition, the distinctions among thrifts, commercial banks, and other financial institutions are gradually disappearing. An important regulatory change in this regard is the creation of financial holding companies under the Financial Services Modernization Act of 1999, invariably referred to as the Gramm, Leach, Bliley Act (GLBA). Under GLBA, healthy depository institutions are allowed either to own or to be affiliated through financial holding companies with any other financial institution, although not with nonfinancial firms. Unitary thrift holding companies that had been affiliated with nonfinancial firms prior to GLBA are allowed to maintain these affiliations, however. As of November 2006, 641 financial holding companies have been created and remain effective.

BANK REGULATION

This section discusses bank chartering, regulatory supervision, and branching. In the "Reserve Requirements" and "Capital Requirements" sections, the two main types of "safety and soundness" regulation of banks, reserve and capital requirements, respectively, are described. Users of financial reports must assess banks' current and expected future reserve and capital levels, because these levels affect the ability of banks to grow. The "Regulatory Cycles" section summarizes the historically cyclical path of bank regulation and recent deregulatory trends.

Chartering, Regulatory Supervision, and Branching

The regulation of banks is a complex patchwork that reflects both historical accident and bureaucratic politics. Many academics and others have argued that a simpler, nonoverlapping system of regulation would be more efficient, to little effect so far.

Both thrifts and commercial banks can be either state or federally chartered, in what is referred to as the dual banking system. Federal charters are granted by the Comptroller of the Currency (COC) for commercial banks and by the Office of Thrift Supervision (OTS) for thrifts. Both the COC and OTS are branches of the Treasury Department. Appropriate state authorities grant state charters.

The Federal Deposit Insurance Corporation (FDIC) regulates any financial institution for which it provides deposit insurance. Regulatory examinations and other general regulation are performed by: the COC for federally chartered commercial banks; the Federal Reserve and state authorities for state-chartered commercial banks; the OTS and FDIC for federally chartered thrifts; and the OTS, FDIC, and state authorities for state-chartered thrifts. The Federal Reserve acts as the umbrella regulator for bank and financial holding companies, which means it must coordinate with functional regulators of their subsidiaries. The extent of this coordination has been increased by GLBA, and it is working out successfully so far.

Foreign banks operating in the United States generally are subject to the same regulation as domestic banks. They are also subject to regulation at the holding company level by the Federal Reserve under Regulation K, which applies to U.S. banks operating abroad as well.

State authorities determine the ability of banks to branch within a state. Most, if not all, states now allow unlimited intrastate branching.

Reserve Requirements

Under reserve requirements, banks must hold vault cash or noninterest-bearing deposits with the Federal Reserve as a percentage of their transaction deposits (interest- and noninterest-bearing checking accounts). For 2007, this percentage is 0% for the first $8.5 million of transaction deposits, 3% for transaction deposits between $8.5 million and $45.8 million, and 10% thereafter. The primary intent of reserve requirements is to ensure that banks have access to enough cash to meet the foreseeable demands of depositors and thus to prevent bank runs. Historically, reserves were required at higher rates and for a broader set of deposits.

For banks with deposits over $207.7 million (which are required to report weekly to bank regulators), reserve requirements must be met on average over two-week reserve maintenance periods. Sometimes banks have to scrounge for reserves on the last days of the period. To meet reserve requirements, larger banks usually borrow in the federal funds market, which involves short-term (usually one-day) uncollateralized borrowing and lending between financial institutions. When a bank's credit risk is an issue, it can borrow in the collateralized securities repurchase market instead. Smaller banks usually borrow from one of the 12 Federal Home Loan Banks (FHLBs), which they jointly own along with some insurance companies. The FHLBs have access to low-cost funding due to their size.

Banks also may borrow at the discount window of the Federal Reserve under three distinct lending programs described in its Regulation A: primary, secondary, and seasonal. The primary program is available to all generally sound banks, but the Federal Reserve sets the primary rate 1% higher than its target federal funds rate to dissuade discount window borrowing by banks that can access other markets. The secondary program is available to banks for which a timely return to market financing is foreseeable and for the orderly resolution of failing banks; the secondary rate is set .5% above the primary rate. The seasonal program is available to banks that have recurring intrayear fluctuations in funding needs; the seasonal rate usually is set close to the target federal funds rate.

Larger banks tend to purchase (borrow) reserves and smaller banks tend to sell (lend) reserves. The Federal Reserve sets a target for the federal funds rate to achieve macroeconomic goals, lowering the rate in depressed or potentially deflationary times and raising the rate in boom or potentially inflationary times. For example, the target federal funds rate is 5.25% in November 2006, having been raised by the Federal Reserve in 17 separate .25% increments from a very low 1% level in June 2004 as the economy improved over this period. The Federal Reserve has various tools at its disposal to keep the actual federal funds rate near the target rate. The most important of these are open market purchases and sales of government securities, which influence the amount of funds available in the economy. The actual federal funds rate can fluctuate considerably around the target in the last days of reserve maintenance periods when there are imbalances in the demand and supply for federal funds.

Capital Requirements

Under regulatory capital requirements, banks must maintain various measures of equity above certain percentages of corresponding measures of assets. The intent of capital requirements is to ensure that banks are and will remain solvent, so that they are able to pay off their liabilities as they come due.

Currently there are three main capital ratios for which requirements exist:

1. The leverage ratio
2. The Tier 1 risk-based capital ratio
3. The total risk-based capital ratio

The leverage ratio pertains solely to banks' credit risk. The risk-based capital ratios pertain to banks' credit risk and for banks with significant market risk, as measured by their trading assets plus trading liabilities exceeding $1 billion or 10% of total assets, to their market risk.

As will be discussed, the two risk-based capital ratios will change in January 2008 when U.S. bank regulators begin the four-year phase-in period for the Basel II Capital Accord (Basel II) for a small set of large banks and refine existing capital requirements for other banks. The leverage ratio will not be affected by Basel II.

This section first describes current capital requirements, and then describes the expected changes in those requirements resulting from the adoption of Basel II. Users of financial reports should understand these capital requirements, because they indicate bank regulators' main concerns regarding risks banks undertake, and these concerns are similar in many respects to those of users.

Leverage Ratio. The leverage ratio is based on a measure of equity called "Tier 1" capital. Tier 1 capital equals common equity with these adjustments:

- Minus other comprehensive income associated with unrealized gains and losses on available-for-sale securities under SFAS No. 115, *Accounting for Certain Investments in Marketable Securities* (1993), and effective cash flow hedges under SFAS No. 133, *Accounting for Derivative Instruments and Hedging Activities* (1998).

- Plus minority interest and noncumulative perpetual preferred stock.
- Plus qualifying cumulative perpetual preferred stock, including trust preferred securities issued by unconsolidated special purpose entities that are accounted for under generally accepted accounting principles (GAAP) as subordinated debt of the bank. This item is subject to a limit of 25% of the sum of common stock, minority interests, and noncumulative and qualifying cumulative perpetual preferred stock for most banks, but it is subject to a tighter limit of 15% of this sum for internationally active banks with greater than $250 billion of assets or $10 billion of on-balance sheet foreign exposures.
- Minus goodwill and certain other disallowed intangible assets (with any associated deferred tax liability optionally netted).
- Minus servicing assets and purchased credit card relationships in excess of 100% of Tier 1 capital and minus disallowed nonmortgage servicing assets and purchased credit card relationships in excess of 25% of Tier 1 capital.
- Minus credit-enhancing interest-only strips (with any associated deferred tax liability optionally netted) in excess of 25% of Tier 1 capital.
- Minus deferred tax assets expected to be realized beyond one year or that exceed 10% of Tier 1 capital, whichever is greater.
- Minus deductions of percentages of nonfinancial equity (i.e., merchant banking) investments with exceptions for investments in Small Business Investment Companies that are less than 15% of Tier 1 capital and for grandfathered investments held continuously since March 13, 2000. These deductions are 8% of the investment for investments less than 15% of Tier 1 capital, 12% for investments from 15 to 25% of Tier 1 capital, and 25% for investments in excess of 25% of Tier 1 capital. Nonfinancial equity investments are not included in assets for any of the capital ratios, and so these percentages reflect the amount of Tier 1 capital that must be held against these investments.

These adjustments to Tier 1 capital reflect in part the reversal of partial fair value accounting for financial instruments, in part the inclusion of long-term, nondebt financing and in part the exclusion of less liquid, more subjectively measured, or riskier assets.

The leverage ratio is Tier 1 capital divided by assets, where the definition of assets reflects adjustments consistent with those to Tier 1 capital. The leverage ratio must be 4% (5%) or above for the bank to be considered adequately (well) capitalized. If the leverage ratio is below 2%, then the bank is considered critically undercapitalized. Under the Federal Deposit Insurance Corporation Improvement Act (FDICIA) of 1991, bank regulators must take specific prompt corrective actions whenever a bank's leverage ratio falls below 5%, and these actions become more intrusive as the ratio becomes lower. When the leverage ratio falls below 2%, a receiver generally should be appointed and the bank sold or liquidated.

Risk-Based Capital Ratios. Under the 1988 Basel Capital Accord (Basel I), banks have been required since 1990 to meet capital requirements that attempt to incorporate the differential risk of various types of assets and also other on– and off–balance sheet exposures. These capital requirements are based on a measure of risk-adjusted assets that has evolved considerably over time, as banks have engaged in an increasingly wide range of activities with considerable risk.

To calculate risk-adjusted assets, each type of on–balance sheet asset is given a risk weight. For example, cash and most obligations of the U.S. government and Ginnie Mae mortgage-backed securities have a 0% risk weight, interbank deposits and Fannie Mae and Freddie Mac mortgage-backed securities have a 20% risk weight, first mortgages on residential property have a 50% risk weight, and commercial and industrial loans have a 100% risk weight.

Off–balance sheet items are multiplied both by the appropriate risk weight and by a credit conversion factor intended to capture the "credit equivalent amount" of the item. For example, direct credit substitute standby letters of credit (i.e., guarantees of outstanding obligations of third parties) have a conversion factor of 100%, performance-related standby letters of credit and loan commitments with an original maturity exceeding one year have a conversion factor of 50%, commercial letters of credit have a conversion factor of 20%, liquidity facilities provided to asset-backed commercial paper conduits with an original maturity less than one year have a conversion factor of 10%, and other loan commitments with a original maturity less than one year have a conversion factor of 0%.

Due to the considerable risk of these instruments, special risk-based capital requirements exist for derivatives, retained interests from securitizations, recourse obligations, and certain direct credit substitutes. For derivatives, the credit equivalent amount equals the fair value of the derivative (if it is positive) plus an additional amount for the potential future credit exposure. This additional amount equals the notional amount of the derivative times a conversion factor that depends on the remaining maturity and type of contract (e.g., interest rate, foreign exchange, or equity). The risk weight for a derivative depends on various factors determined by regulators, such as the type of counterparty.

Residual interests from banks' own securitizations, recourse obligations, and certain direct credit substitutes are given similar special treatment when they involve risk retention that is disproportionate to the face amount of the instrument, as is often the case. This similar treatment reflects the fact that issuers in risky asset securitizations use these alternative means of retaining risk substitutably. Recourse obligations and direct credit substitutes are defined broadly to include credit guarantees, warranties and representations, credit derivatives, purchased residual interests from securitizations, certain loan servicing rights, and clean-up calls in securitizations.

Residual interests, recourse obligations, and direct credit substitutes either qualify for an external ratings-based approach or they do not. They qualify for an external ratings-based approach if they are either traded and rated by a single external rating agency or not traded but rated by more than one external rating agency; if not traded, the lowest rating must be one level below investment grade or better for long-term positions and investment grade or better for short-term positions. A limited set of recourse obligations and direct credit substitutes also may qualify for an internal ratings-based approach for banks with qualified internal ratings systems or for banks using qualifying software that reflects external rating standards.

For residual interests, recourse obligations, and direct credit substitutes that qualify for an external ratings-based approach, the risk weights range from 20% for the highest-rated positions to 200% for the lowest-rated positions. For recourse obligations and direct credit substitutes that qualify for an internal ratings-based approach, the risk weights range from 100 to 200%. For residual interests that do not qualify for any ratings-based approach, the bank must hold capital equal to the face amount of the residual interests (the "dollar-for-dollar" capital requirement). For recourse obligations and direct credit substitutes that do not qualify for any ratings-based approach, banks must hold capital against the face amount of that position and all more senior positions up to the maximum contractually specified loss on those positions less any recourse liability accrued for these positions under GAAP (the "low-level exposure" rule).

Risk-adjusted assets generally equal the weighted sum of on–balance sheet assets using these risk weights and off–balance sheet items using these risk weights and conversion factors, taking into account the special rules for derivatives, residual interests, recourse obligations, and certain direct credit substitutes. An exception exists for asset-backed commercial paper conduits that are sponsored by the bank and are consolidated for GAAP purposes under FASB Interpretation (FIN) No. 46(R), *Consolidation of Variable Interest Entities* (2003), as discussed in Chapter 9; these conduits' assets are not included in risk-weighted assets. The only risk-based capital required to be held by banks sponsoring these conduits arises from credit enhancements or liquidity facilities the banks provide to the conduits.

The Tier 1 risk-based capital ratio is Tier 1 capital divided by risk-adjusted assets. Any minority interest associated with asset-backed commercial paper conduits is not included in Tier 1 capital for the purposes of calculating risk-weighted capital ratios. The Tier 1 risk-based capital ratio must be 4% (6%) or above for the bank to be considered adequately (well) capitalized. If it is below 3%, then the bank is considered significantly undercapitalized.

The total risk-based capital ratio is based on a measure of total capital that equals Tier 1 capital plus Tier 2 capital, where Tier 2 capital cannot exceed Tier 1 capital. Tier 2 capital includes six categories:

1. Any cumulative perpetual preferred stock, including trust preferred securities, not included in Tier 1 capital.
2. Hybrid instruments, perpetual debt, and mandatory convertible debt.

3. Percentages depending on remaining maturity of nonperpetual preferred stock with an original maturity of greater than 20 years. These percentages decline from 100% for instruments with a remaining maturity of five years or more to 20% for instruments with a remaining maturity from one to two years.
4. Percentages depending on remaining maturity of qualifying subordinated debt and nonperpetual preferred stock with an original maturity of at least 5 years (but less than 20 years for preferred stock), subject to a maximum of 50% of Tier 1 capital. These percentages are the same as for the prior item.
5. The allowance for loan and lease losses (not including any allocated transfer risk reserve related to foreign loans and leases and including any allowance for off-balance sheet credit exposures), subject to a maximum of 1.25% of gross risk-adjusted assets.
6. Unrealized gains on available-for-sale equity securities, subject to a maximum of 45% of the unrealized gains on these securities with readily determinable fair values.

The first four of these items reflect intermediate to long-term subordinated financing. The fifth item reflects bank regulators' desire to mitigate banks' incentive not to recognize loan default to maintain capital, since recognizing loan default reduces common equity and thus Tier 1 capital. However, adding the pretax allowance for loan losses to Tier 2 capital implies that recognizing loan default actually increases total capital, since the allowance for loan losses reduces common equity only by its after-tax effect. The sixth item reflects the fact that unrealized gains on equity securities traded in liquid markets are realizable.

Some additional minor deductions from Tier 1 or Tier 2 capital are required for investments in unconsolidated subsidiaries, intentional reciprocal holdings of the capital of other banks, and various other items determined by bank regulators. Normally, half of each of these deductions is made to Tier 1 capital and half to Tier 2 capital, although a higher percentage may be required to be deducted from Tier 1 capital for riskier investments.

The risk-based capital required for market risk is based on the Value-at-Risk (VaR) of the bank's trading positions and nontrading foreign exchange and commodity exposures at a 99% one-tailed confidence level (VaR is discussed in Chapter 12). The VaR measure used is the higher of the VaR for most recent day or three times the average VaR for the past 60 business days. Additional amounts of risk-based capital are required for any specific risk or de minimis exposures not captured in the VaR measure. The risk-based capital required for market risk times 12.5 is added to risk-based assets to calculate the risk-based capital ratios.

A third type of capital, Tier 3, can be allocated solely to market risk. Tier 3 capital is short-term, subordinated, unsecured debt meeting various restrictions; most important, it must include a clause precluding payment of either interest or principal (even at maturity) if the payment would cause the issuing organization's risk-based capital ratio to fall or remain below the minimum required. Any of Tier 1, Tier 2, or Tier 3 capital can be allocated for market risk as long the sum of the Tier 2 and Tier 3 capital allocated for market risk does not exceed 250% of the amount of Tier 1 capital allocated for market risk and the total amount of Tier 2 and Tier 3 capital does not exceed Tier 1 capital.

The total risk-based capital ratio is total capital divided by risk-adjusted assets. It must be 8% (10%) or above for the bank to be considered adequately (well) capitalized. If it is below 6%, then the bank is considered significantly undercapitalized. Exhibit 2.2 summarizes the current capital requirements for banks.

Different types of banks are more likely to be constrained by different capital ratios. For example, banks that hold assets with low risk weights and few off–balance sheet items (i.e., most retail banks) are more likely to be constrained by the leverage ratio than by the risk-based capital ratios. The opposite is true for banks that hold assets with high risk weights and substantial off–balance sheet items (i.e., most wholesale banks). For these banks, the Tier 1 risk-based capital ratio is more likely to bind when the banks have a lot of subordinated debtlike instruments that qualify as Tier 2 capital; otherwise the total risk-based capital ratio is more likely to bind.

Banks can raise regulatory capital ratios in various ways, some of which are purely cosmetic. Asset sales and capital issuance raise capital ratios in an economically descriptive way. In contrast, selling appreciated assets or repurchasing depreciated liabilities while immediately replacing those items raises regulatory capital without increasing economic capital. The same is true for any accounting choice that raises (lowers) a measure of capital proportionately more (less) than it does the corresponding measure of assets.

All three capital ratios are limited as measures of banks' solvency. Each ratio is based on book values of assets and owners' equity, which can differ substantially from the fair values of these items. Each does not account for the actual risk of different types of assets. The leverage ratio does not take into account any differences in the risk of assets. The risk weights and conversion factors used in risk-based capital ratios are ad hoc, and they need not

EXHIBIT 2.2 Bank Capital Requirements

		Capital Status			
		Well Capitalized	**Adequately Capitalized**	**Under-Capitalized**	**Appoint Receiver**
	Leverage	5%	4%	3%	2%
Capital Ratio	Risk-based Tier 1	6%	4%	3%	—
	Risk-based total	10%	8%	6%	—

reflect the risks of different types of assets even on average. Moreover, these risk weights and conversion factors do not take into account variation in risk within categories. For example, some commercial loans are essentially riskless, while subprime residential mortgages can entail considerable risk. Accordingly, regulatory capital requirements provide banks with incentives to hold assets with a high level of risk relative to the capital required, a behavior referred to as capital arbitrage. For example, the growth of Ginnie Mae, Fannie Mae, and Freddie Mac mortgage-backed securities has been positively affected by their 0 or 20% risk weights, well below the 50% risk weight on residential mortgages.

Basel II and Other Forthcoming Changes in Risk-Based Capital Requirements. In part to address concerns about capital arbitrage and in part to include capital requirements for operational risk, in June 2006 the Basel Committee issued a comprehensive revised Basel II risk-based capital framework[1] which it expected to be adopted beginning in January 2007. This framework allows banks to adopt several approaches of varying sophistication to calculating risk-based capital for both credit and operational risk, and it also refines the definition and treatment of trading books subject to credit and market risk requirements.

Of the countries internationally that have indicated that they intend to adopt Basel II and have provided a projected implementation timetable, most plan to phase the framework in some fashion over the 2007–2008 period. For example, the member countries of the European Union plan to adopt Basel II's simpler approaches at the beginning of 2007 and its advanced approaches at the beginning of 2008. These timetables may not be met, however, especially by countries with less developed banking systems. For example, the central bank of India had indicated it intended to adopt Basel II in March 2007, but stated in November 2006 that it had decided to delay mandatory adoption of the framework for two years due to the lack of preparedness of its banking system.

U.S. bank regulators have stated that they will adopt only Basel II's most advanced approaches for credit and operational risk, and they will require those approaches only for about 10 large, internationally active banks whose credit and operational risk management systems are and will remain subject to rigorous evaluation. These regulators have proposed that other banks use a refined version of existing risk-based capital requirements, and they have already proposed a number of specific refinements. The other banks will be allowed to use Basel II's advanced approaches if their risk management systems pass through the same evaluation process as for the large banks, and regulators expect about 10 of these banks to do so. Even for the approximately 20 banks expected to use the advanced approaches, regulators have stated they intend to adopt Basel II with a one-year delay (in January 2008) and a four-year transition period (one-year parallel running with existing capital requirements and three years of floors based percentages on existing capital requirements that decline from 95% in the first year to 85% in the third year). Thus, Basel II will not fully replace existing capital requirements until 2012.

The remainder of this section describes the proposed refinements of existing capital requirements that will apply to the vast majority of banks in the United States. It then briefly describes the advanced and highly complex approaches that will apply to approximately 20 banks, although due to their size these banks constitute a large share of the assets of U.S. banks. The portions of Basel II that will not be adopted in the United States are not described.

In a September 2005 advance notice of proposed rulemaking, the U.S. bank regulators proposed refinements to existing risk-based capital requirements to make them more sensitive to differences in credit risk across exposures.[2] The most important of these refinements are:

- Increasing the number of risk-weight categories to include 35%, 75%, 150%, and 350%.
- Making greater use of external credit ratings from Nationally Recognized Statistical Rating Organizations (NRSROs) as indicators of credit risk. For example, it is proposed that long-term exposures with the highest investment-grade rating have a 20% risk weight, the lowest investment-grade rating have a 100% risk weight, and ratings two or more categories below investment grade have a 350% risk weight.
- Allowing all guarantees from guarantors with investment-grade senior debt and all collateral in the form of all investment-grade securities to reduce required risk-based capital.
- Modifying the risk weights associated with one- to four-family residential mortgages to take into account the loan-to-value ratio and the credit score of the borrower.
- Applying credit conversion factors to short-term, noncancellable loan commitments of 10% and to securitizations with early amortization features of 10% or a percentage related to indictors of the likelihood that early amortization is triggered (such as excess spread).
- Increasing the risk weights on delinquent or nonaccrual loans and risky types of commercial real estate loans.

Basel II's Advanced Internal-Ratings-Based Approach for assessing credit risk requires banks to assess each borrower's probability of default, the expected loss rate given a borrower's default for each exposure to the borrower, and the expected amount of each exposure given the borrower's default. Banks generally will have to deduct from risk-based capital expected credit losses (e.g., through the allowance for loan losses) and will have to set aside capital for unexpected credit losses. Basel II's Advanced Measurement Approach for assessing operational risk requires banks to model the drivers and distribution of losses from operational risk using both internal and external data. Banks generally will have to set aside capital for both expected and unexpected losses from operational risk. In September 2006 the federal bank regulators issued a notice of proposed rulemaking that contains their proposals and requests for comments regarding the implementation of Basel II.[3]

Regulatory Cycles

Historically, bank regulation has cycled between periods of increasing and decreasing regulation; we are currently in a period of deregulation. The main types of regulation subject to these trends have been interest rate ceilings, restrictions on providing nonbanking services (e.g., securities and insurance), and geographical restrictions (interstate banking and intrastate branching). A brief history of the highpoints of legislation affecting bank regulation follows.

From about the time of the Great Depression through the 1970s, bank regulation increased. Three main laws were passed during this period: the McFadden Act (1927), the Banking (Glass-Steagal) Act (1933), and the Bank Holding Company Act (1956). The McFadden Act made branching of nationally chartered banks subject to the same branching regulations as state-chartered banks. At the time, state-chartered banks typically were not allowed to engage in interstate banking, and so this act essentially prohibited interstate banking. The 1994 Riegle-Neal Interstate Banking and Branching Efficiency Act essentially eliminated the McFadden Act's prohibitions against interstate banking, although in 29 states it is necessary to acquire a bank already operating in that state in order to enter the state. Legislation is currently under consideration in the House of Representatives that would allow *de novo* entry into all states.

The Banking Act prohibited commercial banks from underwriting securities, with the exception of municipal and U.S. bonds, private placements, and real estate loans. This portion of the act has been substantially repealed by GLBA. The Banking Act also established the FDIC to insure bank deposits.

The Bank Holding Company Act prohibited bank holding companies from owning or being owned by nonfinancial enterprises. This act also restricted the ability of a bank holding company to acquire banks in other states unless allowed by the state (i.e., it extended the McFadden Act's provisions to bank holding companies). Commercial enterprises effectively circumvented the intent of this act by purchasing banks, renouncing their bank charters, and performing only a subset of normal banking activities, thereby becoming "nonbank banks." The Competitive Equality in Banking Act of 1987 (CEBA) curtailed the creation of new nonbank banks and subjected existing nonbank banks to the same restrictions on interstate banking as apply to banks. CEBA created a loophole for industrial loan companies (ILCs) that at the time were small local institutions that offered loans to industrial workers and did not offer demand deposits or other checking accounts; however, it did allow new ILCs to be created if they remained small *or* did not offer checkable deposits. Some ILCs have been created and grown very large since the passage of CEBA by refraining from offering checkable deposits. The largest is Merrill Lynch Bank USA, which in March 2006 held assets of $62 billion and deposits of $54 billion. Wal-Mart has applied to create an ILC in Utah that would service its huge credit and debit card and check transaction volume and also offer FDIC-insured certificates of deposits (through brokers); if allowed, this ILC presumably would quickly become very large. There has been considerable opposition to ILCs in general and Wal-Mart's application in particular, however, and this political pressure caused the FDIC to decide in July 2006 to delay decisions regarding all ILC applications for six months.

During the 1970s, high inflation combined with interest rate ceilings caused banks to lose deposits to higher-yielding investment products offered by other financial institutions and to securities. Thrifts' cost of funds from nondeposit sources often exceeded the rates they were earning on their long-term, fixed-rate residential mortgage portfolios, causing their widespread ill health and frequent insolvency. These problems motivated the following two deregulatory laws in the early 1980s: the Depository Institutions Deregulation and Monetary Control Act (DIDMCA, 1980) and the Garn-St. Germain Depository Institutions Act (DIA, 1982).

DIDMCA phased out interest rate ceilings by 1986, allowed interest-bearing checking through negotiable order of withdrawal (NOW) accounts, made reserve requirements uniform for all depository institutions, made available Federal Reserve services such as borrowing at the discount window to most financial institutions, increased deposit insurance coverage from $40,000 to $100,000 per account, and allowed federally chartered thrifts to make consumer and commercial loans.

DIA allowed thrifts to issue demand deposits, money market, and super-NOW accounts, with the last two accounts free of interest rate ceilings. It enabled thrifts to hold a broad spectrum of assets, including commercial paper and bonds, even junk bonds.

Together, DIDMCA and DIA eliminated most of the meaningful distinctions between thrifts and commercial banks. Many banking observers view these acts as contributing to the thrift crisis that occurred in the late 1980s. In particular, the extension of deposit insurance coverage made thrifts—and their depositors, who might otherwise have monitored thrifts' asset allocations—insensitive to downside risk. Accordingly, some thrifts took on too much risk in an attempt to increase the probability that they would become or remain solvent.

Although most of the provisions of DIDMCA and DIA still hold, thrifts now are required to hold a less risky set of assets and are subject to risk-based deposit insurance and increased regulatory scrutiny, as specified in FIRREA in 1989 and FDICIA in 1991. The QTL provision of FIRREA (discussed in the "Activities of Depository Institutions" section) limits the ability of thrifts to hold risky assets such as junk bonds. The QTL provision created new distinctions between thrifts and commercial banks.

Also, FIRREA completely revamped the regulation of thrifts. It created the OTS to regulate thrifts, because it was widely believed that thrifts had "captured" their prior regulator, the Federal Home Loan Bank Board. It transferred deposit insurance for savings and loans from the insolvent Federal Savings and Loan Insurance Corporation to the (marginally more solvent) Savings Association Insurance Fund (SAIF). It transferred deposit insurance for savings banks to the Bank Insurance Fund (BIF), the same fund as for commercial banks. The Federal Deposit Insurance Reform Act of 2005 recently combined the SAIF and BIF into the Deposit Insurance Fund, which is administered by the FDIC.

In addition, FIRREA provided a variety of ways to deal with failing thrifts. For example, it allows healthy commercial banks to acquire failing thrifts. It created the Resolution Trust Corporation (RTC) to dispose of the assets of failed thrifts; having performed this task, the RTC disbanded in 1995. FIRREA also allows healthy thrifts to be chartered as commercial banks. In addition, FIRREA imposed uniform capital requirements on thrifts and commercial banks.

As discussed, whenever a bank's leverage capital ratio falls below well capitalized, FDICIA requires bank and thrift regulators to take prompt corrective actions. FDICIA limits the ability of the FDIC to employ its too-big-to-fail policy, in which the FDIC pays off all the depositors of a very big bank regardless of whether their deposits were insured or not. However, FDICIA does allow uninsured depositors of a failed bank to be paid if to do otherwise would "have serious adverse effects on economic conditions or financial stability," referred to as the "systemic risk exception." Also, FDICIA introduced risk-based deposit insurance premiums, and it limits the ability of the Federal Reserve to lend to failing banks.

Reflecting the generally good times in the banking industry since the early to mid-1990s and the consolidation of the financial services industries, the current trend is toward deregulation, as evidenced most notably by GLBA in 1999. This act essentially repeals the portions of the Banking Act, Bank Holding Company Act, and DIA limiting the ability of banks to underwrite securities and insurance and to be affiliated with nonfinancial enterprises. As discussed in the "Activities of Depository Institutions" section, GLBA allows the creation of financial holding companies in which all types of financial services activity may be performed. Financial holding companies are bank holding companies that have filed successfully with the Federal Reserve. Each of their depository institution subsidiaries is required to be well managed and capitalized and to have a satisfactory rating under the Community Reinvestment Act of 1977.

In implementing GLBA, the Federal Reserve and Treasury Department negotiated rules regarding where specific financial services activities must be located within the corporate structure of financial holding companies. Within limits, securities underwriting and insurance agency activities can be performed by subsidiaries of banks, while insurance underwriting and merchant banking must be performed by subsidiaries of financial holding

EXHIBIT 2.3 Schematic Corporate Structure of a Financial Holding Company

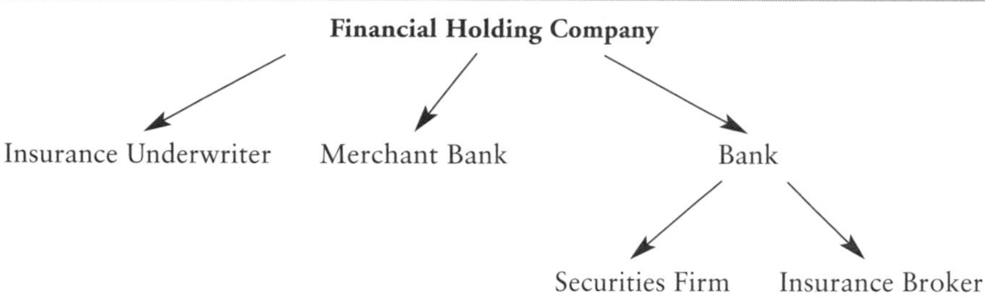

companies, that is, by affiliates of banks. Exhibit 2.3 depicts a schematic corporate structure. The logic behind these rules is that activities that have been performed by many banks for a while without significant problems (securities) or that are low risk (insurance brokerage) may be performed in subsidiaries of banks and so can be integrated with the banks' other activities. Activities that are high risk and for which banks have relatively little experience (merchant banking and insurance underwriting) must be performed in subsidiaries of the financial holding company, which better protects banks from those risks. The Federal Reserve and Treasury Department originally indicated that they would reconsider the possibility of bank subsidiaries performing merchant banking after five years, although they have not provided any indication of undertaking such a reconsideration yet.

Exhibit 2.4 summarizes the evolution and current state of bank regulation. Interest rate ceilings (with the exception of usury restrictions) are gone, geographical restrictions are substantially gone, and healthy banks are free to align with other financial institutions through financial holding companies, subject to Federal Reserve approval.

BANK SUBTYPES

This section introduces some generally useful terminology and distinctions pertaining to various subtypes of banks.

Wholesale versus Retail Banks

On the asset side, wholesale banks make mostly large-denomination loans to businesses, governments, and other large institutions, while retail banks lend predominantly in smaller amounts to households and small businesses. On the liability side, wholesale banks tend to raise funds through larger, higher-interest-bearing deposits and other managed liabilities, while retail banks tend to raise funds from smaller and lower- or noninterest-bearing "core deposits," that is, passbook savings, small time, and checking/NOW

EXHIBIT 2.4 Cyclical Nature of Bank Regulation

	Period			
Type of Regulation	**Pre–1980 (Regulation)**	**1980–1987 (Deregulation)**	**1989–1991 (Regulation)**	**1994–Present (Deregulation)**
Interest Rate Caps	Regulation Q (1993) introduces	DIDMCA (1980) phases out by 1986; DIA (1982) eliminates on money market/ NOW accounts		
Line of Business Restrictions:				
Securities	Banking Act (1933) restricts	CEBA (1987) allows Section 20 affiliates to perform limited activities		GLBA (1999) allows financial holding companies to perform
Insurance	BHCA (1956) restricts			GLBA (1999) allows financial holding companies to perform
Commercial	BHCA (1956) restricts			Still restricted
Geographical Restrictions:				
Intrastate branching	McFadden Act (1927) restricts if state laws restrict	Many states allow		Most or all states allow
Interstate branching	BHCA (1956) restricts if state laws restrict	Many states allow		Riegle-Neal Act (1994) allows

BHCA denotes Bank Holding Company Act. CEBA denotes Competitive Equality in Banking Act. DIDMCA denotes Depository Institutions Deregulation and Monetary Control Act. DIA denotes Depository Institutions Act. GLBA denotes Gramm, Leach, Bliley Act.

accounts. Retail banks typically have extensive branch networks, which yield higher net interest margin but also higher noninterest expenses.

Thrifts and small commercial banks are typically retail, while larger commercial banks tend to be wholesale. There are exceptions, however. For example, Bank of America, the second largest bank in the United States, is substantially a retail bank. Exhibit 2.5 illustrates some of the differences between larger (i.e., more likely to be wholesale) and smaller (i.e., more likely to be retail) commercial banks.

Corporate versus Consumer Banks

This distinction overlaps substantially with the wholesale/retail dichotomy, but it is based on the clientele of the bank rather than the services offered. John Reed, the former chief executive officer of Citibank, described a mindset difference between consumer and corporate banks, with consumer banks focusing on the efficient provision of a standardized product and corporate banks focusing on developing customer-specific products. Citibank is largely a corporate bank.

As a result of the losses incurred by large banks in the period from 2000 to 2002 on wholesale and corporate positions (e.g., Enron), many of these banks have moved aggressively in the retail and consumer direction over the past few years, primarily via mergers and acquisitions. For example, J. P.

EXHIBIT 2.5 Balance Sheet and Income Statement Statistics for U.S. Commercial Banks in 2005

	Bank Size Rank			
	1–10 Largest (Most Wholesale)	11–100	101–1,000	>1,000 Smallest (Most Retail)
Balance Sheet Numbers as a Percent of Average Assets:				
Commercial loans	10.6	12.2	11.8	10.2
One- to four-family residential loans	17.7	21.1	15.2	17.2
Core deposits	40.2	48.2	59.1	67.7
Managed liabilities	40.8	37.0	28.3	21.0
Income Statement Numbers as a Percent of Average Assets:				
Interest revenue	4.47	5.34	5.57	5.78
Interest expense	1.89	1.94	1.84	1.82
Loan loss provision	.20	.52	.24	.21
Noninterest income	2.37	2.75	2.02	1.34
Noninterest expense	2.99	3.55	3.37	3.49

Source: Federal Reserve Board, "Profits and Balance Sheet Developments at U.S. Commercial Banks in 2005," *Federal Reserve Bulletin* (June 2006). This data is for individual banks, not for bank or financial holding companies.

Morgan Chase acquired Bank One, a primarily retail/consumer bank. As a result, certain aspects of retail and consumer banking, such as credit card and mortgage origination and servicing, are now concentrated in a small number of very large and previously wholesale or corporate banks.

Money Center versus Superregional versus Regional versus Local Banks

Money center banks are large banks with a wholesale and international focus, such as Citibank, JPMorgan Chase, and Bank of America, although the latter is primarily domestically focused. Perhaps because the number of true money center banks has dwindled due to mergers and acquisitions, this term has fallen somewhat out of fashion recently. Bank regulators and others are now more likely to refer to banks with money-center–like attributes simply as large and internationally active, and to include in this category very large but almost entirely domestically focused banks such as Wachovia, Wells Fargo, and SunTrust. Superregional banks operate in a number of states and have a retail and domestic focus, such as PNC Financial and Keycorp. Such banks usually grow through acquisitions of regional and local banks. Regional banks are smaller and less geographically extended versions of superregional banks. Local banks are retail banks that operate in a narrowly defined geographical area, usually a single state.

Merchant Banks

Merchant banks take equity positions in nonfinancial firms, and they also provide various corporate finance services, such as advice on mergers and acquisitions, securities underwriting, and bridge financing. Merchant banks' fee income often exceeds their net interest income.

Under GLBA, financial holding companies' investments in nonfinancial firms must be made as a part of a bona fide underwriting or merchant banking or investment banking activity. In particular, these investments may not be made to evade prohibitions on financial holding companies engaging in nonfinancial activities prohibited under the act. Merchant banks are allowed to hold equity investments for up to 10 years, however, and so they do participate in the performance of nonfinancial firms.

Investments in nonfinancial firms must be held by a subsidiary of the financial holding company, not by a bank or its subsidiaries. In contrast, equity positions in financial firms are allowed by the bank and its subsidiaries.

RECENT TRENDS

Some important recent trends affecting banks include:

- Loss of market share
- High profitability and increasing fee income

- Increasing risk tolerance and diversification
- Increasingly backup sources of funds
- Industry consolidation and regulation
- Technological change and cost structure

Loss of Market Share

Various alternative sources of and competitors for funds have arisen since the 1970s, and as a result, banks hold a smaller share of the financial assets in the economy. As illustrated in Exhibit 2.6, financial institutions competing against and growing faster than banks include mutual funds, private pension funds, and life insurers.

This loss of market share can be attributed to specific types of competitors taking away specific types of borrowers from banks, as illustrated in the examples that follow. As shown in Exhibit 2.7, the corporate bond and commercial paper markets and finance companies have taken away large and small commercial and industrial loans, respectively. As shown in Exhibit 2.8, finance companies, mortgage banks, real estate investment trusts (REITs), mortgage-backed securities purchasers, and government-sponsored entities (GSEs) have taken away mortgages. As shown in Exhibit 2.9, finance companies and consumer loan-backed securities purchasers have taken away consumer loans. The last two examples largely reflect the growth of financial asset securitization, an increasingly important market-based source of funds. Although mortgages and consumer loans are the most commonly securitized financial assets, even commercial and industrial loans and junk bonds have begun to be securitized.

Some of these trends have partly reversed over the past decade due to banks' good health, as low interest rates reduced the opportunity cost of holding deposits and as GLBA freed banks to compete in ways not previously

EXHIBIT 2.6 Financial Assets Held by Type of Financial Institution in the United States ($ in trillions)

	Year				
	1970	1980	1990	2000	2005
Commercial banks	.5	1.5	3.4	6.5	9.3
Thrifts	.3	.9	1.5	1.7	2.5
Mutual funds	.1	.1	1.1	6.4	8.3
Private pension funds	.1	.5	1.6	4.5	5.0
Life insurers	.2	.5	1.4	3.1	4.4

Source: Federal Reserve Board Statistical Release Z.1, "Flow of Funds Accounts of the United States," tables L.109, .114, .115, .117, .118, and .121–.123.

EXHIBIT 2.7 Funding Sources for Outstanding Borrowings of Nonfarm, Nonfinancial Corporate Businesses in the United States by Year ($ in billions)

	Year				
	1970	1980	1990	2000	2005
Commercial banks	104	230	546	853	638
Commercial paper	7	28	116	278	94
Corporate bonds	167	366	1,008	2,230	3,006
Finance companies	20	78	241	413	431

Source: Federal Reserve Board Statistical Release Z.1, "Flow of Funds Accounts of the United States," table L.102.

EXHIBIT 2.8 Funding Sources for Outstanding One- to Four-Family Residential Mortgages in the United States by Year ($ in billions)

	Year				
	1970	1980	1990	2000	2005
Commercial banks	42	159	430	966	1,774
Thrifts	165	483	650	719	1,201
Finance companies and REITs	7	23	81	195	624
Mortgage-backed securities and GSEs	18	165	1,162	3,008	5,476

Source: Federal Reserve Board Statistical Release Z.1, "Flow of Funds Accounts of the United States," table L.218.

EXHIBIT 2.9 Funding Sources for Outstanding Consumer Loans in the United States by Year ($ in billions)

	Year				
	1970	1980	1990	2000	2005
Commercial banks	66	180	382	551	707
Thrifts	17	67	141	249	338
Finance companies	32	79	138	234	517
Consumer loan-backed securities	0	0	77	521	597

Source: Federal Reserve Board Statistical Release Z.1, "Flow of Funds Accounts of the United States," table L.222.

available. In addition, during the hedge fund crisis in late 1998 and other times of economic uncertainty, both borrowers and lenders often have transacted with banks rather than skittish securities markets.

High Profitability and Increasing Fee Income

Banks' performance had been very good since 1993, with only a very minor bump during the 2001–2002 recession. Over this period, the average return on equity for chartered commercial banks (i.e., the portion of bank/financial holding companies devoted to commercial banking) was consistently about 15%. In contrast, their return on equity during the banking crisis from 1987 to 1991 averaged about 7%.[4] Thrifts experienced a similar but even more extreme pattern of profitability, although they remain somewhat less profitable than commercial banks, as discussed in Chapter 3. Reflecting this prolonged period of good performance, 98% of chartered commercial bank assets were held by well-capitalized banks in 2005.[5]

Fee income is becoming a relatively bigger determinant of profitability compared to interest margin. For example, noninterest income for chartered commercial banks has risen from 1.81% of interest revenue in 1990 to 2.37% in 2005,[6] with these figures ignoring the fee income earned outside the chartered commercial bank in a subsidiary of the financial holding company, which undoubtedly has grown far more sharply. This rise reflects both lower net interest income and higher noninterest income. Net interest income is low both because generally low interest rates have led to low rates earned on assets and because banks now rely more on managed liabilities, which pay higher rates than core deposits. Fee income is high because banks perform more services of various types, for which they charge higher fees.

Increasing Risk Tolerance and Diversification

After the bank crisis of the late 1980s, banks were very cautious in making lending decisions in the early 1990s. During the period of profitability just described, banks became progressively more willing to accept credit and other risks. For example, commercial banks gradually made more commercial and industrial loans, and they increased the amount of their fixed-rate, long-term lending.

Working to reduce their risk, banks are better diversified than they were before the bank crisis. Although thrifts remain constrained by the QTL provision of FIRREA, this provision has been weakened over time by the broadening of the definition of QTIs.

Increasingly Backup Sources of Funds

Banks are increasingly backup rather than primary sources of funds, for example, issuing standby letters of credit and loan commitments for a fee. During the hedge fund crisis in late 1998, when credit markets tightened, and also during the recession of 2001–2002, many of these commitments were exercised, exposing banks to potentially underpriced credit risk. More generally, banks are becoming more risk managers or credit guarantors and less depository institutions.

Industry Consolidation and Regulation

Banking and the other financial services industries are consolidating through mergers and acquisitions. Some of these combinations are driven by the desire to expand and/or consolidate branch operations (e.g., Chemical with Chase Manhattan and many acquisitions of thrifts by commercial banks) or, recently, to expand retail and consumer banking generally (e.g., JPMorgan Chase with Bank One). Others are driven by the desire to expand across states (e.g., Bank of America with first Nationsbank and then FleetBoston). Others are driven by banks' desire to expand into nonbank activities or nonbanks' desire to expand into banking and their ability to do so under GLBA (e.g., Travelers with Citicorp and UBS with Paine Webber). As of March 2003, the number of financial holding companies (FHCs) engaging in nonbank financial activities under GLBA were: securities underwriting and dealing (57 FHCs), merchant banking (26 FHCs), insurance underwriting (26 FHCs), and insurance brokerage (165 FHCs).[7]

The consolidation and diversification of the financial services industries poses problems for regulators interested in maintaining a level playing field for financial institutions or in assessing their risk. Many of these problems also apply to the analysis of financial institutions.

Technological Change and Cost Structure

Technology (e.g., automated teller machines [ATMs], telephone and Internet banking) is changing the nature of retail banking. Banks now exist that have no branches and for which all transactions are conducted over the telephone or electronically. As a result, noninterest expense (especially for facilities and salaries) is declining.

NOTES

1. Basel Committee on Banking Supervision, "Basel II: International Convergence of Capital Measurement and Capital Standards: A Revised Framework—Comprehensive Version," June 2006.
2. Board of Governors of the Federal Reserve System, Division of Banking Supervision and Regulation, "APNR for Proposed Revisions to the U.S. Risk-Based Capital Rules," September 2005.
3. Board of Governors of the Federal Reserve System, Federal Deposit Insurance Corporation, Office of the Comptroller of the Currency, and Office of Thrift

Supervision, "Risk-Based Capital Standards: Advanced Capital Adequacy Framework," September 2006.

4. Federal Reserve Board, "Profit and Balance Sheet Developments at U.S. Commercial Banks in 2005," *Federal Reserve Bulletin* (June 2006): A77.
5. Ibid., p. A85.
6. Ibid., p. A101.
7. Federal Reserve Board and U.S. Department of the Treasury, "Report to the Congress on Financial Holding Companies under the Gramm, Leach, Bliley Act," November 2003.

CHAPTER 3
Thrifts

This chapter introduces the financial reporting and analysis issues for thrifts, the simplest type of depository institution and similar in most respects to retail commercial banks. The first section describes the structure of thrifts' financial statements, interweaving discussion of the historical and current financial performance of the thrift industry and the financial statements of a representative thrift. The second section outlines the risk-return trade-offs that thrifts face and the financial analysis issues they imply. These trade-offs and analysis issues all apply to commercial banks and most apply to other types of financial institutions. This section leads naturally into Chapters 4, 5, and 6, which describe in detail three fundamental types of financial analysis for thrifts and other financial institutions:

1. Analysis of disclosures of interest rate risk and net interest earnings
2. Analysis of disclosures of credit risk and losses
3. Analysis of fair value accounting and disclosures for financial instruments

The material in Chapter 2 describing thrifts' nature and regulation as depository institutions is not repeated.

As a practical matter, the material in this chapter is most likely to pertain to the thrift component of a diversified financial or thrift holding company. Relatively few undiversified thrifts of any size remain today, for two main reasons. First, under the Savings and Loan Holding Company Act of 1967, unitary thrift holding companies—which hold only one thrift and comprise the vast majority of thrift holding companies—had much more freedom to diversify than did commercial banks prior to the passage of the Gramm, Leach, Bliley Act of 1999 (GLBA). Unitary thrift holding companies could engage in any activity that did not directly threaten the subsidiary thrift, including nonfinancial activities. The ability of thrifts to engage in new nonfinancial activities has been eliminated by GLBA, however. In 1996, approximately 20% of unitary thrift holding companies engaged in nonbanking activities, mostly real estate, insurance, and securities.[1]

Second, the number of thrifts has decreased rapidly (e.g., from 3,677 in 1986 to 1,305 in 2005) for several reasons, all of which are primarily attributable to the thrift industry troubles that spanned from the mid-1970s to the early 1990s, peaking around 1990.[2] These reasons are partially illustrated by data available from 1990 to 2005 for federally chartered thrifts regulated by the Office of Thrift Supervision (OTS).[3] Such regulated thrifts numbered 2,359 or 83% of thrifts in 1990 and 863 or 66% of thrifts in 2005, with the percentage decline attributable to a large number of federally chartered thrifts converting to state charters. From 1990 to 2005, 439 OTS-regulated thrifts failed and 65 voluntarily dissolved, with almost all of the failures occurring from 1990 to 1992. These failure statistics do not reflect the large number that occurred during the late 1980s. As allowed under the Financial Institutions Reform, Recovery, and Enforcement Act of 1989 (FIRREA), 213 healthy thrifts converted to commercial banks and 493 thrifts were acquired by commercial banks from 1990 to 2005.

Historically, the vast majority of thrifts were mutually owned by their depositors; for example, in 1978, 3330 (76%) of the 4,373 thrifts in the United States were mutuals.[4] Due to demutualizations primarily occurring in the mid-1980s to 1990s, however, most thrifts (and all of the largest thrifts) now are stock corporations, with some part of a mutual holding company. In 2005, only 339 (26%) of 1,305 thrifts were mutuals.[5] The largest mutual thrift remaining is Third Federal Savings and Loan, the 28th largest thrift in the United States based on assets, and about 1/40th the size of Washington Mutual, the largest. Since demutualizations of thrifts have diminished in number and significance in the past decade, demutualizations are discussed in more detail in Chapter 14 in the context of insurers.

FINANCIAL STATEMENT STRUCTURE

This section discusses the structure of thrifts' balance sheets, income statements, and cash flow statements. Descriptions of the historical and current financial performance of the thrift industry and of sample financial statements from the Form 10-K filing of Golden West Financial Corporation for the fiscal year ending December 31, 2005, are interwoven to provide context.

Golden West is a large thrift holding company, the second largest in the United States, that remains largely undiversified. Its primary subsidiary is World Savings Bank, a federally chartered savings bank. It also owns two small securities subsidiaries: Atlas Advisors (an investment advisor) and Atlas Securities (a registered broker-dealer). Golden West has a very simple balance sheet even for a thrift, and it is traditional in most respects except that it primarily holds adjustable-rate one- to four-family residential mortgages and mortgage-backed securities, so that it does not incur substantial interest rate risk. Golden West is able to earn a positive interest rate spread primarily because it performs the funds aggregation role discussed in Chapter 1's "Funds Aggregation" section. It also charges fees for various activities, such as account servicing and mortgage origination and servicing. Wachovia agreed to acquire Golden West in May 2006, and this deal was approved by the Federal Reserve in September of that year.

Balance Sheet

The balance sheets of thrifts are unclassified, meaning that there is no distinction between current and noncurrent accounts. This reflects the liquid nature of their mostly financial assets and liabilities. Assets and liabilities typically are listed in order of liquidity, which reflects a combination of intent to hold and term to maturity.

Exhibit 3.1 reports the average percentage balance sheet (all numbers are divided by average total assets) for federally insured thrifts in 2005. Thrifts' primary assets are residential mortgage loans and mortgage-backed securities, which constitute 63% of total assets, reflecting the qualified thrift lender provision of FIRREA, which requires that thrifts hold 65% of their assets in qualified thrift investments. Their primary liabilities are deposits (60% of which are insured by the Federal Deposit Insurance Corporation [FDIC]) and Federal Home Loan Bank (FHLB) advances, which together total 76% of thrifts' financing. Thrifts' core deposit intangible assets—which represent the expected future interest cost benefit from core deposits and is discussed in detail the "Core Deposit Intangibles" section—are generally not recognized on their balance sheets unless acquired in a business combination.

The composition of thrifts' balance sheets has changed in fairly significant ways over time.[6] In the highly regulated period prior to 1975, thrifts' balance sheets were dominated by one- to four-family residential mortgage

EXHIBIT 3.1 Thrift Industry Balance Sheet as a Percentage of Average Industry Assets in 2005

Assets:	
Cash and investment securities	7.3%
Mortgage-backed securities	13.2%
One- to four-family residential mortgages	50.0%
Other assets (fairly diversified)	29.5%
Total assets	100%
Equities:	
Deposits (60.2% insured)	58.1%
FHLB advances	17.7%
Other liabilities	13.0%
Total liabilities	88.8%
Owners' equity	11.2%
Total liabilities and equity	100%

Source: Office of Thrift Supervision, "2005 Fact Book: A Statistical Profile of the Thrift Industry," April 2006, Tables 1.11 and 2.2.1.

assets (about 85% of assets) and core deposit liabilities (about 80% of assets), and thrifts were generally well capitalized. During the late 1970s and especially through the deregulatory period in the 1980s, thrifts moved away from residential mortgages partly into mortgage-backed securities as that market developed and partly into a wide range of other, often credit riskier assets allowed under the Depository Institutions and Monetary Control Act of 1980 and the Garn-St. Germain Depository Institutions Act of 1982, with residential mortgage related assets barely exceeding 50% of thrifts' assets in the mid-1980s. Thrifts also lost core deposits during this period due to higher interest rates and the increasing availability of alternative investments opportunities for depositors, with core deposits declining to about 65% of assets in the mid-1980s. Thrifts replaced these deposits with noncore deposits, FHLB advances, and other wholesale borrowings. Thrifts were undercapitalized throughout the 1980s.

As discussed, the passage of FIRREA in 1989 required thrifts to hold more mortgage-related assets. From 1989 to 2005, these changes in thrifts balance sheet composition have occurred. On the asset side, one- to four-family residential mortgages have risen from 41% to 50% of total assets and cash and investment securities have fallen from 13% to 7% of total assets, reflecting the current dynamic residential mortgage market and also thrifts' recent preference for holding mortgages rather than somewhat lower-yielding mortgage-backed securities. On the liability side, deposits have fallen from 76% to 58% of total assets; moreover, the percentage of deposits that are insured by the FDIC (requiring a balance of less than $100,000, a proxy for core deposits) has fallen from 87% to 60%. These changes reflect the increasing number of alternative investments in which potential depositors can place their money, and it implies that thrifts are continuing to become more wholesale on the liability side. About half of the decrease in deposits has been offset by an increase in FHLB advances from 8% to 18% of total assets, with the remainder being offset by a dramatic increase in owners' equity from an undercapitalized 3.6% of total assets in 1989 to a very well capitalized 11.2% in 2005.

Even now that they are well capitalized, like most types of financial institutions thrifts have high financial leverage compared to nonfinancial firms (i.e., liabilities are approximately eight times owners' equity in 2005). This high leverage is not a problem in a good economy with low and diversifiable credit risk and stable interest rates. It was a problem during the thrift crisis, however, when thrifts were hurt by high levels of default in the residential mortgage market in many areas of the country and by holding much longer duration assets than liabilities given the cumulative effect of interest rate volatility since the mid-1970s.

Golden West's balance sheet at the end of 2005 is reported in Exhibit 3.2. Its balance sheet reflects the liquidity ordering just described. Reflecting Golden West's relative lack of diversification, 96% of its assets are in residential mortgages and mortgage-backed securities. On the liability side, Golden West is somewhat more wholesale than the average thrift, with a lower percentage of deposits (48% of assets) and higher percentage of FHLB advances and other wholesale borrowings (44% of assets). Some of this wholesale character is an artifact of Golden West's large, entirely organic growth in assets over the past few years (e.g., from $58.6 billion in 2001 to $124.6 billion in 2005, 126% growth over four years), which has been difficult to finance solely with deposits, and the still fairly low interest rates on wholesale borrowings

EXHIBIT 3.2 Golden West Financial Corporation and Subsidiaries Consolidated Statement of Financial Condition ($ in thousands)

	December 31	
	2005	**2004**
ASSETS:		
Cash	$ 518,161	$ 292,421
Federal funds sold and other investments	1,321,626	936,353
Securities available for sale, at fair value	382,499	438,032
Purchased mortgage-backed securities available for sale, at fair value	11,781	14,438
Purchased mortgage-backed securities held to maturity, at cost	303,703	376,632
Mortgage-backed securities with recourse held to maturity, at cost	1,168,480	1,719,982
Loans receivable:		
Loans held for sale	83,365	52,325
Loans held for investment less allowance for loan losses of $295,859 and $290,100	117,798,600	100,506,854
Total Loans Receivable	117,881,965	100,559,179
Interest earned but uncollected	392,303	248,073
Investment in capital stock of Federal Home Loan Banks	1,857,580	1,563,276
Foreclosed real estate	8,682	11,461
Premises and equipment, net	403,084	391,523
Other assets	365,299	338,171
Total Assets	$124,615,163	$106,888,541
LIABILITIES AND STOCKHOLDERS' EQUITY:		
Deposits	$ 60,158,319	$ 52,965,311
Advances from Federal Home Loan Banks	38,961,165	33,781,895
Securities sold under agreements to repurchase	5,000,000	3,900,000
Bank notes	2,393,951	2,709,895
Senior debt	8,194,266	5,291,840
Taxes on income	547,653	561,772
Other liabilities	688,844	402,952
Total Liabilities	115,944,198	99,613,665

(continues)

EXHIBIT 3.2 *(Continued)*

	December 31	
	2005	**2004**
Stockholders' equity:		
Common stock, par value $.10:		
Authorized 600,000,000 shares		
Issued and outstanding, 308,041,776 and 306,524,716 shares	30,804	30,652
Additional paid-in capital	338,997	263,770
Retained earnings	8,077,466	6,728,998
	8,447,267	7,023,420
Accumulated other comprehensive income from unrealized gains on securities, net of income tax of $140,482 and $158,347	223,698	251,456
Total Stockholders' Equity	8,670,965	7,274,876
Total Liabilities and Stockholders' Equity	$124,615,163	$106,888,541

in 2005, which made the interest cost benefits of issuing deposits over wholesale borrowings relatively small.

At 7.0%, Golden West has considerably lower owners' equity as a percentage of assets than the average thrift. This reflects the very low level of interest rate risk associated with its mostly adjustable-rate mortgages and mortgage-backed securities as well as relatively low credit risk. This percentage increased slightly from 6.8% in 2004, reflecting a higher growth rate in owners' equity than assets during the year.

Income Statement

The order of thrifts' income statements reflects the historical primacy of net interest income. This primacy has diminished somewhat over time, however, as thrifts, especially the larger ones, have focused relatively more on loan origination and servicing. For example, driven by record mortgage originations due to historically low interest rates and a hot residential real estate market, 2003 was the most profitable year ever in thrift industry history. Washington Mutual, the largest U.S. thrift, issued an earnings warning in December 2003 resulting primarily from a decline in mortgage originations and the fees and gains on sale they generate as interest rates began to rise at the end of the year. Interest revenue is at the top of the income statement, from which interest expense is subtracted to yield net interest income before the provision for loan losses. The provision for loan losses is subtracted to yield net interest income after the provision for loan losses. The provision for loan losses naturally offsets net interest income before the provision for loan losses, since loans subject to greater credit risk should carry higher interest rates, all else being equal. At the bottom of the income statement, other income, usually mostly fees for account servicing and mortgage origination and servicing and gains on the sale and securitization of mortgages, is added. Finally, noninterest expenses, usually primarily the cost of operating a retail banking network, and tax expense are subtracted.

Exhibit 3.3 reports the average percentage income statement (all numbers are divided by interest revenue) for federally insured thrifts in 2005. Thrifts' income statements have changed radically over the past 25 years. Throughout the 1980s, when thrifts had to pay high interest rates to raise funds, they had very low (and in 1981 and 1982 negative) net interest income before the provision for loan losses. Moreover, the provision for loan losses peaked at 12.6% of interest revenue in 1988, a year of unusually frequent mortgage defaults due to a depressed real estate market throughout most of the United States. Industry net income was negative in 6 of the 10 years from 1981 to 1990. In contrast, in 2005, thrifts had net interest income before the provision for loan losses of 53.7% of interest revenue and a provision for loan losses of 4.0% of interest revenue.

Noninterest income also has risen gradually as a percentage of interest revenue over time, from 7.9% in 1981 to 33.0% in 2005, as thrifts have increasingly provided financial services for fees. Working in the opposite direction, however, noninterest expense also has risen as a percentage of interest revenue, from 15.4% in 1981 to 47.4% in 2005, in part because the cost of operating a retail banking network has increased and in part because the provision of services for fees involves noninterest expense. The low interest rates in 2005 compared to 1981 also partly explain the increases in these noninterest items as percentages of interest revenue.

EXHIBIT 3.3 Thrift Industry Income Statement as a Percentage of Interest Revenues in 2005

Interest income	100%
− Interest expense	(46.3)
Net interest income before the provision for loan losses	53.7
− Provision for loan losses	(4.0)
Net interest income after the provision for loan losses	49.8
+ Noninterest income	33.0
− Noninterest expense	(47.4)
− Tax expense	(12.6)
Net income	22.7%

Source: Office of Thrift Supervision, "2005 Fact Book: A Statistical Profile of the Thrift Industry," April 2006, Table 3.3.

Reflecting their relatively small interest-rate spread, thrifts typically have a low return on assets, averaging 1.19% in 2005. Their high leverage leads to a relatively normal return on equity, however, averaging 12.84% in 2005. Thrifts are currently much more profitable than they were during the thrift crisis, as discussed earlier. Despite their current health, however, in most years thrifts' return on equity remains about 85% of commercial banks. The sole exception to this occurred in 2003, when the profitability of the thrift industry rivaled that of banks. For example, the thrift industry's return on assets was 1.29% and return on equity was 14.29% in 2003, well above the quite good levels in 2005.[7]

Exhibit 3.4 reports Golden West's income statement in 2005. Despite its low risk, Golden West is more profitable than the average thrift, with net income equal to 24.0% of interest revenue. It arrives at this level of net income by assuming and managing low-risk assets and liabilities with a high level of efficiency. Reflecting its virtually exclusive focus on adjustable-rate mortgage assets that on average earn lower interest rates than do fixed-rate mortgages, Golden West has below-average net interest income before the provision for loan losses as a percentage of interest revenue of 47.3%. It has very low noninterest income of 7.5% of interest revenue, reflecting a low level of diversification into fee-based businesses. Golden West is able to generate high net income mainly because it has virtually zero credit losses and very low noninterest expenses at 15.5% of interest revenue. It is able to maintain such low noninterest expense in part by generating a high level of deposit volume out of its retail branch network by offering close to market rate transaction accounts and by promoting deposit products that respond to changes in depositor preferences as conditions change. It also added a significant amount of wholesale FHLB advances and senior debt in the past few years to facilitate its growth.

Cash Flow Statement

The distinction of operating, investing, and financing cash flows on the cash flow statement is generally arbitrary for thrifts and most other financial institutions, since most of their activities are financial in nature. For example, Golden West originates some loans that it intends to retain and some that it intends to sell. The loans it retains are potentially identical to the ones it sells, although in fact Golden West tends to retain adjustable-rate mortgages and to sell fixed-rate mortgages. However, the principal cash flows on the loans it intends to retain are classified as investing while the principal cash flows on the loans it intends to resell are classified as operating (like inventory). As a result, a thrift's unverifiable intent to sell a specific percentage of loans in a year can have a huge effect on the composition of its cash flows without affecting its net cash flow. Similar cash flow statement classification issues arise from intent-based classifications of investment securities and various other items. In analyzing thrifts and most other financial institutions,

EXHIBIT 3.4 Golden West Financial Corporation and Subsidiaries Consolidated Statement of Net Earnings ($ in thousands)

	Year Ended December 31		
	2005	**2004**	**2003**
Interest Income:			
Interest on loans	$5,969,566	$3,976,619	$3,178,087
Interest on mortgage-backed securities	92,746	131,720	261,712
Interest and dividends on investments	137,584	70,517	88,545
	6,199,896	4,178,856	3,528,344
Interest Expense:			
Interest on deposits	1,550,517	944,493	938,123
Interest on advances	1,221,795	448,535	269,793
Interest on repurchase agreements	155,511	49,589	9,048
Interest on other borrowings	337,002	117,634	102,996
	3,624,825	1,560,251	1,319,960
Net Interest Income	2,935,071	2,618,605	2,208,384
Provision for loan losses	8,290	3,401	11,864
Net Interest Income after Provision for Loan Losses	2,926,781	2,615,204	2,196,520
Noninterest Income:			
Fees	369,867	210,576	163,306
Gain on the sale of securities and loans	10,514	13,216	72,274
Other	81,755	70,131	77,750
	462,136	293,923	313,330
Noninterest Expense:			
General and administrative:			
Personnel	655,425	547,432	453,476
Occupancy	92,877	86,117	76,649
Technology and telecommunications	89,900	79,453	78,701
Deposit insurance	7,556	7,068	6,683
Advertising	28,633	26,743	22,516
Other	88,024	93,313	82,490
	962,415	840,126	720,515
Earnings before Taxes on Income	2,426,502	2,069,001	1,789,335
Taxes on income	940,338	789,280	683,236
Net Earnings	$1,486,164	$1,279,721	$1,106,099

it is usually wise to ignore cash flow statement classifications and to focus on what the cash flow statement tells us about the institution's new investments and sources of funding during the year. The cash flow statement is usually illuminating in this regard.

Exhibit 3.5 reports Golden West's cash flow statement in 2005. Golden West's net cash provided by operating activities during the year was increased by $429 million larger sale than origination of loans originated for sale. The investing section of the statement indicates that its main investment during the year is a $17.6 billion net increase in loans held for portfolio. The supplementary schedule of noncash transactions indicates that $34.3 billion of loans were securitized into mortgage-backed securities to increase their usefulness as collateral, though because these securities are fully retained by Golden West, they remain classified as loans receivable. Golden West's main sources of funding for this growth are net increases of $7.2 billion in

EXHIBIT 3.5 Golden West Financial Corporation and Subsidiaries Consolidated Statement of Cash Flows ($ in thousands)

	Year Ended December 31		
	2005	2004	2003
Cash Flows from Operating Activities:			
Net earnings	$ 1,486,164	$ 1,279,721	$ 1,106,099
Adjustments to reconcile net earnings to net cash provided by operating activities:			
Provision for loan losses	8,290	3,401	11,864
Amortization of net loan costs	343,710	189,367	100,579
Depreciation and amortization	53,423	48,587	42,379
Loans originated for sale	(363,274)	(428,526)	(2,003,352)
Sales of loans	792,212	552,964	3,217,876
Increase in interest earned but uncollected	(139,507)	(60,812)	(2,114)
Decrease (increase) in deferred interest	(394,200)	(34,157)	41,450
Federal Home Loan Bank stock dividends	(71,366)	(44,458)	(40,854)
Decrease (increase) in other assets	(37,437)	60,415	146,553
Increase (decrease) in other liabilities	248,321	117,431	(10,128)
Increase (decrease) in taxes on income	43,928	(3,963)	84,061
Other, net	948	(1,228)	(1,925)
Net cash provided by operating activities	1,971,212	1,678,742	2,692,488
Cash Flows from Investing Activities:			
New loan activity:			
New real estate loans originated for investment portfolio	(51,153,125)	(48,560,551)	(33,981,369)
Real estate loans purchased	(1,277)	(46,769)	(2,115)
Other, net	213,623	(212,104)	(414,193)
	(50,940,779)	(48,819,424)	(34,397,677)

EXHIBIT 3.5 *(Continued)*

	Year Ended December 31		
	2005	2004	2003
Real estate loan principal repayments	33,375,894	23,258,098	18,034,803
Purchases of mortgage-backed securities held to maturity	-0-	(19,028)	(366,509)
Repayments of mortgage-backed securities	446,322	897,283	2,007,746
Proceeds from sales of foreclosed real estate	43,444	49,284	54,231
Decrease (increase) in federal funds sold, securities purchased under agreements to resell, and other investments	(385,273)	603,152	(1,160,667)
Decrease (increase) in securities available for sale	10,326	(10,511)	202,914
Purchases of Federal Home Loan Bank stock	(227,661)	(369,979)	(37,185)
Additions to premises and equipment	(66,089)	(81,396)	(53,892)
Net cash used in investing activities	(17,743,816)	(24,492,521)	(15,716,236)
Cash Flows from Financing Activities:			
Increase in deposits	$ 7,193,008	$ 6,238,346	$ 5,688,168
Additions to Federal Home Loan Bank advances	14,239,000	16,700,000	10,240,000
Repayments of Federal Home Loan Bank advances	(9,059,730)	(4,918,340)	(6,874,865)
Proceeds from agreements to repurchase securities	9,850,000	6,051,855	4,504,306
Repayments of agreements to repurchase securities	(8,750,000)	(5,173,240)	(2,005,220)
Increase (decrease) in bank notes	(315,944)	(305,959)	1,805,929
Net proceeds from senior debt	2,944,509	4,287,595	-0-
Repayment of subordinated notes	-0-	-0-	(200,000)
Dividends on common stock	(79,911)	(64,157)	(54,159)
Exercise of stock options	35,296	29,277	12,728
Purchase and retirement of Company stock	(57,884)	-0-	(151,230)
Net cash provided by financing activities	15,998,344	22,845,377	12,965,657
Net Increase (Decrease) in Cash	225,740	31,598	(58,091)
Cash at beginning of period	292,421	260,823	318,914
Cash at end of period	$ 518,161	$ 292,421	$ 260,823

(continues)

EXHIBIT 3.5 *(Continued)*

	Year Ended December 31		
	2005	2004	2003
Supplemental cash flow information:			
Cash paid for:			
Interest	$ 3,121,663	$ 1,484,231	$ 1,328,673
Income taxes	896,413	793,373	599,367
Cash received for interest and dividends	5,661,466	4,080,387	3,569,163
Noncash investing activities:			
Loans receivable and loans underlying mortgage-backed securities converted from adjustable rate to fixed-rate	521,820	149,776	1,227,486
Loans transferred to foreclosed real estate	40,676	47,167	57,008
Loans securitized into mortgage-backed securities with recourse recorded as loans receivable	34,332,574	24,535,995	13,663,049
Mortgage-backed securities held to maturity desecuritized into adjustable rate loans and recorded as loans receivable	163,416	1,024,116	-0-
Transfer of loans held for investment from loans held for sale	23,070	69,578	144,323

deposits, $5.2 billion in FHLB advances, and $2.9 billion in senior debt. As noted earlier, Golden West's reliance on FHLB advances and senior debt implies that it became more wholesale on the liability side.

MAIN RISK-RETURN TRADE-OFFS AND FINANCIAL ANALYSIS ISSUES

This section discusses the main risk-return trade-offs for thrifts. The financial report disclosures useful for the assessment of each trade-off are described. Most of this discussion applies in whole or part to other financial institutions.

Interest Rate Risk

Thrifts bear interest rate risk when their financial assets and liabilities are imperfectly matched on duration. As discussed in the "Yield Curve Speculation" section in Chapter 1, historically thrifts tended to have financial assets with longer duration than their liabilities, and so they speculated on an upward-sloping yield curve. When they do this, thrifts are hurt when the yield curve shifts upward in parallel—that is, when interest rates rise by a constant amount for otherwise comparable financial instruments of different maturities—because the loss on their longer-duration assets is greater than the gain on their shorter-duration liabilities due to the greater effects of compound interest on longer-term instruments. The opposite is true when the yield curve shifts down in parallel, although the ability of residential mortgagees to refinance (most without penalty) limits thrifts' gain on their primary assets when interest rates fall.

Because of the thrift crisis, thrifts are now much more sensitive to interest rate risk, and most try to reduce differences in the durations of assets and liabilities. (There are exceptions, such as Washington Federal, which is analyzed in Chapters 4 and 6.) Golden West takes this to an extreme, holding almost entirely adjustable-rate or short-term assets and liabilities. More typically, thrifts sell or securitize a portion of the fixed-rate loans they originate or hedge these loans in some fashion, for example, by financing them using long-term debt or by engaging in receive floating-pay fixed interest rate swaps. Despite this trend, thrifts remain significantly exposed to interest rate risk for two reasons:

1. Thrifts still find the interest rate spread associated with speculating on an upward-sloping yield curve to be worth the risk.
2. It is often difficult or costly for thrifts to eliminate all interest rate risk. For example, the effective duration of certain financial instruments such as mortgages that can be refinanced and core deposits that are not sensitive to market rates depends on the not entirely predictable or even rational behavior of mortgagees and depositors. A thrift may not know its duration mismatch with precision.

Even when the durations of thrifts' assets and liabilities are equal, thrifts still may be exposed to differential changes in interest rates at different maturities—that is, to nonparallel shifts in the yield curve—unless the entire distributions of the timing of cash receipts on their assets and cash payments on their liabilities are identical. Moreover, this identity cannot hold unless thrifts have exactly the same amount of financial assets and liabilities. Thus, thrifts effectively always bear some interest rate risk; the only questions are of what kinds and how much.

Thrifts' financial reports include various disclosures that are useful for the assessment of their interest rate risk. Information about the duration or interest rate sensitivity of assets and liabilities is provided in voluntary repricing gap disclosures and the required market risk disclosures of the Securities and Exchange Commission (SEC). The SEC also requires disclosures describing the level (change) in net interest income in the period in terms of the levels of (changes in) the average balances and interest rates on specific interest-bearing assets and liabilities. Chapters 4 and 12 analyze interest rate risk based on these disclosures.

Liquidity Risk

Thrifts bear liquidity risk insofar as the cash inflows on their assets may come more slowly or less certainly than the withdrawals on their liabilities. Thrifts need to maintain a cushion of cash or reliably marketable investments to pay off liabilities as they come due and to maintain reserve requirements. As discussed in Chapter 2, the Federal Reserve provides liquidity to banks through its discount window lending programs.

Interest rate and liquidity risks tend to go together for imperfectly marketable fixed-rate assets; both risks rise with the maturity of the assets, all else being equal. This is not true for floating-rate assets, however. For example, Golden West bears fairly normal liquidity risk on its mostly adjustable-rate mortgage-related assets despite the fact that their value is largely insensitive to interest rates. Like fixed-rate mortgages, floating-rate mortgages pay principal slowly (ignoring prepayment, which is less interest rate motivated than for fixed-rate mortgages), and so they yield liquidity risk to the extent that these mortgages cannot be sold or pledged if and when Golden West needs liquidity.

Illiquidity occurs most frequently during periods of economic uncertainty, when thrifts may find it difficult to raise new financing or to liquidate their assets at the same time as their deposits are being withdrawn. These periods are not necessarily the same as those of interest rate volatility, since the markets for certain types of financing can become thin or even shut down in periods of economic uncertainty, so that interest rates do not fully adjust to reflect that uncertainty. For example, the markets for credit risky subprime mortgages effectively shut down during the hedge fund crisis in the second half of 1998. In contrast, the markets for prime mortgages generally are highly liquid.

The assessment of thrifts' liquidity risk involves evaluation of the marketability of their assets, differences in the effective terms of their assets and liabilities, the persistence of their cash flows and profitability, and current economic conditions. For example, while Golden West holds cash and various types of available-for-sale or short-term securities of about $2.2 billion, or only about 1.8% of total assets, it holds a very large portfolio of loans receivable securitized into mortgage-backed securities that it uses as collateral for borrowing. Moreover, its loans receivable are almost entirely adjustable rate, so that its interest margin could be squeezed only if interest rates rose sharply beyond any interest rate caps on the loans. Golden West discloses that 60% of its deposits are in amounts below $100,000 and so are likely to be fully insured and thus unlikely to be withdrawn in times of economic turmoil. It has been successful in borrowing both through deposits and wholesale liabilities, such as FHLB advances. Together, these factors suggest it is highly unlikely that Golden West will become illiquid in the foreseeable future.

Credit Risk

Thrifts bear credit risk insofar as their loans and securities may not be repaid. Their credit risk is exacerbated by the fact that they are often not well diversified, in part because of the qualified thrift lender provision of FIRREA. Moreover, thrifts typically have disproportionate mortgage originations and holdings in their local region. For example, in its 2005 Form 10-K filing, Golden West discloses that 62% of its residential mortgage portfolio is collateralized by property in California.

As discussed in Chapter 7, thrifts originate different types of mortgages with different credit risk: prime versus subprime and manufactured home, government versus conventional, first versus home equity, and traditional versus nontraditional interest-only or payment option mortgages with the potential for negative amortization. In addition, thrifts differ in their credit extension policies with respect to factors such as loan-to-value and debt-to-income ratios.

The SEC requires extensive disclosures useful for the assessment of loan credit quality. Since different types of loans have different probability and predictability of future default, the SEC requires that the amount of loans outstanding by major type of loan also must be disclosed. Relatedly, the SEC requires that the allowance for loan losses and the amount of gross loan charge-offs and recoveries of prior charge-offs during the year be broken down by type of loan. The allowance for loan losses and loan charge-offs can be discretionary, however. As a check on this discretion, the SEC also requires the disclosure of a relatively nondiscretionary measure of default called nonperforming loans, which includes loans that are not accruing interest or are more than 90 days past due and restructured troubled debt. Chapter 5 describes the analysis of loan credit quality based on these disclosures.

Persistence of Noninterest Income

Like many other financial institutions, thrifts' profitability increasingly depends on noninterest income, such as account fees, mortgage origination and servicing fees, gains on the sale or securitization of mortgages, and impairment of mortgage servicing rights. Many of these sources of noninterest income are concentrated in periods that exhibit certain interest rate characteristics, and they may be positively or negatively correlated with each other. For example, mortgage origination fees are much larger in periods in which interest rates decline sufficiently to yield mortgage refinancing, as occurred in dramatic fashion in 2003. However, refinancing yields impairment of the preexisting portfolio of mortgage servicing rights. Gains and losses on the sale or securitization or mortgage loans tend to be largest in periods of substantial mortgage origination and when interest rates decline between mortgage origination and sale or securitization. The correlations of these sources of noninterest income are discussed in detail in Chapter 7 in the context of mortgage banks; thrifts and mortgage banks originate the same type of loans, but thrifts hold some or all of mortgages they originate in portfolio while mortgage banks sell or securitize essentially all of the mortgages they originate.

Thrifts' sources of noninterest income are usually disclosed in a disaggregated fashion that is useful for these purposes. For example, on its income statement, Golden West breaks its noninterest income down into fees, gains on sale, and other. Not surprisingly, Golden West's fee income and other noninterest income both appear to be quite persistent while its gains on sale are more volatile.

Interest and noninterest income interact in various ways. Loan originations naturally tend to increase both interest and noninterest income. Implicit service fees often are tucked into the interest rate on a loan or other financial instrument rather than paid as an up-front fee. Thus, some of what should be classified as noninterest income is in fact classified as interest revenue.

Operating Efficiency and Operational Risk

Thrifts typically operate retail branch networks that involve large fixed costs in order to raise low-interest-rate core deposits. The high fixed cost nature of branch networks leads to operating leverage that magnifies the effects of thrifts' other risks.

Branch networks provide places to originate loans and to raise and service deposits. Branch networks should be used as efficiently as possible and should be worth the cost and risk they entail. For example, the benefit of being able to raise low-interest-rate core deposits should not exceed the incremental cost of branch networks that is attributable to that function. Otherwise, a thrift would be better off raising funds at market rates.

Golden West's strategy is to raise core deposits by paying a close approximation to market rates. Although this strategy decreases the benefit it receives from a dollar of core deposits that it would have to be able to raise at lower rates, it increases the amount of funds that Golden West raises through its branch network. Depending on the size and stickiness of potential depositors and the cost of operating retail branches, such a strategy might or might not be efficient. As discussed in the "Income Statement" section, this strategy appears to work for Golden West.

Servicing mortgages and deposits involves repetitive transactions and back-office costs. As with operating branch networks, it is important that these activities be performed efficiently and reliably. Operational risk, manifested in both financial and reputational losses, can result when back-office systems break down, which could occur because the systems are inadequate, employees commit errors or fraud, natural disasters or acts of terrorism occur, or various other reasons.

Thrifts' disclosures of noninterest expense tend to be fairly aggregated, and it is generally impossible to determine the costs attributable to specific functions, such as deposit servicing, loan origination, and loan servicing. For example, on its income statement, Golden West breaks noninterest expense down into personnel, occupancy, deposit insurance, advertising, and other. Thrifts' operating efficiency can be assessed by comparing the amounts of their various operating expenses to net interest income and to noninterest income.

Core Deposit Intangibles

Thrifts' core deposits generally pay lower than wholesale market interest rates. This is particularly likely when interest rates have risen recently, because core deposits are "sticky," meaning that depositors do not withdraw their funds from nonterm deposits immediately when interest rates rise. Moreover, depositors often roll over term accounts at maturity even when those accounts pay less than market rates. Thrifts' expected future benefits in terms of reduced interest costs from their core deposits are often referred to as their core deposit intangibles, which can be viewed either as intangible assets or reductions of deposit liabilities. In either case, they are inseparable from the deposit liabilities.

In valuing a thrift, it is necessary to value its core deposit intangible. This is an inherently difficult task, because the value of the intangible depends on the behavior of both the thrift and its depositors. A thrift that pays closer to market rates on its core deposits, as Golden West does, will have stickier deposits that provide less of an benefit in terms of reduction of interest cost in the current period. Depositors' propensity to keep their funds invested in deposits will vary with their views on the stability of the economy and the desirability of alternative investments.

The OTS posts various documents on its Web site that are useful for estimating the value of core deposit intangibles, including its model for valuing core deposit intangibles, industry-wide deposit rollover rates, and the sensitivity of the value of core deposit intangibles to interest rate changes.[8]

Other Financial Analysis Issues

Thrifts are subject to intense competition from other, often much larger, financial institutions. Although geographically focused thrifts may derive economic rents from their superior knowledge of or presence in local loan and deposit markets, these rents are difficult to maintain in the increasingly competitive markets for originating residential mortgages and raising retail deposits, thrifts' main assets and liabilities. Such rents are more likely to survive for less commodity-like loans not large enough to attract the interest of larger banks (e.g., commercial or commercial real estate loans of small to medium size) and for deposits from underserved groups (e.g., non-English speaking ethnic groups). Users of financial reports should attempt to assess thrifts' exposure to competition, in particular to competitors cherry-picking their most profitable activities (e.g., better credit risks and core depositors).

Thrifts' growth can be constrained by reserve and capital requirements that bind currently or that are likely to bind in the future. Users of financial reports should attempt to assess thrifts' ability to grow, by assessing both their reserve and capital adequacy and their ability to raise capital. As discussed in Chapter 6, disclosures of the fair values of financial instruments are useful in identifying thrifts that may not currently be capital constrained but might become so, since capital ratios largely reflect amortized cost accounting that can overstate the economic value of their capital.

Management quality is always an important consideration in interpreting the results of any financial analysis. Management quality is particularly important in the competitive and rapidly changing environment facing thrifts and other financial services firms.

NOTES

1. Office of Thrift Supervision, "Holding Companies in the Thrift Industry Background Paper," April 1997, executive summary.
2. Office of Thrift Supervision, *2005 Fact Book: A Statistical Profile of the Thrift Industry,* April 2006, Table 1.1.
3. Ibid., Table 7.1. (Data for 1990 are from the *2000 Fact Book.*)
4. Ibid., Table 1.1.
5. Ibid.
6. Ibid., Tables 2.2, 2.3.1, and 2.4.1.
7. Ibid., Table 3.1.
8. Office of Thrift Supervision, *The OTS Net Portfolio Value Model Manual,* Chapters 3 and 6, www.ots.treas.gov/Handbooks/OTS Net Portfolio Value Model, and Office of Thrift Supervision, "Selected Asset and Liability Price Tables," www.ots.treas.gov/Statistical Releases/Asset and Liability Price Tables.

CHAPTER 4

Interest Rate Risk and Net Interest Earnings

Interest rates are prices for borrowing money for defined periods of time, usually a year. Interest rates depend on many factors, some of which are macroeconomic and some of which are specific to the borrowing or borrower. Macroeconomic factors include the economy-wide preference for current versus future consumption, which determines "real" interest rates, and expected inflation, which determines "nominal" interest rates. Economic policymakers, most notably the Federal Reserve, influence these macroeconomic factors. Specific factors include the term of fixed-rate borrowings; the repricing characteristics of floating-rate borrowings; any subordination, collateralization, or guarantee of the borrowing; and the credit risk of the borrower.

Changes in interest rates yield changes in the values of financial instruments whose cash flows do not vary in perfect proportion with interest rates. Financial institutions holding portfolios of such instruments are subject to interest rate risk to the extent that the construction of their portfolios does not perfectly hedge the risks of the constituent instruments. Interest rate risk is the most pervasive type of risk across financial institutions, significantly affecting thrifts and commercial banks (banks) and also many nonbank institutions, such as lessors and life insurers.

The first two sections of this chapter contain intuitive treatments of financial economic theory relevant to the assessment of interest rate risk. The first section evaluates the relative appropriateness of two common but inconsistent views of interest rate risk—the variability of value and the variability of cash flows attributable to changes in interest rates. Value variability is argued to be the more conceptually correct and workable view for most financial institutions. This section also describes the ways that value variability can be reduced. The second section defines various concepts necessary to understand interest rate risk: maturity, repricing interval, duration, yield curves, and spot interest rates. Simple examples are used to demonstrate the application of these concepts to the evaluation of interest rate risk.

The third and fourth sections describe the analysis of disclosures of the level and change in net interest earnings required for banks under Securities and Exchange Commission (SEC) Industry Guide 3. The third section examines banks' "analysis of net interest earnings" disclosures, which decompose net interest earnings into the average balance and average interest rate during the year for each type of interest-earning asset and interest-paying liability. The fourth section examines their "rate-volume analysis" disclosures, which decompose the change in net interest earnings during the year into the effects associated with the changes in the average balance and the average interest rate for each type of interest-earning asset and interest-paying liability.

The fifth section describes the analysis of interest rate risk using banks' voluntary repricing gap disclosures. These disclosures report the entire book value of the main types of financial assets and liabilities that reprice in various time intervals. These disclosures indicate the sensitivity of banks to movements in interest rates at these intervals on the yield curve.

Until 1998, virtually all banks disclosed repricing gap. Since then, most banks have eliminated these disclosures because they overlap with the SEC's market risk disclosures which became required around that time. These market risk disclosures are now the primary source of information for assessing firms' interest rate and other market risks, especially for nonbanks. Discussion of these disclosures is deferred to Chapter 12, since they are motivated by and better understood in the context of derivatives and hedging activities that are discussed in Chapter 11. The analysis of repricing gap disclosures described in this chapter applies straightforwardly to market risk disclosures in the tabular format, one of three possible disclosure options. In the absence of a voluntary repricing gap disclosure, this analysis can also be applied to measures of repricing gap pieced together by the analyst from required disclosures of the maturity or repricing interval of the main types of financial assets and liabilities for banks.

Sample disclosures from Golden West Financial Corporation's 2005 Form 10-K filing are used to demonstrate the analysis of interest rate risk and net interest earnings. As discussed in Chapter 3, Golden West originates and holds mostly adjustable-rate financial assets and liabilities, so the average durations of its financial assets and liabilities are both very low, rendering Golden West almost immune to interest rate risk. Accordingly, the 2005 repricing gap disclosure of a thrift exposed to parallel shifts in the yield curve, Washington Federal, also is examined.

VIEWS OF INTEREST RATE RISK

There are two alternative views of interest rate risk. Under the first view, interest rate risk is defined as the variability of the *value* of a financial instrument or firm that results from uncertainty about interest rates. For value variability to arise, the future net cash flows of the financial instrument or firm must not vary in perfect proportion to interest rates, and there also must be some time until cash flows occur. In particular, if future net cash flows are fixed or vary in less than precise proportion to interest rates, then their value moves inversely with interest rates. This correlation becomes more negative as the time until the occurrence of the net cash flows increases.

For example, consider the obligation to pay a fixed nominal amount of \$100 10 years from today. Assume that the appropriate annual interest rate for this instrument, denoted r, is currently 10%, but this rate will change immediately to a new level that is plus or minus 2% of the current level. The current value of this obligation is $\$100/1.1^{10} = \$38.55$. If r rises to 12% (falls to 8%), then the value of the obligation decreases (increases) to $\$32.20 = \$100/1.12^{10}$ ($\$46.32 = \$100/1.08^{10}$). In contrast, obligations that pay a perfectly floating nominal amount of $\$38.55 \times (1 + r)^{10}$ 10 years from today or that pay \$38.55 immediately have a value of \$38.55 today, regardless of r.

Under the second view, interest rate risk is defined as the variability of the *cash flows* of a financial instrument or firm that result from uncertainty about future interest rates. In the examples just given, the obligation to pay \$100 10 years from today has no cash flow variability, but the obligation to pay $\$38.55 \times (1 + r)^{10}$ 10 years from today does. This view of interest rate risk is commonly observed in everyday life. For example, most people buying houses believe that fixed-rate mortgages involve lower interest rate risk than do floating-rate mortgages, even though the value of a fixed-rate mortgage varies with interest rates while the value of a perfectly floating-rate mortgage does not. The underlying rationale for this view is that most people's salaries do not vary much if at all with interest rates, and so they view their entire portfolio as less risky with the addition of a fixed-rate rather than floating-rate mortgage. Even these people really conceptualize interest rate risk as the variability of the value of their portfolios, however. Fixed-rate mortgages act as hedges of the values of their salaries, thereby reducing the variability of the values of their portfolios.

The variability of value is clearly the more conceptually correct and workable view of interest rate risk for the types of financial institutions that hold sizable portfolios of financial instruments, such as banks. Implicit in cash flow variability as a measure of interest rate risk is the idea that liquidity is a primary concern. In contrast to individuals' salaries, financial instruments are usually fairly liquid. If financial institutions require liquidity, they do not need to wait for their liquid financial assets to pay cash over time but rather can sell them and receive fair value. Thus, even regarding liquidity, value variability generally provides the better measure of interest rate risk for financial institutions. From a workability perspective, the values of financial institutions' financial instruments, which often are correlated in ways that hedge or accentuate risk at the portfolio level, can be analyzed far more easily than can their streams of cash flows. For example, this workability is evidenced in the "Duration and Parallel Shifts in Flat Yield Curves" section in the portfolio aggregation properties of duration, a concept directly related to value variability.

Value variability may not be the best measure of interest rate risk for financial institutions that primarily hold illiquid financial assets and/or generate volatile streams of fee income, such as mortgage banks originating credit-risky types of subprime mortgages, or for nonfinancial firms that primarily hold illiquid real assets, however. For these firms, it may make sense to conceptualize their interest rate risk in terms of cash flow variability, especially if their borrowing opportunities are or might be limited.

A financial institution can reduce its interest rate risk as defined by the variability of value in two ways.

1. The financial institution could hold only short-term or floating-rate financial assets and liabilities, so that interest rate fluctuations have a minimal effect on the value of each of its financial instruments. For example, it could hold only floating-rate mortgages on its asset side and short-term deposits or money market instruments on its liability side, as Golden West does to a close approximation.
2. The institution could try to match the amount and timing of its cash inflows on fixed-rate assets with those of its fixed-rate liabilities. For example, the institution could hold fixed-rate mortgages and issue long-term debt with the same duration. Relatedly, the institution could use derivatives, such as interest rate swaps, to eliminate any mismatch remaining after any asset-liability matching.

In practice, financial institutions that try to insulate themselves from interest rate risk usually combine these techniques.

INTEREST RATE RISK CONCEPTS

This section defines three frequently used measures of the period of time over which a financial instrument is outstanding and thus exposed to interest rate risk: maturity, repricing interval, and duration. Yield curves are described in the "Yield Curves" section. The "Duration and Parallel Shifts in Flat Yield Curves" section shows that duration fully determines the change in the value of a financial instrument or institution resulting from a small parallel movement in a flat yield curve. Spot interest rates are defined in the "Spot Interest Rates" section. The "Nonparallel Shifts in Nonflat Yield Curves" section describes the steps involved in assessing the exposure of financial institutions to any type of change in the yield curve. The "Interest Rate Risk and the Effect of Repricing on Net Interest Income" section discusses an alternative but more limited approach to assessing interest rate risk based on the effect on net interest income of financial instruments maturing or repricing during the period.

Maturity, Repricing Interval, and Duration

Maturity is the remaining time until the final payment on a financial instrument. For example, a 30-year mortgage has a maturity of 30 years at its origination. Maturity has two obvious limitations as a measure of interest rate risk:

1. The values of many financial instruments are attributable in part or even predominantly to cash flows prior to maturity. Maturity overstates the interest rate risk associated with these cash flows.
2. Many financial instruments accrue interest using a floating interest rate, which reduces or even eliminates interest rate risk, regardless of maturity.

Repricing interval addresses the second limitation of maturity. Repricing interval is the time until the interest rate on a financial instrument next resets or its maturity, if the instrument does not reprice before maturity. For example, a 30-year floating-rate mortgage that resets its interest rate every six months has a six-month repricing interval at its origination. If repricing is complete when it occurs, then the value of the financial instrument does not vary with movements in interest rates beyond its next repricing date. Complete repricing may not occur, however, because floating-rate financial instruments often include contractual provisions (e.g., interest rate caps or floors) that restrict the magnitude of repricings or involve repricing using interest rates that lag market rates. If repricing is not complete, then repricing interval underestimates interest rate risk.

Duration addresses both limitations of maturity. Assuming repricing is complete when it occurs, duration is the weighted-average repricing interval of the individual expected net cash flows on a financial instrument. (Incomplete repricing can be taken into account in the calculation of duration, although such complex calculations are beyond the scope of this book, and the remaining discussion assumes any repricing is complete.) The net cash flow at the next repricing date of a financial instrument is defined to include the entire remaining principal on the instrument if it completely reprices at that date. This treats all expected cash flows on perfectly floating-rate instruments as occurring no later than the next repricing date. Each expected cash flow is weighted in proportion to its percentage contribution to the value of the instrument.

Maturity is weakly greater than repricing interval, which is weakly greater than duration. The difference between repricing interval and duration increases with interest rates, since higher interest rates decrease the weights on more distant cash flows in the duration calculation but do not affect repricing interval. Repricing interval is a conceptually more correct measure of interest rate exposure than maturity, and duration is a conceptually more correct measure of interest rate exposure than is repricing interval. In fact, as demonstrated in the "Duration and Parallel Shifts in Flat Yield Curves" section, duration completely determines the change in the value of a financial instrument or institution resulting from a small parallel shift in a flat yield curve.

Since duration is the most conceptually correct of the three measures of interest rate risk, it is defined mathematically and its properties are described. Some assumptions are necessary to provide a simple mathematical characterization of duration. Assume that expected cash flows are realized only at the end of each period, and denote the s-period ahead expected cash flow by CF_s. Assume that CF_s is known and exogenous, in particular, that it is not subject to prepayment or other options whose probability of exercise depends on interest rates. Assume that the periodic market interest rate used to discount CF_s to its current value, denoted r, does not depend on s, the number of periods until the realization of the cash flows. This is equivalent to assuming a flat yield curve. Using these assumptions and notation, the duration of a financial instrument that reprices in n periods is:

$$\frac{\left(\frac{CF_1}{1+r}\times 1\right)+\left(\frac{CF_2}{(1+r)^2}\times 2\right)+\left(\frac{CF_3}{(1+r)^3}\times 3\right)+\ldots+\left(\frac{CF_n}{(1+r)^n}\times n\right)}{\frac{CF_1}{1+r}+\frac{CF_2}{(1+r)^2}+\frac{CF_3}{(1+r)^3}+\ldots+\frac{CF_n}{(1+r)^n}} \text{ periods.} \quad (4.1)$$

The denominator of Equation 4.1 is the current value of the financial instrument, denoted V. The weight on sth period in this calculation is $CF_s/[(1 + r)^s \times V]$, which declines with s for given r and CF_s, since a dollar of expected cash flow farther in the future contributes less to the value and thus to the duration of the financial instrument.

The measure of duration in Equation 4.1 is called simple duration. The equations and statements that follow that are based on this equation apply strictly to shifts in flat yield curves. They generally hold as good first-order approximations for parallel shifts in nonflat yield curves, in which the entire yield curve shifts up or down by a constant amount. Once one admits the possibility of nonflat yield curves, however, shifts in the yield curve need not be parallel, and duration has no direct relation to value changes for nonparallel shifts in yield curves.

Formulas for the durations of two broad classes of financial instruments —loans with constant per-period payments and bonds with constant per-period coupon payments and a single face value payment in the final period —are derived and discussed. These instruments have streams of cash flows with simple mathematical structures, which allow for the derivation of simple expressions for duration.

Consider an n-period fixed-rate loan that pays equal amounts at the end of each period, that is, it has no prepayment or credit risk. Both the maturity and repricing interval of the loan are n periods. Since the periodic cash flows on the loan are constant, Equation 4.1 for the duration of a financial instrument simplifies to duration of n – period loan =

$$\frac{\frac{1}{1+r}\times 1+\frac{1}{(1+r)^2}\times 2+\frac{1}{(1+r)^3}\times 3+\ldots+\frac{1}{(1+r)^n}\times n}{\frac{1}{1+r}+\frac{1}{(1+r)^2}+\frac{1}{(1+r)^3}+\ldots+\frac{1}{(1+r)^n}} \text{ periods.} \quad (4.2)$$

Since both the numerator and denominator in Equation 4.2 can be expressed as power series, this equation can be further simplified to

duration of n-period loan =

$$\left(\frac{1-(n+1)\frac{1}{(1+r)^n}}{1-\frac{1}{(1+r)^n}}+\frac{1}{r}\right) \text{ periods.} \quad (4.3)$$

Equation 4.3 implies that the duration of an n-period loan asymptotes to $1 + 1/r$ as $n \to \infty$, which equals 11 for $r = 10\%$.

Exhibit 4.1 provides calculations of the duration of an n-period loan for various values of n assuming that $r = 10\%$. These calculations indicate that the duration of a loan rises slower with n for larger n and that the duration of a 100-period loan (10.99) is trivially different from the duration of an infinite-period loan. This would not be true if r were sufficiently low, however, as would be the case if periods were short. Intuitively, the weight on the s-period ahead cash flow in the duration calculation declines toward zero with s, reflecting the time value of money.

Consider a bond that includes both constant coupon payments of r_c times the face value F per period and the face value payment of F at maturity. The duration of this bond is a weighted average of the duration of the n coupon

EXHIBIT 4.1 Duration of Fixed-Rate Loans and Bonds, $r = 10\%$, n and r_c Varying

		Duration of Bond		
n	**Duration of Loan**	$r_c = 0\%$	$r_c = 10\%$	$r_c = 20\%$
1	1	1	1	1
2	1.48	2	1.91	1.85
3	1.92	3	2.74	2.58
5	2.81	5	4.17	3.80
10	4.73	10	6.76	5.99
30	9.18	30	10.37	9.79
100	10.99	100	11	11

payments, which is the same as the duration of an n-period loan in Equation 4.3, and the duration of the face value payment, which is n. The weights are the percentages of the value of the bond that are attributable to the coupon payments and the face value payment. The weight on the face value payment, denoted w_F, is $1/[(r_c/r) \times \{(1 + r)^n - 1\} + 1]$ and the weight on the coupon payments is $1 - w_F$. Thus the duration of an n-period bond is

duration of n-period bond =

$$(1 - w_F) \times (\text{duration of } n\text{-period loan}) + w_F \times n \quad (4.4)$$

Exhibit 4.1 provides calculations of the duration of an n-period bond given in Equation 4.4 for various values of n and r_c. The duration of an n-period bond always exceeds the duration of an n-period loan, because the bond's face value payment has a longer duration than its coupon payments. Relatedly, the difference between the durations of an n-period bond and n-period loan is greater when the bond's coupon rate is lower, all else being equal, since a lower coupon rate reduces the percentage of the value of the bond attributable to the coupon payments.

Yield Curves

A financial instrument's yield to maturity is the interest rate (internal rate of return) that equates the current market value of the instrument to the discounted present value of its remaining cash flows to maturity. A yield curve is the function relating the yields to maturity for a well-defined class of financial instruments to their maturities. A well-defined class of financial instruments has comparable noninterest rate risks and cash flow configurations. For example, U.S. Treasury notes and bonds are essentially credit-riskless and pay coupons during their terms and face values at maturity, and so their yields can be plotted meaningfully on a single yield curve. In contrast, U.S. Treasury bills pay no coupons and so are not strictly comparable to U.S. Treasury notes and bonds. In particular, the duration of a U.S. Treasury bill equals its maturity, while the duration of a U.S. Treasury note or bond is less than its maturity. Similarly, yields for U.S. Treasuries and London Interbank Offered Rate (LIBOR) instruments are not strictly comparable because of the slightly greater credit risk in LIBOR instruments. As discussed in Chapter 5, credit risk depends on maturity, so the meaning of comparable credit risk across maturities is somewhat ambiguous.

Yield curves tend to slope upward, with longer-maturity financial instruments having higher yields. For example, on average at year end from 1993 to 2005, 20-year U.S. Treasury bonds yielded about 2.2% more than did three-month U.S. Treasury bills, although this spread varied from 3.64% at the end of 2004 to .23% at the end of 2000.[1] The tendency for yield curves to slope upward reflects the fact that longer-duration instruments have more interest rate risk, consistent with the view of interest rate risk in terms of the variability of value, not the variability of net cash flows.

The expected path of future interest rates affects the slope and shape of the yield curve, however, and sufficiently large expected declines in interest rates cause the yield curve to slope downward. This was the case for the Treasury yield curve over various ranges of maturities during 2000, because the Federal Reserve had raised short-term rates during 1999 and 2000 to cool the economy and long-term rates were low in part because of low inflation and a low supply of long-term Treasury bonds due to budget surpluses run during the Clinton administration. As depicted in Exhibit 4.2, at the end of 2005 the Treasury yield curve was virtually flat over maturities from 6 months to 10 years because of repeated increases in the target federal funds rate by the Federal Reserve during 2004 and 2005 and persistently low long-term rates. In contrast, the Treasury yield curve at the end of 2003 was steeply upward sloping, due to unusually low short-term rates.

Since most of the examples in this book are taken from 2005 financial statements, it is useful to understand how the yield curve moved during that year in some detail. As indicated in Exhibit 4.2, short- and intermediate-term yields rose from the beginning to the end of the year, while long-term yields did not change appreciably. Short-term yields rose fairly continuously, tracking the eight .25% increases in the target federal funds rate dispersed throughout the year. In contrast, long-term yields rose in the first quarter of the year (.27% for 10-year Treasuries), fell in the second quarter (−.51%

EXHIBIT 4.2 Constant Maturity Treasury Yield Curve Year Ends 2003 to 2005

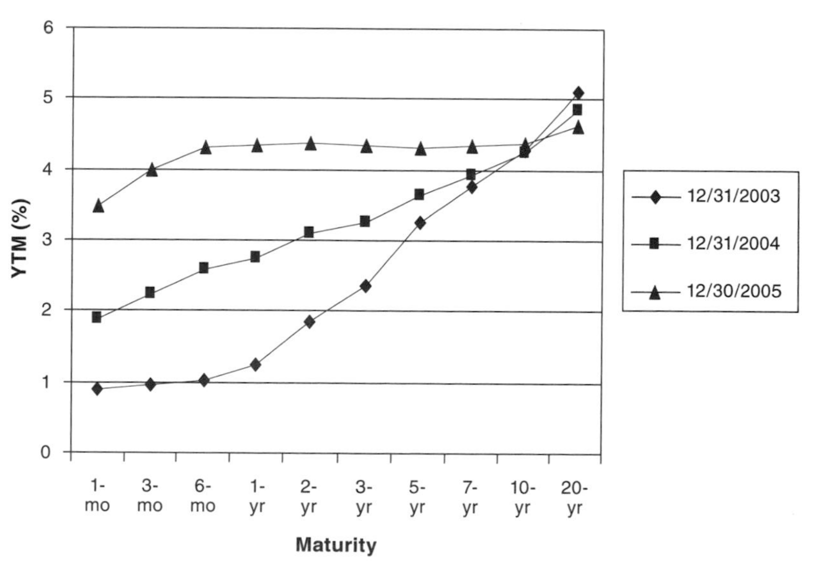

Source: Federal Reserve Board.

for 10-year Treasuries), and then rose in the second half (.39% for 10-year Treasuries). The path of intermediate-term yields during the year was between those of short- and long-term yields.

Duration and Parallel Shifts in Flat Yield Curves

The simple duration of a financial instrument as defined in Equation 4.1 completely determines the percentage change in the value of the instrument resulting from a small parallel shift in a flat yield curve. Specifically, the partial derivative of the value of a financial instrument, V, with respect to the interest rate, r, is $\partial V/\partial r = -CF_1/(1+r)^2 - 2 \times CF_2/(1+r)^3 - \cdots - n \times CF_n/(1+r)^{n+1}$. Substituting the expression for duration in Equation 4.1 into this expression yields $\partial V/\partial r = -\text{duration} \times V/(1+r)$. Rearranging this equation and approximating the partial derivative by a small change in value divided by a small change in r yields

$$\frac{\Delta V}{V} \approx -\text{duration} \times \frac{\Delta r}{1+r}, \text{ for a flat yield curve and small } \Delta r \qquad (4.5)$$

This equation illustrates the analytical simplicity and power of duration as a measure of exposure to parallel shifts in the yield curve. For example, if the duration of a financial instrument is 10, then the percentage change in value to a 1% upward parallel shift in the yield curve is approximately $-10\%/(1+r)$, which is close to -10% as long as r is not too high.

The approximation in Equation 4.5 is good only for fairly small changes in r because duration decreases with r, as discussed in Equation 4.1. For large parallel shifts in a flat yield curve, Equation 4.5 overstates the change in value for an increase in r (since duration decreases) and understates the change in value for a decrease in r (since duration increases). In other words, the effect of r on duration yields "convexity" in the relationship between the change in value and the change in r (i.e., a positive second partial derivative $\partial^2 V/\partial r^2$) that is not captured by the linear approximation based on the first partial derivative.

This convexity results from the earlier assumption that the cash flows do not depend on interest rates. As discussed in Chapter 7, "negative convexity" (i.e., a negative second partial derivative) can result over some range of interest rates for instruments that include options tied to interest rates, such as the prepayment options on residential mortgages.

To illustrate Equation 4.5's application and limitations resulting from convexity, consider a 10-year loan with constant annual payments starting in one year. Exhibit 4.3 reports the value and duration of the loan for various interest rates assuming a flat yield curve, and also the actual and Equation 4.5–estimated changes in the value of the loan to various parallel shifts in the yield curve. The estimated value changes to ±1% parallel shifts in the yield curve from Equation 4.5 are generally close to the actual value changes for these shifts, illustrating the power of the equation with respect to parallel

EXHIBIT 4.3 Actual and Equation 4.5–Estimated Effects of Parallel Shifts in the Yield Curve on the Value of a 10-Year Loan

Interest Rate	Value	Duration	Actual Change in Value to Parallel Shift in Yield Curve of −3%	−2%	−1%	+1%	+2%	+3%	Estimated Change in Value to ±1% Parallel Shift in Yield Curve from Equation 4.5
2%	8.98	5.34	—	1.02	.49	−.45	−.87	−1.26	±.47
4%	8.11	5.18	1.36	.87	.42	−.39	−.75	−1.09	±.40
6%	7.36	5.02	1.17	.75	.36	−.34	−.65	−.94	±.35
8%	6.71	4.87	1.01	.65	.31	−.29	−.57	−.82	±.30
10%	6.14	4.73	.88	.57	.27	−.26	−.49	−.72	±.26
20%	4.19	4.07	.47	.30	.15	−.14	−.27	−.39	±.14

shifts in the yield curve as long as they are not too large. Convexity is evidenced in this table in two ways. First, as the interest rate increases (i.e., moving vertically down the columns of the table), the duration of the loan and thus its sensitivity to a given change in the yield curve decrease. Second, for a given interest rate (i.e., moving horizontally across a row in the table), the value of the loan is progressively more sensitive to the yield curve falling the further it falls and progressively less sensitive to the yield curve rising the further it rises.

The duration of a portfolio is the weighted-average duration of the components of the portfolio, where the weights reflect the relative contributions of the components to the value of the portfolio, with liabilities having negative weights. For example, assume the interest rate is 10% and a bank invests \$10 in the 10-year loans just described (which as reported in Exhibit 4.3 have a duration of 4.73 years for this interest rate) and that it finances those loans with \$9 of deposit liabilities with a one-year duration and \$1 million of owners' equity. In this example, the duration of the bank's portfolio of loan assets and deposit liabilities is $(10/1) \times (4.73 \text{ years}) - (9/1)(1 \text{ year}) = 38.3$ years. Note that the duration and thus interest rate risk of the bank's portfolio far exceeds that of its assets, reflecting the effect of a debt/equity ratio of 9 on the duration of the portfolio. This high duration indicates the substantial interest rate risk associated with thrifts' historical positions in long-duration assets and short-duration liabilities.

The duration of a financial institution can be calculated in the same fashion as that of any portfolio of financial instruments. Specifically, the change in the value of the financial institution to small parallel shifts in a flat yield curve is determined entirely by the difference between the weighted-average durations of the institution's financial assets and liabilities. Denote financial assets by A, financial liabilities by L, and net financial assets $A - L$ by

OE. Substituting the weighted-average durations of the financial institution's net financial assets into Equation 4.5 yields the change in the value of the financial institution to small parallel shifts in a flat yield curve:

$$\frac{\Delta V_{OE}}{V_{OE}} \approx -\left(\left[\text{duration}_A \times \frac{V_A}{V_{OE}}\right] - \left[\text{duration}_L \times \frac{V_L}{V_{OE}}\right]\right) \times \frac{\Delta r}{1+r}, \qquad (4.6)$$

for a flat yield curve and small Δr

The value of a financial institution is insensitive to small parallel shifts in a flat yield curve when the expression in parentheses in Equation 4.6—referred to as the leverage-adjusted duration gap—equals zero. This occurs when the durations of financial assets and liabilities are matched, taking into account the fact that the values of financial assets and liabilities are generally not equal. For example, if the value of financial assets exceeds the value of financial liabilities, then the duration of financial liabilities has to be proportionately longer than the duration of financial assets to immunize the institution against small parallel shifts in a flat yield curve.

More generally, Equation 4.6 indicates the three steps necessary to assess a financial institution's risk to parallel shifts in a flat yield curve, under the assumption that the institution's financial instruments do not have cash flows that depend on interest rates:

1. Assess the weighted-average durations of assets and liabilities.
2. Take into account differences in the value of assets and liabilities.
3. Recognize that Equation 4.6 overstates the effect of large increases in r and understates the effect of large decreases in r under the assumptions just made, which yield convexity (the opposite would be the case with negative convexity).

Spot Interest Rates

In a yield curve for coupon-paying financial instruments, such as U.S. Treasury notes and bonds, the yield on an instrument with a given maturity is not the appropriate interest rate at which to discount expected cash flows that occur at that maturity, since this yield applies in a weighted-average sense to all the cash flows on the instrument. "Spot" interest rates are needed to discount expected cash flows at specific points in time. Spot interest rates can be calculated directly from observable market values for comparable zero-coupon instruments, if such instruments trade in liquid markets. Alternatively, these rates can be inferred from the yields on comparable coupon-paying instruments.

These inferences are made iteratively, starting with spot interest rates for one-period financial instruments and calculating spot interest rates on progressively longer-term instruments. Denote the s-period spot rate by $r_{spot,s}$. The one-period spot rate, $r_{spot,1}$, equals the yield on a comparable one-period coupon-paying instrument, which can be calculated directly from the market value of that instrument. The two-period spot rate, $r_{spot,2}$, can be inferred from the market value of a comparable two-period coupon-paying instrument, by equating this value to the discounted value of the cash flows on the instrument using the previously calculated one-period spot rate, that is, $V_0 = CF_1/(1 + r_{spot,1}) + CF_2/(1 + r_{spot,2})^2$. Similarly, the three-period spot rate, $r_{spot,3}$, can be inferred from the market price of a three-period coupon-paying instrument, by equating this price to the discounted value of the cash flows on the instrument using the previously calculated one-period and two-period spot rates, $V_0 = CF_1/(1 + r_{spot,1}) + CF_2/(1 + r_{spot,2})^2 + CF_3/(1 + r_{spot,3})^3$. And so on.

Spot interest rates are distinct from though related to the "forward" interest rates often appearing in theoretical valuation models. Forward rates are the interest rates applicable to particular forward periods, for example, the period from three to four years out. Forward rates can be derived iteratively from spot rates in a somewhat analogous fashion to how spot rates are derived from yields. The analyses discussed next using spot rates could easily be recast using forward rates.

Nonparallel Shifts In Nonflat Yield Curves

Financial institutions may be exposed to changes in the slope (more or less steep) or shape (more concave or convex) of the yield curve, even when they are not exposed to parallel shifts in the yield curve. Such exposures occur whenever the distributions of the timing of the expected cash flows on the institution's financial assets and liabilities differ. For example, an institution with no exposure to parallel shifts in the yield curve could have financial assets with cash flows that occur over a wide period, while its financial liabilities have cash flows that occur at a specific point in time.

To assess a financial institution's interest rate risk generally, users of financial reports would optimally like to know the net expected cash flows (including the principal on floating-rate financial instruments that completely reprice) in fairly finely sliced time intervals. Users can determine these amounts from the SEC market risk disclosures if the tabular format disclosure option is chosen, as demonstrated in Chapter 12. The value of the expected net cash flows in each time interval is sensitive to changes in the appropriate spot interest rate for that interval. In any time interval for which positive net cash flow is expected, the institution gains when the spot interest rate for that interval falls and loses when the spot rate for that interval rises. Conversely, in any time interval for which negative net cash flow is expected, the institution gains when the spot rate for that interval rises and loses when the spot rate for that interval falls. Naturally, these gains or losses are larger for exposures of larger absolute size and for longer time intervals. The sensitivity of the financial institution to specific yield curve movements is determined by its sensitivity to spot rates in the various time intervals along the yield curve.

Alternatively, repricing gap disclosures provide the amount of financial assets and financial liabilities that reprice in relatively broad intervals, which provides a less accurate indication of a financial institution's interest rate risk. The value of a financial instrument repricing in an interval is sensitive to changes in the appropriate interest rate for that interval given the cash flow characteristics of the instrument. Specifically, in any time interval for which a financial institution has net financial assets repricing, the institution gains when the interest rate for that interval falls and loses when the interest rate rises. Conversely, in any time interval for which a financial institution has net financial liabilities repricing, the institution gains when the interest rate for that interval rises and loses when the interest rate falls. Analysis of repricing gap disclosures using this logic is described in the "Repricing Gap Disclosures" section.

For example, assume a financial institution is immune to parallel shifts in the yield curve because its portfolio has a weighted-average duration of zero but that it has positive expected cash flows or net financial assets repricing at short time intervals (due to a larger amount of floating-rate mortgages than nonterm deposits), it has negative expected cash flows or net financial liabilities repricing at intermediate intervals (due to a larger amount of term deposits than intermediate-term fixed rate assets), and it has positive expected cash flows or net financial assets repricing at long intervals (due to a larger amount of fixed-rate mortgages than long-term fixed-rate borrowings); in fact, this is now a fairly common exposure for banks. This institution benefits when spot interest rates at short and long time intervals fall and when spot interest rates at intermediate intervals rise. Together, these movements imply a more concave (U-shaped downward) yield curve. The institution is hurt by the opposite interest rate movements.

If a financial institution speculates on interest rate movements, then, under the (possibly heroic) assumption of no end-of-period window dressing to obscure this speculation, the user of financial reports can use the sign of the expected net cash flows or net financial instruments repricing in a given time interval to determine which way the institution expects interest rates to move for that interval. The institution will have positive net cash flows or net financial assets repricing in a time interval if it expects the interest rate for that interval to fall and negative net cash flows or net financial liabilities repricing if it expects the interest rate for that interval to rise.

For example, a financial institution that believes that the yield curve will become more steeply positively sloped will hold net financial assets that reprice at short time intervals and net financial liabilities that reprice at long time intervals. Conversely, an institution that believes an upward-sloping yield curve will flatten or invert will hold net financial liabilities that reprice at short time intervals and net financial assets that reprice at long time intervals. An institution that believes that the yield curve will become more convex by rising at short and long time intervals and falling at intermediate time intervals will hold net financial assets repricing at intermediate time intervals and net financial liabilities repricing at short and long time intervals. Conversely, an institution that believes the yield curve will become more concave by falling at short and long time intervals and rising at intermediate time intervals will hold net financial assets repricing at short and long time intervals and net financial liabilities repricing at intermediate time intervals.

The amounts of these gains and losses can be determined through straightforward present value calculations, as illustrated in the next example. Assume that a financial institution holds the following portfolio of fixed-rate assets and liabilities, all of which pay no interest or principal until they mature: \$10 of one-year assets accruing interest at a rate of 5% (that receive $\$10 \times 1.05 = \$10.50$ at maturity), \$20 of two-year liabilities accruing interest at a rate of 7% (that pay $\$20 \times 1.07^2 = \$22.90$ at maturity), and \$12 of three-year assets accruing interest at a rate of 8% (that receive $\$12 \times 1.08^3 = \$15.12$ at maturity). Assume that these interest rates reflect current market spot interest rates but that market spot interest rates change instantaneously to a 6% one-year rate, an 8% two-year rate, and a 9% three-year rate.

These changes in rates constitute a 1% parallel upward shift in the yield curve. The value of the one-year assets is now $\$10.50/1.06 = \$9.91$, for a loss of \$.09. The value of the two-year liabilities is now $\$22.90/1.08^2 = \$19.63$, for a gain of \$.37. The value of the three-year assets is now $\$15.12/1.09^3 = \$11.67$, for a loss of \$.33. The financial institution suffers a small net loss of \$.05, because the loss on the one-year and three-year assets slightly outweighs the offsetting gain on the two-year liabilities. Because of its U-shaped exposure, this institution is relatively insensitive to parallel shifts in the yield curve, despite its high leverage. This institution is not immune to nonparallel shifts in the yield curve, however, and would be hurt considerably more by the one- and three-year spot rates rising 1% while the two-year spot rate fell 1%.

Interest Rate Risk and the Effect of Repricing on Net Interest Income

Interest rate risk has been described thus far in terms of the effects of changes in interest rates on the values of financial instruments and institutions. This is both the simplest and most general way to assess interest rate risk. An alternative and fairly common approach describes interest rate risk in terms of the effects of changes in interest rates on net interest income. Under this approach, financial institutions benefit when net financial assets mature or reprice at times when interest rates are higher than expected and are hurt when net assets mature or reprice at times when interest rates are lower than expected. Similarly, financial institutions are hurt when net financial liabilities mature or reprice at times when interest rates are unexpectedly high and benefit when net financial liabilities mature or reprice at times when interest rates are unexpectedly low.

While this alternative approach is a good way to explain the level and change in net interest income during the period, as discussed in the "Analysis of Net Interest Earnings" and "Rate-Volume Analysis" sections, and it corresponds to one possible disclosure format for the SEC market risk disclosures discussed in Chapter 12, it is highly limited as a way to assess interest rate risk. In particular, it does not incorporate changes in the value of financial instruments that mature or reprice in subsequent periods, and so it does not portray the *most important* effects of changes in the yield curve during the period on the value of financial institutions. This approach does give the correct direction of the exposure of the value of a financial institution to interest rates under two highly restricted conditions, however:

1. If the fact that the institution has more assets repricing than liabilities in the current period implies that it also has more liabilities repricing than assets in *each* subsequent period, and vice versa; and
2. If the shift in the yield curve during the period is parallel.

These conditions ensure that increases in a financial institution's net interest income are associated with increases in its value, and vice versa.

If users of financial reports do not recognize the limitations of this alternative approach, it can lead to incorrect and even dangerous conclusions about how financial institutions can and should operate. It is true that net interest income will be high if financial assets (liabilities) are originated or reprice when interest rates on these instruments are high (low). However, in the absence of capital constraints, there is no reason why such originations can occur only when financial assets and liabilities mature. For example, if funds are needed to originate new financial assets, existing financial assets can be sold or securitized or new financial liabilities issued. More important, it is dangerous to think that financial institutions as a group can time the repricing of their assets and liabilities in anticipation of changes in interest rates, since interest rates are difficult to forecast. Even if a given financial institution has some ability to forecast interest rates, its attempt to time the repricing or maturity of assets and liabilities will usually lead to a mismatch of the durations of its assets and liabilities that will make it more interest rate risky, not less so.

Users of this approach often use the term "asset sensitive" to describe a financial institution for which more assets than liabilities reprice in the current period, implying that net interest income will benefit from a rise in interest rates, and "liability sensitive" to describe an institution for which more liabilities than assets reprice in a period, implying that net interest income will be hurt by a rise in interest rates. This terminology is not used in this book, because the sensitivity of a financial institution's value to interest rates depends on the relative durations of its financial assets and liabilities, not on the amount of these items repricing in the current period.

ANALYSIS OF NET INTEREST EARNINGS

This section and the next analyze banks' two required disclosures about net interest earnings. This section analyzes banks' analysis of net interest earnings disclosures. The "Rate-Volume Analysis" section examines their rate-volume analysis disclosures. These disclosures are useful because they provide a basis for understanding the level and change in current net interest earnings and thus for forecasting future net interest earnings. To illustrate the analysis of these disclosures, Golden West's disclosures in 2005 are examined.

SEC Industry Guide 3 requires that banks disclose three things for each of the past three years for each major category of interest-earning asset and interest-paying liability:

1. The average amount outstanding during the period
2. The average yield earned/paid
3. The interest earned/paid, that is, (1) × (2)

Two useful summary statistics also are disclosed. "Interest rate spread" is the difference between the average yield on interest-earning assets and the average yield on interest-paying liabilities. "Net yield on average interest-earning assets" is net interest earnings divided by average interest-earning assets.

The net yield on average interest-earning assets is usually slightly higher than the interest rate spread, reflecting the fact that banks typically have more interest-earning assets than interest-paying liabilities. Specifically, denote the average yield on interest-earning assets (interest-paying liabilities) by r_A (r_L) and the average book values of interest-earning assets and interest-paying liabilities by BV_A and BV_L, respectively. Then interest rate spread is $r_A - r_L$ and net yield on average interest-earning assets is $(r_A \times BV_A - r_L \times BV_L)/BV_A = r_A - r_L \times BV_L/BV_A$, which is usually bigger than interest rate spread because BV_L/BV_A is usually less than one.

Care should be taken in interpreting the analysis of net interest earnings disclosures, for five reasons. First, average interest rates need not reflect end-of-year rates. End-of-year interest rates are generally better predictors of future rates than are the average rates for the year. Relatedly, average balances need not reflect end-of-year balances. Users of financial reports can attempt to remedy this aspect of the disclosures by using end-of-year balances to the extent that they are reported on the balance sheet or in the footnotes on a sufficiently disaggregated basis.

Second, the yields in these disclosures need not reflect current market interest rates for various reasons. For fixed-rate financial instruments, the yields invariably reflect the historical interest rates used in amortized cost accounting; even for the relatively few financial instruments accounted for at fair value on the balance sheet, interest on these instruments still is calculated on an amortized cost basis. For floating-rate instruments, the interest rates in the disclosure reflects the rate at which interest currently accrues, which need not be the current market rate if the instrument has not repriced recently or if restrictions or lags exist in repricing. Relatedly, the average balances reflect book values, which need not equal fair values. The differences of historical and current interest rates and of amortized costs and fair values are likely to be largest for long-term, fixed-rate financial instruments. Users can attempt to remedy this aspect of the disclosures using footnote disclosures of the fair values of financial instruments required under SFAS No. 107, *Disclosures about Fair Value of Financial Instruments* (1991), as discussed in Chapter 6.

Third, financial institutions can make short-term decisions that affect current net interest earnings in a different way than future net interest earnings. For example, a bank can offer below-market rates on its core deposits. Since core deposits are relatively sticky, doing this will tend to increase the bank's net interest earnings in the short run, but it will make it harder for the bank to raise core deposits in the long run and will lead to attrition of existing core deposits over time. Similarly, banks often offer low introductory "teaser" rates on certain loans, especially credit card receivables and floating-rate mortgages. When the amount of origination of floating-rate loans varies over time, the proportion of loans with low teaser rates varies. For example, when a bank originates a larger amount of loans with low teaser rates in the current year than usual, it depresses net interest income relative to its normal level.

Fourth, interest rates earned on loans should be higher when banks accept more credit risk (or any other type of noninterest rate risk). For example, credit card loans should have higher interest rates than prime residential mortgage loans. Accordingly, this disclosure should be interpreted in conjunction with disclosures of banks' asset quality and credit risk.

Fifth, interest rates paid on liabilities should be lower for banks that bear more noninterest costs of raising funds (i.e., with large branch networks). Accordingly, this disclosure should be interpreted in conjunction with disclosures of noninterest expense.

Golden West's 2005 analysis of net interest earnings disclosure is reported in Exhibit 4.4. This disclosure indicates that Golden West's strategy in 2005 is to invest predominantly in loans receivable and mortgage-backed securities, almost all of which are (backed by) one- to four-family residential mortgages, which constitute $111 billion of its $115 billion of average interest-earning assets and earn an average rate of 5.46%. Golden West finances these investments primarily with savings accounts with an average balance of $20 billion paying an average rate of 1.93%, term accounts with an average balance of $33 billion paying an average rate of 3.34%, and Federal Home Loan Bank (FHLB) advances with an average balance of $37 billion paying an average rate of 3.34%. The rates Golden West pays on savings and especially term accounts are high for core deposits at the end of 2005; its strategy during 2005 was to raise the rates paid on term accounts in anticipation of increases in interest rates, to facilitate growth in those deposits.

Golden West's net interest spread is 2.38% and its net yield on average interest-earning assets is 2.56% in 2005. These are relatively low percentages compared to other banks during this year, and they reflect the fact that Golden West does not speculate on the yield curve or bear much credit risk, and it is highly efficient with respect to noninterest expense. Its spread results almost entirely from its role as a funds aggregator repackaging small, liquid deposits into large, less liquid mortgage loans. Its spread fell considerably during the year from the 2.73 to 2.89% level it earned during the period of very low deposit and wholesale borrowing rates from 2002 to 2004, and it appears to be returning to the 2 to 2.2% level Golden West consistently earned during the decade up to 2000.

Comparison of the 2004 and 2005 average balance columns in Exhibit 4.4 indicates substantial asset growth and some liability composition changes for Golden West during 2005. Golden West's interest-earning assets grew from $92 billion in 2004 to $115 billion in 2005. This growth was almost entirely in loans receivable and mortgage-backed securities, despite the fact that the flattening of the yield curve in 2005 reduced the affordability of Golden West's adjustable-rate mortgages relative to fixed-rate mortgages. This growth was financed primarily by increases in term accounts, which grew from an average balance of $12 billion to $33 billion, and FHLB advances, which grew from an average balance of $28 billion to $36 billion. In contrast, savings accounts dropped from $32 billion to $20 billion.

As noted, Golden West's net interest spread and net yield on average interest-earning assets both declined considerably from 2004 to 2005. For example its spread declined by .35% from 2.73% to 2.38%, reflecting a lesser increase in the average yield on earning assets (.87%) than on interest-bearing liabilities (1.22%). This compression of its spread seems likely to continue in 2006, given the sharper rise in end-of-year yields compared to average yields for interest-bearing liabilities than for earning assets and Golden West's historical much lower spread. Alternatively, the relatively sluggish rise in the end-of-year yield on earning assets may be attributable to lags in the indices Golden West uses in repricing its residential mortgage assets, a temporary effect.

RATE-VOLUME ANALYSIS

The SEC requires in Industry Guide 3 that banks disclose for each of the past two years for each major category of interest-earning asset and interest-bearing liability the change in net interest earnings due to:

- Pure volume effects (i.e., the difference between the current and prior years' average balances times the prior year's average interest rate)
- Pure interest rate effects (i.e., the difference between the current and prior years' average interest rates times the prior year's average balance)
- Interactive volume/rate effects (i.e., the difference between current and prior years' average balances times the difference between current and prior years' average interest rates)

EXHIBIT 4.4 Golden West Financial Corporation, Average Daily Balances, Annualized Yield, and End-of-Period Yield for Earning Assets and Interest-Bearing Liabilities at and for the Years Ended December 31 ($ in thousands)

	2005			2004			2003		
	Average Daily Balances (*a*)	Average Yield	End of Period Yield	Average Daily Balances (*a*)	Average Yield	End of Period Yield	Average Daily Balances (*a*)	Average Yield	End of Period Yield
ASSETS									
Loans receivable and MBS (*b*)	$111,101,985	5.46%	6.05%	$89,149,520	4.61%	4.75%	$69,852,274	4.92%	4.61%
Investments	1,703,970	3.89	4.11 (*c*)	1,475,869	1.77	2.08 (*c*)	3,632,896	1.31	.93 (*c*)
Invest. in capital stock of FHLBs	1,709,786	4.17	n/a (*d*)	1,335,559	3.33	n/a (*d*)	1,125,097	3.63	n/a (*d*)
Earning assets	$114,515,741	5.41%	6.03%	$91,960,948	4.54%	4.73%	$74,610,267	4.73%	4.54%
LIABILITIES									
Deposits:									
Checking accounts	$ 4,868,331	1.46%	1.69%	$ 5,669,317	1.38%	1.35%	$ 5,070,536	1.56%	1.38%
Savings accounts (*e*)	19,507,640	1.93	2.20	31,932,705	1.80	1.94	27,251,850	1.96	1.72
Term accounts	33,030,346	3.34	3.78	11,723,928	2.48	2.74	12,205,343	2.67	2.45
Total deposits	57,406,317	2.70	3.24	49,325,950	1.91	2.08	44,527,729	2.11	1.85
Advances from FHLBs	36,531,354	3.34	4.33	28,372,344	1.58	2.30	19,621,477	1.38	1.28
Reverse repurchases	4,602,694	3.38	4.30	3,279,313	1.51	2.23	803,481	1.13	1.13
Other borrowings (*f*)	9,197,410	3.66	4.55	5,355,996	2.20	2.78	4,921,266	2.09	2.06
Interest-bearing liabilities	$107,737,775	3.03%	3.78%	$86,333,603	1.81%	2.22%	$69,873,953	1.89%	1.67%

EXHIBIT 4.4 *(Continued)*

	2005			2004			2003		
	Average Daily Balances (*a*)	Average Yield	End of Period Yield	Average Daily Balances (*a*)	Average Yield	End of Period Yield	Average Daily Balances (*a*)	Average Yield	End of Period Yield
Average net yield		2.38%			2.73%			2.84%	
Primary spread			2.25%			2.51%			2.87%
Net interest income	$ 2,935,071			$ 2,618,605			$ 2,208,384		
Net yield on average earning assets (*g*)		2.56%			2.85%			2.96%	

(*a*) Includes balances of assets and liabilities that were acquired and matured within the same month.

(*b*) Includes nonaccrual loans (90 days or more past due).

(*c*) Freddie Mac stock pays dividends; no end-of-period interest yield applies.

(*d*) FHLB stock pays dividends; no end-of-period interest yield applies.

(*e*) Includes money market deposit accounts and passbook accounts.

(*f*) As of December 31, 2005, the Company had entered into three interest rate swaps to effectively convert certain fixed-rate debt to variable-rate debt. The effect of the interest rate swaps is reflected in the average yield and end-of-period yield.

(*g*) Net interest income divided by daily average of earning assets.

Applying notation developed earlier, these effects can be represented as follows. The change in net interest revenue during the period is $r_{At}BV_{A,t} - r_{At-1}BV_{A,t-1}$. With some straightforward algebra, this amount can be decomposed into the pure volume effect, $r_{At-1}\Delta BV_{A,t}$, the pure rate effect, $BV_{A,t-1}\Delta r_{At}$, and the interactive effect, $\Delta r_{At}\Delta BV_{A,t}$. The SEC allows the interactive effect to be allocated on a consistent basis to the pure volume and rate effects, which in practice usually means in proportion to the relative magnitudes of the pure effects.

These proportions will not be between zero and 1 if the pure rate and pure volume effects have opposite signs, which can have odd implications for the reported rate and volume effects, especially if the absolute magnitudes of the pure effects are close. For example, assume $BV_{A,t-1} = 8$, $BV_{A,t} = 10$, $r_{At-1} = .06$, and $r_{At} = .05$, so that the pure rate effect is $-.08 = 8 \times -.01$, the pure volume effect is $.12 = .06 \times 2$, the sum of the pure effects is .04, and the interactive effect is $-.02 = -.01 \times 2$. In this example, the portion of the interactive effect applied to the pure rate effect is $.04 = -.02 \times (-.08/.04)$, yielding a reported rate effect of $-.04$, and the portion of the interactive effect applied the pure volume effect is $-.06 = -.02 \times (.12/.04)$, yielding a reported volume effect of .06.

The rate-volume analysis disclosure is merely a convenience, since the user of financial reports could with some tedium construct it from the previously described analysis of net interest earnings earned disclosure and in fact could distinguish the pure and interactive effects in the process. Still, this disclosure makes changes in a bank's strategy for net interest income clear at a glance, with the big numbers in absolute value indicating the big effects.

Golden West's 2005 rate-volume analysis disclosure is reported in Exhibit 4.5. This disclosure clearly indicates the previously described sizable increases in loans receivable and mortgage-backed securities, term accounts, and FHLB advances and the sizable decrease in savings accounts during 2005. One can also see that average yields rose for all assets and liabilities, though less so for assets.

REPRICING GAP DISCLOSURES

Repricing gap disclosures report the entire book value of each main type of interest-earning asset and interest-paying liability that reprices in various intervals. Different banks use different intervals, but the most commonly used are less than one year, one to five years, and beyond five years. Repricing gap disclosures provide a somewhat crude indication of the sensitivity of banks to movements in interest rates at these points on the yield curve.

Prior to 1998, all banks disclosed repricing gap. Although there was no written requirement for these disclosures, their unanimous provision suggests the SEC leaned on banks to make them. A fairly large number of banks eliminated or reduced repricing gap disclosures in 1998 or subsequent years, presumably because they overlap with the SEC's market risk disclosures.

Despite the fact that they are no longer uniformly provided, users of financial reports should understand repricing gap disclosures for three reasons:

1. Many banks still disclose repricing gap, which indicates a bank's strategy regarding interest rate risk in an intuitive way using descriptive terminology. This terminology applies directly to the analysis of interest rate risk using market risk disclosures in the tabular format.
2. Repricing gap disclosures invariably provide incremental information beyond market risk disclosures when these disclosures are not in the tabular format.
3. Under SEC Industry Guide 3, banks must disclose the amount of securities, loans, and deposits in different maturity or repricing intervals in financial reports, and some repricing information is provided in regulatory reports as well; these disclosures provide the user of financial reports with some ability to construct repricing gap, especially for simple banks such as thrifts.

In repricing gap disclosures, "gap" refers to differences in the amounts of financial assets and liabilities repricing in a given interval, and it is used in two different senses:

1. Referring to a specific time interval. In this sense, "negative gap" means more liabilities reprice than assets in that interval, and "positive gap" means that more assets reprice than liabilities in that interval. This is now the more common usage.
2. Referring to early versus late time intervals, or, equivalently, to whether a financial institution's assets reprice quicker or slower than its liabilities. "Negative gap" in this sense means that more liabilities reprice than assets in early intervals, and more assets reprice than liabilities in late intervals. "Positive gap" in this sense means that more assets reprice than liabilities in early intervals, and more liabilities reprice than assets in late intervals. Prior to the thrift crisis, thrifts were invariably negative gap in this sense, although this is no longer the case.

Repricing gap disclosures are limited in at least seven respects:

1. The intervals are generally quite wide, so they provide a crude indication of repricing interval.
2. The entire book value of a given financial instrument typically is placed in a single repricing interval, despite the fact that the instrument may have cash flows that occur in prior intervals. This makes the calculation of duration difficult.
3. Some financial assets, such as residential mortgages and mortgage-backed securities, include prepayment options, and some financial liabilities include put, call, or conversion options. While historical rates of prepayment or other option exercise usually are incorporated into repricing gap disclosures, options whose probability of exercise depends on interest

EXHIBIT 4.5 Golden West Financial Corporation, Volume and Rate Analysis of Interest Income and Interest Expense Average for the Years Ended December 31 ($ in thousands)

				Increase/Decrease in Income/Expense Due to Changes in Volume and Rate (*a*)					
	2005	2004	2003	2005 versus 2004			2004 versus 2003		
	Income/ Expense (*b*)	Income/ Expense (*b*)	Income/ Expense (*b*)	Volume	Rate	Total	Volume	Rate	Total
Interest Income									
Loans receivable and MBS	$6,062,312	$4,108,339	$3,439,799	$1,118,240	$835,733	$1,953,973	$870,816	$ (202,276)	$668,540
Investments	66,218	26,060	47,691	4,579	35,579	40,158	(51,629)	29,998	(21,631)
Invest. in capital stock of FHLBs	71,366	44,457	40,854	14,116	12,793	26,909	6,495	(2,892)	3,603
Total interest income	6,199,896	4,178,856	3,528,344	1,136,935	884,105	2,021,040	825,682	(175,170)	650,512
Interest Expense									
Deposits:									
Checking accounts	71,150	78,417	78,900	(12,125)	4,858	(7,267)	(8,108)	7,625	(483)
Savings accounts (*c*)	377,062	575,039	533,402	(243,972)	45,995	(197,977)	77,900	(36,263)	41,637
Term accounts	1,102,305	291,037	325,821	682,038	129,230	811,268	(12,526)	(22,258)	(34,784)
Total deposits	1,550,517	944,493	938,123	425,941	180,083	606,024	57,266	(50,896)	6,370
Advances from FHLBs	1,221,795	448,535	269,793	158,478	614,782	773,260	133,812	44,930	178,742

EXHIBIT 4.5 *(Continued)*

	2005	2004	2003	Increase/Decrease in Income/Expense Due to Changes in Volume and Rate (*a*)					
				2005 versus 2004			2004 versus 2003		
	Income/ Expense (*b*)	Income/ Expense (*b*)	Income/ Expense (*b*)	Volume	Rate	Total	Volume	Rate	Total
Reverse repurchases	155,511	49,589	9,048	26,098	79,824	105,922	36,482	4,059	40,541
Other borrowings	337,002	117,634	102,996	113,556	105,812	219,368	9,387	5,251	14,638
Total interest expenses	3,264,825	1,560,251	1,319,960	724,073	980,501	1,704,574	236,947	3,344	240,291
Net interest income	$2,935,071	$2,618,605	$2,208,384	$ 412,862	$ (96,396)	S 316,466	$588,735	$ (178,514)	$410,221
Net interest income increase (decrease) as a percentage of average earning assets (*d*)				.36%	(.08%)	.28%	.64%	(.19%)	.45%

(*a*) The change in volume is calculated by multiplying the difference between the average balance of the current year and the prior year by the prior year's average yield. The change in rate is calculated by multiplying the difference between the average yield of the current year and the prior year by the prior year's average balance. The mixed changes in rate/volume are calculated by multiplying the difference between the average balance of the current year and the prior year by the difference between the average yield of the current year and the prior year. This amount is then allocated proportionately to the volume and rate changes calculated previously.

(*b*) The effects of interest rate swap activity have been included in income and expense of the related assets and liabilities.

(*c*) Includes money market deposit accounts and passbook accounts.

(*d*) Includes nonaccrual loans (90 days or more past due).

rates cannot properly be described in a static portrayal of interest rate sensitivity such as repricing gap.

4. Core deposits can have effective duration (i.e., are sticky) without having any maturity. In this regard, different banks classify core deposits differently. Some, like Golden West, classify core deposits as having a zero repricing interval, while others use deposit rollover rates published by the Office of Thrift Supervision (OTS) to classify core deposits statistically into repricing intervals. Conceptually, the treatment of core deposits should reflect the behavior of both depositors and the bank. For example, a bank that has a policy of paying higher rates on core deposits, as Golden West does, effectively renders its core deposits as shorter repricing, regardless of their stickiness. In contrast, a bank that chooses to milk its core deposits will have slower repricing but also may lose depositors at a faster rate than implied by the OTS rollover rates.
5. The interest rate indices on which repricing of floating-rate financial instruments are based often include lags—usually of a month or two, but sometimes longer—that are not reflected in repricing gap disclosures.
6. Repricing may not fully align rates earned or paid with market rates, due to repricing caps or floors.
7. Repricing gap can change quickly, especially through the use of derivatives such as interest rate swaps.

Despite these limitations, research shows that repricing gap is significantly related to banks' interest rate risk and hedging behavior.[2]

Exhibit 4.6 reports Golden West's 2005 repricing gap disclosure. Golden West reports it is positive gap in the zero- to three-month interval and negative gap in all subsequent intervals. Almost all of the action is in the zero- to three-month interval, where $120 billion of Golden West's $123 billion of interest-earning assets reprice due to its reliance on adjustable-rate mortgages and mortgage-backed securities. Similarly, $89 billion of its $115 billion of interest-paying liabilities reprice in this interval. In its discussion of this disclosure, Golden West indicates that its adjustable-rate loans actually reprice somewhat more slowly than its short-duration liabilities, however, due to lags in the repricing indices for its loans.

Golden West's emphasis on very quickly repricing assets and liabilities makes it close to immune to shifts in the yield curve. In this regard, Golden West states in its 2005 Form 10-K filing that "a 200 basis point rate increase sustained over a thirty-six month period would initially, but temporarily, reduce our primary spread [due to the lags in the repricing indices for its loans mentioned above], and would not adversely affect our long-term profitability and financial strength."

It is useful to compare Golden West's modest interest rate risk to that of Washington Federal, a thrift that primarily holds fixed-rate mortgage-related assets that it finances with shorter maturity liabilities. A condensed

EXHIBIT 4.6 Golden West Financial Corporation, Repricing of Interest-Earning Assets and Interest-Bearing Liabilities and Repricing Gaps as of December 31, 2005 ($ in millions)

	Projected Repricing (*a*)				
	0–3 Months	**4–12 Months**	**1–5 Years**	**Over 5 Years**	**Total**
Earning Assets:					
Investments	$ 1,702	$ 2	$ -0-	$ -0-	$ 1,704
MBS:					
Adjustable rate	1,113	-0-	-0-	-0-	1,113
Fixed rate	15	34	150	172	371
Loans receivable:					
Adjustable rate	114,730	1,363	817	-0-	116,910
Fixed rate held for investment	77	165	408	240	890
Fixed rate held for sale	82	-0-	-0-	-0-	82
Other (*b*)	2,080	-0-	-0-	129	2,209
Total	$119,799	$ 1,564	$ 1,375	$ 541	$123,279
Interest-Bearing Liabilities:					
Deposits (*c*)	$ 36,479	$ 20,718	$ 2,960	$ 1	$ 60,158
FHLB advances	37,436	328	692	505	38,961
Other borrowings	12,739	200	2,154	495	15,588
Impact of interest rate swaps	1,900	-0-	(1,900)	-0-	-0-
Total	$ 88,554	$ 21,246	$ 3,906	$1,001	$114,707
Repricing gap	$ 31,245	$ (19,682)	$(2,531)	$ (460)	$ 8,572
Cumulative gap	$ 31,245	$ 11,563	$ 9,032	$8,572	
Cumulative gap as a percentage of total assets	25.1%	9.3%	7.2%		

(*a*) Based on scheduled maturity or scheduled repricing; loans and MBS reflect scheduled amortization and projected prepayments of principal based on current rates of prepayment.

(*b*) Includes primarily cash in banks and Federal Home Loan Bank (FHLB) stock.

(*c*) Deposits with no maturity date, such as checking, passbook, and money market deposit accounts, are assigned zero months.

repricing gap disclosure for Washington Federal is reported in Exhibit 4.7, along with more detailed maturity and repricing information about its loans. Like many traditional thrifts prior to the thrift crisis, Washington Federal's repricing gap disclosure indicates it is strongly negative gap in the zero- to one-year interval and strongly positive gap in intervals beyond four years. This disclosure clearly incorporates assumptions about the prepayment of Washington Federal's fixed-rate mortgages, because its disclosures about the maturity of its loans indicate it has far larger positive gap exposures at long maturities. If prepayment turns out to be slower than assumed (say because interest rates rise and the residential real estate market turns down, events that have already occurred to some extent), then Washington Federal's repricing gap exposures will be larger than disclosed. Moreover, although not reported in Exhibit 4.7, Washington Federal discloses that $1.7 billion of its liabilities (FHLB advances and reverse repurchase agreements) included embedded options (call options exercisable by the counterparty) that exacerbate its repricing gap exposure if interest rates rise. As a result of these exposures, Washington Federal's value would fall considerably if the yield

EXHIBIT 4.7 Washington Federal, Inc.'s Repricing Disclosures for the Year Ending September 30, 2005 ($ in thousands)

Interest Rate Risk

The Company accepts a high level of interest rate volatility as a result of its policy to originate fixed-rate single-family home loans that are longer term than the short-term characteristics of its liabilities of customer accounts and borrowed money. The following table shows the estimated repricing periods for earning assets and paying liabilities.

	Repricing Period			
	Within 1 Year	After 1 Year to Before 4 Years	Thereafter	Total
As of September 30, 2005				
Earning Assets*	$ 2,547,230	$ 2,224,709	$3,294,572	$ 8,066,511
Paying Liabilities	$(4,673,467)	(1,480,044)	(762,994)	(6,916,505)
Excess (Liabilities) Assets	$(2,126,237)	$ 744,665	$2,531,578	
Excess as % of Total Assets	−25.82%			
Policy limit for one year excess	−60.00%			

*Asset repricing period includes estimated prepayments based on historical activity.

EXHIBIT 4.7 *(Continued)*

Loans Receivable

The Company originates adjustable and fixed interest rate loans, which at September 30, 2005, consisted of the following:

Fixed-Rate		Adjustable-Rate	
Term to Maturity	**Book Value**	**Term to Rate Adjustment**	**Book Value**
Within 1 year	$ 49,259	Less than 1 year	$ 976,907
1 to 3 years	103,122	1 to 3 years	246,653
3 to 5 years	35,766	3 to 5 years	102,301
5 to 10 years	221,593	5 to 10 years	5,317
10 to 20 years	509,041	10 to 20 years	8,462
Over 20 years	4,333,854	Over 20 years	—
	$5,252,635		$1,339,640

curve shifted upward. Washington Federal argues that the additional spread it earns from accepting this interest rate risk is worth it, noting that it has never recorded a monthly operating loss. It is important to recognize that the measure of operating income referred to in this statement reflects interest revenue and expense measured on an amortized cost basis and does not include unrealized fair value gains and losses.

NOTES

1. Federal Reserve Board, www.federalreserve.gov/releases/h15/data.htm.
2. M. Flannery and C. James, "The Effect of Interest Rate Changes on the Common Stock Returns of Financial Institutions," *Journal of Finance* 39, No. 4 (1984); and C. Schrand, "The Association between Stock Price Interest Rate Sensitivity and Disclosures about Derivative Instruments," *Accounting Review* 72, No. 1 (1997).

CHAPTER 5

Credit Risk and Losses

Most investments in debt instruments (e.g., loans, leases, debt securities, and retained interests from securitizations) are expected to yield less than the contractually promised payments (i.e., default) with some probability. On default, some portion of the principal and accrued interest invested in the instrument is expected to be lost. The default probability and expected loss conditional on default depend on attributes of the instrument and the borrower as well as economic conditions. To compensate investors for the expected amount and risk of credit losses, the initial yield on a credit-risky debt instrument must include a premium above the yield on a credit-riskless instrument with the same noncredit risks. Contingent lending and financial guarantees (e.g., loan commitments, letters of credit, recourse obligations, and credit derivatives) also expose financial institutions to credit risk, for which they must charge actuarially fair fees, like insurers. After initiation, a credit-risky instrument will likely perform better or worse than expected, so the investor will earn an above- or below-normal return.

Accounting for credit-risky financial instruments not recognized at observed market value generally involves estimating expected future credit losses. This estimation requires judgment, the extent of which varies across instruments. For example, large portfolios of individually small and homogeneous credit card receivables have more statistically predictable credit losses than do individually large and heterogeneous commercial real estate loans. The need for judgment in estimating credit losses allows financial institutions to manage net income, regulatory capital, and other accounting numbers. For example, during the bank crises from the mid-1970s to early 1990s and to a lesser extent the 2001 to 2002 recession, the concern was that banks underreserve for credit losses in an attempt to appear more profitable or solvent. In contrast, during the good economic times from the mid-1990s through 2000 and to a lesser extent from 2003 to the present, the concern was that banks overreserve for credit losses to store income for future periods.

The Securities and Exchange Commission (SEC) and bank regulators and accounting standard setters have addressed these concerns through a number of actions since 1998. Most notably, in November 1998 the SEC required SunTrust Banks to reduce its perceived overstated allowance for loan losses by $100 million (about 11%), with the public nature of this act clearly intended as a signal to the banking industry as a whole. In July 2001, the SEC issued Staff Accounting Bulletin (SAB) No. 102, *Selected Loan Loss Allowance Methodology and Documentation Issues,* which requires banks to have systematic, consistently applied (e.g., across the business cycle), documented, auditable methods for calculating the allowance for loan losses. In July 2002, the SEC agreed to a cease-and-desist order with PNC Financial that dealt with various transactions in which PNC transferred (and treated as sold, despite retaining control over and essentially all of the risk of) nonperforming assets without having adequately reserved for the associated credit losses prior to the transfer. Over this period, the SEC has also explicitly raised its expectations about management's discussion of the allowance for loan losses in financial reports in various significant respects. Although bank regulators publicly disagreed with the SEC around the time of the SunTrust restatement regarding whether banks were overreserved for credit losses,[1] their recent rulemaking largely mirrors SAB No. 102.[2] Accounting standard setters have changed the accounting for acquired impaired loans and have proposed to make broader changes in the accounting for credit losses.

This chapter describes the accounting and disclosure rules for thrifts and commercial banks (banks) regarding credit losses and risk on their loan portfolios. As in Chapter 4, the focus is on banks because of the unusually detailed disclosures required of them under SEC Industry Guide 3, but credit risk is also a significant concern for many other financial institutions, such as subprime mortgage banks, lessors, and life insurers. Loans and other debt instruments are the main source of credit risk for the vast majority of banks, although a few very large banks, such as JPMorgan Chase, assume credit risk primarily through the other types of credit-risky exposures mentioned earlier. For these very large banks, the analyst must assess the aggregate credit risk of their various exposures. The assessment of banks' loan loss reserve adequacy and loan portfolio quality using financial report information is illustrated using disclosures from Golden West's 2005 Form 10-K filing and various other sources.

The first section briefly summarizes the economics of credit risk and related financial economics research. The second section describes the main accounts for loans and loan losses. In the third and fourth sections, the distinct accounting and disclosure rules for estimated credit losses on unimpaired and impaired loans, respectively, are described. The fifth section illustrates the use of standard accounting ratios to assess banks' loan loss reserve adequacy and loan portfolio quality. Empirical research on the management and market valuation of the allowance and provision for loan losses is briefly summarized in the final section. Appendix 5A includes a "classic case" on SunTrust Banks' 1998 restatement of its allowance for loan losses.

ECONOMICS OF CREDIT RISK

For a bank to accept credit risk, it must expect to be paid either interest at a sufficiently large premium above the risk-free rate or an actuarially fair fee. The required credit risk premium or fee depends on four main determinants:

1. The probability that the borrower will default
2. The expected loss conditional on default
3. The variability of the loss
4. The institution's ability to diversify losses within its own portfolio or to transfer them to a third party

The first of these determinants reflects the fact that credit risk has a discrete aspect—a default either occurs or it does not—which is similar to insurance risk. Theoretical research predicts and empirical research finds that the first two of these determinants are positively correlated,[3] reflecting macroeconomic factors and the role of collateral, and the other determinants likely are as well.

Macroeconomic and industry conditions (e.g., interest rates, growth) and attributes of both the financial instrument (e.g., principal amount, maturity, age, collateral, and covenants) and the borrower (e.g., liquidity, solvency, profitability, and operating risk) affect each of the first three determinants, sometimes in subtle ways. For example, the age of a loan affects the probability of default, because borrowers are unlikely to default immediately after receiving cash. As a result, the assessment of credit risk is contextual for individual exposures and involves nontrivial difficulties in aggregating across exposures.

Regarding the fourth determinant, the institution's ability to diversify credit risk in its own portfolio depends on the correlations of default for the financial instruments in its portfolio. Not surprisingly, defaults tend to be correlated in time periods, industry groups, and geographical areas as well as among significant counterparties. The institution's ability to transfer credit risk to a third party depends on the willingness of financial markets to accept credit risk, which varies over time, often but not always tracking the business cycle. For example, credit risk premia rose sharply during the hedge fund crisis in the second half of 1998, when lenders shunned credit risk despite no significant economic downturn. After returning to normal levels in 1999, credit risk premia rose in the second half of 2000 and were high in 2001 and 2002, as financial institutions tightened credit standards as the economy turned down. Credit risk premia have been fairly low from mid-2003 through 2006. Because credit risk premia tend to track the business cycle, they also tend to stay above or below average for relatively long periods; research shows that market average credit risk premia revert to their means over one to four years.[4] Research also shows that changes in the credit risk premia on individual bonds are driven primarily by market-wide demand and supply conditions rather than by observable indicators of changes in the credit risk of the bond's issuer.[5]

Reflecting the difficulties in modeling credit risk, historically credit risk has been estimated primarily using elaborate statistical models developed by academics, banks, bond rating agencies, and others beginning in the mid-1960s.[6] These models explain debt instruments' credit risk measured in various ways, including the probability of default, credit ratings, and loan classifications (e.g., accrual, special mention, substandard, doubtful, and loss). The models examine both the levels of these credit-risk measures and the probabilities with which those levels migrate favorably or unfavorably over time. The explanatory variables in these models are primarily accounting ratios, which typically are chosen through data mining exercises rather than on theoretical grounds. The optimal choice and weighting of explanatory variables depend critically on the assumed "loss function"—for example, on assumptions about the relative costs of incorrectly classifying a good loan as bad versus a bad loan as good.

In the past decade, the theory of credit risk has developed rapidly and is converging in many respects with the theory of interest rate risk (e.g., duration and the yield curve) discussed in Chapter 4.[7] In this theory, the market prices defaultable securities using discount rates that include a premium to compensate for credit risk, generating a separate yield curve for each given level of credit risk. Credit risk interacts in subtle ways with maturity, however, so that yield curves for instruments with different levels of credit risk generally are not parallel. For example, currently low-risk borrowers are unlikely to default quickly, since even if they turn unprofitable it takes them a while to erode their equity and cash reserves. Thus their credit risk premia tend to rise over some range of maturities. In contrast, currently high-risk borrowers are more likely to default relatively quickly. Moreover, if they survive sufficiently long, their credit risk usually moderates. This fact implies that credit risk premia for relatively high-risk borrowers tend to decline with maturity.

Complementing this theoretical development, the recent rise of the markets for credit derivatives and risky asset securitizations has made credit risk premia more observable, resulting in a boom in research on credit risk estimation using market information.[8] An issue in this research is that credit risk premia for one type of financial instrument (e.g., credit derivatives) invariably correspond imperfectly to credit risk premia for other types of financial instruments issued by or referenced to the credit of the same borrower (e.g., bonds), due to differences in the contractual features of the instruments and the demand and supply characteristics of the markets in which they trade. In addition, the practical usefulness of this research naturally hinges on the market's ability to assess credit risk, which varies across types of financial instruments and borrowers. Still, the development of these markets is the primary reason why the Basel Committee decided in the Basel II Capital Accord to allow banks to estimate their risk-based capital using either external or internal credit ratings.

ACCOUNTS FOR LOANS AND LOAN LOSSES

The accounting for banks' loan assets differs depending on whether the bank intends to hold the loans in portfolio or for sale. It also differs for purchased loans for which it was probable at the time of purchase that the bank would receive all the contractual payments on the loans due to the lack of creditworthiness of the borrower (hereafter "acquired impaired loans"). This section first describes in detail the accounting for loans that are held in portfolio and that are not acquired impaired loans (i.e., that were originated by the bank or are acquired unimpaired loans). This section then briefly describes the differences in the accounting for loans held for sale and for acquired impaired loans.

A gross asset, loans outstanding, reports the remaining contractual principal on loans held in portfolio, with a separate interest receivable account reporting interest accrued but not yet received. The sum of loans outstanding and interest receivable equals the present value of the contractually promised future payments on loans. For each loan, this present value is calculated using an "effective interest rate" that is determined at the origination or purchase of the loan. This effective interest rate is the internal rate of return that equates the initial contractual principal to the present value of the contractually promised payments. This rate includes a credit risk premium that reflects both the expected amount of credit losses, which is not risk per se, and the priced (e.g., nondiversifiable) variability of those losses, which is risk. This rate is higher than the internal rate of return that equates the initial contractual principal to the present value of the expected payments on the loan, which reflects only the priced variability of losses.

A contra-asset account, the allowance for loan losses, reports the portion of loans outstanding that the bank's management estimates will not be received, although aspects of accounting rules to be discussed imply that the allowance for loan losses generally will not reflect management's best estimates. The provision for loan losses, typically classified as an expense (although it is more properly viewed as partly a contra-revenue and partly a gain or loss, as will be discussed) records the decrease in income from credit losses on loans in the period.

The loans outstanding, allowance for loan losses, and provision for loan losses accounts articulate in various ways that are depicted in schematic T accounts in Exhibit 5.1. Standard bookkeeping conventions are used in this exhibit and in T accounts and journal entries throughout the book. Under these conventions, some accounts (assets and expenses) increase on the debit (left) side and the other accounts (liabilities, owners' equity, and revenues)

EXHIBIT 5.1 Accounts for Loans and Loan Default

Loans Outstanding (Gross Asset)			**Allowance for Loan Losses (Contra-Asset)**			**Provision for Loan Losses (Contra-Revenue or Expense)**	
beginning balance				beginning balance			
+ loan initiations and purchases	− principal payments			+ provision for loan losses (unimpaired loans)	=	+ provision for loan losses (unimpaired loans)	
	− loan sales and securitizations						
	− net loan charge-offs	=	− net loan charge-offs	+ loan write-downs (impaired loans)	=	+ loan write-downs (impaired loans)	
= ending balance				= ending balance			

increase on the credit (right) side. Contra accounts increase on the side opposite to the accounts they are deductions from (e.g., a contra-asset increases on the credit side). It is not necessary to know these conventions to follow the discussion, however, because increases and decreases in T accounts and journal entries always are indicated using plus and minus signs.

Loans outstanding increase with the principal amount of new loans, whether initiated or purchased by the bank. Loans outstanding decrease with principal payments, with the loan principal that is sold or securitized, and with gross charge-offs of loans net of recoveries of prior charge-offs. The principal cash flows on loans held in portfolio are classified as investing on the cash flow statement. While there is very little authoritative guidance as to when loan charge-offs should be recorded, this should occur only when a loan is deemed to be uncollectible with high probability. Exceptions to this principle are reflected in the requirements of the Federal Financial Institutions Examination Council (FFIEC, a cooperative group of the main bank regulators) for consumer loans, revised in 1999. Under these requirements, revolving loans (e.g., credit card receivables) must be charged off no later than 180 days past due, and closed-end (e.g., installment) loans must be charged off no later than 120 days past due, regardless of the probability of collection.

The allowance for loan losses increases with the provision for loan losses and decreases with net loan charge-offs each period. By reducing both loans outstanding and the allowance for loan losses, the charge-off of a loan essentially removes all traces of that loan from the bank's books.

The allowance for loan losses, provision for loan losses, and net loan charge-offs each provide distinct information about loan default. The allowance for loan losses is a "stock" measure that reflects bank management's estimate of future credit losses on its loans outstanding. This estimate should incorporate the size and composition of the loan portfolio, the default probabilities on loans in the portfolio, and the expected losses conditional on default. The provision for loan losses and net loan charge-offs are both "flow" measures of credit losses during the period, but of very different natures. The provision for loan losses reflects bank management's estimate of the expected credit losses due to initiating and holding loans during the period. It should incorporate the initial estimates of default probabilities and expected losses conditional on default on the loans initiated during the period; this portion of the provision for loan losses is properly viewed as contra to interest revenue earned over the period the loan is held, not as an expense. It also should incorporate the changes in the default probabilities and expected losses conditional on default on the loans held during the period; this portion of the provision is properly viewed as a gain or loss. In contrast, net loan charge-offs should reflect the realization of default on specific loans held during the period.

Because allowances and provisions for loan losses reflect estimates of future credit losses while loan charge-offs reflect the realization of loan default, the former should be more timely but also more judgmental than the latter. In cases where managerial discretion has been used to delay making provisions for loan losses, however, loan loss provisions and loan charge-offs may occur at close to the same time. For example, this was the case with large commercial banks' less developed country (LDC) loans in the 1980s. Despite the fact that these loans often traded in the early 1980s at a fraction of their book value, banks began significantly to provide for and charge off these loans only in 1987. Banks were able to delay making provisions for these loans in part by continuing to lend more to LDC borrowers. Research on these and other discretionary accounting behaviors is summarized in the section "Research on Banks' Loan Loss Reserves."

Loan charge-offs also include a judgmental component, however, as evidenced by nontrivial percentages of charged-off loans often being subsequently recovered. In fact, one way to overreserve for credit losses without being obvious about it is to adopt a fast charge-off policy that keeps the allowance for loan losses at a reasonable level. This possibility is discussed in the "Loan Portfolio Quality and Loan Loss Reserve Adequacy" section.

Loans held for sale are recorded at lower of cost or fair value, like inventory, under the American Institute of Certified Public Accountants Statement of Position (AICPA SOP) No. 01-6, *Accounting by Certain Entities*

(Including Entities with Trade Receivables) that Lend to or Finance the Activities of Others. (AICPA SOPs are issued in the year indicated by their first two digits.) Unrealized losses on these loans are recorded directly as a reduction to the asset, and no allowance for loan losses is recorded. The principal cash flows on loans held for sale are classified as operating on the cash flow statement.

For acquired impaired loans, AICPA SOP No. 03-3, *Accounting for Certain Loans or Debt Securities Acquired in a Transfer*, requires that at acquisition the gross loans outstanding recorded equal the discounted expected (not contractual) payments on the loans, so that no allowance for loan losses is recorded. Consistent with this balance sheet valuation, SOP No. 03-3 requires that the effective interest rate for these loans be the internal rate of return that equates the initial investment to the present value of the expected payments. Subsequent to acquisition, an allowance is recorded if it is probable the expected cash flows on the loans have decreased below those expected at acquisition, and the effective interest rate is recalculated if it is probable that expected payments have increased significantly.

ACCOUNTING AND DISCLOSURE RULES FOR UNIMPAIRED LOANS

Estimated credit losses are calculated differently for unimpaired and impaired loans. Individual loans are deemed impaired when they meet criteria discussed in the "Accounting and Disclosure Rules for Impaired Loans" section; all other loans are unimpaired. The very general rules governing recognition and measurement of credit losses for unimpaired loans are described next. Significant differences in how these general rules are applied across types of loans are discussed in the "Importance of Loan Type" section. Disclosures of credit losses and risk on loans required in SEC Industry Guide 3 are described in the "Disclosures" section.

Recognition and Measurement

The overarching standard that deals with credit losses is Statement of Financial Accounting Standards (SFAS) No. 5, *Accounting for Contingencies* (1975), which states that loss contingencies should be recognized on the balance sheet (as liabilities or contra-assets) if they are "probable" and the amount of the losses can be "reasonably estimated." Neither "probable" nor "reasonably estimated" is defined precisely. "Probable" usually is interpreted to mean more likely than some fairly high threshold probability, such as 50%. "Reasonably estimated" is clarified somewhat in FASB Interpretation (FIN) No. 14, *Reasonable Estimation of the Amount of a Loss* (1976), which states that if a range of loss can be reasonably estimated, then the most likely amount within the range should be chosen if one exists. If no amount within the range is most likely, then the low end of the range should be chosen. SFAS No.

5's (1975) requirement to record allowances only for loss contingencies that are probable and capable of reliable estimation and FIN No. 14's requirement to choose the low end of the range imply that allowances for loan losses are measured in an anticonservative fashion and so will tend to be revised upward over time as uncertainty about loan default resolves. Because this uncertainty generally is greater for credit-riskier loans, such loans tend to yield larger upward revisions in the allowance for loan losses over time.

The imprecise language used in SFAS No. 5 and FIN No. 14 provides ample room for discretion to be applied to the allowance and provision for loan losses. Although the SEC recently has attempted to mitigate this discretion through the issuance of SAB No. 102, it did not alter those two standards in any way.

Importance of Loan Type

In practice, the methods used to estimate credit losses for unimpaired loans vary across two general types of loan:

1. Individually small and homogenous loans (e.g., credit card receivables and other consumer loans) typically are classified into groups, and statistics based on past experience are used to estimate credit losses. SFAS No. 5's criteria that losses be probable and capable of reliable estimation are usually met *at initiation* for large and homogeneous portfolios, and so an allowance for loan losses will be recorded at that time that should be reasonably close to the expected credit losses on those loans based on historical data. Although some judgment about current market conditions often is used to temper these statistical estimates, this judgment is constrained by the availability and historical predictive power of these estimates. Banks need not use equally reliable statistical methods, however, and they can influence the historical data by charging off loans too quickly and various other actions.
2. Individually large and heterogeneous loans (e.g., commercial and industrial loans and commercial real estate loans) typically are evaluated on a loan-by-loan basis primarily by the loan officers responsible for these loans. SFAS No. 5's recognition criteria often are not met until shortly before this type of loan defaults. As discussed in the "Financial Economic Research on Credit Risk" section, models to estimate credit losses for this type of loan are still developing, and even in the absence of discretion by loan officers, banks can badly misestimate credit losses for this type of loan, especially when economic conditions change quickly. More discretion exists in estimating credit losses for this type of loan, however, and empirical research finds that loan officers' incentives are to hide loan default on the loans they originated.[9]

The two general types of loans just described should be thought of as endpoints on a continuum, with specific types of loans falling somewhere in the continuum. For example, in its 2005 Form 10-K filing, Golden West states how it calculates its allowance for loan losses for its mortgages:

> In order to evaluate the adequacy of the allowance, the Company determines an allocated component and an unallocated component. The allocated component consists of reserves on loans that are evaluated on a pool basis, primarily the large portfolio of one- to four-family loans, as well as loans that are evaluated on an individual basis, such as major multi-family and commercial real estate loans. However, the entire allowance is available to absorb credit losses inherent in the total loan receivable balance.
>
> To evaluate the adequacy of the reserves for pooled loans, a model is used that is based on the Company's historical repayment rates, foreclosure rates, and loss experience over multiple business cycles. Data for the model is gathered using an internal database that identifies and measures losses on loans and foreclosed real estate broken down by age of the loan. To evaluate the adequacy of reserves on individually evaluated loans, impairment is measured based on the fair value of the collateral taking into consideration the estimated sale price, cost of refurbishing the security property, payment of delinquent property taxes, and costs of disposal.
>
> The Company has also established an unallocated component to address the imprecision and range of probable outcomes inherent in the estimates of credit losses. The amount of the unallocated reserve takes into consideration many factors, including trends in economic growth, unemployment, housing market activity, home prices for the nation and individual geographic regions, and the level of mortgage turnover. The ratios of allocated allowance and unallocated allowance to total allowance may change from period to period.

As this passage indicates, even Golden West's portfolio of relatively homogeneous residential mortgages yields an allowance for loan losses that reflects some discretion. The degree of discretion is greater for its less homogeneous "major multi-family and commercial real estate loans."

As noted, a large portfolio of homogenous loans usually will have probable loan default of some amount immediately upon initiation, and so SFAS No. 5 effectively requires that a loan loss provision be recorded immediately for these loans. While this implies banks have relatively little discretion over loan loss provisions for these loans, it also yields poor matching of interest revenues and loan loss provisions for these loans, because no interest revenue is recorded at initiation. The problem is not SFAS No. 5 (1975), but rather that the effective interest rate on the loan is based on contractually promised cash payments and thus rises with expected credit losses. A conceptually preferable approach would be to calculate the effective interest rate using the expected payments at initiation, as SOP No. 03-3 requires for acquired impaired loans. Under this approach, the effective interest rate and thus interest revenue would reflect a premium only for priced variability in credit losses, not for expected credit losses. Provisions for loan losses would be recorded only when credit losses are greater than initial expectations.

Disclosures

Since the extent of credit risk and discretion over the allowance for loan losses varies across loan types, SEC Industry Guide 3 requires that banks disclose information about loans and credit losses in aggregate and by major type of loan, distinguishing domestic and foreign loans. These disclosures are most important for banks that hold a diverse mixture of loans. This section describes these disclosures and illustrates their usefulness using sample disclosures from Golden West's 2005 Form 10-K filing as well as the SunTrust case in the appendix.

SEC Industry Guide 3 requires that banks disclose loans outstanding by type for each of the past five years. Because different types of loans have different credit risk that is accounted for differently, this disclosure helps users of financial reports interpret banks' disclosures of credit losses both at the aggregate level and by loan type. Exhibit 5.2 reports Golden West's disclosures about the composition of its loan portfolio from 2001 to 2005. This disclosure is rather dull due to Golden West's almost complete reliance on fairly homogeneous one- to four-family residential mortgages. SunTrust's more diversified loan portfolio disclosed in its 1998 Form 10-K filing is reported in Exhibit 5A.3—37.8% commercial loans (fairly heterogeneous), 47.3% real estate loans (fairly homogeneous), and 14.9% consumer loans (very homogeneous) in 1998.

Industry Guide 3 basically requires that the allowance for loan losses be decomposed into the amount associated with each type of loan and the amount not allocated to any loan type, although this disclosure can be replaced with a narrative discussion of the risk elements in the loan portfolio. When made, as it usually is now, this disclosure is useful because the size of the allowance for loan losses should vary across types of loans based on their differential credit riskiness and also on the speed of charge-offs, if this speed is too fast or slow. For example, the FFIEC's required policies for consumer loans (especially closed-end loans) imply these loans probably are charged off too quickly on average, thereby reducing the allowance for loan losses attributable to those loans.

Exhibit 5.3 reports Golden West's disclosure of the composition of the allowance for loan losses from 2001 to 2005. The allowance for loan losses for the one- to four-family residential loans and the multifamily and commercial loans are roughly proportionate to the loans outstanding for those types of loans, reflecting the generally similar nature of Golden West's various types of real estate loans. Golden West's allowance for one- to four-family residential real estate loans is almost entirely general to the portfolio, while about 7% of the allowance for multifamily and commercial real estate loans is

EXHIBIT 5.2 Golden West's 2005 Form 10-K Loan Portfolio Composition Disclosure ($ in thousands)

	December 31				
	2005	2004	2003	2002	2001
Loans collateralized by primarily first deeds of trust:					
One- to four-family units	$111,394,353	$ 94,449,233	$69,586,604	$54,934,357	$38,326,759
Over four-family units	4,794,359	4,748,335	3,554,715	3,257,389	2,766,888
Commercial real estate	10,205	15,220	18,598	20,465	29,117
Land	-0-	-0-	-0-	114	199
Loans on deposits	10,509	10,734	11,780	13,240	16,672
Other (*a*)	1,672,539	1,335,657	1,033,881	717,751	451,084
Total loans receivable	117,881,965	100,559,179	74,205,578	58,943,316	41,590,719
MBS with recourse collateralized by:					
One- to four-family units	1,168,480	1,719,982	2,579,288	4,458,582	11,821,868
Over four-family units	-0-	-0-	1,070,760	1,412,487	1,747,751
Total MBS with recourse	1,168,480	1,719,982	3,650,048	5,871,069	13,569,619
Loans receivable and MBS with recourse	$119,050,445	$102,279,161	$77,855,626	$64,814,385	$55,160,338

(*a*) Includes loans in process, net deferred loan costs, allowance for loan losses, and other miscellaneous discounts and reserves.

EXHIBIT 5.3 Golden West's 2005 Form 10-K Filing Composition of Allowance for Loan Losses Disclosure ($ in thousands)

	2005	2004	2003	2002	2001
Real Estate					
1 to 4 units					
General	$283,152	$274,660	$273,894	$263,004	$240,135
Specific	-0-	339	-0-	-0-	-0-
	283,152	274,999	273,894	263,004	240,135
5+ units and commercial					
General	12,062	14,095	15,005	16,521	18,166
Specific	645	1,016	1,038	1,572	2,712
	12,707	15,111	16,043	18,093	20,878
Total	$295,859	$290,110	$289,937	$281,097	$261,013
Ratio of allowance for loan losses to total loans held for investment and MBS with recourse	.25%	.28%	.37%	.43%	.47%

specific to individual loans, reflecting the somewhat less homogeneous nature of the latter types of loans.

More interesting differences in the composition of the allowance for loans losses are evident in Exhibit 5A.3 of the SunTrust case in the appendix. For example, SunTrust's consumer loans constitute 14.9% of its loans outstanding but 44.6% of its allowance for loan losses, because of the high credit losses on these loans. The high percentage of the allowance attributable to consumer loans obtains despite speedy charge-offs of these loans.

Historically, the disclosure of the unallocated portion of the allowance was useful because discretion over the allowance for loan losses often was concentrated in that portion of the allowance. For example, the SEC appears to have decided that SunTrust had overstated its allowance for loan losses in part because of the size of its unallocated allowance. SunTrust originally reported an unallocated allowance for loan losses of 45.6% of the total allowance in its 1997 Form 10-K filing. In its amended 1997 Form 10-K filing submitted in November 1998, SunTrust reduced its unallocated allowance percentage to 37.2%. In its 1998 Form 10-K filing, SunTrust reduced its unallocated allowance percentage to 4.5%.

The SEC has induced banks to reduce the unallocated portion of their allowances for loan losses through the SunTrust restatement and SAB No. 102's requirement that banks have systematic methods for calculating the allowance for loan losses. Although this may have helped reduce banks' exercise of discretion over the allowance for loan losses, it also has made any discretionary behavior that remains more difficult to observe.

Industry Guide 3 also requires the disclosure of beginning and ending balances of the allowance for loan losses, the provision for loan losses, and gross loan charge-offs and recoveries of prior loan charge-offs by major type of loan. This disclosure is useful because loan charge-offs are a relatively nondiscretionary measure of loan default that can be used to assess the adequacy of the allowance and provision for loan losses, as discussed in the "Loan Portfolio Quality and Loan Loss Reserve Adequacy" section. Recoveries of loan charge-offs provide an indication of whether loan charge-offs are being recorded at the proper time; too high a percentage of recoveries indicates too fast a charge-off policy, and vice versa.

If a bank reports the composition of the allowance for loan losses, then the provision for loan losses for each loan type can be inferred, since for each type of loan the change in the allowance equals the provision for loan losses minus net loan charge-offs. The change in the unallocated allowance for loan losses equals the portion of the provision for loan losses not attributable to any specific type of loan.

Exhibit 5.4 presents Golden West's disclosures regarding the activity in its allowance for loan losses from 2001 to 2005. As indicated, Golden West recorded a tiny provision for loan losses of $8.3 million and only $2.5 million net loan charge-offs on its $119.1 billion loan portfolio during 2005, reflecting essentially zero default on mortgages due to booming real estate markets and its conservative credit extension policies. Between 2000 and 2003, Golden West built up its allowance for loan losses by 22% by recording loan loss provisions well in excess of its minimal net loan charge-offs. Golden West has experienced almost no loan default in the past five years and has a healthy allowance for loan losses. Notice that Golden West maintains a separate recourse liability for loans sold and loans securitized and retained. SunTrust's 1998 disclosures regarding the activity in its allowance for loan losses are reported in Exhibit 5A.2 and are a focus of the case in the appendix.

Complementing these disclosure requirements, the SEC expects detailed discussion of period-to-period changes in specific elements of the allowance for loan losses in management's discussion and analysis (MD&A). It also expects clear discussion of the methodology for calculating the allowance for loan losses and any changes in that methodology from prior periods.[10]

Disclosures of significant concentrations of economic risks and of significant accounting estimation risks are required by AICPA SOP No. 94-6, *Disclosures of Certain Significant Risks and Uncertainties*. Disclosures of financial instruments with concentrations of credit risk are required under SFAS

EXHIBIT 5.4 Golden West's 2005 Form 10-K Filing Activity in the Allowance for Loan Losses Disclosure ($ in thousands)

	2005	2004	2003	2002	2001
Beginning allowance for loan losses	$290,110	$289,937	$281,097	$261,013	$236,708
Provision for loan losses charged to expense	8,290	3,401	11,864	21,170	22,265
Loans charged off	(4,363)	(4,613)	(3,633)	(1,943)	(2,425)
Recoveries	1,822	1,385	609	857	351
Net transfer of allowance from recourse liability	-0-	-0-	-0-	-0-	4,114
Ending allowance for loan losses	$295,859	$290,110	$289,937	$281,097	$261,013
Ratio of net charge-offs to average loans outstanding and MBS with recourse	.00%	.00%	.00%	.00%	.00%
Ratio of allowance for loan losses to NPAs	77.4%	84.4%	68.4%	66.2%	66.3%

No. 107, *Disclosures about Fair Value of Financial Instruments* (1991), as amended. These disclosure requirements often apply to banks' loan portfolios. In this regard, Financial Accounting Standards Board (FASB) Staff Position (FSP) SOP 94-6-1 (2005) clarifies that nontraditional loan products which allow zero or negative loan amortization for a period of time, a high initial loan-to-value ratio, a subordinated claim to collateral, or artificially low (i.e., teaser) initial interest rates may trigger these disclosure requirements.

ACCOUNTING AND DISCLOSURE RULES FOR IMPAIRED LOANS

The next section discusses the accounting and disclosure rules for credit losses on impaired loans. The "Nonperforming Loans" section covers SEC Industry Guide 3 required nonperforming loans disclosures.

Impaired Loans

SFAS No. 114, *Accounting by Creditors for Impairment of a Loan* (1993), and SFAS No. 118, *Accounting by Creditors for Impairment of a Loan: Income Recognition and Disclosure* (1994), govern accounting and disclosures for impaired loans. These standards do not apply to individually small, homogeneous loans for which loan losses are estimated at the portfolio level, since impairment is assessed only at the individual loan level. These standards also do not apply to lease financing receivables, presumably because the FASB did not want to revisit lease accounting in these standards.

SFAS No. 114 defines a loan as impaired when it is probable that the contractual payments will not be received. Insignificant delays or shortfalls in payments do not require a loan to be deemed impaired. In contrast, a troubled debt restructuring is by its nature impaired. SFAS No. 118 defines a loan as impaired when the present value of the expected cash flows is less than the book value of the loan. The FASB does not directly acknowledge that the SFAS No. 118 definition of impairment is broader than the SFAS No. 114 definition, since expectations reflect averages that are affected by any probability, no matter how low, while "probable" usually is interpreted to mean more likely than some fairly high threshold probability. In any event, banks appear to use convenient proxies for impairment (e.g., number of days past due unless sufficiently well collateralized) rather than the definitions in either of these standards.

When a specific loan is deemed impaired, SFAS No. 114 requires that the loan be written down to the present value of the expected cash flows using the effective interest rate determined at the initiation of the loan. The provision for loan losses should be increased by the amount of the write-down. The market value of the loan or the fair value of any collateral may be used in place of the present value calculation. SFAS No. 118 requires that the firm disclose the amount of interest revenue recognized on impaired loans and how this revenue is calculated.

The accounting for loan impairment is deficient because an impaired loan is by its nature riskier than an unimpaired loan, all else being equal, and so the effective interest rate used is too low. Still, SFAS No. 114 is significantly tougher than its predecessor SFAS No. 15, *Accounting by Debtors and Creditors for Troubled Debt Restructurings* (1977), which required that a restructured loan be written down only if the undiscounted sum of the restructured payments is less than the book value of the loan, and, if so, that the loan be written down only to the undiscounted sum of the payments.

SFAS No. 118 requires that banks disclose the amount of impaired loans, the portion of the allowance for loan losses devoted to impaired loans, and any interest revenue recorded on impaired loans; some banks go further and provide separate accounts for unimpaired and impaired loans. For example, in its 2005 Form 10-K filing, Golden West makes this disclosure:

> The portion of the allowance for loan losses that was specifically provided for impaired loans was \$645 thousand and \$1.4 million at

December 31, 2005 and 2004, respectively. The average recorded investment in total impaired loans was $347 million and $387 million during 2005 and 2004, respectively. All amounts involving impaired loans have been measured based upon the fair value of the related collateral. The amount of interest income recognized during the years ended December 31, 2005, 2004, and 2003 on the total of impaired loans at each year-end was $10 million (2005), $10 million (2004), and $13 million (2003).

Nonperforming Loans

Industry Guide 3 requires banks to disclose the amounts of nonaccrual loans, past-due loans, loans subject to troubled debt restructurings, and potential problem loans for each of the past five years. "Nonaccrual" means not accruing interest, which usually refers to loans that are more than 90 days past due and not sufficiently well collateralized. "Past due" refers to loans that are more than 90 days delinquent with respect to contractual principal and interest payments, but still accruing interest. Troubled debt restructurings are defined in SFAS No. 15 as restructurings made because of the borrower's financial condition that the creditor would not have otherwise considered; the standard provides a noncomprehensive list of indicators of such restructurings. Nonperforming loans are the sum of nonaccrual loans, past due loans, and restructured troubled debt. Potential problem loans include loans that are performing but for which bank management has serious doubts that the borrower will be able to comply with the current terms of the loan. Nonperforming assets are the sum of nonperforming loans and other real estate owned, which is real estate acquired through foreclosure on mortgaged property. (Be aware that bank regulators define other real estate owned somewhat more broadly.)

The criteria used to determine nonperforming loans are likely to be similar to (or even the same as) the criteria used to assess loan impairment discussed in the "Impaired Loans" section, and so this disclosure overlaps considerably with disclosures of impaired loans. The SEC does not require disclosure of nonperforming loans by type of loan, although some banks make this useful disclosure voluntarily. SunTrust does so in its 1998 Form 10-K filing, reported in Exhibit 5A.1, presumably because of the pressure it received from the SEC to justify its allowance for loan losses.

Nonperforming loans are both timely and nonjudgmental compared to the allowance for loan losses. This is not to say that nonperforming loans are completely nondiscretionary in amount of classification, however. For example, a bank can avoid designating a loan as nonperforming by continuing to lend more to the borrower. Judgmental appraisals of collateral affect designations as sufficiently well collateralized, which determine whether loans are nonaccrual versus past due. Decisions to repossess real estate affect other real estate owned and thus nonperforming assets.

A useful feature of the nonperforming loans disclosure is that it enables the user of financial reports to distinguish the existence of problem loans from the determinants of the expected losses on those loans. For example, a simple way to model the expected losses on a loan portfolio is as the amount of nonperforming loans times the probability of default on nonperforming loans times the percentage loss on nonperforming loans given default, plus the amount of performing loans times the probability of default on performing loans times the percentage loss on performing loans given default. The probability of default on nonperforming loans usually is considerably higher than that on performing loans. The percentage loss conditional on default should be the same for the two types of loans, however, since a performing loan usually will become nonperforming before defaulting.

Exhibit 5.5 presents Golden West's disclosures of its nonperforming loans from 2003 to 2005. During 2004, Golden West's nonperforming loans decreased sharply in total amount and as a percentage of total assets, and this percentage remained essentially constant in 2005. The decrease in 2004 primarily reflected booming real estate markets in California and elsewhere in the United States. It also implies, as shown in Exhibit 5.4, that Golden West's allowance for loan losses rose substantially relative to nonperforming loans in that year.

LOAN PORTFOLIO QUALITY AND LOAN LOSS RESERVE ADEQUACY

"Loan portfolio quality" refers to the credit risk of the loan portfolio, in particular, whether the value of the portfolio has deteriorated or is prone to future deterioration. "Loan loss reserve" adequacy refers to the appropriateness of the allowance and provision for loan losses as stock and flow

EXHIBIT 5.5 Golden West's 2005 Form 10-K Filing Nonperforming Assets and Restructured Troubled Debt Composition Disclosure ($ in thousands)

	December 31		
	2005	**2004**	**2003**
Nonaccrual loans	$373,671	$332,329	$410,064
Foreclosed real estate	8,682	11,461	13,904
Total nonperforming assets	$382,353	$343,790	$423,968
TDRs	$ 124	$ 3,810	$ 3,105
Ratio of NPAs to total assets	.31%	.32%	.51%
Ratio of TDRs to total assets	.00%	.00%	.00%
Ratio of NPAs and TDRs to total assets	.31%	.33%	.51%

measures, respectively, of credit losses, given the quality of the loan portfolio. Assessment of a bank's loan portfolio quality and loan loss reserve adequacy begins with a detailed understanding of the types of loans the bank holds, focusing on concentrations of risk and the current economic conditions that are relevant to those loans. For example, Golden West mostly holds adjustable-rate residential mortgages on property in California, and so it is primarily exposed to the California real estate market and economy. The extent of this exposure is affected and generally mitigated by the fact that Golden West usually originates loans that have moderate size (e.g., it discloses that the average size of its mortgage origination in California in 2005 was $338,000) and have loan-to-value ratios lower than 80% or mortgage insurance. This understanding provides the basis for the interpretation of certain standard ratios. Whenever feasible, a bank's ratios should be compared to those of banks that hold comparable loans. For example, Washington Mutual provides a fairly good comparison for Golden West, although it is considerably larger and more diversified geographically and by type of loan than Golden West. In addition, ratios should be calculated to the extent possible by type of loan, because the ratios behave very differently for different types of loan.

The ratios used to assess loan portfolio quality and loan loss reserve adequacy employ the same four measures of credit losses—the allowance for loan losses, the provision for loan losses, loan charge-offs and recoveries, and nonperforming loans—and so raise many of the same interpretational issues. In this regard, the next section discusses the relative strengths and weaknesses of net loan charge-offs and nonperforming loans as nondiscretionary measures of loan losses, which should be considered in the assessment of both loan portfolio quality and loan loss reserve adequacy. The "Loan Portfolio Quality" and "Loan Loss Reserve Adequacy" sections discuss the respective analyses. Although the assessment of loan portfolio quality is logically prior to and in many respects more important than the assessment of loan loss reserve adequacy, more emphasis is placed on the latter due to its higher accounting content.

Alternative Benchmark Measures of Credit Losses

Since the allowance and provision for loan losses are measured with discretion, less discretionary benchmark measures of credit losses are necessary to assess loan portfolio quality and especially loan loss reserve adequacy. The two most common benchmarks are net loan charge-offs and nonperforming loans. Each of these benchmarks has strengths and weaknesses.

Net loan charge-offs are relatively nondiscretionary because they should be recorded when a loan is known to be uncollectible with high probability. An issue with net loan charge-offs is that a bank that wants to store income for future periods without being too noticeable about it might adopt a fast charge-off policy, so that the allowance for loan losses does not build up suspiciously high. A bank adopting such a policy would experience a large amount of recoveries of prior loan charge-offs. The SEC probably decided that SunTrust had overstated its allowance for loan losses in part because it averaged recoveries equal to almost 40% of gross loan charge-offs from 1993 to 1997. SunTrust charged off consumer loans prior to or at a certain number of days past due (in particular, credit card receivables prior to or at 180 days past due and other consumer loans prior to or at 90 days past due). While the FFIEC requires as of June 1999 that banks charge off credit card receivables no later than 180 days past due and other consumer loans no later than 120 days past due, most banks do not recover such a high percentage of loan charge-offs. In any event, such a high recovery rate is inconsistent with the principle that charge-offs should reflect loans that are uncollectible with high probability.

Another issue with net loan charge-offs is that they can be relatively untimely, especially for large, heterogeneous loans for which charge-off decisions are made loan by loan. This untimeliness is a particular concern when economic conditions are changing. For example, at the beginning of a downturn, net loan charge-offs typically remain low for a while even though credit risk is rising. The opposite is true at the beginning of an upturn. The user of financial reports needs to think carefully about what loan charge-offs in the current period imply for future charge-offs.

Nonperforming loans are generally timelier and less discretionary than net loan charge-offs. An issue is that the implications of a dollar of nonperforming loans for future credit losses can vary considerably depending on the context. Some nonperforming loans default with high probability or yield large losses conditional on default while others have less severe or even no negative consequences. Another issue is that when loans are charged off quickly, as occurs for consumer loans, there may be very few nonperforming loans on the bank's books at any given time, even though loans may become nonperforming with high frequency.

Both net loan charge-offs and nonperforming loans are limited benchmarks in that they are associated with problem loans that may or may not indicate credit risk on other loans in the bank's portfolio. The importance of this limitation depends on how related problem loans are to these other loans.

On balance, net loan charge-offs provide a better benchmark for small, homogenous loans that are charged off quickly using number-of-days-past-due rules, such as credit card receivables, since nonperforming loans are likely to be understated for these loans. Nonperforming loans provide a better benchmark for large, heterogeneous loans that are charged off on a loan-by-loan basis using judgment, since loan charge-offs are likely to be untimely and to vary over time for these loans. Thus the best single benchmark for a given bank depends on the primary kinds of loans the bank holds. Even for specific types of loans for which one of the benchmarks is generally superior, the other benchmark often provides distinct and important insights, however.

Loan Portfolio Quality

Loan portfolio quality depends on the bank's credit risk management skill, loan portfolio composition, and applicable economic conditions, which are often region or industry specific, especially for smaller banks. In assessing loan portfolio quality, analysts usually focus on the ratios of the four main measures of credit losses to loans outstanding, with lower ratios implying higher loan portfolio quality, all else being equal. The allowance for loan losses, provision for loan losses, and net loan charge-offs typically provide better measures of loan portfolio quality than nonperforming loans for homogeneous loans, while the opposite usually is true for heterogeneous loans. Be aware that all of the measures of loan portfolio quality, but especially those involving charge-offs of heterogeneous loans, often lag actual loan portfolio quality.

In this regard, loan portfolio quality can also be assessed using information outside the bank's financial report, which is often far timelier. In particular, banks' exposures to specific troubled borrowers often can be gleaned from various sources, including the borrowers' SEC filings.

As shown in Exhibit 5.6, loan quality measured using the ratios of loan charge-offs and delinquencies (loans more than 30 days past due, which is highly correlated with nonperforming loans) to loans outstanding varied considerably from 1991 to 2005 and across loan types. In 1991, still in the bank crisis period, loan quality was poor for many loan types, with commercial real estate being particularly troubled. Loan quality improved dramatically from 1991 to 1994 and remained very good throughout the remainder of the 1990s for most loan types. The notable exception to this rule is credit card receivables, which experienced higher levels of default during the mid- to late 1990s than previously, reflecting the aggressive behavior of banks in extending consumer credit during this period. Loan quality worsened somewhat in the recessionary period from late 2000 through 2002, especially for commercial and industrial loans, before generally improving through 2005.

Inspection of Exhibits 5.2 through 5.5 indicates that Golden West's loan portfolio quality is exceedingly high regardless of the ratio examined. The case in Appendix 5A examines SunTrust's loan portfolio quality, which, while generally good, varies considerably across its loan types, with its credit card and other consumer loans experiencing far higher levels of net charge-offs than its other loans.

Loan Loss Reserve Adequacy

In assessing the adequacy of loan loss reserves, analysts usually focus on three ratios that incorporate the two less discretionary benchmark measures of credit losses in different ways:

1. The ratio of the allowance for loan losses to nonperforming loans (ALL/NPL)

EXHIBIT 5.6 Net Charge-off and Deliquency Rates for Selected Loan Types, U.S. Commercial Banks, 1991–2005

Net Charge-off Rates

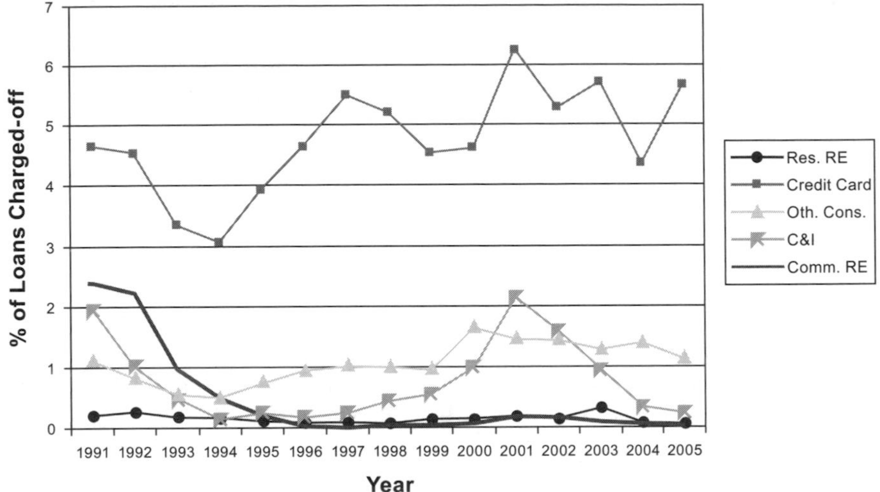

Delinquency Rates

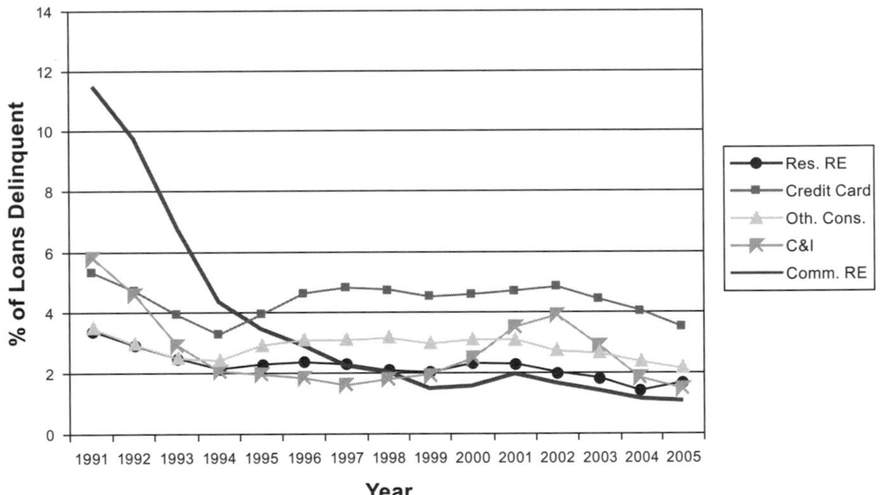

Res. RE refers to residential real estate.
Oth. Cons. refers to other consumer.
C&I refers to commercial and industrial.
Comm. RE refers to commercial real estate.

Source: Federal Financial Institutions Examination Council. Seasonally adjusted annual data for loan charge-offs and delinquencies for the fourth quarter of each year are used to calculate the ratios.

2. The ratio of the allowance for loan losses to net loan charge-offs (ALL/LCO)

3. The ratio of the provision for loan losses to net loan charge-offs (PLL/LCO)

In each ratio, a relatively discretionary variable recognized on the balance sheet or income statement (i.e., the allowance or provision for loan losses) is compared to a relatively nondiscretionary variable that has no direct effect on total assets or income (i.e., nonperforming loans or net loan charge-offs). Each of these ratios is discussed in the text that follows.

The ratio ALL/NPL compares two stock measures of credit losses. In theory, this ratio should rise with the probability that nonperforming loans default and with the expected percentage loss given default on a loan, because the allowance for loan losses should capture expected losses on nonperforming loans, not just the existence of these loans. This ratio should also rise with the ratio of performing to nonperforming loans and with the probability that performing loans default, because the allowance for loan losses should incorporate expected credit losses on all loans, not just nonperforming loans. For most loan types, this ratio should rise in bad economic times and fall in good economic times, because loans are more likely to default and because the expected percentage loss given default on loan is likely to be larger in bad times than in good times. However, the ratio of performing to nonperforming loans tends to be higher in good times than in bad times, offsetting these effects to some extent.

The actual average ALL/NPL for the banking industry exhibits a pattern opposite to that predicted, however. Exhibit 5.7 shows that the ratio of the allowance for loan losses to delinquent loans was very low during the bank crisis period from 1987 to 1991, approximately doubled by 1994 as the condition of banks improved, remained at about this level through 1999, fell during the subsequent economic downturn and bottomed out in 2001, rose through 2004 as economy improved, and then moderated slightly in 2005. This pattern strongly suggests that banks underreserve for loan losses on a relative basis in bad times compared to good times, thereby smoothing their income and Tier 1 capital.

The patterns in this ratio for the banking industry can often be observed at the individual bank level. For example, as reported in Exhibit 5.3, ALL/NPL follows a similar pattern for Golden West from 2001 to 2005, rising from .66 in 2001 to .84 in 2004 and then falling to .77 in 2005. Similarly, the SEC's conclusion that SunTrust was overreserved for loan losses probably reflected in part the increase in SunTrust's ALL/NPL from 3.42 in 1996 to 5.87 in 1997. After the restatement, SunTrust's ALL/NPL declined to 4.56 in 1998. This ratio still seems high, however, since it is consistent with SunTrust losing everything on its nonperforming loans plus $3.56 in performing loans per dollar of nonperforming loans. The alternative view is that this ratio reflects the fact that SunTrust holds a large amount of credit-risky consumer loans that are charged off quickly, thereby reducing nonperforming

EXHIBIT 5.7 Loan Loss Reserve Adequacy Ratios, U.S. Commercial Banks, 1987–2005

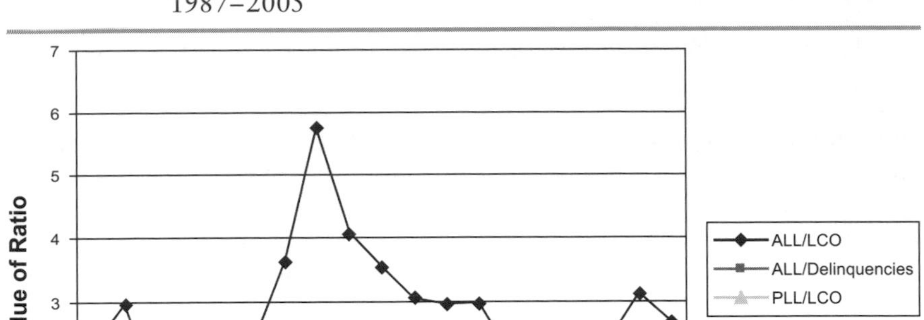

ALL refers to allowance for loan losses.
LCO refers to net loan charge-offs.
PLL refers to provisions for loan losses.

Source: Federal Financial Institutions Examination Council and Federal Reserve Board. Seasonally adjusted annual data for loan charge-offs and delinquencies for the fourth quarter of each year are used to calculate the ratios.

loans and making it an inappropriate benchmark for the allowance for loan losses.

The ratio ALL/LCO compares the allowance for loan losses, a stock measure of credit losses, to net loan charge-offs, a flow measure. In theory, this ratio should rise with the remaining life of the loans currently held by the bank, since the allowance for loan losses should reflect expected credit losses on those loans over their remaining life. This ratio should also rise early in an economic downturn and fall later in the downturn, and it should fall early in an economic upturn and rise later in the upturn, because the allowance for loan losses should reflect credit losses on a timelier basis than do net loan charge-offs, especially for heterogeneous loans.

The actual average ALL/LCO for the banking industry again exhibits a pattern opposite to that predicted, however. Exhibit 5.7 shows that ALL/LCO was low in the bad economic times from 1987 to 1991, approximately tripled by 1994 as the condition of banks improved, moderated somewhat but still remained high from 1995 to 1999, fell during the subsequent economic downturn and bottomed out in 2001, rose through 2004 as the economy improved, and then moderated slightly in 2005. This pattern again strongly suggests that banks underreserve for loan losses on a relative basis in bad times compared to good times.

The ratio PLL/LCO compares two flow measures of credit losses. This ratio captures whether expense recognition this period has kept up with the realization of credit losses and so whether the allowance for loan losses is being drawn up or down. For the same reasons just discussed for the ratio ALL/LCO, the ratio PLL/LCO should rise early in an economic downturn and fall later in the downturn, and it should fall early in an economic upturn and rise later in the upturn.

The actual average PLL/LCO for the banking industry does not follow the predicted pattern, however, and it sometimes follows the opposite pattern. Exhibit 5.7 shows that in most years PLL/LCO closely tracks and slightly exceeds net loan charge-offs. In contrast to the theoretical prediction, this ratio declined from 1999 to 2001, early in the economic downturn, before rising late in the economic downturn in 2002 and then falling subsequently as the economy improved. Moreover, in occasional years, such as 1987, large catch-up provisions for loan losses are recorded, skewing the ratio.

As with loan portfolio quality, loan loss reserve adequacy should be addressed at the level of individual loan types, emphasizing the ratios with the superior benchmark measure of credit losses in the denominator. The SunTrust case in Appendix 5A requires such an assessment.

An important issue in assessing loan loss reserve adequacy is reclassifications of loans and their effects on allowances for loan losses. The SEC requires the allowance for loan losses to reflect credit losses only for items classified as loans on the balance sheet (i.e., loans held in portfolio, including any securitized mortgages for which the mortgage-backed securities are fully retained). Loans held in portfolio can be reclassified as held for sale, in which case banks account for them at the lower of amortized cost or fair value, with decreases in value attributable to credit losses not included in the allowance for loan losses. Loans can be securitized, with the securities either retained or sold. As discussed in Chapter 6, retained securities are accounted for at fair value if they are classified as trading or available for sale, again with decreases in value attributable to credit losses again not included in the allowance for loan losses. Retained securities that are classified as held to maturity are accounted for at cost and are subject to a distinct impairment approach than described earlier for loans.

Allowances for loan losses also can be reclassified, since banks often have distinct allowances for different types of loans (e.g., domestic versus foreign and unimpaired versus impaired). For example, in 1997, J. P. Morgan had $576 million of assets that became nonperforming due to counterparties (mostly on swaps transactions) defaulting in Asia. J. P. Morgan recorded no expense during 1997 for this economic loss, because its beginning-of-year allowance for domestic credit losses was so large it was able to reclassify a portion of this allowance to cover the foreign economic loss. The SEC now states that direct transfers from the allowance for loan losses to other credit loss accounts are inappropriate. Any allowed reclassifications of allowances for loan losses should be clearly disclosed.

Loan sales, other loan transfers, and restructurings of loan terms sometimes are used as a way to reclassify credit losses from the provision for loan losses to realized losses on sale or to defer or avoid recognition of credit losses. PNC Financial's transactions that gave rise to the SEC cease-and-desist order discussed earlier are an example of this.

Overstated allowances for loan losses sometimes are argued to be an acceptable or even beneficial application of accounting conservatism, for example, by reducing banks' tendency to underprice risky loans. Such allowances yield misleading financial reporting, however, as they provide banks with considerable ability to manage their income upward subsequently. Periodic income is poorly measured when economic volatility is suppressed through the creation of excess reserves that are subsequently drawn down as needed.

A manifestation of this argument is often apparent in recent calls by various bank regulators in the United States and abroad for "dynamic," "forward-looking," or "statistical" loan loss provisioning. The subtext of these calls generally is to allow banks to overreserve even more than they do already in good economic times to cushion the blow when the business cycle inevitably turns down, with the goal of reducing systemic risk. Although it is no doubt true that banks could use statistics more extensively and effectively in determining their allowances for loan losses, especially for heterogeneous loans, good accounting requires that the allowance reflect only expected losses on the loans currently in the bank's portfolio over the remainder of their terms based on information available at the time. In particular, allowances should not be "forward-looking" in the sense that they include losses arising from future lending activity, even if such losses are highly probable due to the business cycle or for other reasons.

RESEARCH ON BANKS' LOAN LOSS RESERVES

Empirical research provides two important findings regarding banks' loan loss reserves. First, while the results are not uniform across studies, research generally shows that banks exercise discretion over the allowance and provision for loan losses to smooth earnings across the business cycle, to raise regulatory capital when needed, and to reduce taxes.[11] With regard to income smoothing, banks overstate provisions for loan losses to lower income in good times and understate provisions to raise income in bad times. Banks also make this income smoothing less apparent by accelerating loan charge-offs in good times relative to bad times. With regard to regulatory capital, as discussed in Chapter 2, the allowance for loan losses is included in Tier 2 capital up to a maximum of 1.25% of risk-based assets. Because the allowance is included in Tier 2 capital on a pretax basis, it increases Tier 2 capital by the tax rate times the allowance, because it decreases owners' equity on an after-tax basis. Banks that are in danger of violating Tier 2 capital requirements and are below the maximum allowance raise the allowance. With regard to taxes, until the Tax Reform Act of 1986, tax deductions were highly associated with loan loss provisions, and so banks had the incentive to overstate provisions for loan losses. Since 1986, tax deductions generally are associated with loan charge-offs, so there is an incentive to overstate charge-offs.

Second, the market often reacts positively to increased allowances and provisions for loan losses.[12] For example, Citicorp's market value rose almost 15% on the two days around its several-billion-dollar provision for loan losses for LDC debt in May 1987. One explanation for this phenomenon is that banks record loan loss provisions when they are ratcheting up the strictness of their credit policy or when they believe that their earnings are strong enough to absorb a hit. There is evidence that the market has not reacted positively to loan loss provisions recently, however. This is probably attributable to banks' generally good economic performance since 1993, which implies they have little to signal by increasing loan loss provisions.

Research has shown that banks' loan portfolio composition, profitability, regulatory capital ratios, and fiscal quarter are related to the timeliness of and thus the market reaction to loan loss provisions. For example, provisions for loan losses for small, homogeneous loans are timely information about loan default and are perceived as bad news by the market. The opposite is true for large, heterogeneous loans.

APPENDIX 5A: SUNTRUST BANKS—AFTER THE RESTATEMENT

Background

SunTrust Banks was required by the SEC in November 1998 to reduce its allowance for loan losses by $100 million (about 11% of its allowance). SunTrust amended its 1997 Form 10-K filing, which involved reducing and reallocating the allowance in 1997 and prior years. This restatement was attributed primarily to SunTrust's merger with Crestar, and it was allocated $40 million to 1996, $35 million to 1995, and $25 million to 1994.

SunTrust's original 1997 Form 10-K filing had at least three attributes that suggested overstatement of either its allowance or provision for loan losses.

1. Its ratio of the allowance for loan losses to nonperforming loans increased from 3.42 in 1996 to 5.87 in 1997.
2. It reported an unallocated allowance for loan losses of 45.6% of the total allowance, up from 14.7% in 1992.

3. It had a very high percentage (averaging almost 40% from 1993 to 1997) of recoveries of prior loan charge-offs.

An alternative explanation for the first and third attributes is that SunTrust holds a fairly large amount of consumer loans that are charged off quickly. Under this explanation, nonperforming loans are artificially small and a high rate of recoveries of prior charge-offs are to be expected.

Case Materials

SunTrust's main disclosures regarding its allowance for loan losses and nonperforming loans from its 1998 Form 10-K filing follow. This disclosure is unusually detailed both in its explanations of SunTrust's estimation methods for the allowance for loan losses and in the data it provides about SunTrust's nonperforming loans by type of loan. This disclosure includes only SunTrust's restated numbers.

Case Questions

- Calculate the ratio of the allowance for loan losses to nonperforming loans and the ratio of the allowance for loan losses to net loan charge-offs for each major type of loan for SunTrust in 1998. Explain the differences in the two ratios for each type of loan and in a given ratio across types of loans. Do you believe these differences are primarily attributable to economic differences across types of loan, to SunTrust's provisioning for loan losses, or to SunTrust's loan charge-off policy?
- Calculate the ratio of recoveries of prior charge-offs to gross charge-offs by type of loan. For what type of loan are recoveries highest? Why? Do recoveries indicate anything about discretion over loan charge-offs?
- Which is the better benchmark for the allowance for loan losses for SunTrust for each type of loan: nonperforming loans or net loan charge-offs? Why?
- Calculate the ratio of the provision for loan losses to net loan charge-offs for SunTrust from 1993 to 1998. Do its provisions for loan losses seem excessive?
- Is SunTrust appropriately reserved for loan losses at the end of 1998?

Case Aftermath

In October 2004, SunTrust restated earnings for the first two quarters of 2004, firing its chief credit officer and two other executives, again as a result of an overstated allowance for loan losses.

EXCERPTS FROM SUNTRUST BANK'S 1998 FORM 10-K FILING

ALLOWANCE FOR LOAN LOSSES

SunTrust maintains an allowance for loan losses sufficient to absorb inherent losses in the loan portfolio. The Company is committed to the early recognition of problems and to a strong, conservative allowance and believes the current allowance to be at a level adequate to cover such inherent losses. At year-end 1998, the Company's total allowance was $944.6 million. The allowance for loan losses was impacted by several adjustments in 1998 relating to acquisition, merger, and portfolio management activity over the course of the year. In 1998, Crestar transferred $13.0 million out of the allowance for loan losses related to the sale of credit card loans. Crestar also acquired $3.0 million in additional allowance related to acquisitions. The net result of these transactions was a $10.0 million decrease in the allowance.

The Company's total allowance at year-end equated to approximately 3.5 times the average charge-offs for the last three years and 4.9 times the average net charge-offs for the same three-year period. Because historical charge-offs are not necessarily indicative of future charge-off levels, the Company also gives consideration to other risk indicators when determining the appropriate allowance level.

The allowance for loan losses consists of three elements: (i) allowances established on specific loans, (ii) general allowances based on historical loan loss experience and current trends, and (iii) allowances based on general economic conditions and other risk factors in the Company's individual markets.

The specific allowance element is based on a regular analysis of criticized loans where the internal credit ratings are below a predetermined classification. This analysis is performed at the relationship manager level for those loans with total credit exposure of $250 thousand or greater. The specific allowance established for these criticized loans is based on a careful analysis of related collateral value, cash flow considerations, and guarantor capacity (if applicable).

The general allowance element is determined by an internal loan grading process in conjunction with associated allowance factors. These general allowance factors are updated annually and are based on a statistical loss migration analysis that examines loss experience in relation to internal grading, as well as current loan charge-off trends. The loss migration analysis is performed annually for commercial and commercial real estate loans. Annual charge-off trend analysis is also completed for homogenous (i.e., residential real estate loans, consumer loans, credit card receivables) loan pool classifications. While loss migration and charge-off trend analysis

(continues)

are conducted annually, the Company may revise the general allowance factors whenever necessary in order to address improving or deteriorating credit quality trends or specific risks associated with a given loan pool classification.

The general economic conditions and other risk factors element is primarily determined by management at the individual subsidiary banks and is based on knowledge of specific economic factors in their markets that might affect the collectibility of loans. It inherently involves a higher degree of uncertainty and considers factors unique to the markets in which the Company operates. Other risk factors take into consideration such issues as recent loss experience in specific portfolio segments, loan quality trends and loan volumes, as well as concentration, economic, foreign, and administrative risk. These other risk factors are reviewed and revised by the bank and holding company management where conditions indicate that the estimates initially applied are different from actual results.

Concentrations of credit risk are discussed in Note 13 to the Consolidated Financial Statements and may affect the Company's analysis of other risks and, ultimately, the level of allowance. SunTrust's only significant concentration by collateral type exists in loans secured by residential real estate. At December 31, 1998, the Company had $20.4 billion in loans secured by residential real estate. A geographic concentration of credit risk arises because SunTrust operates primarily in the Southeastern and Mid-Atlantic regions of the United States. Other groups of credit risk may not constitute a significant concentration, but are analyzed based on other evident risk factors for the purpose of determining an adequate allowance level. An example of this would be the Company's credit exposure to the healthcare industry, which includes segments experiencing structural change and market pressures. At year-end 1998, the Company had outstandings of $1.7 billion of loans in various healthcare segments. Problem loan activity in this industry group increased during 1998 and charge-offs in the healthcare segment represented 9% of total net charge-offs during the year. Although SunTrust engages in international banking activities, only minor exposure exists in areas of concern in Latin America or Asia. The Company's total cross border outstandings are less than $500.0 million and no significant changes in trends occurred in that portfolio during the year ended 1998.

A comprehensive analysis of the allowance for loan losses is performed by the Company on a quarterly basis. In addition, a peer review of allowance levels of large banks is conducted on an annual basis. The Company also established at year-end the SunTrust Allowance for Loan Losses Review Committee, which has the responsibility of affirming allowance methodology and assessing the general and specific allowance factors in relation to estimated and actual net charge-off trends. This committee is also responsible for assessing the appropriateness of the allowance for loan losses for each loan pool classification at the Company, state, and bank levels. As a result of this process, the general allowance factor for commercial real estate loans was reduced for fiscal year 1999 and the general allowance factors for credit cards were increased.

Nonperforming assets are defined and discussed in a following section, with totals outlined in Table 9 [reproduced here as Exhibit 5A.1]. Nonperforming assets increased from $236.9 million at December 31, 1997 to $242.1 million at December 31, 1998. Many of these loans are of the size where the Company's allowance for loan loss methodology requires that they be specifically analyzed by a relationship manager as previously described. This analysis results in specific allowance being required for these loans. The ratio for allowance for loan losses to total nonperforming loans (excluding other real estate owned) decreased from 494.6% at year-end 1997 to 456.0% at year-end 1998. As is conservative industry practice, problem credit card receivables are not classified as nonaccrual but are charged off when they become 180 days past due. As shown in Table 8 [reproduced here as Exhibit 5A.2], the majority of SunTrust's charge-offs, both on a gross and net basis, occurred in the Company's credit card portfolio.

The SunTrust charge-off policy is generally consistent with regulatory standards; however, a somewhat more conservative set of policies governs the secured and unsecured consumer loan portfolios. SunTrust typically places a commercial or real estate loan on nonaccrual when principal or interest is due and has remained unpaid for 90 days or more, unless the loan is secured by collateral having realizable value sufficient to discharge the debt in full, and if the loan is in the legal process of collection. Once a loan has been classified as nonaccrual, it also meets the criteria for an impaired loan. Accordingly, the secured loans may be charged down to the estimated value of the collateral and previously accrued unpaid interest is reversed. Subsequent charge-offs may be required as a result of changes in collateral, market values, or repayment prospects. Consistent with industry practices, confirmation of credit card losses is based on a pre-determined number of days that the credit card loan is past due. SunTrust policy for credit cards requires accounts typically to be charged off prior to or at 180 days past due.

With regard to consumer loans, losses on unsecured loans are confirmed at 90 days past due, compared to the regulatory loss criteria of 120 days. Secured installment loans are typically charged off at 90 days past due if all sources of repayment have been determined to be improbable, or at the occurrence of a loss-confirming event (i.e., bankruptcy, repossession).

The Company's provision for loan losses in 1998 was $214.6 million, which was less than total gross charge-offs of $264.3 million and 11% more than net charge-offs of $193.5 million. The comparable provision

(continues)

EXHIBIT 5A.1 SunTrust Banks' 1998 Nonperforming Loans Disclosures (Table 9 in Its Form 10-K Filing)

	AT DECEMBER 31					
(Dollars in Millions)	**1998**	**1997**	**1996**	**1995**	**1994**	**1993**
NONPERFORMING ASSETS						
Nonaccrual loans						
Commercial	$ 50.1	$ 35.1	$ 68.2	$ 58.1	$ 68.0	$ 87.4
Real estate						
Construction	13.5	16.0	23.7	11.0	24.7	42.7
Residential mortgages	83.9	75.2	74.7	111.3	58.9	67.5
Other	46.6	47.6	103.7	127.6	110.2	148.1
Consumer loans	12.5	12.1	13.4	16.9	17.5	16.2
Total nonaccrual loans	206.6	186.0	283.7	324.9	279.3	361.9
Restructured loans	0.6	2.7	9.9	2.9	12.9	14.5
Total nonperforming loans	207.2	188.7	293.6	327.8	292.2	376.4
Other real estate owned	34.9	48.2	71.1	97.8	136.0	212.2
Total nonperforming assets	$ 242.1	$ 236.9	$ 364.7	$ 425.6	$ 428.2	$ 588.6
RATIOS						
Nonperforming loans to total loans	0.32%	0.33%	0.59%	0.71%	0.70%	1.03%
Nonperforming assets to total loans plus other real estate owned	0.37	0.42	0.73	0.92	1.02	1.60
ACCRUING LOANS PAST DUE 90 DAYS OR MORE	$ 108.2	$ 109.0	$ 106.1	$ 79.8	$ 55.7	$ 53.9

EXHIBIT 5A.2 SunTrust Banks' 1998 Activity in the Allowance for Loan Losses Disclosures (Table 8 in Its Form 10-K Filing)

	YEAR ENDED DECEMBER 31					
(Dollars in Millions)	**1998**	**1997**	**1996**	**1995**	**1994**	**1993**
ALLOWANCE FOR LOAN LOSSES						
Balance—beginning of year	$ 933.5	$ 897.0	$ 915.8	$ 887.2	$ 815.9	$ 718.4
Allowance from acquisitions and other activity-net	(10.0)	2.2	0.3	14.7	24.0	30.0
Provision for loan losses	214.6	225.1	171.8	143.4	149.4	252.4
Charge-offs						
Commercial	(49.0)	(30.0)	(44.5)	(37.8)	(45.6)	(81.8)
Real estate						
Construction	(3.2)	(4.0)	(4.0)	(1.5)	(1.5)	(12.9)
Residential mortgages	(13.8)	(11.8)	(10.1)	(8.4)	(9.1)	(13.7)
Other	(5.2)	(6.9)	(11.3)	(21.9)	(33.5)	(61.6)
Credit card	(129.5)	(143.2)	(129.6)	(85.3)	(54.9)	(50.0)
Other consumer loans	(63.6)	(79.3)	(74.8)	(60.1)	(44.8)	(48.8)
Total charge-offs	(264.3)	(275.2)	(274.3)	(215.0)	(189.4)	(268.8)
Recoveries						
Commercial	14.8	22.0	24.2	29.6	28.8	33.6
Real estate						
Construction	0.3	2.5	2.3	4.3	5.1	5.6

(continues)

EXHIBIT 5A.2 *(Continued)*

	YEAR ENDED DECEMBER 31					
(Dollars in Millions)	**1998**	**1997**	**1996**	**1995**	**1994**	**1993**
Residential mortgages	2.7	2.8	2.3	2.1	1.9	1.5
Other	8.4	8.9	12.7	10.9	12.8	6.1
Credit card	14.9	17.7	13.5	12.2	12.0	10.6
Other consumer loans	29.7	30.5	28.4	26.4	26.7	26.5
Total recoveries	70.8	84.4	83.4	85.5	87.3	83.9
Net charge-offs	(193.5)	(190.8)	(190.9)	(129.5)	(102.1)	(184.9)
Balance—end of year	$ 944.6	$ 933.5	$ 897.0	$ 915.8	$ 887.2	$ 815.9
Total loans outstanding at year-end	$65,089.2	$56,765.2	$50,099.7	$46,019.0	$41,976.3	$36,677.7
Average loans	$60,005.2	$52,653.5	$47,322.8	$43,748.8	$38,624.4	$32,484.6
RATIOS						
Allowance to year-end loans	1.45%	1.64%	1.79%	1.99%	2.11%	2.22%
Allowance to nonperforming loans	456.0	494.6	305.5	279.3	303.7	216.8
Net charge-offs to average loans	0.32	0.36	0.40	0.30	0.26	0.57
Provision to average loans	0.36	0.43	0.36	0.33	0.39	0.78
Recoveries to total charge-offs	26.8	30.7	30.4	39.8	46.1	31.2

and net charge-off amounts for 1997 were $225.1 million and $190.8 million respectively. Net charge-offs for 1998 represented .32% of average loans relative to .36% of average loans for 1997. Actual recoveries decreased from $84.4 million at year-end 1997 to $70.8 million at year-end 1998. In addition, the ratio of recoveries to total charge-offs of 30.7% in 1997 also decreased to 26.8% at year-end 1998. The Company believes this downward trend in recoveries is likely to continue consistent with the low levels of charge-offs in recent years.

In connection with the review by the Staff of the SEC of documents related to the Crestar merger, and the Staff's comments thereon, SunTrust lowered its provision for loan losses in 1996, 1995, and 1994 by $40 million, $35 million, and $25 million respectively. The effect of this action was to increase SunTrust net income in those years and to decrease the allowance for loan losses by a total of $100 million.

The allocation of the allowance for loan losses was modified in 1998 as the result of additional analysis of the Company's net charge-off trends, actual loans outstanding, and assessment of other evident risk factors. This analysis resulted in the allocation of 1998 "general economic and other risk reserves" to better match loss experience and distinct risk exposure by loan category. Prior period amounts have also been reclassified using judgments and estimates based on available information. A minimal unallocated allowance was maintained in order to allow for the inherent imprecision in the allowance allocation process. The 1998 allowance for loan losses allocation reflects this direct analysis as shown in Table 7 [reproduced here as Exhibit 5A.3].

NONPERFORMING ASSETS

Nonperforming assets were $242.1 million at year-end 1998, increasing 2.2% from year-end 1997. At December 31, 1998, the ratio of nonperforming assets to total loans plus other real estate owned was 0.37%, the lowest year-end ratio in the Company's history. Included in nonperforming loans are loans aggregating $14.8 million that are current as to the payment of principal and interest but have been placed in nonperforming status because of uncertainty as to the borrower's ability to make future payments.

Loans classified as nonaccrual, except for smaller balance homogenous loans, also meet the criteria for impaired loans. The Company considers a loan to be nonaccrual with the occurrence of one of the following events: (i) interest or principal has been in default 90 days or more, unless the loan is well secured and in the process of collection; (ii) collection of recorded interest or principal is not anticipated; or (iii) the income is

(continues)

TABLE 5A.3 SunTrust Banks' 1998 Allocation of the Allowance for Loan Losses Disclosures (Table 7 in Its Form 10-K Filing)

	AT DECEMBER 31					
(Dollars in Millions)	**1998**	**1997**	**1996**	**1995**	**1994**	**1993**
ALLOCATION BY LOAN TYPE						
Commercial	$ 251.4	$ 247.8	$ 229.9	$ 211.2	$ 261.8	$ 277.3
Real estate	229.8	229.3	262.8	325.5	322.4	306.7
Consumer loans	420.9	406.9	350.5	327.1	247.6	173.1
Unallocated	42.5	49.5	53.8	52.0	55.4	58.8
Total Allowance	$ 944.6	$ 933.5	$ 897.0	$ 915.8	$ 887.2	$ 815.9
ALLOCATION AS A PERCENT OF TOTAL ALLOWANCE						
Commerical	26.6%	26.5%	25.6%	23.1%	29.5%	34.0%
Real Estate	24.3	24.6	29.3	35.5	36.4	37.6
Consumer loans	44.6	43.6	39.1	35.7	27.9	21.2
Unallocated	4.5	5.3	6.0	5.7	6.2	7.2
Total	100.0%	100.0%	100.0%	100.0%	100.0%	100.0%
YEAR-END LOAN TYPES AS A PERCENT OF TOTAL LOANS						
Commercial	37.8%	33.6%	31.5%	30.6%	33.0%	33.4%
Real estate	47.3	49.0	49.0	49.8	45.7	46.2
Consumer loans	14.9	17.4	19.5	19.6	21.3	20.4
Total	100.0%	100.0%	100.0%	100.0%	100.0%	100.0%

recognized on the loan using the cash basis method of accounting due to the deterioration in the financial condition of the debtor. Other consumer loans and residential real estate loans are generally not subject to the above-referenced guidelines and are normally placed on nonaccrual when payments have been in default for 90 days or more.

SunTrust measures the impairment of a loan based on the present value of expected future cash flows discounted at the loan's effective interest rate. The exception to this policy is real estate loans, whose impairment is based on the estimated fair value of the collateral. If the present value of expected future cash flows (or the fair value of the collateral) is less than the recorded investments in the loans (which include principal, accrued interest, net deferred loan fees or costs, unamortized premium, or discount), SunTrust includes this deficiency in evaluating the overall adequacy of the allowance for loan losses.

Interest income on nonaccrual loans, if recognized, is recorded on a cash basis. When a loan is placed on nonaccrual, unpaid interest is reversed against interest income if it was accrued in the current year and is charged to allowance for loan losses if it was accrued in prior years. When a nonaccrual loan is returned to accruing status, any unpaid interest is recorded as interest income after all principal has been collected.

For the year 1998, the gross amount of interest income that would have been recorded on nonaccrual loans and restructured loans at December 31, 1998, if all such loans had been accruing interest at the original contractual rate, was $22.8 million. Interest payments recorded in 1998 as interest income (excluding reversals of previously accrued interest) for all such nonperforming loans at December 31, 1998, were $8.2 million.

NOTES

1. Speech by Federal Reserve Board governor Laurence Meyer, "Moving Forward into the 21st Century," June 3, 1999, www.federalreserve.gov.
2. Federal Financial Institutions Examination Council, "Policy Statement on Allowance for Loan and Lease Losses Methodologies and Documentation for Banks and Savings Institutions," July 6, 2001 (the same day as SAB No. 102 was issued).
3. E. Altman, B. Brady, A. Resti, and A. Sironi, "The Link Between Default and Recovery Rates: Theory, Empirical Evidence, and Implications," *Journal of Business* (November 2005).
4. F. Longstaff and E. Schwartz, "Valuing Credit Derivatives," *Journal of Fixed Income* (June 1995).
5. P. Collin-Dufresne, R. Goldstein, and S. Martin, "The Determinants of Credit Spread Changes," *Journal of Finance* (December 2001).

6. D. Kao, "Estimating and Pricing Credit Risk," *Financial Analysts Journal* (July/August 2000).
7. D. Duffie and K. Singleton, *Credit Risk: Pricing, Measurement, and Management* (Princeton, NJ: Princeton University Press, 2003).
8. Kao, "Estimating and Pricing Credit Risk."
9. G. Udell, "Loan Quality, Commercial Loan Review and Loan Officer Contracting," *Journal of Banking and Finance* (December 1989); A. Berger and G. Udell, "Small Business Credit Availability and Relationship Lending: The Importance of Bank Ownership Structure," *Economic Journal* (February 2002).
10. The SEC's expectations regarding MD&A disclosures of the allowance for loan losses as of December 1, 2005, are available at www.sec.gov/divisions/corpfin/acctdis120105.pdf.
11. S. Moyer, "Capital Adequacy Ratio Regulation and Accounting Choices in Commercial Banks," *Journal of Accounting and Economics* (July 1990); M. Scholes, G. Wilson, and M. Wolfson, "Tax Planning, Capital Planning, and Financial Reporting Strategy for Commercial Banks," *Review of Financial Studies* (October 1990); A. Beatty, S. Chamberlain, and J. Magliolo, "Managing Financial Reports of Commercial Banks: The Influence of Taxes, Regulatory Capital, and Earnings," *Journal of Accounting Research* (Autumn 1995); J. Collins, D. Shackelford, and J. Wahlen, "Bank Differences in the Coordination of Regulatory Capital, Earnings, and Taxes," *Journal of Accounting Research* (Autumn 1995); and A. Ahmed, C. Takeda, and S. Thomas, "Bank Loan Loss Provisions: A Reexamination of Capital Management, Earnings Management, and Signaling Effects," *Journal of Accounting and Economics* (November 1999); and C. Liu and S. Ryan, "Income Smoothing over the Business Cycle: Changes in Banks' Coordinated Management of Provisions for Loan Losses and Loan Charge-offs from the Pre-1990 Bust to the 1990s Boom," *Accounting Review* (March 2006).
12. See W. Beaver, C. Eger, S. Ryan, and M. Wolfson, "Financial Reporting, Supplemental Disclosures, and Bank Share Prices," *Journal of Accounting Research* (Autumn 1989); J. Elliott, D. Hanna, and W. Shaw, "The Evaluation by the Financial Markets of Changes in Bank Loan Loss Reserve Levels," *Accounting Review* (October 1991); P. Griffin and S. Wallach, "Latin American Lending by Major U.S. Banks: The Effect of Disclosures about Non-Accrual Loans and Loan Loss Provisions," *Accounting Review* (October 1991); J. Wahlen, "The Nature of Information in Commercial Bank Loan Loss Disclosures," *Accounting Review* (July 1994); C. Liu and S. Ryan, "The Effect of Bank Loan Portfolio Composition on the Market Reaction to and Anticipation of Loan Loss Provisions," *Journal of Accounting Research* (Spring 1995); W. Beaver and E. Engel, "Discretionary Behavior with Respect to Allowances for Loan Losses and the Behavior of Security Prices," *Journal of Accounting and Economics* (August–December 1996); C. Liu, S. Ryan, and J. Wahlen, "Differential Valuation Implications of Loan Loss Provisions across Banks and Fiscal Quarters," *Accounting Review* (January 1997); and Ahmed, Takeda, and Thomas, "Bank Loan Loss Provisions."

CHAPTER 6

Fair Value Accounting for Financial Instruments: Concepts, Disclosures, and Investment Securities

In Chapter 1's "Fair Value Accounting" section, fair value accounting is argued to be conceptually and practically preferable to amortized cost accounting for most financial instruments, especially for financial institutions holding matched positions in these instruments. The Financial Accounting Standards Board (FASB) and the International Accounting Standards Board (IASB) agree with this argument, and they are working actively and cooperatively to develop fair value accounting for financial instruments. The FASB currently plans to issue a standard in the first quarter of 2007 allowing U.S. firms the option to account for most financial instruments at fair value, i.e., such a fair value option already exists internationally under a June 2005 amendment to International Accounting Standard (IAS) 39, *Financial Instruments: Recognition and Measurement*—while required fair value accounting for these instruments will expand at more measured pace.

This chapter has two primary purposes:

1. To provide users of financial reports with a robust understanding of how fair value accounting works in theory and in relatively simple contexts. Users must have such an understanding in order to grasp fully the application of fair value accounting in the more complex contexts discussed later in the book, such as securitizations (Chapter 8) and derivatives and hedging (Chapter 11), and also to cope with the coming expansion of fair value accounting.
2. To illustrate how users can analyze the information contained in financial institutions' fair value accounting and disclosures to assess their:
   - Solvency and profitability better than is possible using amortized cost accounting information.

- Discretionary "gains trading"—that is, the timing of the sale of securities and other financial instruments recognized at amortized cost to realize gains or losses and thereby manage income and book value. Assessing gains trading is critical for financial institutions that hold matched positions in financial instruments accounted for at amortized cost, since one side of matched positions inevitably appreciates while the other depreciates, allowing these institutions to raise or lower their income by selectively realizing gains or losses on one side of the positions.

The three sections of this chapter collectively address these purposes. The first section describes the FASB's general approach to fair value accounting and disclosures most recently expressed in SFAS No. 157, *Fair Value Measurements* (2006). This standard defines fair value and includes a hierarchy of the types of inputs that may be used to estimate fair values. This fair value hierarchy gives priority to observable market values and other market inputs, but still allows firms to estimate the fair value of an item when the firm must model its fair value and supply any unobservable (i.e., nonmarket) inputs necessary to apply the model. SFAS No. 157 also requires disclosures of fair values by category within the hierarchy, with more detailed disclosures required for fair values estimated using unobservable inputs. This section develops an understanding of the concepts, strengths, and weaknesses of fair value accounting for financial instruments. It elaborates on the discussion of the superiority of fair value accounting over amortized cost accounting in Chapter 1, which should be read prior to this chapter, as repetition of the prior material is kept to a minimum.

The second and third sections describe the first two significant accounting standards that require disclosure or recognition of the fair value of financial instruments: SFAS No. 107, *Disclosures about Fair Value of Financial Instruments* (1991), and SFAS No. 115, *Accounting for Certain Investments in Debt and Equity Securities* (1993). These standards have substantial effects on financial reports of virtually all financial institutions and many nonfinancial firms, and they remain the primary fair value accounting standards affecting relatively simple institutions such as thrifts.

The second section describes SFAS No. 107 (1991) required footnote disclosure of the fair value of most financial instruments. How these disclosures can be used to adjust financial statements to reflect the fair values of financial instruments is demonstrated. These adjusted financial statements often provide a very different and more accurate picture of a financial institution's solvency and profitability than do the reported financial statements. This section also describes the enhanced disclosures of fair values for items recognized at fair value required by SFAS No. 157 (2006).

The third section describes SFAS No. 115 (1993) accounting for investment securities based on the intent of the firm, with investment securities intended to be held for trading purposes or available for sale recognized at fair value in distinct incomplete fashions and investment securities intended to be held to maturity recognized at amortized cost. While such intent-based accounting is problematic, SFAS No. 115's strength in requiring disclosures that clearly indicate gains trading in investment securities is demonstrated.

FAIR VALUE ACCOUNTING FOR FINANCIAL INSTRUMENTS

The next section introduces the definition of fair value and fair value hierarchy in SFAS No. 157 (2006) and describes the main attributes of fair value accounting when applied fully. The "Arguments against Fair Value Accounting for Financial Instruments" section evaluates five specific arguments against fair value accounting for financial instruments, in part using a numerical example that illustrates the differences between fair value and amortized cost accounting. The "Empirical Research" section briefly summarizes empirical research on fair value accounting for financial instruments.

Definition of Fair Value, Fair Value Hierarchy, and Description of Full Fair Value Accounting

SFAS No. 157 (2006) governs the measurement of fair value for any asset or liability for which other accounting standards (with a few exceptions) require fair valuation, not just for financial instruments. SFAS No. 157 defines fair value as the price that would be received to sell an asset or paid to transfer a liability in an orderly transaction between marketplace participants at the measurement date. Fair value defined in this way is referred to as exit value, and it is distinct from the price that would be paid to purchase an asset or received upon issuing a liability, which is referred to as entry value. The transaction is assumed to occur in the principal (i.e., most active) market for the asset or liability or, in the absence of a principal market, in the most advantageous market for the firm holding the asset or liability. An orderly transaction means a period of time is allowed for the firm to conduct usual and customary marketing activities. Market participants mean knowledgeable, unrelated parties that are willing and able to transact. Fair values do not reflect most transactions costs such as bid-ask spreads and commissions, but they do reflect the costs of transporting an item to market. Transportation costs generally are insignificant for financial instruments, but they may be significant for commodity derivatives and other contracts similar to financial instruments that settle physically. Paragraph C34 of SFAS No. 157 is not clear about whether the envisioned knowledgeable, unrelated parties are assumed to have equally good information about an item as the party currently holding it or not, and thus about whether the fair value of the item can be adversely affected by information asymmetry or not.

Because fair value is defined based on the valuation of marketplace participants, in principle the fair value of an item is the same regardless of who currently holds it, ignoring differential transportation costs. The fair value of an asset assumes the highest and best use of the asset by market participants. If the valuc of an asset is highest when used in conjunction with other assets, then the fair value of the asset is determined under the "in-use" premise that the complementary assets are used together. Otherwise, the fair value of the asset is determined under the "in-exchange" premise that the asset is used separately. The in-exchange premise should apply to most or all financial assets. The fair value of a liability should take into account the risk of nonperformance by the firm (and any other involved parties, such as guarantors), which implies that the fair value of liabilities typically will fall as the firm's creditworthiness deteriorates, yielding gains, and vice versa.

SFAS No. 157 (2006) allows fair values to be estimated using one or more of market-based, income-based, and cost-based approaches, as appropriate under the circumstances. Market-based approaches, such as matrix pricing or the use of market multiples, use prices, or other observable information generated by market transactions involving identical or comparable assets or liabilities. Income-based approaches use discounted cash flow, option pricing, or other valuation models. Cost-based approaches use estimates of the cost to replace the service potential of an asset, adjusted for physical deterioration or other obsolescence. Cost-based approaches generally should not be used for financial instruments.

SFAS No. 157 (2006) contains a hierarchy of the types of inputs that may be used to estimate fair value, giving higher priority to observable inputs that use market data more fully. That is, the highest feasible inputs in the hierarchy should be used. From highest (Level 1) to lowest (Level 3), these inputs are:

1. Quoted prices (unadjusted) in active markets for identical assets or liabilities. Blockage factors should not be used for large positions.
2. Other observable market data such as:
   - Quoted prices for similar assets or liabilities in active markets or for identical assets or liabilities in inactive markets
   - Interest rates, yield curves, volatilities, prepayment speeds, loss severities, credit premia, and default rates
   - Inputs derived principally from or corroborated by market data by correlation or other means

   Level 2 inputs should be adjusted as appropriate for factors specific to the asset or liability being fair valued, such as condition and location of the item and the activity level of the market involved.
3. Unobservable inputs reflecting the firm's own assumptions about the assumptions that market participants would use in pricing the asset or liability.

Where the fair value of an item falls in the hierarchy depends on the inputs used to estimate that fair value. A fair value estimated using inputs from different levels in the hierarchy is determined by its lowest-level input.

Unlike prior accounting standards, SFAS No. 157 (2006) does not impose a minimum reliability threshold on the fair value estimate for a gain or loss to be recognized on the income statement at the initiation of a financial instrument when its fair value does not equal the transaction price. The standard does require enhanced disclosures for fair values estimated based on level 3 inputs, however. These disclosures are described in the section "Disclosures of the Fair Value of Financial Instruments."

Full fair value accounting—which is not currently required for any type of financial instrument, as indicated later—has these aspects:

- On the balance sheet, economic gains and losses are recognized through adjustments to the carrying values of assets and liabilities each period. Economic gains occur either when the fair values of assets rise above their carrying values or the fair values of liabilities fall below their carrying values. Economic losses occur in the opposite cases. Without this aspect, accounting could not be referred to as fair value.
- On the income statement, economic gains and losses are recorded as they occur, not when they are realized. This aspect of full fair value accounting is not required for various financial instruments recognized at fair value on the balance sheet but for which gains and losses are recorded in accumulated other comprehensive income (a category of owners' equity).
- On the income statement, interest is recognized on a fair value basis, as the weighted-average fair value of a financial instrument during the period times the corresponding weighted-average market interest rate. This aspect of fair value accounting is not required for any type of financial instrument, and SFAS No. 115 (1993) prohibits it for trading securities that in other respects are recognized at fair value on the income statement.

In addition, to maximize the information conveyed by fair value accounting, fair value interest and fair value gains and losses should be recognized in separate line items on the income statement. Gains and losses are predominantly transitory, affecting expected future net income only by the amount of the gain or loss times the expected rate of return, while interest is predominantly permanent. In practice, these items often are combined with each other or with other items.

Arguments against Fair Value Accounting for Financial Instruments

At least five distinct (although related) arguments have been made against fair valuation of financial instruments. Understanding these arguments is important because they speak directly to the strengths and weaknesses of fair value accounting.

First, it is argued that fair value accounting yields unnecessary income volatility for a firm that intends to retain a financial instrument to maturity, because the firm will receive or make all of the promised payments on the instrument, and so gains and losses will reverse over its life. This argument is completely specious. It is true that any accounting system that properly accounts for cash will record the same net income over the life of a financial instrument, but this implies nothing about the preferred accounting for the instrument. This argument ignores the fact that expected returns on financial instruments change over time and that these changes have economic meaning. For example, if a bank earns interest on a financial asset at a rate of 10% as promised, but the expected return on similar investments falls to 8% (rises to 12%), then the bank has gained (lost), because the benchmark has changed. It is preferable to recognize gains and losses in a consistently timely fashion, as fair value accounting does, rather than in an inconsistently untimely fashion, as amortized cost accounting does. Specifically, under amortized cost accounting, gains and losses are recognized in three distinct untimely ways: when realized at sale, when impairment write-downs are recorded, and gradually over the life of financial instruments through misstated net interest income in each period. It is also preferable to calculate interest using current interest rates, as fair value accounting does, rather than historical interest rates, as amortized cost accounting does, because current interest rates are better predictors of future interest rates and thus future net interest income than are historical interest rates. Moreover, for the portfolios of financial instruments held by financial institutions, it is critical to account for each of the instruments in the portfolio on a comparable basis, and the most natural and best basis uses current market interest rates.

These points are illustrated in the numerical example summarized in Exhibit 6.1. Assume a bank has just purchased a credit-riskless, nonprepayable, zero-coupon bond asset that will pay \$100 in three years and that the initial market interest rate for this bond is 10%, so the bond is worth \$75.13 = \$100/(1.1)^3 at purchase. The bank finances this bond with a one-year zero-coupon debt liability with the same initial value and interest rate. The debt requires a payment of \$82.64 = \$75.13 × 1.1 at the end of year 1. At the end of years 1 and 2, the bank rolls over the principal and accrued interest on the debt at the market interest rates that apply at those times, paying off the debt at the end of year 3 when the bond pays off. If market interest rates remain at the same level over the life of the bond, then the net income from the bond and debt each period and in total over the three years will be zero.

However, market interest rates unexpectedly change instantaneously at the beginning of year 1 to 8%, so that the bond is worth \$79.38 = \$100/(1.08)^3, yielding an economic gain of \$4.25 = \$79.38 − 75.13, and the debt is worth \$76.52 = \$82.64/1.08, yielding a smaller economic loss of \$1.39 = \$76.52 − 75.13 due to the shorter duration of the debt than the bond. The net gain on the bond and debt is \$2.86 = \$4.25 − 1.39. As reported in Exhibit 6.1 this net gain is recognized immediately under full fair value

EXHIBIT 6.1 Fair Value Accounting Example

	Year			
	1	2	3	Total
Bond Asset:				
Beginning amortized cost value*	75.13	82.64	90.91	
Amortized cost interest	7.52	8.26	9.09	24.87
Beginning fair value*	79.38	85.73	92.59	
Fair value gain	4.25			4.25
Fair value interest	6.35	6.86	7.41	20.62
Debt Liability:				
Beginning amortized cost value*	75.13	82.64	89.25	
Amortized cost interest	7.51	6.61	7.14	21.26
Beginning fair value*	76.52	82.64	89.25	
Fair value loss	1.39			1.39
Fair value interest	6.12	6.61	7.14	19.87
Bank Totals:				
Amortized cost net interest income	.00	1.65	1.95	3.60
Beginning amortized cost owners' equity*	0	0	1.65	
Fair value net interest income	.23	.25	.27	.75
Fair value net gain	2.86			2.86
Fair value net income	3.09	.25	.27	3.60
Beginning fair value owners' equity*	2.86	3.09	3.34	

*The beginning balance sheet values in year 1 are after the change in the market interest rate from 10% to 8%.

accounting, which with fair value interest on the net gain of \$.23 = \$2.86 × .08 yields income of \$3.09 in year 1. In contrast, this net gain is ignored under amortized cost accounting, yielding \$0 net income in year 1. In each subsequent year, fair value net interest income equals the beginning fair value of owners' equity that year times 8%, and reinvestment of this income causes fair value net interest income to rise at an 8% rate from year to year, yielding fair value net interest income of \$.25 and \$.27 in years 2 and 3, respectively. In contrast, under amortized cost accounting, the net gain of \$2.86 that occurs in the first year is recognized through overstated net interest income in years 2 and 3 of \$1.65 and \$1.95, respectively. Because the bond and the debt are accounted for inconsistently, amortized cost net interest income actually is volatile compared to fair value net interest income, and it has no meaningful economic relation to the bank's amortized cost owners' equity at the beginning of the corresponding year.

The superiority of fair value accounting in this example is evident in terms of users of financial reports' ability to predict net (interest) income in year 4. Assuming the bank reinvests the net proceeds from the settlement of the bond and debt of \$3.60 at the end of the third year at 8%, its expected net (interest) income under either fair value or amortized cost accounting in year 4 is \$.29, which is 8% more than the year 3 net (interest) income under fair value accounting but has no meaningful economic relation to net (interest) income of \$1.95 in year 3 under amortized cost accounting. This superiority results from fair value accounting for the bond and the debt employing a consistent interest rate, and from that rate being the current market interest rate. In contrast, amortized cost accounting uses inconsistent interest rates to account for the bond and the debt, with the interest rate on the bond not being the current market rate.

Second, it is argued that gains and losses are by their nature nonrecurring, and so they have little or no predictive power over future income. This argument is almost correct but misleading. A dollar of (after-tax) gain is worth a dollar, which if retained by the firm will increase expected future income by a dollar times the expected rate of return on that dollar. In the prior example, the fair value net gain of \$2.86 in year 1 yields additional fair value net interest income of \$.23 = \$2.86 × .08 in year 1. It is true that the effect of a gain or loss in this period on future earnings is significantly less than a dollar, and so users of financial reports need to distinguish gains and losses from recurring items such as net interest income. In this regard, this argument actually favors fair value accounting, since it is capable of distinguishing unrealized gains and losses from interest, while amortized cost accounting combines them, as illustrated in the example.

Third, it is argued that financial instruments often are involved in economic hedging relationships, that fair value accounting inevitably yields cases where a financial instrument is fair valued but the exposure it hedges is not, and that this yields economically unrepresentative volatility in book value and income. This argument is correct in that the only accounting system that would fully capture all economic hedging relationships is complete fair value accounting for all economic assets and liabilities, and such a system would be impossible to develop or apply. The practical question is whether (expanded) fair value accounting for financial instruments (and possibly nonfinancial hedged items) provides a better description of hedging relationships than does the alternative, amortized cost accounting. As discussed in Chapter 1, amortized cost accounting has many limitations; in particular, it suppresses real economic volatility until financial instruments are sold or repurchased, and it provides financial institutions with considerable ability to manage income by gains trading. Reflecting these limitations, most financial analysts and academics have decided that fair value accounting for financial instruments is preferable to amortized cost accounting.[1]

Fair value accounting for all financial instruments largely resolves the problem of hedging relationships for financial institutions, since they mostly hedge financial instruments with other financial instruments. For example, insurers typically hedge their policy liabilities with investment securities of similar duration. To the extent that financial instruments are effective hedges of each other, fair value accounting recognizes gains and losses on these instruments in book value and income in the same period, so these gains and losses offset. Fair value gains and losses properly do not offset for ineffective hedges or speculation. The fair value option proposed by the FASB also would have this effect *if* financial institutions chose to apply the option to both sides of all of their economic hedging relationships involving financial instruments.

In contrast to financial instruments, nonfinancial items (e.g., expected future purchases and sales; property, plant, and equipment; and intangible assets such as goodwill) may not be capable of fair valuation but still may be economically hedged to some extent by financial instruments. While a thorny problem, this possibility is a poor reason not to fair value financial instruments, given the inherent difficulty of assessing the effectiveness of a hedge when the hedged item is not capable of fair valuation.

Fourth, it is argued that fair values are not reliably measurable for some financial instruments. For example, fair valuing a bank's fixed-rate residential mortgage-related assets requires modeling the prepayment options of the borrowers of the mortgages, and application of any theoretically sound prepayment model requires making a host of estimates about interest rate volatility and the behavior of borrowers. Even the best of these models applied as best as possible will be limited, so the required estimates will be noisy or biased. This argument has considerable truth for illiquid, complex, or highly sensitive financial instruments. However, it is diminished by the increasing sale and securitization of many of the same types of financial instruments that have been said to be hard to fair value, such as subprime mortgages, credit card receivables, commercial loans, junk bonds, and core deposits. (As discussed in Chapter 8, however, the ability to securitize a financial instrument does not necessarily imply the ability to fair value it with precision, especially when risky interests are retained.) The ongoing development of both markets and models for financial instruments implies that if fair value accounting is not yet preferable to amortized cost accounting for a given financial instrument, the right question to ask is when markets or valuation models will develop so that it is preferable.

Fifth, some financial instruments—such as credit card receivables, core deposits, leases, and insurance contracts—are inextricably coupled with customer relationships or other nonfinancial items. Fair valuing these instruments requires either including or excluding the nonfinancial item from the fair value calculation, either of which raises comparability and measurement issues. This argument is correct, and the FASB recognizes that it needs to make decisions about which approach is practically preferable for these instruments.

The best approach for a given financial instrument is likely to depend on whether the financial and nonfinancial aspects of the instrument typically trade as a package or separately.

Empirical Research

A considerable amount of empirical research has been done comparing the fair values and amortized costs of financial instruments in terms of their explanatory power over firm market value or returns. A few studies examining settings in which fair valuation is fairly complete and reliable—in particular, the securities and real estate holdings of various types of investment companies; all find that fair value accounting for financial instruments dominates amortized cost accounting.[2] This finding reflects the fact that fair value accounting is theoretically preferable to amortized cost accounting.

In other settings, the evidence is more ambiguous, although generally favorable to fair value accounting. Be aware that most of this research uses disclosed fair values for financial instruments under SFAS No. 107 (1991), and disclosure need not be an adequate substitute for recognition. Firms may not estimate fair values with as much effort if they are disclosed rather than recognized, and their managements invariably do not discuss or analyze fair value disclosures in financial reports. Most of this research examines commercial banks, which is useful because they hold a wide range of financial instruments that differ with respect to the accuracy of fair value estimates. The research question typically asked is whether the fair values of their financial instruments provide information beyond their amortized costs, that is, whether fair values are useful disclosures, not whether fair value is a preferable valuation basis than amortized cost for financial instruments. A consistently significant finding is that fair values provide information beyond amortized costs for traded investment securities, reflecting the fact that they are the instruments for which fair value can be determined most reliably. For other financial instruments, such as loans, model specification (e.g., inclusion of control variables) is critical to finding that fair values provide information beyond amortized costs.[3]

Research suggests that fair value disclosures, like other accounting numbers, are managed to make less solvent banks appear more solvent and that fair values contain a sizable amount of noise that is ignored by the market.[4]

Research shows that partial fair value accounting yields more volatile owners' equity and net income than does amortized cost accounting and that this volatility is partly economically descriptive and partly not.[5] A recent study shows that the volatility of full fair value income derived from SFAS No. 107 (1991) fair value disclosures is incrementally associated with market-based measures of bank risk (return volatility, beta, long-term interest-rate beta, and pricing multiples) controlling for income volatility based on reported net income or comprehensive income.[6] This reflects fair value accounting's greater desirability as it is applied more broadly.

DISCLOSURES OF THE FAIR VALUE OF FINANCIAL INSTRUMENTS

The next section describes the required disclosures of the fair value of most financial instruments under SFAS No. 107 (1991), and the FASB's recent enhancement of those disclosures for items recognized at fair value in SFAS No. 157 (2006). The "Adjusting Financial Statements to Reflect the Fair Value of Financial Instruments" section illustrates how these disclosures can be used to adjust reported balance sheets and income statements to reflect fair values.

SFAS No. 107 and SFAS No. 157

SFAS No. 107 (1991) requires that firms disclose the fair value and the carrying value (usually the amortized cost) of both on– and off–balance sheet financial instruments. If it is not practicable to estimate fair value for a financial instrument, then the firm must disclose why and provide information about the characteristics of the item (e.g., carrying amount, effective interest rate, and maturity). A typical commercial bank discloses the fair values of on–balance sheet cash, securities, loans, derivatives, deposits, other managed liabilities and long-term debt, and the fair values of off–balance sheet loan commitments, letters of credit, and bankers acceptances.

There are some exceptions to the SFAS No. 107 (1991) disclosure requirements. The most important ones are mortgage-servicing rights, core deposit intangibles, leases, insurance contracts, and investments accounted for using the equity method. Although each of these items has some nonfinancial aspects, all either are predominantly financial instruments or are inextricably coupled with financial instruments. The fair value of mortgage-servicing rights must be disclosed under SFAS No. 156, *Accounting for Servicing of Financial Assets* (2006), however, as discussed in Chapter 8.

For each major category of assets and liabilities recognized at fair value, SFAS No. 157 (2006) requires various additional disclosures in each interim and annual accounting period, the most incrementally useful of which are:

- The fair value measurements at the reporting date and the level within the fair value hierarchy where they all must be disclosed. These disclosures indicate the differing level of judgment involved in estimating fair values for different items.
- When fair values are estimated using Level 3 inputs on a recurring basis (e.g., for derivatives and trading and available-for-sale securities), the beginning and ending fair values in the period must be reconciled, indicating the total (realized and unrealized) gain or loss, the net amount of purchases, sales, issuances, and settlements, and transfers in or out of Level 3 measurements during the period. In addition, the amount of the total gain or loss for the period that is attributable to the assets and

liabilities still held at the reporting date and where those gains and losses are reported in the statement of income must be disclosed.

- When fair values are estimated using Level 3 inputs on a nonrecurring basis (e.g., for impaired loans and other financial assets subject to some form of impairment accounting), a description of the inputs and how they are developed.

The additional disclosures required for fair values estimated using Level 3 inputs indicate the most judgmental components of reported earnings for the period arising from fair value accounting.

Adjusting Financial Statements to Reflect the Fair Value of Financial Instruments

Most financial institutions can be viewed in large part as portfolios of financial instruments. Since fair value is the preferred valuation basis for financial instruments, it is generally useful to adjust financial institutions' reported financial statements to reflect the fair value of their financial instruments using SFAS No. 107 (1991) disclosures. This exercise can provide a very different and more accurate picture of financial institutions' solvency and performance than do their reported financial statements, especially in periods of interest rate, credit, or other economic volatility.

The methods for adjusting the balance sheet and income statement to reflect the fair value of financial instruments are discussed in the "Balance Sheet" and "Income Statement" sections, respectively. Golden West's 2005 balance sheet and income statement are adjusted to reflect the fair value of its financial instruments in the "Adjusting Golden West's Financial Statements" section.

Balance Sheet. Denote the fair value of a representative financial instrument by FV and its book value by BV. (If a financial instrument is not recognized on the balance sheet, its book value is zero.) If FV – BV for a financial asset is positive (negative), then there is a cumulative unrecognized pretax gain (loss) on the asset since its inception. If FV – BV for a financial liability is positive (negative), then there is a cumulative unrecognized pretax loss (gain) on the liability since its inception.

These pretax adjustments are necessary to make the balance sheet reflect the fair value of financial instruments:

- Add the difference between the fair and book value of each financial asset or liability (FV – BV) to its book value (BV), which yields the fair value of the instrument, FV.
- The pretax adjustment to owners' equity is the sum of FV – BV for the firm's financial assets minus the sum of FV – BV for the firm's financial liabilities.

A tricky issue is how to estimate the effect of this pretax adjustment on deferred taxes. The tax effects of unrealized capital gains and losses depend on whether and when the corresponding financial instruments are sold, the return on unrealized gains and losses until they are sold, and the firm's tax status when they are sold. (In addition, in a few cases, such as municipal bonds, the income on the item is tax-exempt.) If the firm is expected not to pay taxes, then there is no need for an adjustment to deferred taxes. Assuming the firm is expected to pay taxes, there are two possible ways to estimate the adjustment to deferred taxes. The simple approach is to ignore the benefits of tax deferral and increase (decrease) the deferred tax liability account by the firm's estimated tax rate times the pretax increase (decrease) in owners' equity. Under this approach, the after-tax adjustment to owners' equity is 1 minus the tax rate times the pretax adjustment.

The conceptually correct but far more difficult approach is to estimate the time at which unrecognized gains and losses will be realized and to discount the tax effects on the expected realized gains and losses, including accrued interest in the interim. This estimate depends on the firm's turnover rate of financial instruments, which likely differs for unrecognized gains and losses due to tax and other reasons. This approach reduces the effect on deferred taxes compared to the simple approach. As this approach raises numerous estimation issues that are tangential to this book, the simple approach is employed here.

For example, assume the carrying value of a held-to-maturity (HTM) security is 10 and its fair value is 12, implying a cumulative unrecognized pretax gain of 2. Assume that the firm pays income taxes at a rate of 40%. To adjust the balance sheet to fair value using the simple approach to taxes, add 2 to HTM securities, .8 = 2 × .4 to the deferred tax liability, and 1.2 = 2 × .8 to retained earnings.

Income Statement. Exhibit 6.2 depicts schematic T accounts that illustrate the nature of the adjustments necessary to make the income statement reflect the fair value of financial instruments. For concreteness, the exhibit represents the specific case of a financial asset that is carried on the balance sheet at amortized cost and that has experienced a cumulative unrecognized gain. The logic is the same for cumulative unrecognized losses and financial liabilities, although the signs of the adjustments change for financial liabilities, as is discussed later. These T accounts assume that interest is accrued in separate interest receivable or payable accounts; this is the case for short-term accruals of interest but not for long-term accruals of interest (e.g., for amortization of bond discounts and premia).

The T account for the recognized financial asset at amortized cost increases with originations or purchases, which are assumed to be at their fair value, as is usually the case. This account decreases with principal payments and also with sales (including securitizations) of the financial asset at amortized cost. This account may also increase or decrease from transfers of financial assets across accounts (e.g., available-for-sale securities being transferred to trading); such transfers are not represented in the T account in Exhibit 6.2.

As for the recognized financial asset, the T account for the disclosed financial asset at fair value increases with originations or purchases and

EXHIBIT 6.2 Schematic T Accounts Depicting Adjustments to the Income Statement to Reflect the Fair Value of Financial Instruments

Recognized Financial Asset at Amortized Cost

beginning amortized cost (BV_{beg})	
+ origination or purchases	− principal payments
	− sales (amortized cost)
= ending amortized cost (BV_{end})	

Disclosed Financial Asset at Fair Value

beginning fair value (FV_{beg})	
+ originations or purchases	− principal payments
+ total (realized plus unrealized) gain during period	− sales (fair value)
= ending fair value (FV_{end})	

Cumulative Unrecognized Gain on Financial Asset

beginning cumulative unrecognized gain ($FV_{beg} - BV_{beg}$)	
+ total (realized plus unrealized) gain during period	− realized gain during period
= ending cumulative unrecognized gain ($FV_{end} - BV_{end}$)	

decreases with principal payments. Unlike for the recognized financial asset, the T account for the disclosed financial asset increases with the total (realized plus unrealized) gain on the asset that occurs during the period and decreases with sales of the asset at fair value, including any realized gain. Thus, only the unrealized portion of the total gain remains in the account at the end of the period.

Subtracting the T account for the recognized financial asset from the T account for the disclosed financial asset item by item (e.g., the beginning amortized cost balance is subtracted from the beginning fair value balance) and recognizing that both purchases and originations and principal payments are equal in the two accounts yields the analytically useful T account for the cumulative unrecognized gain on the financial asset. The change in this account during the period—that is, $(FV_{end} - BV_{end}) - (FV_{beg} - BV_{beg})$—is the total (realized plus unrealized) gain during the period minus the realized gain during the period, or, equivalently, the unrealized and thus unrecognized gain during the period. This amount must be added to pretax income to reflect the fair value of financial instruments.

These three pretax adjustments are necessary to make the income statement reflect the fair value of financial instruments:

1. For each financial asset recognized at amortized cost, add $(FV_{end} - BV_{end}) - (FV_{beg} - BV_{beg})$ for the asset to pretax income.
2. For each financial liability recognized at amortized cost, subtract $(FV_{end} - BV_{end}) - (FV_{beg} - BV_{beg})$ for the liability from pretax income.
3. For financial instruments that are recognized on the balance sheet at fair value but for which gains and losses bypass the income statement and are recorded in accumulated other comprehensive income (i.e., available-for-sale securities, as discussed in the "Investment Securities" section, and derivatives that are effective cash flow hedges, as discussed in Chapter 11), adjustments 1 and 2 must be applied replacing BV with the amortized costs of the instruments. The amortized cost of available-for-sale securities is provided in the investment securities footnote. The amortized cost of derivatives that are effective cash flow hedges can be inferred from the accumulated other comprehensive income associated with these items, which is reported in the statement of stockholders' equity.

The adjustment to deferred tax expense is again a tricky issue. Under the simple approach, tax expense should be increased (decreased) by the firm's estimated tax rate times the net increase (decrease) in pretax income just described. Net income should be adjusted to reflect the adjustment to pretax income times one minus the firm's estimated tax rate.

Continuing the example in the "Balance Sheet" section, assume at the beginning of the period the held-to-maturity security had a book value of 10 but a fair value of 13, for a cumulative unrecognized pretax gain of 3. Since there was a cumulative unrecognized pretax gain of only 2 at the end of the period, an unrecognized pretax loss of $1 = -(2 - 3)$ occurred during the period. Thus, to adjust the income statement to reflect the fair value of the security using the simple approach to taxes, subtract 1 from pretax income, .4 from tax expense, and .6 from net income.

Note that these adjustments do not convert interest to a fair value basis, and so the adjustment of the income statement is incomplete in this sense. The total amount of net income is correct, however, because the net pretax unrealized gain adjustment just described is misstated by exactly the amount of the adjustment that should have been made to interest. An example illustrating this point is provided in the "SFAS No. 115's Accounting Requirements" section. Users of financial reports could attempt the difficult task of estimating the appropriate adjustment to interest by estimating the current and original market rates on the firm's financial instruments and make an offsetting adjustment to the gain.

Adjusting Golden West's Financial Statements. Golden West's SFAS No. 107 (1991) fair value disclosures from its 2005 Form 10-K filing are reported in Exhibit 6.3. Its balance sheet and income statement in 2005 are reported in Exhibits 3.2 and 3.4 of Chapter 3, respectively.

Exhibit 6.4 reports the adjustments to Golden West's 2005 balance sheet and income statement necessary to make them reflect the fair value of financial instruments. Financial assets and liabilities that are accounted for at fair value on both the balance sheet and income statement are omitted from this exhibit, since they require no adjustments. As noted, available-for-sale securities are accounted for at fair value on the balance sheet but at amortized cost on the income statement, and it is necessary to obtain their amortized costs from the investment security footnote in order to adjust the income statement to reflect the fair values of those securities. The amortized cost of Golden West's available-for-sale securities other than mortgage-backed securities is $11,968,000 in 2005 and $28,044,000 in 2004, and the amortized cost of its available-for-sale mortgage-backed securities is $11,132,000 in 2005 and $14,624,000 in 2004.

The first and second columns of Exhibit 6.4 report the adjustments to Golden West's 2005 and 2004 balance sheets, respectively. To indicate clearly the effects of each adjustment on owners' equity and net income, positive numbers represent cumulative unrecognized gains and negative numbers represent cumulative unrecognized losses; thus, the numbers for financial liabilities are minus the adjustments to their balances. The third column reports the adjustments to the 2005 income statement. These adjustments are the changes in the cumulative unrecognized gains and losses during 2005. Pretax effects on owners' equity are reported in the second-to-last row of the exhibit. After-tax adjustments to owners' equity and net income are reported in the last row.

Interpreting the cumulative and 2005-specific unrecognized gains and losses for Golden West in 2005 is a bit tricky because of the recent complicated movements in interest rates. Although interest rates generally declined from 2001 to 2003, short- to intermediate-term interest rates rose fairly consistently in 2004 and 2005, and long-term rates fluctuated considerably in 2004 and 2005 while ending both of these years close to where they started. The effects of these interest rate movements likely offset to some extent, but one would need to know how much assets and liabilities of what durations Golden West originated at each point during this period to be able to determine the dominant effects with confidence. (Management is in the best position to make such interpretations, of course, but unfortunately it rarely provides them in financial reports.) Users of financial reports should attempt to understand the reasons for these unrecognized gains and losses as best as possible given the information available.

EXHIBIT 6.3 Golden West's 2005 Fair Value of Financial Instruments Disclosures ($ in thousands)

	December 31, 2005		December 31, 2004	
	Carrying Amount	**Estimated Fair Value**	**Carrying Amount**	**Estimated Fair Value**
Financial Assets:				
Cash	$ 518,161	$ 518,161	$ 292,421	$ 292,421
Federal funds sold and other investments	1,321,626	1,321,626	936,353	936,353
Securities available for sale	382,499	382,499	438,032	438,032
Mortgage-backed securities available for sale	11,781	11,781	14,38	14,438
Mortgage-backed securities held to maturity	1,472,183	1,472,609	2,095,614	2,138,894
Loans receivable	117,881,965	118,987,054	100,559,179	101,261,901
Interest earned but uncollected	392,303	392,303	248,073	248,073
Investment in capital stock of Federal Home Loan Banks	1,857,580	1,857,580	1,563,276	1,563,276
Capitalized mortgage servicing rights	39,134	53,719	53,234	62,273
Interest rate swaps	-0-	-0-	10,309	10,309
Financial Liabilities:				
Deposits	60,158,319	60,260,546	52,965,311	53,022,209
Advances from Federal Home Loan Banks	38,961,165	38,978,241	33,781,895	33,790,789
Securities sold under agreements to repurchase	5,000,000	4,998,367	3,900,000	3,899,607
Bank notes	2,393,951	2,393,907	2,709,895	2,709,742
Senior debt	8,194,266	8,200,022	5,291,840	5,323,968
Interest rate swaps	37,571	37,571	-0-	-0-

The cumulative unrecognized gains on all of the assets and the cumulative unrecognized losses on most of the liabilities generally are more consistent with the decreases in long-term rates rather than with the recent increases in short- to intermediate-term rates, despite the fact that Golden West

EXHIBIT 6.4 Adjustment of Golden West's 2005 Financial Statements to Reflect the Fair Value of Financial Instruments ($ in thousands)

	Balance Sheet Adjustments		Income Statement Adjustments
	2005 Cumulative Unrecognized Gain (Loss)	**2004 Cumulative Unrecognized Gain (Loss)**	**2005 Unrecognized Gain**
Securities available for sale	370,531	409,988	−39,457
Mortgage-backed securities available for sale	649	−186	835
Mortgage-backed securities held to maturity	426	43,280	−42,854
Loans receivable	1,105,089	702,722	402,367
Capitalized mortgage servicing rights	14,585	9,039	5,546
Total assets	1,491,280	1,164,843	326,437
Deposits	−102,227	−56,898	−45,329
Advances from Federal Home Loan Banks	−17,076	−8,894	−8,182
Securities sold under agreements to repurchase	1,633	393	1,240
Bank notes	44	153	−109
Senior debt	−5,756	−32,128	26,372
Total liabilities	−123,382	−97,374	−26,008
Pretax effect on owners' equity or net income	1,367,898	1,067,469	300,429
Aftertax effect on owners' equity or net income	820,738.8	640,481.4	180,257.4

holds primarily short-duration assets and liabilities. The unrecognized losses on securities available for sale and mortgage-backed securities held to maturity and the unrecognized gain on senior debt during 2005 probably reflect the increases in short- to intermediate-term rates during that year. The explanations for the $402 million unrecognized gain on loans receivable and $45 million unrecognized loss on deposits during 2005 are not apparent, however. Golden West's unrecognized gains and losses likely are not entirely attributable to interest rate movements, however. For example, the $371 million cumulative unrecognized gain on its securities available-for-sale resulted almost entirely from Golden West's holdings of Freddie Mac stock, and the

$15 million cumulative unrecognized gain on its capitalized mortgage servicing rights may reflect declining expected prepayment.

Whatever the reasons, at the end of 2005 there is a cumulative unrecognized gain of $1.5 billion on Golden West's assets and a cumulative unrecognized loss of $123 million on its liabilities. The $821 million net after-tax effect of these fair value adjustments on its owners' equity is nontrivial at about 9% of its $8.7 billion of owners' equity. Thus, Golden West's solvency is higher than it appears on its 2005 balance sheet. Similarly, the $180 million net after-tax effect of the fair value adjustments on Golden West's net income is also nontrivial at about 12% of its $1.5 billion net income in 2005. Thus, Golden West's profitability also is better than it appears on its 2005 income statement.

In periods of interest rate volatility or for financial institutions that hold positions with more interest rate risk, fair value adjustments generally will be much larger than they are for Golden West in 2005. Appendix 6A considers the case of Washington Federal in 2005, a thrift that holds much longer duration assets than liabilities, as reported in Exhibit 4.7 of Chapter 4. The fair value adjustment would be very adverse for Washington Federal in a year with substantial increase in long-term rates. The last year with a substantial increase in long-term rates from the beginning to the end of the year was 1994. The first edition of this book included a case on T.R. Financial in 1994, a thrift with an exposure to interest rates similar to Washington Federal; fair value adjustment reduces T.R. Financial's reported net income of $12 million in 1994 by $50 million to $38 million, which is −26% of its adjusted owners' equity of $146 million.

A limitation of SFAS No. 107 (1991) fair value disclosures is that they do not make gains trading apparent. These disclosures only allow the user of financial reports to determine the total gain or loss net of the realized gain or loss, that is, the unrealized gain or loss. Although the income and cash flow statements may provide some clues about realized gains and losses and thus gains trading, the information in these statements is usually too aggregated to indicate gains trading clearly. As discussed in the next section, SFAS No. 115 (1993) remedies this problem for available-for-sale and held-to-maturity securities by requiring disclosures of unrealized and realized gains and losses on those securities.

INVESTMENT SECURITIES

The next section describes the main accounting requirements of SFAS No. 115 (1993). The "Restrictions on Reclassifying Securities and the Possibility of Gains Trading" section describes SFAS No. 115's restrictions on transfers between types of securities and their implications for the possibility of gains trading. The "Other-than-Temporary Impairment" section describes SFAS No. 115's requirements for impairment write-downs of investment securities in certain circumstances. The "Disclosures and Assessment of Gains

Trading" section describes SFAS No. 115's required disclosures and their usefulness for the assessment of gains trading. The "JPMorgan Chase's Available-for-Sale Securities" section analyzes JPMorgan Chase's available-for-sale securities footnote in 2004.

SFAS No. 115's Accounting Requirements

SFAS No. 115 (1993) provides the accounting and disclosure requirements for investment securities, including debt and equity securities. SFAS No. 115 is the first standard that requires financial statement recognition of a significant class of financial instruments at fair value. It is natural that the FASB started fair value accounting with investment securities, since these instruments are most likely to be traded in liquid markets with observable market prices, and so the measurement of fair values is least likely to be a problem. Moreover, gains trading is easiest to accomplish using investment securities because of their liquid nature. Investment securities often are used in economic hedging relationships,[7] however, and so the third argument against fair valuation discussed in the "Arguments against Fair Value Accounting for Financial Instruments" section applies.

SFAS No. 115 (1993) is an inconsistent standard that does not require fair value accounting for all investment securities or full fair value accounting for any security. It requires firms to classify securities into three types — trading, available for sale (AFS), and HTM—based on their ability and intent to hold the securities. Most equity securities cannot be classified as HTM, since they have no fixed maturity. These classes of securities are accounted for very differently, and these differences influence firms' classification choices.[8]

These differences are illustrated in the schematic T accounts for trading/AFS and HTM securities in Exhibit 6.5. Trading/AFS securities are represented in a combined account because the asset is accounted for the same way for the two types of securities, although income and the components of owners' equity are not, as indicated in the schematic T account for the accumulated other comprehensive income from AFS securities in the exhibit. The description of two of the items in this combined account—the increase in the account from the total (realized and unrealized) gain during the period and the reduction of the account from any sale—assumes that trading and AFS securities are written to fair value immediately prior to any sale, as would be the case if fair value accounting is applied continuously. The T accounts in this exhibit again assume that interest is accrued in a separate interest receivable account, and they reflect the effects of other-than-temporary impairment write-downs, which are treated in most respects like realized losses, as discussed in the section "Other-than-Temporary Impairment."

The accounting for trading securities is mostly fair-value based. Trading securities are accounted for at fair value on the balance sheet. Unrealized gains and losses on these securities are recognized on the income statement in the period they occur. Thus, gains trading is not possible with trading securities.

EXHIBIT 6.5 Schematic T Accounts for Investment Securities

Trading and AFS Securities	
beginning balance (fair value)	
+ purchases	− principal payments
+ total (realized and unrealized) gain during period*	− sales (fair value)*
ending balance (fair value)	

HTM Securities	
beginning balance (amortized cost, possibly impaired)	
+ purchases	− principal payments
	− impairment writedown
	− sales (amortized cost, possibly impaired)
ending balance (amortized cost, possibly impaired)	

Accumulated Other Comprehensive Income from AFS Securities	
	beginning cumulative unrecognized gain
− realized gain during period*	+ total (realized and unrealized) gain during period*
	+ impairment write down during period
	ending cumulative unrecognized gain

*These items are in the amounts indicated only if trading and AFS securities are written to fair value immediately prior to any sale.

In contrast, AFS securities are accounted for at fair value on the balance sheet, but unrealized gains and losses on these securities bypass the income statement and are recorded instead in accumulated other comprehensive income, a distinct part of owners' equity. Gains and losses on AFS securities are recognized on the income statement when they are realized at sale, and so gains trading is possible with AFS securities. As gains and losses on these securities are recognized in income, their effect on accumulated other comprehensive income is reversed, a process sometimes referred to as recycling.

Finally, HTM securities are accounted for at amortized cost. Despite this fact, gains trading is generally not possible using HTM securities, because these securities cannot be sold without giving up the right to classify securities as HTM, except in the highly constrained circumstances to be described.

An unappreciated fact is that SFAS No. 115 (1993) requires interest revenue to be accounted for on an amortized cost basis for all investment securities. As illustrated earlier, an implication of this fact is that interest revenue gradually recognizes prior economic gains and losses on securities. As this occurs, the recognition of prior economic gains and losses in net income (for trading securities) or accumulated other comprehensive income (for AFS securities) in prior periods must be reversed. For trading securities, the reversal of prior gains and losses and their recognition in interest both affect income, so that the amount of net income is correct each period, but its gain and loss and interest components have perfectly negatively correlated errors. For AFS securities, the reversal of prior gains and losses affects accumulated other comprehensive income, while their recognition in interest affects income, so that the amount of net income is incorrect.

These points are illustrated through the simple example of a zero-coupon bond asset in the "Arguments against Fair Value Accounting for Financial Instruments" section, allowing the bond to be classified as any of the three types of security. The journal entries in the first year are:

at purchase:

trading, AFS, or HTM securities	75.13	
cash		75.13

when market rate changes from 10% to 8%
(initial recognition or not of unrealized gain):

if trading:

trading securities (+ asset)	4.25	
unrealized gain on trading securities (+ income)		4.25

if AFS:

AFS securities (+ asset)	4.25	
other comprehensive income (+ owners' equity)		4.25

if HTM:

no journal entry

at end of year 1 (accrual of interest and reversal of unrealized gain):

interest receivable (+ asset)	7.51	
interest revenue (+ income)		7.51

if trading:

unrealized loss on trading securities (− income)	1.16	
trading securities (− asset)		1.16

if AFS:

other comprehensive income (− owners' equity)	1.16	
AFS securities (− asset)		1.16

Similar journal entries are recorded in subsequent years.

Assume the bond is classified as a trading security. In year 1, net income includes interest revenue of $7.51, which is overstated by $1.16 relative to fair value interest revenue of $6.35. Net income includes an unrealized gain of $3.09, which is understated by $1.16 relative to the fair value gain of $4.25. Total net income is correct at $10.60, because the errors on its two components offset. Total owners' equity is also correct.

Assume instead the bond is classified as an AFS security. In year 1, net income is the interest revenue of $7.51, which is overstated by $1.16 relative to fair value interest revenue of $6.35. Total net income is understated by $3.09, the remaining unrealized gain on the security at the end of the period. This amount is recognized in accumulated other comprehensive income, however, so that owners' equity is correct.

Assume instead the bond is classified as an HTM security. In year 1, net income is the interest revenue of $7.51, which is overstated by $1.16 relative to fair value interest revenue of $6.35. Total net income is understated by $3.09, the remaining unrealized gain on the security at the end of the period. This amount is not recognized on the balance sheet, so that owners' equity is also incorrect.

Most financial institutions classify most investment securities as AFS, although thrifts and insurance companies sometimes classify a fair amount as HTM, and a few of the largest financial institutions have substantial trading portfolios. As illustrations of two ends of continuum, in 2005, Golden West held $1.5 billion of HTM securities (and much larger amounts of mortgage-backed securities classified as loans receivable and accounted for in a similar way as HTM securities) but only $394 million of AFS securities and no trading securities. In contrast, in 2005, JPMorgan Chase held $249 billion of trading securities but only $48 billion of AFS securities and $77 million of HTM securities.

Restrictions on Reclassifying Securities and the Possibility of Gains Trading

Since the intent to hold securities is unobservable, the classification of securities into the three types under SFAS No. 115 (1993) allows firms to exercise discretion to obtain desired accounting treatments, including gains trading. The FASB attempted to mitigate this discretion in several ways in SFAS No.

115. First, the standard requires disclosures about transfers between portfolios.

Second, the standard allows securities to be transferred out the HTM portfolio only under these conditions:

- When the security's credit rating declines significantly
- When tax law or regulations change significantly
- When a major business combination or disposition takes place that requires transfers to maintain the firm's policies
- When an isolated, nonrecurring, and unusual event that could not have been reasonably anticipated (e.g., Hurricane Katrina) occurs

A firm that transfers securities out of the HTM portfolio under other circumstances loses the ability to classify securities as HTM. These restrictions substantially limit the ability of firms to gains trade using HTM securities. The FASB has allowed firms to transfer securities out of the HTM portfolio on two occasions, however, in late 1995 and upon the initial adoption of SFAS No. 133, *Accounting for Derivative Instruments and Hedging Activities* (1998). The first occasion provided relief to the large number of firms that had classified too many securities as HTM upon the initial adoption of SFAS No. 115 (1993). The second occasion reflects SFAS No. 133's prohibition on the use of hedge accounting for economic hedges of the interest rate risk of HTM securities.

Third, SFAS No. 115 (1993) requires that transfers of securities among the three types be recorded at fair value in some fashion. In particular, a transfer from the AFS portfolio to the HTM portfolio requires that the existing unrealized gain or loss on the security be amortized into income over its remaining life. In other words, pretransfer gains and losses on the security are accounted for as if it had remained AFS, while posttransfer gains and losses on the security are accounted for using the required amortized cost accounting for HTM securities. A transfer from the AFS portfolio to the trading portfolio requires that any unrealized gain or loss on the AFS security flow through income at the time of the transfer. This implies that firms still can gains trade without even selling AFS securities, however, by transferring appreciated or depreciated AFS securities to the trading portfolio.

Other-than-Temporary Impairment

For individual investment securities classified as AFS or HTM that are impaired in the sense that the fair value has declined below the amortized cost, SFAS No. 115 (1993) requires that the firm determine whether the impairment is "other than temporary." If so, the security is written down to fair value, which becomes the new cost basis of the security, and the impairment loss is recorded in income as if it were realized.

The Securities and Exchange Commission (SEC) staff states that the determination of other-than-temporary impairment should depend on the length of time the security has been impaired, the magnitude of the impairment, the financial condition and near-term prospects of the issuer of the security, and the intent and ability of the investor to hold the security until an anticipated recovery of value. For debt securities, SFAS No. 115 (1993) states that an other-than-temporary impairment has occurred if it is probable that the investor will be unable to collect all amounts due according to the contractual terms of the securities, due to default, say. Declines in the fair values of debt securities resulting from market interest rate movements generally do not give rise to other-than-temporary impairments, as stated obliquely in SFAS No. 115 and more clearly in Emerging Issues Task Force (EITF) 99-20, *Recognition of Interest Income and Impairment on Purchased and Retained Beneficial Interests in Securitized Financial Assets,* unless the firm has decided to sell the securities.

EITF 03-1, *The Meaning of Other-than-Temporary Impairment and Its Application to Certain Investments*, now rescinded, constituted a recent attempt to provide more concrete and stringent guidance regarding what constitutes other-than-temporary impairment. This attempt was quashed by the banking industry and other constituents concerned that they would have to record impairment write-downs associated with interest rate movements based on the size or duration of the impairments or their histories of selling securities at a loss.

The rescission of EITF 03-1 was effected by FASB Staff Position (FSP) FAS 115-1 and FAS 124-1, *The Meaning of Other-than-Temporary Impairment and Its Application to Certain Investments* (2005), which provides procedural guidance regarding the assessment of impairment. Despite having the same title as EITF 03-1, this FSP does not provide any new guidance regarding what constitutes other-than-temporary impairments, however. It carries along EITF 03-1's requirements for tabular disclosures of the fair value and unrealized losses on impaired securities by category, distinguishing securities that have and have not been in a continuous loss position for 12 months or longer, accompanied by discussion of the nature of the impairments and the reason why they have not been deemed other than temporary. It also requires some additional disclosures for cost-method investments for which the assessment of fair value may not have been conducted. These disclosures provide users of financial reports with some sense as to whether impairment write-downs are being recorded properly.

Disclosures and the Assessment of Gains Trading

Gains trading may take place in two senses:

1. The firm holds a portfolio of securities that have appreciated or depreciated *since purchase,* from which it chooses to sell selected securities. (This sense is what most people have in mind when they refer to gains trading.)
2. The firm holds securities that appreciate or depreciate *during the year,* but its realization of gains and losses during the year is not representative

of this appreciation or depreciation. (This sense is actually more important from the perspective of measuring net income.)

SFAS No. 115 (1993) requires various disclosures that allow the user of financial reports to assess gains trading in each of these senses. Specifically, for each major type of security classified as either AFS or HTM, the firm must disclose the fair value, amortized cost, gross unrealized gains, and gross unrealized losses. The firm also must disclose realized gains and losses on AFS securities and on HTM securities in the infrequent cases they are sold. The user of financial reports can assess gains trading in the first sense by comparing the distributions of cumulative unrealized gains and losses and realized gains and losses during the year for each type of security. The user can assess gains trading in the second sense by calculating the total gain or loss during the year and comparing it to the realized gain during the year for each type of security.

Assuming that information about purchases and sales of securities is provided in a sufficiently disaggregated fashion on the cash flow statement and there are no mergers and acquisitions during the year, SFAS No. 115 (1993) disclosures allow the analyst to determine each of the additions to and subtractions from the T accounts for investment securities in Exhibit 6.5. Specifically, information about beginning and ending balances can be obtained from the investment securities footnote. Information about purchases and principal and interest payments can be obtained from the cash flow statement. Information about realized and unrealized gains and losses can be obtained from the investment securities footnote.

SFAS No. 115 (1993) also requires disclosures of fair value and amortized cost by four maturity categories—less than 1 year, 1 to 5 years, 5 to 10 years, and beyond 10 years—that refine the SEC's Industry Guide 3 disclosure requirements for securities discussed in Chapter 4.

JPMorgan Chase's Available-for-Sale Securities

As an illustration of the disclosures provided under SFAS No. 115 (1993), excerpts from JPMorgan Chase's 2004 footnote disclosures for AFS securities are reported in Exhibit 6.6, omitting its disclosures by type of AFS security and various other items for simplicity and adding certain historical information from its 2002 footnote disclosures to enable the assessment of gains trading over a longer period than is possible with a single disclosure. Be aware that the 2004 amounts reported in this exhibit are affected by J. P. Morgan Chase's merger with Bank One (thereby creating JPMorgan Chase), which became effective July 1, 2004, and that this may contaminate some of calculations for that year.

These disclosures indicate that JPMorgan Chase realized net gains on AFS securities of $100 million in 2004, $769 million in 2003, and $1,222 million in 2002, or $2,091 million over the three-year period. This is despite it having net unrealized losses on these securities of $429 million at the end

EXHIBIT 6.6 Excerpts from JPMorgan Chase's 2004 Available-for-Sale Security Footnote Disclosures ($ in millions)

The following table presents realized gains and losses from AFS securities:

	Year Ended December 31		
	2004	**2003**	**2002**
Realized gains	$ 576	$2,123	$1,904
Realized losses	(238)	(677)	(341)
Net realized securities gains	338	1,446	1,563

The amortized cost and estimated fair value of AFS securities were as follows for the dates indicated:

December 31	**Amortized Cost**	**Gross Unrealized Gains**	**Gross Unrealized Losses**	**Fair Value**
2004	$94,821	$ 570	$989	$94,402
2003	$60,422	$ 445	$799	$60,068
2002*	$82,952	$1,395	$315	$84,032
2001*	$59,534	$ 472	$722	$59,284

*The amounts for 2001 and 2002 are from J. P. Morgan Chase's 2002 annual report.

The following table presents the fair value and unrealized losses for AFS securities by aging category:

December 31, 2004	**Fair Value**	**Gross Unrealized Losses**
Securities with unrealized losses		
Less than 12 months	$54,449	$532
12 months or more	$14,018	$457
Total	$68,467	$989

Included in the $989 million of gross unrealized losses on AFS securities at December 31, 2004, was $457 million of unrealized losses that have existed for a period greater than 12 months. These securities are predominately rated AAA, and the unrealized losses are due to overall increases in market interest rates and not due to underlying credit concerns of the issuers. Substantially all of the securities with unrealized losses aged greater than 12 months have a market value at December 31, 2004, that is within 3% of their amortized cost basis.

The Firm believes that all aged unrealized losses, as described above, are expected to be recovered within a reasonable time through a typical interest rate cycle. Accordingly, the Firm has concluded that none of the securities in its investment portfolios are other-than-temporarily impaired at December 31, 2004.

(continues)

EXHIBIT 6.6 *(Continued)*

The following table presents the amortized cost, estimated fair value and average yield at December 31, 2004, of JPMorgan Chase's AFS securities by contractual maturity:

	Available-for-Sale Securities		
Maturity Schedule of Securities December 31, 2004	**Amortized Cost**	**Fair Value**	**Average Yield**
Due in one year or less	$ 8,641	$ 8,644	2.44%
Due after one year through five years	19,640	19,600	3.18
Due after five years through 10 years	9,270	9,278	3.77
Due after 10 years	57,270	56,880	4.48
Total securities	$94,821	$94,402	3.95%

of 2004, $354 million at the end of 2003, and $250 million at the end of 2001, although it did have net unrealized gains of $1,080 million at the end of 2002. These calculations appear generally consistent with it gains trading in the first sense in most or all of the years from 2002 to 2004. In addition, JPMorgan Chase experienced unrealized losses of $75 million = $429 million − $354 million during 2004 and $1,434 million = $354 million + $1,080 million during 2003, and an unrealized gain of $1,330 million = $1,080 million + $250 million during 2002 on AFS securities. This is consistent with it gains trading in the second sense in 2004 and 2003 but not in 2002. The amounts involved are particularly significant in 2003 and 2002, even for a bank as large as JPMorgan Chase. In particular, the net realized gain in 2002 is almost half of its pretax net income of $2,519 million in that year.

JPMorgan Chase did not record any impairment write-downs on its impaired AFS securities in 2004, noting that they are predominantly AAA rated and that the unrealized losses are expected to be recovered over "a typical interest rate cycle." This reflects the fact that firms generally do not record impairment losses for impairments caused by interest rate movements unless the firm has decided to sell the impaired securities.

APPENDIX 6A: WASHINGTON FEDERAL'S BIG GAP

Washington Federal's repricing gap disclosure is provided in Exhibit 4.7 of Chapter 4 and its fair value of financial instruments disclosure is provided in Exhibit 6A.1 for the fiscal year ending September 30, 2005 (fiscal 2005).

Case Questions

1. Do Washington Federal's reported owners' equity and net income in 2005 differ from its fair value of owners' equity and net income? Can you explain the reasons for any differences?

EXHIBIT 6A.1 Washington Federal's 2005 Fair Value of Financial Instruments Disclosures ($ in thousands)

	September 30, 2005		September 30, 2004	
	Carrying Amount	Estimated Fair Value	Carrying Amount	Estimated Fair Value
Financial Assets:				
Cash and cash equivalents	$ 637,791	$ 637,791	$ 508,361	$ 508,361
Repurchase agreements	—	—	200,000	200,000
Available-for-sale securities	1,077,856	1,077,856	899,525	899,525
Held-to-maturity securities	212,479	211,596	156,373	158,792
Loans receivable and securitized assets	6,008,932	6,086,613	5,093,443	5,203,650
FHLB stock	129,453	129,453	137,274	137,274
Financial Liabilities:				
Customer accounts	5,031,505	5,037,419	4,610,358	4,615,616
FHLB advances and other borrowings	1,885,000	1,871,474	1,300,000	1,357,405

2. Does Washington Federal's statement that it has never recorded a monthly operating loss imply it is not very interest rate risky?
3. How large would Washington Federal's economic loss be if the yield curve experienced a parallel upward shift of 1%?

NOTES

1. For the views of analysts, see P. Knutson and G. Napolitano, "Criteria Employed by the AIMR Financial Accounting Policy Committee in Evaluating Financial Accounting Standards," *Accounting Horizons* (June 1998). For the views of academics, see American Accounting Association Financial Accounting Standards Committee, "Response to the FASB Preliminary Views: Reporting Financial Instruments and Certain Related Assets and Liabilities at Fair Value," *Accounting Horizons* (December 2000).
2. T. Carroll, T. Linsmeier, and K. Petroni, "Fair Value vs. Historical Cost Accounting: Evidence from Closed-End Mutual Funds," *Journal of Accounting, Auditing, and Finance* (Winter 2003); J. Danbolt and W. Rees, "Mark-to-Market Accounting and Valuation: Evidence from UK Real Estate and Investment Companies," Working Paper, University of Glasgow (2003).
3. M. Barth, W. Beaver, and W. Landsman, "Value-Relevance of Banks' Fair Value Disclosures under SFAS No. 107," *Accounting Review* (October 1996);

E. Eccher, K. Ramesh, and R. Thiagarajan, "Fair Value Disclosures by Bank Holding Companies," *Journal of Accounting and Economics* (August–December 1996); K. Nelson, "Fair Value Accounting for Commercial Banks," *Accounting Review* (April 1996); M. Venkatachalam, "Value-Relevance of Banks' Derivatives Disclosures," *Journal of Accounting and Economics* (June 1996); and M. Wong, "The Association between SFAS No. 119 Derivatives Disclosures and the Foreign Exchange Risk Exposure of Manufacturing Firms," *Journal of Accounting Research* (Autumn 2000).

4. W. Beaver and M. Venkatachalam, "Differential Pricing of Discretionary, Nondiscretionary and Noise Components of Loan Fair Values," *Journal of Accounting, Auditing, and Finance* (Winter 2003); and D. Nissim, "Reliability of Banks' Fair Value Disclosures for Loans," *Review of Quantitative Finance and Accounting* (June 2003).
5. J. Francis, "Accounting for Futures Contracts and the Effect on Earnings Variability," *Accounting Review* (October 1990); M. Barth, W. Landsman, and J. Wahlen, "Fair Value Accounting: Effects on Banks' Earnings Volatility, Regulatory Capital, and Value of Contractual Cash Flows," *Journal of Banking and Finance* (June 1995); and V. Bernard, R. Merton, and K. Palepu, "Mark-to-Market Accounting for Banks and Thrifts: Lessons from the Danish Experience," *Journal of Accounting Research* (Spring 1995).
6. L. Hodder, P. Hopkins, and J. Wahlen, "Risk-Relevance of Fair Value Income Measures for Commercial Banks," *Accounting Review* (April 2006).
7. A. Beatty, S. Chamberlain, and J. Magliolo, "An Empirical Analysis of the Economic Implications of Fair Value Accounting for Investment Securities," *Journal of Accounting and Economics* (December 1996).
8. N. Godwin, K. Petroni, and J. Wahlen, "Fair Value Accounting for Property-Liability Insurers and Classification Decisions under FAS 115," *Journal of Accounting, Auditing, and Finance* (Summer 1998).

CHAPTER 7

Mortgage Banks

Like thrifts, mortgage banks mainly originate or purchase one- to four-family residential mortgages, although some do significant business in multifamily and commercial real estate mortgages. Unlike thrifts, mortgage banks usually hold mortgages only to accumulate enough to sell efficiently and sometimes to provide evidence that they are creditworthy. Mortgage banks often sell mortgages through securitizations, in which case they usually retain the right to service the mortgages and sometimes retain mortgage-backed securities (MBS). When the securitized mortgages are risky, in order to induce investors to purchase the MBS, the retained securities usually are residual or otherwise subordinated claims that concentrate the risk of the underlying mortgages.

Mortgage banking is primarily a fee-based rather than interest rate spread–based business. Mortgage banks earn fees from originating and servicing mortgages. Mortgage banks also generate gains (and sometimes losses) when they sell mortgages. The amount they receive (in cash, other proceeds, and retained securities) from securitizations usually exceeds the amount they pay to obtain mortgages, because MBS have desirable features, such as liquidity or cash flow characteristics, for which investors are willing to pay. Mortgage banks' fee-driven nature naturally leads to an income statement focus in valuing these firms, rather than the balance sheet focus for thrifts.

Because prime fixed-rate residential mortgages usually are prepayable without penalty (and other types of fixed-rate mortgages may also be prepayable without penalty or with a penalty that is smaller than the realized value of the prepayment option), mortgage banks are exposed to interest-rate-motivated prepayment risk on their fixed-rate mortgage-related assets. Specifically, mortgagees often prepay and refinance their fixed-rate mortgages when mortgage commitment rates fall sufficiently to make this decision economically attractive given the costs involved in refinancing. Prepayment yields large percentage impairment losses on mortgage banks' mortgage servicing rights, interest-only strips, and residual securities that have little or no value upon prepayment of the underlying mortgages, and it yields smaller percentage impairment losses on most of mortgage banks' other types of mortgage-related assets. Offsetting these effects, mortgage banks' origination fees and gains on sale are strongly positively affected by refinancing of fixed-rate mortgages. Understanding interest-rate-motivated prepayment sensitivity is thus a primary focus in the analysis of mortgage banks. Non–interest-rate-motivated prepayment (e.g., moving and cash-out refinancing) has less pervasive but still quite significant effects on mortgage banks.

This chapter examines most aspects of mortgage banks' financial reporting and analysis, with two main exceptions. First, detailed discussions of the accounting and disclosure rules for securitizations, prepayment-sensitive retained securities, and mortgage servicing rights under Statement of Financial Accounting Standards (SFAS) No. 140, *Accounting for Transfers and Servicing of Financial Assets and Extinguishments of Liabilities* (2000), and SFAS No. 156, *Accounting for Servicing of Financial Assets* (2006), are deferred to Chapter 8. Since the information provided under these rules is of critical importance in the analysis of mortgage banks, the type of financial institution most affected by securitizations, these two chapters should be read as a matched set. Second, mortgage banks actively use derivatives to hedge their prepayment and other risks, and their fixed-rate interest rate lock commitments usually are accounted for as derivatives. Discussion of the accounting and disclosure rules for derivatives is deferred to Chapter 11.

The next section provides background information about the mortgage banking industry, its major players, and mortgage banks' activities. The "Financial Statement Structure" section describes the structure of mortgage banks' financial statements, using Countrywide Financial Corporation (Countrywide) as a representative mortgage bank. The "Main Risk-Return Trade-Offs and Financial Analysis Issues" section outlines the risk-return trade-offs that mortgage banks face and the corresponding financial analysis issues that these trade-offs imply. The final section briefly describes accounting requirements regarding fee revenue and associated costs on mortgage banking activities.

MORTGAGE BANKING INDUSTRY, MAJOR PLAYERS, AND ACTIVITIES

The federal government essentially created the mortgage banking industry, which began in the 1950s originating mortgages insured by federal government agencies. Mortgage banking took off in 1970, when the Government National Mortgage Association (commonly referred to as Ginnie Mae), a federal government agency within the Department of Housing and Urban Development (HUD), sponsored the first securitization of government-insured mortgages. The Federal National Mortgage Association (Fannie Mae) and the Federal Home Loan Mortgage Corporation (Freddie Mac), previously government agencies and now private corporations with $2.25 billion conditional lines of credit from the U.S. Treasury, also facilitated the spectacular growth of the MBS market and mortgage banks. Freddie Mac sponsored the first securitization of conventional (not government-insured) mortgages in 1971.

Ginnie Mae currently sponsors securitizations of mortgages insured by these government agencies:

- Federal Housing Administration (FHA) within HUD
- Department of Veterans Affairs (VA)
- Rural Housing Service (RHS) within the Department of Agriculture
- Office of Public and Indian Housing (PIH) within HUD

Ginnie Mae sponsored residential MBS with a value of $377 billion outstanding at the end of 2005. During 2005, Ginnie Mae securitized $90 billion of mortgages, of which 68% were FHA mortgages and 29% were VA mortgages. Ginnie Mae securitizes most government-insured mortgages (e.g., 93% of all FHA and VA mortgages outstanding in 2005 had been securitized by Ginnie Mae).[1] Ginnie Mae is decreasing fairly rapidly in size as fewer government-insured mortgages are issued.

Fannie Mae and Freddie Mac are federally chartered and referred to as government-sponsored enterprises (GSEs). Reflecting restrictions specified in their charters, Fannie Mae and Freddie Mac primarily purchase and sponsor securitizations of conforming conventional mortgages. For a mortgage to be conforming, it must meet certain criteria including a maximum principal that changes annually based on the mean home price and is $417,000 for 2006, a maximum principal-to-property value ratio, a debt-to-income cap, and mortgage documentation. In July 2006, Fannie Mae held $731 billion of mortgages in portfolio and guaranteed $1.7 trillion of outstanding MBS held by others, while Freddie Mac held $711 billion of mortgages in portfolio and guaranteed $1.1 trillion of outstanding MBS.[2]

Fannie Mae and Freddie Mac are regulated under the Federal Housing Enterprise Safety and Soundness Act of 1992, which imposes capital requirements. Their regulator is the Office of Federal Housing Enterprise Oversight (OFHEO) within HUD. OFHEO's statutory powers and staffing are less than those of bank regulators, although its staffing has increased considerably since the well-publicized accounting problems identified in the summer of 2003 at Freddie Mac, which led OFHEO to publish a special report on Freddie Mac in December 2003 and subsequently to investigate Fannie Mae. OFHEO published a special report on Fannie Mae in September 2004, and it classified Fannie Mae as significantly undercapitalized in December 2004. Legislation is currently being considered in Congress to replace OFHEO and the regulator of the Federal Home Loan Banks (FHLBs) with a regulator with the same statutory powers as bank regulators.

The FHLBs, while also GSEs, are not actively involved in mortgage securitization. They are actively involved in the mortgage market, however, primarily by providing funding to their member institutions that is collateralized by the mortgages those institutions hold, but also by holding mortgages that they acquire from those institutions. At the end of 2005, the FHLBs held $105 billion of mortgages.[3] In the remainder of this chapter, "the GSEs" refers to Fannie Mae and Freddie Mac.

The U.S. residential MBS market, with $5.4 trillion outstanding in June 2006, is now somewhat larger than the $4.8 trillion U.S. Treasury securities market.[4] The MBS market has had a profound effect on home ownership in the United States (and thereby on the U.S. economy as a whole) by making fixed-rate mortgages lower cost and more widely available.

The GSEs claim on their Web sites that they reduce the interest rate on the fixed-rate conforming mortgages they securitize by .25 to .5% compared to the fixed-rate jumbo mortgages they do not securitize. While the GSEs clearly facilitated the development of the MBS market and play major roles in that market today, a lively public policy debate is ongoing regarding how much the GSEs reduce mortgage rates, the extent to which they benefit from an implicit subsidy resulting from investors' perception that their debt is effectively guaranteed by the federal government, and whether their retained portfolios are so large as to constitute a systemic risk. In particular, economists at the Federal Reserve have argued that the interest rate premium on jumbo prime mortgages over the interest rate on the conforming prime mortgages does not primarily indicate the GSEs' effect on the cost of fixed-rate mortgages, but rather is largely an artifact of the segmentation and lesser liquidity of the market for jumbo mortgages that results from the existence of an arbitrary ceiling on the principal amount of conforming mortgages.[5] While he was Federal Reserve Board Chairman, Alan Greenspan argued that the enormous size of the GSEs' retained portfolios: (1) has resulted from their cost of debt capital being reduced by .4% because of investors' perception of a federal government guarantee of their debt, a huge advantage in the highly competitive mortgage market, (2) constitutes a systemic risk, and (3) could be reduced without significant effect on the mortgage market because these portfolios are financed by debt that from investors' perspective is similar to MBS.[6] As part of a capital restoration program approved by OFHEO, Fannie Mae reduced its retained portfolio considerably from its peak at $917 billion in September 2003 to $715 billion in November 2005. In contrast, Freddie Mac's retained portfolio grew rapidly over this period. As part of its comprehensive settlement with OFHEO and the Securities and Exchange Commission in May 2006, Fannie Mae has agreed to increase its portfolio only moderately and with OFHEO approval in the future.

The size of the MBS market derives from the huge amount of residential mortgages in the United States. In March 2006, $9.5 trillion of one- to four-family residential mortgages were outstanding, with about 56% held in the form of MBS.[7] In each year from 2001 to 2005, over $2 trillion of one- to four-family residential mortgages were originated. In 2003, originations were a record $3.8 trillion, with an unusually high 66% of these originations being refinancings due to historically low interest rates in the middle of the year.[8] Even now that long-term interest rates have crept up, originations remain fairly high for non–interest-rate-motivated reasons. For example, Freddie Mac estimated that 88% of mortgages refinanced in its portfolio in the second quarter of 2006 involved the mortgagee taking out cash in excess of 5% of the mortgage principal[9]; this level of cash-out refinancing has been made possible by the dramatic appreciation in the value of real estate over the past decade, a run that apparently has ended.

There are various distinct types of residential mortgages. Government-insured mortgages are guaranteed in whole or part by an agency of the federal government, while private firms bear the credit risk on conventional mortgages. Approximately 8% (92%) of mortgages outstanding are government-insured (conventional); the percentage of government-insured mortgages has declined substantially over time; for example, it was 17% in 1990.[10]

Prime mortgages (rated A if conforming and Alt-A otherwise) are made to individuals with essentially unimpaired credit usually measured using the Fair Isaac Corporation's (FICO) credit scores; these mortgages generally must also have loan-to-value ratios that are not too high given the borrower's credit score or private mortgage insurance and other desirable attributes. Subprime mortgages (rated A− to D) generally are made to individuals with somewhat to very troubled credit histories as measured by FICO scores; these mortgages may also reflect higher loan-to-value ratios for a given credit score or other less desirable attributes. No industry standard determines the classification of mortgages from A to D, although their relative riskiness is indicated by the usual premia above the interest rate paid on A-rated mortgages for lower-rated mortgages: A−, 1 to 2%; B, 2 to 3%; C, 3.5 to 4.5%; and D, 5 to 6%.[11] Manufactured home mortgages usually are subprime; moreover, the value of their collateral depreciates relatively quickly.

Subprime mortgages first became significant in the mid-1990s due to a number of regulatory and economic events. The Depository Institutions Deregulation and Monetary Control Act of 1980 overrode state-mandated ceilings on interest rates and fees, making high-cost subprime mortgages possible. The Alternative Mortgage Transaction Parity Act of 1982 allowed variable-rate and balloon mortgages, common features of subprime mortgages, especially the lower grades. The Tax Reform Act of 1986 eliminated the tax deductibility of interest on consumer debt; while this act has made all types of mortgages tax preferred to other forms of consumer debt, it is particularly important for subprime mortgages due to their high pretax interest rates and because subprime mortgagees often engage in cash-out refinancing or take out home equity mortgages to avoid assuming consumer debt. Finally, by the mid-1990s, the securitization markets for credit-risky assets had developed sufficiently so that these mortgages did not have to be held in full by the originator.

In 2003, subprime mortgages constituted about 27% of the number of residential mortgages outstanding in the United States but only about 9% of the dollar amount of mortgage originations,[12] due to the considerably smaller average principal amount of subprime mortgages. Subprime mortgage originations have fallen from their peak of 15% of the dollar amount of mortgage originations in 1997 for two main reasons. First, the lower grades of subprime mortgages are issued less frequently now, due to the illiquidity of and default on these mortgages and the bankruptcies or distress of the originators of these mortgages during and after the hedge-fund crisis in the second half of 1998. However, originations of subprime mortgages rated A− continue to grow, in part because the GSEs now purchase these mortgages and in part because the largest mortgage originators, such as Countrywide, primarily originate this grade of subprime mortgages. Reflecting this fact, mortgages rated A− constituted 84% of subprime mortgage originations by number in 2003 but only 62% in 1997.[13] Second, subprime mortgages are less susceptible to the interest-rate-motivated prepayment and refinancing that has led to historically high levels of originations of prime mortgages in recent years, 2003 in particular.

As discussed, mortgages must meet a number of criteria in order to be conforming. Being too large to meet the maximum principal requirement ("jumbo") is the most common reason why an otherwise conforming mortgage is nonconforming. Jumbo mortgages are approximately 15% of the dollar amount of conventional mortgages.[14] The vast majority of nonjumbo prime conventional mortgages are conforming.

Home equity mortgages are second mortgages in which the first mortgagor has a senior claim on the mortgaged property. Compared to first mortgages, the credit risk of home equity mortgages depends more on the creditworthiness of the borrower and less on the value of the collateral. Home equity mortgages are often in the form of lines of credit that can be drawn on as desired by the borrower.

In 1997, mortgage banks originated 56.3%, commercial banks originated 24.8%, and thrifts originated 18.3% of one- to four-family residential mortgages.[15] Banks and other financial institutions recently have acquired most mortgage banks, however, so the analysis of mortgage banks now is usually as a part of a diversified financial institution. Countrywide is somewhat of an exception as the sole remaining large independent mortgage bank, although it has diversified into non–mortgage-banking activities, as discussed in the next section. In 2005, Countrywide was the largest residential mortgage originator and servicer in the United States, originating about 16% of the $3.1 trillion residential mortgages originated that year and servicing about 12% of the mortgages outstanding.[16] The second through seventh largest players in these markets, based on their volume of activity in 2005, are Wells Fargo Home Mortgage, Washington Mutual, Chase Home Finance, Bank of America, CitiMortgage, and GMAC Residential Holdings. Residential mortgage origination and servicing are both concentrated markets, with these seven firms together having over 50% market share of these markets.[17]

Mortgage servicing entails various activities, such as billing, collecting, and processing payments; dealing with defaulted mortgages; and providing customer service. Servicers also have to advance cash in two circumstances.

1. They advance property taxes and insurance on delinquent accounts in order to maintain the value of the collateral in the securitization trust.

2. They advance principal and interest payments on delinquent accounts, unless it is determined that these amounts are not recoverable from the collateral of the accounts.

As compensation for performing these activities, servicers receive servicing fees, which are usually between .25% and .5% of the outstanding principal on the mortgages. In addition to the normal servicing fee, an excess servicing fee often results from Ginnie Mae and the GSEs issuing MBS at half-percentage-point increments; the excess servicing fee is the yield on the underlying mortgages minus the yield on the MBS minus the guarantee fee paid to Ginnie Mae or the GSEs minus the normal servicing fee.

Servicers can reinvest the float arising from borrowers' monthly mortgage, tax, and insurance payments for a period of time before these payments need to be passed along to the parties entitled to receive the payments. Servicers also receive late fees.

There is usually a fairly active market in the sale of mortgage servicing and subservicing rights. Subservicers perform servicing activities for a contracted period of time, but the servicer remains legally obligated to provide the service. Special servicers often deal with defaulted accounts. Mortgage banks often securitize excess servicing fees to raise funds and reduce risk.

FINANCIAL STATEMENT STRUCTURE

The next three subsections describe the structures of mortgage banks' balance sheets, income statements, and cash flow statements, respectively, using Countrywide's 2005 Form 10-K filing. As a mortgage bank, Countrywide primarily originates, securitizes, and services prime first mortgages, although now about 10% of its origination volume is in each of subprime and prime home equity mortgages. Although Countrywide still is primarily a mortgage bank, the Federal Reserve approved its application to become a financial holding company in 2001, and Countrywide has diversified into warehouse lending to other mortgage banks, banking, various securities activities related to MBS markets, and insurance. Countrywide's non–mortgage-banking businesses are not described in this chapter.

Balance Sheet

Mortgage banks have three main assets:

1. Mortgages and MBS held for sale, which are valued at the lower of cost or market, like inventory
2. Retained securities from securitizations
3. Mortgage servicing rights (MSRs)

MSRs are accounted for separately from the underlying mortgages only when the principal is sold or securitized to third parties, or when MSRs are purchased from third parties. Mortgage banks also often hold a wide range of derivatives and other financial instruments that hedge the considerable prepayment and other risks of their mortgage-related assets. Because these assets contain embedded written prepayment options, mortgage banks' hedging instruments are predominantly purchased options, and thus assets.

Countrywide's 2005 balance sheet is reported in Exhibit 7.1. At the end of 2005, Countrywide holds $175.1 billion of assets, of which $11.0 billion are trading securities held by its broker-dealer subsidiary, $70.1 billion are mortgages held for investment primarily by its banking and warehouse lending subsidiaries, and $24.3 billion are generic liquid instruments. Of the remaining $69.7 billion of assets that may relate to mortgage banking, $36.8 billion (53%) are mortgages or MBS held for sale, $11.4 billion (16%) are other financial instruments—a footnote indicates this amount includes hedging instruments of $.8 billion (1%), a variety of senior retained securities and other securities of $7.9 billion (11%), and residual, subordinated, or otherwise risky retained securities of $2.7 billion (4%)—and $12.6 billion (18%) are MSRs.

The percentage of assets attributable to mortgages and MBS held for sale depends on if and when securitizations and sales of these instruments occur during the year, which depends on the timing and volume of mortgage originations and the liquidity of the markets to sell mortgages.

The percentage of assets attributable to retained securities usually rises with the credit risk of the mortgages that are securitized. To induce investors to purchase MBS when the underlying mortgages are credit risky, the issuer invariably has to provide some form of credit enhancement, the most common of which is the retention of residual or otherwise subordinated securities. Since Countrywide primarily securitizes prime mortgages and the subprime mortgages it securitizes appear to be primarily or solely rated A−, it holds a relatively small amount of residual or otherwise subordinated securities. Specifically, Countrywide discloses that it retains $2.0 billion of residual or otherwise subordinated securities from its securitizations of subprime and prime home equity mortgages and that the size of the residual interest usually ranges from 1 to 5.5% of the principal balance of the mortgages securitized.

Mortgage servicing rights have constituted an increasingly smaller percentage of mortgage banks' assets over the past few years, because unusually high mortgage prepayment rates have shortened their average life. Some portion of this increase in prepayment rates is attributable to the unusually low and generally declining long-term rates in recent years, although Freddie Mac reports that 30-year conventional, conforming, fixed-rate mortgage commitment rates were about 1.1% higher in October 2006 than their historic low in June 2003. However, some portion appears to be attributable to mortgagees' increased tendency to refinance mortgages for non–interest-rate-motivated reasons, which may persist.

EXHIBIT 7.1 Countrywide Financial Corporation and Subsidiaries
Consolidated Balance Sheets

	Years Ended December 31,	
	2005	**2004**
	(in thousands)	
ASSETS		
Cash	$ 1,031,108	$ 751,237
Mortgage loans and mortgage-backed securities held for sale	36,818,688	37,350,149
Trading securities owned, at fair value	10,314,384	10,558,387
Trading securities pledged as collateral, at fair value	668,189	1,303,007
Securities purchased under agreements to resell, securities borrowed, and federal funds sold	23,317,361	13,456,448
Loans held for investment, net of allowance for loan losses of $189,201 and $125,046, respectively	70,071,152	39,661,191
Investments in other financial instruments, at fair value	11,455,745	10,091,057
Mortgage servicing rights, net	12,610,839	8,729,929
Premises and equipment, net	1,279,659	985,350
Other assets	7,518,245	5,608,950
Total assets	$175,085,370	$128,495,705
LIABILITIES		
Notes payable	$ 76,187,886	$ 66,613,671
Securities sold under agreements to repurchase and federal funds purchased	34,153,205	20,465,123
Deposit liabilities	39,489,256	20,013,208
Accounts payable and accrued liabilities	6,307,818	5,594,764
Trading securities sold, not yet purchased, at fair value	2,285,171	2,912,620
Income taxes payable	3,846,174	2,586,243
Total liabilities	162,269,510	118,185,629
Commitments and contingencies	—	—
SHAREHOLDERS' EQUITY		
Common stock	30,008	29,085
Additional paid-in capital	2,954,019	2,570,402
Accumulated other comprehensive income	61,114	118,943
Retained earnings	9,770,719	7,591,646
Total shareholders' equity	12,815,860	10,310,076
Total liabilities and shareholders' equity	$175,085,370	$128,495,705

Reflecting their fee-based nature, mortgage banks' total assets tend to be small compared to their volume of originations during the year and, for mortgage banks that actively service mortgages, compared to the principal in their servicing portfolios. For example, Countrywide discloses that it originated $428 billion in 2005 and serviced $1.1 trillion of mortgages at the end of 2005.

Unlike thrifts, which raise a large portion of their funds from core deposits, mortgage banks raise funds in securities markets or from banks, and so are wholesale on the liability side. For example, at the end of 2005, Countrywide's primary financing liabilities are $76.2 billion of notes payable with a remaining maturity from 1 month to 30 years, $34.2 billion of short-term MBS repurchase agreements, and $39.5 billion of deposits in its banking subsidiary.

As a large, successful mortgage bank with A-rated long-term debt, Countrywide has considerable access to securities markets. Despite this fact, it has $7.3 billion of unsecured and $9.2 billion of secured unused revolving credit financing from banks and a $6.0 billion reusable commitment from a multi-seller asset-backed commercial paper conduit to purchase its conforming mortgages. Countrywide pays fees to maintain these backup sources of financing, because mortgage banks require a steady flow of capital to originate or purchase mortgages or MSRs in order to maintain their flow of fees. If capital flows dry up, mortgage banks decline very quickly, as happened to subprime mortgage banks in the hedge-fund crisis in the second half of 1998.

To facilitate the sale of mortgages, mortgage banks may provide recourse to the purchasers of their mortgages and MBS, which yields a recourse liability. Recourse is not generally required to sell prime mortgages and MBS, but it may be required to sell subprime or home equity MBS. Countrywide primarily originates prime mortgages and so has a relatively small recourse liability of $175.7 million, which is entirely attributable to its subprime and home equity mortgage securitizations. It also discloses that it has a maximum loss in excess of the recorded recourse liability of $349.9 million.

Mortgage banks are typically less leveraged than thrifts, both because they do a relatively large amount of volume off a relatively small capital base and because MSRs and certain other of the positions they hold are risky. In its 2002 annual report, Countrywide disclosed its internal financial leverage (debt:equity) guidelines were: 15:1 for mortgage origination, which is similar to a bank; 40:1 for capital market activities, which is similar to the GSEs; and 3:1 for mortgage servicing, which is similar to a property-casualty insurance company. In part because it now holds a substantial amount of mortgages in its banking and warehouse lending subsidiaries and in part because MSRs are a smaller portion of its total assets, Countrywide's leverage ratio has increased over time and now is similar to that of a bank.

Income Statement

Mortgage banks' main revenues are usually fees for mortgage origination and servicing as well as gains on the sale of mortgages. Although amortization and impairment of MSRs are logically expenses and losses, respectively, mortgage banks often deduct these items directly from mortgage servicing fees as if they are contra-revenues. This yields the net effect of mortgage servicing (ignoring back-office costs) in a single line on the income statement.

Gains on sale tend to be larger for securitizations than for whole mortgage sales, in part because of the desirability of MBS to investors and in part because investors in MBS tend to have less market power than do investors in whole mortgages. In favorable markets for risky asset sales, gains on sale tend to be much smaller for prime mortgages than for credit-riskier mortgages, reflecting the less developed state of the markets for credit-riskier assets as well as accounting measurement and risk retention considerations discussed in Chapter 8. For example, Countrywide discloses that during 2005 it recorded gains as a percentage of principal amount sold of .82% for prime mortgages, 2.01% for subprime mortgages, and 2.10% for prime home equity mortgages. Countrywide's largest percentage gains on sale were 2.75% for "reperforming" mortgages that had been nonperforming but returned to performing status.

Countrywide's income statement for 2005 is reported in Exhibit 7.2. In that year, it has total revenues net of MSR amortization and impairment of $10.0 billion, of which $6.3 billion is primarily due to mortgage banking activities discussed in detail later, $2.2 billion is net interest income after the provision for loan losses that is primarily due to banking and warehouse lending activities, $1.0 billion is net premiums earned due to insurance activities, and $.5 billion is commissions that is primarily due to capital markets activities. Of the primarily mortgage banking revenue, $4.9 (78%) billion is origination fees and gain on sale of mortgages combined and $1.5 billion (22%) is the net effect of mortgage servicing.

Since 2002, Countrywide has not disclosed mortgage origination fees separately from gains on sales of mortgages; this presumably is because the vast bulk of mortgage banks' origination fees are recognized as revenue at the date of sale of the mortgages, as discussed later in the section "Accounting for Fees and Costs." Countrywide's aggregation of these items makes its financial analysis more difficult, however, because the primary determinants of mortgage origination fees—the volume and mix of mortgages sold—do not include a primary determinant of the gain on sale of mortgages—the change in interest rates between the origination and sale of mortgages.

Countrywide discloses that of its mortgage origination fees and gains on sale of mortgages combined, $2.8 billion (57%) is attributable to prime first mortgages, $1.5 billion (31%) is attributable to subprime and prime home equity mortgages, and $.6 billion (12%) is attributable to reperforming mortgages and various other types of loans. The gains on sale of prime mortgages are less than twice that for subprime/prime home equity mortgages despite the fact that Countrywide originates about five times as many prime first mortgages as subprime/prime home equity mortgages, reflecting the much higher percentage gains on credit-riskier mortgages discussed earlier.

EXHIBIT 7.2 Countrywide Financial Corporation and Subsidiaries Consolidated Statement of Earnings

	Years Ended December 31,		
	2005	2004	2003
		(in thousands)	
REVENUES			
Gain on sale of loans and securities	$4,861,780	$4,842,082	$5,887,436
Interest income	7,970,045	4,645,654	3,347,801
Interest expense	(5,616,425)	(2,608,338)	(1,940,207)
Net interest income	2,353,620	2,037,316	1,407,594
Provision for loan losses	(115,685)	(71,775)	(48,204)
Net interest income after provision for loan losses	2,237,935	1,965,541	1,359,390
Loan servicing fees and other income from retained interests	4,281,254	3,269,587	2,804,338
Amortization of mortgage servicing rights	(2,288,354)	(1,940,457)	(2,069,246)
Recovery (impairment) of retained interests	23,345	(648,137)	(1,432,965)
Servicing hedge (losses) gains	(523,078)	(215,343)	234,823
Net loan servicing fees and other income (loss) from retained interests	1,493,167	465,650	(463,050)
Net insurance premiums earned	953,647	782,685	732,816
Other revenue	470,179	510,669	462,050
Total revenues	10,016,708	8,566,627	7,978,642
EXPENSES			
Compensation	3,615,483	3,137,045	2,590,936
Occupancy and other office	879,680	643,378	525,192
Insurance claims	441,584	390,203	360,046
Advertising and promotion	229,183	171,585	103,902
Other operating	703,012	628,543	552,794
Total expenses	5,868,942	4,970,754	4,132,870
Earnings before income taxes	4,147,766	3,595,873	3,845,772
Provision for income taxes	1,619,676	1,398,299	1,472,822
NET EARNINGS	$2,528,090	$2,197,574	$2,372,950

Countrywide's net revenue from mortgage servicing and other retained interests reflects $4.3 billion of mortgage servicing and other fees less $2.3 billion of MSR amortization, less a $23 million recovery of prior impairments of its MSRs and other retained interests, and less a $.5 billion loss on its MSR servicing hedge.

Mortgage banks' main revenue line items are highly and differentially associated with fixed-rate mortgage commitment rates, in particular with the sufficiently large decreases in or historically low levels of rates that yield substantial prepayment and refinancing of fixed-rate mortgages. These associations are discussed in detail in the "Interest Rate and Prepayment Risks" section.

Mortgage banks' main pretax expenses are the labor and occupancy costs associated with operating retail networks to acquire mortgages and back offices to service mortgages. Mortgage banks that securitize mortgages also may pay substantial guarantee fees to the agencies, other MBS sponsors, or credit insurers that guarantee their securitizations. Countrywide classifies guarantee fees as a reduction of mortgage servicing revenue, not as an expense, which makes considerable sense, because the guarantee fee is effectively paid out of the gross servicing fee, leaving only a net servicing fee. In 2005, Countrywide has $5.5 billion of pretax expenses not including $.4 billion insurance claims expense, $3.6 billion (65%) of which is for salaries, $.9 billion (16%) of which is for occupancy, and $.9 billion (16%) is advertising and other. Countrywide is a unique independent mortgage bank in the extensive scale of its retail network and back offices.

Cash Flow Statement

Mortgage banks' main adjustment to net income in the operating section of the cash flow statement is usually the change in mortgages and MBS held for sale, which are treated like inventory with respect to cash flow statement classification. This adjustment can be very large compared to income and so can yield huge variations in cash from operations. Cash from operations tends to be low in periods in which there is an increase of mortgages and MBS available for sale, and vice versa. These variations in cash from operations are generally not a concern as long as the change in mortgages and MBS held for sale does not reflect difficulty in selling or originating mortgages. For example, a buildup of mortgages may reflect lags associated with the need to accumulate enough to securitize efficiently or to hold these mortgages for a period of time to prove their creditworthiness. However, if a buildup reflects an inability to sell mortgages, as was the case with subprime mortgage banks during the hedge-fund crisis, then it is a signal of illiquidity. A decrease in mortgages and MBS may reflect an inability or unwillingness to originate mortgages, although this is less likely to be a concern.

Countrywide's 2005 cash flow statement is reported in Exhibit 7.3. Its cash from operations is negative in each of each of the three years presented but fluctuates considerably over time, from $(10.6) billion in 2003, to $(5.5) billion in 2004, to $(11.7) billion in 2005. The main contributor to these fluctuations are the larger excess of originations of mortgages and MBS held for sale over proceeds from selling or receiving principal payments on those instruments in 2003 and 2005 ($10.5 billion and $12.6 billion, respectively) versus 2004 ($7.0 billion).

Mortgage banks' main investing cash flows are typically their investments in MSRs and retained securities from securitizations, assuming these securities are not classified as trading, in which case they affect cash from operations. For example, in 2005, Countrywide's cash for investment of $(41.8) billion is attributable in part to a $.3 billion net addition to MSRs, although its main investment is a $33.7 billion investment in mortgages held for investment in its banking and warehouse lending subsidiaries.

Mortgage banks' financing cash flows straightforwardly reflect their sources of funds, either from issuing securities or borrowing from other financial institutions. For example, to finance its large increases in mortgages held for investment and MSRs during 2005, Countrywide's cash from financing is positive at $53.7 billion. Its cash from financing is primarily attributable to net increases in short-term borrowings of $8.1 billion, long-term debt of $12.6 billion, securities sold under agreements to repurchase and federal funds purchased of $13.7 billion, and deposits of $19.5 billion.

It is often important for users of mortgage banks' financial reports to examine their supplemental disclosures about noncash transactions. Certain of their activities, such as securitizing but not (yet) selling mortgages or desecuritizing MBS into mortgages, have no effect on the cash flow statement but may have implications for financial analysis. Desecuritizations are a concern if they reflect an inability to sell the MBS.

MAIN RISK-RETURN TRADE-OFFS AND FINANCIAL ANALYSIS ISSUES

Interest Rate and Prepayment Risks

Mortgage banks are exposed to interest rate risk on their mortgage-related assets through prepayment and discounting effects that are not entirely distinct. The prepayment effect reflects the fact that most residential mortgages give mortgagees a call option to prepay. Prime residential mortgages usually are prepayable without penalty. Subprime residential mortgages usually are prepayable, although penalties often apply. In contrast, commercial mortgages either are not prepayable or include prepayment penalties.

The prepayment call option is valuable primarily for fixed-rate mortgages, and so mortgages are assumed to be fixed-rate in the remainder of this subsection. The value of the option rises as interest rates fall, sharply so over the range of interest rates for which the probability of prepayment rises substantially. Since the value of the prepayment call option comes out of the mortgage, the value of the mortgage falls with interest rates over approximately the same range.

EXHIBIT 7.3 Countrywide Financial Corporation and Subsidiaries Consolidated Statement of Cash Flow

	Years Ended December 31,		
	2005	2004	2003
		(in thousands)	
Cash flows from operating activities:			
Net earnings	$ 2,528,090	$ 2,197,574	$ 2,372,950
Adjustments to reconcile net earnings to net cash used by operating activities:			
Gain on sale of loans and securities	(4,861,780)	(4,842,082)	(5,887,436)
Accretion of discount on securities	(386,322)	(422,683)	(474,302)
Accretion of discount and fair value adjustments on notes payable	(58,397)	(32,783)	(32,062)
Net change in fair value of hedged notes payable and related interest-rate and foreign-currency swaps	(2,777)	370	330
Amortization of deferred fees on time deposits	13,706	4,928	—
Provision for loan losses	115,685	71,775	48,204
Amortization of mortgage servicing rights	2,288,354	1,940,457	2,069,246
(Recovery) impairment of mortgage servicing rights	(601,017)	279,842	1,326,741
Change in fair value of mortgage servicing rights attributable to hedged risk	213,166	—	—
(Recovery) impairment of other retained interests	(346,121)	404,226	208,387
Interest capitalized on loans held for investment	(123,457)	(1,503)	—
Depreciation and other amortization	243,101	151,159	110,082
Stock-based compensation expense	39,909	32,776	23,176
Provision for deferred income taxes	1,469,093	492,188	344,189

(continues)

EXHIBIT 7.3 *(Continued)*

	Years Ended December 31,		
	2005	**2004**	**2003**
		(in thousands)	
Tax benefit of stock options exercised	115,117	93,057	88,031
Origination and purchase of loans and mortgage-backed securities held for sale	(448,686,210)	(335,890,238)	(406,775,069)
Proceeds from sale and principal repayments of loans and mortgage-backed securities	436,083,977	328,901,595	396,319,952
Decrease (increase) in trading securities	933,354	(517,263)	(2,595,373)
Decrease in investments in other financial instruments	1,422,310	517,200	1,369,928
Increase in other assets	(1,970,798)	(893,398)	(11,996)
Increase (decrease) in accounts payable and accrued liabilities	679,285	795,106	(129,315)
(Decrease) increase in trading securities sold, not yet purchased, at fair value	(627,449)	1,442,976	1,023,414
(Decrease) increase in income taxes payable	(181,598)	(184,439)	49,224
Net cash used by operating activities	(11,700,779)	(5,459,160)	(10,551,699)
Cash flows from investing activities:			
Increase in securities purchased under agreements to resell, federal funds sold, and securities borrowed	(9,860,913)	(3,008,346)	(4,450,734)
Additions to loans held for investment, net	(33,697,649)	(13,355,505)	(20,193,110)
Sales of loans held for investment	2,678,737	—	—
Additions to investments in other financial instruments	(6,071,163)	(7,042,716)	(11,506,640)
Proceeds from sale and repayment of investments in other financial instruments	5,961,014	14,894,871	10,965,252
Additions to mortgage servicing rights	(302,441)	(385,459)	(49,607)

EXHIBIT 7.3 *(Continued)*

	Years Ended December 31,		
	2005	**2004**	**2003**
		(in thousands)	
Purchase of premises and equipment, net	(475,907)	(341,738)	(260,639)
Net cash used by investing activities	(41,768,322)	(9,238,893)	(25,495,478)
Cash flows from financing activities:			
Net increase in short-term borrowings	8,142,815	9,772,156	16,552,092
Issuance of long-term debt	21,873,808	16,535,096	8,202,650
Repayment of long-term debt	(9,282,361)	(10,518,279)	(5,245,209)
Issuance of Company-obligated mandatorily redeemable capital pass-through securities	—	—	500,000
Net increase (decrease) in securities sold under agreements to repurchase and federal funds purchased	13,688,082	(11,548,289)	9,378,573
Net increase in deposit liabilities	19,462,342	10,680,609	6,213,400
Issuance of common stock	213,303	111,176	542,075
Payment of dividends	(349,017)	(209,362)	(80,376)
Net cash provided by financing activities	53,748,972	14,823,107	36,063,205
Net increase in cash	279,871	125,054	16,028
Cash at beginning of year	751,237	626,183	610,155
Cash at end of year	$ 1,031,108	$ 751,237	$ 626,183

As discussed in the "Duration and Parallel Shifts in Flat Yield Curves" section in Chapter 4, the value of nonprepayable fixed-rate assets varies inversely with interest rates due to the effect of discounting, more so for longer duration assets. In addition, the relationship between the value of such assets and interest rates exhibits convexity. That is, their value falls proportionately less with interest rates for higher interest rates, because higher interest rates reduce the weights on more distant payments in the calculation of duration.

The discounting effect for prepayable mortgages is more complex than for nonprepayable fixed-rate assets. The duration of mortgages rises with interest rates over a range of rates, as the declining probability of prepayment works to stretch out payments. The increase of duration with interest rates is said to yield negative convexity (although "concavity" is a simpler and more correct term) in the relationship between the value of mortgages and interest rates. That is, the value of mortgages rises slower or falls faster with interest rates for higher rates. The extent of negative convexity varies substantially across types of mortgage-related assets, as discussed in Chapter 8.

For sufficiently low interest rates, the value of a prepayable mortgage rises with interest rates, because the decreasing value of the prepayment call option dominates. The prepayment effect weakens as interest rates rise, and the discounting effect exactly equals it at some interest rate. Above that rate, the value of the mortgage falls with interest rates, because the discounting effect dominates. The interest rate for which the prepayment and discounting effect exactly offset, and thus for which the value of the mortgage is highest, depends on the prepayment sensitivity of the mortgage.

The prepayment sensitivity of a portfolio of mortgages depends on the contract interest rates, remaining terms, demographics, and refinancing history of the portfolio. An important aspect of the refinancing history is whether the most prepayment-sensitive borrowers have been "burned out" of the portfolio by refinancing due to prior interest rate decreases.

Mortgage banks have three main types of exposures to interest rate and prepayment risks. These exposures tend to offset each other when interest rates fall sufficiently to induce substantial prepayment and refinancing, but to reinforce each other when interest rates rise sufficiently so that the discounting effect dominates the prepayment effect.

First, mortgage banks usually have an inventory of unsold fixed-rate mortgages and MBS as well as a pipeline of mortgage commitments at fixed interest rates. These instruments are exposed to interest rates through the prepayment and discounting effects discussed earlier. In the case of mortgage commitments, prepayment should be interpreted as nonexercise or renegotiation of the commitments. As depicted in Exhibit 7.4, the values of mortgages and MBS held for sale fall as interest rates move in either direction away from the interest rate for which the discounting and prepayment effects are exactly equal. The value function for mortgage commitments has a similar shape to but is lower than that for mortgages, because prepayment causes mortgage banks to receive the principal plus any prepayment penalty on mortgages, while they receive nothing if unfunded mortgage commitments expire unexercised. (As discussed in Chapter 11, fixed-rate mortgage commitments usually are accounted for as derivatives by the issuer.)

Second, mortgage banks' mortgage origination fees reflect a base level that occurs due to people moving or refinancing for non–interest-rate-motivated reasons, such as moving and cash-out refinancing. Mortgage origination fees rise steeply when interest rates fall sufficiently to induce substantial prepayment and refinancing, as depicted in Exhibit 7.5.

Gains on the sale of mortgages reflect both of the first two exposures, being affected by both the percentage gain on mortgages sold, which depends on interest rate movements between the origination and sale of mortgages, and the volume of mortgages sold in a period, which tends to be close to

EXHIBIT 7.4 Interest Rate Sensitivity of Mortgages and MBS Held for Sale

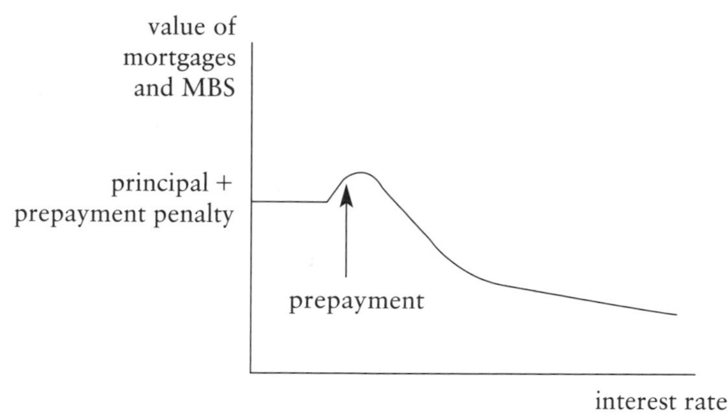

the volume of mortgages originated in the period. As discussed in the section "Accounting for Fees and Costs," mortgage banks recognize essentially all mortgage origination fees when the mortgages involved are sold, along with the gain on sale.

Third, mortgage banks hold MSRs and two types of retained securities discussed in detail in Chapter 8—interest-only strips and residual securities—that have minimal or no principal amount that is paid upon prepayment of the underlying mortgages. For simplicity, only MSRs are discussed here, although the interest rate and prepayment risks of these retained securities is similar. The valuation of MSRs is complex in part because their value comes from a number of sources, as discussed in the section "Mortgage Banking Industry, Major Players, and Activities." It has been estimated that the value

EXHIBIT 7.5 Interest Rate Sensitivity of Mortgage Origination Fees

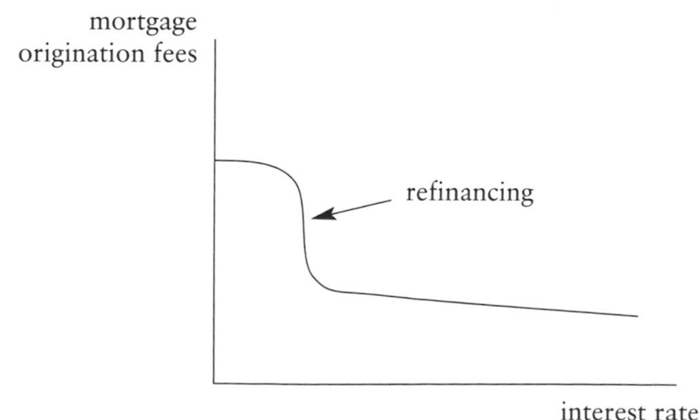

of MSRs is, on average, largely attributable to only two elements, however: (1) 70% to the servicing fee stream and (2) 26% to reinvestment of the float.[18] Both servicing fees and the benefits of reinvesting float cease if mortgages prepay. This fact causes the value of MSRs to exhibit a far more pronounced sensitivity to interest rates than does the value of fixed-rate mortgages and mortgage commitments. Specifically, as depicted in Exhibit 7.6, the value of mortgage banks' existing MSRs is zero if interest rates fall sufficiently to induce prepayment on the underlying mortgages. As interest rates rise above the rate that induces prepayment, the value of MSRs first rises sharply and then eventually falls with interest rates as the discounting effect dominates. The discounting effect begins to dominate the prepayment effect for a higher interest rate than for mortgages, however, due to the larger percentage losses associated with prepayment on MSRs.

Mortgage banks' interest rate and prepayment risks reflect the sum of these three exposures. Comparison of Exhibits 7.5 and 7.6 indicates that MSRs are strong natural hedges of mortgage origination fees (and also gains on sale to the extent that gains on sale are driven by origination volume) when interest rates decrease but not when interest rates increase enough so that the discounting effect dominates the prepayment effect. Specifically, when interest rates decrease sufficiently to induce substantial interest-rate-motivated prepayment and refinancing, mortgage origination fees and gains on sale rise, while MSRs suffer impairment losses. (This natural hedge exists only to the extent that a mortgage bank is able to originate mortgages that refinance and make a profit on mortgage originations, of course.) When interest rates rise, mortgage origination fees and gains on sale fall, while MSRs first rise in value as the likelihood of prepayment declines but ultimately fall in value once the discounting effect outweighs the prepayment effect.

EXHIBIT 7.6 Interest Rate Sensitivity of MSRs

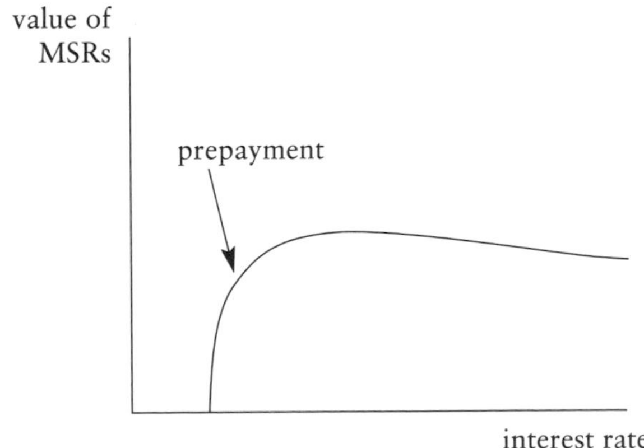

Despite this natural hedge, mortgage banks remain substantially exposed to interest rate movements in the absence of additional hedging, although the nature and direction of their net exposure has changed over time. Historically, mortgage banks with large servicing portfolios would suffer larger impairment losses on their MSRs than they garnered in incremental mortgage origination fees and gains on sale when interest rates decreased sufficiently to induce substantial prepayment and refinancing. Reflecting lower valuations of MSRs recently, the opposite is usually now the case.

Exhibit 7.7 illustrates these associations by reporting Countrywide's main mortgage-banking-related income statement line items for each the fiscal years 1997 to 2005. To indicate the extent of interest-rate-motivated prepayment and refinancing during the year, the exhibit points out the years in which the 30-year fixed-rate mortgage commitment rate dropped by more than .5% during some portion of the year or reached a three-year historic low, and it also reports the amount of residential mortgage originations in the United States and the percentage of those originations that are refinancings each year. The years of highest (growth trend–adjusted) mortgage originations and refinancing percentage are 1998 and 2003, both years in which mortgage commitment rates reached historic lows. Compared to a normal year, mortgage originations and refinancing percentage are high in every year from 2001 to 2005, however, reflecting both low interest rates and the continuing strength of the residential housing market.

While Countrywide only reports mortgage origination fees separately from gains on sale for the years up to 2001, as discussed, both origination fees and gains on sale clearly rise with refinancing activity, being largest in the years that mortgage commitment rates fall to historically low levels, with 1998 and 2003 being the standout years. Mortgage servicing rights suffer impairment losses when mortgages prepay, with the standout years being 1998 and 2002, not 2003. The main reason for this is that by the beginning of 2003, valuations of MSRs were low due to shortened estimated lives, reflecting low interest rates at the time and mortgagees' demonstrated increased propensity to prepay.

Because this natural hedge is not perfect, most mortgage banks attempt to economically hedge the interest rate and prepayment risks of their MSRs and/or their net exposures. Some MBS or options on MBS are virtually tailor-made hedges for mortgage banks' exposures. For example, a principal-only strip rises in value as interest rates fall sufficiently to induce prepayment, which effectively hedges their MSRs. Similarly, options to sell MBS effectively hedge their mortgages, MBS, and mortgage commitments.

It can be difficult for mortgage banks to hedge their exposures effectively, however, for three reasons. First, mortgage banks' various exposures are each distinctly nonlinear, as depicted in Exhibits 7.4, 7.5, and 7.6, giving rise to an even more nonlinear net exposure. Second, prepayment is not a deterministic function of interest rates, being affected by various economic and behavioral factors. Third, mortgages banks' exposures are essentially

EXHIBIT 7.7 Countrywide Financial Corporation Abridged Income Statement, 1997 to 2005 (Indicating Major 30-Year Fixed-Rate Mortgage Commitment Rates Decreases and Historic Lows and Residential Mortgage Originations in the United States)

(Dollars in billions) *(a)*	**2005**	**2004**	**2003**	**2002**	**2001**	**2000**	**1999**	**1998**	**1997**
Mortgage origination fees	?	?	?	?	.8	.4	.3	.6	.3
Gain on sale of mortgages (including origination fees from 2002 on)	4.9	4.8	5.9	3.7	.9	.6	.6	.7	.4
Mortgage servicing fees and other income from retained interests	4.8	3.3	2.8	2.0	1.4	1.2	1.0	.8	.7
– Amortization of MSRs	(2.3)	(1.9)	(2.1)	(1.3)	(.8)	(.5)	(.5)	(.6)	(.3)
– Impairment of MSRs and other retained interests	0	(.6)	(1.4)	(3.4)	(1.5)	(.9)	.2	(.5)	(.2)
+ Servicing hedge gain	(.5)	(.2)	.2	1.8	.9	.8	(.3)	.4	.2
= Net loan servicing income	1.5	.5	(.4)	(.9)	.0	.6	.6	.2	.4
30-year mortgage commitment rates fall by .5% during year *(b)*	no	yes	no	yes	yes	yes	no	no	yes
30-year mortgage commitment rates fall to level lower than in prior three years *(b)*	no	no	yes	yes	yes	no	no	yes	no
Total residential mortgage originations during year in U.S. (dollars in trillions) *(c)*	2.9	2.8	3.8	2.7	2.1	1.0	1.3	1.5	.9
Refinancing percentage *(c)*	48%	53%	66%	62%	57%	21%	36%	69%	29%

(a) For fiscal years up to and including 2000, the fiscal year-end is February 28 of the subsequent year. The 2001 fiscal year is the 10 months ending December 31, 2001. Subsequent fiscal years are the calendar year.

(b) Average 30-year fixed-rate mortgage commitment rates fell from 8.14% in April 1997 to 7.10% in December 1997, fell from 7.14% in May 1998 to 6.71% in October 1998 (a historic low), fell from 8.52% in May 2000 to 7.38% in December 2000, fell from 7.16% in June 2001 to 6.62% in October 2001 (a historic low), fell from 7.00% in January 2002 to 6.05% in December 2002 (a historic low) and then fell further to 5.26% in June 2003 (a 40-year low), and fell from 6.29% in June 2004 to 5.72% in October 2004. *Source:* Freddie Mac.

(c) *Source:* Mortgage Bankers Association.

written options and most common types of hedges are purchased options, and it is necessary for the exercise prices of these options to match precisely. Otherwise, mortgage banks are subject to the "whiplash" risk that interest rates will move in one direction and then reverse, causing the options underlying their exposures to be exercised while the options underlying their hedges are not, or vice versa.

The effectiveness of Countrywide's hedging of its MSRs can be assessed by examining the correlation of the MSR impairments and servicing hedge gains from 1997 to 2005 reported in Exhibit 7.7. Although Countrywide's servicing hedge is clearly not perfectly effective, in years of larger MSR impairment, such as 2002, it experiences larger servicing hedge gains, while in years of smaller MSR impairment, such as 2005, it experiences smaller servicing hedge gains or servicing hedge losses. Countrywide does not appear to try to completely hedge the variability of the value of its MSRs, however; this likely reflects the fact that its mortgage origination fees naturally hedge its MSRs.

It is easier and cheaper to hedge interest rate and prepayment risks on lower-credit-risk prime mortgages and MBS than on higher-risk subprime mortgages and MBS, because the most liquid available hedging instruments have very low credit risk. In the hedge fund crisis in the second half of 1998, some subprime mortgage banks that hedged their credit-risky exposures with low-credit-risk hedges were hurt when the value of both the exposure and the hedge fell, because credit-risky rates rose and low-credit-risk rates fell during the period.

Either because they find it necessary to induce investors to purchase their MBS or because their business model involves retaining the yield spread of subprime mortgages over subprime MBS, subprime mortgage banks often retain highly prepayment-risky residual or interest-only securities from their securitizations. This exposes subprime mortgage banks to high prepayment risk.

Prepayment risk interacts with credit risk, because borrowers with lower creditworthiness generally find it more difficult to refinance their mortgages, especially in periods when markets shy away from credit risk, as occurred during the hedge-fund crisis. In addition, subprime mortgages may include prepayment penalties, which deter prepayment.

Mortgage banks commonly provide several useful statistics about their prepayment risk. The average interest rate earned and term to maturity of fixed-rate mortgages are both positively associated with prepayment rates. Historical prepayment rates also may indicate future prepayments, since demographics vary across mortgage banks.

Various models are used to assess prepayment risk in order to value mortgage-related assets such as MBS. An options-pricing model is the theoretically correct approach, since prepayment is an option. These models are discussed in Chapter 8.

Credit Risk

Mortgage banks bear credit risk on their mortgages and MBS held for sale, mortgage commitments, retained interests from securitizations, including MSRs, and any recourse obligations they assume. The effect of credit risk on the value of MSRs could go in either direction, because servicers receive late fees that far exceed their incremental costs when borrowers pay late. Mortgage servicing rights clearly decrease in value if borrowers default, however, since the stream of servicing fees stops, and servicers lose cash they advanced in certain circumstances.

Because of the government's guarantee of all or part of the principal, government-insured mortgages are generally less credit risky than conventional mortgages. Despite higher collateral requirements, subprime and manufactured home mortgages are considerably credit riskier than prime mortgages. For example, in an analysis based on GSE prime and subprime mortgages originated from 1995 to 1998 for which the subprime mortgages all have the highest rating (A−), credit losses on subprime mortgages were estimated to be five to six times higher than for prime mortgages.[19] Because of their less valuable collateral, home equity mortgages are more credit risky than first mortgages on the same property; more generally, their credit risk is less determined by the collateral and more determined by the borrower. Commercial mortgages are typically nonrecourse to the general credit of the mortgagee, which increases their credit risk.

Mortgages that are neither government-insured nor prime and conforming usually require some level of credit enhancement to be sold or securitized. Credit enhancement comes in various forms, including retention of residual or subordinated securities, overcollateralization of the securitization trust, contribution of a cash reserve, assumption of a recourse liability, and purchase of third-party credit insurance.

Liquidity Risk

Mortgage banking is a cash flow–based business. Funds must be available to lend, because mortgage origination fees, mortgage servicing fees, and gains on sale all follow from the mortgage origination. A major source of funds comes from the sale of mortgages, which has been facilitated by the dramatic rise of the MBS market since 1970. In periods when it is hard to sell mortgages, however, mortgage banks' cash flow and liquidity can be compromised. Although this has never occurred for prime mortgages in modern times, it did for subprime mortgages during the hedge-fund crisis in the second half of 1998, because investors did not want to hold risky investments. Many subprime mortgage banks could not securitize their mortgages and so had to try to sell them in a very unfavorable wholesale market. Moreover, as a result of subprime mortgage banks' distress, most of their usual forms of borrowing dried up. Virtually all pure subprime mortgage banks became illiquid during this period, and many declared bankruptcy.

Government-insured and prime conforming conventional mortgages are easier to securitize and thus more liquid than other types of mortgages. Ginnie Mae sponsors only government-insured mortgage securitizations, and the GSEs primarily sponsor prime conforming conventional mortgage securitizations.

Persistence and Growth of Fee Income

The various sources of fee income for mortgage banks tend to be concentrated in distinct economic conditions, and so they have different persistence. As discussed in the "Interest Rate and Prepayment Risks" section, mortgage origination fees tend to be large in periods in which interest rates fall sufficiently to induce refinancing, and so can be transitory. Although servicing fee revenue tends to be fairly persistent, impairment losses on existing mortgage servicing rights occur in periods in which interest rates fall sufficiently to induce prepayment. Moreover, servicing fee revenue persists only if the mortgage bank refinances its share of mortgages, and the mortgage origination market is very competitive. Gains on sale of mortgages tend to be largest in periods in which interest rates drop sufficiently to induce large amounts of mortgage origination and in which interest rates drop between the time of origination and the time of sale. Gains on the sale of mortgages can be manipulated by managing the inventory of mortgages and MBS held for sale.

Mortgage banks' growth prospects are tied to the health of the residential real estate market. Mortgage banks also are affected by general economic factors, such as gross national product and unemployment rates, and by specific factors, such the mortgagees' probability of moving, immigration rates, and the age and overall desirability of the existing housing stock. The amount of mortgage commitments is a forward-looking indicator of growth that is similar in many respects to an order backlog.

Cross-Selling and Diversification

Many mortgage banks, including Countrywide, attempt to cross-sell other products that are related to mortgages and real estate, such as title insurance, appraisals, home equity mortgages, and homeowners' insurance. These cross-selling opportunities exist because obtaining or refinancing a mortgage is a relatively infrequent but very important decision for their customers. It is less clear whether mortgage banks' customer relationships can be extended to nonmortgage-related services, although this belief usually has been part of the rationale behind banks' recent acquisitions of mortgage banks.

Mortgage banks' activities lead naturally to diversification into certain other financial services businesses related to mortgages, MBS, or real estate. For example, Countrywide has diversified into securities through a broker-dealer business that focuses on the MBS market and an asset management business focusing on distressed mortgage assets and into insurance through an insurance subsidiary that writes creditor-placed property insurance.

Operating Efficiency

Mortgage banks have different cost structures depending on how they originate or acquire mortgages. Mortgage banks may originate mortgages directly from mortgagees through retail branches or the Internet or indirectly through independent brokers, or they may purchase mortgages originated by other financial institutions. Countrywide uses all these methods of obtaining mortgages. Naturally, more revenue is generated from origination of mortgages through retail branches or the Internet, but retail branches involve large and substantially fixed operating costs. As with thrifts, efficient use of costly retail branches by mortgage banks is critical.

Mortgage banks usually handle the high volume of mortgage originations that occur in periods when interest rates decline significantly through the use of temporary employees. Reflecting a decline in mortgage originations that it expects to persist, in October 2006 Countrywide announced that it planned to lay off more than 2,500 employees, about 4% of its workforce.

For mortgage banks that service mortgages, technologically advanced and efficient back offices are also critical, because mortgage servicing is a competitive business. Although Countrywide prefers to originate mortgages through its retail branches, it obtains mortgages from other sources in large part to ensure sufficient servicing volume to employ its back offices efficiently.

ACCOUNTING FOR FEES AND COSTS

The most important accounting issues affecting mortgage banks pertain to securitizations, MSRs, and retained securities, which are covered in Chapter 8. This section briefly summarizes accounting issues related to the recognition of fee revenue and the matching of related costs.

Under SFAS No. 65, *Accounting for Certain Mortgage Banking Activities* (1982), fees for reimbursing specific costs associated with a mortgage application (e.g., the cost of an appraisal) are recognized as revenue and the costs are expensed when the service is provided.

Under SFAS No. 91, *Accounting for Nonrefundable Fees and Costs Associated with Originating or Acquiring Loans and Initial Direct Cost of Leases* (1986), most other fees (e.g., the cost of a mortgage application) are netted against the incremental direct cost of providing the service and deferred, with a net cost yielding an asset and a net fee yielding a liability. If the mortgage is held for sale, then the net asset or liability remains unamortized on the balance sheet until the mortgage is sold. If the mortgage is held in portfolio, then—assuming that prepayment is probable and capable of reasonable estimation at the portfolio level, as is usually the case—the net asset or liability is amortized into interest income to maintain a constant effective yield on the mortgages over their expected remaining life taking into account prepayment. Mortgage commitment fees are deferred in the same fashion as other fees if the commitment is exercised but are recognized in income if and when the commitment expires unexercised. Costs paid to acquire mortgages are added directly to their principal.

The unamortized portion of deferred fees is recognized in income when mortgages are sold. Since mortgage banks typically sell the mortgages they originate quickly, leaving little time to amortize deferred fees, the vast bulk of deferred fees is recognized upon the sale of mortgages. This implies that mortgage sales have a double effect on income, through recognition of both a gain on sale and the unamortized portion of deferred fees.

Although generally not a significant issue for mortgage banks that sell their mortgages quickly, SFAS No. 91 (1986) requires that if actual prepayment turns out to be different from expected prepayment, then the effective yield must be recalculated as of inception of the mortgages in the portfolio, taking into account actual prepayment and revised expectations of future prepayment. This gives rise to "catch-up" adjustments being recorded in interest income; for example, unexpectedly high prepayment yields a reduction of interest income being recorded in the case of a net asset/cost and an increase in interest income being recorded in the case of a net liability/fee. In its special reports mentioned earlier, OFHEO criticized both Freddie Mac and Fannie Mae for not properly recording catch-up adjustments for unexpected prepayment in order to smooth income.

NOTES

1. Ginnie Mae 2005 annual report.
2. Fannie Mae, Monthly Summary, May 2006, www.fanniemae.com, and Freddie Mac, Monthly Volume Summary, May 2006, www.freddiemac.com.
3. Facts at a Glance: FHLBanks, www.fhlbanks.com.
4. Federal Reserve Board Statistical Release Z.1, "Flow of Funds Accounts of the United States," tables L.209 and L.218.
5. W. Passmore, S. Sherlund, and G. Burgess, "The Effect of Housing Government-Sponsored Enterprises on Mortgage Rates," Finance and Economics Discussion Series, 2005-06, Federal Reserve Board, Washington, D.C., www.federalreserve.gov.
6. Remarks by Federal Reserve Board chairman Alan Greenspan, "Government-Sponsored Enterprises," May 19, 2005, www.federalreserve.gov.
7. Federal Reserve Board Statistical Release Z.1, table L.218.
8. Mortgage Bankers Association of America (www.mbaa.org).
9. Freddie Mac news release, August 2, 2006.
10. F. Pafenberg, "Single-Family Mortgages Originated and Outstanding, 1990–2004," Office of Federal Housing Enterprise Oversight, Washington, D.C.
11. L. Hayre, "Guide to Mortgage-Backed Securities," Salomon Smith Barney, March 1999.

12. S. Chomsisengphet and A. Pennigton-Cross, "The Evolution of the Subprime Mortgage Market," *Federal Reserve Bank of St. Louis Review* (January/February 2006).
13. Ibid.
14. Pafenberg, "Single-Family Mortgages Originated and Outstanding."
15. Mortgage Bankers Association of America.
16. Countrywide Financial, February 9, 2006, press release.
17. www.mortgageservicingnews.com and www.nationalmortgagenews.com.
18. S. Aldrich, W. Greenberg, and B. Payner, "A Capital Markets View of Mortgage Servicing Rights," *Journal of Fixed Income* (June 2001).
19. A. Pennington-Cross, "Subprime & Prime Mortgages: Loss Distributions," Working Paper 03-1, Office of Federal Housing Enterprise Oversight, Washington, D.C.

CHAPTER 8

Securitizations

This chapter describes the accounting and disclosure requirements for securitizations, a type of transfer of financial assets governed by Statement of Financial Accounting Standards (SFAS) No. 140, *Accounting for Transfers and Servicing of Financial Assets and Extinguishments of Liabilities* (2000), as amended. In securitizations, the issuer generally transfers financial assets to a special-purpose entity (SPE) that sells asset-backed securities (ABS) representing claims to the cash flows generated by those assets to investors and that conveys the cash it receives from investors back to the issuer. The focus is on securitizations in which the issuer retains contractual interests in the transferred financial assets, such as servicing rights, ABS—which may have the same or different rights as the ABS sold to outside investors, and recourse obligations. In some securitizations, the issuer may also provide implicit recourse, a noncontractual understanding that is not directly accounted for or otherwise considered in SFAS No. 140 (2000).

This chapter also discusses an August 2005 Exposure Draft, *Accounting for Transfers of Financial Assets* (the Transfers ED), that proposes significant amendments to SFAS No. 140 (2000). Although it is not clear at this point which of the Transfers ED's proposals will be adopted, and the Financial Accounting Standards Board (FASB) has already backed away from some of them, these proposals indicate the FASB's concerns with the implementation in practice of SFAS No. 140's (2000) concepts, especially the control concept. Finally, this chapter discusses the accounting for servicing rights under SFAS No. 156, *Accounting for Servicing of Financial Assets* (2006), and prepayment sensitive securities under SFAS No. 140 (2000), because these assets usually result from securitizations.

The required accounting treatment for securitizations under SFAS No. 140 (2000) is determined by whether the issuer surrenders control over the financial assets or not. For control over the financial assets to be deemed surrendered, the assets must be legally isolated from the issuer, the transferee must be able to pledge or exchange the assets, and the issuer must not retain effective control over the assets. SPEs are used to legally isolate the financial assets and for other reasons. SFAS No. 140 (2000) defines "qualifying" SPEs (QSPEs) as those meeting various criteria intended to ensure they are substantially passive entities distinct from the transfer or that basically just hold financial assets and distribute the cash flows generated by those assets. QSPEs are used to satisfy SFAS No. 140's (2000) effective control requirements. QSPEs are exempted from consolidation by the issuer, which is important because such consolidation would reverse any sale accounting for the securitization.

SFAS No. 140 (2000) requires securitizations in which the issuer does not surrender control over the underlying financial assets to be accounted for as secured borrowings. It requires securitizations in which the issuer surrenders control over underlying financial assets to be accounted for as sales to the extent that the issuer receives consideration other than beneficial interests in those assets. In other words, securitizations that qualify for sale accounting but for which the issuer retains some beneficial interests in the underlying financial assets are treated as partial sales of those assets.

Whether a firm's securitizations meet SFAS No. 140's (2000) control-based requirements for sale accounting or not can have significant effects on its financial statements. Compared to secured borrowing accounting, sale accounting reduces reported leverage, raises reported income when a gain on sale is recognized, and classifies the cash received as operating or investing rather than financing.

Accounting for securitizations under SFAS No. 140 (2000) is a limited attempt to describe complex transactions that are structured to yield desired economic and accounting outcomes. This accounting raises three issues for users of financial reports.

1. Despite SFAS No. 140's (2000) focus on control, it is not clear that issuers are affected substantially by whether they surrender control over the underlying financial assets. In particular, the surrender of control over the underlying financial assets need not correspond to the transfer of the risks and rewards of those assets.
2. Certain retained interests—such as residual and subordinated ABS and recourse obligations—concentrate the risk of the underlying financial assets, yielding unreported economic leverage when sale accounting is used. These retained interests are economically similar to (and may be or contain) derivatives.
3. Some retained interests are sensitive or illiquid instruments that require expertise and judgment to value, with considerable possibility for error even when expertise is high and judgment is applied faithfully and even more when they are not. Overvaluation of retained interests leads dollar-for-dollar to overstatement of gains on sale, and vice versa.

The first and second issues imply that, even in the absence of measurement issues, no single accounting approach fully describes securitizations. Most securitizations constitute real transfers of control, value, risks, and rewards, although often to very different extents. For example, issuers frequently transfer much of the value of financial assets to the investors in senior

ABS while retaining residual or subordinated ABS that bear the risk of loss on the assets from the first dollar up to a cap less than the maximum loss. Although such securitizations truncate some of the issuer's downside risks, the issuer retains far more of the assets' risks and rewards than of their value. Sale accounting better captures certain aspects of these securitizations, such as the realization of most of the value of the financial assets and the truncation of downside risk. Secured borrowing accounting better captures others, such as the disproportionate retention of risk. Neither method fully describes these securitizations. In this regard, accounting is simply not a substitute for clear disclosure. Unfortunately, securitization disclosures are typically boilerplate, and users of financial reports need to sift carefully through the available information to determine the economic characteristics of securitizations and to evaluate the inevitable limitations of the accounting for them.

Still, certain securitizations are better described by sale accounting than secured borrowing accounting, and vice versa. This chapter illustrates this point by analyzing disclosures from two very different mortgage banks in two different time periods: Countrywide Financial Corporation (Countrywide) in 2005 and Aames Financial Corporation (Aames) during the hedge-fund crisis in the second half of 1998. Countrywide primarily securitizes prime conforming residential mortgages, for which it retains only mortgage servicing rights (MSRs). Although highly prepayment sensitive, Countrywide's MSRs have relatively verifiable fair values that are a small percentage of the cash proceeds from the securitization. Sale accounting better describes its securitizations. In contrast, Aames primarily securitized subprime home equity mortgages, for which it retained a much larger amount of riskier and less liquid interest-only strips. Aames recorded losses on these securities during its fiscal years 1999 to 2003 that in total exceeded the gains on sale it had recorded over its entire prior life. Secured borrowing accounting would have better described its securitizations.

The third issue pertains to measurement. Aames constitutes an extreme case of overvalued retained interests yielding overstated gains on sale that were subsequently reversed. A subtler but still highly significant example of this issue examined in the case in Appendix 8A is Doral Financial Corporation, which in February 2006 restated its 2001 to 2004 results because of several problems with its securitization accounting, a primary one being overvaluation of its retained interests resulting from the use of a conceptually unsupportable valuation model.

This chapter relies on and continues the discussion of mortgage securitizations in Chapter 7, which should be read first by any reader not familiar with these securitizations. The first section explains why firms securitize financial assets and describes what kinds of financial assets are securitized. The two main securitization structures are described in the second section. The third section describes the accounting and disclosure requirements for securitizations under SFAS No. 140 (2000) as well as the Transfer ED's proposals to amend that standard. The fourth section illustrates the financial analysis issues for securitizations using the examples of Countrywide and

Aames. The fifth section summarizes recent research on securitizations using disclosures that are required under SFAS No. 140 (2000). The sixth section describes the recently changed accounting and disclosure requirements for financial asset servicing rights under SFAS No. 156 (2006) and the accounting for prepayment-sensitive retained securities under SFAS No. 140 (2000). The appendix contains a "classic case": Doral Financial's Interesting Interest-Only Strips.

Certain economic and accounting considerations with general relevance to structured finance transactions, including securitizations, are deferred to Chapter 9. Of particular salience to securitizations accounted for as sales are the rules governing the consolidation of SPEs other than QSPEs.

WHY AND WHAT?

Motivations for and Alternatives to Securitizations

Issuers have various motivations for securitizations. Securitizations provide funds for future originations of financial assets. They allow issuers to diversify their holdings of financial assets and to transfer or transform the risk of those assets in diverse ways. They also allow issuers to focus on the generation of fee income. Securitizations accounted for as sales enable issuers to obtain off–balance sheet financing, to record income immediately as gain on sale rather than over the life of the securitized financial assets as interest income, and to record the cash received as operating or investing rather than financing.

Loan sales and syndications are common alternatives to securitizations. Loans have been sold between financial institutions for well over a century in the United States. Loan sales are an essential part of "correspondent banking," in which a smaller bank has an ongoing relationship with a larger bank. Both sides of correspondent banking relationships benefit through more diversified loan portfolios and improvements in operating efficiency. Smaller banks may originate loans that are too big for them to hold that they sell in part or whole to their larger correspondent banks, while larger banks may sell part of the loans they originate to their smaller correspondent banks. Conducting complex transactions such as securitizations requires incurring costs to develop expertise and systems; smaller banks avoid these costs by selling their loans to larger banks, which enables them to spread these costs across a higher volume of transactions.

Subdivision of loans and sale of the pieces around the time of loan origination is called loan syndication. In loan syndications, various financial institutions effectively lend money to a single borrower. Loan syndications are most likely for large and risky commercial loans, such as the highly leveraged transaction (HLT) loans associated with leveraged buyouts.

Loan syndications can be structured legally either as participations or assignments. A participation is an undivided interest in a single loan that is controlled by the loan originator. The legal status of loan participations can be murky, depending on whether the loan originator is viewed as providing recourse (even implicitly) to the purchasers of participations. If recourse is assessed, then a participation could legally be viewed as a secured borrowing by the loan originator. In contrast, an assignment creates legally separate loans out of the original loan, so that the purchaser of the assignment has a direct claim on the borrower. In this regard, loan assignments are similar to properly structured securitizations. Assignments are currently the primary way in which individually large, heterogeneous loans are divided among financial institutions.

Credit derivatives (discussed in more detail in Chapter 11) are a now fairly established alternative to securitization as a means to transfer credit risk. Credit derivatives may be used by themselves or combined with debt instruments in "synthetic" securitizations. Investors in synthetic securitizations purchase securities issued by entities that typically hold portfolios of low-credit-risk debt instruments (e.g., government or AAA-rated securities) and write credit derivatives referenced to one or more creditors. In the absence of default by the creditors, the investors receive the return on the debt instruments plus the premiums received on the written credit derivatives. In the event of default by the creditors, the debt instruments are used to pay off the purchasers of the credit derivatives. Synthetic securitizations are in certain respects more flexible than ordinary securitizations with respect to the transfer of credit risk, since the credit derivatives employed can be customized to meet the preferences of the parties involved.

These alternatives are generally not as efficient or as flexible as securitizations for the sale of individually small, homogeneous loans, such as residential mortgages, credit card loans, and other consumer loans. In particular, securitizations allow the issuer to spread the risk of the underlying financial assets across a liquid and competitive financial market rather than across a few financial institutions with market power. Securitizations also allow the issuer to retain certain interests in the underlying financial assets and sell others.

Residential Mortgages

This section extends the discussion of residential mortgage securitizations in Chapter 7. Residential mortgages were the first and remain by far the most important type of securitized financial asset, due to the huge number of these mortgages, their ability to be classified into homogeneous groups, and the existence of a unique set of facilitating institutions. Most residential mortgage securitizations are sponsored (i.e., guaranteed in some fashion) or issued (i.e., the mortgages are owned) by Ginnie Mae or one of the government-sponsored enterprises (GSEs). Ginnie Mae sponsors but does not issue securitizations of mortgages for which the principal is guaranteed in whole or part by other federal government agencies. Ginnie Mae provides "timing insurance," which guarantees that principal and interest is paid in a timely fashion to the holders of mortgage-backed securities (MBS). Reflecting these federal government guarantees, Ginnie Mae–sponsored MBS are generally considered credit riskless.

The GSEs also sponsor securitizations of government-insured mortgages, although they usually sponsor and often issue securitizations of conventional conforming mortgages. For the securitizations they sponsor, the GSEs guarantee full and timely principal and interest payments, and so they legally bear the credit risk on the underlying mortgages. The GSEs usually charge issuers about .2% of the outstanding principal per year to provide this guarantee, although they may have arrangements to share credit risks with the issuers in exchange for a reduction of this fee. The MBS sponsored by the GSEs historically have been viewed as having minimal credit risk, in part because most of their MBS are secured by prime conforming mortgages, and in part because of investors' perception that the federal government would step in were the GSEs unable to honor their credit guarantees. For these reasons, GSE-sponsored MBS trade at a negligible yield premium to those of Ginnie Mae.

Various private firms (mostly commercial, investment, and mortgage banks) also issue MBS, usually with some form of credit enhancement. Private MBS may have some credit risk, especially those collateralized by subprime mortgages, but they are usually highly rated at issuance.

Virtually all prime and some subprime residential mortgages are prepayable. Fixed-rate prepayable residential MBS are exposed to prepayment risk, as discussed in Chapter 7's "Interest Rate and Prepayment Risks" section.

Securitizations of Other Financial Assets

Securitizations are important to a wide class of financial institutions that securitize an increasingly wide range of loans, securities, and lease receivables. For example, $458 billion (23%) of commercial mortgages and $618 billion (28%) of consumer loans were held in securitized form at the end of 2005.[1] In principle, almost any type of financial asset can be securitized, although the creation of large pools of homogeneous financial assets whose risks can be assessed by potential ABS investors is difficult for some types. Moreover, some types require active management to maximize the value of defaulted accounts or to maintain their principal balances.

For example, commercial mortgages are individually larger and more heterogeneous than residential mortgages, and so their value is less determinable based on statistics or other information that could be reliably conveyed to investors. These mortgages can be credit risky, in part because they are usually nonrecourse to the general credit of the borrower. These features make securitizations of commercial mortgages subject to adverse selection (lemons) problems, because issuers likely know more about the credit quality of these mortgages than do the potential buyers of the commercial mortgage-backed securities (CMBS). Because of their size and nonrecourse nature, it is often optimal that defaulted commercial mortgages be renegotiated or otherwise worked out.

Like commercial mortgages, credit card receivables are individually credit risky. However, their much smaller size implies that this risk can be diversified considerably within the portfolio securitized and that they are less likely to be renegotiated or worked out. Credit card securitizations involve revolving credit, so that the borrowers may borrow more or pay off their accounts faster than expected, and there typically are seasonal variations in account balances as well. In order to maintain the collateral in the securitization trusts at the desired level, issuers may have to remove or add accounts over time.

In securitizations of commercial mortgages and credit card receivables, the issuers typically retain sizable residual, subordinated, or other interests that insulate investors in the ABS from credit risk and uncertainty about principal balances. For example, in credit card securitizations the issuer typically retains an "excess spread" account, a type of residual interest, which receives the excess of the yield on the credit card receivables less the yield paid on the ABS and all other expenses of the securitization trust. Because payment of the balance of the excess spread account to the issuer is restricted until the ABS investors are paid, this account credit enhances the securitization. The issuer also retains a "seller's interest" that does not credit enhance the securitization but rather absorbs variation in the principal in the trust. In addition, credit card securitizations often contain other contractual or noncontractual features to protect investors, such as early amortization provisions and implicit recourse. The size and risk of the retained interests, the need for active management of defaulted accounts and/or principal balances, and these other features imply that commercial mortgage and credit card securitizations tend to have more of the economic attributes of secured borrowings than do prime conforming residential mortgage securitizations.

A distinctive feature of credit card securitizations is the use of "master trusts" that issue multiple series of securities backed by the same underlying receivables. In each securitization, the issuer contributes additional receivables to the master trust, which then issues a new series of securities. The receivables in the master trust are not segregated in any fashion, and all the receivables collectively support all the series of securities issued.

Asset-Backed Commercial Paper

Asset-backed commercial paper (ABCP) is a type of short-term financing (less than 270 days in the United States) that is employed by both financial institutions and nonfinancial firms. Of the $1.6 trillion of commercial paper outstanding at the end of 2005, $926 billion (57%) is ABCP resulting from securitizations.[2] Either single or multiple issuers may contribute financial assets to ABCP conduits. In the typical case where the assets in the ABCP conduit have longer duration than the short-term ABCP issued by the conduit, the ABCP needs to be reissued in order to pay off the maturing ABCP and maintain funding for the underlying assets. Because it may not be possible for the conduit to reissue the ABCP either for issuer-specific or macroeconomic reasons, external liquidity support is required in ABCP securitizations unless the issuer is very highly rated. Liquidity support is not credit enhancement per se but rather addresses mismatches in the timing of the cash generated by the underlying assets and the cash needed to pay off the maturing ABCP. Such support may involve the liquidity provider agreeing either to lend to the ABCP conduit or to purchase its assets in the event it cannot reissue ABCP. Depending on the credit riskiness of the underlying assets, ABCP securitizations may also involve credit enhancement in a similar fashion as other securitizations.

SECURITIZATION STRUCTURES

Securitizations occur using a number of general structures and variations within those structures; this section describes simplified forms of the two main structures. Pass-through securitizations are described in the section that follows. Pass-through securities represent proportional interests in the underlying financial assets. Common approaches to estimate prepayment risk on pass-through MBS are described and evaluated in the "Estimation of Prepayment Risk" section. The "Tranched Securitizations" section describes such securitizations. Tranched securities represent nonproportional interests in the underlying financial assets, that is, the risks and rewards of those assets are partitioned differently across the tranches.

Although many types of financial assets are securitized, this section emphasizes residential mortgage securitizations due to their importance and developed state. Securitizations of fixed-rate residential mortgages raise the issue of prepayment risk, which affects other securitizations to a much lesser extent, if at all.

Pass-Through Securitizations

The simplest form of securitization is the creation of pass-through ABS by means of a legally separate SPE, usually a trust. Ginnie Mae sponsored the first pass-through securitization of government-insured mortgages in 1970, and Freddie Mac sponsored the first pass-through securitization of conventional conforming mortgages in 1971. In these securitizations, the issuer (often indirectly through the sponsor, as occurs in securitizations sponsored by the GSEs) places financial assets in the SPE, which issues pass-through ABS that entail a proportional interest in the principal and interest payments on the financial assets, after fees are paid to the securitization sponsor and mortgage servicer. Because of these fees and the enhanced liquidity of pass-through ABS compared to the underlying financial assets, pass-through ABS yield less than the underlying financial assets; for example, MBS tend to yield about .5% less than the underlying mortgages. The SPE collects payments on the financial assets and pays them out to the appropriate parties. When substantially all the payments are collected and disbursed, the SPE typically is dissolved.

Exhibit 8.1 depicts the main flows between the various parties to a simple residential mortgage pass-through securitization at issuance and subsequently.

EXHIBIT 8.1 Flows between Parties in a Pass-through Securitization (Only Mortgage Servicing Rights Retained by Issuer) Example

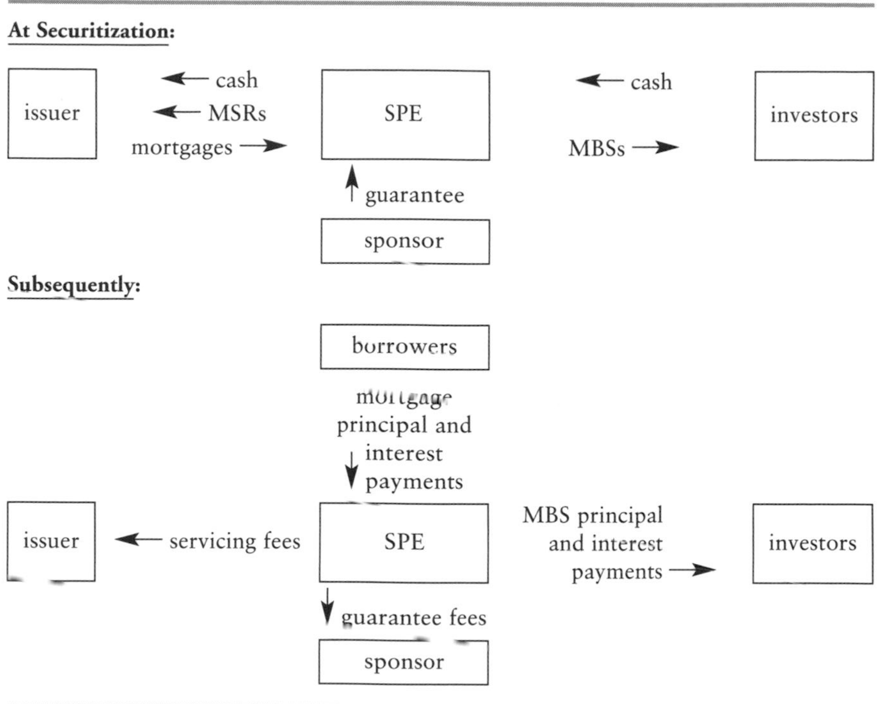

For simplicity, the issuer is assumed to retain none of the MBS and to assume no recourse liability, but to retain the servicing rights, similar to Countrywide's prime mortgage securitizations.

As a numerical example of a pass-through securitization, assume at initiation the issuer places \$100 million of mortgages yielding 6% into an SPE, which issues pass-through MBS yielding 5.5% with a fair value of \$99 million to investors for cash. The issuer retains MSRs that pay a servicing fee of .355% of outstanding principal per year and have a fair value of \$2 million. The sponsor provides a credit guarantee for a fee of .2% of the outstanding principal per year. The .5% lower yield on the pass-through MBS than on the underlying mortgages reflects the increased liquidity of the MBS, the stripping out of the MSRs which are riskier than the underlying mortgages and require the servicer to incur operating costs, and the credit guarantee. To simplify the calculations, all principal payments are assumed to occur at the end of the year. In the first year of the securitization, the mortgagees pay and the SPE receives \$6 million interest along with \$5 million of scheduled and (mostly) prepaid principal on the underlying mortgages. The SPE pays the MBS holders \$5.445 million interest (\$99 million × .055) plus the \$5 million principal, the issuer a servicing fee of \$355,000 (\$100 million ×

.00355), and the sponsor a guarantee fee of \$200,000 (\$100 million × .002). The total payments by the SPE to its various claimants sum to the payments the SPE receives on the underlying mortgages.

Estimation of Prepayment Risk

Since interest and principal payments on pass-through residential MBS generally are guaranteed by a government agency or a GSE or are credit-enhanced, credit risk is usually not a concern for investors in these MBS. Fixed-rate residential MBS are exposed to essentially the same interest-rate motivated prepayment risk as the underlying mortgages, however. As depicted in Exhibit 7.4, the value of fixed-rate residential MBS is reduced by the value of the mortgagees' prepayment call options. The value of this option increases as interest rates decrease toward the rate for which the prepayment effect dominates the discounting effect.

Various imperfect models are used to estimate the value of this prepayment option. A commonly used approach is based on benchmark prepayment rates that vary with mortgage age originally published by the Public Securities Association (PSA), a trade group representing bond dealers that is now called the Bond Market Association. The PSA rates start at 0% per year for a 0-month-old mortgage, rise by .2% per year for each additional month of age up to a 30-month old mortgage, and then remain 6% per year for mortgages older than 30 months. Constant annual prepayment rates (CPR) that do not vary with mortgage age are also commonly used.

Both PSA and CPR prepayment rates have many limitations. For example, the PSA rates are based on historical data on Federal Housing Administration (FHA) mortgages from the 1980s, and so they are not representative of current prepayment rates on any type of mortgage. The type of mortgage and the demographics of the mortgagees in the pool have significant effects on the probability of prepayment. The PSA rates are too low for most mortgages, because prepayments have become more common over time. These rates do not incorporate the fact that pools of mortgages with lower contract interest rates, or for which interest rates have previously dropped leading to pre-payment by the most interest-rate-sensitive borrowers ("burnout"), are less likely to prepay, all else being equal. These rates do not distinguish interest-rate-motivated prepayment (i.e., to refinance at lower rates) from prepayment for other reasons (e.g., moving or cash-out refinancing), despite the fact that interest-rate-motivated prepayment yields larger losses to the holders of MBS. In an ad hoc adjustment for these limitations, prepayment options often are valued using multiples of the PSA rates; for example, 200% PSA means that twice the benchmark prepayment rate for each mortgage age is assumed. The Bond Market Association publishes on its Web site the consensus projected PSA multiples and CPR prepayment rates for mortgages with different contract interest rates for different levels of interest rate movements derived from a bimonthly survey of major mortgage-market participants.

The PSA multiples and revised CPR rates do not capture the option-like nature of prepayment, however. In theory, an option-pricing approach is the correct way to estimate the value of the prepayment call option. The most common such approach is called option-adjusted spread (OAS), which involves estimating the average yield premium required to offset the effect of prepayment on the value of MBS across the distribution of possible interest rate paths and associated prepayment behavior. Although theoretically correct, the application of the OAS approach is very sensitive to the assumptions made about prepayment behavior, and so different analysts applying this approach can and do arrive at very different yield premia for given MBS. It has been suggested that OAS is more useful as an indicator of expected prepayments than as a risk premium.[3]

Tranched Securitizations

Tranched securitizations yield distinct tranches of securities with different prepayment, interest rate, credit, or other risks. Tranched securitizations for residential mortgages are called collateralized mortgage obligations (CMOs), for other loans are called collateralized loan obligations (CLOs), for bonds are called collateralized bond obligations (CBOs), and for other types or mixtures of debt instruments are called collateralized debt obligations (CDOs). In the remainder of this chapter, the more general term CDOs also refers to CLOs and CBOs, but not to CMOs.

CMO securitizations usually involve two steps. The issuer places pass-through MBS created in a number of first-step securitizations into a second-step SPE. The second-step SPE sells claims to various nonproportional partitions of the principal and interest payments made on the pass-throughs. In contrast, CDO securitizations more frequently involve one step and individual pools of financial assets.

Since the Tax Reform Act of 1986, the second-step SPE in CMO securitizations is usually a real estate mortgage investment conduit (REMIC). Although the holders of their residual interests are like stockholders, REMICs do not pay tax at the entity level. Legal and tax rules require REMICs to pay out essentially all cash within a specified time after receipt. The taxation of the SPE in CDO securitizations is very complicated, depending on the nature and location of the SPE, the type of assets securitized, and the type of CDOs issued. The SPE may or may not be a tax-exempt financial asset securitization investment trust (FASIT).

The basic CMO securitization structure, developed in 1983 by Freddie Mac and First Boston, focuses on the prepayable nature of most prime residential fixed-rate mortgages by creating sequential-pay tranches designated A, B, C . . . With two exceptions (discussed later), each tranche receives a scheduled portion of the principal payments received on the underlying pass-through MBS until its principal is fully paid off. Each tranche's principal is paid off at different times, however, because the tranches receive unscheduled prepayments in sequence. Specifically, prepayments are first used to pay off tranche A in full, then tranche B in full, and so on. Exhibit 8.2 depicts the flows between parties in the second step of a CMO securitization, assuming the issuer retains only residual securities referred to as R tranche CMOs, which are described later.

Reflecting this sequential-pay structure, tranche A CMOs have the shortest duration, tranche B CMOs have the next shortest duration, and so on. While tranche A CMOs experience prepayments first, it is generally incorrect to say that they have the most prepayment risk, since their prepayments are often predictably quick. Similarly, the last-tranche CMOs often have predictably slow prepayments. One of the middle tranches usually has the most uncertain prepayments, since these tranches pay off slowly if interest rates rise and quickly if interest rates fall sufficiently.

The differences in the valuation of A and B tranche CMOs as a function of interest rates are depicted in Exhibit 8.3, assuming for pictorial simplicity that these CMOs have the same value for all interest rates above and below certain levels. As interest rates fall below this level, prepayment kicks in later for the B tranche CMOs, and so the discounting effect begins to dominate the prepayment effect for lower interest rates for those CMOs.

EXHIBIT 8.2 Flows between Parties in Second-Step of a CMO Securitization (Only R Tranche CMOs Retained by Issuer) Example

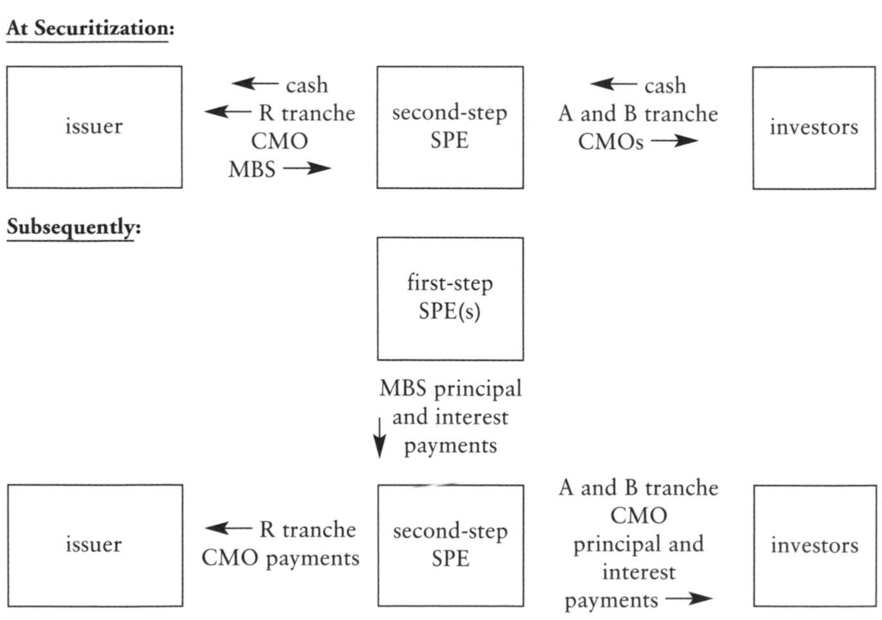

EXHIBIT 8.3 Different Values of CMO Tranches as a Function of Interest Rates (Assuming Values Identical for High and Low Interest Rates)

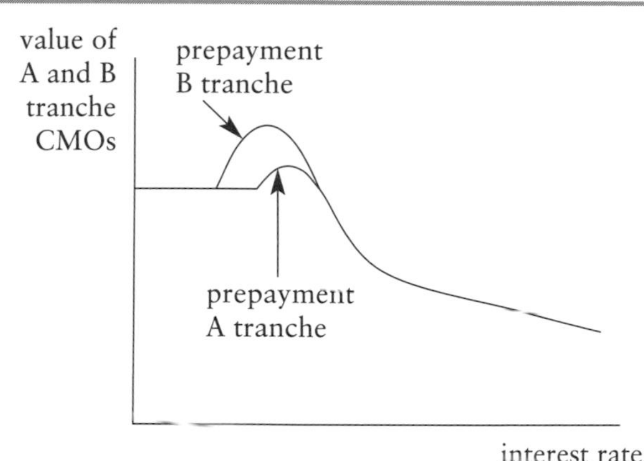

Collateralized mortgage obligation securitizations sometimes create two special tranches: Z and R. Both of these tranches are paid after other tranches are paid off, and so they bear the brunt of default. The Z (for zero, because it has some similarities to a zero-coupon bond) tranche pays neither interest nor principal until the preceding (A, B, C . .) tranches are paid, after which it receives accrued interest and principal payments as they are received by second-step SPE. The Z tranche naturally has longer duration than the preceding tranches.

The R (for residual) tranche gets what is left over after all other tranches are paid, and so bears the first risk of loss on the underlying assets after any third-party credit enhancement. R tranche CMOs derive value from at least three sources.

1. An implicit interest rate spread equal to the difference between the weighted-average spreads on the CMOs and the underlying pass-through MBS. This spread is essentially an interest-only strip, which is described later.
2. Interest on the reinvested float between receipts on the underlying pass-through MBS and payments to the CMO holders.
3. Any excess assets in the trust at the end of the securitization, which could result either from overcollateralization of the trust or from unexpectedly good performance of the securitized assets.

R tranche securities typically rise in value as interest rates rise (i.e., exhibit negative convexity), because the value of the interest-only strip rises as prepayments fall, and the interest on float rises with interest rates.

As a numerical example of a CMO securitization, assume at initiation the issuer places the $99 million of pass-through MBS yielding 5.5% from the prior numerical example into a REMIC, which issues $80 million of A tranche CMOs yielding 5%, and $19 million of B tranche CMOs yielding 7%. The weighted-average yield on the CMOs is 5.38% = [(80 × .05) + (19 × .07)]/99, which is below the 5.5% yield on the underlying pass-through MBS because the distinct cash flow characteristics of the two types of CMOs are desirable to different classes of investors. Both the A and B tranche CMOs have scheduled principal payments of 2% in the first year, with unexpected prepayments going first to the A tranche until it is paid off and then to the B tranche. The issuer retains an R tranche CMO that receives the accumulated spread with interest between the yield on the pass-through MBS and the weighted-average yield on the CMOs. In the first year of the securitization, the A tranche CMO holders receive $4 million interest ($80 million × .05) plus $1.6 million scheduled principal ($80 million × .02) plus $3.02 million prepaid principal. The B tranche CMO holders receive $1.33 million interest ($19 million × .07) plus $380,000 scheduled principal ($19 million × .02). The $115,000 difference between the $5.445 million interest received on the pass-through MBS and the $5.33 million interest paid on the A and B tranche CMOs accumulates to the benefit of the issuer's R tranche CMO, although this cash remains in the securitization trust credit enhancing the other tranched CMOs, which are senior to the R tranche. The total payments by the REMIC to its various claimants sum to the payments it receives on the underlying pass-through MBS.

Securitizations sometimes are structured with only two classes: one that receives only principal payments, principal-only strips (POs), and one that receives only interest payments, interest-only strips (IOs). Any tranche of securities can be separated into its PO and IO components. The POs and IOs have high and very different sensitivity to interest rates and prepayment. As depicted in Exhibit 8.4, POs rise in value steeply as interest rates decline, inducing prepayment, because prepayment accelerates but does not reduce the magnitude of principal payments. As discussed in Chapter 7's "Interest Rate and Prepayment Risks" section, mortgage banks often use POs to hedge their MSRs.

In contrast, IOs rise in value as interest rates fall (i.e., exhibit negative convexity) up to the rate at which increases in prepayment probabilities are sufficient to dominate the discounting effect. Since prepayment truncates interest payments, IOs decline in value very steeply toward zero as interest rates fall beyond this point, like the MSRs depicted in Exhibit 7.6.

CMO securitizations are motivated by the fact that some investors prefer securities with shorter duration (e.g., traditional depository institutions often want to reduce their negative repricing gap), while other investors prefer securities with longer duration (e.g., insurers like to hold securities that match the duration of their policy liabilities). In addition, some investors are more willing to accept uncertainty about prepayments and the resulting negative convexity in the valuation function than are other investors. The issuer of

EXHIBIT 8.4 Valuations of Principal-Only Strips as a Function of Interest Rates

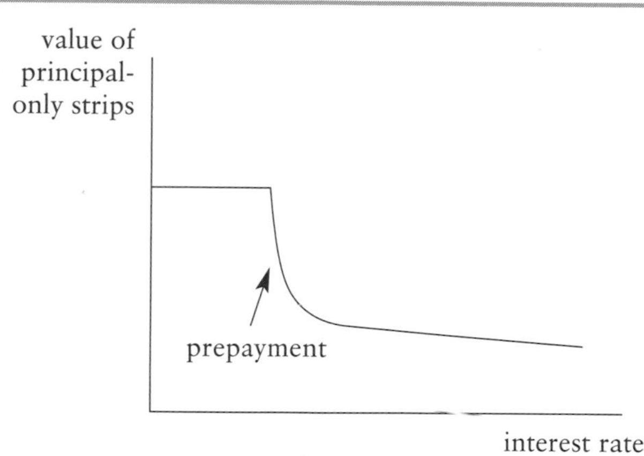

a CMO securitization profits if it can sell the various tranches for more than the cost of the underlying pass-through securities.

CMO securitizations typically are structured to facilitate the estimation of prepayment by being collateralized by many (several hundred is common) separate pools of pass-through MBS. Moreover, variations on CMOs called planned amortization class (PAC) bonds remove prepayment risk provided that prepayments stay within a given range. Support or companion bonds absorb prepayment risk within this range, by jumping ahead of the corresponding PAC bonds in the payment sequence if prepayments are high and behind them if prepayments are low. These PAC securitizations do not remove all prepayment risk, however, since the support bonds may be fully paid off before the corresponding PAC bonds when prepayments are high, and they do not provide cash to pay off the PAC bonds when prepayments are low. "Busted" PACs have occurred in periods of high interest rate volatility. Despite this limitation, PACs and their various offshoots have dominated CMO issuance since 1989.[4]

In the discussion of CMO securitizations thus far, credit risk has been ignored. This is fine if the underlying pass-through MBS are created in agency-sponsored securitizations or are otherwise credit enhanced and so have minimal credit risk. However, credit risk is a significant issue in other types of CMO and most CDO securitizations. The issuer is likely to have considerable informational advantage over investors regarding the credit risk of the underlying financial assets in these securitizations, which would make it difficult to sell securities without some form of credit enhancement. The most common form of credit enhancement is to subordinate some classes of tranched securities that are retained by the issuer (or sold to sophisticated investors) to the senior securities that are sold to investors.

SFAS NO. 140

SFAS No. 140 (2000) defines transfers of financial assets as conveyances of noncash financial assets by and to someone other than the issuer of the assets. Such transfers include securitizations, the focus of this chapter, as well as repurchase agreements, pledges of collateral, and other transactions involving previously issued financial assets. They do not include the original issuance of financial assets or the normal cash flows between the issuer and holder of the assets, for which the accounting is straightforward.

This section discusses the main concepts underlying SFAS No. 140 (2000) and how they apply to securitizations. Although the concepts underlying the standard are clear in most respects and work together fairly well, their application in specific contexts can be subtle and judgmental, and so diversity in practice exists. These application issues led the FASB staff to issue in February 2001 and twice revise a lengthy implementation guide for SFAS No. 140 (2000) and are a primary reason why the FASB published the Transfers ED in August 2005. This section also discusses certain of the Transfer ED's proposals to amend SFAS No. 140 (2000), in particular those involving the control concept.

SFAS No. 140 (2000) uses these general terms to describe the transactions governed by the standard and the parties involved in those transactions: "transfers of financial assets," "transferors," and "transferees." In the context of securitizations, the analogs for these terms are "securitizations," "issuers," and "investors," respectively. Both sets of terms are used later, depending on whether the context is specific to securitizations or not; the terms specific to securitizations can always be substituted for the more general terms, but the converse is not necessarily true.

Scope Exclusions

The scope of SFAS No. 140 (2000) excludes transfers of some important types of financial assets and close approximations to financial assets. Specifically, transfers of financial assets associated with pension and other postemployment benefit plans, leveraged leases, and insurance contracts are excluded. Transfers of unrecognized financial assets (e.g., operating lease receipts) and recognized nonfinancial assets (e.g., servicing rights) are excluded, even when they are virtually identical to transfers of recognized financial assets. These scope exclusions affect banks less than they do lessors and insurance companies.

Concepts and Accounting Requirements

Transfers in which the issuer has no continuing involvement in the financial assets are accounted for as complete sales. The issuer records an increase in cash and other net assets for the amount received or fair value, a decrease in financial assets at their carrying value, and a gain or loss for the difference between these two amounts, using this journal entry:

cash and other net assets (+ assets)	amount received or fair value = a
loss (− income)	$b - a$, if positive, 0 otherwise
financial assets (− assets)	carrying value of financial assets = b
gain (+ income)	$a - b$, if positive, 0 otherwise.

Transfers in which the issuer has some continuing involvement in the financial assets raise the question of whether the transfer is a sale or a secured borrowing. SFAS No. 140 (2000) applies these three concepts to determine whether a given transfer should be accounted for as a sale or secured borrowing, and, if as a sale, how the transferor should record the sale:

1. Financial assets involved in transfers accounted for as sales should be broken down into their retained and transferred components.
2. Transfers in which the transferor surrenders control over the financial assets should be accounted for as sales. Transfers in which the transferor retains control over the financial assets should be accounted for as secured borrowings.
3. The transferor should recognize the "net proceeds" of the securitization at fair value and retained beneficial interests in the securitized financial assets at the carrying value of those assets times the proportion of the fair value of those assets that is attributable to the retained beneficial interests.

These concepts are referred to here as the financial components, control, and fair value concepts, respectively. The application of each of these concepts is discussed in detail next.

Financial Components Concept. The financial components concept reflects the idea that the sequence of transactions leading up to a given position should not affect the current accounting for that position. For example, a firm that sells loans with recourse has exactly the same position as a third-party insurer of the loans. Thus, the firm should derecognize the loans and recognize a recourse liability in the same way as the third-party insurer does. This concept allows securitizations in which the issuer retains some but not all interests to be accounted for as partial sales, reflecting the fact that these securitizations meaningfully partition claims to the underlying financial assets. Without this concept, securitizations would have to be accounted for either as complete sales or as secured borrowings, as was the case prior to SFAS No. 125, *Accounting for Transfers and Servicing of Financial Assets and Extinguishments of Liabilities* (1996), the predecessor of SFAS No. 140 (2000).

Although the financial components concept is very attractive in theory, in practice it can work only as well as the accounting for retained interests were they held by third parties. For example, in the case of the recourse obligation already discussed, one could argue that sufficiently complete guarantees of financial assets by third parties would be better accounted for by the guarantor recognizing those assets in their entirety on its books rather than just recognizing a guarantee or derivative liability as is required under current generally accepted accounting principles (GAAP).

If applied more broadly, the financial components concept could have profound implications for the development of accounting for (structured) financial transactions and hybrid financial instruments. Many financial transactions other than securitizations involve partitioning claims on an underlying set of financial instruments or nonfinancial items; for example, reinsurance partitions rights and obligations with respect to underlying insurance policies between the ceding insurer and the reinsurer, as discussed in Chapter 16. Leases involve partitioning claims on underlying real assets among the lessee, lessor, and various types of third parties, a point emphasized in a February 2000 special report on leasing by the G4+1 group of accounting standards setters (the standards setters of Australia, Canada, New Zealand, the United Kingdom, the United States, and, as an observer, the International Accounting Standards Committee) and discussed in Chapter 13.[5] Many financial instruments have embedded options or other components, a point recognized in SFAS No. 133, *Accounting for Derivative Instruments and Hedging Activities* (1998), discussed in Chapter 11, and in SFAS No. 155, *Accounting for Certain Hybrid Financial Instruments* (2006) and the FASB's current project on liabilities and equity, discussed in Chapter 9.

Control Concept. The definition of control in SFAS No. 140 (2000) reflects both legal and effective notions. For the transferor to have surrendered control over financial assets:

- The assets must be legally isolated from the transferor, even in the case of its bankruptcy or receivership.
- The transferee must have the legal right to pledge or exchange the assets without any constraint that provides a more than trivial benefit to the transferor.
- The transferor does not maintain effective control over the assets through either
  - An agreement that both entitles and obligates the transferor to repurchase or redeem them before their maturity.
  - The unilateral ability to repurchase specific assets, other than through a cleanup call of the residual assets in the SPE at the end of the life of the transfer.

To meet the effective control condition, the transferor may remove only financial assets randomly or conditional on a third-party action, such as default on or cancellation of the debt by the borrower. If the transferor has the right to remove specific assets conditional on default or any other event, then once that event occurs, the transferor regains control over the affected assets and any prior sale accounting regarding those assets must be reversed.

Since securitizations and many other types of transfers of financial assets involve SPEs, and SPEs usually are precluded from pledging or transferring assets, some tweaking of the control concept is necessary to allow these transactions to be accounted for as sales. In this regard, SFAS No. 140 (2000) defines a "qualifying SPE" (QSPE) as an SPE meeting certain conditions intended to insure that it is not effectively controlled by the transferor. Specifically, a QSPE must

- Be demonstrably distinct from the transferor
- Have significantly limited and entirely specified activities
- Hold only passive financial assets that are appropriate given the restrictions on its activities (e.g., it may not hold derivatives with notional amounts greater than the beneficial interests held by parties other than the transferor)
- Be able to dispose of noncash assets only in automatic response to specified conditions

For example, a QSPE cannot use discretion in disposing of defaulted loans, although the transferor or third parties (such as servicers that specialize in defaulted loans) can be granted an option to purchase defaulted loans either for a fixed price or for fair value. Because they cannot be effectively controlled by the transferor, QSPEs are used only in transfers where active management of assets by the transferor is not critical. The Transfers ED proposes that QSPEs can hold equity only temporarily in conjunction with the collection of assets.

QSPEs are transparent to the accounting process, so that the investors in the ABS issued by the QSPE are viewed as the transferees subject to the requirement that they are able to pledge or exchange the transferred assets. Under SFAS No. 140 (2000), transferors do not consolidate QSPEs, since that would reverse sale accounting for the transfer. This decision is upheld in FASB Interpretation (FIN) No. 46(R), *Consolidation of Variable Interest Entities: An Interpretation of ARB No. 51* (2003), discussed in Chapter 9. SPEs that are not QSPEs generally are subject FIN No. 46(R)'s consolidation rules, however.

In transfers involving QSPEs in which the transferor retains disproportionate risk in the assets held by the QSPE, a direct transfer from the transferor to the QSPE generally would not be legally isolated from the transferor. To overcome this problem, transfers involving QSPEs often are accomplished using two-step structures. In the first step, the transferor places the assets into a wholly owned, bankruptcy-remote entity that meets the legal isolation requirement. In the second step, this entity transfers the assets to a QSPE, which issues beneficial interests to investors, possibly including the transferor, and may engage in other contractual relationships with the transferor such as recourse.

The Transfers ED proposes to tighten the definition of control in that SFAS No. 140 (2000) in a number of ways. Although these proposals clearly are intended to ensure that the transferor surrenders control over the transferred assets and to remedy diversity in application of SFAS No. 140's control conditions in practice, many of them would be onerous for transferors interested in obtaining sale accounting, and the FASB appears to be reconsidering some of them. The most important of these proposals are:

- To meet the legal isolation condition
  - A legal analysis of whether the transfer achieves legal isolation must be performed, likely including analyses of whether the transfer is a legal true sale and whether the SPE must be consolidated by the transferor.
  - The assessment of legal isolation must consider any arrangement or agreement made in connection with a transfer even if not contemporaneous with the transfer.
  - If the transferee is a QSPE, then no arrangements could be made between the transferor and QSPE's beneficial interest holders that would jeopardize isolation if they were between the issuer and the QSPE.
- To meet the pledge or exchange condition
  - If the transferee is a QSPE, each holder of beneficial interests in the transferred assets, including transferors retaining such interests, must have the right to pledge or exchange their interests.
  - Each entity in a multistep structure must have the right to pledge or exchange the beneficial interests it receives.
- To meet the effective control condition
  - For SPEs with the ability to roll over beneficial interests, such as most ABCP conduits, to be QSPEs, no party could have two or more of the following involvements with the SPE—liquidity support, credit enhancement, or the right to specify the terms, conditions, or timing of reissuances of beneficial interests—that enable the party to obtain a more-than-trivial incremental benefit.

In June 2006, the FASB decided to proceed with redeliberations of the proposals regarding the legal isolation condition. In October 2006, the FASB decided that to meet the legal isolation condition, legal isolation from each entity represented in the consolidated financial statements must be achieved. In July 2006, the FASB decided to proceed with redeliberations of the proposals regarding the effective control condition but to defer redeliberations of the proposals regarding the pledge or exchange condition until completion of redeliberations on the permitted activities of QSPEs and the effects of continuing involvements on isolation.

If the transferor does not surrender control over the transferred financial assets, then the transfer is treated as a secured borrowing. In secured borrowing accounting, the transferor recognizes a liability for the cash received and reclassifies the transferred assets as pledged collateral, as represented in these journal entries:

cash and other net assets (+ assets)	amount received or fair value
debt (+ liabilities)	amount received or fair value
pledged financial assets (+ assets)	carrying value
financial assets (− assets)	carrying value

Fair Value Concept. SFAS No. 140 (2000) uses fair values in two distinct ways in accounting for transfers of financial assets for which the transferor has surrendered control over the assets as (partial) sales. First, the transferor recognizes the "net proceeds" from the transfer at fair value. SFAS No. 156 (2006) recently broadened the definition of net proceeds to include servicing assets, so that net proceeds now are defined as receipts of cash and other net assets that are not related to the transferred financial assets plus retained servicing assets minus retained servicing liabilities and other liability interests in the transferred financial assets (e.g., recourse obligations). Second, the transferor recognizes retained beneficial interests in the transferred assets (i.e., ABS) at the carrying value of the transferred financial assets times the percentage of the fair value of those assets attributable to the retained beneficial interests. Together, these uses of fair values imply that the extent to which a transfer is accounted for as a partial rather than complete sale rises with the percentage of the fair value of the transferred financial assets attributable to the retained beneficial interests. For example, a gain on sale is recorded equal to that percentage times the difference between the fair value and the carrying value of the transferred financial assets.

Reflecting the fair value concept, the transferor's journal entry for a transfer of financial assets accounted for as a (partial) sale is:

cash and other net assets (+ assets)	amount received or fair value $= a$
servicing rights (+ assets)	fair value of retained servicing rights $= b$
securities (+ assets)	$d \times$ (fair value of retained securities/fair value of financial assets) $= c$
loss (− income)	$d + e - a - b - c$, if positive, 0 otherwise
financial assets (− assets)	carrying value of financial assets $= d$
recourse liability (+ liabilities)	fair value of recourse liability $= e$
gain (+ income)	$a + b + c - d - e$, if positive, 0 otherwise

For example, assume a portfolio of loans is securitized, the carrying value of the loans is \$100 (item d in the last journal entry), securities backed by these loans are sold for \$98 cash (item *a*), and servicing rights with a fair value of \$3 (item *b*), securities with a fair value of \$6 (related to item *c*), and a recourse obligation with a fair value of \$2 (item *e*) are retained by the issuer. The net proceeds of the securitization are \$99 = \$98 + 3 − 2. The fair value of the loans is the net proceeds plus the fair value of the retained securities (i.e., \$105 = \$99 + 6) so that the percentage of the fair value of the loans that is attributable to the retained securities is 5.71% = \$6/\$105. Reflecting this percentage, the portion of the carrying value of the loans allocated to the retained securities is \$5.71 = \$100 × 5.71%. The gain on sale is the \$99 net proceeds plus the \$5.71 allocated to the retained securities minus the \$100 carrying value, or \$4.71. This gain is 94.29% = 100% − 5.71% of the \$5 difference of the fair value and carrying value of the loans.

As discussed in the next section, SFAS No. 140 (2000) requires that issuers disclose the cash received from and the gain or loss on the securitizations of the period. The remainder of the journal entry for securitizations generally can be estimated with reasonable confidence using information provided in the issuer's financial report.

Disclosures

Concerns as to whether gains on the securitization of financial assets were being properly recorded under SFAS No. 125 (1996) arose shortly after that standard was adopted. These concerns were realized in striking fashion in the huge losses recorded by subprime mortgage banks such as Aames on their retained interests from securitizations as a result of the hedge-fund crisis in the second half of 1998. Reflecting this experience, SFAS No. 140 (2000) requires a long list of disclosures for securitizations accounted for as sales. These disclosures help users of financial reports to assess whether issuers have recorded gains on sale in the proper amount and to evaluate the value, risks, and rewards of retained interests.

SFAS No. 140 (2000) requires minimal disclosures for securitizations accounted for as secured borrowings, however. This is unfortunate because a number of securitizers of risky assets, such as Conseco prior to disposing of its finance businesses in 2003, intentionally (and easily) structure their securitizations to "flunk" sale accounting. Despite the problematic nature of sale accounting for their securitizations, users of financial reports may be worse off when these firms intentionally flunk sale accounting, due to the loss of informative disclosures.

A brief description of the most important of these disclosures, most of which apply to securitizations accounted for as sales during both the current period and any prior period presented in the financial statements, follows. The issuer must disclose:

- A description of the economic characteristics of securitizations, including the nature of each retained interest

- The policies used to account for and the methodology and significant assumptions used to estimate the fair values of each retained interest, or the reason why it is not practicable to estimate their fair values
- Sensitivity tests indicating the hypothetical change in the fair value of each retained interest to two or more unfavorable changes in each significant assumption used to estimate its fair value
- The gain or loss on sale during the period
- The various cash flows between the issuer and the securitization SPEs during the period—most important, the amount received from the current period's securitizations

Various disclosures are also required about the issuer's portfolio of managed (i.e., owned plus sold but managed) financial assets.

Excerpts from Countrywide's loan sale (primarily securitizations) footnote for 2005 are provided in Exhibit 8.5. With some effort and residual uncertainty, a user can piece together information from this footnote and elsewhere in Countrywide's financial report to estimate its journal entry for securitizations and other loan sales during the year.

Specifically, Countrywide discloses in its loan-sale footnote that the cash proceeds from its securitizations during 2005 are $364.7 billion and the gain on sale of loans is $4.0 billion, which is relatively small at 1.1% of the cash proceeds.

In its MSR footnote reported in Exhibit 8.6, Countrywide discloses that its net addition to MSRs is $5.8 billion during 2005. Not all of this is attributable to securitizations, however, since Countrywide separately purchases MSRs. Countrywide discloses in its supplemental-cash-flow-information footnote

EXHIBIT 8.5 Countrywide Financial Corporation, Excerpts from Securitization Footnote: December 30, 2005 Form 10-K Filing

The Company routinely originates, securitizes, and sells mortgage loans into the secondary mortgage market. Prime mortgage loan securitizations are generally structured without recourse to the Company. However, the Company generally has limited recourse on the Prime Home Equity and Nonprime Mortgage Loans it securitizes, through retention of a subordinated interest or through its issuance of a corporate guarantee of losses up to a negotiated maximum amount. While the Company generally does not retain credit risk on the Prime Mortgage Loans it securitizes, it has potential liability under representations and warranties it makes to purchasers and insurers of the loans. The Company had a liability for losses relating to representations and warranties included in other liabilities totaling $169.8 million and $139.9 million at December 31, 2005 and 2004, respectively. The Company recognized gains of $4.0 billion, $4.3 billion, and $5.5 billion from sales of mortgage loans in securitizations in the years ended December 31, 2005, 2004, and 2003, respectively.

(continues)

EXHIBIT 8.5 *(Continued)*

Key economic assumptions used in determining the fair value of MSRs at the time of securitization are as follows:

	Years Ended December 31,		
	2005	2004	2003
Weighted-average life (in years)	4.4	4.7	6.0
Weighted-average annual prepayment speed	23.0%	21.2%	16.9%
Weighted-average OAS (1)	6.5%	5.9%	4.6%

(1) Option-adjusted spread over LIBOR.

Key economic assumptions used in determining the fair value of other retained interests at the time of securitization are as follows:

	Years Ended December 31,		
	2005	2004	2003
Weighted-average life (in years)	3.5	3.5	2.4
Weighted-average annual prepayment speed	30.2%	32.9%	28.0%
Weighted-average annual discount rate	20.1%	25.0%	2.6%
Weighted-average lifetime credit losses	2.0%	2.7%	1.5%

The following table summarizes cash flows between the Company and securitization special purpose entities:

	Years Ended December 31,		
	2005	2004	2003
	(dollar amounts in thousands)		
Proceeds from new securitizations	$364,669,509	$259,102,621	$346,180,875
Proceeds from collections reinvested in securitizations	3,329,840	1,836,796	1,844,332
Service fees received	1,877,780	1,586,166	1,461,747
Purchases of delinquent loans	(3,786,551)	(3,387,739)	(3,715,193)
Servicing advances	(2,524,067)	(3,334,357)	(2,519,583)
Repayment of servicing advances	2,352,253	3,576,598	2,124,564
Other cash flows received on retained interests (1)	1,309,437	704,813	1,237,183

(1) Represents cash flows received on retained interests other than servicing fees.

EXHIBIT 8.5 *(Continued)*

Key assumptions used in measuring the fair value of the Company's MSRs at December 31, 2005 and 2004 and the effect on the fair value of those MSRs from adverse changes in those assumptions, are as follows:

	December 31,	
	2005	2004
	(dollar amounts in thousands)	
Fair value of mortgage servicing rights	$12,720,755	$8,882,917
Weighted-average life (in years)	5.6	6.1
Weighted-average annual prepayment speed	22.8%	22.0%
Impact of 5% adverse change	$ 238,131	$ 236,789
Impact of 10% adverse change	$ 463,010	$ 452,705
Impact of 20% adverse change	$ 877,291	$ 859,520
Weighted-average OAS	6.4%	6.0%
Impact of 5% adverse change	$ 94,600	$ 106,519
Impact of 10% adverse change	$ 187,660	$ 156,338
Impact of 20% adverse change	$ 367,225	$ 306,544

Key assumptions used in subsequently measuring the fair value of the Company's other retained interests at December 31, 2005 and 2004, and the effect on the fair value of those other retained interests from adverse changes in those assumptions are as follows:

	December 31,	
	2005	2004
	(dollar amounts in thousands)	
Fair value of other retained interests	$ 2,675,461	$1,908,504
Weighted-average life (in years)	2.4	2.5
Weighted-average annual prepayment speed	38.3%	34.8%
Impact of 5% adverse change	$ 57,329	$ 112,851
Impact of 10% adverse change	$ 110,297	$ 211,947
Impact of 20% adverse change	$ 214,392	$ 394,330
Weighted-average annual discount rate	17.9%	18.1%
Impact of 5% adverse change	$ 25,646	$ 24,022
Impact of 10% adverse change	$ 54,844	$ 46,376
Impact of 20% adverse change	$ 117,472	$ 88,818
Weighted-average net lifetime credit losses	1.7%	2.0%
Impact of 5% adverse change	$ 44,834	$ 41,437
Impact of 10% adverse change	$ 90,552	$ 80,833
Impact of 20% adverse change	$ 177,589	$ 158,730

(continues)

EXHIBIT 8.5 *(Continued)*

These sensitivities are hypothetical and should be used with caution. As the figures indicate, changes in fair value based on a given percentage variation in individual assumptions generally cannot be extrapolated. Also, in the preceding tables, the effect of a variation in a particular assumption on the fair value of the retained interest is calculated independently without changing any other assumption. In reality, changes in one factor may result in changes in another which might compound or counteract the sensitivities.

EXHIBIT 8.6 Countrywide Financial Corporation, Excerpts from Mortgage Servicing Rights Footnote, December 31, 2005, Form 10-K Filing

The activity in Mortgage Servicing Rights ("MSRs") is as follows:

	Years Ended December 31,		
	2005	**2004**	**2003**
	(dollar amounts in thousands)		
Mortgage Servicing Rights			
Balance at beginning of period	$ 9,820,511	$8,065,174	$7,420,946
Additions	5,835,946	4,142,641	6,138,569
Securitization of MSRs	(54,533)	(56,038)	(1,263,890)
Amortization	(2,288,354)	(1,940,457)	(2,069,246)
Change in fair value attributable to hedged risk	(213,166)	—	—
Application of valuation allowance to write down impaired MSRs	(69,045)	(390,809)	(2,161,205)
Balance before valuation allowance at end of period	13,031,359	9,820,511	8,065,174
Valuation Allowance for Impairment of Mortgage Servicing Rights			
Balance at beginning of period	(1,090,582)	(1,201,549)	(2,036,013)
Recoveries (additions)	601,017	(279,842)	(1,326,741)
Application of valuation allowance to write down impaired MSRs	69,045	390,809	2,161,205
Balance at end of period	(420,520)	(1,090,582)	(1,201,549)
Mortgage Servicing Rights, net	$12,610,839	$8,729,929	$6,863,625

The estimated fair values of mortgage servicing rights were $12.7 billion, $8.9 billion, and $6.9 billion as of December 31, 2005, 2004, and 2003, respectively.

that its MSRs increased by $5.5 billion due to loan sales, which is about 1.5% of the cash proceeds. Even if this disclosure were not provided, as is typically the case, it usually can be inferred from other disclosures. For example, Countrywide discloses in its loan-servicing footnote that its servicing portfolio increased by $491 billion due to new loan production and by $51 billion due to purchases of MSRs during 2005. This suggests that approximately 91% or $5.3 billion of the increase in its MSRs is attributable to securitizations.

Countrywide discloses in its supplemental-cash-flow-information footnote that its other retained interests increased by $1.9 billion due to loan securitizations, which is about .5% of the cash proceeds. Again, even if this disclosure were not provided, as is typically the case, it usually can be inferred from other disclosures. For example, Countrywide's securitization footnote indicates that the balances of its other retained interests are $2.7 billion at the end of 2005 and $1.9 billion at the end of 2004, for an average balance and net increase in 2005 of $2.3 billion and $.8 billion, respectively. This footnote also discloses that the estimated life of its other retained interests is 2.4 years, so that these interests amortized by about $960 million during 2005 (i.e., the average balance of $2.3 billion divided by the average life of 2.4 years). In addition, in its management's discussion and analysis Countrywide discloses that its other retained interests experienced a $365 million impairment loss during 2005. These disclosures yield an estimate of $2.1 billion for the increase in Countrywide's other retained interests from its securitizations in 2005 (i.e., $.8 billion + $960 million + $365 million).

Finally, Countrywide discloses a recourse liability of $176 million at the end of 2005 and $152 million at the end of 2004 in its schedule for valuation and qualifying accounts. The average balance and net change in these disclosed liabilities in 2005 are $164 million and $24 million, respectively. Assuming they amortize at the same rate as Countrywide's MSRs (for which an average life of 5.6 years is disclosed in the loan-sale footnote), amortization of these liabilities during 2005 is estimated to be $29 million (i.e., the average balance of $164 million divided by 5.6 years). This yields an estimated increase in these liabilities of $.1 billion due to loan sales during 2005 (i.e., $24 million + $29 million).

These disclosures and estimates collectively yield this estimate of Countrywide's journal entry for its securitizations and other loan sales (in $ billions):

cash (+ assets)	364.7 (disclosed)
MSRs (+ assets)	5.5 (estimated)
other retained interests (+ assets)	1.9 (estimated)
financial assets (− assets)	368.0 (plug)
recourse liability (+ liabilities)	.1 (estimated)
gain (+ income)	4.0 (disclosed)

In general, any estimation issues for Countrywide's securitizations seem minor, given the relatively small amount of its retained interests, over 70%

of which are fairly liquid MSRs, and its small percentage gain on sale. Still, its retained interests are almost twice as large as its gain on sale, so any overvaluation of these interests would have a larger percentage effect on the gain on sale and could eliminate the gain on sale if sufficiently large.

Countrywide's loan-sale footnote contains a variety of other information of some usefulness. Countrywide discloses the assumed prepayment speeds and discount rates used to value its MSRs and other retained interests, which provides indications of their nature and risk. For example, it discloses a weighted-average life of 5.6 years for its MSRs, which primarily result from securitization of prime conforming mortgages, that is over twice as long as the weighted-average life of 2.4 years it discloses for its other retained interests, which primarily result from securitizations of subprime and home equity mortgages. This difference reflects a lower expected level of prepayments on prime mortgages than on subprime and home equity mortgages. These assumptions can be compared to those of comparable firms to assess the degree of conservatism Countrywide uses in valuing its retained interests. In fact, based on such an analysis, in February 2003 Fitch Ratings put Countrywide on a negative credit rating watch for potentially overvalued MSRs (a concern that Countrywide emphatically refuted).[6]

Countrywide also discloses sensitivity to 10 and 20% adverse changes in prepayment and interest rate assumptions for MSRs and other retained interests. Although these disclosures faithfully follow requirements of SFAS No. 140 (2000)—in fact, virtually all issuers report sensitivity disclosures in the same boilerplate format, which is modeled after an example in an appendix to the standard—they are limited in three respects:

1. Changes of 10 and 20% in an estimated prepayment rate of 22.8% for MSRs and 38.3% for other retained interests are small relative to actual changes in prepayment that occur when interest rates drop substantially.
2. Separate sensitivity disclosures for prepayment rates and interest rates do not reflect the fact that sufficiently large interest rate decreases drive prepayment increases. Relatedly, it is not clear how the two chosen changes in interest rates correspond to the two chosen changes in prepayment rates.
3. The probability of prepayment is a highly nonlinear function of interest rates, rising steeply when interest rates drop sufficiently.

These limitations imply that users of financial reports have to think carefully about the available information to assess the risk of retained interests.

FINANCIAL ANALYSIS ISSUES

There are three main financial analysis issues for securitizations:

1. Is sale accounting applied when the issuer still bears most of the risks and rewards on the financial assets?

2. Are the amounts recorded for retained interests and thus gains on sale appropriate?
3. Are these gains persistent, or are they timed to manage income?

These issues are discussed next, contrasting Countrywide today with Aames during the hedge-fund crisis, and they also are illustrated in the case in Appendix 8A.

Is Sale Accounting Appropriate?

SFAS No. 140 (2000) requires securitizations to be accounted for as sales if the issuer surrenders control over the securitized financial assets. This requirement raises two related issues. First, securitizations involve SPEs with limited powers that typically are specified by the issuers. Thus, it is not clear that issuers are affected substantially by surrendering control over the financial assets. Moreover, SFAS No. 140 (2000) requires sale accounting to be applied even if issuers hold repurchase options on the securitized financial assets, as long as the issuer surrenders control over the assets for the period prior to their repurchase and these options do not provide a more than trivial benefit to the issuer.

Second, for most financial analysis purposes, the main concern is whether the issuer retains the risks and rewards of the underlying financial assets, not whether it retains control over those assets. The issuer can retain disproportionate credit and other risks through residual or subordinated securities and recourse obligations, which effectively yield unreported economic leverage by concentrating the risks and rewards of the securitized assets. As depicted in Exhibit 8.7, from a risks-and-rewards perspective, securitizations that transfer the value and the risk and rewards of the underlying assets proportionally from the issuer to the purchasers of the securities are pure partial sales, while securitizations that transfer none of the risks and rewards are pure secured borrowings. As discussed, however, most securitizations transfer more of the value than of the risks and rewards of the underlying assets, and so from this perspective these securitizations are neither pure partial sales nor pure secured borrowings, although they usually are closer to one or the other or these pure cases.

The salience of this second issue and thus the most descriptive accounting method from a risks-and-rewards perspective varies substantially across types of securitizations. At one end of the continuum, Countrywide primarily securitizes prime conforming mortgages, retaining MSRs only, to which the company currently allocates about 1.5% of the value of the underlying mortgages. These securitizations are clearly better accounted for as sales from a risk-and-rewards perspective. At the other end of the continuum, subprime mortgage banks such as Aames and other securitizers of risky assets retain large amounts of residual or subordinated securities, to which they allocate a much larger fraction of the carrying values of the underlying assets. These securitizers may also provide explicit or implicit recourse. These securitizations

EXHIBIT 8.7 Accounting for Securitization from a Risks-and-Rewards Perspective*

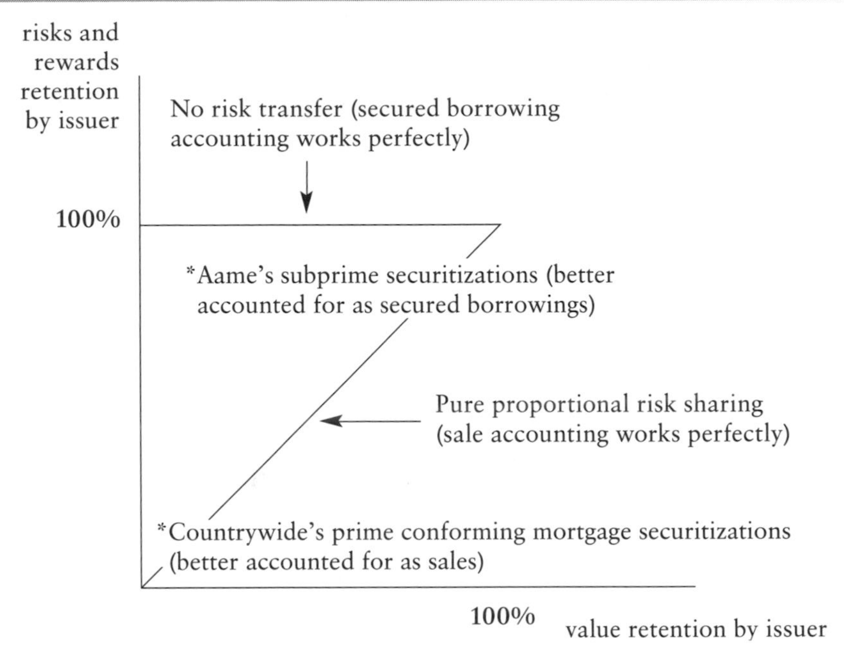

*Indicates roughly where the designated firms' securitizations fall.

are clearly better accounted for as secured borrowings from a risk-and-rewards perspective. Exhibit 8.7 depicts roughly how Countrywide and Aames's securitizations are best accounted for under a risks-and-rewards perspective.

Is the Amount of the Gain on Sale Correct?

The accuracy of an issuer's reported gain on sale depends on its ability to estimate the fair value of its retained interests. This ability is highest when these interests trade in liquid markets. When they do not, the issuer's expertise and judgment in using models to estimate the value of these interests determines whether the gain on sale is measured accurately.

The salience of this point again varies across types of securitizations. At one end of the continuum, Countrywide mainly retains MSRs on prime conforming residential mortgages. There is a moderately active resale market in these fairly homogeneous assets. There is also publicly available information on the main inputs (e.g., prepayment rates) that major market participants use to value MSRs. These conditions allow the fair value of MSRs to be observed or estimated with some reliability and for these estimates to be refined over time and compared across firms. By comparison, the residual or subordinated securities retained by subprime mortgage banks and other securitizers of credit risky assets are less liquid and more heterogeneous. Illiquidity is a particular problem during periods when the market shies away from credit risk, such as the hedge-fund crisis.

Are Gains on Sale Persistent or Managed?

Sale accounting for securitizations accelerates the recognition of income compared to secured borrowing accounting or simply holding the financial assets, so issuers can increase or decrease current period income by timing securitizations accounted for as sales. Users of financial reports should examine the intertemporal correlation of gains on sale with the issuer's level of income before these gains. Income smoothing is suggested if gains on sale are high when income prior to gains on sale is low, and vice versa. Users also should examine the intertemporal correlation of the amount of potentially securitizable financial assets with the amount actually securitized. For example, an issuer that wants to increase (decrease) gains on sale will deplete (build up) its stock of potentially securitizable financial assets, assuming the fair value of these assets exceeds their carrying value.

This point is not usually a major concern for mortgage banks, since they tend to securitize everything they originate as quickly as is feasible and efficient. However, it can be a significant issue for banks and other financial institutions that hold portfolios of financial assets, from which they sometimes choose to securitize selected assets.

A Cautionary Tale: Aames Financial in the Hedge-Fund Crisis*

From its founding in 1991 up to the hedge-fund crisis in the second half of 1998, Aames was a fast-growing, apparently profitable subprime home equity lender. Unlike Countrywide and other large residential mortgage originators today, which generally lend only to prime (A rated) and the highest quality (A- rated) subprime borrowers, Aames originated loans to essentially the whole spectrum of (A to D rated) borrowers, with 35% and 38% of the loan originations in its fiscal year ending June 1998 being to A- rated borrowers and B or lower-rated borrowers, respectively. Moreover, as a home equity lender, Aames generally did not have the first claim to the real property collateralizing the loan. For both these reasons, most of its loans were much credit riskier than prime first residential mortgages.

In its securitizations, Aames retained IOs (essentially residual interests) and MSRs. These IOs credit-enhanced and reduced the prepayment risks of the senior securities sold in its securitizations. In June 1998, the $491 million carrying value of Aames's IOs was over 15 times the $32 million carrying value of its MSRs, and for this reason Aames's retained interests as a percent-

*This section is derived from the case in the appendix of Chapter 8 in the first edition of this book. The original version of this case was coauthored with Mohan Venkatachalam.

age of the cash proceeds from its securitizations were considerably greater than those of Countrywide. For its securitizations in fiscal year 1998, Aames discloses that it received cash proceeds of $2.4 billion and that it retained MSRs of $19.5 million (.8% of the cash proceeds) and IOs of $182 million (7.6% of the cash proceeds), for total retained interests of 8.4% of the cash proceeds, four times greater than Countrywide's 2.0% calculated earlier. Moreover, the June 1998 balances of its MSRs and IOs noted earlier imply that Aames retained interests in prior years' securitizations that were even larger percentages of the cash proceeds from those securitizations. Although its securitizations qualified for sale accounting under SFAS No. 125's (1996) control-based approach, due to the size and riskiness of its IOs, Aames's securitizations would have been better accounted for as secured borrowings under a risks-and-rewards perspective.

During the first two weeks of the hedge-fund crisis in August 1998, the financial markets spurned credit-risky positions, causing immediate sharp decreases in credit-riskless rates and increases in credit-risky rates, and as a consequence causing credit risk premia to spike dramatically (e.g., the spread of high-yield debt securities over U.S. Treasuries of comparable maturity approximately doubled).[7] In fact, certain risky debt markets virtually shut down, with the result being that Aames was unable to securitize its loans for a nine-month period. In addition, many of Aames's better/improving-quality borrowers prepaid their loans and refinanced elsewhere at the low interest rates then available to prime and near-prime borrowers, while many of its worse/deteriorating-quality borrowers defaulted because they could not refinance their loans, a strategy subprime borrowers often use to avoid defaulting.

In its fiscal year ending June 1999, Aames recorded write-downs of $6 million on its MSRs and $186 million on its IOs. It attributed these write-downs as approximately equally attributable to these three factors: unexpectedly high prepayment, unexpectedly high realized credit losses, and an increase in the rate used to discount future cash flows. Also in that fiscal year, Aames recorded losses of $37 million on funds advanced as servicer (which credit-enhanced its securitizations), $15 million on credit-riskless hedges of its subprime loan commitments (short positions in U.S. Treasuries that lost value when credit-riskless rates fell), and $64 million from a retrospective write-down of its IOs from changing its accounting method for credit enhancements from the conceptually unsupportable cash-in method to the cash-out method. The cash-in method effectively treated cash held in the trust that credit enhanced the senior securities sold by the trust as Aames's cash, while the cash-out method properly treated this cash as possibly being distributed to Aames in the future. In June 1998, the cash-in method was not explicitly disallowed under GAAP and was also used by a number of other issuers. The cash-in method was disallowed in an implementation guide for SFAS No. 125 (1996) issued by the FASB staff in December 1998. The collective effect of these write-downs was for Aames's retained earnings to decrease from $54 million at the end of June 1998 to $(197) million at the end of June 1999. That is, Aames recorded losses during its fiscal year 1999 that were approximately five times the retained earnings it accumulated over its eight-year history up to then.

Moreover, at least one of these write-downs appears to have been insufficient at the time it was made. The write-down of its IO strip associated with the increase in the discount rate resulted from an increase in the discount rate from the weighted-average rate on the underlying loans (which Aames disclosed in its 1998 filing to be about 10%, roughly a 5% premium over riskless rates for comparable maturities at the time) to 15%. Even the revised 15% rate was too low given that Aames's IOs concentrated most of the risk of the underlying loans into a position an order of magnitude smaller. Consistent with this view, Aames continued to write down its IOs in the fiscal years 2000 to 2003, with these additional write-downs summing to $179 million. By the end of 2003, Aames's retained earnings had decreased further to $(365) million.

During the hedge-fund crisis, Aames and other subprime mortgage banks securitizers of credit-risky assets were accused by financial analysts and in the business press of misestimating retained interests and thereby overstating gains on sale.[8] Although this accusation certainly is consistent with much of the analysis herein, it should also be noted that even after the fact, it is difficult to assess how much of Aames's losses was attributable to lack of expertise versus willful misjudgment in their *ex ante* estimation of the value of their retained interests and how much was attributable to their *ex post* bad luck in running up against the hedge-fund crisis, a credit crunch of surprising force given the overall good performance of the economy at the time.

Perhaps the most striking aspect of Aames's losses was the complete absence of any offsetting gains, indicating a total failure to manage their exposure to a credit crunch like the hedge-fund crisis. When such a credit crunch occurred, as they do periodically, Aames was bound to be badly hurt.

Unlike many other subprime mortgage banks that failed as a result of the hedge-fund crisis, Aames managed to survive despite its huge losses. In 2004 it converted into a real estate investment trust and in May 2006 it reached agreement to be acquired by Accredited Home Lenders.

EMPIRICAL RESEARCH ON SECURITIZATIONS

Enabled by the enhanced disclosures for securitizations now available under SFAS No. 140 (2000) and similarly expanded disclosures in bank regulatory filings, empirical researchers have begun to ask whether securitizations economically are sales or secured borrowings and whether securitizations are used to manage earnings and regulatory capital. This research is crude in that it generally does not distinguish securitizations by either the type of assets securitized or the nature and magnitude of the retained interests. (It is difficult to distinguish securitizations along these dimensions while retaining samples of size sufficient to conduct statistical tests with adequate power, due to the limited number of issuers and years since SFAS No. 140 [2000] became effective.) In particular, this research does not distinguish securitizations of prime conforming residential mortgages, which are relatively close to sales economically, from other securitizations, which are economically closer to and sometimes indistinguishable from secured borrowings.

This research finds that, on average, securitizations appear to be more like secured borrowings, with the assets and liabilities of the securitization trust having the same valuation and risk implications for the issuer as its own assets and liabilities.[9] The research also finds that issuers time securitizations, cherry-pick the assets to be securitized, and manipulate the assumptions use to value retained interests to manage income and regulatory capital.[10]

SERVICING RIGHTS AND PREPAYMENT-SENSITIVE SECURITIES

Servicing Rights

SFAS No. 156 (2006) recently amended SFAS No. 140's (2000) accounting and disclosure requirements for the rights to service financial assets, of which MSRs are one example. Servicing rights are recognized separately from the remainder of the financial assets only when those rights are retained in a securitization or other transfer or are purchased in the open market. At initiation, all servicing rights are measured at fair value if practicable. Although servicing rights are usually assets, servicing liabilities result if the cost of servicing exceeds the fees, as might be the case if the credit risk of a portfolio rises or if the principal in the portfolio is low.

Subsequent to initiation, firms can choose one of two approaches to accounting for each class of servicing assets and liabilities. Classes should be identified based on the inputs available to measure servicing assets and liabilities or the firm's method of managing the risks of those assets and liabilities or both.

The first approach is to amortize each class of servicing rights over the period of and in proportion to the estimated net servicing income or loss for that class. If this approach is used, servicing assets (liabilities) are subject to a fair value impairment (increased obligation) test. Servicing assets within a class must be stratified based on their predominant risk characteristics (e.g., prepayment risk for MSRs), with the asset for each stratum being written down to fair value if it is below the carrying value. Servicing liabilities must be similarly stratified and written up to fair value if it is above the carrying value. Impairments deemed not other than temporary are recorded in a valuation allowance contra to the servicing asset, while those deemed other than temporary directly reduce the servicing asset. Previously recorded impairments and increased obligations can be reversed if not deemed other than temporary. Impairment standards applied to strata within a portfolio are more conservative than those applied to the portfolio, since gains on one stratum cannot be used to offset losses on another stratum. This approach is essentially the same as was previously required under SFAS No. 140 (2000).

The second approach is to irrevocably fair value each class of servicing rights. This "fair value option" approach was motivated (i.e., made politically feasible) in large part by mortgage banks' difficulty in obtaining hedge accounting for imperfectly effective hedges of their MSRs. Fair valuing MSRs avoids the need for special hedge accounting by accounting for MSRs in the same fashion as the derivatives used to hedge them. Countrywide and most of the other large mortgage servicers chose this approach for their MSRs in the first quarter of 2006.

SFAS No. 156 (2006) expanded the disclosure requirements for servicing rights, which are in addition to those required for all retained interests from securitizations already discussed. It is particularly important for users to analyze these disclosures for servicing-oriented mortgage banks, for which MSRs are a primary asset. Firms must disclose how they determine classes of servicing rights, the risks of servicing rights, the amount of contractually specified servicing and other fees, where each type of fee is reported in the income statement, and how they estimate the fair value of servicing rights. Firms also must disclose essentially the entire activity in the T accounts for each separate class of servicing assets and liabilities, with different disclosures naturally required depending on the approach chosen to account for the class after initiation.

If the amortization/impairment approach is chosen, firms must disclose the balances and the fair values at the beginning and end of the period as well as the additions, disposals, amortization, and impairments during the period. These disclosures are similar to those previously required under SFAS No. 140 (2000), and those from Countrywide's 2005 Form 10-K filing are presented in Exhibit 8.6. If the fair value approach is chosen, firms must disclose the beginning and ending fair values, additions, disposals, and the changes in fair value resulting from changes in valuation inputs and for other reasons. Like most large mortgage banks, Countrywide has chosen the fair value approach for all its MSRs, and its disclosures in its Form 10-Q filing for the first quarter of 2006 are presented in Exhibit 8.8. This disclosure improves upon Countrywide's prior disclosures by distinguishing the additions to MSRs due to purchases and due to securitizations and other transfers of financial assets, thereby allowing users to reconstruct the journal entry for the securitizations of the period with greater accuracy.

Prepayment-Sensitive Securities

SFAS No. 140 (2000) requires that retained prepayment-sensitive securities for which the issuer might not recover substantially all its investment be held as either trading or available-for-sale securities under SFAS No. 115, *Accounting for Certain Investments in Debt and Equity Securities* (2003), which is discussed in Chapter 6. The motivation for this is to ensure that these securities are carried at fair value on the balance sheet. In contrast, under SFAS No. 134, *Accounting for Mortgage-Backed Securities Retained After the*

EXHIBIT 8.8 Countrywide Financial Corporation, Excerpts from Mortgage Servicing Rights Footnote, March 31, 2006, Form 10-K Filing

The Company adopted SFAS 156 effective January 1, 2006. As a result of adopting SFAS 156, all separately recognized MSRs created in the securitization of, or in the sale of loans after December 31, 2005, are recognized initially at fair value. All MSRs are subsequently carried at fair value with changes in fair value recognized in current period earnings.

The activity in MSRs carried at fair value is as follows:

	Quarter Ended March 31, 2006
	(in thousands)
Mortgage Servicing Rights	
Balance at beginning of period	$12,610,839
Remeasurement to fair value upon adoption of SFAS 156	109,916
Fair value at beginning of period	12,720,755
Purchases of servicing assets	1,911
Servicing resulting from transfers of financial assets	1,209,424
Change in fair value:	
Due to changes in valuation inputs or assumptions in valuation model (1)	978,281
Other changes in fair value (2)	(738,567)
Balance at end of period	$14,171,804

(1) Principally reflects changes in discount rates and prepayment speed assumptions, primarily due to changes in interest rates.

(2) Represents changes due to realization of expected cash flows.

Securitization of Mortgage Loans Held for Sale by a Mortgage Banking Enterprise (1998), these securities could have been classified as any of the three classes of securities under SFAS No. 115 (1993), depending on management's intent to hold these securities. SFAS No. 134's (1998) guidance still holds for non–prepayment-sensitive securities.

APPENDIX 8A: DORAL FINANCIAL'S INTERESTING INTEREST-ONLY STRIPS

Case Overview

This case examines Doral Financial Corporation (Doral), the largest residential mortgage lender in Puerto Rico. When Doral originates governmental or conventional conforming mortgages, it usually securitizes them through Ginnie

Mae or the GSEs in securitizations that raise few issues. When it originates nonconforming mortgages, however, Doral usually sells them to other financial institutions. Although these sales are not securitizations per se, they have many of the same features as securitizations. In particular, Doral retains mortgages servicing rights and IO strips and provides partial recourse, while the purchasers of the remaining interests in the loans receive a variable rate (three-month London Interbank Offered Rate [LIBOR] plus a spread) on their investment similar to purchasers of variable-rate pass-through mortgage-backed securities. Doral's retained IOs receive the fixed rate earned on its nonconforming mortgages less the variable rate paid to the purchasers less the mortgage servicing fee. Doral's nonconforming mortgages appear to be good credit quality, so its credit enhancement of the sales of these mortgages is a relatively minor issue.

Doral filed its Form 10-K for 2004 on March 15, 2005. In that filing, Doral recorded an impairment loss of $102 million on its IOs as a result of short-term rates rising. In the three days following that write-down, Doral's share price fell by about 45%, and market participants began to pressure it for more information about its IOs. On April 19, 2005, Doral issued a press release indicating that it planned to correct its methodology for valuing its IOs. A subsequent independent investigation into its accounting unearthed other problems in its accounting for nonconforming mortgage sales—most important, a significant portion were determined not to have legally isolated the assets and thus not to qualify for sale accounting under SFAS No. 140 (2000)—as well as various other accounting problems that are not the subject of this case. Four of Doral's top managers or directors resigned under pressure or were dismissed in August 2005. Doral's share price declined almost 80% from its peak in January 2005 to the filing of its amended Form 10-K/A for 2004 on February 27, 2006. Two Puerto Rican mortgage lenders that engaged in transactions with Doral and/or each other, R&G Financial and FirstBank, have experienced similar accounting problems and share price effects as Doral.

These materials are attached:

- Excerpts from Doral's Amended Form 10-K/A for 2004 filed on February 27, 2006
- Excerpts from Doral's Form 10-K for 2004 filed on March 15, 2005

Although most of these excerpts focus on Doral's nonconforming mortgage sales, some relate to all its mortgage securitizations and sales.

Case Questions

- Determine as fully as possible how Doral originally accounted for and restated its accounting for its mortgage securitizations and sales during 2004 (e.g., reconstructing the journal entries would be a good way to do this).

- What are the nature and magnitude of the risks of Doral's IOs?
- How reasonable and significant are these aspects of Doral's valuation of its IOs in its original filing for 2004:
  - Its use of the current LIBOR rate rather than the forward LIBOR yield curve to project the future cash flows on its IOs and to discount those cash flows
  - Its estimates of prepayment
- Does Doral providing recourse by itself necessarily cause the nonconforming mortgages sold not to be legally isolated? When recourse is provided or risk otherwise retained over transferred assets in securitizations, how is legal isolation usually ensured?
- Compare the economic descriptiveness of the sale accounting used by Doral to secured borrowing accounting for its nonconforming mortgage sales? Is the problem in these sales risk retention by Doral or error in measuring the value of retained interests or both?
- How much of Doral's pretax restatement of retained earnings at the end of 2004 is attributable to
  - The incremental effect of reversing sale accounting for some of its nonconforming mortgage sales
  - The incremental effect of writing down its IOs
  - The common effect of these items
- Which and how much of Doral's accounting problems could have been determined or suspected from careful analysis of its original Form 10-K filing for 2004?

DORAL FINANCIAL CORPORATION AMENDED FORM 10-K/A FILING EXCERPTS FISCAL YEAR ENDING DECEMBER 31, 2004, FILED ON FEBRUARY 27, 2006

SALE OF LOANS AND SECURITIZATION ACTIVITIES

Residential Mortgage Loan

Doral Financial customarily sells or securitizes a significant portion of the residential mortgage loans that it originates and purchases. The Company generally strives to sell mortgage loans that do not conform to GNMA, FNMA or FHLMC requirements (nonconforming loans) in bulk to local financial institutions or to FNMA or FHLMC and other financial institutions in negotiated transactions. Doral Financial's bulk sales historically have operated very similar to securitization transactions because when Doral Financial sells a pool of loans to an investor it retains the servicing rights and agrees to pay the purchaser a specified pass-through rate for the entire pool. Any amounts received on the mortgages above the pass-through rate are retained by Doral Financial. The pass-through rate paid to the investors may be a fixed rate, but more often is a variable rate generally based on a spread over the three-month London Interbank Offered Rate (LIBOR). The present value of the future cash flows retained by Doral Financial above any contractual servicing fees are recognized on Doral Financial's financial statements as interest-only strips.

Doral Financial's nonconforming loan sales are generally made on a limited recourse basis. As of December 31, 2004 and 2003, Doral Financial was servicing mortgage loans with an aggregate principal amount of $1.8 billion and $1.5 billion, respectively, on a recourse basis. As of December 31, 2004 and 2003, Doral Financial's maximum contractual exposure relating to its portfolio of loans sold with recourse, including recourse obligations to FNMA and FHLMC, was approximately $884.8 million and $692.8 million, respectively. As of December 31, 2004 and 2003, Doral Financial recognized an estimated recourse liability of $11.4 million and $5.9 million, respectively, to absorb potential losses from such recourse arrangements.

NON-INTEREST INCOME

Set forth next is certain information regarding the Company's loan sale and securitization activities and resulting IO and MSR capitalization.

	For the Years Ended December 31,		
($ in thousands)	**2004 (As Restated)**	**2003 (As Restated**	**2002 (As Restated)**
Total loan sales and securitizations	$2,531,345	$2,308,070	$1,987,317
Total loans sales resulting in the recording of IOs	1,063,052	342,560	291,992
IOs capitalized	53,624	30,258	33,864
MSRs capitalized	27,520	31,690	28,290

NOTES TO CONSOLIDATED FINANCIAL STATEMENTS YEARS ENDED DECEMBER 31, 2004, 2003, AND 2002

1. Restatement of Previously Issued Financial Statements

Summary of Accounting Adjustments by Category

The Company has classified the accounting practices and related adjustments that were affected by the restatement into six categories. The classification involves subjective judgments by management, and particular accounting errors may fall within more than one category. The cumulative

(continues)

impact of the changes to retained earnings through December 31, 2004 is summarized as:

($ in thousands)	**Cumulative Increase (Decrease) of Retained Earnings Through December 31, 2004**
Pretax Restatement Adjustments:	
Recharacterization of mortgage loan sales transactions as secured borrowings	$ (595,525)
Valuation of IOs	(283,082)
Accounting for servicing assets	(23,144)
Accounting for derivative instruments and investment securities	(24,381)
Provision for loan and lease losses	7,195
Other accounting adjustments	(1,863)
Total pretax restatement adjustments	(920,800)
Income tax impact of restatement adjustments	226,396
Total retained earnings and legal surplus impact	$ (694,404)

Following is a summary, by category, of each of the principal accounting adjustments made in connection with the restatement.

Recharacterization of Mortgage Loan Sales Transactions as Secured Borrowings

The existence of certain recourse provisions in the Company's mortgage loan sales to local financial institutions was not captured by the Company's financial reporting process. In particular, the independent investigation found that it is likely that the former treasurer and the former director emeritus of the Company inappropriately entered into oral agreements or understandings with FirstBank, providing recourse beyond the limited recourse established in the written contracts. Based on an analysis of these findings and other evidence reviewed by the Company, the Company concluded that the mortgage loan sales to FirstBank did not qualify as sales under SFAS No. 140, because these sales did not satisfy the "reasonable assurance" standard of SFAS No. 140 regarding the isolation of assets in bankruptcy.

The impact of the revised accounting treatment of these mortgage loan sales as loans payable as of December 31, 2004, 2003, and 2002 was an increase in Doral Financial's mortgage loans held for sale portfolio, excluding any necessary adjustment related to deferred loan origination fees and direct costs, of $3.3 billion, $1.7 billion, and $1.1 billion, respectively, and an increase in loans payable to creditors by similar amounts. The cumulative effect of the conclusion that the transactions discussed above should not have been accounted as sales but rather as secured borrowings on Doral Financial's pretax income through December 31, 2004, was a decrease of $595.5 million. This includes cumulative decreases of $582.5

million for 2002, 2003, and 2004 and decreases of $13.0 million for periods prior to 2002. The impact in earnings was principally attributable to the reversal of gains on sale recognized and the reversal of subsequent valuation and amortization adjustments related with the associated IOs and MSRs.

Valuation of IOs

IOs represent the estimated present value of the cash flows, retained by Doral, generated by the underlying fixed-rate mortgages (as adjusted for expected losses and prepayments, as well as by the estimated market value of caps, if applicable, as explained below) after subtracting: (1) the interest rate payable to the investor and (2) a contractual servicing fee. The contractual rate payable to investors can be either fixed or variable, while the underlying mortgages generate interest at a fixed rate. When the contractual rate payable to investors is variable, Doral is required to pay to the investor a floating rate based on a spread over the three-month LIBOR, which resets quarterly. Generally, the mortgage loan sale contracts with a variable contractual rate are subject to either interest rate caps or calls that are set at or below the weighted-average coupon (less the servicing fee) of the underlying mortgages loans and, to a lesser extent, based on a spread above the initial contractual pass-through rate at the time of sale (which generally does not exceed the weighted-average coupon of the underlying mortgage loans). For a very small portion of the portfolio, the contracts are also subject to a floor or minimum rate. In substance, Doral Financial sells its legal rights over the mortgage loans to counterparties and is entitled to retained interests on the underlying mortgage loans at a fixed rate and is required to pay to the counterparty a floating rate based on three-month LIBOR, subject to a call or a cap and, in certain instances, a floor provision. IOs are classified as securities held for trading.

The Company has determined that the previous IO valuation was not in accordance with GAAP. The Company corrected its methodology for the valuation of its IOs based on these factors:

Use of forward LIBOR rates. Under the previous methodology, Doral incorrectly determined the estimated fair value of its portfolio of IOs based on an internal static cash flow model that incorporated internally generated prepayment and discount rate assumptions and an expected interest rate spread based on existing three-month LIBOR rates at the close of the reporting period without taking into account projected changes in LIBOR rates. In addition, to value its IOs for financial reporting purposes, Doral Financial historically obtained two valuations from third parties, compared them to the valuation produced by its internal model, and recorded the IOs in its consolidated financial statements at the lowest of the three valuations. Doral has concluded, based on its internal review,

(continues)

that to properly value the Company's portfolio of floating rate IOs, the valuation model (the "New Model") should use an expected interest rate spread based on implied LIBOR rates derived from the yield curve at the date of the valuation.

Market-based prepayment and discount rate determination. Under Doral's previous internal valuation model, prepayment assumptions were generally determined quarterly by management on the basis of prior prepayment experiences on Doral's mortgage portfolio and future prepayment expectations. Discount rates were historically determined by applying a premium to an interest rate at the end of the period based on a mortgage index average. Under the new model, Doral Financial bases its prepayment and discount rates on information derived from publicly available market sources. For example, Doral Financial's new IO valuation model establishes prepayment assumptions by reference to prepayment forecasts published on Bloomberg by a predetermined number of mortgage-backed securities dealers. These forecasts are then adjusted using a regression analysis designed to correlate the prepayment experiences of the mortgage loans underlying Doral Financial's IOs to a generic pool of U.S. mainland FNMA mortgages. In addition, to calculate discount rates, Doral Financial uses a zero volatility spread ("Z-spread") approach, which is the market recognized spread over the swap curve that takes into consideration additional yield requirements based on the risk characteristics of a particular instrument. Doral Financial obtains the Z-spread from major investment banking firms. Accordingly, the prepayment assumptions and discount rates incorporated into Doral Financial's valuation model will no longer incorporate management's internal assumptions regarding the future, but will be based on publicly available and independently verifiable market benchmarks and statistically derived relationships.

The cumulative effect of changes in the value of the Company's IOs that resulted from the above-mentioned changes in the valuation model and certain reclassifications of retained assets, including the reclassification of certain IO sales as secured borrowings, on Doral's pretax income through December 31, 2004, was a decrease of $283.1 million. This includes cumulative decreases of $72.0 million for 2002, 2003, and 2004 and $211.1 million for periods prior to 2002.

Sales and Securitizations of Mortgage Loans

At December 31, 2004, fair values of the Company's retained interests were based on internal and external valuation models that incorporate market driven assumptions, adjusted by the particular characteristics of the Company's servicing portfolio, regarding discount rates, mortgage prepayment rates, and implied forward LIBOR rates. The weighted averages of the key economic assumptions used by the Company in its internal and external valuation models and the sensitivity of the current fair value of residual cash flows to immediate 10% and 20% adverse changes in those assumptions for mortgage loans at December 31, 2004, were:

($ in thousands)	**Servicing Assets (as Restated)**	**Interest-Only Strips (as Restated)**
Carrying amount of retained interest	$123,586	$127,361
Weighted-average expected life (in years)	5.1	4.7
Constant prepayment rate (weighted-average annual rate)	14.12%	17.04%
Decrease in fair value due to 10% adverse change	$ (4,902)	$ (4,964)
Decrease in fair value due to 20% adverse change	$ (9,355)	$ (9,597)
Residual cash flow discount rate (weighted-average annual rate)	9.60%	10.50%
Decrease in fair value due to 10% adverse change	$ (4,054)	$ (2,582)
Decrease in fair value due to 20% adverse change	$ (7,857)	$ (5,057)

These sensitivities are hypothetical and should be used with caution. As the figures indicate, changes in fair value based on a 10% variation in assumptions generally cannot be extrapolated because the relationship of the change in assumption to the change in fair value may not be linear. Also, in this table, the effect of a variation in a particular assumption on the fair value of the retained interest is calculated without changing any other assumption; in reality, changes in one factor may result in changes in another (e.g., increases in market interest rates may result in lower prepayments), which may magnify or counteract the sensitivities.

The activity in interest-only strips is shown next:

($ in thousands)	**2004 (As Restated)**	**2003 (As Restated**	**2002 (As Restated)**
Balance at beginning of year	$128,566	$142,835	$105,780
Capitalization of IOs from loan sales	53,624	30,258	33,864
Amortization	(58,340)	(46,985)	(43,150)
Gains on the IO value	3,511	2,458	46,341
Balance at end of year	$127,361	$128,566	$142,835

In 2004, 2003, and 2002, the Company recognized gains of $83.6 million, $94.7 million, and $70.2 million, respectively, on the sales and

(continues)

securitization of residential mortgage loans. Total loan sales and securitizations amounted to $2.5 billion, $2.3 billion, and $2.0 billion for 2004, 2003, and 2002, respectively.

DORAL FINANCIAL CORPORATION FORM 10-K FILING EXCERPTS: FISCAL YEAR ENDING DECEMBER 31, 2004, FILED ON MARCH 15, 2005

Total loan sales and securitizations were $6.8 billion for 2004, compared to $5.0 billion for 2003 and $4.0 billion for 2002. Loan sales and securitizations that resulted in the recording of IOs amounted to $3.5 billion during 2004, compared to $2.0 billion for 2003 and $1.6 billion for 2002. Doral Financial retained IOs as part of its sales activities of $509.3 million for 2004, compared to $281.3 million for 2003 and $197.9 million for 2002. During 2004, Doral Financial also recorded $66.9 million in connection with the recognition of MSRs as part of its loan sale and securitization activities, compared to $47.0 million for 2003 and $40.1 million for 2002.

Sale of Mortgage Loans

In 2004, 2003, and 2002, the Company recognized gains of $598.8 million, $390.1 million, and $220.6 million, respectively, on the sales and securitization of residential mortgage loans. Values used in measuring the retained interests at the date of the sales of the loans resulting from transactions completed during the year were:

Servicing Assets from Loan Sales. The Company measures the servicing assets at the date of the sales based on current market rates in similar transactions ranging from 1.40% to 2.30% per annum during 2004 and 2003, depending on the type of loan.

Interest-Only Strips. The Company measures the interest-only strips at the date of the transaction based on market values computed based on interest rate spreads on loans sold multiplied by a market multiple. These market multiples ranged from 4.95 to 5.50 during 2004 (2003 – 4.75 to 5.50).

At December 31, 2004, fair values of the Company's retained interests were based on prices provided by dealers as well as external and internal discounted cash flow models that incorporate assumptions regarding discount rates, mortgage prepayment rates, and spot LIBOR rates. The key economic assumptions used by the Company in its internal valuation models and the sensitivity of the current fair value of residual cash flows to immediate 10% and 20% adverse changes in those assumptions for mortgage loans at December 31, 2004, were:

($ in thousands)	**Servicing Assets**	**Interest-Only Strips**
Carrying amount of retained interest	$203,245	$878,732
Weighted-average remaining life (in years)	7	8
Constant prepayment rate (annual rate)	9.45%	7.20%

($ in thousands, Continued)	Servicing Assets	Interest-Only Strips
Impact on fair value of 10% adverse change	$ 5,984	$ 24,134
Impact on fair value of 20% adverse change	$ 11,590	$ 45,785
Residual cash flow discount rate (annual)	9.70%	7.63%
Impact on fair value of 10% adverse change	$ 7,853	$ 31,111
Impact on fair value of 20% adverse change	$ 15,175	$ 60,354

These sensitivities are hypothetical and should be used with caution. As the figures indicate, changes in fair value based on a 10% variation in assumptions generally cannot be extrapolated because the relationship of the change in assumption to the change in fair value may not be linear. Also, in this table, the effect of a variation in a particular assumption on the fair value of the retained interest is calculated without changing any other assumption; in reality, changes in one factor may result in changes in another (e.g., increases in market interest rates may result in lower prepayments), which may magnify or counteract the sensitivities.

The next table summarizes the estimated change in the fair value of the Company's IOs, net of embedded caps, as of December 31, 2004, given several hypothetical (instantaneous and parallel) increases in the three-month LIBOR and does not consider hedging strategies used by the Company.

($ in millions)		Change in Fair Value		
Change in 3-month LIBOR (basis points)	+25	+50	+100	+200
Change in fair value of IOs	$(69.9)	$(138.8)	$(274.7)	$(542.2)

The analysis in the above table is limited in that it was performed at a particular point in time and does not incorporate changes in other factors or assumptions that would impact the sensitivity of the IO valuation in such scenarios.

The activity in interest-only strips is shown next:

($ in thousands)	2004	2003	2002
Balance at beginning of year	$578,124	$359,185	$218,848
Capitalization of IOs from loan sales	509,349	281,273	197,919
Amortization	(101,550)	(79,622)	(40,527)
(Losses) gains on the IO value	(131,007)	7,314	(6,465)
Purchases of IOs	23,816	9,974	10,720
Sales of IOs	—	—	(21,310)
Balance at end of year	$878,732	$578,124	$359,185

NOTES

1. Federal Reserve Board Statistical Release Z.1, "Flow of Funds Accounts of the United States," tables L.220 and L.222.
2. Ibid., table L.208.
3. S. Chen, "Understanding Option-Adjusted Spreads: The Implied Prepayment Hypothesis," *Journal of Portfolio Management* (Summer 1996).
4. L. Hayre, Salomon Smith Barney United States Fixed Income Research Report, "Guide to Mortgage Backed Securities," March 1999.
5. G4+1 Group of Accounting Standards Setters, *Leases: Implementation of a New Approach* (Norwalk, CT: Financial Accounting Standards Board, February 2000).
6. See Countrywide's February 20, 2003, press release at www.countrywide .com.
7. "Profit and Balance Sheet Developments at U.S. Commercial Banks in 1998," *Federal Reserve Bulletin* (June 1999).
8. L. Scism, "Some Analysts Seek Accounting Rule Changes That Would Slash Profits of Sub-prime Lenders," *Wall Street Journal,* September 29, 1998.
9. W. Landsman, K. Peasnell, and C. Shakespeare, "Are Asset Securitizations Sales or Loans?" Working Paper, University of North Carolina at Chapel Hill, 2006; F. Niu and G. Richardson, "Are Securitizations in Substance Sales or Secured Borrowings: Capital Market Evidence," Working Paper, Wilfrid Laurier University, 2005.
10. P. Dechow, J. Myers, and C. Shakespeare, "Playing with Assumptions to Report a Rosy Future Today: The Role of Corporate Governance in the Reporting of Asset Securitizations," Working Paper, University of Michigan, 2004; C. Shakespeare, "Do Managers Use Securitization Volume and Fair Value Estimates to Hit Earnings Targets?" Working Paper, University of Michigan, 2004; E. Karaoglu, "Regulatory Capital and Earnings Management in Banks: The Case of Loan Sales and Securitizations," Working Paper, University of Southern California, 2005.

CHAPTER 9

Elements of Structured Finance Transactions

This chapter discusses important and common elements of structured finance transactions and the accounting issues they raise. Although these elements—special-purpose/variable-interest entities, netting agreements, transactions entered into contemporaneously and in contemplation of one another, hybrid financial instruments, and financial guarantees—may seem diverse, they are all used in bundling, unbundling, and transforming traditional financial claims, the essential activities of structured finance. These elements are often found in the securitization, leasing, and reinsurance transactions discussed in Chapters 8, 13, and 16, respectively, or are combined with derivatives, which are discussed in Chapter 11. This chapter also discusses a final rule recently issued by the Securities and Exchange Commission (SEC) that requires disclosures of off–balance sheet financing and also a special report recently issued by the SEC that expresses its views on accounting-motivated structured finance transactions.

For the first four of the elements of structured finance transactions just listed, the primary accounting question is whether to account for a bundle as a unit in some fashion or instead as the constituent elements of the bundle. In particular, should the primary beneficiary of a variable-interest entity consolidate that entity or not? Should multiple transactions between two counterparties that are subject to a netting agreement or are engaged in contemporaneously and in contemplation of one another be accounted for as a single net transaction or as multiple gross transactions? Should a hybrid financial instrument (e.g., convertible debt) that pays off in one of two or more forms be accounted for as a single instrument (e.g., debt, equity, or something in between) or as components that reflect each of its potential payoff forms (e.g., debt with some probability and equity with some probability)? Regardless of how we account for a bundle, some aspects of its economics usually are lost. For example, if we account for multiple transactions between two counterparties that are engaged in contemporaneously and in contemplation of one another but are not subject to a netting agreement as a net transaction, then the credit risk inherent in the individual transactions is suppressed. Conversely, if we account for these transactions individually, then their relationship from a business perspective may not be as apparent.

Financial guarantees transfer the credit or specified other risks of financial instruments to the guarantor. Financial guarantees raise the issue of risk concentration in much the same way as do residual and subordinated interests created in securitizations discussed in Chapter 8.

The first section of this chapter discusses the economic purposes of special-purpose entities and the recently developed consolidation rules for variable-interest entities in FASB Interpretation (FIN) No. 46(R), *Consolidation of Variable Interest Entities: An Interpretation of ARB No. 51* (2003). The second section discusses the economic purposes of netting agreements and the circumstances under which contracts subject to netting agreements may be presented net on the balance sheet under FIN No. 39, *Offsetting of Amounts Related to Certain Contracts: An Interpretation of APB Opinion No. 10 and FASB Statement No. 105* (1992). This section also discusses when and in what respects transactions that are entered into contemporaneously and in contemplation with one another must be accounted for as unit versus separately under four very narrowly framed accounting rules. The third section discusses the developing accounting for hybrid financial instruments. The fourth section discusses the financial reporting requirements for financial guarantees under FIN No. 45, *Guarantor's Accounting and Disclosure Requirements for Guarantees, Including Indirect Guarantees of Indebtedness of Others* (2002).

SPECIAL-PURPOSE/VARIABLE-INTEREST ENTITIES

The next section discusses economic purposes of special-purpose entities (SPEs) and the accounting issues they raise that until recently had been addressed unsatisfactorily by accounting standards. The "FIN No. 46(R)" section explains the current accounting rules governing the consolidation of variable-interest entities (VIEs), a newly defined class of entities that includes almost all SPEs. An interesting example of a VIE newly consolidated under FIN No. 46(R) (2003) is provided in the "Example: Dell Financial Services" section.

Economic Purposes and the Ineffectiveness of Prior Consolidation Rules

SPEs are entities that are restricted by contract or corporate charter to engage in specified and generally limited economic activities. Because of these restrictions, SPEs do not have the same ongoing control issues as ordinary firms, and their equity holders' voting rights often are of little or no importance. In addition, the primary bearers of SPEs' risks and rewards frequently are not their equity holders but rather parties with other contractual relationships with them. For example, this is likely to be the case when SPEs serve as conduits for some form of debt financing and so do not require much if any equity financing, as occurs in most securitizations and leasing arrangements.

SPEs are used to isolate assets in bankruptcy-remote entities so that all of the parties to transactions are as insulated as possible from the bankruptcy of any party to the transaction, with the main concerns usually being the bankruptcy of the transferor of assets to the SPE (e.g., in a securitization) or the user of the SPE's assets (e.g., a lessee). SPEs also serve as nexuses of contracts; that is, all parties involved in a transaction contract with the SPE rather than bilaterally with each other, thereby improving the efficiency and robustness of the contracting. In these respects, SPEs are better thought of as contractual devices than as firms.

Assuming that an SPE is not consolidated by the firms involved with it, the SPE enables those firms to obtain off–balance sheet financing of the assets held by the SPE and to recognize income on transactions with the SPE. Accordingly, the main accounting issue raised by SPEs is whether they should be consolidated by the firm with the most significant economic relation to them, which might be the sponsor that set up the SPE, the primary transferor of assets to the SPE, the primary user of the SPE's assets, or various other parties. Consolidation of ordinary firms is governed by Accounting Research Bulletin (ARB) No. 51, *Consolidated Financial Statements* (1959), which requires an investor firm to consolidate an investee firm in which it has a "controlling financial interest." A controlling financial interest means that the investor firm controls the investee firm's ongoing operations and has a sufficiently large residual claim on the investee firm. In practice applying ARB No. 51 (1959), a controlling financial interest is almost always defined as ownership of a majority voting equity interest.

The controlling-financial-interest-based approach employed in ARB No. 51 (1959) rarely yields consolidation of SPEs. This is partly because no party needs to exercise ongoing control over SPEs due to their restricted purposes and partly because the equity holders often are not the primary bearers of SPEs' residual risks and rewards. Reflecting this fact, special consolidation rules have been applied to SPEs since no later than the issuance of Emerging Issues Task Force (EITF) 90-15, *Impact of Nonsubstantive Lessors, Residual Value Guarantees, and Other Provisions in Leasing Transactions*, in 1990. EITF 90-15 adopted a solely risk-and-rewards-based approach to the consolidation of SPEs. Although EITF 90-15's language and conditions for consolidation pertain to the leasing setting, it was applied to consolidation of SPEs generally until it was superseded by FIN No. 46, *Consolidation of Variable Interest Entities* (2003). Simplifying and generalizing EITF 90-15's language somewhat, under this standard a firm was required to consolidate an SPE if *all* of these three conditions were met:

1. Substantially all of the SPE's assets resulted from transactions with that firm.
2. The firm bore substantially all of the residual risks and rewards of the SPE.

3. The SPE had insufficient equity at risk over the term of the transaction.

In practice, equity at risk usually was deemed insufficient if it was less than 3% of the SPE's assets. EITF 90-15 rarely led to the consolidation of any SPE unless one of the parties involved desired it.[1] There are various reasons for this, including the difficulty of applying the standard outside the leasing setting (which involves indivisible real assets, not divisible financial assets) and the relative ease of meeting the 3% equity ownership threshold.

EITF 90-15's ineffectiveness, apparent since its issuance, became widely recognized as a result of Enron's implosion. Enron used thousands of SPEs but rarely consolidated them under EITF 90-15, often consistent with the standard, but sometimes violating that standard's intent or letter by using related parties to appear to not meet the criteria for consolidation or by meeting all of the criteria for consolidation but not consolidating anyway.

FIN No. 46(R)

Recognizing EITF 90-15's ineffectiveness, in January 2003 the Financial Accounting Standards Board (FASB) issued FIN No. 46 to govern the consolidation of SPEs and other entities whose equity holders do not bear the risk and rewards of or exercise control over the entity. FIN No. 46 was superseded by the largely consistent but somewhat more specific and implementable FIN No. 46(R) in December 2003. Like EITF 90-15, FIN No. 46(R) (2003) adopts a risk-and-rewards-based approach to consolidation, but it includes considerably more stringent criteria for consolidation and more generally applicable language than the prior standard. Although FIN No. 46(R)'s (2003) title states (misleadingly) that it is an interpretation of ARB No. 51 (1959), FIN No. 46(R) does not include control as a condition for consolidation. The only way that control appears in FIN No. 46(R) is that the equity holders' *lack of* control factors into whether the entity is a variable-interest entity subject to that standard's provisions, as discussed later. In this regard, FIN No. 46(R) (2003) should be viewed as an extension, not an interpretation, of ARB No. 51 (1959); FIN No. 46(R) applies to entities for which ARB No. 51's controlling-financial-interest-based approach does not work.

FIN No. 46(R) (2003) pertains to the consolidation of VIEs rather than SPEs per se. VIEs are defined as entities meeting *any* of these conditions:

- The equity investment at risk is insufficient to permit the entity to finance its activities without additional financial support from any party. This condition is presumed to be met if the equity investment at risk is 10% or less of the entity's assets, a much higher threshold than the 3% previously used in applying EITF 90-15 in practice. Equity investments cannot be provided or guaranteed by other parties.
- The equity investors do not bear either the expected losses or the residual return of the entity or both.

- The equity investors do not have the ability to make decisions about an entity's activities that have a significant effect on the entity's success. Instead, the activities of the entity involve or are conducted on behalf of an investor (or its related parties) with a voting interest that is disproportionately small compared to its financial interest. "An investor" means any party that absorbs the entity's losses or benefits from its residual returns through any variable interest (defined later).

FIN No. 46(R) (2003) specifically exempts certain types of entities that may meet these conditions from its provisions. Qualifying SPEs (QSPEs) under Statement of Financial Accounting Standards (SFAS) No. 140, *Accounting for Transfers and Servicing of Financial Assets and Extinguishments of Liabilities* (2000), which are not consolidated, are the main exception pertaining to structured finance transactions.

The vast majority of SPEs are VIEs, because the equity investors in SPEs usually lack substantive control rights and often for other reasons. However, VIEs need not be SPEs, because the definition of a VIE does not include restrictions on business activities. In this regard, FIN. No. 46(R) (2003) distinguishes businesses—defined as "a self-sustaining integrated set of activities and assets conducted and managed for the purpose of providing a return to investors . . . [that] consists of (a) inputs, (b) processes applied to those inputs, and (c) resulting outputs that are used to generate revenues"—from other potential VIEs. Only businesses that meet certain criteria that suggest they likely are VIEs need to be evaluated for whether they are VIEs.

Under FIN No. 46(R) (2003), consolidation of VIEs is based not on (voting) equity ownership but rather on the broader notion of variable interests. Variable interests are ownership, contractual, or other pecuniary interests in an entity whose values vary positively with the fair value of the entity's net assets exclusive of variable interests. Equivalently, variable interests absorb (rather than create) the variation in the fair value of the entity's net assets exclusive of variable interests. Examples of potential variable interests include the equity, risky debt, or beneficial interests of the entity, guarantees of the entity's assets, derivatives that absorb rather than create risk for the entity, and the portion of management or other fees that are based on the performance of the entity (i.e., removing the portions of fees that reflect normal compensation for services provided). FASB Staff Position (FSP) No. FIN 46(R), *Implicit Variable Interests under FASB Interpretation No. 46* (2005), states that variable interests may be explicit (i.e., direct and contractual) or implicit (i.e., indirect through related or unrelated parties or not contractual).

Variable interests in specified assets of the entity are considered variable interests of the entity if the fair value of the specified assets is more than half the total fair value of the entity's assets or if the investor holding those variable interests also holds other variable interests in the entity. Specified assets of a VIE are treated as a separate VIE from the host VIE (making the host VIE a "silo") if those assets are essentially the only source of payment for specified variable interests.

Unless it is apparent that a firm's variable interests in a VIE are not significant and the firm did not participate in the design of the VIE, the firm is required to determine whether an entity with which it is involved is a VIE at the time the firm becomes involved with the entity. The firm must reconsider that determination whenever there are significant changes in the entity's governance, activities, or variable interests. A decline in the value of an entity's equity resulting from accumulated losses does not by itself make the entity a VIE.

A firm must consolidate a VIE if it or its related parties is expected to absorb a majority of the VIE's expected losses or to receive a majority of the VIE's expected residual returns or both. If one firm will absorb a majority of the VIE's expected losses and another firm will receive a majority of the VIE's expected residual returns, then the firm that absorbs the losses should consolidate the VIE. As discussed, control plays no role in the consolidation decision. Reflecting this fact, the firm that consolidates a VIE is called its "primary beneficiary."

Losses and residual returns are discounted and measured relative to the expected value of the VIE, not zero. Hence, losses and residual returns each should occur about half the time if the distribution of the VIE's outcomes is fairly symmetric. Expected losses equal the probability of a loss of a given magnitude times the magnitude of that loss summed across all possible levels of losses. Expected residual returns are defined analogously.

To illustrate, assume the cash flows on an SPE's investments are \$0 with 40% probability, \$10 with 30% probability, \$20 with 20% probability, and \$40 with 10% probability. These cash flows are to be received in one year and the interest rate is 10%. The value of the SPE's investments is $(\$10 \times .3 + \$20 \times .2 + \$40 \times .1)/1.1 = \$10$. The firm experiences losses if the cash flows are either \$0 or \$10, which yield discounted values of \$0 and \$9.09 and thus losses of \$10 and \$.91, respectively. The expected loss is $\$10 \times .4 + \$.91 \times .3 = \$4.27$. The firm experiences residual returns if the cash flows are either \$20 or \$40, which yield discounted values of \$18.18 and \$36.36 and thus residual returns of \$8.18 and \$26.36, respectively. The expected residual return is $\$8.18 \times .2 + \$26.36 \times .1 = \$4.27$. Expected losses equal expected residual returns because both losses and residual returns are measured relative to expectations. If an investor in the SPE expects to incur losses exceeding \$2.14 or to receive residual returns exceeding \$2.14 or both, then it should consolidate the SPE under FIN No. 46(R) (2003).

As mentioned, a firm's related parties can affect whether an entity with which the firm is involved is a VIE and, if so, whether the firm is the primary beneficiary of the VIE. Undoubtedly reflecting Andy Fastow's extensive use of Enron employees (and their significant others) as equity investors in Enron's SPEs, related parties of a firm are defined more broadly in FIN No. 46(R) than elsewhere in generally accepted accounting principles (GAAP). They include parties that:

- Depend on financial support from the firm

- Received the funds for their investment in a VIE as a contribution or loan from the firm
- Cannot dispose of their investment in a VIE without the approval of the firm
- Have a close business relationship with the firm
- Are officers, employees, or directors of the firm

If two or more related parties hold variable interests in a VIE that collectively make the related party group the primary beneficiary of the VIE, then the related party most clearly associated with the VIE is the primary beneficiary.

FIN No. 46(R) (2003) has led to more frequent consolidation of SPEs than was the case under EITF 90-15. The most significant type of SPE that must be consolidated under the new standard is asset-backed commercial paper conduits. These conduits typically must be consolidated by the financial institution that provides them with liquidity facilities and credit enhancement. Entities issuing collateralized bond, loan, and debt obligations, if not QSPEs, will be consolidated by the holders of sufficiently large risky (e.g., residual or subordinated) interests. Federal Reserve economists inferred from weekly changes in bank credit data (for chartered banks, not bank holding companies) that FIN No. 46 and FIN No. 46(R) (2003) together caused large U.S. commercial banks to consolidate conduits holding $67 billion of assets in 2003.[2] This amount appears to be much lower than the actual effect of these interpretations on the holding companies that own these banks. For example, JPMorgan Chase disclosed that that it consolidated VIEs holding $27 billion of assets and Bank One disclosed it consolidated VIEs holding $39.6 billion of assets as a result of adopting FIN No. 46 and FIN No. 46(R) (2003) in 2003. Moreover, some holding companies such as Citigroup adopted FIN No. 46(R) (2003) in 2004.

In some cases, FIN No. 46 or FIN No. 46(R) (2003) led to the deconsolidation of SPEs previously consolidated under EITF 90-15, however, because the variable interests held by other parties absorbed more than 50% of the losses and residual returns. An example of this are trusts issuing preferred securities that banks use to raise regulatory capital while maintaining tax deductibility of interest payments that were deconsolidated when FIN No. 46(R) (2003) was adopted.

As discussed in Chapter 2, U.S. bank regulators ignore the implications of FIN No. 46(R) (2003) for the consolidation of asset-backed commercial paper conduits and the entities issuing trust preferred securities for the purposes of capital regulation.

The bookkeeping for consolidating VIEs based on variable interests required by FIN No. 46(R) (2003) is modeled after the bookkeeping for consolidating ordinary firms based on equity ownership required by SFAS No. 141, *Business Combinations,* (2001). Differences arise, however, because the primary beneficiary generally will not have recognized certain of its variable interests (e.g., future management fees based on the VIE's performance) prior to consolidation of the VIE and so these interests cannot be eliminated in consolidation in the same fashion as equity interests. For the same reason, certain of the variable interests held by other firms involved with the VIE cannot be accounted for as minority interests in consolidation.

Under FIN No. 46(R) (2003), at the time of initial consolidation by the primary beneficiary, assets and liabilities of the VIE are recognized at (possibly adjusted) fair values unless:

- Those assets and liabilities were transferred by the primary beneficiary to the VIE at or shortly prior to the time it became the primary beneficiary.
- The VIE is under common control with the primary beneficiary.

In both of these cases, the valuations of assets and liabilities do not change upon either their transfer to the VIE or the consolidation of the VIE, so that no gain or loss is recorded. In other cases, the fair values of assets are adjusted downward pro rata if the fair value of the consideration paid is below the amount consistent with those fair values, taking into account the reported amount of previously held interests and the fair value of liabilities and noncontrolling interests. Conversely, if the fair value of consideration paid is above the amount consistent with the fair values of assets, then goodwill is recognized if the VIE is a business and an extraordinary loss is recognized otherwise. In this respect, VIEs that are businesses are treated more like ordinary firms in consolidation.

The bookkeeping required by FIN No. 46(R) (2003) after the initial consolidation of VIEs is also modeled after that for ordinary firms based on equity ownership required under ARB No. 51 (1959).

FIN No. 46(R) (2003) requires disclosures about VIEs by primary beneficiaries and other firms holding significant variable interests. These disclosures include:

- The nature, purpose, size, and activities of the VIE
- The carrying amount and classification of consolidated assets that are collateral for the VIE's obligations and any lack of recourse to the general credit of the primary beneficiary (primary beneficiaries only)
- The nature of the firm's involvement with the VIE, when it began, and the maximum exposure to loss as a result of that involvement (other firms only)
- Why information necessary to apply FIN No. 46(R) (2003) is not available

These disclosures are useful for a number of reasons. Perhaps most important, in many cases FIN No. 46(R) (2003) requires firms to record assets on their balance sheet that they do not control, such as financial institutions and the assets in commercial paper conduits that those institutions provide with liquidity support or credit enhancement. Also important, the distinctions between the firms that are required to consolidate VIEs and those that are meaningfully involved with VIEs but are not so required can be relatively slight, as the next example demonstrates.

Example: Dell Financial Services

Dell Financial Services (DFS), a joint venture between Dell (a manufacturing company) and CIT (a lessor), provides an interesting example of a VIE for which FIN No. 46's (2003) proper application initially was in dispute. DFS's purpose is to help Dell's customers finance purchases of Dell products, as described in Dell's Form 10-K filing for the fiscal year ending January 31, 2004 (fiscal 2004).

> The joint venture allows Dell to provide its customers with various financing alternatives while CIT provides the financing for the transaction between DFS and the customer. In general, DFS facilitates customer financing transactions through either loan or lease financing. For customers who desire loan financing, Dell sells equipment directly to customers who, in turn, enter into loans with CIT to finance their purchases. For customers who desire lease financing, Dell usually sells the equipment to DFS, and DFS enters into direct financing lease arrangements with the customers.
>
> Dell currently owns a 70% equity interest in DFS. In accordance with the partnership agreement between Dell and CIT, losses generated by DFS are fully allocated to CIT. Net income generated by DFS is allocated 70% to Dell and 30% to CIT, after CIT has recovered any cumulative losses. If DFS is terminated with a cumulative deficit, Dell is not obligated to fund any losses, including any potential losses on receivables transferred to CIT. Although Dell has a 70% equity interest in DFS, prior to the third quarter of fiscal 2004 the investment was accounted for under the equity method because the company historically could not, and currently does not, exercise control over DFS.

Subsequent to the issuance of FIN No. 46 (2003), both Dell and CIT said they were not the primary beneficiary of DFS.[3] Dell argued that CIT bore all losses on DFS (until such time if any that CIT recouped these losses from subsequent profits) and that losses are more important than residual returns in determining the primary beneficiary of a VIE. In contrast, CIT argued that Dell received 70% of all income on DFS (after reimbursing CIT for prior cumulative losses), and DFS was profitable and so unlikely to generate losses. Neither of these arguments clearly incorporates the fact that losses and residual returns are defined relative to expectations not zero under FIN No. 46(R) (2003). Under this definition, Dell very likely bears more than half the expected losses and residual returns of DFS, along with being considerably more affected by the success or failure of DFS from a business perspective. Likely for these reasons, Dell consolidated DFS in August 2003, although Dell states that it does not control DFS, presumably because it shares control with CIT. The consolidation of DFS increased Dell's consolidated assets and liabilities by $588 million.

Although FIN No. 46(R) (2003) generally made consolidation of SPEs more likely than under EITF 90-15, the initial dispute between Dell and CIT over which should consolidate DFS, despite the fact that it was an asymmetrically structured joint venture, illustrates that by no means did the new standard ensure that SPEs are consolidated. Consolidation does not occur in symmetrical joint ventures, and it is less likely to occur when three or more parties are each significantly involved with an SPE.

RELATED TRANSACTIONS

Structured finance often involves taking (and subsequently unwinding) multiple transactions that are related in some fashion. The next section discusses the accounting issues and rules for multiple transactions contractually linked by netting agreements. The "Transactions Entered into Contemporaneously and in Contemplation of One Another" section discusses the accounting issues and rules for multiple transactions that are related in a business sense but not contractually. The "Example: Structured Prepay Transactions" section provides an interesting example in which both of these sets of issues may arise.

Netting Agreements and FIN No. 39

Netting agreements are the most common form of contractual relationship relating multiple transactions. In these agreements, multiple transactions among two or more counterparties settle by net rather than gross payments being made among the counterparties in some or all circumstances. For example, if Firm A owes firm B $10 on Transaction X, Firm B owes Firm A $40 on Transaction Y, and the two transactions are subject to a netting agreement that covers all circumstances, then Firm B pays Firm A $30 net for the two transactions. Netting agreements reduce credit and other performance risks. For example, if Firm B defaults on its $40 gross obligation to Firm A, then Firm A would not have to pay the $10 gross it owes Firm B, so that Firm A bears credit risk only on its $30 net receivable not its $40 gross receivable from Firm B.

Netting agreements are most useful when counterparties engage in repeated transactions with each other that offset economically. This occurs frequently among firms trading derivatives and other financial and commodity instruments. Trading firms typically engage in a high volume and wide variety of transactions with a limited set of counterparties, and they often modify their trading positions over time by taking offsetting positions rather than by directly settling positions in order to maximize the speed and minimize the cost of trading. For these reasons, frequent trading counterparties are likely to have master netting agreements that cover wide classes of transactions.

There are various types of netting agreements with distinct effects. Close-out netting agreements specify that if a counterparty to the agreement defaults on one transaction covered by the agreement, then all the transactions covered by the agreement terminate and net payments are made. Payment netting agreements specify that payments to be made at the same time be made net. Novation netting agreements legally replace economically offsetting contracts with new contracts whose payment terms reflect the net amounts of the offsetting contracts.

FIN No. 39 (1992) requires gross balance sheet presentation of contracts unless the right of setoff exists. The right of setoff is defined as the enforceable legal right to set off determinable amounts accompanied by the intent to set off. Close-out and novation netting agreements usually constitute an enforceable legal right to set off. If the right of setoff exists, then FIN No. 39 (1992) allows but does not require the contracts involved to be presented net on the balance sheet, with its rationale being that gross presentation more transparently indicates the credit risks of contracts that settle individually.

FIN No. 39 (1992) substantially increased the size of trading-oriented firms' balance sheets. For example, due solely to the adoption of FIN No. 39 (1992) in 1994, U.S. chartered commercial banks' reported assets and liabilities rose about $90 billion, or 2.3% of assets.[4] The vast bulk of that increase was attributable to the 10 largest and most trading-oriented banks, whose assets and liabilities rose by about 9% of assets. This increase primarily resulted from large commercial banks' more limited ability to report their derivatives positions net.

Transactions Entered into Contemporaneously and in Contemplation of One Another

Four accounting rules—EITF 98-15, *Structured Notes Acquired for a Specific Investment Strategy*; EITF 00-4, *Majority Owner's Accounting for a Transaction in the Shares of a Consolidated Subsidiary and a Derivative Indexed to the Minority Interest in That Subsidiary*; Derivatives Implementation Group (DIG) K1 (1999); and DIG F6 (2000)—consider the possibility that a firm engages in multiple transactions that economically offset in whole or part (rather than a single or no transaction) in order to circumvent accounting rules in some fashion. Each of these rules considers one or more very narrowly framed fact patterns. EITF 98-15 considers two structured notes with mirror-image contractual terms, so that when one note experiences a gain, the other note experiences a loss of the same amount. EITF 00-4 considers minority interest in a subsidiary and a sold put option on that minority interest. The two DIG issues consider several specific examples of offsetting instruments that are individually or collectively derivatives.

These four rules all require that the multiple transactions in the fact patterns under consideration be accounted for "as a unit" for some specified accounting purpose if the transactions meet all of these four conditions:

1. Are entered into contemporaneously and in contemplation of one another
2. Are executed with the same counterparty or are structured through an intermediary
3. Relate to the same risk
4. Have no apparent economic need or substantive business purpose that could not have been accomplished in a single transaction

(These are the conditions stated in EITF 00-4, DIG K1 (1999), and DIG F6 (2000); EITF 98-15 contains similar but not identical conditions.) The specified purposes of accounting for multiple transactions as a unit in the four rules are all different. EITF 98-15 prohibits recognizing a gain on one structured note without recognizing the offsetting loss on the other note, and vice versa. EITF 00-4 requires treating the minority interest as if it has been acquired by the firm. DIG K1 requires treating offsetting nonderivative instruments as a single derivative. DIG F6 prohibits using either of offsetting derivatives as accounting hedges.

As noted, these rules consider very narrowly framed fact patterns and require accounting for multiple transactions meeting the four conditions as a unit in quite different ways. As a result, it is difficult to determine whether and how multiple transactions that meet the four conditions but are not covered in the fact patterns under consideration or for which accounting for the transactions as a unit would have different effects are subject to these rules. All four of the rules consider cases where the measurement of owners' equity and net income are affected, and so it seems reasonable to restrict their application to situations in which such measurement issues are involved. In addition, three of the four rules (all but EITF 00-4, which deals with consolidation issues) consider cases where amortized cost accounting is being abused or fair value accounting potentially avoided in some fashion, and so they are consistent with the FASB's expressed preferences for fair value accounting discussed in Chapters 1 and 6. None of these rules considers financial statement classification or disclosure, even though these issues often arise with multiple transactions that economically offset.

Recognizing the difficulties in deciding when and how to apply these rules, the EITF attempted in EITF 02-2, *When Certain Contracts that Meet the Definition of Financial Instruments Should Be Combined for Accounting Purposes,* to provide guidance that applied to multiple financial instruments that economically offset generally. However, the EITF's discussion of this issue was discontinued in March 2003 when it realized that the issue conflicted with decisions reached in the FASB's liabilities and equity project and could not decide on the issue's boundaries. The EITF did preliminarily agree on a more inclusive version of the third condition that would have required that the transactions exhibit only one or more economically offsetting risks, not necessarily the same risk on all dimensions. It also preliminarily agreed that a substantive business purpose could not result from accounting effects in the fourth condition.

Example: Structured Prepay Transactions

Prepays are hybrid instruments with embedded derivatives. Prepays both provide financing from one counterparty to another and transfer market price risk between the counterparties. One counterparty pays cash at the inception of the prepay while the other counterparty pays cash or other consideration later with a value that depends on the movements in some market price or prices since initiation. For example, in a commodity prepay, the first counterparty pays a fixed amount of cash up front to the second counterparty in exchange for the second counterparty's promise to provide a specified amount of commodities or cash with the same value later. Although commodity prepays are the most common type, prepays have been structured where the second counterparty's payments depend on interest rates, stock prices, and probably other market prices.

Enron and a number of other firms engaged in structured prepay transactions involving prepays and other financial instruments that hedged the market price risks of the prepays. If each counterparty to one of these prepay transactions performed on each instrument, then the realizations of the market risks of the prepays and other financial instruments would offset economically, rendering the outcomes of the transaction similar to that of a loan. The prepay and other financial instruments usually were not subject to netting agreements, however, so that the instruments did not exhibit the right of setoff. As a result, if any counterparty did not perform on any instrument, then the realizations of market price risk on the instruments would not offset and the transaction would yield outcomes very different from that of a loan.

The next example of a structured commodity prepay transaction involving one prepay and one hedging instrument is depicted in Exhibit 9.1. The instruments are engaged in contemporaneously and in contemplation of one another but are not subject to a netting agreement. For simplicity, the example ignores the time value of money. The first instrument, a prepaid commodity forward, requires Firm A to pay \$80 up front to Firm B in exchange for the promise of 10 units of a commodity to be delivered in one year with an expected value of \$8/unit. The second instrument, a commodity swap to be settled in one year, requires Firm B to provide Firm A with units of the commodity having a value of \$80 while Firm A promises to provide Firm B with 10 units of the commodity. If both firms perform on both instruments, then their net effect is Firm A pays cash of \$80 up front to Firm B in exchange for commodities with a value of \$80 delivered in one year, much the same outcome as an \$80 one-year loan from Firm A to Firm B. However, if there is no netting agreement and either firm defaults on either instrument, then the outcome may be quite different from that for a loan. For example, if firm B defaults on the prepaid forward, then Firm A might have to pay Firm B on the commodity swap, depending on the value of the commodity at the settlement date. To illustrate, if the value of the commodity turns out to be \$10/unit, then Firm A has to pay \$20 = 10 units × \$10/unit

EXHIBIT 9.1 Structured Commodity Prepay Transaction Example

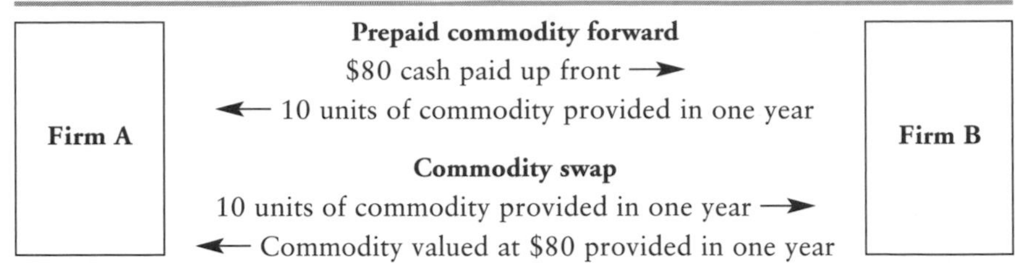

– $80 to Firm B on the commodity swap. Thus the structured prepay transaction is very different from a loan in this default scenario, because in a loan the lender does not pay a borrower when it defaults and the amount of the lender's loss on default is not tied to commodity prices. Similar conclusions apply in the default scenario in which Firm A defaults on the commodity swap and the scenario in which Firm B defaults on the commodity swap but not the prepaid forward.

How should this structured prepay transaction be accounted for and analyzed by users of financial reports? Due to the lack of a right of offset, FIN No. 39 (1992) requires that the two instruments involved the transaction be presented gross on the balance sheet, not on a combined basis as a loan. For example, Firm B will record some type of financial liability for the prepay and a derivative asset or liability for the commodity swap. Given the absence of a netting agreement, gross balance sheet presentation captures the instruments' distinct credit risks as well as their market risks to the extent that those risks interact with their credit risks. Reflecting this fact, for the purposes of assessing credit risk and also the interaction between commodity price risk and credit risk, users should evaluate this transaction gross. Assuming there is no substantive business purpose for structuring the transaction using multiple instruments for the purposes of assessing most aspects of the transaction other than credit risk, such as commodity price risk, users should evaluate this transaction net.

Structured prepay transactions have very different effects than loans on financial statement classifications, and these effects yield accounting motivations for these transactions. Such classification issues are discussed next in the broader context of hybrid financial instruments.

HYBRID FINANCIAL INSTRUMENTS

Although not a financial instrument due to its physical settlement, the prepaid commodity forward in the last example is a hybrid instrument; that is, it is neither a loan nor a derivative but rather a mixture of the two that settles as a single instrument. There are many types of hybrid financial instruments and also hybrid nonfinancial instruments that are similar to hybrid financial instruments (hereafter hybrid financial instruments). The risky beneficial interests created in securitizations (e.g., residual securities and principal-only and interest-only strips) can be viewed as hybrid financial instruments. Convertible debt, mandatorily redeemable stock, and puttable stock are other examples.

Hybrid financial instruments constitute a type of structured finance product. In order to be successful, these products must be desirable to a sufficiently large set of investors. These instruments often are components of larger structured finance transactions, as in the case of the prepay example.

Hybrid financial instruments serve two general economic purposes. First, they bundle desired features of multiple simple instruments into a single instrument and/or eliminate the undesired features of single instruments. By such bundling, hybrid financial instruments can reduce transaction costs, including the costs of monitoring and settling multiple simple instruments, and can mitigate the need to assume undesired market risks. Second, by settling as a single net instrument, hybrid financial instruments can mitigate credit risks compared to multiple single instruments in much the same way as a netting agreement.

Hybrid financial instruments raise two sets of accounting issues with which the FASB currently is grappling. First, should hybrid financial instruments be decomposed into their constituent components? For example, should the prepaid commodity forward in the last example be decomposed into a host loan and an embedded commodity price swap? Decomposing hybrid financial instruments is a daunting task both because it can be difficult to identify meaningful and understandable components associated with the various features of the instruments and because the measurement of the identified components can be judgmental. Decomposing hybrid financial instruments in this fashion also ignores their mitigation of credit risk discussed earlier, but, when it can be done reliably, it helps with the next set of issues.

Second, hybrid financial instruments in their entirety do not fall neatly into the usual characteristic-based classifications of financial instruments, yielding both accounting measurement and financial statement classification issues that accounting standard setters have not resolved in a comprehensive fashion. For example, if the prepay in the last example is not decomposed into its components, then how should it be classified on the contracting firms' balance sheets, as a loan or a derivativelike instrument? Should the classification depend on whether the prepay is measured at amortized cost, like a loan, or fair value, like a derivative, or should the measurement depend on the classification? Relatedly, how should the cash flow at the inception of the prepaid commodity forward be classified on the firms' cash flow statements? If the prepay is classified as a loan, then the cash flow must be classified as investing by the payor and financing by the payee, but if the prepay is classified as a derivativelike instrument, then the cash flow usually would have been classified by both firms as operating prior to the issuance of SFAS

No. 149, *Amendment of Statement 133 on Derivative Instruments and Hedging Activities* (2003), but as financing by the payee subsequently, as discussed in Chapter 11.

In part because the accounting for hybrid financial instruments is developing as this book is being written and in part because certain aspects of current accounting for these instruments are discussed in Chapter 11, only the three main approaches taken in current accounting standards and the current status of the FASB's ongoing project on liabilities and equity are described in this chapter. The three main approaches taken in current accounting standards are:

- Decomposition into components
- Fair value option
- Improved financial statement classification or enhanced disclosure

Decomposition into Components Approach

As discussed in Chapter 11, under SFAS No. 133, *Accounting for Derivative Instruments and Hedging Activities* (1998), firms must unembed and separately account for derivatives embedded in a host hybrid financial instrument if the derivatives are not "clearly and closely related to" the host instrument and that instrument is not already measured at fair value on both the balance sheet and income statement under GAAP. SFAS No. 155, *Accounting for Certain Hybrid Financial Instruments* (2006), provides exceptions to this requirement for plain vanilla principal-only and interest-only strips.

Fair Value Option Approach

SFAS No. 155 (2006) allows firms to choose irrevocably at the inception of certain hybrid financial instruments to fair value those instruments throughout their lives on both the balance sheet and income statement, thereby avoiding decomposition of hybrid financial instruments into their host instruments and embedded derivatives under SFAS No. 133 (1998). Fair valuation of hybrid financial instruments in their entirety is the simplest approach to the measurement issues posed by these instruments, although it does not address the classification issues they raise. Also, because it is a fair value option, not requirement, firms are likely to exercise this option differently, yielding noncomparable financial reports.

Improved Financial Statement Classification or Enhanced Disclosure Approach

SFAS No. 150, *Accounting for Certain Instruments with Characteristics of both Liabilities and Equity* (2003), requires that certain instruments with characteristics of both liabilities and equity—mandatorily redeemable stock, obligations to repurchase shares that require settlement in assets, and obligations to issue a variable number of shares with a value unrelated or inversely related to the value of a fixed number of shares—that previously had been classified as equity or in the mezzanine between liabilities and equity be classified as liabilities, reflecting the obligations inherent in these instruments. For firms whose outstanding stock is all mandatorily redeemable, SFAS No. 150 (2003) requires that the liability for this stock be clearly labeled on the balance sheet.

SFAS No. 150 (2003) also requires enhanced disclosures for instruments with characteristics of both liabilities and equity, including the nature and terms of the instruments, the amounts paid under each settlement alternative, and how changes in the value of shares affect the settlement amounts. Regardless of how the FASB decides to account for hybrid financial instruments, their complex economic nature clearly makes such enhanced disclosure desirable. When provided, these disclosures should be considered carefully by users of financial reports.

In its ongoing liabilities and equity project, the FASB currently is considering whether to account for instruments with characteristics of both equity and nonequity using one or more of the "ownership-settlement," "ownership," and "reassessed expected outcomes" approaches. The ownership-settlement approach views equity as resulting either from direct ownership instruments or from indirect ownership interests that have payoffs that are based on and vary in the same direction as direct ownership instruments. This is distinct from the ownership approach, which views equity more narrowly as resulting only from direct ownership instruments. The FASB's decision to choose one of the ownership settlement and ownership approaches would affect whether and how hybrid financial instruments are decomposed into components and also how (the components of) the instruments are classified on the financial statements. The reassessed expected outcomes approach considers the probabilities that an instrument settles in its various possible forms. The FASB's decision to choose this approach would primarily affect how hybrid financial instruments are decomposed into components.

FINANCIAL GUARANTEES

FIN No. 45, *Guarantor's Accounting and Disclosure Requirements for Guarantees, Including Indirect Guarantees of Indebtedness of Others* (2002), defines financial guarantees as contracts that contingently require the guarantor to transfer assets or provide services to the guaranteed party or a creditor of the guaranteed party:

- Based on changes in an underlying (i.e., a price, an index, lawsuit, tax judgment, or other variable) related to an asset, a liability, or an equity security held by the guaranteed party
- Based on another entity's failure to perform under an agreement with the guaranteed party

- As a result of indirect guarantees of the indebtedness of the guaranteed party to one of its creditors

Examples of financial guarantees under FIN No. 45 (2002) include financial and performance-related standby letters of credit and guarantees of the market value of a financial or nonfinancial asset owned by the guaranteed party or equity issued by the guaranteed party. FIN No. 45 (2002) provides exceptions for lessees' residual value guarantees in capital leases, most insurance contracts, guarantees that are derivatives accounted for at fair value, and various other items.

Certain contracts that effectively function as financial guarantees will not be accounted for as such because they do not meet the characteristic-based definition of a guarantee in FIN No. 45 (2002). Most important, FIN No. 45 (2002) states that commercial loan commitments, which are commonly used to provide liquidity support and/or credit enhancement for asset-backed commercial paper conduits and various other types of debt financing, do not to meet this definition. The FASB reasons that these commitments do not guarantee payment of a *specific* financial obligation of the holder of the commitment in the event it defaults on that obligation. Although this is true, in most cases the primary role of commercial loan commitments clearly is to support commercial paper issuances by the holders of the commitments, because of the size and short duration of these issuances. In supporting its decision, the FASB notes that these commitments usually include material adverse change provisions that in principle allow the writer of the loan commitment to back out in the face of deterioration of the holder of the commitment. Although this also is true, the financial institutions making commercial loan commitments rarely invoke material adverse change provisions in practice even in the face of significant deterioration of the creditworthiness of the holder of the commitments (e.g., WorldCom), for both legal liability and business relationship reasons. The author argues in more depth elsewhere that commercial loan commitments supporting commercial paper issuances in this fashion would be properly accounted for in the same fashion as financial guarantees under FIN No. 45 (2002).[5]

FIN No. 45 (2002) requires financial guarantees to be measured at fair value at inception, but it does not provide significant guidance regarding the measurement of the guarantee after inception. It requires the recognition of financial guarantees that went unrecognized under SFAS No. 5, *Accounting for Contingencies* (1975), due to that standard's "probable" criterion for recognizing loss contingencies.

FIN No. 45 (2002) requires firms to disclose relevant information about their guarantees, including the nature, terms, performance triggers, recourse provisions, collateral, and maximum potential amount of future payments on those guarantees. Users of financial reports should evaluate these disclosures carefully. As mentioned, financial guarantees raise the issue of risk concentration, which is discussed in considerable detail in Chapter 8 on securitizations. For example, if a firm by guaranteeing the value of an asset bears most of the risk of that asset, then for most purposes users should treat that asset as if it were the firm's asset. More generally, financial guarantees raise the issue of the nature and magnitude of the involvement of the guarantor with the guaranteed party or guaranteed items. This issue is most significant when the guarantor owned or had some other business relationship with the guaranteed party or guaranteed items prior to the issuance of the guarantee.

RECENT SEC DECISIONS REGARDING STRUCTURED FINANCE TRANSACTIONS

Structured finance transactions often have accounting motivations, such as off–balance sheet financing and income management. If improperly accounted for or inadequately disclosed, these transactions can impair the transparency of financial reports. The SEC issued a final rule in 2003 that expands mandated disclosure of off–balance sheet financing arrangements, and it issued a special report in 2005 that puts forth proposals for the development of accounting standards and provides cautionary words about accounting-motivated structured transactions.

In January 2003, the SEC issued the final rule, *Disclosure in Management's Discussion and Analysis about Off–Balance Sheet Arrangements and Aggregate Contractual Arrangements.* In this rule, the SEC views off–balance sheet arrangements as "means through which companies typically structure off–balance sheet transactions or otherwise incur risks of loss that are not fully transparent to investors." The SEC specifically mentions financial guarantees, risky retained interests in securitizations, derivatives, and variable interests as examples of such off–balance sheet financing arrangements. This rule requires disclosures of off–balance sheet arrangements that provide a clear understanding of the material effects of those arrangements on financial condition, operating performance, liquidity, and other related topics required to be covered in the management's discussion and analysis section of financial reports. This rule requires disclosure of the nature and purpose of the arrangements and any known condition that might cause the arrangements to be terminated. The disclosures of off–balance sheet financing provided under this rule are far more voluminous and better integrated then previously had been the case, and they should be carefully evaluated by the user of financial reports. By no means do these disclosures capture all off–balance sheet financing, however. In particular, these disclosure requirements apply only when an "unconditionally binding definitive agreement exists" between the parties. Many off–balance sheet financing arrangements, such as synthetic leases discussed in Chapter 13, include cancellation provisions or renewal options in which such an agreement does not exist.

In June 2005, the SEC issued the special report, *Report and Recommendations Pursuant to Section 401(c) of the Sarbanes-Oxley Act of 2002 on Arrangements with Off–Balance Sheet Implications, Special Purpose Entities, and Transparency of Filings by Issuers.* This report includes many suggestions for future accounting standards with respect to structured finance transactions. It also contains strong criticism of accounting-motivated structured transactions, by which it means

> transactions that are structured in an attempt to achieve reporting results that are not consistent with the economics of the transaction, and thereby impair the transparency of financial reports . . . . [W]e include not only those transactions that would not have been undertaken but for the perceived "benefits" of the resultant financial reporting, but also those that adopt a more complex form than would otherwise be the case, in order to achieve an accounting result.

Relatedly, in a December 6, 2004 speech, Scott Taub, the deputy chief accountant of the SEC, states that

> where registrants seek to structure transactions for financial reporting purposes, we will expect disclosures even if the accounting goal is achieved, and we can expect to see restatement where we don't believe the literature has been fully complied with.

Finally, in May 2006, the SEC and the primary bank regulators jointly issued a proposed statement concerning the elevated risk, including reputational risk, that may result from banks' complex structured finance activities.[6] Firms and individuals engaging in structured finance transactions should consider these statements carefully.

NOTES

1. See A. Hartgraves and G. Benson, "The Evolving Accounting Standards for Special Purpose Entities and Consolidations," *Accounting Horizons* (September 2002).
2. M. Carlson and R. Perli, "Profits and Balance Sheet Developments at U.S. Commercial Banks in 2003," *Federal Reserve Bulletin* (Spring 2004).
3. J. Weil and G. McWilliams, "Dell-CIT Venture May Remain an Orphan Despite New Rules," *Wall Street Journal,* March 27, 2003.
4. W. English and B. Reid, "Profits and Balance Sheet Developments at U.S. Commercial Banks in 1994," *Federal Reserve Bulletin* (June 1995).
5. B. Lev and S. Ryan, "Accounting for Commercial Loan Commitments," Working Paper, New York University, November 2004.
6. Board of Governors of the Federal Reserve System, Federal Deposit Insurance Corporation, Office of the Comptroller of the Currency, Office of Thrift Supervision, and Securities and Exchange Commission, "Interagency Statement on Sound Practices Concerning Elevated Risk Complex Structured Finance Activities," May 9, 2006.

CHAPTER 10

Commercial Banks

The commercial banking industry in the United States comprises a diverse array of financial institutions that individually and collectively offer a wide range of financial services. A primary reason for this diversity is the fact that healthy commercial banks can create financial holding companies (FHCs) that engage in any financial activity under the Gramm, Leach, Bliley Act of 1999 (GLBA). The health requirement of this act has not been a constraint on the formation of FHCs by commercial banks, as almost the entire industry currently is profitable and well capitalized and has been so for over a decade. As of November 2006, 641 FHCs remain effective, the vast majority of which were created by institutions that are primarily commercial banks.[1] In addition, frequent mergers and acquisitions involving commercial banks and other financial institutions have blurred the boundaries between commercial banking and the other financial services industries. Mergers and acquisitions also have dramatically increased industry concentration; from 1990 to 2005, the number of commercial banking organizations in the United States decreased from more that 12,000 to less than 8,000, and the 10 largest banks' share of the industry's assets rose from about 20% to 50%.[2]

Although this short chapter provides a sense for commercial banks' diversity, all of the topics covered in this book apply in some fashion to either them or the FHCs to which they belong. Readers primarily interested in commercial banking should not begin with this chapter; at a minimum, they should first read Chapter 2, which describes the nature and regulation of depository institutions, and Chapter 3's "Main Risk-Return Trade-Offs and Financial Analysis Issues" section, which discusses the analysis issues for thrifts, all of which apply to commercial banks' traditional activities as depository institutions.

Compared to thrifts, larger and more wholesale commercial banks tend to be more like securities firms in two ways. First, they focus more on generating fee or other noninterest income and less on generating interest income. Although both thrifts and commercial banks earn noninterest income on traditional banking activities—such as deposit servicing, loan origination, trust, and asset management—larger and more wholesale commercial banks increasingly earn fee income on nontraditional activities usually conducted by securities firms previously—such as investment banking, financial advisory services, brokerage, trading (including dealing), and merchant banking. Their trading positions (and often their merchant banking investments) are accounted for at fair value on both balance sheet and income statement, yielding gains and losses that are recognized in income as they occur, as discussed in Chapter 6. Their interest income is reduced by securitizations of financial assets, as discussed in Chapter 8.

Second, the largest U.S. commercial banks are extensively involved with derivatives as dealers, traders, and hedgers. For example, the Bank of International Settlements reports that over-the-counter (OTC) derivatives with a notional amount of $285 trillion were outstanding in December 2005, while the Office of Thrift Supervision reports that $85 trillion (30%) of this amount was held by the three largest U.S. commercial banks—JPMorgan Chase ($44 trillion), Bank of America ($21 trillion), and Citigroup ($20 trillion)—with an additional $9 trillion (3%) being held by the next 22 largest U.S. commercial banks.[3] It is critical for financial analysts to understand commercial banks' derivatives use, in part because derivatives trading is a significant source of noninterest income for the largest banks and in part because the use of derivatives could increase or decrease their exposure to market and other risks, depending on whether they use derivatives for speculation or hedging. Chapters 11 and 12 describe financial report information about derivatives provided under the accounting standards for derivatives and hedging and the required market risk disclosures of the Securities and Exchange Commission (SEC), respectively.

Because of commercial banks' focus on generating noninterest income, compared to the balance sheet focus of the analysis of thrifts, the analysis of commercial banks places more weight on income or cash flow statement–based valuation approaches. These approaches require users of financial reports to assess the risk and persistence of commercial banks' various noninterest income streams. Users depend on the quality of the management's discussion and analysis and other disclosures in performing this task, since sources of noninterest income with differential risk and persistence often are reported together in the financial statements.

The remainder of this chapter provides descriptive analysis of financial statement data for the commercial banking industry as a whole and for a representative bank holding company, SunTrust Banks, Inc. (SunTrust), in 2005. SunTrust is a large commercial bank—the ninth largest in the United States in terms of assets—that primarily operates in the Southeast. SunTrust is representative of the industry in many respects, combining traditional consumer and corporate banking activities with a diverse set of other activities, including investment banking, brokerage, and investment management. With $117 billion notional amount outstanding at the end of 2005, SunTrust is a moderately active dealer ($76 billion) and user ($41 billion) of derivatives. The next three sections describe commercial banks' balance sheets, income statements, and cash flow statements, respectively.

BALANCE SHEET

As with thrifts, the balance sheets of commercial banks are unclassified, with no distinction made between current versus noncurrent accounts. This reflects the liquid nature of most financial assets and liabilities. Assets and liabilities generally are listed in order of liquidity, which reflects a combination of intent to hold and term to maturity.

Exhibit 10.1 reports an average percentage balance sheet (all numbers are divided by average industry assets) for U.S. commercial banks in 2005. To provide a sense for differences between larger, more wholesale and smaller, more retail commercial banks, the exhibit also reports this data for the 10

EXHIBIT 10.1 Commercial Bank Industry Balance Sheet as a Percentage of Average Industry Assets in 2005

	All Banks	10 Largest Banks	101–1,000 Largest Banks
Assets:	100%	100%	100%
Bank deposits, federal funds sold, and reverse RPs	6.9	7.2	4.6
Trading account	4.2	7.8	.1
Investment Securities:	17.9	15.6	21.5
U.S. Treasuries, agency backed-MBS, and debt	12.1	10.2	15.9
Other	5.8	5.4	5.6
Loans and leases outstanding, net:	57.9	51.4	65.2
Commercial and industrial	11.2	10.6	11.8
Consumer	9.1	8.8	5.4
One- to four-family real estate	18.3	17.7	15.2
Other real estate	14.1	6.8	30.7
Other	6.0	8.1	3.1
– Allowance for loan losses	(.8)	(.7)	(.9)
Noninterest-earning assets	13.2	16.0	8.7
Liabilities:	89.9	90.8	89.1
Deposits:	67.0	64.0	73.3
Core (transaction deposits, savings, small time)	47.5	40.2	59.1
Other (large time and foreign)	19.5	23.8	14.2
Federal funds purchased and RPs	7.1	8.4	5.5
Other managed liabilities	9.7	8.7	8.6
Other liabilities	6.1	9.8	1.7
Owners' Equity	10.1%	9.2%	10.9%

Source: "Profits and Balance Sheet Developments at U.S. Commercial Banks during 2005," *Federal Reserve Bulletin* (June 2006).

Note: RP denotes securities repurchase agreements.

largest (assets greater than $88 billion) and the 101 to 1,000 largest (assets between $457 million and $7 billion) banks. These data are taken from regulatory call reports, which reflect only the chartered bank and its subsidiaries, not the nonbank subsidiaries of the holding company. Some commercial banks' securities activities appear to remain in subsidiaries of the financial or bank holding company, despite the fact that the GLBA now allows these activities to be performed in subsidiaries of the chartered bank. Moreover, two of commercial banks' other nonbanking activities, insurance underwriting and merchant banking, must be conducted in subsidiaries of FHCs.

Compared to thrifts, which hold 64% of their assets in one- to four-family residential mortgages and mortgage-backed securities (MBS), commercial banks hold a wide range of assets. Two broad classes, loans (including leases) and securities, together constitute about 80% of their assets. The 57.9% of assets attributable to loans is spread across commercial and industrial loans (11.2%), consumer loans (9.1%), one- to four-family real estate mortgages (18.3%), other real estate loans (14.1%), and other loans and leases (6.0%). Over the past five years, the percentage of real estate loans has risen by over 5%, reflecting the robustness of real estate markets. Commercial loans have fallen by a similar percentage over this period, first due to commercial banks' reluctance to make these loans as a consequence of the corporate bankruptcies and recession of 2001–2002 and subsequently reflecting firms' ability to finance their investments either through accumulated profits or securities issuance. The 22.1% of commercial banks' assets attributable to securities is spread across trading securities (4.2%), essentially credit-riskless U.S. Treasury, agency-backed MBS, and agency debt securities (12.1%), and credit-riskier other securities (5.8%).

Commercial banks' asset mix varies somewhat across size classes, although by less than it did five years ago, because the 10 largest banks have become more retail/consumer-oriented, reducing their holdings of commercial loans and increasing their holdings of consumer loans and one- to four-family residential mortgages over this period. Within loans, the most significant remaining difference is the 10 largest banks hold far less other real estate loans (6.8% of assets) than the 101 to 1,000 largest banks (30.7% of assets), reflecting the fact that multifamily and commercial real estate loans tend to be fairly heterogeneous and too small individually to attract the largest banks' attention. Within securities, the 10 largest banks hold more trading securities and less investment securities, reflecting their blurring with securities firms. The 10 largest banks hold a credit-riskier mix of investment securities, with proportionately less U.S. Treasury and agency securities and more other securities. The 10 largest banks hold more noninterest-earning assets and less loans as a percentage of total assets compared to the 101 to 1,000 largest banks, reflecting the 10 largest banks' focus on noninterest income and larger goodwill.

The differences in goodwill are likely to become larger over time. Since SFAS No. 141, *Business Combinations* (2001), became effective, commercial banks' mergers and acquisitions can no longer be accounted for as poolings of interests that do not yield reported goodwill, as usually was the case previously. SFAS No. 141 (2001) requires a version of purchase accounting that typically yields large amounts of reported goodwill for the acquirer in the most significant bank mergers and acquisitions, which not surprisingly usually is one of the largest banks. For example, J. P. Morgan Chase's acquisition of Bank One in 2004 gave rise to $34 billion of reported goodwill for the resulting subtly renamed JPMorgan Chase, a large amount even for bank of its huge size.

On the liability side, much like thrifts, commercial banks primarily raise funds through deposits (67.0% of assets), although a larger fraction of these clearly are noncore (e.g., large time and foreign) deposits (19.5%). The remaining liabilities are wholesale, raised mainly in the federal funds, securities repurchase, and corporate debt markets. In contrast, thrifts' wholesale funds are raised almost entirely from the Federal Home Loan Banks.

Commercial banks' liability mix varies substantially with bank size. The 10 largest banks hold less total and core deposits but more noncore deposits than the 101 to 1,000 largest banks. The 10 largest banks also raise more funds in nondeposit wholesale markets.

Like thrifts, commercial banks are highly leveraged, with owners' equity equaling 10.1% of assets. The 10 largest banks hold less owners' equity as a percentage of assets (9.2%) than the 101 to 1,000 largest banks (10.9%). This reflects larger banks' greater ability to diversify risks across their portfolios and possibly higher risk tolerance.

The balance sheet composition of commercial banks has remained fairly stable over time. There has been a gradual movement toward holding securities rather than loans on the asset side and toward raising funds from wholesale sources rather than core deposits on the liability side. Both of these trends are rather subtle and are dominated by fluctuations around the trend in specific years, however. For example, due to low interest rates and investor concerns about the securities markets, it was relatively easy for banks with retail networks to raise core deposits from 2001 to 2004.

As noted, SunTrust conducts a diverse set of traditional and nontraditional activities that are represented on its 2005 balance sheet reported in Exhibit 10.2. Reflecting its traditional activities, SunTrust has a relatively large loan portfolio at 63% of assets. Although loan types are not broken out on the balance sheet, SunTrust reports in its loan footnote that 59% of its loans are real estate, 29% are commercial, and 12% are consumer. SunTrust raises significant amounts of funds from both core and noncore deposits and from a varied set of wholesale markets. Deposits are high for such a large bank at 68% of assets. Although core deposits are not cleanly broken out on the balance sheet, SunTrust's regulatory disclosures indicate that 72% of its deposits are core.

Reflecting its less traditional activities, SunTrust has moderate-size trading positions on both sides of the balance sheet. About $1 billion of each of its trading assets and trading liabilities are matched derivatives SunTrust engages in as a derivatives dealer.

EXHIBIT 10.2 SunTrust Banks, Inc., Consolidated Balance Sheets

	As of December 31	
(Dollars in thousands)	**2005**	**2004**
Assets		
Cash and due from banks	$ 4,659,664	$ 3,876,741
Interest-bearing deposits in other banks	332,444	15,929
Funds sold and securities purchased under agreements to resell	1,313,498	1,596,269
Trading assets	2,811,225	2,183,645
Securities available for sale	26,525,821	28,941,080
Loans held for sale	13,695,613	6,580,223
Loans	114,554,895	101,426,172
Allowance for loan and lease losses	(1,028,128)	(1,050,024)
Net loans	113,526,767	100,376,148
Premises and equipment	1,854,527	1,860,415
Goodwill	6,835,168	6,806,013
Other intangible assets	1,122,967	1,061,451
Customers' acceptance liability	11,839	12,105
Other assets	7,023,308	5,559,765
Total assets	$179,712,841	$158,869,784
Liabilities and Shareholders' Equity		
Noninterest-bearing consumer and commercial deposits	$ 26,327,663	$ 24,878,314
Interest-bearing consumer and commercial deposits	71,244,719	67,231,381
Total consumer and commercial deposits	97,572,382	92,109,695
Brokered deposits	15,644,932	6,100,911
Foreign deposits	8,835,864	5,150,645
Total deposits	122,053,178	103,361,251
Funds purchased and securities sold under agreements to repurchase	10,374,533	9,342,831
Other short-term borrowings	1,937,624	2,062,549
Long-term debt	20,779,249	22,127,166
Acceptances outstanding	11,839	12,105
Trading liabilities	1,529,325	1,098,563
Other liabilities	6,139,698	4,878,420
Total liabilities	162,825,446	142,882,885
Common stock, $1.00 par value	370,578	370,578

EXHIBIT 10.2 *(Continued)*

	As of December 31	
(Dollars in thousands)	**2005**	**2004**
Additional paid in capital	6,761,684	6,749,219
Retained earnings	9,310,978	8,118,710
Treasury stock, at cost, and other	(493,936)	(528,558)
Accumulated other comprehensive income	938,091	1,276,950
Total shareholders' equity	16,887,395	15,986,899
Total liabilities and shareholders' equity	$179,712,841	$158,869,784

INCOME STATEMENT

As with thrifts, the order of commercial banks' income statements reflects the historical (although not necessarily current) primacy of net interest income. Interest revenue is at the top, from which interest expense is subtracted to yield net interest income before the provision for loan losses. The provision for loan losses is subtracted to yield net interest income after the provision for loan losses. The provision for loan losses naturally offsets net interest income before the provision for loan losses, since loans subject to more credit risk should carry higher interest rates, all else being equal. At the bottom of the income statement, noninterest income is added and noninterest expenses and tax expense are subtracted.

Exhibit 10.3 reports average percentage income statements (all numbers are divided by average industry assets) in 2005 for all U.S. commercial banks and for the same size classes as before. Despite a trend toward noninterest income, commercial banks' net income remains driven primarily by net interest income. Reflecting the still-low interest rates during 2005, interest revenue is 4.98%, interest expense is 1.89%, and the provision for loan losses is .30% of assets. These amounts yield net interest income after the loan loss provision of 2.79% of assets, which exceeds noninterest income of 2.33% of assets. Noninterest expenses are 3.19% of assets. These amounts yield a return on assets of 1.31%. Although this level of return on assets may seem low, in conjunction with their high leverage, commercial banks earned a fairly normal return on equity of 13.0% in 2005.

Commercial banks' income statement composition varies somewhat across size classes. The 10 largest banks have lower interest revenue than the 101 to 1,000 largest banks, for three reasons.

1. As noted, a lower percentage of their assets earn interest.
2. Their loans yield only 6.16% compared to 6.90% for the 101 to 1,000 largest banks.

EXHIBIT 10.3 Commercial Bank Industry Income Statement as a Percentage of Average Industry Assets in 2005

	All Banks	10 Largest Banks	101–1,000 Largest Banks
Interest revenue	4.98%	4.47%	5.57%
− Interest expense	(1.89)	(1.89)	(1.84)
= Net interest income	3.09	2.58	3.73
− Loan loss provision	(.30)	(.20)	(.24)
= Net interest income after loan loss provision	2.79	2.38	3.49
− Noninterest income:	2.33	2.37	2.02
Service charges on deposits	.39	.42	.36
Income from fiduciary activities	.31	.27	.35
Trading income	.17	.31	.01
Other noninterest income	1.47	1.38	1.30
− Noninterest expense	(3.19)	(2.99)	(3.37)
= Net noninterest expense	(.86)	(.62)	(1.35)
= Income before taxes	1.93	1.75	2.13
− Tax expense	(.62)	(.57)	(.68)
= Net income	1.31%	1.18%	1.45%

Source: "Profits and Balance Sheet Developments at U.S. Commercial Banks during 2005," *Federal Reserve Bulletin* (June 2006). These data are taken from regulatory call reports and represent commercial banks, not bank holding companies.

Note: Totals may not sum exactly because small amounts for realized gains and losses and extraordinary items are omitted.

3. They hold more low-yielding bank deposits, federal funds sold, and reverse repurchase agreements.

Interest expense is similar across size categories, with the 10 largest banks having a slightly lower cost of funds than the 101 to 1,000 largest banks. This fact mainly reflects the still-low-interest-rate environment in 2005, which yields a relatively small spread between the rates paid on core deposits and wholesale funds. In a higher-interest-rate environment, larger, more wholesale commercial banks typically have a higher cost of funds than smaller, more retail banks.

Total noninterest income rises somewhat with bank size, at 2.37% of assets for the 10 largest banks and 2.02% for the 101 to 1,000 largest banks. Given the prior discussion, one might expect the 10 largest banks to have relatively more noninterest income. The reason for this is that some of the 10 largest banks' noninterest income from nontraditional activities is not reflected in the regulatory call report data, because this income is located in subsidiaries of the holding company rather than in the chartered bank or its subsidiaries. Commercial banks' noninterest income composition varies with bank size, with the 10 largest banks having higher trading income than the 101 to 1,000 largest banks.

Noninterest expense falls somewhat with bank size, at 2.99% of assets for the 10 largest banks and 3.37% of assets for the 101 to 1,000 largest banks. This reflects the fact that the smaller, more retail banks have greater costs associated with operating retail banking networks. However, the 10 largest banks tend to have more highly trained and thus higher-salaried employees.

Over time, aside from largely offsetting changes in interest revenue and expense that track changes in interest rates, the main change in commercial banks' income statement composition has been an increase in noninterest income from 1.67% of assets in 1990 to 2.33% in 2005. Again, the call report data understate this trend, because of the business conducted in subsidiaries of holding companies.

SunTrust's 2005 income statement is reported in Exhibit 10.4. Its amount of net income is slightly below average, with a return on assets of 1.17% and

EXHIBIT 10.4 SunTrust Banks, Inc., Consolidated Statements of Income

(Dollars in thousands except per share data)	Year Ended December 31		
	2005	**2004**	**2003**
Interest Income			
Interest and fees on loans	$5,961,122	$3,947,231	$3,593,630
Interest and fees on loans held for sale	485,724	281,292	448,322
Interest and dividends on securities available for sale			
Taxable interest	1,032,785	844,526	609,500
Tax-exempt interest	35,733	26,340	17,971
Dividends	104,215	72,580	66,671
Interest on funds sold and securities purchased under agreements to resell	43,206	18,577	15,673
Interest on deposits in other banks	867	178	146
Other interest	67,657	27,658	16,929
Total interest income	7,731,309	5,218,382	4,768,842
Interest Expense			
Interest on deposits	1,832,975	766,188	771,631
Interest on funds purchased and securities sold under agreements to repurchase	312,193	108,591	106,174

(continues)

EXHIBIT 10.4 *(Continued)*

(Dollars in thousands except per share data)	Year Ended December 31 2005	2004	2003
Interest Expense			
Interest on other short-term borrowings	94,965	30,195	33,511
Interest on long-term debt	912,210	628,253	537,223
Total interest expense	3,152,343	1,533,227	1,448,539
Net Interest Income	4,578,966	3,685,155	3,320,303
Provision for loan losses	176,886	135,537	313,550
Net interest income after provision for loan losses	4,402,080	3,549,618	3,006,753
Noninterest Income			
Service charges on deposit accounts	772,519	700,022	643,103
Trust and investment management income	673,720	586,783	502,409
Retail investment services	213,274	192,811	161,753
Other charges and fees	456,481	390,494	326,311
Investment banking income	216,530	206,730	192,480
Trading account profits and commissions	145,120	127,799	109,878
Card fees	210,779	153,439	119,585
Net gain on sale of RCM assets	23,382	—	—
Other noninterest income	450,394	288,059	123,606
Securities (losses)/gains	(7,155)	(41,691)	123,876
Total noninterest income	3,155,044	2,604,446	2,303,001
Noninterest Expense			
Employee compensation	2,117,156	1,804,911	1,585,919
Employee benefits	417,055	363,402	358,644
Net occupancy expense	312,070	268,248	237,266
Outside processing and software	357,387	286,270	246,654
Equipment expense	204,038	184,865	178,443
Marketing and customer development	156,711	128,291	100,280
Amortization of intangible assets	118,964	77,582	64,515
Merger expense	98,642	28,401	—
Other noninterest expense	908,706	755,068	628,895
Total noninterest expense	4,690,729	3,897,038	3,400,616
Income before provision for income taxes	2,866,395	2,257,026	1,909,138
Provision for income taxes	879,156	684,125	576,841
Net Income	$1,987,239	$1,572,901	$1,332,297

a return on equity of 12.1%. SunTrust partly makes up for below-average net interest income and noninterest income by having below-average noninterest expense. SunTrust provides quite good disaggregation of its noninterest income in its income statement. Most of its noninterest income is from fairly traditional activities, although it reports $217 million investment banking income and $145 million trading account income.

CASH FLOW STATEMENT

As with thrifts, the distinction among operating, investing, and financing cash flows is arbitrary on commercial banks' cash flow statements, since most of their cash flows relate to financial instruments. SunTrust's cash flow statement in 2005 is reported in Exhibit 10.5. The arbitrary nature of this distinction is reflected, for example, in its classification of cash flows on loans held for sale as operating but the cash flows on loans held in portfolio as investing, even though these cash flows arise from transactions in the same sort of financial assets. SunTrust's $7.1 billion net increase in loans held for sale during 2005 reduced its cash flow from operations by that amount. The same cash flow statement classification issue arises for commercial banks' trading portfolios.

In analyzing a commercial bank, it is usually wise to ignore its cash flow statement classifications and focus instead on what the cash flow statement indicates about the bank's new investments and sources of funding during the year. The cash flow statement is usually quite illuminating in this regard. For example, as indicated in the financing section of its cash flow statement, SunTrust's main source of new financing during 2005 was a net increase in deposits of $18.7 billion. Given that 72% of SunTrust's deposits are core, one might expect this financing to be raised from core deposits, but in fact $13.2 billion of this amount was raised from noncore foreign and brokered deposits, so that SunTrust raised funds primarily from wholesale sources during 2005. In its investing section, SunTrust's main investment during 2005 is a $13.7 billion net increase in loans.

NOTES

1. www.federalreserve.gov/generalinfo/fhc/.
2. E. Klee and G. Weinbach, "Profits and Balance Sheet Developments at U.S. Commercial Banks in 2005, *Federal Reserve Bulletin* (June 2006).
3. Bank of International Settlements, "Semiannual OTC Derivatives Statistics," June 2006, www.bis.org/statistics/otcder/dt1920a.pdf; Comptroller of the Currency, "OCC's Quarterly Report on Bank Derivatives Activities: Fourth Quarter 2005," Washington, D.C.

EXHIBIT 10.5 SunTrust Banks, Inc., Consolidated Statements of Cash Flow

	Year Ended December 31		
(Dollars in thousands)	**2005**	**2004**	**2003**
Cash Flows from Operating Activities:			
Net income	$ 1,987,239	$ 1,572,901	$ 1,332,297
Adjustments to reconcile net income to net cash (used in) provided by operating activities:			
Net gain on sale of RCM assets	(23,382)	—	—
Depreciation, amortization, and accretion	783,084	667,145	881,542
Origination of mortgage servicing rights	(341,694)	(196,118)	(384,198)
Provisions for loan losses and foreclosed property	179,294	137,032	314,667
Deferred income tax provision	178,318	144,988	179,905
Amortization of compensation element of performance and restricted stock	9,190	8,515	5,475
Stock option compensation	26,375	17,443	8,722
Securities losses/(gains)	7,155	41,691	(123,876)
Net gain on sale of assets	(4,411)	(11,175)	(12,596)
Originated loans held for sale	(48,516,792)	(30,194,087)	(43,816,219)
Sales of loans held for sale	41,401,402	29,516,696	46,011,952
Net increase in other assets	(1,874,683)	(616,943)	(451,686)
Net increase in other liabilities	1,470,187	91,496	168,490
Net cash (used in) provided by operating activities	(4,718,718)	1,179,584	4,114,475
Cash Flows from Investing Activities:			
Proceeds from maturities, calls, and repayments of securities available for sale	4,783,789	5,083,485	10,841,607
Proceeds from sales of securities available for sale	4,367,480	8,875,126	7,633,468

(continues)

EXHIBIT 10.5 *(Continued)*

	Year Ended December 31		
(Dollars in thousands)	**2005**	**2004**	**2003**
Purchases of securities available for sale	(7,221,819)	(12,264,430)	(19,933,984)
Loan originations net of principal collected	(14,070,420)	(9,555,401)	(5,533,737)
Proceeds from sale of loans	337,902	357,785	392,412
Capital expenditures	(201,650)	(238,009)	(157,608)
Proceeds from the sale of other assets	42,841	37,427	39,324
Other investing activities	5,311	2,584	13,932
Net cash used for acquisitions	—	(1,265,650)	(34,261)
Net cash used in investing activities	(11,956,566)	(8,967,083)	(6,738,847)
Cash Flows from Financing Activities:			
Net increase in consumer and commercial deposits	5,470,301	5,254,911	2,404,052
Net increase (decrease) in foreign and brokered deposits	13,229,240	1,135,626	(1,328,925)
Net increase (decrease) in funds purchased and other short-term borrowings	906,777	(1,439,497)	(1,120,063)
Proceeds from the issuance of long-term debt	1,974,987	4,728,616	3,281,676
Repayment of long-term debt	(3,233,688)	(1,203,676)	(189,686)
Proceeds from the exercise of stock options	135,701	96,457	27,945
Acquisition of treasury stock	(196,396)	(14,064)	(182,152)
Dividends paid	(794,971)	(603,309)	(505,396)
Net cash provided by financing activities	17,491,951	7,955,064	2,387,451
Net increase (decrease) in cash and cash equivalents	816,667	167,565	(236,921)
Cash and cash equivalents at beginning of period	5,488,939	5,321,374	5,558,295
Cash and cash equivalents at end of period	$ 6,305,606	$ 5,488,939	$ 5,321,374

CHAPTER 11

Derivatives and Hedging

This chapter describes SFAS No. 133, *Accounting for Derivative Instruments and Hedging Activities* (1998), as amended in significant ways by SFAS No. 138, *Accounting for Certain Derivatives and Certain Hedging Activities* (2000), SFAS No. 149, *Amendment of Statement 133 on Derivative Instruments and Hedging Activities* (2003), and SFAS No. 155, *Accounting for Certain Hybrid Financial Instruments* (2006), and in lesser ways by various other standards. SFAS No. 133 (1998) also has been interpreted and in some respects altered by 145 Derivatives Implementation Group (DIG) issues that remain effective as of November 2006 and do not pertain to the initial adoption of the standard. In this chapter, "SFAS No. 133 (1998)" refers to the standard as originally written, while "SFAS No. 133 (1998), as amended" refers to the entire literature, which comprises an exceedingly complex and detailed set of accounting and disclosure requirements. This chapter focuses on the essential elements and the strengths and weaknesses of these requirements from the perspective of users of financial reports.

Although derivatives have been used for centuries, derivatives markets first developed in earnest in the 1970s, and the widespread use of derivatives took off in the early 1990s. The global derivatives markets are now huge, and they continue to grow rapidly. Based on its semiannual surveys of major market participants, which do not capture all derivatives, the Bank for International Settlements (BIS) reports that the notional amount of over-the-counter derivatives at the end of 2005 was $285 trillion, with $215 trillion of interest rate derivatives ($173 trillion of interest rate swaps, by far the most common type of derivative), $32 trillion of foreign exchange derivatives, $10 trillion of credit derivatives, $5 trillion of equity-linked derivatives, $4 trillion of commodity derivatives, and $19 trillion of other derivatives. BIS also reports that the notional amount of exchange-traded derivatives at the end of 2005 was $58 trillion, with $52 trillion of interest rate derivatives, $5 trillion of equity-linked derivatives, and $174 billion of foreign exchange derivatives.[1] Although the notional amounts of derivatives usually far exceed their fair values, these amounts generally do indicate the risk transferred by derivatives.

SFAS No. 133 (1998) was motivated by desire of the Financial Accounting Standards Board (FASB) to make firms' use of derivatives more transparent in their financial reports. Once derivatives became widely used in the early 1990s, policymakers became concerned that the value and risks of derivatives were not well understood by less sophisticated firms or transparent to users of financial reports. This concern was particularly strong during 1993–1994, a period in which interest rates first fell then rose sharply, foreign exchange rates and commodity prices fluctuated considerably, and a number of well-publicized and very large losses on derivatives and hybrid financial instruments occurred, such as Orange County, California; Gibson Greetings; Procter & Gamble; and Metallgesellschaft. For example, the Orange County bankruptcy was caused mainly by its leveraged investment in "inverse floaters," hybrid debt instruments with embedded interest rate swaps that pay interest at a rate that floats inversely with interest rates. This investment suffered huge losses when interest rates rose sharply in 1994. The Asian financial crisis in the second half of 1997, which segued into the Russian debt/hedge fund crisis in the second half of 1998, raised concerns about derivative counterparty risks and the systemic risks posed by hedge funds' opaque and highly leveraged positions in derivatives that are still being debated by policymakers today.[2]

Although flawed in a number of respects, SFAS No. 133 (1998) succeeds in making firms' derivatives usage more transparent than under prior accounting rules and practices, through both its accounting and its disclosure requirements. Most notably, the standard requires that all derivatives be fair valued on the balance sheet as gross assets and liabilities. In contrast, under prior accounting rules and practices, derivatives used for hedging usually were either netted against the hedged items or not recognized on the balance sheet. The standard also requires that unrealized gains and losses on derivatives that do not qualify for cash flow hedge accounting or that result from most types of hedge ineffectiveness be recorded in net income as they occur. These accounting requirements are not universally beloved by firms that use hedge accounting, however, because they cause the firms to have larger balance sheets (which reduces return ratios and may raise capital requirements) and more volatile net income than they would have had for the same positions under prior hedge accounting rules and practices.

Hedge accounting means that gains and losses on exposures and effective hedges of those exposures are recognized in net income in the same periods, which can be accomplished by conforming either the accounting for the hedged item to that for the hedge or the accounting for the hedge to that for the hedged item. Without hedge accounting, hedged items and derivatives-based hedges typically would be accounted for using different valuation bases —amortized cost for most hedged items and fair value for derivatives—with the economically nondescriptive consequence that effective hedging would increase volatility in net income compared to no hedging.

SFAS No. 133 (1998) restricts hedge accounting to effective derivatives-based hedges of specific exposures or portfolios of highly correlated exposures, despite the fact that hedging often can be accomplished more efficiently and effectively using nonderivatives-based hedges or at the level of aggregate net exposures. These restrictions are intended to ensure that hedge accounting is used only for hedging relationships that are clearly documented and determined to be effective on an ongoing basis.

SFAS No. 133's (1998) weakest feature is it allows for two distinct and basically inconsistent approaches to hedge accounting: fair value and cash flow hedge accounting. Fair value hedge accounting applies to hedges of exposures that exhibit fair value variability. It conforms the accounting for the hedged item to the fair value accounting for the derivative hedge on both the balance sheet and the income statement. In this regard, fair value hedge accounting is essentially an expansion of fair value accounting to the hedged item. In contrast, cash flow hedge accounting applies to hedges of exposures that exhibit cash flow variability. It conforms the accounting for the derivative hedge to the accounting for the hedged item on the income statement, but not on the balance sheet, since the standard requires that all derivatives be recorded at fair value on the balance sheet. To accommodate the inconsistent treatment of cash flow hedge derivatives on the balance sheet and income statement, unrealized gains and losses on these derivatives are initially recorded in accumulated other comprehensive income on the balance sheet, where they remain until they are recycled into net income to smooth the income statement effects on the hedged item.

Fair value and cash flow hedge accounting have very different effects on the financial statements. An important difference between the two approaches is that cash flow hedge accounting ignores hedge ineffectiveness due to underhedging while fair value hedge accounting captures all hedge ineffectiveness. Largely for this reason, firms often prefer cash flow hedge accounting and devise hedging strategies to obtain it. Although it may appear that firms cannot choose whether to use fair value or cash flow hedge accounting for a given hedge, since the hedged items in fair value hedges must exhibit fair value variability while the hedged items in cash flow hedges must exhibit cash flow variability, this is often not the case for financial institutions. These institutions hold portfolios of financial instruments, some of which exhibit fair value variability and others cash flow variability, and so they often are able to choose the hedged item and thus the hedge accounting method for a given hedge.

As discussed in Chapters 1 and 6, fair value is the proper valuation basis for liquid financial instruments held by financial institutions, and so fair value hedge accounting is preferable to cash flow hedge accounting for these institutions' hedges of financial instruments. In this regard, the FASB is working toward requiring fair value accounting for all financial instruments. If and when this occurs, hedge accounting for hedges of financial instruments, which constitute most of financial institutions' hedging, will no longer be allowed under SFAS No. 133 (1998). It will also no longer be needed, because consistent fair value accounting for both the derivative hedge and the hedged item will occur without hedge accounting.

SFAS No. 133's (1998) strongest feature is that it makes hedge ineffectiveness more apparent than under prior accounting rules and practices, which generally ignored the ineffective portion of hedges altogether. As noted, gains and losses resulting from most types of hedge ineffectiveness are recorded in net income as they occur; moreover, required disclosures indicate the amount of gains and losses by type of hedge ineffectiveness and in what income statement line item those gains or losses appear. Two significant types of hedge ineffectiveness are ignored under SFAS No. 133 (1998), as amended, however. First, as noted, SFAS No. 133 (1998) ignores ineffectiveness associated with cash flow underhedges. Second, SFAS No. 138 (2000) allows firms to hedge close to riskless benchmark (U.S. Treasury or London Interbank Offered Rates [LIBOR]) interest rates within credit or prepayment risky exposures, in most respects ignoring the potentially substantial "basis risk" involved with these hedges.

For practical reasons, the portions of SFAS No. 133 (1998), as amended, that pertain solely to foreign exchange derivatives and hedges of foreign exposures are not discussed in this chapter. To do this properly requires explaining SFAS No. 52, *Foreign Currency Translation* (1981), which would require a chapter of its own. With a few significant exceptions that are mentioned in this chapter, the accounting requirements for foreign exchange derivatives and for hedging of foreign exposures are consistent with those discussed in this chapter.

The first two sections of this chapter provide intuitive overviews of derivatives and hedging, respectively. Readers well acquainted with these topics can skip these sections. The accounting and disclosure requirements for derivatives and hedging in SFAS No. 133 (1998), as amended, are described in the third section. The last section discusses the strengths and weaknesses of this standard and the issues it poses for financial analysis. A framework for analyzing financial institutions' derivatives and hedging is developed that emphasizes the need for users of financial reports to interpret financial institutions' disclosures of derivatives and hedging jointly with their market risk disclosures. Market risk disclosures are described in Chapter 12, and the financial analyses recommended by the framework that involve those disclosures are demonstrated in that chapter as well, so these two chapters should be viewed as a matched set. In both chapters, excerpts from SunTrust Banks' 2005 Form 10-K filing are used to illustrate the accounting and disclosure requirements and the financial analysis techniques.

DERIVATIVES

Definition

There is no unambiguous definition of derivatives from an economic perspective. Any security derived from one or more primitive securities could be referred to as a derivative; the practical application of this view of a derivative would require identification of the set of primitive securities, however, since otherwise derivatives could be the primitive securities. Rather than attempting to make such an arbitrary and static identification, SFAS No. 133 (1998) defines derivatives for accounting purposes as instruments that possess three characteristics common in contracts primarily used to manage risks.

Modifying SFAS No. 133's (1998) language somewhat to correspond to that used by market participants, the standard's first condition for a contract to be a derivative is that its settlement amounts are jointly derived from the notional amounts and prices of one or more underlying variables (hereafter called "underlyings"). Underlyings are usually economic goods, such as financial assets or commodities, although they could be almost anything. For example, derivatives exist that are based on weather-related underlyings, such as hurricanes and temperature. Notional amounts are principal or other monetary amounts for most derivatives and physical quantities for commodity derivatives. Prices could be interest rates, exchange rates, market prices for securities or commodities, indicators of default, credit indices, or virtually any other variable.

SFAS No. 133 (1998) uses the term "underlying" to mean "price"; this usage is both nonstandard and nondescriptive, so it is not adopted in this chapter. It probably reflects the fact that price is not always a descriptive term either, since the prices that determine the settlement payments on derivatives sometimes are not prices in the conventional sense.

Derivatives generally can be viewed as combining offsetting long and short positions in more primitive financial instruments. For example, a receive-fixed/pay-floating interest rate swap is a long position in a fixed-rate financial asset and a short position in a floating-rate financial asset. This feature implies that the fair values of derivatives at inception are typically zero or small relative to the notional amounts of their underlyings. Derivatives' small initial fair values reduce the liquidity requirements and counterparty risks that firms face by engaging in risk management activities. Subsequent gains and losses on derivatives can be very large relative to their initial fair values, however, since the risk transferred by derivatives depends on their notional amounts, not their fair values.

Consistent with this offsetting-positions feature, SFAS No. 133's (1998) second condition for a contract to be a derivative is that it must require a smaller initial net investment that other types of contracts that would be expected to have a similar response to changes in market factors. This condition is weaker than a relatively small initial net investment condition the FASB considered imposing during its deliberations of SFAS No. 149 (2003); for example, a contract that has an initial value that is 90% of other contracts that would be expected to have a similar response to changes in market prices would meet this condition, even though its initial value would be relatively large.

Most derivatives settle net, meaning that only the net value of the offsetting positions changes hands at settlement, thereby reducing firms' exposures to the credit risk of their derivatives counterparties. Most simple derivatives settle in cash, even commodity derivatives for which the notional amounts are physical quantities. Most compound derivatives, such as swaptions (an option on a swap), settle in another derivative or a nonderivative financial instrument.

Consistent with this net-settlement feature, SFAS No. 133's (1998) third and final condition for a contract to be a derivative is that its terms must require or permit net settlement, or the contract must be readily settled net by a means outside the contract. For example, a commodity forward that requires the commodity to be delivered to the purchaser would still meet this condition if the purchaser could easily sell the commodity for cash in a liquid market. The FASB decided in SFAS No. 149 (2003) that commitments to originate mortgages that will be held for sale should be accounted for by the potential lender as derivatives if they meet SFAS No. 133's (1998) three conditions to be derivatives, but other loan commitments should not be accounted for as derivatives even if they meet those conditions. The primary reason why the FASB distinguishes mortgage commitments from other loan commitments in this fashion is the liquidity of the mortgaged-back securities (MBS) market and the lender's contractual right to resell mortgages makes net settlement of mortgages by a means outside the contract more feasible.

SFAS No. 133 (1998), as amended, exempts various sizable classes of contracts that may exhibit all three characteristics from being accounted for as derivatives. These exceptions include contracts indexed to the firm's own equity that it classifies in owners' equity, employee stock options, contingent consideration in business combinations, normal forward purchases and sales, most insurance contracts, financial guarantees in which the guaranteed party is exposed to default by the party referenced in the guarantee, and plain vanilla interest-only and principal-only strips.

Some instruments that market participants generally do not refer to as derivatives, such as financial guarantees in which the guaranteed party is not exposed to default by the party referenced in the guarantee, exhibit all of SFAS No. 133's (1998) three characteristics and are not exempted, and so are derivatives for accounting purposes. Conversely, some instruments that market participants refer to as derivatives and that are commonly used for risk management purposes, such as physically settled commodity forwards that cannot readily be settled net, do not exhibit all three characteristics and so are not derivatives for accounting purposes.

SFAS No. 133 (1998) requires that a derivative embedded in a hybrid financial instrument be separated from the host instrument if the hybrid financial instrument is not accounted for at fair value on the balance sheet and income statement under otherwise applicable generally accepted accounting principles (GAAP)—including SFAS No. 155's (2006) fair value option discussed in Chapter 9—and the embedded derivative is not "clearly and closely related" to the host instrument. Whether an embedded derivative is "clearly and closely related" to the host instrument is a matter of judgment that should take in account whether the economic characteristics of the host instrument and embedded derivative are similar in nature and whether the presence of the embedded derivative changes the return on the hybrid financial instrument sufficiently. For example, a convertible bond includes an embedded equity call option that is not clearly and closely related to the host bond both in terms of their economic characteristics and by the ability of the call option to change the return on the convertible bond. Holders of convertible bonds should separate the equity call option from the host bond. Issuers of the same bonds should not separate the option and the bond, however, because the option is indexed to the issuer's stock and would on a stand-alone basis be recognized in the issuer's owners' equity, and so is exempted from being a derivative.

There are many specific types of derivatives, although they fall into three main types that are discussed next:

1. Futures and forwards
2. Options
3. Swaps

Futures and Forwards

A futures or forward contract obligates one party to buy and another party to sell something at a future date for a specified price. Futures are standardized exchange-traded instruments that settle in cash daily and that involve guarantees of the performance of both parties by the clearinghouse of the exchange. Since futures settle in cash daily, their fair value at any point in time tends to be small. Futures involve relatively low transaction costs and credit risk but often allow only imperfect risk management due to their standardized nature.

In contrast, forwards are customized to the needs of specific clients. Forwards trade over the counter (OTC) and usually settle at the end of the contract period. Forwards are not guaranteed by a clearinghouse and so may involve substantial credit risk, depending on the creditworthiness of the counterparties. Increasingly, derivative dealers require their counterparties to post collateral in forward contracts and other OTC derivatives in an amount that reflects their current fair value. Collateral does not fully protect the dealer against default, however, since the value of derivatives can change quickly. Derivatives dealers must have very good internal control systems to monitor changes in the value of their derivatives and the posting of collateral by their counterparties, since a clearinghouse does not perform these functions. Derivatives dealers use master netting agreements, which net the cash flows on the covered contracts between the dealer and a given counterparty, to mitigate credit risk, as discussed in Chapter 9.

For example, a commodities forward contract involves a notional amount that is a physical quantity (e.g., bushels of wheat) and the price of a well-defined commodity (e.g., the price of a bushel of wheat of a given grade to be delivered in a given place). Assuming net cash settlement, if the spot price of the commodity at termination rises above the forward price, then the seller of the forward contract pays the purchaser the notional amount times the difference between the spot and forward prices. Conversely, if the spot price of the commodity falls below the price specified in the forward contract, then the purchaser of the forward contract pays the seller the notional amount times the difference between the forward and spot prices. To illustrate, if the notional amount is 100 bushels of wheat, the forward price is $2 per bushel, and the spot price of wheat at the maturity of the forward contract is $2.50, then the seller pays the purchaser $50 = ($2.50 − 2) × 100.

The payoff on a purchased (long) forward contract is depicted in Exhibit 11.1. The payoff on the corresponding sold (short) forward contract is minus the payoff on the purchased forward contract. The cumulative payoff on a futures contract is the same as the payoff on a forward contract with the same terms, ignoring reinvestment of gains and losses from daily settlement of futures contracts.

A purchaser (seller) of a forward contract is often a user of or holder of a short position in (supplier of or holder of a long position in) the underlying good that is attempting to hedge changes in the price of the good. The payoff from the contract adjusts the effective price paid or received for the good in the spot market to the forward price for both parties. Alternatively, a purchaser (seller) of a forward contract may be speculating on increases (decreases) in the price of the good.

Options

An option contract provides the purchaser with the right but not the obligation to buy or sell the underlying at a specified strike price over a specified

EXHIBIT 11.1 Payoff on a Purchased Forward Contract

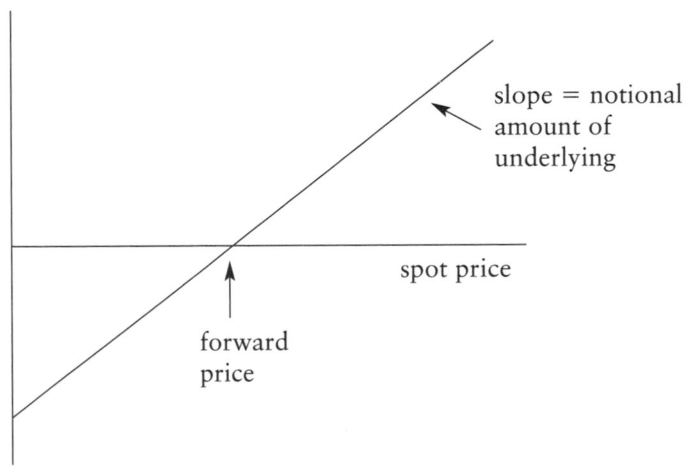

term. An option to buy is referred to as a call option and an option to sell is referred to as a put option. Unlike most other derivatives, the purchaser of an option must pay the seller (called the "writer") a premium, so that options have initial value. This premium is recognized initially as an asset by the purchaser and as a liability by the writer. In this regard, options are similar to insurance contracts.

Assuming net cash settlement, an exercised call option yields a payment from the writer to the purchaser for the notional amount times the difference between the spot price at exercise and the strike price. An exercised put option yields a payment from the writer to the purchaser for the notional amount times the difference between the strike price and the spot price at exercise. For example, a stock put option involves a notional amount that is a number of shares and a price that is the market price per share. The purchaser of a stock put option is paid the number of shares times the difference between the strike price and the share price at the exercise date when the price per share is below the strike price, and zero otherwise. To illustrate, if the notional amount is 10 shares of stock, the strike price is \$30, and the share price is \$22 at the exercise date, then the writer of the put option pays the purchaser \$80 = (\$30 − 22) × 10.

The "intrinsic value" of an unexercised option is the amount that would be received by the purchaser if the option were exercised immediately. The intrinsic value is:

- Zero if the option is currently "out of the money"—that is, the spot price is below (above) the strike price for a call (put) option
- Zero if the option is currently "at the money"—that is, the spot price equals the strike price
- Positive if the option is currently "in the money"—that is, if the spot price is above (below) the strike price for a call (put) option.

The value of an option prior to its expiration date is its intrinsic value plus its time value, which is the incremental value associated with the right to exercise the option later.

Under the assumptions made in standard option pricing theory (most relevantly, independent and identically distributed returns on the underlying), the time value of an option is greatest when the option is at the money. Intuitively, an out-of-the-money option requires the price to move a certain amount in the favorable direction for the purchaser before it has intrinsic value, and so it has less time value than an at-the-money option. Similarly, an in-the-money option loses intrinsic value if the price moves in the unfavorable direction, and so it also has less time value than an at-the-money option. Holding the spot price constant, the time value of the option decreases as the time to expiration shortens, so as the exercise date approaches, the value of the option converges to its intrinsic value (i.e., its payoff). The net of premium value of and payoff at exercise to a purchased call option are depicted in Exhibit 11.2.

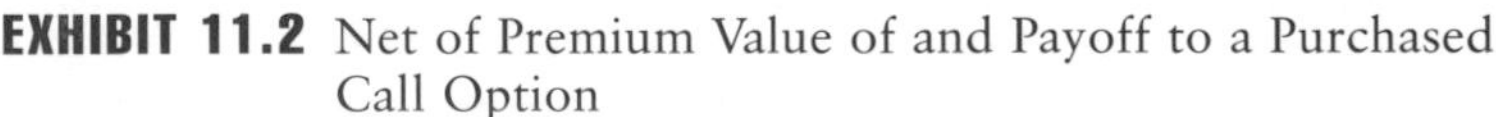

EXHIBIT 11.2 Net of Premium Value of and Payoff to a Purchased Call Option

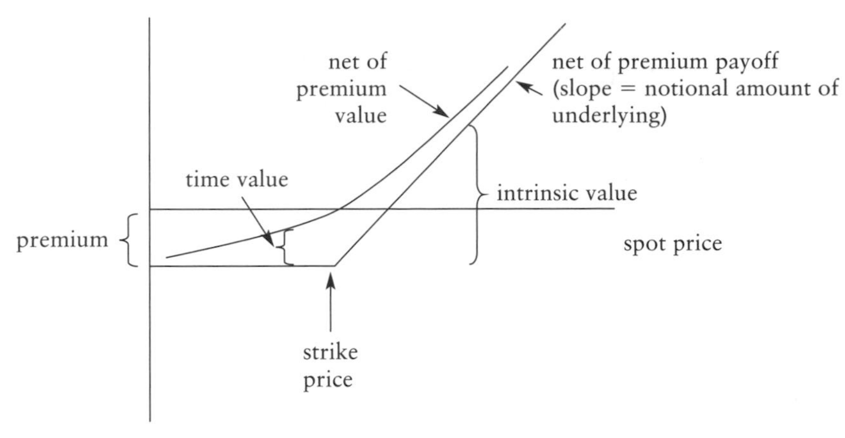

A previously unexercised purchased call (put) option will be exercised at the expiration date if and only if the spot price is above (below) the strike price at that date. Assuming the option can be exercised early, various factors—most important, the dividend or interest yield on the underlying—determine how deep in the money an option has to be before it is optimal for the purchaser to exercise the option early. Under the assumptions of option-pricing theory, a call option on an underlying that will not pay interest or dividends prior to the expiration date of the option will never be exercised early, since such an option always will have some time value. In contrast, a put option on the same underlying may be exercised early, because the strike price is the upper bound of the value of such an option.

Because of the differential incentives for the early exercise of put and call options, a central relation in option pricing theory referred to as put-call parity holds only for "European" options that cannot be exercised early. Put-call parity means that European put and call options on the same underlying with the same exercise price are related in value in this way: A portfolio of one European put option plus one unit of the underlying has the same value as a portfolio of one European call option plus cash in the amount of the strike price discounted from the expiration date of the option to the present. At the expiration date, both portfolios yield the underlying if the spot price exceeds the strike price and the strike price otherwise.

Unlike most other derivatives, options involve payoffs only for spot prices on one side of the strike price, and so they are used to hedge or speculate in one direction. Hedging with options usually involves reducing the downside risk of an existing position by purchasing a put option (and paying a premium), although it could involve reducing the upside risk of an existing position by selling a put option (and receiving a premium). The purchaser of a put option who owns the underlying is said to be "covered," meaning hedged against decreases in the price of the underlying. The purchaser of a put option who does not own the underlying is said to be "naked," meaning speculating on decreases in the price of the underlying.

Options can be combined with other options or derivatives to yield two-sided effects. For example, purchased call and put options on the same underlying yield a straddle, which pays off if the spot price either rises above the strike price of the call or falls below the strike price of the put. Options often are embedded in lending agreements, either by giving the borrower the option to borrow on predetermined terms (e.g., loan commitments) or by restricting the interest rates in some fashion (e.g., caps, floors, and collars).

Options yield a variety of problems for hedge accounting and market risk disclosures. As depicted in Exhibit 11.2, the value of an option is a nonlinear function of the spot price, and options pay off only for spot prices on one side of the strike price. These attributes imply that it is difficult to assess and maintain options' effectiveness as economic hedges, unless the hedged item exhibits exactly the same nonlinearity. SFAS No. 133 (1998) skirts this problem for hedge accounting purposes by allowing the nonlinear time value of an option to be ignored (i.e., only the piecewise linear intrinsic value to be used) in determining hedge effectiveness. Market risk disclosures often provide linear characterizations of exposures and so do not describe nonlinear exposures, such as options, well, as discussed in Chapter 12.

Swaps

A swap contract is a generally net cash settled exchange of recurring payments between two parties. Ignoring transactions costs, a swap is equivalent to a sequence of forward contracts, one for each recurring payment. In this regard, swaps are really not a separate type of derivative.

The most common type of swap is the "plain vanilla" interest rate swap, in which one party pays fixed interest payments to and receives floating-rate payments from its counterparty. The party that receives floating (fixed) and pays fixed (floating) payments is sometimes referred to as the purchaser (seller) of the swap, although more commonly swaps are referred to based on what is received and paid, as in a receive-fixed/pay-floating swap. This language is more general, because "basis swaps" both receive and pay at (different) floating rates. The floating interest rates most commonly used in plain vanilla dollar-denominated swaps are three-month and six-months LIBOR. The fixed rates in these swaps are referred to as swap rates.

Interest rate swaps have notional amounts that are principal amounts. Although the price that drives the settlement payments on these swaps is the floating interest rate (or, for basis swaps, rates), for plain vanilla interest rate swaps it is simpler to view this price as the value of the fixed-rate financial instrument that constitutes one side of the swap. This simplicity results from the fact that the value of the swap rises or falls approximately dollar for dollar with the value of that fixed-rate financial instrument, as depicted in Exhibit 11.3, because the value of the floating-rate instrument that constitutes the other side of the swap does not vary significantly with interest rates. This simpler view of the price of an interest rate swap is used later in this chapter.

A receive-floating/pay-fixed interest rate swap is effectively a long position in a floating-rate financial asset and a short position in a fixed-rate financial asset. A firm engaging in a receive-floating/pay-fixed interest rate swap may be attempting to transform a fixed-rate asset into a floating-rate asset, to transform a floating-rate liability into a fixed-rate liability, or to speculate that interest rates will increase. Similarly, a receive-fixed/pay-floating interest rate swap is effectively a long position in a fixed-rate financial asset and a short position in a floating-rate financial asset. A firm engaging in a receive-fixed/pay-floating interest rate swap may be attempting to transform a floating-rate asset into a fixed-rate asset, to transform a fixed-rate liability into a floating-rate liability, or to speculate that interest rates will decrease.

At the firm level, interest rate swaps effectively move repricing gap between the 0-1 interval and the interval equal to the tenor of the swap. (The tenor of a derivative is analogous to the maturity of a cash instrument; a different term is used for derivatives because they generally do not deliver the underlying.) For example, a receive-fixed/pay-floating swap with a five-year tenor creates positive gap in the five-year interval from the receive-fixed leg, and it creates the same amount of negative gap in the <1-year

EXHIBIT 11.3 Value of Plain Vanilla Received-Fixed/Pay-Floating Interest Rate Swap

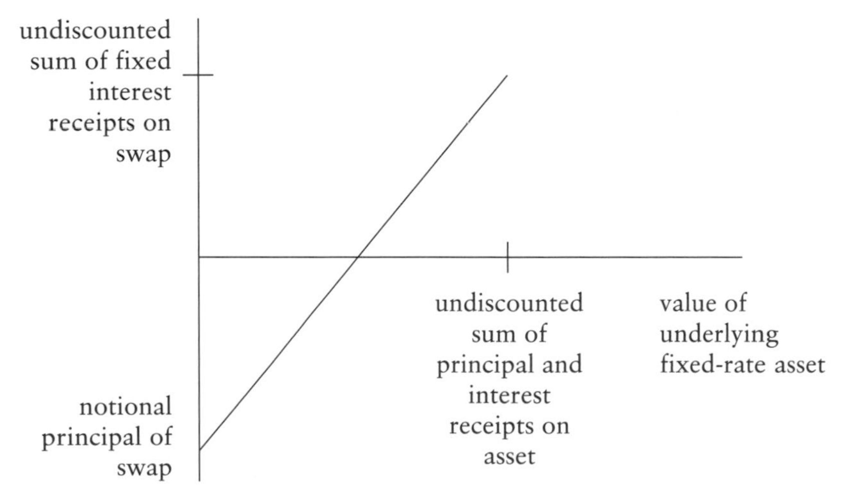

interval from the pay-floating leg. A receive-floating/pay-fixed swap with the same tenor would do the opposite.

Users of financial reports should be aware that plain vanilla interest rate swaps have this subtle economic aspect that affects the accounting for them in practice: When the yield curve slopes upward, as is usually the case, the fixed payments on these swaps are expected to exceed the floating payments early in their life; in fact, the first payment on these swaps typically is determined to be such at inception. To offset these expected early cash flows and be issued with zero initial value, receive-fixed/pay-floating interest rate swaps must be expected to experience unrealized losses and receive-floating/pay-fixed interest rate swaps to experience unrealized gains early in their life. In accounting practice, firms usually classify the cash flows on interest rate swaps in interest income but the fair value gains and losses on swaps in another line item on the income statement. Under this practice, by engaging in interest rate swaps, firms can manage the classification of their income without affecting their net income on average. For example, a financial institution that wants to raise interest income while lowering other income in a period engages in a receive-fixed pay floating swap. Moreover, if the institution obtains hedge accounting for the swap, it can manage the classification of net income in this fashion without increasing the variability of net income, since unexpected unrealized gains and losses on the swap will be offset by unrealized losses and gains on the hedged item for effective fair value hedges and be recorded in accumulated other comprehensive income for effective cash flow hedges. Empirical research finds that banks engage in this discretionary behavior when their interest income is above or below their target level (defined as the prior years' net interest margin percentage times the current year's average interest-earning assets).[3]

Because plain vanilla interest rate swaps are the most common type of derivative, especially for commercial banks, they are emphasized in subsequent portions of this chapter devoted to accounting and analysis.

Compound Derivatives

Compound derivatives combine futures and forwards, options, and swaps with each other or with nonderivative financial instruments. For example, structured notes are debt instruments with embedded options or swaps. Complex swaps are swaps with leverage or embedded options. Swaptions are options to purchase or sell swaps.

Credit Derivatives

The types of derivatives just described are used to manage market risks. In contrast, credit derivatives are used to manage credit or other counterparty risks, an important consideration for commercial banks and many other types of financial institution. As discussed in Chapter 8, credit derivatives are used in synthetic securitizations.

The most common type of credit derivative is credit default swaps, in which the purchaser pays a periodic premium to the seller in exchange for the right to receive payment if a specified credit event (e.g., default) for the referenced creditor occurs. Credit derivatives are essentially a type of financial guarantee, although the purchaser of these derivatives need not be exposed to the credit risk of the referenced creditor.

Credit derivatives have a notional amount that is a principal amount. The price that determines the settlement payments on credit default swaps is a discrete indicator of a credit event by a referenced creditor or, in the case of multiname swaps, by more than one referenced creditor. For other credit derivatives, these prices may be based on continuous variables, such as default indices or credit risk premia.

An issue for credit derivatives is the relative lack of observability of a referenced creditor's default, which need not be an unambiguously discrete event. To address this issue, the International Swaps and Derivatives Associations (ISDA) published its Credit Derivatives Definitions in 1999, which it updated in 2003. These definitions standardized the contractual terms of credit derivatives, most important what constitutes a credit event that requires payment by the sellers of these derivatives. These events involving the referenced creditor are included in ISDA's definition of a credit event:

- Bankruptcy
- The acceleration of, default/other failure to pay on, or repudiation of/imposition of moratorium on payment of an obligation
- The restructuring of an obligation in a manner unfavorable to the holders

The ISDA definitions have facilitated the development, use, and liquidity of credit derivatives, currently the fastest-growing type of derivative. For example, BIS reports $10.3 trillion of credit derivatives outstanding globally in December 2005, compared to $4.7 trillion outstanding in December 2004, a 119% increase. The Office of the Comptroller of the Currency reports credit derivatives held by U.S. commercial banks of $5.8 trillion in December 2005 compared to $287 billion in December 1999, a 20-fold increase in six years since the ISDA definitions were first published. The rapid growth of credit derivatives recently has led to operational issues for dealers in confirming and settling trades that market participants and policymakers have taken steps to resolve.[4]

HEDGING

Hedging means taking a position in a hedging instrument, often but not always a derivative, that offsets risks on hedged exposures in whole or part. A perfect hedge has risks that are perfectly negatively correlated with and of the same magnitude as those of the hedged exposure, so that the hedge "immunizes" the firm against the risks of the hedged exposure.

Few hedges are perfect, for these and other reasons:

- Firms may not understand their specific exposures or be able to model their aggregate exposure perfectly, and they cannot hedge what they cannot understand or model. Firms may not understand their individual exposures due to behavioral or other complex effects. For example, banks' prepayment-sensitive residential mortgage–related assets and core deposits are subject to the not entirely predictable behavior of mortgagees and depositors, respectively. Firms may not be able to model their aggregate exposures because of the number and variety of their individual exposures or because of the complexity of the interactions among these exposures. For example, mortgage banks have a number of mortgage-related exposures that are highly and distinctly affected by interest rates, as discussed in Chapter 7.
- Firms often hedge specific exposures rather than their aggregate exposures, in part because SFAS No. 133 (1998) only allows hedge accounting for hedges of specific exposures. Small imperfections in hedging specific exposures can add up to large imperfections in hedging aggregate exposures, especially if the different business units of the firm adopt the same hedging strategy.
- Perfect hedges may not be available or the cost of obtaining them may outweigh the benefits, so firms make do with less costly but imperfect hedges. For example, standardized futures contracts are used frequently even though customized forward contracts allow for fuller hedging. Similarly, interest rates swaps based on LIBOR or U.S. Treasury rates are used even though the hedged exposure may reflect a credit-risky interest rate.
- Hedging instruments are subject to credit or other counterparty risks. If the counterparty to a hedging instrument defaults, then the hedge will be ineffective.

In addition, firms that make profits by accepting risk often choose not to hedge fully because it reduces their expected profits.

The next two sections discuss two important and understandable concepts that pertain to hedge effectiveness, delta and basis. The assessment of hedge effectiveness in practice is discussed in the third section.

Delta and Delta Hedging

The delta of a derivative is the ratio of the change in the price of the derivative to the change in the price of the underlying, for small changes in the price of the underlying. In other words, it is the tangent to or first derivative of the function relating the value of the derivative to the price of the underlying at a given price for the underlying. Delta is a local measure of risk sensitivity. The change in the value of a derivative for a small change in the price of the underlying is approximately equal to the delta of the derivative times its notional amount times the change in the price of the underlying.

As depicted in Exhibits 11.1 and 11.3, purchased forwards and receive-fixed/pay-floating swaps have deltas of 1. (This assumes the derivatives are unleveraged; the absolute values of the deltas of derivatives rise with their leverage.) Sold forwards and receive-floating/pay-fixed interest rate swaps have deltas of minus 1. Since the value functions of forwards and interest-rate swaps are linear in the price of the underlying, delta is a global measure of risk sensitivity for those contracts.

As depicted in Exhibit 11.2, purchased call options have deltas between zero and 1 depending on the relation of the current price of the underlying to the strike price of the option. When a purchased call option is far out of the money, the value of the option changes little with the price of the underlying, and its delta is close to zero. Conversely, when the purchased call option is deep in the money, the value of the option changes by almost the same amount as the price of the underlying, and its delta is close to 1. Written call options and purchased put options have deltas between zero and minus 1, while written put options have deltas between zero and 1.

Delta hedging reduces the absolute value of the delta of the combination of the hedged item and hedge (the hedging relationship) toward zero, so that the value of that relationship does not vary much with the price of the underlying. Since delta is defined only for small changes in the price of the underlying, a zero delta hedging relationship may be susceptible to sudden large changes in the price of the underlying. For example, consider a mortgage bank hedging its portfolio of mortgage servicing rights with securities whose value does not exhibit the same highly nonlinear relationship with interest rates. In general, a zero delta hedging relationship will not stay zero delta without portfolio rebalancing.

Delta hedging strategies can be improved on in two general and non-mutually exclusive ways. First, dynamic delta hedging strategies attempt to maintain approximately zero delta hedging relationships over time by rebalancing one or both sides of the relationship with some frequency. These strategies must trade off increased hedge effectiveness against potentially sizable transactions costs. Second, better static hedges can be constructed by reducing the second or higher derivatives of the value function of the hedging relationship toward zero. For example, gamma hedging strategies—gamma is the change in delta divided by the change in the value of the underlying for a small change in the value of the underlying—reduce the sensitivity of the delta of hedging relationship to changes in the value of the underlying. These strategies may require sophisticated modeling of both the hedged item and the hedge and also intricately constructed hedges, as occurs with mortgage banks' hedging of mortgage servicing rights.

Basis and Basis Risk

Basis is the difference between the prices that drive the settlement payments on the hedged item and the hedge. Basis risk arises from volatility in basis. The example of Aames Financial in the hedge fund crisis discussed Chapter

8 involves a striking example of basis risk; Aames used short positions in U.S. Treasury securities to hedge the interest rate risks of its credit-risky subprime mortgages. The basis of Aames's hedge is the large credit risk premium for subprime mortgages over U.S. Treasury securities. While credit risk premia may be stable over long periods, they invariably rise in times of high economic uncertainty, such as the hedge fund crisis, when they approximately doubled. Basis risk usually occurs in less dramatic fashion, of course, as when mortgage banks hedge their prime residential mortgage–related assets with LIBOR or Treasury-based hedges. Even the basis between U.S. Treasury and LIBOR rates exhibits basis risk because of the slight credit risk in LIBOR and because of fluctuations in the demand and supply conditions in both markets.

A basis hedge is an attempt to mitigate basis risk. An example of a derivative used for basis hedging is a basis swap, where variable interest payments based on one floating rate (e.g., LIBOR) are swapped for interest payments based on another floating rate (e.g., the prime rate).

Assessment of Hedge Effectiveness

Since most hedges are imperfect, in practice a less stringent notion than perfection is used to decide when hedges are sufficiently effective to allow hedge accounting. The assessment of hedge effectiveness depends on whether the designated hedged item exhibits variability of fair value or cash flows. A hedge usually is said to be effective if changes in the fair value (cash flows) of the hedge are expected to be between 80 and 125% of changes in the fair value (cash flows) of the hedged item. Various statistical methods, such as regression, are used in this assessment. These methods necessarily use historical data. In this regard, the user of financial reports should keep in mind that historical hedge effectiveness does not imply future hedge effectiveness. For example, Aames's hedging strategy worked well during the 1990s right up to August 1998, when it failed abysmally. Infrequent but sometimes huge breakdowns of hedge effectiveness occur for hedging relationships that are static (e.g., zero delta) or involve substantial basis risk.

SFAS NO. 133 (1998), AS AMENDED

This section describes SFAS No. 133 (1998), as amended, the primary accounting standard governing derivatives and hedging. The definition of a derivative in this standard is provided in the "Definition" section, and the assessment of hedge effectiveness in practice is discussed in the "Assessment of Hedge Effectiveness" section; this material is not repeated here. The "Restricted Scope of Hedge Accounting" section describes the restricted scope of SFAS No. 133 (1998), as amended. The basic principles of the standard and the two hedge accounting methods it allows are described in the "Basic Accounting Principles" section. The "Bookkeeping" section works through the bookkeeping for an example of a bank that hedges the interest rate risk of its aggregate exposure using an interest rate swap. This swap can be designated as either a fair value hedge or a cash flow hedge of different portions of the aggregate exposure, so the example illustrates the inconsistencies of fair value and cash flow hedge accounting. The "Required Disclosures" section describes the required disclosures under these standards.

Restricted Scope of Hedge Accounting

This section summarizes how SFAS No. 133 (1998), as amended, by generally allowing hedge accounting only for effective derivatives-based hedges of specific exposures, prohibits hedge accounting for most economic hedging relationships. It also indicates some exceptions to these prohibitions the FASB allowed for practical or political reasons.

SFAS No. 133 (1998) generally allows hedge accounting only for hedges using derivatives. This feature prohibits hedge accounting for natural hedges, such as a traditional depository institution hedging fixed-rate deposits that are recognized at amortized cost on the balance sheet using trading or available-for-sale securities that are recognized at fair value.

The standard allows exceptions to this prohibition for nonderivatives-based hedges of net investments in foreign operations and unrecognized firm commitments designated in foreign currencies.

Relatedly, the standard allows hedge accounting for hedges using whole derivatives or proportional pieces of derivatives, but generally prohibits hedge accounting for hedges using nonproportional pieces of derivatives. An exception to this prohibition is that the time value of an option can be excluded from (i.e., only the intrinsic value of the option can be used as) the hedge.

SFAS No. 133 (1998) generally allows hedge accounting only for hedges of specific exposures. This requirement is motivated by the FASB's desire for unambiguous hedge documentation—which is inherently more difficult to attain for aggregate exposures—and hedge effectiveness tests that are clearly linked to that documentation, as discussed in the "Hedge Documentation, Hedge Effectiveness Testing, and the Shortcut Method" section. However, this requirement poses two problems for firms that economically hedge exposures at a more aggregate level for cost, hedge effectiveness, or internal management reasons, and also for users of financial reports.

1. A firm may hold a derivative that constitutes an effective economic hedge of its aggregate exposure but not of any of its specific exposures, and so be prohibited from using hedge accounting, yielding economically nondescriptive volatility in its owners' equity and net income. This problem is most likely to arise when the firm's natural hedging eliminates risks that cannot be hedged using available derivatives. For example, the firm might hold partly offsetting long and short positions in a commodity in a specific location that are too large to be hedged individually using available derivatives, but that net to a position that can be hedged in this way.

2. Conversely, a firm may hold a derivative that is an economic antihedge of the firm's aggregate exposure but that is an effective hedge of one of the firm's specific exposures. This firm would be allowed to use hedge accounting, suppressing economic volatility in net income.

The second problem is pervasive for financial institutions that hold partly offsetting positions and so is illustrated in detail using this numerical example. Assume a bank holds \$50 of fixed-rate assets, \$50 of floating-rate assets, and \$100 of fixed-rate liabilities. Ignoring credit risk, \$50 of the bank's fixed-rate assets and liabilities offset, so that the bank's aggregate exposure is the mismatch between its remaining nonoffsetting \$50 of floating-rate assets and \$50 of fixed-rate liabilities. The bank could economically hedge this aggregate exposure using a receive-fixed/pay-floating interest rate swap with a \$50 notional principal. This swap would be an effective hedge of the bank's specific exposures of \$50 of floating-rate assets or \$50 of fixed-rate liabilities, and so the first problem mentioned above does not arise in this example. However, the bank could instead designate its \$50 of fixed-rate assets as the hedged item and effectively hedging this specific exposure with a receive-floating/pay-fixed interest rate swap with a \$50 notional principal. The bank would use fair value hedge accounting for this designated hedging relationship, despite the fact that this swap is an antihedge of the bank's aggregate exposure. Also problematically, the bank could designate more than \$50 of its fixed-rate liabilities as the hedged item, hedge this exposure using a receive-fixed/pay-floating interest rate swap with a corresponding notional amount, and use fair value hedge accounting for the hedging relationship. The portion of the swap exceeding \$50 in notional amount would be an antihedge of the bank's aggregate exposure.

These problems are mitigated by two fairly narrow exceptions to the prohibition on hedging aggregate exposures.

1. SFAS No. 133 (1998) allows exposures to be aggregated into portfolios if they involve substantially the same risks. Although it is not clear exactly what this means, SFAS No. 133 includes an example that if the value or cash flows of one exposure in a portfolio are expected to change 10%, then the value or cash flows of the other exposures should change between 9% and 11%. SFAS No. 133 also states that it is not acceptable to take fixed-rate loans with different historical rates and thus different prepayment characteristics and aggregate them into a portfolio.
2. SFAS No. 138 (2000) allows hedge accounting for foreign currency cash flow hedges using internal derivatives (e.g., derivatives traded between the companies within a consolidated firm and the firm's risk management center), if the firm enters into derivative contracts with unrelated third parties that offset, on a net basis for each foreign currency, the foreign exchange risk arising from the internal derivatives.

SFAS No. 133 (1998) does not allow hedge accounting for hedges of the interest rate risk associated with held-to-maturity securities. The idea is that firms that classify securities as held to maturity have decided that fair value is not a relevant measure of the securities' value, consistent with the intent-based classification of securities in SFAS No. 115, *Accounting for Certain Investments in Debt and Equity Securities* (1993), discussed in Chapter 6. The FASB did not want to provide firms with the option to fair value held-to-maturity securities by choosing to fair value hedge the interest rate risk of these securities.

Finally, SFAS No. 133 (1998) does not allow hedge accounting for hedged items that are already measured at fair value on the balance sheet and income statement under otherwise applicable GAAP; in this case, gains and losses on both hedge and hedged items will offset in income without special hedge accounting.

Basic Accounting Principles

SFAS No. 133 (1998) requires that all derivatives be recognized at fair value on the balance sheet as gross assets or liabilities, not netted against hedged items. Derivatives not designated as accounting hedges are also fair valued on the income statement.

The standard allows two distinct and basically inconsistent types of hedge accounting for derivatives-based hedges that meet requirements regarding the documentation of the hedge and hedge effectiveness: fair value and cash flow hedge accounting. This section describes the distinct nature of the two hedge accounting methods, the hedge documentation and effectiveness testing requirements that must be met to use hedge accounting, and various other specific aspects of hedge accounting.

Fair Value Hedge Accounting. Fair value hedges are hedges of changes in the fair value of an exposure. For example, a bank may hold fixed-rate loans (i.e., assets) whose fair value varies inversely with interest rates. The bank can hedge this fair value variability by engaging in a receive-floating/pay-fixed interest rate swap. More generally, a firm can designate a derivative as a fair value hedge of an on–balance sheet asset or liability or an off–balance sheet firm commitment, such as a take-or-pay contract.

For an effective fair value hedge, both the hedge and the hedged item are fair valued on the balance sheet with unrealized gains and losses recorded in income as they occur. Although this is the normal accounting for a derivative, it is not for the hedged item, the accounting for which is altered to conform to that for the derivative hedge. This alteration is most apparent for a fair value hedge of a firm commitment, in which a previously off–balance sheet item appears on the balance sheet at fair value.

The income effects (cash flows and unrealized gains or losses) of the derivative hedge and the hedged item offset to the extent that the hedge is effective, but not otherwise. Because these income effects do not offset for the ineffective portion of the hedge, volatility in owners' equity and net income results from hedge ineffectiveness.

Cash Flow Hedge Accounting. Cash flow hedges are hedges of changes in the cash flows of an exposure. For example, a bank may have floating-rate debt the cash flows of which vary with interest rates. The bank can hedge this cash flow variability by engaging in a receive-floating/pay-fixed interest rate swap. More generally, a firm can designate a derivative as a cash flow hedge of an on–balance sheet asset or liability or an off–balance sheet forecasted transaction, such as expected future purchases or sales.

For an effective cash flow hedge, the accounting for the hedged item does not change, and the derivative hedge is fair valued on the balance sheet but the after-tax gain or loss on the effective portion of the hedge is immediately recognized in accumulated other comprehensive income (i.e., bypasses the income statement and is recorded directly in owners' equity). The accumulated other comprehensive income effect is reversed and recognized in net income (i.e., recycled) in the same periods as and in proportion to the income effect of the hedged item, thereby smoothing net income. For example, in the case of an interest rate swap, the accumulated other comprehensive income effect is reversed into interest income to smooth the interest income on the hedged floating-rate instrument.

Unlike under fair value hedge accounting, under cash flow hedge accounting the accounting for the derivative hedge is altered to conform to that for the hedged item. This conformity occurs only on the income statement, however, not the balance sheet. As a result, cash flow hedge accounting really is not hedge accounting with respect to other comprehensive income or owners' equity, which are volatile, as illustrated in the "Bookkeeping" section, but it is hedge accounting with respect to net income.

In contrast to the natural and immediate recognition of hedge ineffectiveness in fair value hedge accounting, cash flow overhedges require modifications to the bookkeeping to capture hedge ineffectiveness, while hedge ineffectiveness is ignored for cash flow underhedges. A cash flow overhedge (underhedge) occurs when the absolute cumulative change in the value of the hedge since the inception of the hedge is greater (less) than necessary to offset the cumulative change in the expected future cash flows on the hedged item. For cash flow overhedges, the change during the period in the amount by which the cumulative change in the value of the hedge is greater than necessary to offset the cumulative change in the expected future cash flows of the hedged item is recognized in net income that period. In contrast, for cash flow underhedges, no hedge ineffectiveness is recorded in net income, although the smoothing of net income associated with such underhedges will be incomplete, as illustrated in the "Bookkeeping" section.

This discussion indicates that cash flow hedge accounting under SFAS No. 133 (1998) is conceptually unsound, yielding nonarticulation of the balance sheet and income statement, volatility in accumulated other comprehensive income, and asymmetric treatment of overhedging and underhedging. Relatedly, cash flow hedge accounting is conceptually inferior to fair value hedge accounting, especially for financial institutions' hedges of their financial instruments for which fair value accounting is preferred, as discussed in Chapters 1 and 6. Cash flow hedge accounting reflects a political compromise between the FASB and its constituents made in order to gain general acceptance of SFAS No. 133 (1998). This compromise accommodates both the FASB's desire to fair value all derivatives on the balance sheet and firms' desire to report smooth net income for effective cash flow hedges.

Inconsistency of Fair Value and Cash Flow Hedge Accounting. The inconsistency of hedge accounting under SFAS No. 133 (1998) is illustrated in the two prior examples of banks engaging in receive-floating/pay-fixed interest rate swaps. In these examples, the banks receive either fair value or cash flow hedge accounting, depending on whether the hedged item is fixed-rate loans or floating-rate debt. Both banks are hedging liquid financial instruments using the same derivative. The first bank uses the swap to reduce the fair value variability but increase the cash flow variability of its fixed-rate loans. In contrast, the second bank uses the swap to reduce the cash flow variability but increase the fair value variability of its floating-rate debt. That is, the two banks appear to be making opposite risk transformations, yet SFAS No. 133 (1998) allows hedge accounting of different forms in both cases.

This inconsistency becomes even more apparent if one recognizes that the two examples could involve the same bank, a traditional depository institution, which holds fixed-rate loans and floating-rate debt in roughly the same amounts. As discussed in Chapter 4, this bank will experience economic losses (gains) on this aggregate exposure if interest rates rise (fall). The bank can eliminate this risk by engaging in a receive-floating/pay-fixed swap, since the swap will experience economic gains (losses) if interest rates rise (fall). Under SFAS No. 133 (1998), the bank's management has the unconstrained choice whether to designate the swap either as a fair value hedge of the fixed-rate loans or as a cash flow hedge of the floating-rate debt. Thus, the accounting for same derivative and same aggregate exposure varies significantly depending on the economically meaningless designation of the specific hedging relationship.

Income Statement Presentation. SFAS No. 133 (1998), as amended, contains few requirements regarding income statement presentation, in particular, regarding the gross versus net presentation of the hedge and hedged item and the line item classification of their various income effects. In practice, the recurring income effects of a hedge and hedged item (e.g., interest revenue or expense in hedges of interest rate risk) usually are netted and recorded in the usual income statement line item for the hedged item (e.g., interest revenue if the hedged item is an asset and interest expense if the hedged item is a liability). Insofar as a fair value hedge is effective, unrealized gains and losses on the hedged item and hedge usually are netted and recorded in the same line item, which may or may not be the same line item as for the recurring income on the hedged item. Unrealized gains and losses arising from the ineffective portion of a hedge usually are reported in a separate line item. Additional income statement line item classification practices specific to hedges of interest rate risk using interest rate swaps are discussed in the "Bookkeeping" section.

Hedge Documentation, Hedge Effectiveness Testing, and the Shortcut Method. To receive hedge accounting, SFAS No. 133 (1998) requires formal and unambiguous documentation of the hedge, the hedged item, and the hedging strategy at the inception of the hedge. Unambiguous documentation is particularly important for cash flow hedges of forecasted transactions, because the dates, amounts, and terms of these transactions generally are not known prior to their occurrence, which may not happen. The documentation must specify forecasted transactions in sufficient detail so that as transactions occur, it is apparent whether they are the hedged forecasted transactions or not. For example, a firm can hedge the first but not last *n* transactions in a period, because the last *n* transactions can only be determined with certainty at the end of the period.

SFAS No. 133 (1998) requires that documented hedging relationships be expected to be effective at initiation and on an ongoing basis. In general, the standard requires at least quarterly assessment of hedge effectiveness, considering both the past and expected future performance of the hedge. Reflecting the onerous nature of this requirement, especially for financial institutions with many hedging relationships, this is often referred to as long-haul hedge effectiveness testing.

Exceptions to most or all of the activities involved in long-haul hedge effectiveness testing exist when the critical terms of the hedge and the hedged item are identical, not just close, for which the hedge can be assumed to be effective. SFAS No. 133 (1998) provides two separate sets of conditions under which the hedge can be assumed to be effective. One set applies to forward contracts and is listed in paragraph 65 of the standard, while the other set applies to interest rate swaps used to hedge (possibly benchmark) interest rate risk and appears in paragraph 68. Although the two sets of conditions are very similar in nature, the conditions in paragraph 68 are considerably more numerous and detailed than those in paragraph 65. Perhaps for this reason—although with no clear justification given the very similar language used in the two paragraphs—the FASB staff concludes in DIG E4 (2003) and DIG G9 (2000) that firm may assume hedge effectiveness without any ongoing hedge effectiveness testing and record no gains or losses from hedge ineffectiveness only if the conditions in paragraph 68 are met. In contrast, if only the conditions in paragraph 65 are met, the FASB staff states that the firm must continue to assess whether the critical terms of the hedge and the hedged item remain identical and record any gains or losses associated with hedge ineffectiveness. Reflecting this distinction, in these and other DIG issues the FASB staff refers to application of the criteria in paragraph 68 (but not paragraph 65) as the shortcut method. Meeting the conditions in paragraph 65 also substantially reduces the onerous nature of long-haul hedge effectiveness testing, however.

SFAS No. 133 (1998) does not provide specific guidance regarding how to assess hedge effectiveness. It requires the subsequent assessment of hedge effectiveness to be consistent with the initial strategy; for example, a firm cannot redesignate a fair value hedge as a cash flow hedge at a later date. As noted in the "Assessment of Hedge Effectiveness" section, in practice a hedge usually is considered to be effective if changes in the value (cash flows) of the hedge are expected to be between 80 and 125% of changes in the value (cash flows) of the hedged item. To meet this requirement, the documentation may specify proportions of the derivatives used to hedge or of the exposure to be hedged. To illustrate, a firm that desires to hedge less than the full extent of an exposure while obtaining hedge accounting usually will specify a proportion of the exposure as the hedged item.

SFAS No. 133's (1998) hedge documentation and effective testing requirements place significant burdens on firms that want to use hedge accounting. These burdens are heaviest for firms that engage in many hedging transactions for which the shortcut method cannot be used. Reasonable people can disagree as to whether these requirements are worth their undoubtedly considerable cost. The FASB likes the idea that these requirements impose a strict discipline on the use of hedge accounting, and it is possible that this discipline yields internal control benefits for firms. However, it is also possible that these requirements deter the use of hedge accounting or even hedging altogether.

Hedges of Benchmark Interest Rates. In order to facilitate the use of hedge accounting for hedges using the most common interest rate derivatives, SFAS No. 138 (2000) allows hedge accounting for some hedges of near-riskless benchmark interest rates within the risky market rates that drive hedged items. The allowed benchmark interest rates currently are U.S. Treasury and LIBOR rates, although this list likely would change if these rates were replaced as the primary ones used in interest rate derivatives. SFAS No. 138 (2000) allows hedge accounting for effective fair value hedges of the benchmark interest rate risk of fixed-rate assets and liabilities and firm commitments, and also for effective cash flow hedges of the benchmark interest rate risk of forecasted transactions involving fixed-rate instruments. However, the standard prohibits cash flow hedge accounting for hedges of the benchmark interest rate risk of existing or forecasted purchases or sales of floating-rate instruments that are indexed to other rates.

When hedge accounting is allowed for hedges of benchmark interest rates, the basis risk between the risky market rates that drive the hedged item and the benchmark interest rate is ignored for the purpose of assessing hedge effectiveness. The shortcut method may even be used for hedges of benchmark interest rates that meet the conditions in paragraph 68 of SFAS No. 133 (1998). There is no good conceptual reason to ignore basis risk in the assessment of hedge effectiveness, however. For example, Aames's previously discussed use of short positions in U.S. Treasuries to hedge exposures to subprime mortgages would qualify as effective hedges under SFAS No. 138 (2000), regardless of the volatility of credit risk premia.

For fair value hedges of benchmark interest rates, the hedged item is recognized not at fair value but rather at a pseudo–fair value that does not take into account the change in the basis between the market interest rate that drives the hedged item and the benchmark interest rate since the inception of the hedge. Specifically, at any point during the hedge term, the hedged item is recognized at the net present value of the remaining contractual cash flows on the entire hedged item (i.e., not just the portion of these cash flows attributable to the benchmark interest rate) where the discount rate used in this calculation is the market rate driving the hedged item at the inception of the hedge plus the change in the benchmark rate from the inception of the hedge to the current point in time. The use of this discount rate implies that the hedged item will be recognized at fair value only if the basis of the hedge has not changed since the inception of the hedge. Thus unrealized gains and losses arising from basis risk generally are not recognized immediately in net income.

Hedge Termination. Adequately documented and effective accounting hedging relationships may be terminated either because the firm no longer desires hedge accounting or because the relationship no longer meets hedge effectiveness requirements. The latter reason is particularly likely for dynamic hedges of nonlinear or otherwise complicated exposures that must be rebalanced over time. When an accounting hedging relationship is terminated for reasons other than misapplication of hedge accounting, SFAS No. 133 (1998) requires that past statements not be restated but that hedge accounting be dropped going forward. For a fair value hedge, the fair value of the hedged item at termination usually becomes its carrying value, and thereafter the item is accounted for using normal accounting rules. However, at the termination of a fair value hedge of a firm commitment, the firm commitment is derecognized and the entire gain or loss on the firm commitment is recorded in net income. For a cash flow hedge, any gain or loss recognized in accumulated other comprehensive income at termination usually is reclassified into net income over time in the same fashion as if the hedge still existed. However, if a cash flow hedge of a forecasted transaction is discontinued because it is probable that the transaction will not occur, then the entire gain or loss on the hedge is recognized immediately in net income.

When a hedging relationship is terminated, both hedged items and hedges in discontinued hedging relationships can be redesignated in new hedging relationships. Again, this is particularly likely for dynamic hedges of nonlinear or otherwise complicated exposures that must be rebalanced over time.

Misapplication of Hedge Accounting. Firms sometimes use hedge accounting for hedging relationships they have not properly documented or for which they have not conducted adequate hedge effectiveness testing. Such misapplications of hedge accounting are accounting errors that, if material, require retroactive restatement of financial statements to reverse the use of hedge accounting. Restatement is required even if the hedging relationship could have satisfied the conditions for hedge accounting.

Glass Lewis & Co. reports that, during 2005, 57 firms restated their past financial statements for misapplication of hedge accounting, and at least 10 more announced that such restatements were forthcoming.[5] Most of these restatements involved improper documentation of the hedging relationship, inadequate hedge effectiveness testing, or other unmet requirements for hedge accounting. About a quarter of the restatements involved misapplication of the shortcut method. SunTrust also misapplied the shortcut method, but did not restate its prior financial statements and is not in the Glass Lewis list because the effects of this misapplication were immaterial; instead, SunTrust recorded a cumulative adjustment in the fourth quarter of 2005 to reverse its prior use of the shortcut method. Bank of America's 2005 restatement for the misapplication of the shortcut method is examined in the case in the appendix to Chapter 12. The remaining restatements involved incorrect valuation of derivatives or bookkeeping errors.

Impairment. SFAS No. 133 (1998) includes various rules regarding impairment of the hedged item, both individually and in conjunction with the hedge. These rules are most important for cash flow hedges, because the hedged item is not fair valued. Hedged items are subject to normal impairment accounting rules. If an impairment loss is recognized on a hedged item in a cash flow hedge, then any corresponding gain on the hedge is reclassified from accumulated other comprehensive income to net income to offset the impairment loss. If a net loss on the hedged item and hedge in a cash flow hedge is expected because of a loss on the hedge (e.g., if hedged inventory is expected to be sold at a net loss because of a loss on the hedge), then the corresponding amount of the loss in accumulated other comprehensive income is reclassified to net income.

Bookkeeping

This section works through and intuitively explains the accounting for an example of a partly ineffective hedge of a financial institution's aggregate exposure using an interest rate swap. To illustrate the differences between the two types of hedge accounting, the swap is designated first as a fair value hedge and then as a cash flow hedge of different portions of this aggregate exposure. The financial statements that result from the two types of hedge accounting are compared, and general conclusions are drawn about the nature and relative economic descriptiveness of the two types. Finally, the bookkeeping burdens imposed by SFAS No. 133 (1998) are discussed.

The example is based on these assumptions. ANTIDI (designating an antitraditional depository institution) Bancorp holds this balance sheet at the end of year 0: floating-rate loans of $100, fixed-rate debt of $90, and owners' equity of $10. The floating-rate loans cannot be prepaid, are credit riskless, have a three-year term, and earn interest in each year at CIBOR (designating a computationally convenient interbank offered rate, the simple properties of which are described later) during that year. Accrued interest is received at the end of each year, and the principal of $100 is received at the end of year 3. The fixed-rate debt cannot be prepaid, is credit riskless, has a three-year term, and pays interest at a 10% annual rate. Accrued interest is paid at the end of each year, and the principal of $90 is paid at the end of year 3. ANTIDI engages in a receive-fixed/pay-floating interest rate swap at the beginning of year 1. The swap is credit riskless, and it has a three-year term and a notional principal of $95. The floating payments out each year are based on CIBOR during the year. The fixed payments in are based on a fixed-rate of 10%. The swap has no initial value.

Changes in CIBOR occur only at the end of each year, and so the end-of-year rate applies during the next year. The realizations of CIBOR are: end year 0, 10%; end year 1, 12%; and end year 2, 11%. The yield curve is flat, so that the current CIBOR can be used to discount all the future payments on the swap, the floating-rate loans, and the fixed-rate debt for the purposes of fair valuing these items. Relatedly, expected future rates equal the current rate, so that the current CIBOR can be used to forecast the interest receipts on the floating-rate loans and the cash flows on the swap.

ANTIDI can designate the receive-fixed/pay-floating swap either as a fair value hedge of its fixed-rate debt or as cash flow hedge of its floating-rate loans. In both cases, the swap would be designated as an effective hedge, but it would be partly ineffective because the notional amount of the swap ($95) is more than the principal of the fixed-rate debt ($90) and less than the principal of the floating-rate loans ($100). This example is very simple because hedge ineffectiveness results only from mismatches of the (notional) principal amounts of the hedged items and the swap. As a result, hedge ineffectiveness as assessed for accounting purposes easily could be eliminated by specifying the fair value hedge to be 90/95 of the swap or the cash flow hedged item to be 95% of the floating-rate loans, although this would not change the accounting in either of these cases. Specifically, fair value hedge accounting would not change because the excess 5/95 of the swap would be fair valued on both the balance sheet and income statement. Similarly, cash flow hedge accounting would not change, because the accounting for the hedged item is unaffected and hedge ineffectiveness due to underhedging is not recognized.

The reader should be aware that, in other settings, rescaling the hedged item or hedge either may not eliminate hedge ineffectiveness as assessed for accounting purposes or may change the accounting, however. Specifically, hedge ineffectiveness results from various sources other than mismatched principal amounts—such as nonlinearity, basis risk, and mismatched maturity or other terms—and rescaling the hedged item or hedge generally will not eliminate these sources of hedge ineffectiveness. Moreover, in the setting of a fair value underhedge resulting only from a principal mismatch, rescaling the hedged item to the size of the hedge changes the accounting, because the excess of the hedged exposure over the hedged item would not be fair valued.

Taxes are ignored in this example. In practice, the effects on net income, accumulated other comprehensive income, and owners' equity are all after-tax.

Fair Value Hedge of the Fixed-Rate Debt. If ANTIDI designates the swap as a fair value hedge of the fixed-rate debt, then both the swap and the fixed-rate debt are fair valued on both the balance sheet and the income statement. The floating-rate loans are accounted for as usual.

As noted, SFAS No. 133 (1998), as amended, contains few requirements regarding income statement line item classification, and practice appears diverse. With regard to the fair value hedge of fixed-rate debt using an interest rate swap in this example, the standard does not specify whether interest expense and gains or losses on the hedged debt and swap should be calculated on an amortized cost or fair value basis, although Appendix B of SFAS No. 133 (1998) contains an example in which these items are calculated on a fair value basis for the swap but on an inconsistent amortized cost basis for the hedged debt. Ideally, these items would be calculated on a consistent fair value basis for both the hedged debt and the swap, with interest on the debt and swap being classified in interest expense and with gains and losses on the debt and swap both being classified in the same noninterest line item (e.g., other income). Unlike either the example in Appendix B of the standard or this ideal, in practice most firms, including SunTrust, measure interest expense for the hedged debt on an amortized cost basis and interest on the swap as its settlement cash flows.[6] This practice yields interest income that equals fair value interest income for the combination of the hedged debt and swap only if the hedge is perfectly effective; when there is hedge ineffectiveness, this practice yields smoother interest income than fair value interest income. The mismeasurement of interest income under this approach is perfectly offset by mismeasurement of unrealized gains and losses of the opposite amount, however, so that net income is unaffected.

In the exposition of the example, the ideal approach of calculating interest and gains and losses on a fair value basis is used for both the hedged debt and the swap. The differences of this approach from the practice described earlier are summarized at the end of the example.

These journal entries are recorded by ANTIDI in years 1 through 3. In year 1, ANTIDI records the interest revenue on the floating-rate loans ($\$100 \times 10\% = \$10$), the interest expense on the fixed-rate debt ($\$90 \times 10\% = \$9$), and the loss on the swap and the partly offsetting gain on the fixed-rate debt that result from CIBOR rising to 12%. The expected payments on the swap are $\$95 \times (12\% - 10\%) = \$1.9$ in years 2 and 3, so the loss on the swap is $\$1.9/1.12 + \$1.9/(1.12)^2 = \$3.21$. The fair value of the fixed-rate debt is $\$9/1.12 + \$99/(1.12)^2 = \$86.96$, so the gain on the fixed-rate debt is $\$90 - \$86.96 = \$3.04$. This gain is smaller than the loss on the swap, because the fixed-rate debt has a lower principal of \$90. Both the loss on the swap and the gain on the fixed-rate debt are recorded in net income, so the hedge ineffectiveness yields volatility in net income.

interest on floating-rate loans:		
cash (+ asset)	10	
interest revenue (+ income)		10
interest on fixed-rate debt:		
interest expense (− income)	9	
cash (− asset)		9
loss on swap:		
loss (− income)	3.21	
swap (+ liability)		3.21
gain on fixed-rate debt:		
debt (− liability)	3.04	
gain (+ income)		3.04

Although in this example the swap is a 5/90 overhedge of the fixed-rate debt, an underhedge would be treated symmetrically under fair value hedge accounting.

In year 2, ANTIDI records the interest revenue on the floating-rate loans ($100 × 12% = $12), the fair value interest expense on the fixed-rate debt ($86.96 × 12% = $10.44), and the fair value interest expense on the swap liability ($3.21 × 12% = $.39). The balances of both the debt and the swap are adjusted for differences between interest expense and cash paid. Finally, the gain on the swap and the offsetting loss on the fixed-rate debt the result from CIBOR falling to 11% are recorded. Since CIBOR decreases to 11%, the expected payment on the swap in year 3 is now $95 × (11% − 10%) = $.95. The ending balance of the swap liability is $.86 = $.95/1.11, and the gain on the swap is $.84 = $1.9/1.12 − $.86. The loss on the fixed-rate debt is $99/1.11 − $99/1.12 = $.80.

interest on floating-rate loans:		
cash (+ asset)	12	
interest revenue (+ income)		12
interest on fixed-rate debt:		
interest expense (− income)	10.44	
debt (+ liability)		1.44
cash (− asset)		9
interest on swap:		
interest expense (− income)	.39	
swap (− liability)	1.51	
cash (− asset)		1.9
gain on swap:		
swap (− liability)	.84	
gain (+ income)		.84
loss on fixed-rate debt:		
loss (− income)	.8	
debt (+ liability)		.8

In year 3, ANTIDI records the interest revenue ($100 × 11% = $11) and principal payment ($100) on the floating-rate loans, the fair value interest expense ($89.19 × 11% = $9.81) and principal payment ($90) on the fixed-rate debt, and the fair value interest expense on the swap liability ($.86 × 11% = $.09). The balances of both the debt and the swap must be adjusted for differences between interest expense and interest paid.

interest and principal on floating-rate loans:		
cash (+ asset)	111	
interest revenue (+ income)		11
loans (− asset)		100
interest and principal on fixed-rate debt:		
interest expense (− income)	9.81	
debt (− liability)	89.19	
cash (− asset)		99
interest on swap:		
interest revenue (− income)	.95	
cash (− asset)		.95

The ending balances in the loans, debt, and swap accounts are all $0.

Cash Flow Hedge of the Floating-Rate Loans. If ANTIDI instead designates the receive-fixed/pay-floating swap as a cash flow hedge of the floating-rate loans, then both the hedged loans and the fixed-rate debt are accounted for as if there were no hedge. The swap is fair valued on the balance sheet, and the change in the fair value of the swap each period initially is recorded in accumulated other comprehensive income, because this swap is a 5% underhedge. If the swap were an overhedge, however, then the portion of the gains or losses on the swap associated with the overhedge would be recognized immediately in net income. Prior gains (losses) on the swap are recognized in net income as the swap receives (pays) cash. Specifically, cash receipts (payments) increase (decrease) interest revenue on the hedged loans, which in this example works to smooth 95% of the volatility of interest revenue on these loans.

These journal entries are recorded in years 1 through 3. In year 1, ANTIDI records the interest revenue on the floating-rate loans ($100 × 10% = $10), the interest expense on the fixed-rate debt ($90 × 10% = $9), and the loss on the swap when CIBOR rises to 12%. This loss is calculated above to be $3.21 and is recorded in accumulated other comprehensive income.

interest on floating-rate loans:		
cash (+ asset)	10	
interest revenue (+ income)		10

interest on fixed-rate debt:		
interest expense (− income)	9	
cash (− asset)		9
loss on swap:		
acc. other comp. income (− owner's equity)	3.21	
swap (+ liability)		3.21

If the swap had a notional principal of $105 instead, then it would be a 5% overhedge of the floating-rate loans. The loss on the swap would have been $3.55. Of this amount, $3.38 is associated with the effective hedge and so would be recognized in accumulated other comprehensive income, while $.17 is associated with the 5% overhedge and so would be recognized in net income.

In year 2, ANTIDI records the interest revenue on the floating-rate loans ($100 × 12% = $12), the interest expense on the fixed-rate debt ($90 × 10% = $9), and the cash payment on the swap ($1.9), which offsets 95% of the $2 increase in interest revenue on the floating-rate loans. The net change in the value of the swap liability, which as calculated earlier decreases by $2.36 from a beginning balance of $3.21 to an ending balance of $.86, is recorded in accumulated other comprehensive income. This amount logically is attributable to three economically distinct items: (1) the cash payment on the swap ($1.9), (2) plus the gain on the swap attributable to the decline in CIBOR from 12% to 11% ($1.9/1.12 − $.95/1.11 = $.84), and (3) minus the fair value interest on the beginning swap liability balance ($3.21 × 12% = $.39).

interest on floating-rate loans:		
cash (+ asset)	12	
interest revenue (+ income)		12
interest on fixed-rate debt:		
interest expense (− income)	9	
cash (− asset)		9
cash on swap, adjustment of interest on loans:		
interest revenue (− income)	1.9	
cash (− asset)		1.9
change in fair value of swap:		
swap (− liability)	2.36	
acc. other comp. income (+ owner's equity)		2.36

In year 3, ANTIDI records the interest revenue ($100 × 11% = $11) and principal receipt ($100) on the floating-rate loans, the interest expense ($90 × 10% = $9) and principal payment ($90) on the fixed-rate debt, and the cash payment on the swap ($.95), which offsets 95% of the $1 increase in interest revenue on the floating-rate loans over the original amount of $10. The net decrease in the value of the swap liability is $.86, which is recorded in accumulated other comprehensive income.

interest and principal on floating-rate loans:		
cash (+ asset)	111	
interest revenue (+ income)		11
loans (− asset)		100
interest and principal on fixed-rate debt:		
debt (− liability)	90	
interest expense (− income)	9	
cash (− asset)		99
cash on swap, adjustment of interest on loans:		
interest revenue (− income)	.95	
cash (− asset)		.95
change in fair value of swap:		
swap (− liability)	.86	
acc. other comp. income (+ owner's equity)		.86

Since there are no further cash flows, the ending balances in the loans, debt, swap, and accumulated other comprehensive income accounts are all $0.

Comparison of Fair Value and Cash Flow Hedge Accounting. Exhibit 11.4 summarizes the effects on net income, accumulated other comprehensive income, and owners' equity of using fair value versus cash flow hedge accounting for the preceding example. In interpreting this exhibit, recognize that ANTIDI's net exposure after the swap is the same as if it had $5 of floating-rate assets (the $100 of floating-rate loans minus the $95 notional value on the receive-fixed/pay-floating interest rate swap) and $5 of fixed-rate assets (the $95 notional value of the swap minus the $90 of fixed-rate debt). Thus, ANTIDI has $5 positive repricing gap in the 0–1 year interval and $5 positive repricing gap in the 2–3 year interval, low net exposures compared to ANTIDI's gross loan, debt, and swap exposures. Economically, ANTIDI loses mildly when CIBOR rises and benefits mildly when CIBOR falls.

When the swap is designated as a fair value hedge of the fixed-rate debt and full fair value accounting is used for both the hedge and the hedged item, interest income and net income both fluctuate mildly, as one would expect, given that the swap is a highly effective but not perfect hedge of ANTIDI's net exposure. Interest income rises and falls with CIBOR. Net income is lowest in year 1, when ANTIDI experiences net losses of $.17 associated with the rise in CIBOR to 12%. Net income is highest in year 2, when ANTIDI experiences net gains of $.04 associated with the decline in CIBOR to 11%. Income is normal in year 3, when ANTIDI has no remaining interest rate risk. The volatility in owners' equity is determined entirely by the mild volatility in net income. Fair value hedge accounting clearly describes this hedge of this aggregate exposure properly.

The practice of measuring interest expense on the hedged debt on an amortized cost basis and the cash flow on the swap to offset that interest

EXHIBIT 11.4 Comparison of Fair Value and Cash Flow Hedge Accounting Example

	Year 1	Year 2	Year 3
Fair value hedge of fixed-rate debt (using fair value interest for debt and swap):			
Interest income	1	1.17	1.1
Gains and losses	(.17)	.04	0
Net income	.83	1.21	1.1
Owners' equity	10.83	12.04	13.15
Fair value hedge of fixed-rate debt (using amortized cost interest for debt and cash flow for interest on swap):			
Interest income	1	1.1	1.05
Other income (misstated gains and losses)	(.17)	.11	.05
Cash flow hedge of floating-rate loans:			
Interest income = net income	1	1.1	1.05
Other comprehensive income	−3.21	2.36	.86
Owners' equity	7.79	11.25	13.15

expense does not affect the total amount of net income or owners' equity, but it mismeasures interest income and other income by offsetting amounts. For example, Exhibit 11.4 indicates that a gain of $.05 is recorded in year 3 even though the ANTIDI had no interest rate risk in that year.

In contrast, when the swap is designated as a cash flow hedge of the floating-rate assets, interest income, which equals net income, is quite smooth, since cash flow hedge accounting removes 95% of the fluctuations in interest revenue on the floating-rate loans. The fluctuations in net income are entirely attributable to the swap being a 5% underhedge of the floating-rate loans. Cash flow hedge accounting does not recognize the interest rate risk from ANTIDI's slight positive gap exposure in the 2–3 year interval, however, and so this income smoothing understates the economic volatility of ANTIDI's net position. However, accumulated other comprehensive income and owners' equity are highly and misleadingly volatile, since only the swap is fair valued.

The differences in net income under the two hedge accounting methods in this example result solely from hedge ineffectiveness. In contrast, differences in accumulated other comprehensive income and owners' equity under the two hedge accounting methods would result even if the hedge was perfectly effective.

Bookkeeping Burdens. Hedge accounting under SFAS No. 133 (1998), as amended, involves a lot of journal entries, far more than under prior hedge accounting. By itself, the need to record more journal entries does not constitute a significant burden, since most of the bookkeeping process is automated. Moreover, prior hedge accounting was economical with journal entries because it kept most derivatives used for hedging off–balance sheet and did not distinguish the effective and ineffective portions of hedges, neither of which is a good thing.

Required Disclosures

This section describes SFAS No. 133's (1998) disclosure requirements. Using SunTrust's disclosures in its 2005 Form 10-K filing, this section also demonstrates the inferences users of financial reports can make about the accounting effects of firm's derivatives and hedging from these required disclosures. The case examining Bank of America's 2005 restatement for misapplication of the shortcut method in the appendix of Chapter 12 also focuses, in part, on making such inferences.

SFAS No. 133 (1998) requires firms to discuss their hedging objectives and strategy and their use of derivatives to meet these objectives. Although these disclosures often are very general, they invariably provide users of financial reports with a sense for the firm's approach to hedging. Moreover, some firms, including SunTrust, voluntarily disclose the notional amounts and tenors of the various types of derivatives they use for hedging. These disclosures provide users with a much greater understanding of the firm's hedging, especially if the firm also provides market risk or other disclosures that indicate the nature and extent of its exposures being hedged, as SunTrust also does. Chapter 12 demonstrates how such an understanding can be developed using SunTrust's disclosures.

Firms must disclose, separately for fair value hedges and cash flow hedges, the net gain or loss on derivatives recognized in net income or other comprehensive income due to:

- Exclusion from the test for hedge effectiveness
- Hedge ineffectiveness
- Termination of the designation of derivatives as hedges

Firms must disclose where on the income statement these net gains or losses appear. These disclosures help the user of financial reports observe ineffective hedging or speculation.

SunTrust makes these disclosures about its fair value and cash flow hedges in 2005.

> **Fair Value Hedges**
>
> The Company enters into interest rate swaps to convert fixed rate assets and liabilities to floating rates. For the years ended December 31, 2005 and 2004, the Company recognized additional income in the net interest income of $89.2 million and $197.7 million, respectively, related to

cash payments from net settlements and income accrued from inteest rate swaps accounted for as fair value hedges. This hedging strategy resulted in zero ineffectiveness for the years ended December 31, 2005 and 2004.

The Company maintains a risk management program to manage interest rate risk and pricing risk associated with its mortgage lending activities. The risk management program includes the use of forward contracts that are recorded in the financial statements at fair value and are used to offset changes in value of the mortgage inventory due to changes in market interest rates. A portion of the forward contracts have been documented as fair value hedges of specific pools of loans that meet the similar assets test as described in SFAS No. 133, and the qualifying pools of hedged loans are recorded in the financial statements at their fair value. The pools of loans are matched with a certain portion of the forward contracts so that the expected changes in market value will inversely offset within a range of 80% to 125%. This hedging strategy resulted in ineffectiveness that reduced earnings by $40.4 million and $50.0 million for the years ended December 31, 2005 and 2004, respectively. The impact of the hedge ineffectiveness is substantially offset by higher levels of net interest income from holding first mortgage loans.

Cash Flow Hedges

The Company uses various interest rate swaps to convert floating rate assets and liabilities to fixed rates. Specific types of funding and principal amounts hedged were determined based on prevailing market conditions and the current shape of the yield curve. The terms and notional amounts of the swaps are determined based on management's assessment of future interest rates, as well as other factors.

For the years ended December 31, 2005 and 2004, the Company recognized interest income of $15.2 and interest expense of $46.2 million, respectively, related to interest rate swaps accounted for as cash flow hedges. This hedging strategy resulted in ineffectiveness that reduced earnings by $2.4 million for the year ended December 31, 2005 and resulted in zero ineffectiveness for the year ended December 31, 2004.

SunTrust states its interest rate swaps, whether fair value or cash flow hedges, convert fixed- or floating-rate assets or liabilities to the opposite type, reflecting the fact that hedge accounting is applied at the level of specific exposures. For the purpose of assessing SunTrust's risk management, however, users of financial reports should view these swaps as working together to move SunTrust's firm-level repricing gap between the 0–1 interval and the various intervals corresponding to the tenors of the swaps, as discussed in the "Swaps" section. SunTrust's disclosures discussed in Chapter 12 indicate the tenors of its swaps vary from less than 1 year to beyond 10 years.

SunTrust discloses that fair value hedges of fixed-rate assets and liabilities using interest rate swaps increased its net interest income by $89.2 million during 2005, related to cash receipts from net settlements and also income accrued from the swaps. SunTrust clearly uses the common practice of recording interest on fair value hedged items on an amortized cost basis and interest on interest rate swaps as the settlement cash flows (plus some additional amount for accrued income). SunTrust states that there was no ineffectiveness for these hedges during 2005, implying that the unrealized gains and losses on the swaps and the hedged items perfectly offset during the year. SunTrust's net journal entries for these fair value hedges during 2005 are (in millions):

increase in interest income as cash is received on swaps:		
cash (+ asset)	89.2	
interest income (+ income)		89.2
offsetting unrealized gains and losses on perfectly effective hedge:		
hedged fixed-rate assets and liabilities (+ asset or − liability)	x	
interest rate swaps (− asset or + liability)		x

Users of financial reports usually cannot determine the amount of the offsetting gains and losses on the hedge and hedged item for the effective portion of fair value hedges, which is why x rather than a specific number appears in the last journal entry. Unusually, however, SunTrust discloses the fair value of its swaps by type of hedge at the beginning and end of the year, as well as the fair value of derivatives that are terminated or dedesignated as hedges during the year. In conjunction with the $89.2 million cash receipt on the swaps discussed earlier, these disclosures yield an estimate for x of $72.8 million (the disclosed ending fair value hedge swap liability of $216 million minus the disclosed beginning fair value hedge swap liability of $38 million minus cash interest received on fair value hedge swaps during year of $89.2 million minus $16 million positive fair value on terminated/dedesignated fair value hedge swaps).

SunTrust states that its forwards are fair value hedges of pools of similar mortgages held for sale. These forwards most likely are contracts to sell MBS that have a tenor equal to the expected holding period of the hedged pools, which disclosures discussed in Chapter 12 indicate is about four weeks on average. The ineffectiveness of this hedging relationship reduced earnings by a fairly sizable $40.4 million (though only 2% of SunTrust's net income during 2005), most likely because the actual holding periods of the mortgages in the pools did not exactly match the tenor of the forwards, although there may also be some basis risk in these hedges. Assuming the disclosed effect on earnings is after-tax and denoting the corporate tax rate by τ, SunTrust's net journal entry for these fair flow hedges during 2005 is (in millions):

imperfectly offsetting unrealized gains and losses on forwards hedge and hedged mortgages:

earnings (− income)	40.4	
mortgages	x	
tax expense (+ income)		$40.4\tau/(1-\tau)$
forwards		$x + 40.4/(1-\tau)$

(If the disclosure is pretax, then the journal entry is the same as when $\tau = 0$.) Again, users usually cannot determine the offsetting gains and losses on the hedge and hedged item for the effective portion of fair value hedges. Although an estimate of x for SunTrust's swap-based fair value hedges was made above using its disclosures of the fair value and cash flows on those swaps, SunTrust does not disclose the cash flows on its forward-based fair value hedges. Moreover, because these hedges turn over about 12 times a year, these cash flows likely are large compared to the fair values of the forwards. Hence, x cannot be reliably estimated for these hedges.

SunTrust states that its cash flow hedges of floating-rate assets and liabilities using interest rate swaps increase interest income by $15.2 million during 2005, reflecting the settlement cash flows on the swaps. These hedges had hedge ineffectiveness (i.e., overhedging) that reduced earnings by $2.4 million, a relatively small amount. Assuming the disclosure of the effect of hedge ineffectiveness is after-tax, SunTrust's net journal entries for these cash flow hedges during 2005 are (in millions):

increase in interest income from cash receipts on swaps:

cash (+ asset)	15.2	
interest income (+ income)		15.2

hedge ineffectiveness:

earnings (− income)	2.4	
tax expense (+ income)		$2.4\tau/(1-\tau)$
interest rate swaps (− asset or + liability)		$2.4/(1-\tau)$

There would also be a journal entry for the unrealized gain or loss on the effective portion of the cash flow hedge swaps that is recorded in accumulated other comprehensive income. Disclosures that indicate this journal entry are discussed later.

SFAS No. 133 (1998) requires additional disclosures for cash flow hedges, in part because the FASB views cash flow hedge accounting as a less desirable form of hedge accounting than fair value hedge accounting, and in part because firms are allowed to cash flow hedge forecasted transactions, which are not existing exposures of the firm and may never occur. Firms must disclose the beginning and ending balances in accumulated other comprehensive income associated with cash flow hedges, the change in the balance attributable to unrealized gains and losses on cash flow hedges during the period, and the change in the balance attributable to reclassifications into net income during the period. The gross additions and subtractions from accumulated income during the current period indicate the smoothing of net income in that period resulting from the use of cash flow hedge accounting. The balance of other comprehensive income indicates the amount that net income will be smoothed in future periods as a result of gains on cash flow hedge derivatives that have already occurred.

SunTrust makes the following disclosures in 2005:

Comprehensive income for the years ended December 31, 2005, 2004, and 2003, is:

($ in thousands)	**2005**	**2004**	**2003**
Unrealized (loss) gain on derivative financial instruments, net, recognized in other comprehensive income:			
Before income tax	(17,329)	16,402	45,366
Income tax	6,585	(5,741)	(15,878)
Net of income tax	(10,744)	10,661	29,488

The components of accumulated other comprehensive income at December 31 were:

($ in thousands)	**2005**	**2004**	**2003**
Unrealized (loss) on derivative financial instruments	(17,339)	(6,595)	(17,257)

These disclosures indicate that a $17.3 million pretax and $10.7 million after-tax net unrealized loss on SunTrust's cash flow hedges was recorded in accumulated other comprehensive income during 2005. The journal entry for the net unrealized loss recorded in accumulated other comprehensive income for its cash flow hedges during 2005 is ($ in millions):

acc. other comp. income (− owners equity)	10.7	
deferred taxes (+ asset or − liability)	6.6	
interest rate swaps (− asset or + liability)		17.3

As discussed, SunTrust also disclosed a $15.2 million net increase in interest income for its cash flow hedges during 2005, implying that a $2.1 = $17.3 − $15.2 million gross pretax unrealized loss occurred on cash flow hedges during 2005.

These disclosures allow users of financial reports to undo the net effects of effective cash flow hedge accounting during the period if they desire, by reversing the change in accumulated other comprehensive income and recording it instead in income. The journal entry to do this for SunTrust during 2005 is ($ in millions):

net interest income (− income)	17.3	
tax expense (+ income)		6.6
acc. other comp. income (+ owners' equity)		10.7

In addition, firms must disclose how much of the gains and losses on cash flow hedges currently recognized in accumulated other comprehensive income will be amortized into net income in the next year, indicating how much net income is expected to be smoothed in that year from the cash flow hedges currently in place. For example, SunTrust discloses

> Gains and losses on derivative contracts that are reclassified from accumulated other comprehensive income to current period earnings are included in net interest income. As of December 31, 2005, $16.8 million, net of taxes, of the deferred net losses on derivative instruments that are recorded in accumulated other comprehensive income are expected to be reclassified to interest expense in the next twelve months as derivatives mature or as payments are made.

Finally, firms must disclose the maximum length of time over which the firm is cash flow hedging forecasted transactions. Given that forecasted transactions far in the future are not certain to occur, this disclosure enables analysts to identify one of the most problematic uses of cash flow hedge accounting, the period over which net income is being smoothed by these hedges, and to anticipate the effect if these transactions do not occur. SunTrust does not mention any outstanding hedges of forecasted transactions.

While enhancing required disclosures of derivatives in the respects indicated, SFAS No. 133 (1998) also eliminated useful disclosures of the notional amounts and credit risks of derivatives that had been required under SFAS No. 105, *Disclosures of Information about Financial Instruments with Off–Balance Sheet Risk and Financial Instruments with Concentrations of Credit Risk* (1990), and SFAS No. 119, *Disclosure about Derivative Financial Instruments and Fair Value of Financial Instruments* (1994). Disclosures of notional amount had been criticized as meaningless, because the value and risk of a derivative are generally not determinable from its notional amount alone. Moreover, notional amounts do not aggregate easily across the derivative holdings of a firm, because risk sensitivities vary across derivatives, and because derivatives often net economically in ways that are not apparent from notional amounts.

The elimination of the notional amount disclosures was unfortunate, however, because the simplest and often best way to determine the nature and extent of firm's hedging is to compare the notional amounts and tenors of its derivatives to the size and maturities of its exposures. Moreover, research has shown notional amount disclosures to be relevant for the assessment of market risk beyond disclosures of the fair value of the derivatives and summary market risk measures such as Value-at-Risk.[7] Intuitively, the initial fair values of derivatives are small relative to the risk transferred and so indicate little about the risk associated with holding derivatives, whereas the notional amounts of derivatives indicate more, especially when combined with disclosures of the tenors and other contractual features of derivatives. As noted, some firms, including SunTrust, voluntarily disclose the notional amounts of derivatives.

The FASB has recognized the drawbacks of eliminating these disclosures and has an ongoing project to improve disclosures of derivatives. The FASB's goals are to require disclosures that provide users of financial reports with a clear understanding of how and why firms use derivatives, how firms account for derivatives and hedged items, and how derivatives affect firms' financial statements. As of November 2006, the FASB has decided to require these disclosures, with the first two required to be made by primary underlying risk (e.g., interest rate, foreign currency, and commodity), accounting designation (nonhedge, fair value hedge, and cash flow hedge), and purpose:

- The notional amounts, leverage factors, and fair values of derivatives on a gross basis even if a netting agreement exists that allows derivatives to be presented net on the balance sheet under FASB Interpretation (FIN) No. 39, *Offsetting of Amounts Related to Certain Contracts: An Interpretation of APB Opinion No. 10 and FASB Statement No. 105* (1992), as discussed in Chapter 9.
- Where fair values of derivatives are recorded on the balance sheet and where gains and losses on derivatives are recorded on the income statement.
- The effects of the effective and ineffective portions of gains and losses on cash flow hedge derivatives on net income.
- Counterparty credit risk on derivatives and the fair value of uncollateralized derivative exposures.
- The existence and nature of contingent features (e.g., payment acceleration) and the fair value of derivatives containing those features.

FRAMEWORK FOR ASSESSING FINANCIAL INSTITUTIONS' DERIVATIVES AND HEDGING

Despite some form of fair value accounting for derivatives and fairly extensive required disclosures of derivatives and hedging under SFAS No. 133 (1998), as amended, evaluating financial institutions' usage of derivatives for hedging and other purposes can be difficult, for three reasons:

1. SFAS No. 133 (1998), as amended, has various weaknesses that have been summarized throughout the chapter. Most notably, hedge accounting is applied only to hedges of specific exposures, and so it is often difficult for users of financial reports to determine how these hedges modify

financial institutions' aggregate exposures, which is usually the primary concern. It is possible that effective hedges of specific exposures are anti-hedges of the firm's aggregate exposure.

2. Financial institutions often use many derivatives for various purposes, and this usage typically is described in highly aggregated disclosures, such as the excerpts provided from SunTrust's financial reports (which are, in fact, unusually detailed).
3. It is very rare for financial institutions to discuss the threats to their hedging policies, even at the level of specific exposures, except after the fact when these policies fail.

These points are exacerbated by the fact that firms' disclosures regarding derivatives and hedging often are not clearly tied to their market risk disclosures.

The user of financial reports should try to answer four questions to assess a financial institution's derivatives and hedging:

1. What is its aggregate exposure?
   - What is the magnitude and nature of the sensitivity of this aggregate exposure to changes in market prices?
   - What is the remaining life of the exposure?
2. What derivatives does it use to modify the risk of its aggregate exposure?
   - Is it economically hedging or speculating?
   - Is any hedge or speculation one-sided or two-sided?
   - Is it attempting to modify fair value or cash flow variability? If cash flow variability, does this make sense?
   - Are the amounts, sensitivities, and tenors of its derivatives reasonable given its aggregate exposure?
3. What are the threats to hedge effectiveness?
   - Nonlinearity?
   - Basis risk?
   - Exposure not known (e.g., prepayment depends on behavior)?
4. How does accounting describe its derivatives and hedging?
   - Do its derivatives qualify as accounting hedges?
   - If so, are they fair value hedges or cash flow hedges?
   - What are the limitations of the accounting?

In addition to whatever information firms voluntarily provide about derivatives and hedging in the management discussion and analysis (MD&A), users of financial reports are provided with three required disclosures to answer these questions.

1. Disclosures of the fair value of financial instruments under SFAS No. 107, *Disclosures about Fair Value of Financial Instruments* (1991), allow

users to calculate the current and prior period changes in the fair value of the financial institution's financial instruments, including derivatives. Correlation of these fair value changes with market price movements in those periods provides a backward-looking but fairly objective indication of the institution's risk exposures.

2. Accounting and disclosures under SFAS Nos. 133 (1998), as amended, provide an indication of the institution's derivatives usage and the effectiveness of its hedges of specific exposures.
3. Market risk disclosures provide a forward-looking but often more subjective, aggregated, or nondirectional indication of the institution's risk exposures.

Users of financial reports need to construct as coherent a story as possible about a financial institution's derivatives and hedging from these sources. Market risk disclosures and financial analyses techniques that help users complete this task are discussed in Chapter 12.

NOTES

1. Bank for International Settlements, *BIS Quarterly Review*, Statistical Annex, June 2006, www.bis.org/publ/qtrpdf/r_qa0606.pdf.
2. Speech by Federal Reserve Board chairman Ben Bernanke, "Hedge Funds and Systemic Risk," May 16, 2006, www.federalreserve.gov/boarddocs/speeches/2006/200605162/default.htm.
3. T. Linsmeier and C. Song, "Are Interest-Rate Swaps Used to Manage Banks' Earnings?" Working Paper, Michigan State University, 2006.
4. "Toward Greater Financial Stability: A Private Sector Perspective: The Report of the Counterparty Risk Management Group II," July 2005, www.crmpolicygroup.org/docs/CRMPG-II.pdf.
5. Glass Lewis & Co., "The Hocus Pocus of Hedge Accounting," January 19, 2006; "Getting It Wrong the First Time," March 2, 2006.
6. Linsmeier and Song, "Are Interest-Rate Swaps Used to Manage Banks' Earnings?"
7. M. Wong, "The Association between SFAS 119 Derivatives Disclosures and the Foreign Exchange Risk of Manufacturing Firms," *Journal of Accounting Research* (Autumn 2000); C. Liu, S. Ryan, and H. Tan, "How Banks' Value-at-Risk Disclosures Predict Their Total and Priced Risk: Effects of Bank Technical Sophistication and Learning over Time," *Review of Accounting Studies* (June/September 2004).

CHAPTER 12

Market Risk Disclosures

This chapter has two complementary purposes. First, it describes the market risk disclosures required under Securities and Exchange Commission (SEC) Financial Reporting Release (FRR) No. 48, *Disclosure of Accounting Policies for Derivative Financial Instruments and Derivative Commodity Instruments and Disclosure of Quantitative and Qualitative Information about Market Risk Inherent in Derivative Financial Instruments, Other Financial Instruments, and Derivative Commodity Instruments* (1997).[1] These are the main required disclosures of firms' exposures to changes in market prices, including interest rates, exchange rates, commodity prices, and equity prices. These disclosures are useful in the analysis of financial institutions regardless of whether they engage in derivatives and hedging or not. Second, this chapter demonstrates how these market risk disclosures, in conjunction with the accounting for and disclosures of derivatives and hedging required under Statement of Financial Accounting Standards (SFAS) No. 133, *Accounting for Derivative Instruments and Hedging Activities* (1998) discussed in Chapter 11, allow users of financial reports to evaluate how financial institutions' derivatives and hedging affect their market risk.

The first section provides an overview of the salient features of FRR No. 48's (1997) disclosure requirements and their usefulness in understanding how financial institutions use derivatives for hedging or speculative purposes. The second through fourth sections discuss the three main approaches among which firms may choose to disclose their market risk: the tabular format, the sensitivity approach, and the Value-at-Risk (VaR) approach. In each of these three sections, the disclosure approach under consideration is described, its strengths and weaknesses are explained, and analyses based on actual disclosures by Golden West Financial, Countrywide Financial, and JPMorgan Chase are conducted. The fifth section compares the three disclosure approaches. The sixth section draws together the two purposes of this chapter by using SunTrust Banks' market risk and other disclosures to analyze the effect of its derivatives used for hedging purposes on its market risk. The final section summarizes recent empirical research on the usefulness of FRR No. 48's (1997) market risk disclosures. The appendix contains a case examining Bank of America's derivatives and market risk disclosures. This case also examines Bank of America's 2005 restatement of prior years' financial statements to reverse hedge accounting for misapplication of the shortcut method, which pertains to material presented in Chapter 11.

OVERVIEW OF FRR NO. 48 (1997)

Like the Financial Accounting Standards Board's (FASB's) motivations for issuing SFAS No. 133 (1998) discussed in Chapter 11, the SEC issued FRR No. 48 (1997) to address the concern that the market and other risks of firms' derivatives were not well understood by firms' managements or transparently presented in their financial reports. FRR No. 48's (1997) disclosure requirements apply to derivatives that must settle financially, to commodity derivatives that by custom settle financially, and to most nonderivative financial instruments, although leases, insurance contracts, and various other financial instruments are exempted. Although FRR No. 48 (1997) encourages voluntary disclosures of the market risk of exempted financial instruments and nonfinancial items not subject to the rule, in practice firms rarely provide such disclosures.

FRR No. 48 (1997) defines risk as the possibility of loss, not gain. Possibility of loss is a one-sided notion of risk that translates into overall risk (variance) only when the returns on the item under consideration are distributed symmetrically. Derivatives and other financial instruments that are or include options are particularly likely to exhibit asymmetric return distributions.

FRR No. 48 (1997) requires that market risk disclosures be made once a year in firms' Form 10-K filings. Given the infrequency of these disclosures, they are unlikely to be useful for firms that speculate, since speculative positions tend to change frequently. In this regard, FRR No. 48 (1997) requires separate disclosures for instruments held for trading purposes and those held for other purposes.

A significant limitation of market risk disclosures made under FRR No. 48 (1997) is that they need not be comparable across firms, exposures for a given firm, or time, for four reasons. First, firms may define loss in terms of reduction of value, earnings, or cash flow, and the three definitions of loss are not identical and can be inconsistent. For example, a perfectly floating-rate asset's earnings and cash flows vary with interest rates, but its value does not. A fixed-rate asset's value varies with interest rates, but its cash flows (and earnings, if the asset is accounted for at amortized cost on the income statement) do not.

Second, firms may disclose their exposure to each type of market risk using any of these approaches:

- *Tabular format.* This approach reports fair values and information sufficient to estimate the expected cash flows over each of the next five years and beyond five years for derivatives and other financial instruments grouped based on common characteristics. With respect to interest rate risk, this approach is similar to but generally more detailed and standardized than disclosures of repricing gap discussed in Chapter 4.

- *Sensitivity approach.* This approach reports the loss of value, earnings, or cash flow attributable to a specific adverse market price movement chosen by management, subject to the constraint that the movement be at least 10% of the beginning value of the market price.
- *Value-at-risk approach.* This approach reports the loss of value, earnings, or cash flow that occurs over a certain period with a certain probability, usually 5%. When loss is defined in terms of earnings or cash flow, the measure is properly termed earnings at risk (EaR) or cash flow at risk (CFaR). In this chapter, "pure" VaR refers to VaR where loss is defined in terms of value, while VaR refers collectively to pure VaR, EaR, and CFaR. Pure VaR and EaR are close to the same thing when earnings include most or all fair value gains and losses, as would be the case for a trading-oriented financial institution, but not otherwise.

These approaches have distinct strengths and weaknesses. The tabular format provides less processed and more disaggregated data than the other approaches, and so it allows users of financial reports considerable freedom to develop their own risk measures. However, this approach does not clearly convey the nature of option exposures or the covariances among exposures, so users typically have to make assumptions about these exposures to use these disclosures. The sensitivity and VaR approaches provide aggregate risk measures that embed management's knowledge of option exposures and covariances among exposures. However, they are hard to interpret without a full understanding of the assumptions involved in the aggregation. Moreover, the VaR approach does not indicate the direction of market price movements that causes loss, so it does not help users estimate the effects of subsequent changes in market prices. This is also a problem for the sensitivity approach when the market price movement is more complex than or otherwise differs from the chosen movement in the risk disclosure. For example, firms using the sensitivity approach for interest rate risk usually report the loss to parallel shifts in the yield curve, not to changes in the slope or shape of the yield curve. Even when firms do disclose losses to changes in the slope or shape of the yield curve, these disclosures do not and logically cannot cover all possible change in the yield curve. FRR No. 48 (1997) requires that firms discuss the assumptions and limitations of their chosen approaches, though in practice these disclosures tend to be boilerplate.

Firms need not choose the same approach for each type of market risk. This makes it difficult for users of financial reports to develop measures of firms' aggregate market risk, since different types of market risk may be correlated. For example, interest rates are correlated with exchange rates.

Third, the period over which loss is measured in the sensitivity and VaR approaches varies across firms and across different risks for a given firm. Earnings and cash flow sensitivity usually are measured over a relatively long period, most commonly one year. In a pure VaR approach or in an EaR approach when earnings include most fair value gains and losses, loss usually is measured over a short period, such as a day or a week. In contrast, in an EaR approach when earnings do not include most fair value gains and losses or in a CFaR approach, loss usually is measured over a longer period, such as a quarter or year. Sensitivity and VaR estimates need not rise linearly or in any other simple fashion with the length of the measurement time period, due to portfolio changes over time and for other reasons, although under simplifying assumptions it usually is possible to make these estimates more comparable through appropriate transformations. For example, under the assumption that returns to the portfolio are independent and identically distributed over time, VaR estimates can be made comparable by dividing the estimates by the square root of the number of days in the measurement time period.

Fourth, the size of the market price movements in the sensitivity approach and the confidence level used in the VaR approach vary across firms. Different-size market price movements in the sensitivity approach do not raise comparability problems if exposures are linear, but they do if exposures are nonlinear. Different confidence intervals in the VaR approach are easily adjusted for if the shapes of the lower tails of the distributions of returns on the portfolios under consideration are known (e.g., this would be the case if these returns are normally distributed), but not otherwise.

As discussed in Chapter 11, derivatives often have small fair values but high sensitivity to market price movements. This sensitivity could either increase or decrease a firm's market risk. For example, if the sensitivity of the firm's derivatives to market price movements has the opposite sign and the same or smaller absolute magnitude than the sensitivity of its prederivatives exposures to those movements, then these derivatives decrease the firm's market risk. Conversely, if the sensitivities of the firm's derivatives to market price movements have the same sign as the sensitivity of its prederivatives exposures to those movements, then these derivatives increase the firm's market risk.

To evaluate the effect of a firm's derivatives usage on its market risk, users of financial reports need to jointly analyze its accounting for and disclosures of derivatives and hedging provided under SFAS No. 133 (1998) and its market risk disclosures provided under FRR No. 48 (1997). Users are confronted with two related difficulties in this task, however.

1. Under SFAS No. 133 (1998), hedge accounting is applied and disclosures of derivatives and hedging are required at the level of individual hedging relationships in which the hedged item must be a specific exposure or portfolio of highly correlated exposures. In contrast, FRR No. 48 (1997) requires market risk disclosures at the (in most cases) more aggregated level of the firm's exposure to specific types of market risk. Thus, users must determine whether and how individual hedging relationships affect market risks at the firm level.

2. Market risk disclosures provided using the sensitivity or VaR approaches generally do not distinguish market risks prederivatives and postderivatives. Thus, additional information about derivatives usage is necessary to assess how the firm's derivatives modify its market risks.

Although FRR No. 48 (1997) is the primary source of market risk disclosures, other specific disclosure requirements related to market risk exist, which were discussed in prior chapters. As discussed in Chapter 4, banks sometimes voluntarily disclose repricing gap in their financial reports, and even if they do not, their repricing gap can be estimated from piecemeal disclosures of the maturity or repricing intervals of their loans, securities, and deposits. As discussed in Chapter 8, SFAS No. 140, *Accounting for Transfers and Servicing of Financial Assets and Extinguishments of Liabilities* (2000), requires disclosures of the sensitivity of the valuation of retained interests from securitizations to changes in significant assumptions, including market prices such as interest rates. As discussed in Chapter 11, SFAS No. 133 (1998) requires hedge effectiveness disclosures that usually pertain to market risk.

TABULAR FORMAT

The tabular format requires that fair values and information sufficient to estimate the expected cash flows over each of the next five years and beyond five years (i.e., six time intervals) be disclosed for derivatives and other financial instruments grouped based on common characteristics for each market risk. Users of financial reports should be aware that this information is not always tabulated in the same way by different firms, and so it is critical to read their textual discussions of the construction of the tables. For example, in presenting this information for the interest rate risk of floating-rate instruments, most banks—including Golden West, whose disclosure is analyzed herein—use a maturity-based format in which these instruments are classified into the six time intervals based on their maturity, while some banks use a repricing-based format in which these instruments are classified into the time intervals based on their repricing intervals. Analyzing these data appropriately given the form of presentation chosen, users can make the same inferences regardless of that form, however. For simplicity, only the maturity-based presentation is described herein. In addition, banks may treat differently mortgage prepayment and the stickiness of core deposits with no maturity.

The information necessary to estimate the cash flows in the six time intervals depends on the type of financial instrument. For example, for fixed-rate debt instruments, this information includes the expected principal payment and the weighted-average historical interest rate that applies to the principal paid in each of the intervals. For floating-rate debt instruments, this information includes the expected principal payment and the applicable weighted-average estimated forward interest rate in each of the intervals.

For interest rate swaps, this information includes the notional principal amount that expires and the weighted-average pay and receive rates in each of the intervals. For forwards and options, this information includes the notional principal amount that expires and the applicable forward or strike prices in each of the intervals. Ideally, the underlyings of forwards and options would be described with specificity, although this frequently is not the case, and when this is so users of financial reports must make assumptions about their underlyings in order to analyze the information. An example of this issue arises for SunTrust's hedges of its mortgage inventory using forwards with unspecified underlyings that is discussed later.

FRR No. 48 (1997) includes some guidance as to how to group financial instruments. Firms must distinguish:

- Fixed- and floating-rate debt instruments
- Long and short positions in futures and forwards
- Written and purchased put and call options with different strike prices
- Receive fixed and pay fixed interest rate swaps
- Foreign exchange instruments that have different currencies as underlyings or for which the functional currency differs under SFAS No. 52, *Foreign Currency Translation* (1981) (with the ability to aggregate disclosures across currencies that are economically related, managed together, and highly correlated)
- Commodity instruments that have different commodities as underlyings
- Derivatives used in hedging forecasted transactions

Depending on the firm's exposures and its use of derivatives, these disclosures could be voluminous; for example, consider a multinational firm hedging exposures in many countries whose currencies are not highly correlated.

Regarding interest rate risk, tabular format disclosures under FRR No. 48 (1997) generally are more detailed and standardized than repricing gap disclosures by banks. This fact should allow users of financial reports to estimate repricing gap and duration with greater precision and more comparability across banks and to estimate these variables with precision for the first time for other financial institutions. This precision is attributable in part to the use of annual time intervals from one to five years in the tabular format, whereas these four intervals are typically combined in repricing gap disclosures. It is also attributable to the provision of information about expected principal receipts or payments in each interval for fixed-rate instruments. In contrast, repricing gap disclosures typically treat these instruments as repricing completely at their maturity. Regarding other types of market risk, the tabular format disclosures substantially expand on the notional amount disclosures previously required by SFAS Nos. 105, *Disclosure of Information about Financial Instruments with Off–Balance Sheet Risk and Financial Instruments with Concentrations of Credit Risk* (1990) and 119, *Disclosures about Derivative Financial Instruments and Fair Value of Financial Instruments* (1994), which were superseded by SFAS No. 133 (1998).

Exhibit 12.1 presents Golden West's tabular format disclosure from its 2005 Form 10-K filing. This disclosure is manageable, because Golden West is a simple financial institution with fairly aggregated groupings of assets by balance sheet line item; for example, all its deposit liabilities are summed. As required, Golden West distinguishes fixed- and floating-rate assets and liabilities. Golden West's sole type of derivative is receive-fixed/pay-floating interest rate swaps, which it discloses it uses to convert debt from fixed-rate to floating-rate. For each group of financial instruments and each of the six time intervals, Golden West reports the fair value; the amount of (notional) principal expected to be received, paid, or otherwise expire; and the weighted-average interest rate or rates that apply to (notional) principal payments. Golden West discloses that it takes into account expected prepayments on its long-term mortgage-related assets and that it classifies the entire principal of deposits with no maturity in the 0- to 1-year interval.

Golden West's tabular format disclosure indicates the effect of its use of derivatives on its repricing gap. Its receive-fixed/pay-floating swaps increase its repricing gap in the 2- to 4-year interval and reduce its repricing gap in the 0- to 1-year interval. Golden West's swaps reduce its repricing gap in both intervals, because in its 2005 Form 10-K filing it reports a positive repricing gap after derivatives in the 0- to 1-year interval and a negative repricing gap in the 1- to 5-year interval.

Tabular format disclosures provide a disaggregated set of information that can be used for many analytical purposes. Although analysis of these disclosures often involves many calculations for many different financial instruments, given the standardized format of the disclosures, these calculations can be easily conducted using spreadsheet programs. The next two sections use Golden West's tabular format disclosure in Exhibit 12.1 to demonstrate how these disclosures can be used to estimate repricing gap and duration, respectively.

Estimating Repricing Gap

Three steps are involved in estimating repricing gap using tabular format disclosures of interest rate risk. These steps generally yield a more accurate measure of repricing gap than standard repricing gap disclosures described in Chapter 4, because they allow a finer treatment of fixed-rate instruments in the 1- to 5-year interval.

1. Treat fixed-rate financial instruments as a set of zero-coupon instruments with repricing intervals that correspond to the timing of principal cash flows reported in the tabular format disclosure. For example, of Golden West's fixed-rate mortgage-backed securities (MBS), $72 million reprice the 0- to 1-year interval, $58 million reprice in the 1- to 2-year interval, and so on. This approach is more economically descriptive than

EXHIBIT 12.1 Tabular Format Market Risk Disclosures, Golden West Financial Corporation, 2005 Form 10-K Filing

	Expected Maturity Date as of December 31, 2005 (*a*) (Dollars in Millions)							
	2006	**2007**	**2008**	**2009**	**2010**	**2011 and Thereafter**	**Total Balance**	**Fair Value**
Interest-Sensitive Assets:								
Federal funds sold and other investments	$ 1,322	$ -0-	$ -0-	$ -0-	$ -0-	$ -0-	$ 1,322	$ 1,322
Weighted average interest rate	4.11%	.00%	.00%	.00%	.00%	.00%	4.11%	
Securities Available for Sale (*b*)	$ 2	$ -0-	$ -0-	$ -0-	$ -0-	$ -0-	$ 2	$ 2
Weighted average interest rate	4.24%	.00%	.00%	.00%	.00%	.00%	4.24%	
MBS								
Fixed Rate	$ 72	$ 58	$ 50	$ 40	$ 31	$ 120	$ 371	$ 373
Weighted average interest rate	5.86%	5.79%	5.68%	5.64%	5.60%	5.47%	5.65%	
Variable Rate	$ 238	$ 184	$ 156	$ 120	$ 99	$ 316	$ 1,113	$ 1,112
Weighted average interest rate	5.65%	5.63%	5.61%	5.60%	5.58%	5.55%	5.60%	
Loans Receivable (*c*)								
Fixed Rate	$ 291	$ 151	$ 113	$ 86	$ 67	$ 245	$ 953	$ 958
Weighted average interest rate	7.01%	6.92%	6.77%	6.67%	6.60%	6.46%	6.77%	
Variable Rate	$32,007	$23,434	$16,678	$12,432	$ 9,146	$21,559	$115,256	$116,355
Weighted average interest rate	6.53%	6.51%	6.49%	6.47%	6.45%	6.40%	6.48%	
Total	$33,932	$23,827	$16,997	$12,678	$ 9,343	$22,240	$119,017	$120,122
Interest-Sensitive Liabilities:								
Deposits (*d*)	$57,197	$ 1,876	$ 495	$ 435	$ 154	$ 1	$ 60,158	$ 60,261
Weighted average interest rate	3.20%	4.17%	3.45%	3.80%	4.09%	3.31%	3.24%	

EXHIBIT 12.1 *(Continued)*

	Expected Maturity Date as of December 31, 2005 *(a)* (Dollars in Millions)							
	2006	**2007**	**2008**	**2009**	**2010**	**2011 and Thereafter**	**Total Balance**	**Fair Value**
FHLB Advances								
Fixed Rate	$ 2,368	$ 185	$ 460	$ 41	$ 125	$ 346	$ 3,525	$ 3,556
Weighted average interest rate	3.65%	4.88%	4.66%	5.46%	4.96%	5.74%	4.12%	
Variable Rate	$ 6,958	$11,600	$ 8,505	$ 4,029	$ 4,249	$ 95	$ 35,436	$ 35,422
Weighted average interest rate	4.31%	4.35%	4.34%	4.36%	4.41%	4.34%	4.35%	
Other Borrowings								
Fixed Rate	$ 4,569	$ 299	$ 688	$ 1,167	$ -0-	$ 495	$ 7,218	$ 7,216
Weighted average interest rate	4.36%	4.31%	4.61%	4.78% *(e)*	.00%	4.93%	4.49%	
Variable Rate	$ 2,925	$ 3,248	$ 1,049	$ 1,148	$ -0-	$ -0-	$ 8,370	$ 8,376
Weighted average interest rate	4.40%	4.48%	4.49%	4.60%	.00%	.00%	4.47%	
Interest Rate Swaps (notional values)								
Receive Fixed Swaps	$ -0-	$ -0-	$ 700	$ 1,200	$ -0-	$ -0-	$ 1,900	$ 38
Weighted average receive rate	.00%	.00%	4.15%	4.19%	.00%	.00%	4.18%	
Weighted average pay rate	.00%	.00%	4.42%	4.47%	.00%	.00%	4.45%	
Total	$74,017	$17,208	$11,897	$ 8,020	$ 4,528	$ 937	$116,607	$114,869

(a) Based on scheduled maturity or scheduled repricing: Loans and MBS reflect scheduled amortization and projected prepayments of principal based on current rates of prepayment.

(b) Excludes equity securities.

(c) Excludes loans in process, net deferred loan costs, allowance for loan losses, and other miscellaneous discounts.

(d) Deposits with no maturity are included in the 2006 column.

(e) The effect of the interest rate swaps is reflected in the weighted average interest rate.

treating the entire principal of these instruments as repricing at their maturity, as is done in standard repricing gap disclosures.

2. Treat floating-rate financial instruments as repricing within the next year, unless there is reason to believe these instruments reprice more slowly. For example, Golden West discloses that 96% of its floating-rate mortgages and MBS reprice monthly. Assuming for simplicity that all of its MBS reprice no slower than annually, $1,113 million of Golden West's floating-rate MBS reprice in the 0- to 1-year interval.
3. Treat derivatives as the closest available portfolio of cash instruments, and apply steps 1 and 2. This is particularly easy to do for interest rate swaps, whose tenor corresponds directly to their effect on repricing gap. For example, Golden West's receive fixed interest rate swaps are equivalent to a portfolio of fixed-rate assets and floating-rate liabilities, each with a book value of $1,900 million. Of the fixed-rate leg of these swaps, $700 million reprice in the 2- to 3-year interval and $1,200 million in the 3- to 4-year interval. All $1,900 million of the floating-rate leg of these swaps reprices in the 0- to 1-year interval.

In contrast, to perform this step for interest rate forwards and options, it is usually necessary to know the maturity of the underlying fixed-rate asset. For example, SunTrust hedges its mortgage inventory with sold forwards that have an average tenor of about four weeks. The closest available portfolio of cash instruments for these forwards is an asset reflecting the right to receive the forward price in four weeks and a liability reflecting the obligation to deliver the underlying asset in four weeks. The asset creates positive repricing gap in the 0- to 1-year interval, while the liability creates negative repricing gap in the interval equal to the four-week tenor of the forward plus the maturity of the underlying asset. Given that mortgage inventory is the hedged item, the underlying asset in the forwards most likely is 30-year fixed-rate MBS, and so ignoring prepayment these forwards create negative repricing gap in the beyond-10-year interval.

Applying these steps across all the instruments it holds, Golden West's repricing gap in the 0- to 1-year interval is $1,322 (federal funds sold and other investments) + 2 (securities available for sale) + 72 (fixed-rate MBS) + 1,113 (floating-rate MBS) + 291 (fixed-rate loans receivable) + 115,256 (floating-rate loans receivable) − 57,197 (deposits) − 2,368 (fixed-rate [Federal Home Loan Bank] FHLB advances) − 35,436 (floating-rate FHLB advances) − 4,569 (fixed-rate other borrowings) − 8,370 (floating-rate other borrowings) − 1,900 (floating leg of receive-fixed/pay-floating swaps) million = $8,216 million. This amount is fairly close to Golden West's positive repricing gap of $11,563 million in this interval reported in its 2005 repricing gap disclosure; it is lower primarily because Golden West has larger principal payments on its fixed-rate liabilities than on its fixed-rate assets in this interval. Similar calculations yield Golden West's repricing gap in other time intervals.

In its 2005 Form 10-K filing, SunTrust discloses the notional amount and tenor of its derivatives by type of hedge. These disclosures are used to determine how SunTrust's derivatives affect its repricing gap in the section "Effect of SunTrust's Derivatives and Hedging on Its Market Risk."

Estimating Duration

As discussed in Chapter 4, duration determines the change in the value of a financial instrument, portfolio, or firm to a small change in a flat yield curve. Three steps are involved in estimating duration using tabular format disclosures:

1. Estimate the expected cash flows in each interval for each type of fixed-rate financial instrument. This amount equals the principal maturing in that interval plus the expected interest cash flow in that interval. The expected interest cash flow is the sum of the principal cash flows in that and subsequent intervals times the weighted-average interest rates that apply to these principal cash flows. Unless there is reason to believe otherwise, assume that the principal cash flow in an interval occurs halfway through the interval, so that half the reported weighted-average interest rate applies to that principal cash flow.

   For example, the expected principal receipt on Golden West's fixed-rate MBS in 2008 is $50 million, which is assumed to occur halfway during the year, and so the applicable weighted-average interest rate is .0568/2. Similarly, in 2009, the principal receipt is $40 million with a weighted-average interest rate of .0564, in 2010, the principal receipt is $31 million with a weighted-average interest rate of .0560; and beyond 2010, the principal receipt is $120 million with a weighted-average interest rate of .0547. Thus, the expected interest receipt on Golden West's fixed-rate MBS during 2008 is $(50 × .0568/2) + (40 × .0564) + (31 × .0560) + (120 × .0547) million = $12 million, and the expected total cash receipt is $50 + 12 million = $62 million.
2. Unless there is reason to believe otherwise, assume that floating-rate financial instruments pay off in full in the 0- to 1-year interval and that payment of principal and half a year's accrued interest occurs halfway through the interval. For example, under this assumption the expected cash flow on Golden West's variable-rate MBS in the 0- to 1-year interval is $1,113 million (the entire principal) × (1 + .0565/2), or $1,144 million. (Although 96% of Golden West's floating-rate mortgages and MBS reprice monthly, lags in the repricing index make the assumption of a half-year repricing interval approximately correct.)
3. Again treat derivatives as the closest available portfolio of cash instruments and apply steps 1 and 2.

The expected cash flows determined in steps 1 through 3 can be used to estimate duration using the formulas provided in Chapter 4 and are also useful for various other purposes, such as liquidity analysis.

Strengths and Weaknesses

The tabular format's main strength is that it provides relatively unprocessed and disaggregated data that can be used both to assess market risk on an *ex ante* basis and to estimate the *ex post* effect of changes in market prices on the firm, assuming the firm's exposures have not changed since the time of its last disclosure. For example, users of financial reports can use these data to assess the effect of a change in the shape of the yield curve on the firm using the techniques described in Chapter 4. As discussed later, the ability to estimate the effect of subsequent changes in market prices using the tabular format is much greater than for the sensitivity and especially the VaR approaches.

The tabular format has two main weaknesses. First, it is a static portrayal of firms' exposures based on current market conditions and expectations. It is particularly limited in the way it portrays options, since these exposures are nonlinear in their sensitivity to market prices. The correct way to model the market risks of options is by averaging across the various possible future paths of market prices. For example, Golden West indicates that the expected principal payments on its fixed-rate mortgages in the table include expected prepayment. Prepayment is particularly sensitive to sufficiently large downward movements in interest rates. Users of financial reports have to characterize the firm's options and how they behave across the future paths of market prices. This is a difficult task involving many assumptions, which the reporting firm is generally in a far better position to perform.

Second, the tabular format often does not clearly indicate the covariances across different exposures or market risks. Specific financial instruments held by firms may be exposed to the risks of (domestic) interest rate movements, various foreign exchange movements, various commodity price movements, and so on. These risks may covary. Users of financial reports have to characterize the firm's exposures and how they interact with each market price or rate and how market prices covary. Again, this is a difficult task involving many assumptions, which the reporting firm is generally in a far better position to perform.

SENSITIVITY APPROACH

The sensitivity approach requires that the firm provide an estimate of the loss of value, earnings, or cash flow caused by a specific adverse movement in each market price or rate. The firm can choose the size of the movement, although it should be at least 10% of the current market price or rate. For example, in its 2005 Form 10-K, Golden West voluntarily discloses using the sensitivity approach in addition to the previously discussed tabular format.

> We estimate the sensitivity of our net interest income, net earnings, and capital ratios to interest rate changes and anticipated growth based on simulations using an asset/liability model. The simulation model

> projects net interest income, net earnings, and capital ratios based on a significant interest rate increase that is sustained for a thirty-six month period. The model is based on the actual maturity and repricing characteristics of interest-rate sensitive assets and liabilities which takes into account the lags [in the repricing of mortgages] previously described. For mortgage assets, the model incorporates assumptions regarding the impact of changing interest rates on prepayment rates, which are based on our historical prepayment information. The model also factors in projections for loan and liability growth. Based on the information and assumptions in effect at December 31, 2005, a 200 basis point rate increase sustained over a thirty-six-month period would initially, but temporarily, reduce our primary spread, and would not adversely affect our long-term profitability and financial strength.

Golden West chooses three measures of loss: net interest earnings, net earnings, and capital ratios. Golden West indicates that its interest rate spread would temporarily decline from a 2% parallel upward shift in the yield curve but that none of the measures of loss would be permanently affected if this shift were sustained for 36 months. Its choice of a 36-month period is unusually long, and likely reflects the fact that Golden West's repricing gap exposure is affected by lags in repricing its mortgages. As discussed in Chapter 4, Golden West is somewhat sensitive to changes in the shape of the yield curve, and this disclosure obscures this aspect of its exposure.

The sensitivity approach is by far the most common form of market risk disclosure. For example, most banks use the sensitivity approach for their interest rate risk disclosures, most commonly choosing net interest income measured over one year as the measure of loss. When this is the case, users of financial reports can only determine the direction and approximate amount of the bank's repricing gap in the 0- to 1-year interval. As discussed in Chapter 4, if interest rates rise during the following year, net interest income will rise for banks with positive repricing gap and fall for banks with negative repricing gap in the 0- to 1-year interval. Similarly, if interest rates fall during the following year, net interest income will rise for banks with negative repricing gap and fall for banks with positive repricing gap in the 0- to 1-year interval. Assuming a static portfolio, the percentage change in the bank's net interest income over the following year from an instantaneous parallel shift in the yield curve is $\Delta r \times GAP/NII$, where Δr denotes the shift in the yield curve, *GAP* denotes repricing gap in the 0- to 1-year interval, and *NII* denotes net interest income. An example of how this expression can be used to estimate repricing gap in the 0- to 1-year interval is provided in the "Effect of SunTrust's Derivatives and Hedging on Its Market Risk" section.

Some banks reporting using the sensitivity approach choose the value of equity as the measure of loss instead of or, more commonly, in addition to net interest earnings. When value of equity is the measure of loss chosen, users of financial reports can determine the weighted-average duration of the bank's owners' equity using equation 4.5 of Chapter 4. An example of how this equation can be used to estimate the duration of the banks' owners' equity, and thereby make inferences about long-term repricing gap, is provided in the "Effect of SunTrust's Derivatives and Hedging on Its Market Risk" section. As discussed in Chapter 4, banks whose owners' equity has positive duration benefit when interest rates fall and are hurt when interest rates rise, and banks with negative duration benefit when interest rates rise and are hurt when interest rates fall.

When a bank reports its interest rate risk using the sensitivity approach and chooses both net interest earnings and the value of equity as measures of loss, users of financial reports usually can make fairly good inferences about the bank's repricing gap in 0- to 1-year, intermediate, and long-term intervals. The net interest earnings sensitivity directly indicates the bank's 0-to-1-year repricing gap. The bank's value of equity sensitivity usually is dominated by the gap at the repricing interval of its longest-term exposures (hereafter long-term repricing gap). The bank's intermediate-term repricing gap usually can be inferred from its estimated repricing gaps in the 0-to-1-year and long-term intervals, since the amounts of a bank's average interest-earnings assets and interest-paying liabilities must be disclosed in its analysis of net interest income disclosure described in Chapter 4. Such inferences are made using SunTrust as example in the "Effect of SunTrust's Derivatives and Hedging on Its Market Risk" section.

Countrywide provides an uncommonly useful sensitivity disclosure in its 2005 Form 10-K filing, which is presented in Exhibit 12.2. Countrywide reports the sensitivities of the value of each of its financial assets (including mortgage servicing rights), financial liabilities, and derivatives to four parallel shifts in the yield curve: .5% and 1% shifts both up and down. This disclosure indicates the sensitivities of Countrywide's various interest rate sensitive exposures (not including future loan origination fees, of course, which are not financial instruments) to these shifts. It also indicates the correlations of these exposures, how these correlations differ for interest rate increases and decreases, as well the extent of Countrywide's hedging. For example, this disclosure indicates that:

- The values of Countrywide's mortgage servicing rights and mortgages are negatively correlated.
- Countrywide's mortgage servicing rights decline more in value than its mortgages rise in value when interest rates decrease, being dominated by the effect of prepayment rather than discounting.
- Countrywide's mortgage servicing rights rise in value less than its mortgages fall in value as interest rates rise, being dominated by the effect of discounting rather than prepayment.
- Countrywide hedges substantially all of the impairment of its mortgage servicing rights when interest rates fall, but only about half of the appreciation of those rights when interest rates rise.
- Countrywide overhedges its mortgage loan inventory to interest rate movements in both directions, though more so for interest rate increases.

EXHIBIT 12.2 Sensitivity Approach Market Risk Disclosure, Countrywide Financial Corporation, 2005 Form 10-K Filing

Change in Interest Rate (basis points)	Change in Fair Value (in millions)			
	−100	**−50**	**+50**	**+100**
MSRs and other financial instruments:				
MSR and other retained interests	$(2,812)	$(1,302)	$ 1,009	$ 1,714
Impact of Servicing Hedge:				
Mortgage-based	261	130	(130)	(260)
Swap-based	2,626	991	(429)	(598)
MSRs and other retained interests, net	75	(181)	450	856
Interest rate lock commitments	190	136	(218)	(489)
Mortgage Loan Inventory	1,135	691	(862)	(1,842)
Impact of associated derivative instruments:				
Mortgage-based	(1,454)	(890)	1,117	2,387
Treasury-based	187	74	6	74
Eurodollar-based	(97)	(53)	77	166
Interest rate lock commitments and Mortgage Loan Inventory, net	(39)	(42)	120	296
Countrywide Bank:				
Securities portfolio	147	88	(108)	(227)
Mortgage loans	555	299	(376)	(739)
Deposit liabilities	(255)	(131)	136	275
Federal Home Loan Bank advances	(235)	(115)	156	264
Countrywide Bank, net	212	141	(192)	(427)
Notes payable and capital securities	(824)	(412)	393	759
Impact of associated derivative instruments:				
Swap-based	95	48	(48)	(95)
Notes payable and capital securities, net	(729)	(364)	345	664
Insurance company investment portfolios	52	27	(28)	(56)
Net change in fair value related to MSRs and other financial instruments	$ (429)	$ (419)	$ 695	$ 1,333
Net change in fair value related to broker-dealer trading securities	$ (18)	$ (3)	$ (11)	$ (33)

It would be helpful to users of financial reports if other financial institutions provided sensitivity disclosures as useful as this one.

Strengths and Weaknesses

The main strength of the sensitivity approach is its simplicity and ease of interpretation compared to the tabular format. These disclosures are usually a paragraph or two long and easy to understand.

The main weakness of this approach is it may not provide users of financial reports with a good sense for complex or nonlinear exposures. For example, many banks disclose only the sensitivity of their net interest income to parallel shifts in the yield curve, and thereby provide users with virtually no information about the banks' repricing gap beyond one year. As a result, users cannot assess the sensitivity of these banks' value to parallel shifts in the yield curve or evaluate most aspects of their exposures to changes in the slope or shape of the yield curve. Similarly, many banks disclose only the effect of a single adverse market price movement on their net interest income or value. This does not clearly portray nonlinear exposures, such as options. For example, consider a mortgage bank hedging nonlinear exposures to interest rates and prepayment in its mortgage servicing rights or retained residual interests, as discussed in Chapters 7 and 8. A relatively small interest rate decrease might yield a proportionally smaller possible loss than would a larger interest rate decrease. Relatedly, firms that hold prepayment-sensitive assets often lose if interest rates either rise or fall sufficiently, so one cannot assume that a firm that loses when interest rates move in one direction will gain if they move in the other direction.

This weakness could be mitigated easily if firms disclosed sensitivity to multiple changes in market prices, as Countrywide does. SFAS No. 140 (2000) already requires disclosure of the hypothetical change in the fair value of each retained component in securitizations to two or more unfavorable changes in each significant assumption used to estimate the fair value of that component. There is no reason why firms could not provide tables or graphs that indicate the expected gain or loss to multiple movements in market prices in both directions.

The tabular and sensitivity approaches provide complementary information, and ideally financial institutions would provide both. In particular, the sensitivity approach provides the direction of market price movements of greatest concern and an easily understood summary statistic for the magnitude of the possible loss. Thus, it provides a starting place and calibration for analysis of the tabular format disclosure. Golden West is rare in voluntarily disclosing using both approaches, however.

VALUE-AT-RISK APPROACH

The VaR approach requires that the firm provide an estimate of the loss of value, earnings, or cash flow that is expected to result with a specified probability (usually 5%) over a specified time interval for each market risk. Unlike the prior two approaches, the VaR approach is statistical, providing a confidence bound on the lower tail of the distribution of future realizations of market risk. This confidence bound sometimes is said to distinguish normal from abnormal realizations of risk; this phrasing is unfortunate, since realizations of risk outside this bound are normal but infrequent. Users of financial reports should not ignore the possibility of the realization of risks outside the confidence bound, because such realizations are the most likely to damage the firm.

Three main statistical methods are used to estimate VaR. Each method uses historical data on the variances and covariances of the returns to the firm's exposures in some fashion.

1. *Delta-normal method.* The firm assumes that the return to each of the financial instruments it holds is distributed normally, so the returns to all its financial instruments are linearly related. (Under this assumption, delta, normally a local measure of risk sensitivity, is a global measure, explaining the name of this method.) Historical data over some period are used to estimate the variances and covariances of the returns to the firm's financial instruments, and the variance of the returns to its portfolio is solved for numerically. For firms with many exposures, some simplifying assumptions are usually made in this calculation. Most commonly, a portfolio of "standardized positions" in zero-coupon bonds is used to approximate the firm's portfolio of exposures.[2]
2. *Historical simulation method.* The firm observes the multivariate empirical distributions of the returns to its exposures and, through repeated sampling from these distributions, simulates the distribution of the returns to its portfolio of exposures. Since this method does not require the assumption of normality, it is, in principle, more robust than the delta-normal method. Both methods depend critically on the future behaving consistently with the past, however, and the second method is more likely to reflect the idiosyncrasies of the historical data.
3. *Monte Carlo method.* The firm assumes return distributions that it believes apply to its various exposures—most commonly, smooth distributions that resemble the empirical distributions but abstract from the idiosyncrasies of the historical data—and uses these distributions to simulate the distribution of returns to its portfolio. This method combines aspects of the delta-normal and historical simulation methods.

Exhibit 12.3 reports the disclosure in JPMorgan Chase's 2005 Form 10-K filing of the VaRs of its trading activities, which primarily involve market risk, and its credit portfolio, which refers to its credit derivatives not to its loan portfolio. JPMorgan Chase defines VaR in terms of loss of value over a one-day period with 1% probability, as determined using historical simulation. Average, minimum, and maximum VaRs during the current and prior year are disclosed.

EXHIBIT 12.3 Value-at-Risk Approach Market Risk Disclosures for Trading Activities and Credit Portfolio, JPMorgan Chase & Co., 2005 Form 10-K Filing

	Trading VAR Investment Bank (IB) Trading VAR by Risk Type and Credit Portfolio VAR (*a*)							
	2005				**2004** (*e*)			
As of or for the year ended December 31, (in millions)	**Average VAR**	**Minimum VAR**	**Maximum VAR**	**At December 31**	**Average VAR**	**Minimum VAR**	**Maximum VAR**	**At December 31**
By Risk Type:								
Fixed income	$67	$37	$110	$ 89	$74	$45	$118	$57
Foreign exchange	23	16	32	19	17	10	33	28
Equities	34	15	65	24	28	15	58	20
Commodities and other	21	7	50	34	9	7	18	8
Less: portfolio diversification	(59) (*c*)	NM (*d*)	NM (*d*)	(63) (*c*)	(43) (*c*)	NM (*d*)	NM (*d*)	(41) (*c*)
Total trading VAR	$86	$53	$130	$103	$85	$52	$125	$72
Credit portfolio VAR (*b*)	14	11	17	15	14	11	17	15
Less: portfolio diversification	(12) (*c*)	NM (*d*)	NM (*d*)	(10) (*c*)	(9) (*c*)	NM (*d*)	NM (*d*)	(9) (*c*)

EXHIBIT 12.3 *(Continued)*

	Trading VAR Investment Bank (IB) Trading VAR by Risk Type and Credit Portfolio VAR (*a*)							
	2005				2004 (*e*)			
As of or for the year ended December 31, (in millions)	**Average VAR**	**Minimum VAR**	**Maximum VAR**	**At December 31,**	**Average VAR**	**Minimum VAR**	**Maximum VAR**	**At December 31,**
Total trading and credit portfolio VAR	$88	$57	$130	$108	$90	$55	$132	$78

(*a*) Trading VAR excludes VAR related to the Firm's private equity business and certain exposures used to manage MSRs. Trading VAR includes substantially all mark-to-market trading activities in the IB, plus available-for-sale securities held for the IB's proprietary purposes (included within Fixed Income); however, particular risk parameters of certain products are not fully captured, for example, correlation risk.

(*b*) Includes VAR on derivative credit valuation adjustments, credit valuation adjustment hedges, and mark-to-market hedges of the accrual loan portfolio, which are all reported in Trading revenue. This VAR does not include the accrual loan portfolio, which is not marked to market.

(*c*) Average and period-end VARs are less than the sum of the VARs of its market risk components, which is due to risk offsets resulting from portfolio diversification. The diversification effect reflects the fact that the risks are not perfectly correlated. The risk of a portfolio of positions is therefore usually less than the sum of the risks of the positions themselves.

(*d*) Designated as not meaningful ("NM") because the minimum and maximum may occur on different days for different risk components, and hence it is not meaningful to compute a portfolio diversification effect.

(*e*) 2004 results include six months of the combined Firm's results and six months of heritage JPMorgan Chase results.

The disclosure for its trading activities reports the VaRs of its fixed income (interest rate), foreign exchange, equities, and commodities and other positions, both individually and combined. The individual average VaRs in 2005 sum to $145 million, while the total average VaR is 59% of that amount at $86 million. The various types of market risks of JPMorgan Chase's trading positions diversify significantly, because it is unlikely that they will all experience losses in the lower 1% of their distributions on the same day. VaR is the only disclosure format in which such diversification across types of market risk is apparent.

The disclosure reports the VaR for JPMorgan Chase's credit portfolio individually and combined with its trading activities. The average VaR of the credit portfolio is $14 million, $12 of which diversified away when combined with the trading activities, so that the total VaR of the trading activities and credit portfolio is $88 million. Although $88 million is a large number, it is only about .08% of JPMorgan Chase's owners' equity, so it would take 12 realizations of this loss without offsetting gain for it to lose 1% of its capital.

Strengths and Weaknesses

The main strength of the VaR approach compared to the other approaches is that it does not require users of financial reports to assess the probability of given movements in market prices or correlations among exposures. More generally, the VaR approach should reflect management's modeling of the firm's aggregate exposure and the multivariate distribution of changes in market prices.

The approach has two main limitations. First, VaR estimates are very sensitive to the methods used to calculate them, in particular, to the length of the prior period over which variances and covariances are estimated or empirical distributions are sampled. This is true even for very low-risk, liquid exposures, such as portfolios of Treasury securities.[3] The implication is that comparability of VaR estimates across firms and time is low. Relatedly, users of financial reports should attempt to determine whether and how the firm stress tests its VaR estimates for possible ways in which the future is not like the past and to understand the ways and extents to which these estimates are affected by such tests. For example, do the estimates reflect the possibility of an abrupt downward movement in riskless interest rates and upward movement in credit risk premia, such as occurred during the hedge fund crisis in the second half of 1998? Bank regulators have frequently expressed similar concerns about VaR as a regulatory tool, but despite these concerns VaR is the basis for the assessment of market risk using the internal models approach of the Basel II regulatory capital framework discussed in Chapter 2.

JPMorgan Chase makes this disclosure about its stress tests.

> While VaR reflects the risk of loss due to unlikely events in normal markets, stress testing captures the Firm's exposure to unlikely but plausible events in abnormal markets. The Firm conducts economic-value

> stress tests for both its trading and its nontrading activities using multiple scenarios for both types of activities. Periodically, scenarios are reviewed and updated to reflect changes in the Firm's risk profile and economic events. Stress testing is as important as VaR in measuring and controlling risk. Stress testing enhances the understanding of the Firm's risk profile and loss potential, and is used for monitoring limits, one-off approvals and cross-business risk measurement, as well as an input to economic capital allocation.
>
> Based upon the Firm's stress scenarios, the stress test loss (pre-tax) in the IB's [investment bank's] trading portfolio ranged from $469 million to $1.4 billion, and $202 million to $1.2 billion, for the years ended December 31, 2005 and 2004, respectively.

JPMorgan Chase's stress test losses are an order of magnitude larger than its average VaR.

Second, unlike the tabular format and the sensitivity approach, VaR does not provide the direction of the exposure; for example, the firm could be hurt by increases or decreases in interest rates, and users of financial reports will not know which from the VaR disclosures. In general, the nondirectional nature of the VaR disclosures makes them essentially useless for assessing the impact of a given market shock when it occurs. For these reasons, VaR makes a better risk management tool than it does a periodic disclosure device. VaR's main effect on improving risk disclosures is probably through helping management to understand and describe its risk exposures better.

Given these limitations, one might ask why VaR is an allowed disclosure option. Firms argued to the SEC that the direction of the bets they take on market movements are proprietary, so they should not be required to disclose them. It is hard to argue with this point. For example, one of the contributing factors to Long Term Capital Management's insolvency in 1998 was that other market participants became aware of its highly leveraged out-of-the-money bets and bet against it, driving its bets farther out of the money.

COMPARISON OF DISCLOSURE APPROACHES

The three disclosure approaches of FRR No. 48 (1997) differ along three important dimensions:

1. The three approaches provide disclosures that differ in the degree of aggregation. A certain level of disaggregation is usually necessary for the user of financial reports to be able to estimate the gain or loss resulting from specific movements in market prices. The tabular format provides by far the most disaggregated information.
2. The disclosures may indicate the direction or just the volatility of firms' exposures. Value-at-Risk provides a nondirectional measure of volatility, while the other approaches are directional.

3. The disclosures may or may not incorporate management's information about the correlation of its various exposures or the distribution of future market price movements, so the user of financial reports may have to supply this information to assess firm risk. Value-at-Risk embeds far more of management's information about these factors than other approaches.

The relative importance of these attributes depends on the financial analysis question of interest. If the question relates to the firm's sensitivity to future volatility in market prices, then a nondirectional measure such as VaR is fine. Moreover, VaR embeds more total information than any other approach. If one wants to interpret the effect of a specific movement of a market risk factor that has happened or might happen, then a directional measure is necessary. The sensitivity measure is likely to be best for simple and linear exposures, such as exposures to movements in commodity prices, while the tabular format is likely to be best for complex or nonlinear exposures, such as exposures to changes in the shape of the yield curve.

EFFECT OF SUNTRUST'S DERIVATIVES AND HEDGING ON ITS MARKET RISK

SunTrust provides two types of disclosures that allow users of financial reports to develop a good understanding of the effect of its derivatives and hedging on its market risk.

1. Tabular disclosures of the notional amounts and tenors of its derivatives by type of hedging relationship. These disclosures indicate the effect of SunTrust's derivatives used for hedging purposes on its repricing gap. (These disclosures help users of financial reports understand SunTrust's use of hedge accounting.)
2. Interest rate sensitivity disclosures using both net interest income and value of equity as measures of loss. These disclosures provide a fairly good sense for SunTrust's repricing gap after the use of derivatives.

Together the two types of disclosures allow users of financial reports to make reasonably good inferences about whether and the ways that SunTrust uses derivatives for hedging or speculation. These disclosures and the inferences they allow are explained in detail in this section.

SunTrust's tabular disclosures of the notional amounts and tenors of its derivatives by type of hedging relationships are reported in Exhibit 12.4. Note that these are not in exactly the same format as required for tabular format market risk disclosures under FRR No. 48 (1997). Specifically, the time intervals from 2 to 5 years are combined, while the time intervals beyond 5 years are subdivided into 5 to 10 years and beyond 10 years. This alternative partitioning is preferable because SunTrust has a sizable exposure in the beyond-10-year interval due primarily to its (incomplete hedging of its)

EXHIBIT 12.4 Tabular Format Disclosures of Risk Management Derivatives by Type of Hedging Relationship, SunTrust Banks, 2005 Form 10-K Filing

	As of December 31, 2005					
(Dollars in millions)	**1 Year or Less**	**1–2 Years**	**2–5 Years**	**5–10 Years**	**After 10 Years**	**Total**
Cash Flow Asset Hedges						
Notional amount—swaps	$ 300	$4,400	$ 600	$ 500	$ —	$ 5,800
Net unrealized loss	(4)	(68)	(11)	(5)	—	(88)
Weighted average receive fixed rate (*a*)	3.17%	3.62%	3.35%	4.22%	—%	3.68%
Weighted average pay floating rate (*a*)	4.29%	4.29%	4.29%	4.29%	—%	4.29%
Fair Value Asset Hedges						
Notional amount—forwards	$14,384	$ —	$ —	$ —	$ —	$14,384
Net unrealized (loss)/gain	(78)	—	—	1	—	(78)
Cash Flow Liability Hedges						
Notional amount—swaps	$ 1,500	$ 500	$3,065	$ —	$ —	$ 5,065
Net unrealized gain	9	6	64	—	—	79
Weighted average receive floating rate (*a*)	4.46%	4.33%	4.30%	—%	—%	4.35%
Weighted average pay fixed rate (*a*)	2.31%	3.94%	3.37%	—%	—%	3.41%
Fair Value Liability Hedges						
Notional amount—swaps	$ 250	$ 400	$ 767	$4,900	$1,150	$ 7,467
Net unrealized gain/(loss)	(2)	(31)	(189)	5	(216)	
Weighted average receive fixed rate (*a*)	4.78%	4.48%	3.24%	4.02%	5.14%	4.16%
Weighted average pay floating rate (*a*)	4.15%	4.05%	4.29%	4.21%	4.38%	4.23%

(*a*) All interest rate swaps have variable pay or receive rates with resets of six months or less.

mortgage assets. In addition, these disclosures are only for SunTrust's derivatives used for hedging purposes.

Four distinct types of hedging relationships using derivatives are listed in these disclosures.

1. *Cash flow asset hedges using swaps.* These are hedges of floating-rate assets using receive-fixed/pay-floating interest rate swaps with $5.8 billion notional amount and tenors ranging from less than 1 year to 5 to 10 years.
2. *Fair value asset hedges using forwards.* These are hedges of fixed-rate assets (mortgages) using sold forwards, in which the underlying is probably 30-year fixed-rate MBS, as discussed earlier. The notional amount of these forwards is $14.4 billion, and their tenors are less than one year; SunTrust discloses elsewhere in its 2005 Form 10-K filing that their average tenor is .08 year, or about four weeks.
3. *Cash flow liability hedges using swaps.* These are hedges of floating-rate liabilities using receive-floating/pay-fixed interest rate swaps with $5.1 billion notional amount and tenors ranging from less than one year to two to five years.
4. *Fair value liability hedges.* These are hedges of fixed-rate liabilities with $7.5 billion notional amount and tenors ranging from less than 1 year to beyond 10 years.

The effects of these four types of derivatives on SunTrust's repricing gap —using the techniques described in the "Estimating Repricing Gap" section and assuming the underlying of the forwards is fixed-rate mortgages with a repricing interval beyond 10 years—are presented in Exhibit 12.5. The net effect of these derivatives is to increase SunTrust's repricing gap in the 0- to 1-year interval by $5.3 billion, in the 1- to 2-year interval by $4.3 billion, and in the 5- to 10-year interval by $5.4 billion, and to decrease its repricing gap in the 2- to 5-year interval by $1.7 billion and in the beyond-10-year interval by $13.2 billion.

SunTrust's interest rate sensitivity disclosures are reported in Exhibit 12.6. SunTrust reports that its net interest income is expected to decrease by .1% if interest rates rise 1% gradually over the following year and to increase by .7% if interest rates fall 1% gradually over the following year. This disclosure implies that SunTrust is negative gap in the 0- to 1-year interval, more so if interest rates fall than if they rise. The extent of this negative gap can be estimated using the relationship discussed in the "Sensitivity Approach" section that the percentage change in net interest income over the following year from an instantaneous parallel shift in the yield curve equals $\Delta r \times GAP/NII$. In applying this relationship to SunTrust, Δr should be set to $\pm.5\%$ not $\pm 1\%$, since in its simulation the latter rate changes occur gradually over the following year. SunTrust's net interest income (NII) is $4.6 billion in 2005. To explain the reported .1% decrease in its net interest income when interest rates rise 1% gradually during the following year, SunTrust's

EXHIBIT 12.5 Effect of SunTrust's Derivatives on Its Repricing Gap

	Tenor of Derivatives plus Repricing Gap of Underlying of Forwards (in years)				
Notional amounts ($ in billions)	<1	1–2	2–5	5–10	>10
Cash flow asset hedges (receive-fixed/pay-floating swaps)	−5.5	4.4	.6	.5	—
Fair value asset hedges (sold forwards)	14.4	—	—	—	−14.4
Cash flow liability hedges (receive-floating/pay-fixed swaps)	3.6	−.5	−3.1	—	—
Fair value liability hedges (receive-fixed/pay-floating swaps)	−7.2	.4	.8	4.9	1.2
Net effect of derivatives on repricing gap	5.3	4.3	−1.7	5.4	−13.2

0- to 1-year repricing gap (GAP) must be about −.001 × $4.6 billion/.005 = −$.9 billion in that event. This is only −.6% of its $147 billion of average interest-earning assets. Similarly, to explain the reported .7% increase in its net interest income when interest rates fall 1% gradually over the following year, SunTrust's 0- to 1-year repricing gap must be about .007 × $4.6 billion/−.005 = −$6.4 billion in that event, or −4.4% of its average interest-earnings assets. Although SunTrust does not explain these negative repricing gaps in the 0- to 1-year interval, they likely primarily reflect repricing of its deposit liabilities that is faster if interest rates decrease than if they increase.

SunTrust's value of equity disclosure indicates that its value declines by 5.9% if interest rates rise 1% instantaneously and rises by 3.2% if interest rates fall 1% instantaneously. The duration of SunTrust's owners' equity can be estimated using equation 4.5 of Chapter 4. To explain the reported changes in value, SunTrust's owners' equity must have positive duration of about $5.9/(1+r)$ years if interest rates rise and of about $3.2/(1 + r)$ years if interest rates fall. Although SunTrust does not explain these positive durations, they likely are primarily due to SunTrust's large holdings of residential mortgages that prepay at higher rates if interest rates decrease than if they increase.

This analysis implies that SunTrust has negative repricing gap in the 0- to 1-year interval and positive repricing gap in the beyond-10-year interval. These repricing gaps do not by themselves allow the sign or amount of SunTrust's repricing gap in the various intervals from 1 to 10 years to be estimated with certainty. However, because SunTrust has $27 billion more average interest-earning assets than interest-paying liabilities and its derivatives increase its repricing gap in the 1- to 2- and 5- to 10-year intervals by $8 billion more than they reduce its repricing gap in the 2- to 5-year interval, unless SunTrust's positive repricing gap in the beyond-10-year interval is over

EXHIBIT 12.6 Sensitivity Approach Market Risk Disclosures for Nontrading Activities, SunTrust Banks, 2005 Form 10-K Filing

The following table reflects the estimated sensitivity of net interest income to changes in interest rates. The sensitivity is measured as a percentage change in net interest income due to gradual changes in interest rates (25 basis points per quarter) compared to forecasted net interest income under stable rates for the next twelve months.

Rate Change (Basis Points)	Estimated % Change in Net Interest Income over 12 Months	
	December 31, 2005	**December 31, 2004**
+100	(0.1)%	0.3%
−100	0.7%	(0.1)%

The valuation of the balance sheet, at a point in time, is defined as the discounted present value of asset cash flows and derivative cash flows minus the discounted present value of liability cash flows, the net of which is referred to as EVE. In contrast to the net interest income simulation, which assumes interest rates will change over a period of time (ramp), EVE uses instantaneous changes in rates (shock).

Rate Shock (Basis Points)	Estimated % Change in EVE	
	December 31, 2005	**December 31, 2004**
+100	(5.9)%	(3.1)%
−100	3.2%	0.6%

$35 billion, its repricing gap in some or all of the various intervals from 1 to 10 years must also be positive.

Combining these analyses, SunTrust hedges its repricing gap exposures in the 0- to 1-year and beyond-10-year intervals, as the effect of derivatives is to reduce its negative repricing gap in the 0- to 1-year interval and to reduce its positive gap in the beyond-10-year interval. Although it is not certain whether SunTrust's derivatives hedge its repricing gap in the various intervals from 1 to 10 years, it seems likely that they worsen its repricing gap in at least some of those intervals. To the extent that SunTrust is determined to be hedging its aggregate repricing gap exposure, its use of hedge accounting and the smoothing of income that result from that accounting, as described in Chapter 11, raises less concern for users of financial reports.

SunTrust's disclosure of its derivatives, hedging, and market risk are more informative than those provided by most financial institutions. For financial institutions providing less useful disclosures, such as Bank of America in the case in the appendix to this chapter, only cruder analyses of the institution's exposure before derivatives and how its derivatives modify that exposure are possible.

RESEARCH

Empirical research has examined the usefulness of FRR No. 48 (1997) market risk disclosures for both financial institutions and nonfinancial firms. Although this research provides some evidence that these disclosures have improved the market's overall ability to assess differences in market risk across firms, most studies have not been able to develop cross-sectional samples of sufficient homogeneity and size to yield powerful statistical tests, due to the varied approaches and other choices firm make in their market risk disclosures discussed in the "Overview of FRR No. 48" section. Accordingly, the main conclusion of this research is that the usefulness of these disclosures is diminished by their lack of comparability and also by the low quality of firms' disclosures of their exposures before derivatives.[4]

The most significant findings in this research are obtained for small samples of trading-oriented banks that report the market risk of their trading portfolios using fairly comparable VaR disclosures. This research finds that these banks' VaR disclosures explain cross-sectional differences in banks' unsystematic risk as measured by the volatilities of their trading income and stock returns as well as cross-sectional differences in banks' systematic risk as measured by their betas. These results are more significant for the largest, more technically sophisticated banks that are better able to estimate VaR, and they have strengthened over time as VaR becomes better measured by firms and understood by users of financial reports.[5]

Due to its cross-sectional nature, this research does not speak to whether these disclosures are useful for the analysis of individual firms. They certainly can be, as illustrated in the prior section using SunTrust's disclosures.

In addition, behavioral researchers have argued that the limitations of market risk disclosures are exacerbated by various well-known cognitive biases regarding risk evaluation and that the biases interact with the disclosure alternative.[6]

APPENDIX 12A: BANK OF AMERICA'S DERIVATIVES, HEDGING, AND MARKET RISK

This case is based on excerpts from Bank of America's Form 10-K filing for the fiscal year ending December 31, 2005. These excepts include Bank of America's interest rate risk disclosures for its nontrading financial instruments and tabular disclosures of the notional amounts and tenors of its derivatives. The main purpose of the case is to evaluate, as best as possible given these disclosures, how Bank of America's hedging using interest rate swaps affects its interest rate risk. Because Bank of America only provides net interest income sensitivity disclosures, its interest rate exposure after derivatives is not close to fully described, and so significant questions will remain after this evaluation is completed. A related purpose of this case is to determine what additional information about Bank of America's interest rate exposure users of financial reports need to obtain from the bank's management to answer these remaining questions.

These excerpts also include disclosures of the cumulative effects on Bank of America's 2004 balance sheet of its restatement of its financial statements for the years 2001 to 2004 for misapplication of hedge accounting, primarily the shortcut method. (The bank also restated its quarterly financial statements for 2005.) As discussed in Chapter 11, the shortcut method allows firms to assume rather than periodically test for the effectiveness of hedges of interest rate risk using interest rate swaps when certain criteria are met. Bank of America's misapplication of the shortcut method resulted primarily from its operating units engaging in internal interest rate swaps with its trading desk; these swaps were not derivatives or anything else for financial accounting purposes. The trading desk then engaged in identical swaps with the outside market, which are derivatives for financial accounting purposes, but did not do so in a sufficiently timely fashion for the operating units' hedges to qualify for the shortcut method. Bank of America could not retroactively conduct long-haul effectiveness testing for these hedges and so had to reverse its prior application of hedge accounting even though these hedges were effective. Because of Bank of America's disclosures about this restatement, one can see the workings, in reverse, of hedge accounting in more detail than usual. The final purpose of the case is to determine how Bank of America's hedge accounting worked for its various types of hedges. Since these hedges were effective, for analytical purposes users of financial reports might want to and could reinstate hedge accounting for some or all of these hedges.

Case Questions

Regarding the interest rate risk of Bank of America's nontrading financial instruments after its hedging using derivatives at the end of 2005:

- What are the directions and amounts of Bank of America's repricing gap in the 0-to-1-year, intermediate, and long-term intervals after hedging using derivatives?
- What are the effects of Bank of America's receive-fixed/pay-floating and receive-floating/pay-fixed interest rate swaps on its repricing gap?
- How do these interest rate swaps hedge or exacerbate Bank of America's interest rate risk?

Regarding Bank of America's misapplication of hedge accounting up to December 31, 2004:

- Why does Bank of America's restatement yield no adjustment to the valuation of derivatives?
- What types of interest rate swap did Bank of America use to hedge its loans and leases and also its long-term debt subject to the restatement? Have interest rates risen or fallen from the inception of those hedges

to December 31, 2004? Were these swaps fair value hedges or cash flow hedges?

- Which balance sheet accounts were affected by the reversal of fair value hedge accounting? Quantify the effects on those accounts as of December 31, 2004.
- Which balance sheet accounts were affected by the reversal of cash flow hedge accounting? Quantify the effects on those accounts as of December 31, 2004.

EXCERPTS FROM BANK OF AMERICA'S FORM 10-K FILING FOR THE FISCAL YEAR ENDING DECEMBER 31, 2005

INTEREST RATE RISK MANAGEMENT

Interest rate risk represents the most significant market risk exposure to our nontrading financial instruments. Our overall goal is to manage interest rate risk so that movements in interest rates do not adversely affect Net Interest Income. Interest rate risk is measured as the potential volatility in our Net Interest Income caused by changes in market interest rates. Client-facing activities, primarily lending and deposit-taking, create interest rate–sensitive positions on our balance sheet. Interest rate risk from these activities as well as the impact of changing market conditions is managed through the ALM [Asset and Liability Management] process.

Sensitivity simulations are used to estimate the impact on Net Interest Income of numerous interest rate scenarios, balance sheet trends, and strategies. These simulations estimate levels of short-term financial instruments, debt securities, loans, deposits, borrowings, and derivative instruments. In addition, these simulations incorporate assumptions about balance sheet dynamics such as loan and deposit growth and pricing, changes in funding mix, and asset and liability repricing and maturity characteristics. In addition to Net Interest Income sensitivity simulations, market value sensitivity measures are also utilized.

The Balance Sheet Management group maintains a Net Interest Income forecast utilizing different rate scenarios, with the base case utilizing the forward market curve. The Balance Sheet Management group constantly updates the Net Interest Income forecast for changing assumptions and differing outlooks based on economic trends and market conditions. Thus, we continually monitor our balance sheet position in an effort to maintain an acceptable level of exposure to volatile interest rate changes.

We prepare forward looking forecasts of Net Interest Income. The following table [Exhibit 12A.1] reflects the pre-tax dollar impact to forecasted Core Net Interest Income over the next 12 months from December 31, 2005 and 2004, resulting from a 100 bp [basis point] gradual parallel

(continues)

increase, a 100 bp gradual parallel decrease, a 100 bp gradual curve flattening (increase in short-term rates) and a 100 bp gradual curve steepening (increase in long-tem rates) from the forward curve.

EXHIBIT 12A.1 Bank of America's 2005 Estimated Net Interest Income at Risk

			December 31 (Dollars in millions)	
Curve Change	**Short Rate**	**Long Rate**	**2005**	**2004 (Restated)**
+100 Parallel shift	+100	+100	\$(357)	\$(183)
−100 Parallel shift	−100	−100	244	(126)
Flatteners				
Short end	+100	—	(523)	(462)
Long end	—	−100	(298)	(677)
Steepeners				
Short end	−100	—	536	497
Long end	—	+100	168	97

The above sensitivity analysis [Exhibit 12A.1] assumes that we take no action in response to these rate shifts over the indicated years.

Beyond what is already implied in the forward curve, we are modestly exposed to rising rates primarily due to increased funding costs. Conversely, we would benefit from falling rates or a steepening of the yield curve beyond what is already implied in the forward curve.

As part of the ALM process, we use securities, residential mortgages, and interest rate and foreign exchange derivatives in managing interest rate sensitivity.

Interest Rate and Foreign Exchange Derivative Contracts

Interest rate and foreign exchange derivative contracts are utilized in our ALM process and serve as an efficient tool to mitigate our risk. We use derivatives to hedge the changes in cash flows or market values of our balance sheet.

Our interest rate contracts are generally nonleveraged generic interest rate and basis swaps, options, futures, and forwards. In addition, we use foreign currency contracts to mitigate the foreign exchange risk associated with foreign currency–denominated assets and liabilities, as well as our equity investments in foreign subsidiaries. Table 29 [Exhibit 12A.2] reflects the notional amounts, fair value, weighted average receive fixed and pay fixed rates, expected maturity, and estimated duration of our open ALM derivatives at December 31, 2005 and 2004.

The changes in our swap and option positions reflect actions taken associated with interest rate risk management. The decisions to reposition our derivative portfolio are based upon the current assessment of economic and financial conditions including the interest rate environment, balance sheet composition and trends, and the relative mix of our cash and derivative positions. The notional amount of our net receive fixed swap position (including foreign exchange contracts) decreased $328 million to $22.8 billion at December 31, 2005, compared to December 31, 2004. The notional amount of our net option position decreased $266.6 billion to $57.2 billion at December 31, 2005, compared to December 31, 2004. The vast majority of the decrease in the option notional amount was related to terminations and maturities of short duration options which were hedging short-term repricing risk of our liabilities.

Included in the futures and forward rate contract amounts are $35.0 billion of forward purchase contracts of mortgage-backed securities and mortgage loans at December 31, 2005, settling from January 2006 to April 2006 with an average yield of 5.46 percent and $46.7 billion of forward purchase contracts of mortgage-backed securities and mortgage loans at December 31, 2004, that settled from January 2005 to February 2005 with an average yield of 5.26 percent. There were no forward sale contracts of mortgage-backed securities at December 31, 2005, compared to $25.8 billion at December 31, 2004, that settled from January 2005 to February 2005 with an average yield of 5.47 percent.

The following table [Exhibit 12A.2] includes derivatives utilized in our ALM process, including those designated as SFAS 133 hedges and those used as economic hedges that do not qualify for SFAS 133 hedge accounting treatment. The fair value of net ALM contracts decreased from $3.4 billion at December 31, 2004, to $(386) million at December 31, 2005. The decrease was attributable to decreases in the value of options, foreign exchange contracts and futures and forward rate contracts, partially offset by increases in the value of interest rate swaps. The decrease in the value of options was due to reduction in outstanding option positions due to terminations, maturities, and decreases in the values of remaining open options positions. The decrease in the value of foreign exchange contracts was due to the strengthening of the U.S. dollar against most foreign currencies during 2005. The decrease in the value of futures and forward rate contracts was due to the impact of increases in interest rates during 2005 on long futures and forward rate contracts.

MORTGAGE BANKING RISK MANAGEMENT

Interest rate lock commitments (IRLCs) on loans intended to be sold are subject to interest rate risk between the date of the IRLC and the date the loan is funded. Loans held-for-sale are subject to interest rate risk from the date of funding until the loans are sold to the secondary market. To

(continues)

EXHIBIT 12A.2 Bank of America's 2005 Asset and Liability Management Interest Rate and Foreign Exchange Contracts

		Expected Maturity							
December 31, 2005 (Dollars in millions, average estimated duration in years)	**Fair Value**	**Total**	**2006**	**2007**	**2008**	**2009**	**2010**	**Thereafter**	**Average Estimated Duration**
Receive fixed interest rate swaps (1)	$(1,390)								4.17
Notional amount		$108,985	$ 4,337	$13,080	$ 6,144	$39,107	$10,387	$35,930	
Weighted average fixed rate		4.62%	4.75%	4.66%	4.02%	4.51%	4.43%	4.77%	
Pay fixed interest rate swaps (1)	(408)								3.85
Notional amount		$102,281	$ 5,100	$55,925	$10,152	$ —	$ —	$31,104	
Weighted average fixed rate		4.61%	3.23%	4.46%	4.24%	—%	—%	5.21%	
Basis swaps	(644)								
Notional amount (3)		$ 17,806	$ 514	$ 174	$ 884	$ 2,839	$ 3,094	$10,301	
Option products (2)	1,349								
Notional amount (3)		57,246	—	—	57,246	—	—	—	
Foreign exchange contracts	909								

EXHIBIT 12A.2 *(Continued)*

December 31, 2005 (Dollars in millions, average estimated duration in years)	Fair Value	Expected Maturity							
		Total	2006	2007	2008	2009	2010	Thereafter	Average Estimated Duration
Notional amount (3)		57,246	—	—	57,246	—	—	—	
Foreign exchange contracts	909								
Notional amount		16,061	1,335	51	1,436	1,826	3,485	7,928	
Futures and forward rate contracts (4)	(202)								
Notional amount (3)		34,716	34,716	—	—	—	—	—	
ALM contracts	$ (386)								

(1) At December 31, 2005, $46.6 billion of the receive fixed swap notional amount and $41.9 billion of the pay fixed swap notional amount represented forward starting swaps that will not be effective until their respective contractual start dates. At December 31, 2004, $39.9 billion of the receive fixed swap notional amount and $75.9 billion of the pay fixed swap notional amount represented forward starting swaps that will not be effective until their respective contractual start dates.

(2) Option products include caps, floors, swaptions, and exchange-traded options on index futures contracts. These strategies may include option collars or spread strategies, which involve the buying and selling of options on the same underlying security or interest rate index.

(3) Reflects the net of long and short positions.

(4) Futures and forward rate contracts include Eurodollar futures, U.S. Treasury futures, and forward purchase and sale contracts.

hedge interest rate risk, we utilize forward loan sale commitments and other derivative instruments including purchased options. These instruments are used either as an economic hedge of IRLCs and loans held-for-sale, or designated as a cash flow hedge of loans held-for-sale, in which case their net-of-tax unrealized gains and losses are included in Accumulated OCI [other comprehensive income]. At December 31, 2005, the notional amount of derivatives hedging the IRLCs and loans held-for-sale was $26.9 billion. The notional amount of the IRLCs adjusted for fallout in the pipeline at December 31, 2005, was $4.3 billion. The amount of loans held-for-sale at December 31, 2005, was $6.1 billion.

We manage changes in the value of MSRs [mortgage servicing rights] by entering into derivative financial instruments and by purchasing and selling securities. MSRs are an intangible asset created when the underlying mortgage loan is sold to investors and we retain the right to service the loan. As of December 31, 2005, the MSR balance in Consumer Real Estate was $2.7 billion, or 13 percent higher than December 31, 2004.

We designate certain derivatives such as purchased options and interest rate swaps as fair value hedges of specified MSRs under SFAS 133. At December 31, 2005, the amount of MSRs identified as being hedged by derivatives in accordance with SFAS 133 was approximately $2.3 billion. The notional amount of the derivative contracts designated as SFAS 133 hedges of MSRs at December 31, 2005, was $33.7 billion. The changes in the fair values of the derivative contracts are substantially offset by changes in the fair values of the MSRs that are hedged by these derivative contracts.

In addition, we hold additional derivatives and certain securities (i.e., mortgage-backed securities) as economic hedges of MSRs, which are not designated as SFAS 133 accounting hedges. At December 31, 2005, the amount of MSRs covered by such economic hedges was $250 million.

Note 1—Summary of Significant Accounting Principles: Restatement

The Corporation is restating its historical financial statements for the years 2004 and 2003, for the quarters in 2005 and 2004, and other selected financial data for the years 2002 and 2001. These restatements and resulting revisions relate to the accounting treatment for certain derivative transactions under the Statement of Financial Accounting Standards (SFAS) No. 133, "Accounting for Derivative Instruments and Hedging Activities, as amended" (SFAS 133).

As a result of an internal review completed in the first quarter of 2006 of the hedge accounting treatment of certain derivatives, the Corporation concluded that certain hedging relationships did not adhere to the requirements of SFAS 133. The derivatives involved were used as hedges principally against changes in interest rates and foreign currency rates in the Asset and Liability Management (ALM) process.

A number of the transactions included in the restatement did not meet the strict requirements of the "shortcut" method of accounting under SFAS

133. Although these hedging relationships would have qualified for hedge accounting if the "long haul" method had been applied, SFAS 133 does not permit the use of the "long haul" method retroactively. Consequently, the restatement assumes hedge accounting was not applied to these derivatives and the related hedged item during the periods under review. A majority of these transactions related to internal interest rate swaps whereby the Corporation used its centralized trading desk to execute these trades to achieve operational effectiveness and cost efficiency. These interest rate swap trades were executed internally between the Corporation's treasury operations and the centralized trading desk. It has been the Corporation's long standing policy to lay these internal swaps off to an external party within a three-day period. In almost all cases, cash was exchanged (either paid or received) with the external counterparty to compensate for market rate movements between the time that the internal swap and the matching trade with the external counterparty were executed. Although the overall external trade, including the cash exchanged, was transacted at a fair market value of zero, the cash exchanged offset the fair market value of the external swap which was other than zero. Swaps with a fair market value other than zero at the inception of the hedge cannot qualify for hedge accounting under the shortcut method. Accordingly, the shortcut method was incorrectly applied for such derivative instruments.

The Corporation also entered into certain cash flow hedges which utilized the centralized trading desk to lay off the internal trades with an external party. The key attributes, including interest rates and maturity dates, of the internal and external trades were not properly matched. The Corporation performed the effectiveness assessment and measure of ineffectiveness on the internal trades instead of the external trades. As a result, such tests were not performed in accordance with the requirements of SFAS 133. Accordingly, hedge accounting was incorrectly applied for such derivative instruments.

The Corporation used various derivatives in other hedging relationships to hedge changes in fair value or cash flows attributable to either interest or foreign currency rates. Although these transactions were documented as hedging relationships at inception of the hedge, the up-front and ongoing effectiveness testing was not performed, documented, or assessed in accordance with SFAS 133. Adjustments to correct the accounting for those hedging relationships are included in the restated results. We do not believe that these adjustments are material individually or in the aggregate to our financial results for any reported period.

The following table [Exhibit 12A.3] sets forth the effects of the restatement adjustments on affected line items within our previously reported Consolidated Balance Sheet as of December 31, 2004.

(continues)

EXHIBIT 12A.3 Bank of America's Restatement of Its 2004 Balance Sheet for Misapplication of Hedge Accounting

	December 31, 2004	
(Dollars in millions)	**As Previously Reported**	**Restated**
Loans and leases, net of allowance for loan and lease losses	$ 513,211	$ 513,187
Total assets	1,110,457	1,110,432
Accrued expenses and other liabilities	41,243	41,590
Long-term debt	98,078	97,116
Total liabilities	1,010,812	1,010,197
Retained earnings	58,006	58,773
Accumulated other comprehensive income (loss)	(2,587)	(2,764)
Total shareholders' equity	99,645	100,235
Total liabilities and shareholders' equity	$1,110,457	$1,110,432

NOTES

1. 17 CFR 229.305.
2. T. Linsmeier and N. Pearson, "Value at Risk," *Financial Analysts Journal* (March/April 2000).
3. T. Beder, "VaR: Seductive But Dangerous," *Financial Analysts Journal* (September/October 1995).
4. S. Rajgopal, "Early Evidence on the Informativeness of the SEC's Market Risk Disclosures: The Case of Commodity Price Risk Exposures of Oil and Gas Producers," *Accounting Review* (July 1999); L. Hodder, "Reliability and Relevance of SEC Market Risk Disclosures by Commercial Banks," Working Paper, Stanford University, 2002; T. Linsmeier, D. Thornton, M. Venkatachalem, and M. Welker, "The Effect of Mandated Market Risk Disclosures on Trading Volume Sensitivity to Interest Rate, Exchange Rate, and Commodity Price Movements," *Accounting Review* (April 2002); and V. Sribunnak and M. Wong, "Foreign Exchange Sensitivity-Analysis Disclosures and Market-Based Risk Measures," Working Paper, University of Toronto June 2004.
5. P. Jorian, "How Informative Are Value-at-Risk Disclosures," *Accounting Review* (October 2002); C. Liu, S. Ryan, and H. Tan, "How Banks' Value-at-Risk Disclosures Predict their Total and Priced Risk: Effects of Bank Technical Sophistication and Learning over Time," *Review of Accounting Studies* (June/September 2004).
6. L. Hodder, L. Koonce, and M. McAnally, "SEC Market Risk Disclosures: Implications for Judgment and Decision Making," *Accounting Horizons* (March 2001).

CHAPTER 13

Lessors and Lease Accounting

This chapter describes lease accounting and disclosures as governed by Statement of Financial Accounting Standards (SFAS) No. 13, *Accounting for Leases* (1976), and its many amendments. The primary focus is on the limitations of the required accounting from the perspective of the financial analysis of lessors and how users of financial reports can remedy these limitations using the required disclosures. Specifically, SFAS No. 13 (1976) requires the application of one of two very different lease accounting methods depending on criteria pertaining to the extent to which the risk and return on the leased asset is borne by the lessee versus the lessor. Operating lease accounting treats leases as rental arrangements and so portrays lessors as capital asset management companies rather than as the financial institutions that they generally are. In contrast, capital lease accounting—which for lessors is more precisely referred to as either direct financing or sales-type lease accounting, depending on the nature of the leased asset and lease arrangements—treats leases as the joint sale and financing of all or a portion of the leased asset. The first step in the analysis of lessors is usually to recast their financial statements to treat operating leases as financing transactions. These adjusted financial statements are amenable to the financial analyses described in prior chapters for other financial institutions, although lessors are exposed to various distinct risk-return trade-offs that are discussed in this chapter.

For individuals and firms that desire to finance the acquisition of capital assets (i.e., land, buildings, and equipment), leasing is a common alternative to raising funds and purchasing the assets separately. According to the Equipment Leasing Association (ELA), $199 billion, or 27.6%, of the $722 billion of capital assets purchased in 2004 in the United States was financed through leases. The dollar volume of capital assets leased has decreased from a peak of $247 billion in 2000, and the percentage leased has decreased from an average level of 30.5% from 1990 to 2002.[1] These declines are primarily attributable to potential lessees avoiding the enhanced disclosure requirements for off–balance sheet financing and the pressure exerted by the Securities and Exchange Commission (SEC) on firms regarding accounting-motivated structured finance transactions discussed in Chapter 9. This percentage varies substantially across industries and types of capital assets, however, with leasing volume in 2004 being dominated by information technology (21%), transportation equipment (19%), construction equipment (10%), office machines (9%), medical equipment (7%), and agricultural machinery (6%), due to the mobility and commodity-like nature of and liquid resale markets for these assets.[2] To a lesser extent, leases also have been used to finance the acquisition of intangible assets, such as computer software.

Extrapolating from required footnote disclosures of minimum lease payments for a sample of 200 publicly traded firms in the United States (the 100 largest firms in terms of December 31, 2003, market capitalization and 100 randomly chosen firms, a sample dominated by lessees), the SEC estimates that $1.25 trillion of undiscounted operating lease commitments were not recognized on the balance sheets of publicly traded firms in the United States. This compares with the SEC's estimate of only $45 billion of undiscounted lease commitments under capital leases, implying a ratio of operating to capital leases of almost 28 to 1 and thus a strong preference of lessees for operating leases.[3] In contrast, the ELA estimates from its survey of lessors that only 10% of new business volume in 2004 was operating leases.[4] The dramatic differences in the SEC and ELA's statistics undoubtedly are attributable in part to firms' recent movement away from off–balance sheet financing, although one suspects that lessees may be more likely than lessors to record leases as operating and/or that the SEC and ELA's samples are inconsistent.

Dividing leases into micro ticket (<$25,000), small ticket ($25,000 to $250,000), middle market ($250,000 to $5 million), and large ticket (>$5 million), the ELA estimates that the volume of lease originations during 2004 was 6% micro ticket, 29% small ticket, 61% middle market, and only 4% large ticket. The percentage of leasing volume from large-ticket leases has declined dramatically from 37% in 2002, as potential large-ticket lessees have opted for on–balance sheet financing.[5] The larger the lease, the more likely its contractual terms are to be customized to meet the desires of the lessee and other parties to the lease contract. Large-ticket leases can be complex, structured transactions, although there has been a recent movement away from such structuring.

Virtually all leases mitigate risks for or partition risks among the parties to the lease contracts in ways that depend on the contracts' terms. The lessor (or a special-purpose entity [SPE]) retains legal title to the asset that is used by the lessee over the lease term. The lessee is obligated to make periodic payments over the lease term. Although these payments often are fixed and constant, like those on a fixed-rate loan, they may rise or fall deterministically, float with interest rates or specific price indices, be contingent on the revenue or profit generated on the leased property, or depend on the usage of the leased assets. Leases also frequently contain provisions that determine who bears the risk and return on the leased asset at the end of the lease term (the "residual value"), such as renewal or purchase options, nonrenewal penalties, and residual value guarantees. Third parties often provide financing or guarantee residual values.

Lessors are a type of finance company. As such, leasing is primarily an interest-rate-spread business, although this fact is often not clearly reflected in financial statements due to operating lease accounting. Lessors are frequently subject to substantial credit risk, because subprime borrowers often find leasing the most attractive or even the only way to finance capital asset purchases and because repossessing a leased asset often involves a substantial loss of value, especially when the asset is customized to the needs of the lessee. In this regard, lessors typically specialize in remarketing (i.e., releasing or selling) the assets they lease. Lessors also frequently provide services related to the assets they lease.

There are three broad types of lessor: (1) banks, (2) captives (usually subsidiaries of capital asset manufacturers), and (3) independents. In 2004, commercial banks generated 38% of lease originations, captives 25%, and independents 37%.[6] Banks engage almost exclusively in direct financing leases (including leveraged leases). In 2005, $136 billion, or 1.58%, of commercial bank assets were direct financing lease receivables, with the 100 largest banks holding almost all of these receivables.[7] IBM Global Financing, a segment of IBM, is a captive that primarily leases IBM products. Captives typically issue sales-type and operating leases. For example, IBM reports that IBM Global Financing holds a net investment in sales-type leases of $9.9 billion and equipment under operating leases of $1.8 billion in 2005. Independent lessors usually specialize in leasing and remarketing particular kinds of products, and they often provide business services related to the products they lease. For example, GATX Corporation primarily leases transportation equipment (railcars, jets, and ships). Independents typically primarily engage in operating leases. For example, GATX reports that it holds $3.5 billion of assets under operating leases compared to $337 million of finance lease receivables in 2005.

The distinction between the three types of lessor can be blurry. Most notably, General Electric Capital Services (GECS), a wholly owned subsidiary of General Electric, is the largest lessor in the United States. In its 2005 Form 10-K filing, GECS reports that it held $64 billion of lease receivables and $47.9 billion of assets under operating lease and had $11.6 billion of operating lease rentals in 2005. Although GECS might seem likely to be a captive of its parent General Electric, in fact it leases a broad range of capital assets, most of which are not produced by General Electric, and so it is an independent lessor. It also holds $228 billion of loans and so is a very large, bank-like financial institution.

It can be difficult for users of financial reports to observe the leasing activities of banks and captives in financial reports, due to aggregation with their other activities. Even wholly-owned captives must file separate public financial reports, however, if they have publicly traded debt securities. Moreover, parent companies often break out captives' performance in their financial reports to distinguish the financial and nonfinancial aspects of their business. Reflecting users' greater ability to observe the leasing activities of independents, GATX is the primary example used in this chapter.

Lessors, lessees, and other parties involved in leasing arrangements have been significantly affected by two recent standards discussed in Chapter 9: FASB Interpretation (FIN) No. 45, *Guarantor's Accounting and Disclosure Requirements for Guarantees, Including Indirect Guarantees of Indebtedness of Others—an Interpretation of FASB Statements No. 5, 57, and 107 and Rescission of FASB Interpretation No. 34* (2002) and FIN No. 46(R), *Consolidation of Variable Interest Entities—an Interpretation of ARB No. 51* (2003). FIN No. 45 (2002) requires that guarantors of residual values of leased assets and lease payments record these guarantees at fair value at inception and provide enhanced disclosures of these guarantees. FIN No. 46 (R) (2003) makes it much more likely that SPEs used in synthetic and other structured leases will be consolidated by the lessees. Even if a synthetic or other structured lease qualifies for operating lease accounting under SFAS No. 13 (1976), a close approximation to capital lease accounting results if the lessee consolidates the SPE, because the leased asset is recorded on the lessee's balance sheet.

The first section of this chapter describes the competitive advantages of leasing versus conventional financing of capital assets. The second section describes lease structures and contractual terms. The third section discusses risk-return trade-offs for lessors. The fourth section describes the main lease accounting methods. Although the primary focus in this section is on the accounting for lessors, the accounting for lessees also is described because the ability to accommodate lessees' desires for specific accounting treatments is one of the main competitive advantages of leasing. The fifth section discusses analysis issues raised by the differences between the main lease accounting methods for lessors. The sixth section briefly describes the nature of and accounting for three special types of lease transaction: (1) leveraged leases, (2) sale-leasebacks, and (3) synthetic leases. The seventh section analyzes the financial statements of GATX. The eighth section discusses disclosure requirements for lessors and shows how these disclosures can be used to recast accounting for operating leases to better capture the financial aspects of these leases, using GATX as an example. The final section briefly discusses a proposal in 2000 to capitalize essentially all leases and the 2006 decision of the Financial Accounting Standards Board (FASB) to undertake a project to comprehensively reconsider lease accounting that likely will attempt to refine that proposal.

COMPETITIVE ADVANTAGES OF LEASING

Leasing has at least five possible competitive advantages versus conventional financing of the cost of capital assets. First, leases deemed to be true leases rather than conditional sales under federal tax law (Rev. Proc. 2001-28, discussed in detail in the "Synthetic Leases" section) allow lessees that cannot efficiently use the tax benefits associated with the purchase of capital assets (e.g., due to net operating loss carryforwards or insufficient taxable income) to sell those benefits to lessors. Lessors defer taxes through accelerated depreciation of the capital assets. Tax deferral is naturally more valuable when inflation is higher, since higher inflation implies that taxes paid later are paid with lower value dollars. To the extent that lease markets are competitive, lessees recapture the tax benefits through lower lease payments.

As recently as 1985, tax benefits were the main competitive advantage of leasing. From 1981 to 1983, lessors could retain tax benefits while retaining essentially no other risk associated with capital assets (so-called safe harbor leasing), tax depreciation of capital assets was more accelerated than it is now, the purchase of virtually all capital assets received a 10% investment tax credit, the statutory federal corporate tax rate was 52%, and inflation was high. In 1984, safe harbor leasing was eliminated. The Tax Reform Act of 1986 made tax depreciation less accelerated and eliminated the investment tax credit. The corporate tax rate is now 35%, and inflation is low. For these reasons, the tax benefits associated with leasing are now much smaller than they were then. These tax benefits might reappear in the future, however, because they tend to be reinstated in economic downturns, when the government wants to stimulate capital spending in the economy. However, recent economic stimulus packages have been devoid of incentives favorable to the leasing industry. In fact, recent changes in tax law have reduced or eliminated the tax benefits from certain sale-leaseback-type transactions, referred to as sale-in/lease-out (SILO) and lease-in/lease-out (LILO) transactions, which are deemed to convey only a future interest in the capital asset to the purchaser, not the asset itself.

Second, leasing mitigates risks for or partitions risks among lessees, lessors, and third parties that provide financing or guarantee the residual value of the leased assets. Relatedly, it can yield efficiency gains regarding the management and disposal of the leased asset, especially when the asset is not firm specific. Some specific ways leasing does these things are:

- As a form of secured financing, leases protect lessors and third parties against default, which lowers lessees' cost of capital. This is important because lessees are often subprime credits.
- If the term of the lease is less than the whole life of the leased asset and the lessee does not guarantee the residual value in any fashion, then the lessee bears the risk and return on the asset only during the lease term, while the lessor or third parties bear the risk and return on the residual value of the asset.
- Since lessors usually actively engage in remarketing the products they lease, they are generally better able to manage the risk and return on the residual value of the leased asset than are lessees.
- Lease payments may be contingent in various ways that yield risk sharing.

Risk mitigation or partitioning is now one of the two primary competitive advantages of leasing. Eades and Marston provide evidence that options to renew or cancel leases and to purchase leased assets and the efficiency gains from leasing are primary incentives for leasing.[8]

Third, leasing often provides 100% financing of the cost of capital assets. This is possible in part because of the secured nature of lease financing. In addition, captive lessors have the incentive to move the product of their parents. This aspect of leasing conserves cash for lessees, who often are cash constrained.

Fourth, leasing provides a variety of conveniences for lessees. Lessees obtain access to the latest technology without having to dispose of their old technology. Lessors often provide expertise or services related to the leased assets. For example, transportation equipment of various sorts is commonly leased, in part because logistical and maintenance requirements for such equipment are relatively high.

Finally, leasing arrangements often are structured to obtain desired accounting treatments for the lessee (and to a lesser extent the lessor and third parties), usually but not always operating lease accounting. Operating lease accounting allows lessees to record no liability on the balance sheet for the financing of capital assets, which is particularly attractive in highly leveraged industries, such as airlines. In this regard, a considerable body of theoretical and empirical research demonstrates that the market views operating leases as economic liabilities of lessees, implying that operating lease accounting is economically nondescriptive.[9] In contrast, lessees in industries in which a preamortization earnings number (such as earnings before interest, taxes, depreciation, and amortization) is used to measure firm performance often prefer capital lease accounting, because amortization expense on the capital lease asset and interest expense on the capital lease liability are not included in this measure, while rental expense on operating leases is so included. Operating and capital lease accounting also have significantly different effects on the timing and classification of net income and on the classification of cash flow both for lessors and lessees.

LEASE STRUCTURES AND CONTRACTUAL TERMS

Large-ticket leases often are structured to obtain desired economic effects and to exploit tax and financial reporting rules for the lessee, lessor, and possibly a number of third parties, and so they can be very complex contractually. To manage these complexities, these leases often involve the creation of SPEs that hold legal title to the leased assets and that function as the nexus of contractual and financial relationships among the parties to the lease.

SPEs have two main roles in leasing. First, SPEs help protect the parties to the lease against the bankruptcy or nonperformance of any of the other parties. For example, if the lessor declares bankruptcy, then the lessee still can use the asset for the lease term without being subject to the bankruptcy proceedings of the lessor. If the lessee declares bankruptcy, then the lessor and third parties' claims are on the SPE, and so they are both effectively accorded (equal) status as secured lenders in the lessee's bankruptcy proceedings.

Second, SPEs can be structured in various ways to yield desired economic, tax, and financial reporting outcomes for the various parties to the lease. For instance:

- Lessors securitize minimum lease payments, which effectively requires SPEs. Lease securitization volume was $6.3 billion in 2004, with most of this volume resulting from private placements and commercial paper issuances.[10] Securitizations of capital lease payments fall under SFAS No. 140, *Accounting for Transfers and Servicing of Financial Assets and Extinguishments of Liabilities* (2000), and may yield sale accounting for the lessor, as discussed in Chapter 8.
- In "leveraged leasing," the SPE issues nonrecourse (to the lessor) debt to a third-party lender and passes the cash received from the third party to the lessor. As discussed in the "Leveraged Leases" section, the financial accounting rules for these leases allow the lessor to record the nonrecourse debt as a reduction of its lease receivable asset rather than as a liability, so that this financing is off–balance sheet for the lessor.
- Historically, SPEs were used in most "synthetic leases," in which the lessee retains the tax depreciation deductions associated with the leased asset but accounts for the lease an operating lease for financial reporting purposes. As discussed in the "Synthetic Leases" section, these leases exploit differences in tax and financial reporting rules. Synthetic leasing is less likely to involve SPEs after the issuance of FIN No. 46(R) (2003), however, because it is likely that lessees would have to consolidate the SPEs under that standard.
- The ownership and other variable interests of the SPE also can be partitioned in a way such that none of the parties to the lease contract consolidates the SPE for financial reporting purposes, so that the leased asset appears on no party's books. Since the issuance of FIN No. 46(R) (2003), nonconsolidation of the SPE by any party is likely to occur only for leases in which three or more parties (e.g., lessor, lessee, third-party financing, and residual value guarantor) bear significant portions of the expected losses and residual returns of the SPE, so that no party is deemed the primary beneficiary of the SPE.

Despite the significant roles that SPEs play in leasing, lessors' financial reports often provide little insight into their nature or even their existence. For example, in its 2005 Form 10-K filing, GATX provides this disclosure of its variable interest entities.

> GATX has ownership interests in certain investments that are considered Variable Interest Entities ("VIEs"). . . . GATX does not believe it is the primary beneficiary with respect to any of the VIEs. As a result, GATX does not consolidate these entities. GATX's maximum exposure to loss with respect to these VIEs is approximately $235.8 million of which $208.5 million was the aggregate carrying value of these investments recorded on the balance sheet at December 31, 2005.

Leases can result from two sequences of events. In standard leases, the lessor owns the asset originally and leases it to the lessee. In sale-leasebacks, the lessee owns the asset originally, sells it to the lessor, and then leases it back. In principle, the two sequences of events yield the same outcome. In practice, they tend to involve different types of lessees, assets, and lease terms. In particular, sale-leasebacks often involve assets that are constructed by or specialized to the needs of the lessee, and so the leasebacks are likely to be for the entire life of the leased assets. Sale-leasebacks also frequently involve lessees who need immediate liquidity or whose ability to use tax benefits has decreased. As discussed in the "Sale-Leasebacks" section, the accounting for these transactions limits the ability of the lessee to record an immediate gain on sale.

Leases involve payments over some term. The application of lease accounting standards generally depends on the minimum lease payments and term that are reasonably assured. The expected lease payments and term may be much greater than these minimum lease payments and term, however, for two main reasons:

1. Leases may include renewal options, and various aspects of the lease contract, the lessee, and the nature and market for the leased asset may work individually or together to make the exercise of renewal options probable but not necessarily reasonably assured. These aspects include declining real lease payments over time, nonrenewal penalties, residual value or other guarantees by the lessee, and the lessee's business need for the asset.
2. Leases may involve various kinds of contingent payments.

Residual value guarantees play a particularly important role in lease contracts, because they determine who bears the risk of the value of the asset at the end of the lease term. The guarantor may be the lessee or a third-party insurer paid an insurance premium by the lessee. These guarantees come in various forms. The guarantee may start from the first dollar of loss or be triggered only by a greater loss. For example, consider an asset that is expected to have a residual value of $100 but turns out to have a lower value. A first-dollar-of-loss guarantee might pay the lessor $100 minus the current value up to a maximum of $50. A less easily triggered guarantee might pay the lessor $50 minus the current value up to a maximum of $50. In both cases, the maximum guarantee is $50, but the first-dollar-of-loss guarantee is much more likely to be triggered, and so it subjects the guarantor to much more of the risk of the leased asset. For the most part, lease accounting rules do not distinguish different types of residual value guarantees by a given party, however.

In summary, users of financial reports should attempt to determine, to the extent possible, the nature of the structures and contractual terms of a lessor's leases. These factors affect how risks are partitioned among the parties to its lease contracts. They also may render the accounting nondescriptive.

LESSORS' RISKS

Lessors are exposed to various risks:

- The residual value of leased assets can be highly uncertain.
- The tax advantages of leasing are susceptible to unexpected changes in the tax code and inflation.
- Lease receivables whose payments do not float with interest rates yield interest rate risk in the same way as do fixed-rate loans.
- Lessors' ability to securitize lease receivables to raise funds and recognize gains on sale vary with economic conditions.
- Lease receivables are subject to credit risk, since lessees are often subprime credits and since the lessee is more likely to default when the leased asset value deteriorates
- Lessors are exposed to industry and macroeconomic cycles.
- Leasing is a competitive business.

Each of these risks is described next.

Lessors' primary risk is often uncertainty about the residual value of leased assets, which has a similar nature and importance as uncertainty about the value of residual securities for issuers in securitizations discussed in Chapter 8. Frequently a large part of lessors' profit comes from remarketing the asset at the end of the lease term. In a competitive leasing market, higher estimates of residual values yield lower lease payments, so the accurate estimation of residual values is often the key to long-term survival and profit ability. In this regard, residual value estimates can be subjective and highly uncertain, especially for assets that are sensitive to technological change and macroeconomic or industry conditions. The lessor is usually better off remarketing the asset in place to the existing lessee and in many cases loses on the lease if it cannot do so. Lessors also may guarantee residual values for third parties.

The importance of residual value estimates is illustrated by the recent experience of automobile lessors. The Association of Consumer Vehicles Lessors estimates that the average loss experienced by these lessors when vehicles were returned at the end of the lease (about 50% of the time) was \$1,672, \$2,592, and \$2,212 per vehicle in the years 1998, 1999, and 2000, respectively.[11] The industry recorded over \$10 billion on the residual values of leased automobiles in 2000 alone.[12] As a result of these losses, lessors have increased lease payments and lease terms. The ongoing travails of U.S. automobile manufacturers have recently led to enhanced lease incentives, however, which could augur a new round of losses. In this regard, General Motors (GM) states in a March 17, 2006 Form 8-K filing that it:

> intends to make certain adjustments to restate previously reported 2005 financial results. The restatement of quarterly financial results will primarily result from a material misstatement in the accounting for GM's

> portfolio of vehicles on operating lease with daily rental car entities, which occurred in the first quarter of 2005. This mis-statement related to the fact that GM's portfolio of vehicles on operating lease with daily rental car entities, which was impaired at lease inception, was prematurely revalued in 2005 to reflect increased anticipated proceeds upon disposal.

Other risks include the fact that the tax advantages of leasing are susceptible to unexpected changes in the tax code and inflation. As discussed, the tax benefits of leasing are currently relatively low, so they may constitute more of an upside than downside risk to lessors at this point.

Lease receivables that do not float with interest rates yield interest rate risk in the same way as do fixed-rate loans. Some lessors sell or securitize some or all of the minimum lease payments to third parties immediately or after a holding period, in part to mitigate interest rate risk.

Lessors also securitize lease receivables to raise funds and to recognize gains on sale. Insofar as they do this, they become fee-based rather than interest rate spread–based, in much the same way as mortgage banks discussed in Chapter 7.

Lessors' lease receivables are subject to the credit risk of lessees, who are often subprime credits. As a type of secured lender, lessors are protected by the value of the leased asset. However, the lessor's expected loss given default can be high despite the existence of collateral because default by the lessee often is associated with deterioration in the value of the leased asset and because technology assets subject to rapid obsolescence and intangible assets such as software are sometimes leased. Moreover, the extent of lessor's protection depends on whether the lease is deemed to be a true lease rather than security interest as specified in the Uniform Commercial Code (UCC), with the former giving greater rights to the lessor in the event of the lessee's bankruptcy. To be a true lease under the UCC, the lessee must have certain rights to terminate lease payments, the lessor must retain a meaningful residual interest in the leased asset, and the lease must meet an economic realities test.[13] Independent lessors' tendency to concentrate in specific industries reduces their ability to diversify credit risk.

Lessors may also be exposed to the credit risk of residual value guarantors and other parties. This is most likely for captive lessors whose parents guarantee residual values or provide other incentives. An example of such a lessor is General Motors Acceptance Corporation (GMAC), which states in its 2005 Form 10-K filing that it:

> bear[s] the risk of loss to the extent that the value of a leased vehicle upon remarketing is below the projected residual value of the vehicle at the time the lease contract is signed. However, these projected values may be upwardly adjusted as a marketing incentive if General Motors considers an above-market residual appropriate to encourage consumers to lease vehicles. Such residual support by GM results in a lower monthly lease payment by the consumer. General Motors reimburses

> us to the extent remarketing sales proceeds are less than the residual value set forth in the lease contract at lease termination. In addition to GM residual support, in some cases, GMAC may provide residual support on leases to further encourage consumers to lease certain vehicles.
>
> In addition to the residual support arrangement, GM shares in residual risk on all off-lease vehicles sold by auction. We and GM share a portion of the loss when resale proceeds fall below the contract residual values on vehicles sold at auction. GM reimburses us for a portion of the difference between proceeds and the contract residual value (up to a specified limit).
>
> Under what we refer to as pull ahead programs, consumers are encouraged to terminate leases early in conjunction with the acquisition of a new GM vehicle. As part of these programs, we waive the customer's remaining payment obligation and, under most programs, GM compensates us for the foregone revenue from the waived payments. Additionally, since these programs generally accelerate our remarketing of the vehicle, the sale proceeds are typically higher than otherwise would have been realized had the vehicle been remarketed at lease contract maturity. The reimbursement from GM for the foregone payments is, therefore, reduced by the amount of this benefit.

Lessors are exposed to industry and macroeconomic cycles. To the extent that lessors provide industry-specific services, they are exposed to the performance of these industries. Aggregate investment in capital assets tends to follow macroeconomic cycles.

Finally, leasing is a competitive business. Cost efficiency in obtaining and processing business is critical, especially in the high-transactions-volume, small-ticket market.

LEASE ACCOUNTING METHODS

Lease accounting is primarily governed by SFAS No. 13 (1976), although this standard has been repeatedly amended by subsequent standards, interpretations, and technical bulletins published by the FASB and by consensuses, issues, and topics published by the FASB's Emerging Issues Task Force (EITF). Most accounting observers view lease accounting as an unsatisfactory patchwork that sometimes yields complex lease transactions structured to obtain nondescriptive accounting outcomes. This section describes the main lease accounting methods, focusing on the accounting by lessors. The accounting by lessees is also described, since their desire for certain accounting treatments is one of the main competitive advantages of leasing. Unless stated otherwise, SFAS No. 13 (1976) is the source of the accounting rules discussed.

In some cases it can be difficult to determine whether contracts constitute leases of capital assets governed by SFAS No. 13 (1976) or service contracts governed by other accounting standards. For example, do contracts to transport energy or provide telecommunications services over networks constitute leases of portions of those networks? EITF 01-8, *Determining Whether an Arrangement Contains a Lease,* states that leases involve the use of specific capital assets, while service contracts allow the provider to employ substitute means to provide the services.

Leases of capital assets are often bundled with the provision of maintenance and other services by the lessor to the lessee. This raises issues regarding the proper timing and amount of revenue recognition by the lessor, because the separate elements of the bundle may be provided at different times and the contractually specified payments by the lessee for these elements generally are substitutable. SFAS No. 13 (1976) requires minimum lease payments and payments for executory costs such as maintenance to be distinguished and accounted for separately, as discussed in the next section. EITF 00-21, *Revenue Arrangements with Multiple Deliverables,* generally requires that the payments for other services be distinguished from the payments for lease and maintenance based on their relative fair values, and accounted for separately.

Lease Term and Minimum Lease Payments

Definitions of the lease term and minimum lease payments determine which lease accounting method to apply to a given lease. SFAS No. 98, *Accounting for Leases* (1988), defines the lease term as the fixed noncancellable term of the lease plus all periods up to and including those:

- Covered by bargain renewal options (i.e., renewal options that involve rentals sufficiently below the fair market value of the leased asset so that renewal is reasonably assured).
- For which failure to renew the lease imposes a penalty such that renewal is reasonably assured at inception. This penalty includes factors outside the lease, including a pressing business need for the leased asset.
- Governed by renewal options in which the lessee guarantees, directly or indirectly, the lessor's debt associated with the leased property.
- In which the lease can be renewed at the lessor's option.

A lease is deemed noncancellable if it is cancellable only upon the occurrence of a remote contingency, only with the permission of the lessor, only if the lessee enters into a new lease with the same lessor, or only if the lessee incurs a cancellation penalty such that continuation of the lease is reasonably assured at inception. This definition implies that the lease term includes renewal options for which exercise is reasonably assured but not those for which exercise is only probable. Thus, the lease term for accounting purposes may be far shorter than the expected life of the leasing relationship.

Minimum lease payments for the lessee are defined as the payments the lessee is required to make over the lease term in connection with the leased property. These minimum lease payments include guarantees by the lessee of the residual value of the leased asset and penalties the lessee is required to make at the end of the lease term if the lease is not renewed. These minimum lease payments do not include contingent rentals, guarantees by the lessee of the lessor's debt, or executory costs such as maintenance, taxes, and insurance, and so they may be much lower than expected lease payments. Minimum lease payments for the lessor are minimum lease payments for the lessee plus third-party guarantees of residual values and rental payments beyond the lease term.

Determining the Lease Accounting Method

The criteria for determining whether operating or capital lease accounting should be applied to a lease are based on the idea that real assets are not divisible and that the party that bears most of the risk and rewards of the leased asset should have the real asset on its balance sheet. Specifically, capital lease accounting should be applied when the lessee predominantly bears the risk and return on the leased asset, and operating lease accounting should be applied otherwise. SFAS No. 13 (1976) attempts to apply this idea by distinguishing operating and capital leases using bright-line criteria described next.

Specifically, lessees should classify leases that meet one or more of these four criteria as capital leases:

1. The lease transfers ownership of the leased asset to the lessee at the end of the lease term.
2. The lease contains a bargain purchase option.
3. The lease term is 75% or more of the estimated remaining economic life of the leased asset, unless the lease term begins in the last 25% of the total estimated economic life of the leased asset. This condition does not apply to leases of land, since land has infinite life.
4. The present value of the minimum lease payments is 90% or more of fair value of the leased asset. This condition also does not apply to leases of land, presumably because capital land leases with finite term would cause (the right to use) land to be amortized. This criterion also does not apply to leases initiated in the last 25% of the life of the leased asset.

Lessees should account for all other leases as operating leases.

All of these criteria also apply to lessors' lease classifications. The 90% of fair value criterion may lead to different conclusions by the lessee and lessor as to whether the lease should be accounted for as an operating lease or a capital lease, however, because:

- Guarantees of minimum lease payments by third parties are included in minimum lease payments for lessors but not for lessees. This could lead to the lessor accounting for the lease as a capital lease while the lessee accounts for the lease as an operating lease, so that the leased asset appears on neither of the parties' books.

- The interest rate used to estimate the present value may differ for the lessee and the lessor. The lessor should use the implicit interest rate that equates the present value of the minimum lease payments and the estimated unguaranteed residual value of the leased asset to the fair value of the leased asset. This implicit interest rate is not necessarily known to the lessee, since it may not know either the fair value or the estimated unguaranteed residual value of the asset; if not, the lessee should use its incremental borrowing rate instead.

Lessors should classify any lease that meets one or more of the four criteria above and both of the following criteria as a capital lease:

1. The collectibility of the minimum lease payments is reasonably predictable.
2. No significant uncertainties exist about unreimbursable costs for the lessor.

Lessors should classify all other leases as operating. The addition of these two criteria for lessors implies that lessors are less likely to treat leases as capital leases than lessees, all else being equal.

The bright-line nature of the 75% of economic life and 90% of fair value criteria allows leases to be structured to obtain the desired accounting treatments. For example, if the lessee desires operating lease accounting but also to lease the asset for most of its life, then the lease will be structured so that it has a term of no more than 74.9% of the life of the asset and a present value of the cash payments of no more than 89.9% of the fair value of the asset. This lease is economically almost identical to a lease of the same asset for 75% of its life or with cash payments for 90% of its fair value, which would receive capital lease accounting.

Operating Lease Accounting

Accounting. Operating lease accounting treats leases essentially like rent. Assuming that rental payments are a constant amount per period over the life of a lease, the lessor (lessee) records rent revenue (expense) in each period equal to the amount of the lease payments attributable to the lessee's use of the leased asset that period. The lessor (lessee) makes normal deferrals or accruals of lease revenue (expense) depending on the timing of lease payments relative to the recognition of income in each period. Ignoring such minor accruals of lease expense, operating leases provide off–balance sheet financing for lessees.

Lessors retain the fixed assets under lease on their balance sheets. They depreciate these assets over time using their normal depreciation methods. This aspect of operating lease accounting is unnecessary and unfortunate, because lessors must estimate the residual value of the leased assets in order to determine the lease payments they require. It would be preferable to require lessors to depreciate leased assets to their residual values over the lease term.

Some minor accounting complexities arise if lease payments are not constant over the lease term. If lease payments change in a deterministic fashion (e.g., there are scheduled rent increases or "rent holidays" in which the lessee is not required to make lease payments), then FASB Technical Bulletin (FTB) No. 85-3, *Accounting for Operating Leases with Scheduled Rent Increases* (1985), states that lessors (lessees) should record revenue (expense) in equal amounts each period unless "another systematic and rational allocation basis is more representative of the time pattern in which the leased property is physically employed. Using factors such as the time value of money, anticipated inflation, or expected future revenues to allocate scheduled rent increases is inappropriate because these factors do not relate to the time pattern of the physical usage of the leased property." This requirement implies that lessors (lessees) record deferred revenues (prepaid assets) when lease payments decline over the life of the lease and accrued revenues (accrued expenses) when lease payments rise over the life of the lease.

At least 144 lessees (mostly retailers and hospitality firms) restated their financial statements during late 2004–early 2005 for misapplication of FTB No. 85-3 to rent holidays.[14] Most of these restatements occurred shortly after a February 7, 2005, letter from the chief accountant of the SEC to the American Institute of Certified Public Accountants (AICPA).

Lessors (lessees) should record lease revenue (expense) for contingent rental payments when the factors causing these payments occur. In this respect, the portion of a lease associated with contingent rentals is always treated as an operating lease, even if the portion of the lease associated with minimum lease payments is accounted for as a capital lease.

Example. Assume that an automobile with a fair value of $30,000 and an expected useful life of 10 years is leased on January 1 for $5,000 per year payable at the beginning of each year for two years. There is no transfer of ownership or bargain purchase option. Clearly, none of the conditions for capital lease accounting for the lessee is met. Thus, the lease is accounted for as an operating lease. Ignoring deferrals of lease expense and revenue during each year, the journal entries in each of the two years of the lease term are:

for the lessee:		
lease expense (− income)	5000	
cash (− asset)		5000
for the lessor:		
cash (+ asset)	5000	
lease revenue (+ income)		5000
depreciation expense (− income)	x	
automobile (− asset)		x

No specific amounts are recorded for depreciation expense, since the lessor applies the same methods for depreciating assets as if it held the asset for its own use, and these methods have not been specified. Moreover, the lessor's cost has not been specified; this cost would be the $30,000 fair value if the lessor acquired the automobile in the open market and the lessor's production cost if it manufactured the automobile.

Capital Lease Accounting

Capital lease accounting treats a lease like separate purchase and financing of the asset. The accounting for lessees and lessors is less symmetrical than it is under operating lease accounting for several reasons, the main one being that the lessor has to account for the estimated unguaranteed residual value of the leased asset at the end of the lease term while the lessee does not.

Lessees. At the initiation of the lease, the lessee records a lease asset and a lease liability on its balance sheet equal to the present value of the minimum lease payments, or the fair value of the asset if it is known and less than that amount. Over the life of the lease, the lessee amortizes the leased asset to its expected value at the end of the lease term (this value includes guarantees of the residual value by the lessee, among other items) using its normal amortization policies. The lessee also records interest expense on the lease liability on its income statement. Cash payments in excess of interest expense reduce the principal of the lease liability. Exhibit 13.1 depicts the T accounts for lessees' capital lease assets and liabilities.

Lessors. Strictly speaking, the term "capital lease accounting" does not apply to lessors; it has been used up to this point as convenient shorthand for two lease accounting methods for lessors that treat leases as financing transactions: direct financing and sales-type lease accounting. Which method

EXHIBIT 13.1 Lessees' Capital Lease T Accounts

Lease Asset		Lease Liability	
beginning balance			beginning balance
+ npv of minimum lease payments on new leases	− amortization expense	− cash payments	+ npv of minimum lease payments on new leases
= ending balance			+ interest expense
			= ending balance

applies depends on the nature of the leased asset and the lease arrangements. If the leased asset is new and not produced by the lessor, then direct financing lease accounting applies, and the lease is treated as a pure financing transaction. Under direct financing lease accounting, the lessor removes the fixed asset from its books and replaces it with a net lease receivable of the same amount. As noted, the implicit interest rate on the lease is calculated as the rate for which the net lease receivable equals the present value of the minimum lease payments and the expected unguaranteed residual value of the lease asset. Because expected contingent rentals during the lease term are not included in this calculation, the implicit rate is lower than the economic rate that applies to the lease to the extent that contingent rentals have value. Using the implicit rate, the lessor records interest revenue on the net lease receivable over the term of the lease. Cash receipts in excess of interest revenue reduce the principal of the lease receivable.

In contrast, lessors that lease their own products or that are releasing previously leased assets apply sales-type accounting. Sales-type accounting treats the lease as a sale of the asset by the lessor to the lessee. The lessor records sales and cost of goods sold when the lease is initiated. The lessor also records a lease receivable and interest revenue in the same way as for a direct financing lease, although the net lease receivable exceeds the leased inventory removed from the lessor's books by the amount of gross margin recorded.

SFAS No. 13 (1976) requires lessors to report separately the gross lease receivable (the undiscounted minimum lease payments and unguaranteed residual value) and unearned interest income (the difference between the gross lease receivable and the discounted lease payments and unguaranteed residual value). Although this presentation conceivably provides some information about the duration of the lease, far superior information about lease duration is provided in the footnotes, as discussed in the "Lease Disclosures" section. Accordingly, for simplicity, this section describes only the accounting for the net lease receivable.

SFAS No. 13 (1976) also requires lessors to review the estimated unguaranteed residual value at least annually. If the estimate has decreased and the decrease is other than temporary, then the lessor must write down the lease receivable and record the loss immediately.

The T account for lessors' net lease receivables is depicted in Exhibit 13.2. For simplicity, the effects of credit losses, residual value write-downs, and sales or securitizations of lease receivables are ignored. These effects are the similar to those described for loans in Chapters 5 and 8.

Example. Assume that the same automobile in the earlier operating lease example is leased for eight years, so that the 75% of economic life criterion for capital lease accounting applies. Assume that the interest rate on the lease is 10% and the estimated unguaranteed residual value of the automobile at the end of the lease term is $4,287.18, so that the present value of the

EXHIBIT 13.2 Lessors' Net Lease Receivable T Account

Net Lease Receivable	
beginning balance	
+ npv of minimum lease payments and estimated unguaranteed residual value on new leases	− cash receipts
+ interest revenue	− receipt of residual value
= ending balance	

estimated unguaranteed residual value at the beginning of the lease term is $2,000. Assume the annual lease payment is $4,771.32, so that the present value of these payments is $28,000. The sum of the present values of the payments and the residual value is $30,000, the fair value of the automobile. The lessee amortizes the lease asset on a straight-line basis over the eight-year life of the lease, or $3,500/year. The accounting is described both for the case when the lessor is the automobile manufacturer with a cost of producing the automobile of $25,000 (so that sales-type accounting applies) and for the case when the lessor is an unaffiliated finance company (so that direct financing lease accounting applies).

The lessee's journal entries over the first two years of the lease are:

for the lessee:

Date	Account	Debit	Credit
1/1/1	lease asset (+ asset)	28000	
	lease liability (+ liability)		28000
	lease liability (− liability)	4771.32	
	cash (− asset)		4771.32
	(*note:* lease liability balance = 23,228.68)		
12/31/1	amortization expense (− income)	3500	
	lease asset (− asset)		3500
	interest expense (− income)	2322.87	
	lease liability (+ liability)		2322.87
1/1/2	lease liability (− liability)	4771.32	
	cash (− asset)		4771.32
	(*note:* lease liability balance = 20,780.23)		
12/31/2	amortization expense (− income)	3500	
	lease asset (− asset)		3500
	interest expense (− income)	2078.02	
	lease liability (+ liability)		2078.02

The journal entries for the remaining six years have the same structure. The lease asset and lease liability amortize over time just like any other fixed asset and financial liability, respectively, and they both have zero balances at the end of the eight-year term of the lease.

The journal entries for a direct financing lessor are:

direct financing lessor:

1/1/1	lease receivable (+ asset)	30000	
	equipment (− asset)		30000
	cash (+ asset)	4771.32	
	lease receivable (− asset)		4771.32
	(*note:* net lease receivable balance = 25,228.68)		
12/31/1	lease receivable (+ asset)	2522.87	
	interest revenue (+ income)		2522.87
1/1/2	cash (+ asset)	4771.32	
	lease receivable (− asset)		4771.32
	(*note:* net lease receivable balance = 22,980.23)		
12/31/2	lease receivable (+ asset)	2298.02	
	interest revenue (+ income)		2298.02

The journal entries for the remaining six years have the same structure. The net lease receivable is amortized over time in the same way as any other interest-earning financial asset, even though the balance of this receivable includes the present value of the estimated unguaranteed residual value of the leased asset, which is not really a financial asset. The value of the net lease receivable at the end of the lease term but prior to the receipt of the residual value is $4,287.18, the estimated unguaranteed residual value of the leased asset.

The journal entries at initiation for a sales-type lessor are:

sales-type lessor:

1/1/1	lease receivable (+ asset)	30000	
	sales (+ income)		28000
	inventory (− asset)		2000
	cost of goods sold (− income)	23000	
	inventory (− asset)		23000
	cash (+ asset)	4771.32	
	lease receivable (− asset)		4771.32

The journal entries after the initiation of the lease are the same for direct financing and sales-type lessors, because they have identical net lease receivables, all else being equal.

At the initiation of the lease, the leased asset is the inventory of the sales-type lessor, whereas it was equipment for the direct financing lessor. The $25,000 cost of the inventory is divided into the $2,000 present value of the estimated unguaranteed residual value and the remaining $23,000. The

$23,000 is recorded as cost of goods sold, and the $2,000 is recorded as an addition to the net lease receivable. Thus, margins on sale are very sensitive to estimates of unguaranteed residual values for sales-type lessors.

Other Recent Restatements by Lessees for Misapplication of Lease Accounting

In addition to the restatements for rent holidays mentioned earlier, during late 2004–early 2005 at least 96 lessees restated their financial statements for recording construction allowances provided by lessors as a reduction of leasehold assets rather than as deferred income, as required by SFAS No. 13 (1976) and FTB No. 88-1, *Issues Relating to Accounting for Leases*. At least 93 lessees restated for amortizing leasehold improvements over a period longer than the lease term, in violation of SFAS No. 13 (1976).[15] Most of these restatements also occurred shortly after a February 7, 2005, letter from the chief accountant of the SEC to the AICPA.

ANALYSIS ISSUES REGARDING LEASE ACCOUNTING METHODS

This section describes the effects of different lease accounting methods on lessors' financial statements. For simplicity, the fact that generally accepted accounting principles (GAAP) nominally require a given lease to be accounted for as one of operating, direct financing, or sales-type is ignored, and the effects of accounting for the same lease using different methods are demonstrated. This is a reasonable exercise, because slight changes in lease structure around the bright-line criteria described in the "Determining the Lease Accounting Method" section cause a lease to be accounted for using different methods. The primary comparison made in this section is between operating and direct financing lease accounting, which are the possible lease accounting methods for leases of new assets by lessors that do not produce the leased asset. Operating and sales-type lease accounting, which are the possible lease accounting methods for lessors who produce the leased asset or for leases of previously leased assets, are compared more briefly.

Balance Sheet Amounts

The balance sheet of a lessor using operating lease accounting includes a fixed asset, while the balance sheet of a lessor using direct financing lease accounting includes a net lease receivable. At lease initiation, the amounts of the fixed asset and net lease receivable will normally equal the fair value of the new leased asset, but afterward the amounts of the fixed asset and net lease receivable differ. Specifically, fixed assets under operating leases are never depreciated slower than on a straight-line basis. In contrast, assuming constant lease payments, the lease receivable amortizes slowly at the beginning of the life of the lease and faster at the end of the life of the lease. Thus, direct financing lessors generally have larger assets than do operating lessors, all else being equal.

Exhibit 13.3 graphs a lessor's net asset for a single lease of a new asset with constant payments each period during the lease term that is treated as either an operating lease or a direct financing lease. In this exhibit, the operating lease asset is assumed to be depreciated to its residual value over the life of the lease; this assumption has an important implication for the amount of income recognized over the lease term. The operating lease asset also is assumed to be depreciated on a straight-line basis, although in practice it could be depreciated on a more accelerated basis, which would accentuate the difference in the balances of the operating lease asset and the net lease receivable.

If the lessor produces the leased asset, then operating lease accounting yields a fixed asset that is initially recorded at production cost. In contrast, sales-type lease accounting yields a net lease receivable at fair value at the initiation of the lease. Thus, the balance sheet amount of the net lease receivable in a sales-type lease exceeds the amount of the operating lease fixed asset even at initiation, assuming the fair value of the leased asset exceeds its production cost.

Income Statement Amounts

The assumption depicted in Exhibit 13.3—that the operating lessor depreciates the leased asset to its residual value over the lease term—implies that

EXHIBIT 13.3 Lessor's Book Value of Net Assets over Lease Term (Assuming Operating Lease Asset Depreciated to Residual Value on a Straight-Line Basis over Lease Term)

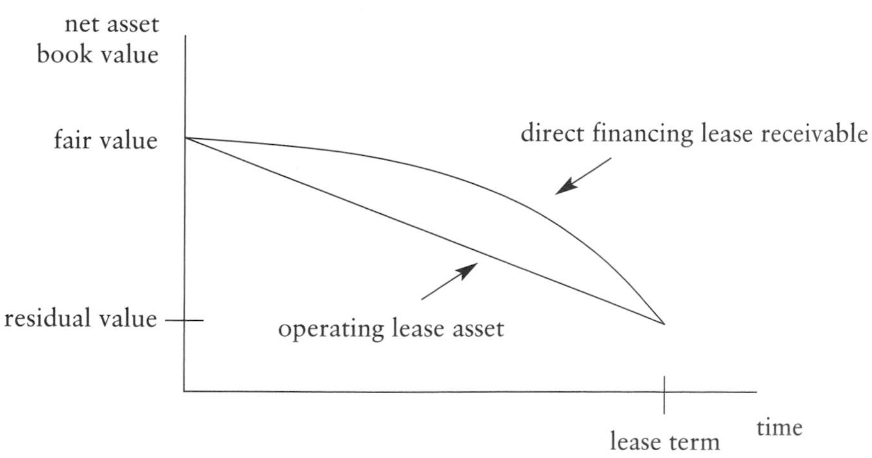

the total amount of net income recognized over the lease term is the same for operating and direct financing lessors, all else being equal. Specifically, the total income for an operating lessor equals the sum of the cash receipts minus the sum of the depreciation on the leased asset. The total income for a direct financing lessor equals the sum of the interest revenue on the lease receivable. The assumption implies that the total depreciation on the operating lessor's fixed asset is the same as the total principal reduction on the direct financing lessor's lease receivable. Thus, interest revenue under direct financing lease accounting equals rental revenue minus depreciation expense under operating lease accounting. As noted, operating lessors' actual depreciation policies are not constrained by this assumption, so the total amount of income recognized over the lease term generally differs for operating and direct financing lessors. An operating lessor that depreciates the asset above (below) its residual value over the lease term will record more (less) total income over the lease term than a direct financing lessor.

The total income over the life of the lease is also the same under operating and sales-type lease accounting under the same assumption already discussed. This assumption implies the gross profit on the asset is recorded gradually over the lease term under operating lease accounting, because depreciation expense on the operating lease asset is less than the principal reduction on the net lease receivable for the sales-type lease by exactly the amount of the gross profit.

Income Statement Timing

Operating lessors record lease revenue equal to the lease receipts applicable to the period as well as depreciation expense on the leased asset. Assuming that lease payments are constant over the lease term and recognizing that depreciation is never slower than straight line, net income is recognized evenly or is back-loaded over the lease term. In contrast, direct financing lessors record interest revenue on the net lease receivable. Unless the lease has balloon features, interest revenue is greatest in the first period of the lease and decreases over time as the net lease receivable amortizes. Thus, lessors recognize net income earlier under direct financing lease accounting than operating lease accounting, all else being equal. Exhibit 13.4 graphs a lessor's net income for a single lease of a new asset with constant payments each period during the lease term that is treated as either a direct financing lease or an operating lease. In this exhibit, the operating lease asset is assumed to be depreciated to its residual value over the life of the lease, so that the total amount of net income is the same under the two lease accounting methods.

The only difference between income for sales-type and direct financing lessors is the gross profit recognized by sales-type lessors at the initiation of leases. Thus, sales-type lease accounting further front-loads net income relative to operating lease accounting, assuming positive gross profit.

EXHIBIT 13.4 Lessor's Net Income over Lease Term (Assuming Operating Lease Asset Depreciated to Residual Value on a Straight-Line Basis over Lease Term)

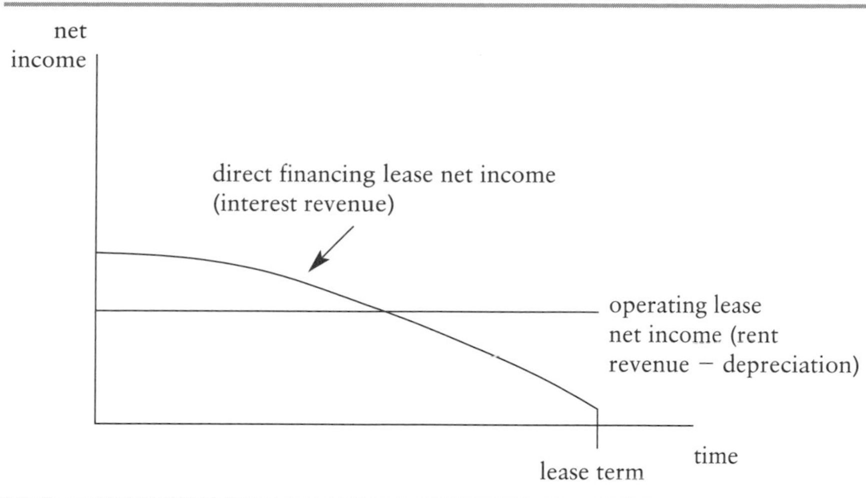

Cash Flow Statement Classification

The lease accounting method used for financial reporting (as opposed to tax reporting) does not affect the amount or timing of cash flows, but it has a dramatic effect on the classification of cash flows. Lease receipts on operating leases are classified as operating cash flows. Lease receipts on direct financing and sales-type leases are classified as operating for the interest revenue portion and as investing for the principal portion. Thus, operating lessors have higher operating cash flow than do direct financing lessors, all else being equal. This difference widens over the term of the lease as more of the lease receipt is classified as principal. In addition, for sales-type leases, at lease initiation there is an operating cash flow for the amount of the gross margin recognized and a net investing cash outflow for exactly the same amount. Due to the classification of gross margin within operating cash flow, sales-type lessors also may have high operating cash flow, especially lessors of high-margin assets.

There are substantial comparability issues in analyzing lessors that use operating, direct financing, and sales-type lease accounting to different extents. Users of financial reports can recast the financial statements to reflect an approximation to capital lease accounting for operating leases using the required disclosures discussed in the "Lease Disclosures" section.

SPECIAL LEASE TRANSACTIONS

This section briefly describes the nature and accounting for three special lease transactions—leveraged leases, sale-leasebacks, and synthetic leases—without going into the numerous structural details and accounting complexities involved. The interested reader can find examples of the accounting for leveraged leases and sale-leasebacks in GAAP guides.

Leveraged Leases

A leveraged lease is a direct financing lease in which the lessor obtains financing collateralized by the leased asset from a third party. In a typical leveraged lease, an SPE holds title to the leased asset and has the right to receive the minimum lease payments from the lessee. The third-party financing has recourse to the SPE that holds title to the leased asset but not to the lessor. The lessor usually retains all the tax benefits on the leased asset, may retain some portion of the minimum lease payments, and usually retains most or all of the unguaranteed residual value. Leveraged leasing is essentially a way for the lessor to diminish the financing aspects of leasing and to concentrate on the tax benefits and residual value aspects. Leveraged leasing also raises funds for future lease originations in much the same way as securitization of lease receivables. All else being equal, lessees are unaffected by whether their leases are leveraged.

For accounting purposes, a leveraged lease is a direct financing lease that meets these three criteria:

1. The third-party financing must be for at least 50% of the fair value of the leased asset (it is usually for considerably more).
2. The third-party financing must be nonrecourse to the lessor.
3. The lessor's net investment in the lease must first fall and then rise over the lease term, as will be described.

Leases meeting these criteria are accounted for using special leveraged lease accounting. On the balance sheet, the lessor's lease receivable is recorded net of the nonrecourse financing. This off–balance sheet treatment of the third-party financing generally is not problematic, given its nonrecourse nature. In addition, a separate asset is recorded for the expected unguaranteed residual value that is retained by the lessor (and, prior to its elimination, for the investment tax credit), in order to highlight the relative importance of this aspect of the lease for the lessor.

The requirement that the lessor's net investment in the lease must decrease early in the life of the lease and increase late in the life of the lease reflects the idea that leveraged lease accounting applies only when tax benefits and residual values dominate the value of the lease to the lessor. Depreciation tax benefits (and previously investment tax credits) are realized early in the life of the lease, while the residual value is received at the end of the lease. The value of the lease receivable decreases over the period that the tax benefits are realized and then increases as the present value of the residual value increases with the passage of time. A negative net investment may result during the lease term, which means the value of the nonrecourse financing exceeds the value of the lessor's remaining benefits on the lease. It also implies that the lessor must contribute funds to the SPE at some point during the lease.

Net income on leveraged leases is recognized in proportion to the lessor's net investment on the lease, but only in the periods the net investment is positive; in other periods, the lease has no effect on net income. Complex, iterative calculations are required to calculate both net income and the net investment on the lease. Two main steps are involved in this calculation:

1. The lessor must calculate the net cash flows on the lease, taking into account the tax benefits. The total net cash flows equal the total net income that will be recognized over the lease.
2. The lessor must calculate the yield on the net investment in the periods that it is positive that allocates the total net cash flows to net income over the life of the lease.

There is no good conceptual reason for the positive net investment condition in the second step, which implies that the calculated yield deviates from a market interest rate and the net investment on the lease differs from the present value of the remaining net cash flows. Unfortunately, it is very difficult for users of financial reports to undo this conceptually problematic accounting.

Regarding the second step, SFAS No. 13 (1976) and FASB Staff Position (FSP) No. FAS 13-2, *Accounting for a Change or Projected Change in the Timing of Cash Flows Relating to Income Taxes Generated by a Leveraged Lease Transaction* (2006), state that the estimated residual value and other important assumptions affecting total net income, including the timing of the cash flows related to taxes, should be reviewed at least annually. If the estimated residual value is other-than-temporarily impaired or other important assumptions change, then the yield on the net investment should be recalculated as of the inception of the lease using actual cash flows up to the date of recalculation and projected cash flows therefter.

Sale-Leasebacks

Lessors often buy the leased asset from lessees and then lease it back to them. No accounting problems are posed by sale-leasebacks for lessors in their role as lessors. Lessors account for purchases and leasebacks separately, using normal lease accounting rules discussed earlier. In contrast, accounting rules restrict when and how the lessee can recognize a gain on the sale. In this regard, lessors often become lessees by selling and leasing back the assets that they lease. They do this to raise financing or to sell tax benefits they cannot use to third parties.

The general rule is that any gain or loss on sale for the lessee is deferred and recognized over the life of the lease in proportion to amortization expense if the leaseback is classified as a capital lease and in proportion to lease payments if the leaseback is classified as an operating lease. Exceptions exist when the leaseback is for less than substantially all of the property sold. The entire gain or loss is recognized immediately if the leaseback is for 10% or less of the assets sold, while a pro rata portion of the gain or loss is recognized immediately if the leaseback is for less than 90% of the assets sold. Sale-leaseback accounting involves many specific rules regarding the reasonableness of the leaseback payments and guarantees by the lessee to the lessor that further constrain the recognition of gains on sale. In this regard, sale-leaseback accounting is considerably tougher regarding recognition of gains on sale than is the accounting for securitizations discussed in Chapter 8.

Synthetic Leases

The tax accounting and financial accounting for lessors are usually but not always the same. The most important difference between tax and financial accounting is embodied in "synthetic leasing." Synthetic leases are accounted for as operating leases for financial reporting purposes, so that the lessee receives off–balance sheet financing, and as conditional sale agreements (the analogue of capital leases) for tax purposes, so that the lessee retains the tax benefits. Lessors are mainly facilitators of synthetic leasing transactions, for which they receive fees, although they also may participate in the residual values of the leased assets to some extent. Synthetic leases have been used since the late 1970s for leases of vehicle fleets. Currently, synthetic leases are most common for large real estate leases, although like other structured accounting-motivated lease transactions, they have recently become less common.

Synthetic leasing is possible because of differences between the criteria for a true lease (the analog of an operating lease) under the tax code and an operating lease under financial accounting rules. The tax code ultimately is based on a judgmental "benefits and burdens of ownership" test, essentially a substance over form test, but it also contains guidelines for distinguishing true leases from conditional sale agreements that sound similar to SFAS No. 13's (1976) criteria for distinguishing operating leases from capital leases. Specifically, instead of the less-than-90% net present value criterion in SFAS No. 13 (1976), the tax code (Rev. Proc. 2001-28) contains these two guidelines for a lease to be a true lease:

1. The lessor has more than 20% of the cost of the leased asset invested and "at risk" at all times during the lease term
2. The residual value is greater than 20% of the cost of the leased asset.

These guidelines are sometimes referred to as the 20/20 tests.

These criteria might seem to make it easy to get synthetic lease accounting, since the tax code's 20%-at-risk criterion would seem to be breached more easily than SFAS No. 13's (1976) 90%-of-fair-value criterion. For example, one might think it would suffice to make the net present value of the payments 85% of the cost of the asset. However, the SFAS No. 13 (1976) criterion is not risk based, while the tax code criterion is risk based, as reflected in the term "at risk."

Synthetic leases are structured in various complex ways to exploit this difference between financial reporting and tax rules. One common approach involves the lessee either purchasing residual value insurance from a third party or guaranteeing the lessor's loss from the first dollar up to a maximum not large enough to yield capital lease accounting for financial reporting purposes but large enough for the lessee to bear most or all of the residual value risk. This approach reduces the amount that the lessor has "at risk," so the lease is classified as a conditional sale agreement for tax purposes. Another common approach involves the inclusion of renewal options in the lease that are highly likely to be exercised by the lessee. These renewal options are structured so that they are not included in the lease term for financial reporting purposes but are viewed as reducing the amount at risk for the lessor for tax purposes.

Since the issuance of FIN No. 46 (R) (2003), synthetic leases usually do not involve the use of SPEs, since the lessee will likely be deemed the primary beneficiary of the SPE and thus have to consolidate the SPE, yielding accounting similar to capital lease accounting. This may be a reason why synthetic leases are less common now. For example, General Motor's 2005 Form 10-K filing contains this disclosure of its synthetic leases as a lessee.

> *Synthetic Leases*—GM leases real estate and equipment from various special purpose entities (SPEs) that have been established to facilitate the financing of those assets for GM by nationally prominent, creditworthy lessors. These assets consist principally of office buildings, warehouses, and machinery and equipment. The use of SPEs allows the parties providing the financing to isolate particular assets in a single entity and thereby syndicate the financing to multiple third parties. This is a conventional financing technique used to lower the cost of borrowing and, thus, the lease cost to a lessee such as GM. There is a well-established market in which institutions participate in the financing of such property through their purchase of interests in these SPEs. Certain of these SPEs were determined to be VIEs under FIN 46. For those leases where GM provides a residual value guarantee of the leased property and is considered the primary beneficiary under FIN 46, GM consolidated these entities as of July 1, 2003. This resulted, for Auto & Other, in an initial increase in assets and debt of $917 million and a cumulative effect of accounting change recorded in cost of sales of $27 million after-tax. As of December 31, 2004, the carrying amount of assets and liabilities consolidated under FIN 46R amounted to $883 million and $1.0 billion respectively. Assets consolidated are classified as "Property" in GM's consolidated financial statements. GM's maximum exposure to loss related to consolidated VIEs amounts to $888 million. For other such lease arrangements involving VIEs, GM holds significant variable interests but is not considered the primary beneficiary under FIN 46R. GM's maximum exposure to loss related

to VIEs where GM has a significant variable interest, but does not consolidate the entity, amounts to $592 million.

Synthetic leases can be structured without SPEs, however.

LESSORS' FINANCIAL STATEMENTS

This section describes the 2005 financial statements of GATX Corporation. GATX engages in both operating and direct financing leases as a lessor and in both operating and capital leases as a lessee. Thus, its financial statements illustrate the nature of and differences between these lease accounting methods, in particular, the limitations of operating lease accounting. GATX has no sales-type leases.

Balance Sheet

Exhibit 13.5 presents GATX's 2005 balance sheet. Most of GATX's assets are either some form of receivable, such as finance leases, or fixed assets leased under operating leases. Finance lease receivables (6% of assets) are gross finance lease receivables net of nonrecourse debt for leveraged leases. Net operating lease assets (66% of total assets) include fixed assets that GATX either owns or leases as a lessee under capital leases. Note that net operating lease assets are over 10 times finance lease receivables, despite the fact that operating lease assets amortize more quickly than do lease receivables. This situation primarily reflects lessees' preference for operating leases, GATX's status as an independent lessor rather than a bank, and the netting of nonrecourse third-party financing of GATX's leveraged leases. The sizable amount of fixed assets that GATX leases as a lessee under operating leases is not reflected on its balance sheet but is indicated in disclosures discussed in the "Lease Disclosures" section.

Most of GATX's liabilities are some form of financing liability. GATX divides debt into recourse and nonrecourse debt. The nonrecourse debt reflects third-party financing of operating leases or direct financing leases that do not qualify for leveraged lease accounting. GATX also reports its capital lease liability as a lessee under capital leases. GATX's economic liability to make payments as a lessee under operating leases is not reflected on its balance sheet. Like banks and other finance companies, GATX is fairly highly leveraged, with shareholders' equity equal to 19.5% of assets, a percentage that is overstated due to the nonrecognition of its assets and liabilities for its operating leases as a lessee.

Income Statement

Exhibit 13.6 presents GATX's 2005 income statement. "Lease income" includes rental revenue on operating leases plus interest revenue on capital leases, despite the fact that these items are very different in nature. "Asset remarketing income" includes the gains from remarketing assets at the end

EXHIBIT 13.5 GATX Corporation Consolidated Balance Sheets

IN MILLIONS/DECEMBER 31	2005	2004
ASSETS		
CASH AND CASH EQUIVALENTS	$ 106.0	$ 63.4
RESTRICTED CASH	53.1	60.0
RECEIVABLES		
Rent and other receivables	87.2	77.0
Finance leases	336.5	285.9
Loans	38.7	89.2
Less—allowance for possible losses	(13.1)	(22.1)
	449.3	430.0
OPERATING LEASE ASSETS, FACILITIES AND OTHER		
Rail	3,728.1	3,847.9
Air	1,298.9	1,724.1
Specialty	90.8	65.4
Other	234.9	212.3
Less—allowance for depreciation	(1,891.1)	(1,924.1)
	3,461.6	3,925.6
INVESTMENTS IN AFFILIATED COMPANIES	667.3	718.6
GOODWILL	86.0	93.9
OTHER ASSETS	421.1	321.4
TOTAL ASSETS	$5,244.4	$5,612.9
LIABILITIES AND SHAREHOLDERS' EQUITY		
ACCOUNTS PAYABLE AND ACCRUED EXPENSES	$ 177.4	$ 171.1
DEBT		
Commercial paper and bank credit facilities	57.0	72.1
Recourse	2,715.4	2,887.1
Nonrecourse	37.7	93.5
Capital lease obligations	62.5	79.4
	2,872.6	3,132.1
DEFERRED INCOME TAXES	683.4	721.0
OTHER LIABILITIES	488.7	407.8
TOTAL LIABILITIES	4,222.1	4,532.0
SHAREHOLDERS' EQUITY		
Common stock, par value	36.5	35.9
Additional paid in capital	424.6	401.7
Retained earnings	696.0	750.3
Accumulated other comprehensive (loss) income	(6.3)	21.6
Treasury shares, at cost	(128.5)	(128.6)
TOTAL SHAREHOLDERS' EQUITY	1,022.3	1,080.9
TOTAL LIABILITIES AND SHAREHOLDERS' EQUITY	$5,244.4	$5,612.9

of leases. These gains are fairly consistent across the three years and average close to $40 million per year, but they do not include more variable impairment charges that sum to a similar amount across the three years. Most significant, GATX recorded an asset impairment charge of $83.4 million in 2005, primarily on old aircraft that are to be sold. These impairment charges reflect the fact that the airline industry, GATX's second largest concentration of customers, is currently troubled; presumably the aircraft involved could have been leased on acceptable terms if the industry was doing better. Depreciation includes depreciation on the fixed assets GATX owns and amortization of capital lease assets it leases as a lessee under capital leases. Interest expense includes interest on debt and interest on its capital lease obligation as a lessee.

Economically, the way GATX generates income is very similar to a bank, leasing being in large part an interest rate spread business. Despite GATX's bank-like nature, its income statement is dominated by rental revenue and depreciation expense on its operating leases, because it has substantially more operating leases than direct financing leases.

Cash Flow Statement

Exhibit 13.7 presents GATX's 2005 cash flow statement. GATX's operating lease receipts as a lessor and payments as a lessee are classified as operating cash flows; they are included in net income with adjustments for short-term accruals and deferrals. GATX's lease receipts on direct financing leases are classified as operating for the interest revenue portion, which is included in net income, and as investing for the principal portion, which is included in "portfolio proceeds" along with cash received from remarketing leased assets. GATX's lease payments on capital leases are classified as operating for the interest expense portion, which is included in net income, and as financing for the principal portion, which is included in "repayment of capital lease obligations."

Since most of GATX's leases are operating leases, the company has very positive operating cash flow and very negative investing cash flow, although investing cash flow was enhanced by $201 million in 2005 due to a sale-leaseback of approximately 2,900 railcars. If GATX had accounted for its operating leases as direct financing leases, then its operating cash flow would have been lower and its investing cash flow higher by the principal portion of the lease payment, and vice versa. In this regard, GATX discloses that "portfolio proceeds" on its direct financing leases (including some payoffs from joint ventures) is $250 million in 2005, which is 88% of its reported operating cash flow. GATX has far more operating leases than direct financing leases, so its operating cash flow would likely be negative if its operating leases were accounted for as direct financing leases.

Although the signing of a lease does not by itself yield net cash flows, in principle the signing of a capital, direct financing, or sales-type lease implies that two cash flows that perfectly offset have occurred. For example, the

EXHIBIT 13.6 GATX Corporation Consolidated Statements of Operations

IN MILLIONS, YEAR ENDED DECEMBER 31	2005	2004	2003
GROSS INCOME			
Lease income	$ 878.4	$ 790.3	$ 762.2
Marine operating revenue	138.3	111.8	85.0
Interest income on loans	10.0	17.8	41.4
Asset remarketing income	43.7	36.5	37.9
Fees	17.7	20.9	18.0
Other	75.3	189.6	76.3
Revenues	1,163.4	1,166.9	1,020.8
Share of affiliates' (losses) earnings	(28.8)	65.2	66.8
TOTAL GROSS INCOME	1,134.6	1,232.1	1,087.6
OWNERSHIP COSTS			
Depreciation	202.7	194.6	188.0
Interest expense, net	164.7	162.4	175.4
Operating lease expense	187.0	173.6	176.0
TOTAL OWNERSHIP COSTS	554.4	530.6	539.4
OTHER COSTS AND EXPENSES			
Maintenance expense	194.9	189.2	166.0
Marine operating expenses	108.9	87.7	68.9
Selling, general and administrative	167.5	163.3	163.6
Asset impairment charges	83.4	3.4	24.6
Other	53.3	31.2	47.2
TOTAL OTHER COSTS AND EXPENSES	608.0	474.8	470.3
(LOSS) INCOME FROM CONTINUING OPERATIONS BEFORE INCOME TAXES	(27.8)	226.7	77.9
INCOME TAX (BENEFIT) PROVISION	(12.7)	68.2	16.2
(LOSS) INCOME FROM CONTINUING OPERATIONS	(15.1)	158.5	61.7
DISCONTINUED OPERATIONS, NET OF TAXES	0.8	11.1	15.2
NET (LOSS) INCOME	$ 14.3)	$ 169.6	$ 76.9

signing of a direct financing yields an increase in capital lease receivables that by itself would require an investing cash outflow and a corresponding reduction in equipment that by itself would generate an investing cash inflow. Since these cash effects offset, the signing of direct financing and sales-type

EXHIBIT 13.7 GATX Corporation Consolidated Statements of Cash Flow

IN MILLIONS/ YEAR ENDED DECEMBER 31	2005	2004	2003
OPERATING ACTIVITIES			
Net (loss) income	$ (14.3)	$ 169.6	$ 76.9
Less: Income from discontinued operations	0.8	11.1	15.2
(Loss) income from continuing operations	(15.1)	158.5	61.7
Adjustments to reconcile (loss) income from continuing operations to net cash provided by operating activities of continuing operations:			
Gains on sales of assets and securities	(43.3)	(112.0)	(42.2)
Depreciation	212.7	207.8	202.6
(Reversal) provision for possible losses	(6.3)	(13.7)	4.7
Asset impairment charges	83.4	3.4	24.6
Deferred income tax (benefit) provision	(36.5)	39.8	(6.9)
Share of affiliates' losses (earnings), net of dividends	97.2	(32.4)	(47.4)
Decrease in recoverable income taxes	7.3	63.8	107.2
(Decrease) increase in operating lease payable	(17.2)	(2.8)	3.9
Increase in aircraft maintenance reserves	33.8	27.5	20.8
Increase in prepaid pension	(5.2)	(12.9)	(11.9)
Decrease in reduction in workforce accrual	(1.2)	(2.5)	(15.0)
Other	(24.8)	(23.0)	(34.7)
Net cash provided by operating activities of continuing operations	284.8	301.5	267.4
INVESTING ACTIVITIES			
Additions to equipment on lease, net of nonrecourse financing for leveraged leases, and facilities	(416.6)	(705.1)	(397.0)
Loans extended	—	(14.2)	(49.5)
Investments in affiliated companies	(29.9)	(7.8)	(99.6)
Other	(74.0)	(32.9)	(82.5)
Portfolio investments and capital additions	(520.5)	(760.0)	(628.6)
Portfolio proceeds	249.5	355.5	540.6
Proceeds from sale-leaseback	201.3	—	—
Proceeds from sale of other assets	46.0	130.3	23.0
Net decrease (increase) in restricted cash	6.9	0.9	(28.4)
Effect of exchange rate changes on restricted cash	—	—	17.7

EXHIBIT 13.7 *(Continued)*

IN MILLIONS/ YEAR ENDED DECEMBER 31	2005	2004	2003
Net cash used in investing activities of continuing operations	(16.8)	(273.3)	(75.7)
FINANCING ACTIVITIES			
Net proceeds from issuance of debt	549.5	127.8	616.7
Repayment of debt	(736.4)	(500.5)	(796.0)
Net (decrease) increase in commercial paper and bank credit facilities	(12.8)	57.8	(0.7)
Net decrease in capital lease obligations	(16.8)	(27.4)	(21.3)
Issuance of common stock and other	23.6	5.8	3.8
Cash dividends	(40.0)	(39.4)	(62.8)
Net cash used in financing activities of continuing operations	(232.9)	(375.9)	(260.3)
EFFECT OF EXCHANGE RATES ON CASH AND CASH EQUIVALENTS	(1.4)	2.9	1.4
CASH FLOWS OF DISCONTINUED OPERATIONS (SEE NOTE 19)			
Operating cash flows	(0.2)	35.0	140.9
Investing cash flows	9.1	222.7	(27.5)
Financing cash flows	—	(61.0)	(65.8)
NET INCREASE (DECREASE) IN CASH AND CASH EQUIVALENTS	$ 42.6	$ (148.1)	$ (19.6)

leases for lessors and capital leases for lessees generally are treated as noncash transactions with no effect on the cash flow statement. SFAS No. 95, *Statement of Cash Flows* (1987), requires that offsetting cash effects of noncash transactions either be reported in the cash flow statement or be disclosed in some fashion, such as reported in the schedule of significant noncash transactions. Despite this requirement, like most lessors, GATX does not make this disclosure.

LEASE DISCLOSURES

Description

Lessors' lease footnotes must include a variety of disclosures, the most important of which are listed next.

Lessors must disclose:

- The type of property leased
- The classification of the leases

- The dates of expiration of the leases

For capital leases, lessors must disclose:

- The net investment in the lease
- The undiscounted future minimum lease payments to be received
- The unguaranteed residual value
- The amount of unearned income
- Minimum future lease receipts in the aggregate and for each of the five succeeding years

For operating leases, lessors must disclose:

- The cost and carrying amount of the property on lease or held for lease
- The amount of accumulated amortization on these assets
- Minimum future lease receipts in the aggregate and for each of the five succeeding years

These disclosures help users of financial reports to assess the nature and risk of the leases.

The minimum lease receipt disclosures help users understand the financing nature of lessors' operating leases, by indicating the duration of these leases. These disclosures do not allow full reconstruction of direct financing or sales-type lease accounting for lessors, however, because they do not include estimates of the amount or timing of the estimated unguaranteed residual values on operating leases. Minimum lease receipt disclosures do allow the user to estimate the present value of those lease receipts, however, which is a measure of the economic receivable associated with operating leases, although it ignores expected receipts that are not included in minimum lease receipts, such as contingent rentals. The fact that minimum lease receipts beyond five years are lumped together makes this determination somewhat difficult for long-term operating leases, however. Users who capitalize operating lease receipts for analytical purposes typically assume either that the payments beyond five years are the same amount as the payment in the fifth year or that these payments decay at some rate over time. No theoretically correct approach applies to all firms.

GATX's Disclosures

Exhibit 13.8 presents GATX's 2005 footnote disclosures regarding leases. Note 2 indicates that GATX primarily leases long-lived transportation equipment; for example, its railcars have a life of 30 to 38 years. Like most lessors, GATX does not disclose the dates of expiration of its leases, even though these disclosures are required under SFAS No. 13 (1976), presumably because lessors have many leases and because the minimum lease payment disclosures provide similar information.

EXHIBIT 13.8 GATX Corporation, Lease Disclosures

NOTE 2. SIGNIFICANT ACCOUNTING POLICIES

OPERATING LEASE ASSETS AND FACILITIES—Operating lease assets and facilities are stated principally at cost. Assets acquired under capital leases are included in operating lease assets and the related obligations are recorded as liabilities. Provisions for depreciation include the amortization of capital lease assets. Operating lease assets and facilities listed below are depreciated over their respective estimated useful life to an estimated residual value using the straight-line method. The estimated useful lives of depreciable new assets are as follows:

Railcars	30–38 years
Locomotives	40 years
Aircraft	25 years
Buildings	40–50 years
Leasehold improvements	5–40 years
Marine vessels	10–50 years

NOTE 3. LEASES

The following information pertains to GATX as a lessor:

FINANCE LEASES—GATX's finance leases are comprised of direct financing leases and leveraged leases. Investment in direct finance leases consists of lease receivables, plus the estimated residual value of the equipment at the lease termination dates, less unearned income. Lease receivables represent the total rent to be received over the term of the lease reduced by rent already collected. Initial unearned income is the amount by which the original sum of the lease receivable and the estimated residual value exceeds the original cost of the leased equipment. Unearned income is amortized to lease income over the lease term in a manner that produces a constant rate of return on the net investment in the lease.

Finance leases that are financed principally with nonrecourse borrowings at lease inception and that meet certain criteria are accounted for as leveraged leases. Leveraged lease receivables are stated net of the related nonrecourse debt. Initial unearned income represents the excess of anticipated cash flows (including estimated residual values, net of the related debt service) over the original investment in the lease. The Company recognized income from leveraged leases (net of taxes) of $4.3 million, $6.1 million, and $10.7 million in 2005, 2004, and 2003, respectively.

In 2003, GATX disposed of a leveraged lease commitment on passenger rail equipment. $184.9 million of assets were sold, including $108.4 million of restricted cash and $48.0 million of progress payments. In addition, $183.4 million of liabilities, primarily nonrecourse debt, were assumed by the acquirer.

The components of the investment in finance leases at December 31 were (in millions):

(continues)

EXHIBIT 13.8 *(Continued)*

	LEVERAGED LEASES		DIRECT FINANCING		TOTAL FINANCE LEASES	
	2005	**2004**	**2005**	**2004**	**2005**	**2004**
Total minimum lease payments receivable	$1,031.4	$1,146.4	$318.0	$171.1	$1,349.4	$1,317.5
Principal and interest on third-party nonrecourse debt	(889.1)	(965.5)	—	—	(889.1)	(965.5)
Net minimum future lease receivable	142.3	180.9	318.0	171.1	460.3	352.0
Estimated non-guaranteed residual value of leased assets	93.0	108.2	62.6	31.0	155.6	139.2
Unearned income	(84.5)	(114.9)	(194.9)	(90.4)	(279.4)	(205.3)
Investment in finance leases	150.8	174.2	185.7	111.7	336.5	285.9
Deferred taxes	(111.4)	(91.4)	—	—	(111.4)	(91.4)
Net investment	$ 39.4	$ 82.8	$185.7	$111.7	$ 225.1	$ 194.5

OPERATING LEASES—Rental income from operating leases is generally reported on a straight-line basis over the term of the lease. Rental income on certain leases is based on equipment usage. Rental income from usage rents was $22.3 million, $31.7 million, and $33.4 million, in 2005, 2004, and 2003, respectively.

MINIMUM FUTURE RECEIPTS—Minimum future lease receipts from finance leases, net of debt payments for leveraged leases, and minimum future rental receipts from noncancelable operating leases at December 31, 2005 were (in millions):

	FINANCE LEASES	OPERATING LEASES	TOTAL
2006	$ 43.5	$ 826.7	$ 870.2
2007	34.3	600.0	634.3
2008	31.8	441.7	473.5
2009	32.5	318.9	351.4
2010	31.7	197.7	229.4
Years thereafter	286.5	351.5	638.0
	$460.3	$2,736.5	$3,196.8

The following information pertains to GATX as a lessee:

EXHIBIT 13.8 *(Continued)*

CAPITAL LEASES—GATX assets that are financed with capital lease obligations and subsequently leased to customers under either operating or finance leases, or otherwise utilized in operations at December 31 were (in millions):

	2005	2004
Railcars and locomotives	$ 82.6	$116.4
Marine vessels	98.0	98.0
	180.6	214.4
Less—allowance for depreciation	(138.3)	(158.1)
	42.3	56.3
Finance leases	6.2	7.5
	$ 48.5	$ 63.8

Depreciation of capital lease assets is classified as depreciation in the consolidated statement of operations. Interest expense on the above capital leases was $5.3 million, $8.4 million, and $12.0 million, in 2005, 2004, and 2003, respectively.

OPERATING LEASES—GATX has financed railcars, aircraft, and other assets through sale-leasebacks that are accounted for as operating leases. A subsidiary of GATX has provided a guarantee for a portion of the residual value related to two operating leases. Operating lease expense was $187.0 million, $173.6 million, and $176.0 million, in 2005, 2004, and 2003, respectively. Certain operating leases provide options for GATX to renew the leases or purchase the assets at the end of the lease term. The specific terms of the renewal and purchase options vary.

In 2005, GATX completed a sale leaseback transaction for approximately 2,900 of its railcars (net book value of $170.0 million) for net proceeds of $201.3 million. The transaction resulted in a gain of $31.3 million, which was deferred and is being amortized as a component of operating lease expense over the 21-year term of the resulting operating lease.

FUTURE MINIMUM RENTAL PAYMENTS—Future minimum rental payments due under noncancelable leases at December 31, 2005 were (in millions):

	CAPITAL LEASES	RECOURSE OPERATING LEASES	NONRECOURSE OPERATING LEASES
2006	$ 11.8	$ 160.5	$ 42.1
2007	11.1	144.8	38.7
2008	11.0	145.0	38.9
2009	10.7	142.8	41.0
2010	8.1	140.6	42.2
Years thereafter	36.4	952.3	356.6
	$ 89.1	$1,686.0	$559.5
Less—amounts representing interest	(26.6)		
Present value of future minimum capital lease payments	$ 62.5		

(continues)

EXHIBIT 13.8 *(Continued)*

The payments for these leases and certain operating leases do not include the costs of licenses, taxes, insurance, and maintenance that GATX is required to pay.

The amounts shown for nonrecourse operating leases primarily reflect rental payments of three bankruptcy remote, special-purpose corporations that are wholly owned by GATX. These rentals are consolidated for accounting purposes, but do not represent legal obligations of GATX.

NOTE 15. CONCENTRATIONS, COMMITMENTS, AND OTHER CONTINGENCIES

CONCENTRATIONS

CONCENTRATION OF CREDIT RISK—Under its lease agreements with lessees, GATX retains legal ownership of the asset except where such assets have been financed by sale-leasebacks. For most loan financings to customers, the loan is collateralized by specifically related equipment. GATX performs credit evaluations prior to approval of a lease or loan contract. Subsequently, the creditworthiness of the customer and the value of the collateral are monitored on an ongoing basis. GATX maintains an allowance for possible losses to provide for potential losses that could arise should customers become unable to discharge their obligations to GATX. The Company did not derive revenues in excess of 10% of consolidated revenues from any one customer for any of the years ended December 31, 2005, 2004, and 2003.

COMMITMENTS

UNCONDITIONAL PURCHASE OBLIGATIONS—At December 31, 2005, GATX's unconditional purchase obligations of $412.0 million consisted primarily of railcar and aircraft acquisitions over the period of 2006 through 2008. GATX had commitments of $234.4 million related to the rail committed purchase program, entered into in 2002. GATX also had commitments of $96.0 million for orders on three new aircraft to be delivered in 2006 and 2007. Unconditional purchase obligations also include $68.4 million of other rail related commitments.

The following table shows GATX's commercial commitments for continuing operations (in millions):

DECEMBER 31	2005	2004
Affiliate guarantees	$ 29.5	$ 34.7
Asset residual value guarantees	368.6	437.6
Lease payment guarantees	27.3	30.3
Other guarantees	77.8	77.8
Total guarantees	503.2	580.4
Standby letters of credit and bonds	23.6	28.9
	$526.8	$609.3

At December 31, 2005, the maximum potential amount of lease, loan, or residual value guarantees under which GATX or its subsidiaries could be required

EXHIBIT 13.8 *(Continued)*

to perform was $503.2 million. The related carrying value of the guarantees on the balance sheet, including deferred revenue primarily associated with residual value guarantees entered into prior to the effective date of FASB Interpretation No. 45 (FIN 45), *Guarantor's Accounting and Disclosure Requirements for Guarantees, Including Indirect Guarantees of Indebtedness to Others,* was a liability of $2.1 million. The expirations of these guarantees range from 2006 to 2017. Any liability resulting from GATX's performance pursuant to the residual value guarantees will be reduced by the value realized from the underlying asset or group of assets. Historically, gains associated with the residual value guarantees have exceeded any losses and were recorded in asset remarketing income in the consolidated statements of operations. Based on known facts and current market conditions, management does not believe that the asset residual value guarantees will result in any significant adverse financial impact to the Company. Accordingly, the Company has not recorded any accrual for contingent losses with respect to the residual value guarantees as of December 31, 2005. GATX believes these asset residual value guarantees will likely generate future income in the form of fees and residual sharing proceeds.

Asset residual value guarantees represent GATX's commitment to third parties that an asset or group of assets will be worth a specified amount at the end of a lease term. Revenue is earned for providing these asset value guarantees in the form of an initial fee (which is amortized into income over the guaranteed period) and by sharing in any proceeds received upon disposition of the assets to the extent such proceeds are in excess of the amount guaranteed (which is recorded when realized).

Lease payment guarantees represent GATX's guarantees to financial institutions of finance and operating lease payments of an unrelated party in exchange for a fee.

Note 3 in Exhibit 13.8 reports GATX's estimated unguaranteed residual values on direct financing leases, which are significant at about 65% of the undiscounted lease receivable after nonrecourse debt, although this overstates the residual value's contribution to the discounted lease receivable. Given the substantial magnitude of GATX's unguaranteed residual values, it is important for users of financial reports to ascertain their nature and risk. This note also reports GATX's minimum lease receipts for its operating leases, of which about 13% are expected to be received after more than five years. In this regard, GATX's operating leases are fairly long-term financing arrangements. Note 3 also reports GATX's minimum operating lease payments as a lessee. Like many lessors, GATX sells and leases back many of its assets as a way to obtain financing and transfer tax benefits that it cannot use efficiently.

Note 15 in Exhibit 13.8 reports GATX's $396 million guarantees of residual values or lease payments to third parties. These guarantees are significant relative to GATX's $1,022 million of owners' equity. As in risky asset securitizations, guarantees of this type are often necessary to obtain third-party financing, and they raise the question of how much risk is retained by the lessor.

Re-Creating Capital Lease Accounting

Minimum operating lease receipt or payment disclosures can be used to recast operating lease accounting into an approximation to capital (for lessors, direct financing or sales-type) lease accounting. Doing this is somewhat easier for lessees than for lessors, since estimated unguaranteed residual values are not disclosed for lessors' operating lessees, so capital lease accounting cannot be re-created fully. In this section, calculations using the minimum lease payment disclosures for GATX's operating leases as a lessee (ignoring its nonrecourse operating leases) illustrate how to perform this type of analysis.

GATX's minimum operating lease payments in each of the next five years and beyond five years is provided in Note 3 in Exhibit 13.8. Its expected minimum operating lease payments decay fairly slowly over the next five years, decreasing from $203 million in 2006 to $183 million in 2010, with virtually all of the decrease occurring from 2006 to 2007. GATX's aggregate payments beyond five years are $1,309 million. Some assumption needs to be made about when payments beyond five years occur. Given the slow decay of the payments through five years, for simplicity payments beyond five years are assumed to be $180 million per year for 7.27 years.

The interest rate to determine the present value of these payments also needs to be estimated. If a lessee's operating and capital leases are fairly similar, then the most natural way to determine this rate is as follows. As required, GATX discloses that interest expense on its capital lease liability is $5.3 million. Given an average capital lease liability of $70.9 million during the year, this interest expense implies an interest rate of 7.5%. Alternatively, this interest rate could be estimated using measures of the firm's cost of debt capital. Discounting the minimum lease payments on operating leases using a 7.5% rate yields an estimated economic liability for operating leases of $1,443 million. This amount is about half of GATX's reported financing liabilities of $2,873 million. This economic lease liability should imply a similar economic lease asset.

Given the magnitudes of this economic liability and asset, it is important for users of GATX's financial reports to recast its operating leases as financing transactions on all the financial statements, not just the balance sheet. This exercise is a fairly straightforward one. On the income statement, the interest expense on GATX's estimated economic lease liability for its operating leases in 2001 is .075 × $1,443 million = $108 million. GATX's disclosures of its minimum lease payments on its operating leases suggest that the life of these leases is about 12.27 years, so annual straight-line amortization expense on its economic lease asset for its operating leases is approximately $1,443 million/12.27 = $118 million. These income statement amounts are classified differently and in sum exceed the rental expense of $203 million that GATX will record for its minimum operating lease payments in 2006 by $23 million.

On the cash flow statement, the $203 million minimum operating lease payment in 2006 economically includes an operating cash outflow of $108 million for interest and a financing cash outflow of $95 million for principal (instead of all $203 million being classified as an operating cash flow, as it is under operating lease accounting).

POSSIBLE FUTURE CHANGES IN LEASE ACCOUNTING

In February 2000, the G4+1 (the standards setters of Australia, Canada, New Zealand, the United Kingdom, the United States, and, as an observer, the International Accounting Standards Committee) published a special report, *Leases: Implementation of a New Approach,* advocating major changes in lease accounting. The special report views leases as exchanges of rights and obligations, which is in contrast to the SFAS No. 13 (1976) view of a lease as a possible exchange of an indivisible real asset. In this respect, the proposal is consistent with the financial components view of SFAS No. 140 (2000) discussed in Chapter 8. The special report supports eliminating the distinction between operating and capital leases and proposes initially capitalizing all material leases at the present value of a defined set of lease payments over a defined lease term. The bulk of the special report tries to deal with the difficult question of how to determine the set of lease payments to be capitalized, given that leases may contain various complicated contractual features.

In July 2006, the FASB decided to comprehensively reconsider lease accounting. This project will be conducted jointly with the International Accounting Standards Board. This project likely will attempt to refine the approach proposed in the G4+1's report. Given the complexity of the issues involved, some of which are described next, the project likely will take a number of years to complete.

The development of a new lease accounting standard faces two main difficulties. First, as with securitizations, a trade-off is involved in adopting a financial components view, because the fair value of leased assets can be partitioned in very different ways than their risk. In fact, leases probably partition risks in more complex and customized ways than do securitizations. No accounting method will fully capture both the partitioning of fair value and risks in all circumstances, and so good disclosure of these transactions will remain critical regardless of the accounting. Moreover, unlike financial instruments, real assets are indivisible in a physical sense. Some accounting observers argue that applying a financial components perspective to real assets makes little economic sense.[16]

Second, if operating lease accounting is eliminated, lessees that want to perpetuate off–balance sheet financing will have the incentive to structure leases in which a large portion of the expected lease payments are excluded from the set to be capitalized. The G4+1's proposal would allow this to be done fairly easily through its treatment of renewal options, whose exercise generally would not be anticipated. A definition of lease term and payments that is robust to such behavior is critical to developing an accounting standard that is a conceptual and practical improvement over existing accounting rules.

NOTES

1. Equipment Leasing Association, "Trends and Forecasts for Equipment Leasing in the U.S." November 2005.
2. Equipment Leasing Association, Presentation at 1st Annual ELA/SEC Meeting, September 8, 2005.
3. Securities and Exchange Commission, *Report and Recommendations Pursuant to Section 401(c) of the Sarbanes-Oxley Act of 2002 on Arrangements with Off-Balance Sheet Implications, Special Purpose Entities, and Transparency of Filings by Issuers,* June 15, 2005.
4. Equipment Leasing Association, "Presentation at 1st Annual ELA/SEC Meeting."
5. Ibid.
6. Ibid.
7. "Profits and Balance Sheet Developments at U.S. Commercial Banks in 2005," *Federal Reserve Bulletin,* June 14, 2006.
8. K. Eades and F. Marston, "Incentives for Leasing: Evidence from the Largest U.S. Lessees and Lessors," Working Paper 04-03, Darden Business School, October 11, 2002.
9. American Accounting Association Financial Accounting Standards Committee, "Evaluation of Lease Accounting Proposed in the G41 Special Report," *Accounting Horizons* (September 2001).
10. Equipment Leasing and Finance Foundation, *2005 State of the Industry,* October 2005.
11. Association of Consumer Vehicle Lessors, "Lease Residual Losses Finally on the Decline," press release, August 3, 2001.
12. M. Maynard, "Favorable Lease Deals May Be Fading Fast," *New York Times,* December 15, 2000.
13. D. Mayer, "True Leases Under Attack: Lessors Face Persistent Challenges to True Lease Transactions," *Journal of Equipment Lease Financing* (Fall 2005).
14. J. Ciesielski, AAO Weblog, www.accountingobserver.com/blog/category/restatement-zoo/leasing-makeovers/.
15. Ibid.
16. D. Monson, "The Conceptual Framework and Accounting for Leases," *Accounting Horizons* (September 2001).

CHAPTER 14

Insurers and Insurance Accounting

This chapter discusses the accounting and disclosure rules governing property-casualty (PC) and life and health (life) insurance and the issues they raise for the analysis of PC and life insurers. The discussion focuses on Statement of Financial Accounting Standards (SFAS) No. 60, *Accounting and Reporting by Insurance Companies* (1982), which governs the accounting for all PC insurance and for traditional types of life insurance, such as term life and whole life, and SFAS No. 97, *Accounting and Reporting by Insurance Enterprises for Certain Long-Duration Contracts and Realized Gains and Losses from the Sale of Investments* (1987), which governs the accounting for primarily investment-oriented types of life insurance policy, such as universal life and most annuities. Although PC and life insurance differ in certain respects, they share many economic features and are both subject to SFAS No. 60 (1982). In addition, many insurers engage in both PC and life insurance. For these reasons, both types of insurance and insurers are covered in this chapter, although the discussion frequently veers off to examine issues that pertain to one type.

Insurance policies are financial option-like contracts that require the insurer to pay the insured party some amount if an insured event occurs during the policy term. When an insured event of a given type occurs, the payoff to the policyholder could be either a fixed amount (as is common in life insurance) or depend on the assessed amount of the loss (as is common in PC insurance), with deductibles and caps usually applying. Insured events usually are discrete and have a fairly low probability of occurring in a given year, such as a hurricane causing damage on a property covered by a PC insurance policy or the death of a person covered by a life insurance policy. In this regard, insurance policies are similar to credit derivatives that pay off on discrete indicators of default. Increasingly, however, insured events reflect the realization of continuous variables, such as the number of hurricanes that form in a given year, which renders insurance policies virtually indistinguishable from financial options. For example, a PC insurance policy that pays off based on the realization of the number of hurricanes that form in a given year essentially is a weather derivative.

Insurers are first and foremost risk managers that assume policyholders' risks by underwriting insurance policies. They may retain and diversify the risks they underwrite internally, relying on the law of large numbers, or they may cede them in part or entirely to reinsurers, a wholesale type of insurer. Reflecting the latter possibility, this chapter should be read in conjunction with Chapter 16, which describes the significant economic and accounting effects that reinsurance has on insurers.

To assume policyholders' risks, insurers are paid a fee, called a premium, which is usually paid at or near the beginning of the policy term. Ignoring the up-front costs of obtaining policies, which can be large for some types of policies, the up-front receipt of premiums makes insurance underwriting self-financing and insurers into investment companies as well as risk managers. Insurers invest premiums for the float period between the receipt of premiums and the payment of claims. The amount of investment income they earn increases with the float period and the rate of return they earn on their assets. To the extent that insurance markets are competitive, insurers' underwriting and investment income should be negatively correlated; that is, when their investment income is higher, their underwriting income should be lower, and vice versa, yielding a normal level of net income.

The expected float period for an insurance policy rises with both its "tail" —the length of time between the occurrence of an insured event covered by the policy and the insurer paying the claim—and its "duration"—the length of time that coverage is provided on fixed terms, taking into account the probability that the holder maintains the policy over time. In PC insurance, variation in the length of the float period across policy types depends primarily on tail, because the duration of PC insurance policies is usually one year. For example, tail is usually a few days or weeks for automobile property policies but can be decades for product liability policies. In life insurance, variation in the length of the float period across policy types depends primarily on duration, because life insurance policies generally have short tails. For example, duration is usually one year for group term life and health policies but can be the entire remaining life of the insured individual for investment-oriented policies, such as whole life.

This chapter emphasizes that users of financial reports should distinguish tail and duration as drivers of the float period and, relatedly, they should separately analyze lines of business with different tails and durations. There are two reasons for this. First, SFAS No. 60 (1982) does not require the liability for unpaid claims to be discounted for short-duration policies, regardless of their tails, and in practice this liability is not discounted for most types of short-duration policies. When this is the case, interest expense is not accrued on this liability and, as a result, the underwriting and investment income net of interest expense generated by these policies are mismeasured, misclassified, and poorly matched in time. This concern arises primarily for long-tailed PC insurance policies.

Second, while SFAS No. 60 (1982) requires discounting of the liability for unpaid claims for long-duration life insurance policies, the economic interest on this liability over time is misclassified as claim expense. In addition, the financial statement classifications for traditional long-duration life insurance policies accounted for under SFAS No. 60 (1982) are inconsistent with and less descriptive than those for primarily investment-oriented life insurance policies accounted for under SFAS No. 97 (1987).

The primary difference between PC and life insurers is the generally higher level of underwriting risk for PC insurers. In this regard, this chapter should be read in conjunction with Chapter 15, which describes PC insurers' highly detailed mandated disclosures about the revisions of and payments on their liabilities for unpaid claims and claim adjustment, which users of their financial reports must analyze carefully. In contrast, because of their lesser underwriting risk, the analysis of life insurers focuses on the credit quality of their assets and the duration matching of their assets and liabilities. In this respect life insurers are more like banks than PC insurers, and the financial analyses described in Chapters 4 and 5 are particularly important for life insurers. These analyses are not repeated here. It should be noted, however, that insurers' financial report disclosures regarding interest rate and credit risk are usually not as informative as those of banks, although insurers' statutory reports contain very detailed disclosures useful for assessing their credit risk. In addition, the fair value of insurance policies other than investment contracts and financial guarantees need not be disclosed under SFAS No. 107, *Disclosures about Fair Value of Financial Instruments* (1991), as discussed in Chapter 6.

The first section of this chapter describes insurance products. The second section describes insurers' risk-return trade-offs. The third section describes insurance regulation. The fourth section explains the primary accounting standards governing insurance, SFAS Nos. 60 (1982) and 97 (1987). The fifth section describes several recently issued standards that govern the accounting for embedded derivatives and other features of investment-oriented life insurance policies. The sixth section describes the effects of SFAS Nos. 60 (1982) and 97 (1987) on the financial statements reported in the 2005 Form 10-K filing of Hartford Financial Services Group (The Hartford), the tenth-largest PC insurer and fourth-largest life insurer in the United States. The seventh section discusses disclosures by segment mandated by Regulation S-X that are useful for conducting separate analyses by line of business. The final section discusses statutory accounting principles (SAP) that underlie insurance regulation and tax accounting rules for insurers.

PRODUCTS

The products offered by PC and life insurers include both traditional insurance policies and products that combine insurance with the investment or risk management features found in standard financial instruments such as securities and derivatives.

Property-Casualty Insurance

Property insurance covers loss or damage to real property (e.g., buildings, automobiles, or other valuables) from specified events (e.g., fire, theft, accident, or catastrophe). Casualty insurance is a catchall term that encompasses almost all coverage that is not property, life, or health insurance. The most important category of casualty insurance, liability insurance, covers the legal liability to third parties (e.g., drivers, passengers, employees, or customers) from specified events. Both property and casualty insurance claims may result from the same insured event; for example, automobile accidents and environmental damage often yield claims under both types of coverage. Reflecting this fact, PC insurers offer policies that cover both property and casualty, called multiple peril insurance.

Personal lines of PC insurance are sold to individuals or households, while commercial lines are sold to businesses. Insurers may position certain products as loss leaders to obtain other lines. For example, insurers often price homeowners' insurance low in an attempt to obtain more profitable automobile insurance.

Net premiums earned (revenue from underwriting insurance policies) for all PC insurance products were $426 billion in the United States in 2005.[1] The 10 largest types of PC insurance in order of the amount of net premiums earned in 2005 were:

1. Personal automobile liability ($88 billion)
2. Personal automobile property ($62 billion)
3. Homeowners' multiple peril ($47 billion)
4. Workers' compensation ($40 billion)
5. Other liability ($29 billion)
6. Commercial multiple peril ($28 billion)
7. Commercial automobile ($25 billion)
8. Reinsurance ($14 billion)
9. Medical malpractice ($7 billion)
10. Inland marine ($7 billion)[2]

Although the three largest lines of business are personal, personal and commercial insurance are roughly equal in terms of net premiums earned, reflecting the far greater number of commercial lines. Property and casualty insurance are also roughly equal in terms of net premiums earned.

Compared to the industry totals, The Hartford's PC insurance activities in 2005 were tilted toward commercial lines of business. Its net premiums earned of $6.6 billion from commercial lines of business—$1.8 billion from its specialty segment (coverage for large businesses and nonstandard products) and $4.8 billion from its business insurance segment (coverage for middle market and small businesses)—were almost twice its $3.6 billion from personal lines.

A recent trend is the development of products that combine features of traditional PC insurance policies and traditional financial instruments used to raise capital. Collectively, these products (along with nontraditional or structured reinsurance products discussed in Chapter 16) fall under the rubric "alternative risk transfer" (ART). Such products include catastrophe bonds whose face value need not be repaid if a specified catastrophe occurs, catastrophe options for which the writer pays the holder a specified amount if a specified catastrophe occurs, and contingent equity that provides the issuer with the option to raise equity if a specified event occurs. These ART products essentially securitize risks that could have been absorbed by insurers.

More generally, the distinctions among PC insurance, banking, and securities products are disappearing, in part because of the development of ART products but also because of the development of the diversified financial services firms allowed by the Gramm, Leach, Bliley Act of 1999 (GLBA) discussed in Chapter 2. For example, all three types of financial institution provide financial guarantees increasingly in substitutable forms and to the same types of customers.

Life Insurance

Life insurance policies are more heterogeneous both across and within types of policies than are PC insurance policies. Most important, life insurance policies are located at various points along a continuum from pure insurance to pure investments. This source of heterogeneity makes it difficult to compare types of policies based on a single measure of size, such as net premiums earned, which pertains to the insurance aspect of the policy. Life insurance policies also exhibit more different combinations of features within a given policy type.

Net premiums earned for all life insurance products were $537 billion (including $273 billion of annuity considerations) in the United States in 2005.[3] The amount insured is naturally higher than premiums, more so for policies with a smaller probability of paying off in a given period. For example, the life insurance in force at the end of 2005 was $31 trillion, with $3.1 trillion of that amount newly issued in 2005.[4] These amounts do not reflect the balances of pure investment-oriented policies, which constitute a large portion of the industry's $4.2 trillion of assets in 2005, $1.4 trillion of which is in separate accounts for policies offering variable returns, described shortly.[5]

Life insurance provides coverage in the case of death ("mortality"). Ordinary life policies are offered to individuals. Group life policies are offered to groups, usually of employees, which reduces the costs of policy sales and administration and also mitigates problems with adverse selection discussed in the "Risk-Return Trade-Offs" section. As a result, group life is considerably cheaper than ordinary life. In the United States in 2005, net premiums earned were $111 billion for ordinary life policies and $30 billion for group life policies.[6] In 2005, ordinary life insurance in force in the United States was $14.7 trillion, while group life insurance in force was $8.7 trillion.[7]

Term life policies are relatively close to pure insurance. They pay a certain amount if a covered individual dies during the policy term, which often is 1 year but may be up to 30 years. One-year term life policies usually are guaranteed renewable at the end of the term for some number of years or up to some age, with the premium rising in a predetermined fashion over time reflecting the higher probability of death as a person ages, but not reflecting changes in the health of the insured party. Multiyear policies usually have level premiums throughout some or all of the term, in which case a portion of the premiums early in the term subsidize the coverage later in term, giving the policies some investment aspect (but usually little or no surrender value). Group life typically is term life. The payouts on term life insurance are usually exempt from income taxes.

Investment-oriented policies can put the investment risk on the insurer, the policyholder, or both. Policies that offer fixed returns put the investment risk on the insurer. Policies that offer variable returns (generally on a separate pool of assets held by the insurer) put the investment risk on the policyholder. Not surprisingly, variable policies exploded during the stock market boom in the 1990s. In an attempt to maintain this growth, life insurers have incorporated minimum benefits and other contractual features into these policies that protect policyholders from downside investment risk or otherwise make the policies desirable. These features are discussed in more detail in the "Accounting Standards Governing Embedded Derivatives and Other Life Insurance Policy Features" section. Investment-oriented insurance products are tax advantaged relative to bank accounts, since the accumulated interest not yet paid out (the inside buildup) is not taxed until paid, although there can be tax penalties and surrender charges imposed for early withdrawals from these policies.

Whole life policies require the holder to make fixed premium payments each period during the holder's life. If the covered individual dies during a given period, then the insurer pays the face value of the policy. If the covered individual does not die during the period, then an investment value remains to the policy. If the policy is surrendered prior to the covered individual's death, then the investment value less any surrender charges (the surrender value) is paid to the holder of the policy. Endowment life is a variation on whole life that has a maturity date at which the balance of the policy is paid out if the covered individual has not died before that date. The absence of surrender charges at the maturity date increases the investment aspects of the policy. In the United States in 2005, whole and endowment life insurance in force was $7.3 trillion.[8]

Universal life policies are similar to whole life policies but have premium payments or a policy maturity that are not fixed, which renders these policies even more investment oriented.

Annuities pay out gradually, usually a constant amount per period. Payments on traditional annuities are triggered by the occurrence of an insured event, such as the insured individual's death, and so these annuities include an insurance component. Most annuities are now primarily investment products, however, not unlike bank accounts or mutual funds.

Life insurers offer a variety of pure investment products, including pension plans and structured settlements. These products are often based on guaranteed investment contracts (GICs) that guarantee both the rate at which interest is credited to the pension plan and the interest rate on current beneficiaries' annuity payments. Aetna, Travelers, and a number of other insurers were significantly hurt by guaranteeing interest at rates that turned out to be too high given the general decline in interest rates from the early 1980s to 2003. Given the gradual payments on GICs, problems can linger on for years; for example, at the beginning of 2001, Equitable Life in the United Kingdom, the world's oldest life insurer, stopped underwriting new business due to problems from GICs written in the 1980s and 1990s.

Accident and health insurance provides coverage in the case of disability or illness (morbidity). Accident and certain types of health insurance are similar to PC insurance, so PC insurers frequently offer these policies. With the exception of long-term care insurance, traditional health insurance has increasingly been replaced over time by the offerings of health maintenance organizations. In the United States in 2005, group accident and heath premiums were $88 billion and other accident and health premiums were $41 billion.[9]

Compared to the industry totals, The Hartford's life insurance activities tilt toward investment-oriented lines of business, especially annuities. It provides summary performance measures for these life insurance segments in its 2005 Form 10-K filing, in rough order from closest to pure insurance product to closest to pure investment product:

- "Group benefits" (primarily term life and accident and health): $3.8 billion of net earned premiums and $.4 billion of investment income
- "Individual life" (primarily universal life): $.8 billion fee income, $.3 billion investment income, and $10.3 billion assets under management
- "Retail" (primarily variable annuities and mutual funds): $2.3 billion fee income, $.9 billion investment income, and $145.9 billion assets under management
- "International" (primarily variable annuities): $.5 billion fee income and $26.1 billion assets under management
- "Retirement plans": $.2 billion fee income, $.3 billion investment income, and $20.4 billion assets under management
- "Institutional" (primarily structured settlements): $.2 billion fee income, $.3 billion investment income, and $20.4 billion assets under management
- "Other" (primarily investments): $.1 billion fee income and $4.0 billion investment income

RISK-RETURN TRADE-OFFS

A pervasive concern faced by all insurers is adverse selection, or the lemons problem. Purchasers of insurance generally know more about their risk than do insurers, and higher-risk individuals are more likely to seek to be insured. For example, early in the spread of the AIDS disease, a disproportionate share of death claims was on policies initiated shortly before death. Eventually, insurers incorporated blood testing and preexisting condition clauses into policies that reduced but did not entirely eliminate this exposure, since blood testing is imperfect and the legal process is costly and uncertain.

Insurers also are susceptible to newly developed risks or, more generally, to risks for which historical data provides less ability to model the distribution of the risk. For example, PC insurers are susceptible to terrorism and global warming, which are or may be reflected in the two largest insured catastrophe losses in history: the terrorist acts of September 11, 2001 ($36 billion of insured losses)[10] and Hurricane Katrina ($41 billion of insured losses).[11] Although it is difficult to attribute any one weather-related event such as Katrina to global warming, it is plausible and perhaps likely that global warming was involved in 7 of the 10 costliest hurricanes in history occurring in 2004 (Charley, Ivan, Frances, and Jeanne) and 2005 (Katrina, Wilma, and Rita).[12] Life insurers are susceptible to pandemics, although the last major one occurred almost ninety years ago with the Spanish flu of 1918–1919, which killed about 500,000 people in the United States alone. (This statement does not reflect the ongoing AIDS disease, which AVERT estimates has killed over 25 million people worldwide since 1981, disproportionately uninsured persons in sub-Saharan Africa.)

The federal government has recently acknowledged the difficulty of (re)insuring for terrorism losses by passing the Terrorism Risk Insurance Extension Act of 2005, which renews most aspects of the Terrorism Risk Insurance Act of 2002 through the end of 2007. Under this act, the federal government absorbs most losses from terrorist acts above a certain threshold amount on most commercial lines of business, while requiring primary insurers to offer this insurance. Compared to the original act, the renewal shifts some risk back onto the insurance industry, however, with the goal being to encourage the development of markets to spread this risk.

PC insurers have responded to increased catastrophe losses from hurricanes by not renewing policies in the most affected areas or by renewing them only at considerably higher premiums. They have also specified in policies that exclusions for flood damage include that resulting from wind-driven storm surge.

Property-Casualty Insurance

Underwriting Risk. Underwriting risk in many lines of PC insurance is high in absolute terms and relative to life insurance, because PC insurers have less ability to diversify risks for these reasons:

- Claims in some PC insurance lines, such as homeowners' insurance in a given area, are highly correlated.
- Claims in other lines, such as product liability, are simply uncertain, being infrequent and idiosyncratic but very large when they occur.
- Catastrophe claims are both correlated and uncertain.

Although all insurers are subject to uncertainties of the legal process, PC insurers underwriting certain casualty lines such as product liability and medical malpractice are especially so. For example, they have been significantly hurt by:

- Juries awarding increasingly large damages, especially in class action lawsuits. There have been periodic rumblings in Congress to pass legislation limiting such damages, but no substantive movement on this front has occurred.
- Unexpectedly broad court interpretations of insurance policies.
- Unexpectedly wide targeting of insured defendants.

For example, in the early 1980s, courts interpreted environmental and asbestos policies much more expansively than intended by insurers. These rulings led to claims on environmental and asbestos policies written decades earlier that almost destroyed Lloyd's of London. Another round of asbestos litigation commenced in the late 1990s targeting defendants that never manufactured asbestos but rather transported, stored, or otherwise had some relationship to the material (e.g., 3M Company manufactured inexpensive masks to filter out dust that did not protect from asbestos). Over time, PC insurers have learned to write policies more tightly, although they are sometimes restricted in this endeavor by state regulators, and it is impossible to anticipate all legal outcomes.

Of course, PC insurers also receive favorable court rulings. This occurred in a federal court of appeals ruling in September 2003 and a jury ruling in May 2004 that the terrorist attacks on the World Trade Center on September 11, 2001, constituted one event, not two, and in a federal district court ruling in August 2006 that wind-driven storm surge from Hurricane Katrina fell under the flood exclusions in most homeowners' policies.

Underwriting Income versus Investment Income. Because underwriting PC insurance is risky, PC insurers typically invest in low-risk, liquid assets and hold considerably more capital than do life insurers. Since PC insurers' investment income is relatively certain, analysis of PC insurers focuses on the adequacy and accuracy of their liabilities for unpaid claims and claims adjustment. A particular concern is that PC insurers that underestimate this liability also tend to underprice insurance, which leads to future losses and potentially to insolvency. A. M. Best estimates that such underestimation and underpricing was the most common cause of PC insurer impairment (defined as an insurance regulator taking an action that adversely affects the insurer's ability to conduct insurance operations or expressing concern about the insurer's solvency or financial condition) from 1969 to 2005, and the primary cause of 38% of those insolvencies.[13]

The amount of investment income that insurers expect to generate from underwriting a policy increases with the length of its float period, which depends on its duration and tail. Since most PC policies have durations of a year, duration does not yield much variation in the float period across these policies. In particular, on average insured events typically occur halfway through a year covered, and so if the premium is paid in full at the beginning of the year, the duration of the policy yields float for half a year.

In contrast, tail varies considerably across PC policies. Tail results from three distinct sources:

1. It takes some amount of time to ascertain whether an insured event occurred during the term of a policy. For example, environmental damage may take decades to become apparent.
2. It takes some amount of time for insurers to determine or negotiate/litigate with policyholders the amount of claims for policies for which the responsibility for or amount of damages is hard to assess. For example, in medical malpractice cases, there is often dispute regarding whether and how a doctor covered was incompetent or negligent in treating a patient and whether the patient's injury resulted from such treatment.
3. Workers' compensation and some other PC policies tend to pay out as annuities rather than as lump sums.

These sources of tail generally are more significant for casualty than property insurance.

The amount of investment income that insurers generate also increases with the rate of return they earn on their investments. In periods in which the rate of return on investment is high, as was the case in the early 1980s and much of the 1990s, competition tends to cause premiums to fall. In such cases, PC insurers are subject to the risk that their rate of return on investment will fall so that investment income will not make up for underwriting losses. PC insurers that rely excessively on investment income to make up for underwriting losses are said to engage in cash flow underwriting. One could argue that the entire industry was engaging in this practice during the period of strong investment returns in the 1990s. As a result of the stock market bust from 2000 to 2001 and also the terrorist events of September 11, 2001, PC premiums rose considerably from 2001 to 2004, largely eliminating this practice at present.

Underwriting Cycle. PC insurance is a highly cyclical business. Underwriting income primarily drives the PC underwriting cycle, since PC insurers' investment income is not particularly cyclical, although it does track interest rates and other determinants of the rate of return on investments. The underwriting cycle is evident in the time-series of the combined ratio, which, roughly speaking, is the ratio of PC insurers' underwriting expenses (i.e., for claim losses, claim loss adjustment, and acquisition of policies) to net premiums earned. More precise definitions of the various versions of the combined ratio are provided in Chapter 15. Holding tail and the expected rate of return on investments and thus expected investment income constant, a lower combined ratio implies higher underwriting income, referred to as harder markets. When markets are sufficiently hard, competitors tend to enter the market, which works to lower premiums and thus to raise the combined ratio. Conversely, a higher combined ratio implies lower underwriting income, referred to as softer markets. When markets are sufficient soft, insurers exit the market or fail, which works to raise premiums. The presence of fewer insurers lowers the combined ratio, and the cycle continues.

Historically, a complete PC underwriting cycle has tended to last about seven to eight years. The predictable nature of the cycle can be seen in the path of the combined ratio from 1967 to 2004 for the PC insurance industry in the United States depicted in Exhibit 14.1. In interpreting this exhibit, it is important to recognize that interest rates fell fairly consistently from the early 1980s to 2003, so that for PC insurers' expected net income to be constant, the combined ratio had to fall correspondingly during this period. In addition, it would be somewhat easier to see the underwriting cycle in the figure if "nonrecurring" catastrophe losses and revisions of loss reserves for prior years were removed from the numerator of the combined ratio; these items yield noticeable increases in the combined ratio in 1984 and 1985 (upward revisions of loss reserves for asbestos, environmental, and other long-tailed policies), 1992 (Hurricane Andrew), and 2001 (September 11). There were also large catastrophe losses in 1994 (Northridge earthquake) and 2004 (four hurricanes) that have less perceptible effects on the path of the combined ratio depicted in the exhibit. Taking these considerations into account, Exhibit 14.1 indicates an unusually long soft market during the 1990s and a hard market from 2001 to 2004.

The length of the underwriting cycle depends on both the state and type of insurance under consideration, since the regulatory climate in a state and the risk management or marketing expertise needed to sell specific types of insurance affect the ease of entry into and, more importantly, exit from a particular market. The length of the cycle also depends on the amount of excess capital collectively held by PC insurers. As discussed in the "Regulation" section, PC insurers generally can underwrite premiums only up to a given multiple of the amount of statutory capital plus surplus that they hold. Excess capital implies that PC insurers have the capacity to grow and tends to lead to price competition that prolongs soft markets. Moreover, excess capital prolongs the time it takes for insurers to exit the market or fail, which also prolongs soft markets.

Given the predictable nature of the underwriting cycle, maintaining underwriting discipline throughout the cycle is both important and feasible. PC insurers should attempt to grow in hard markets when premiums are high but be more restrained and possibly even accept market share loss

EXHIBIT 14.1 Property-Casualty Industry Combined Ratio, 1967–2004

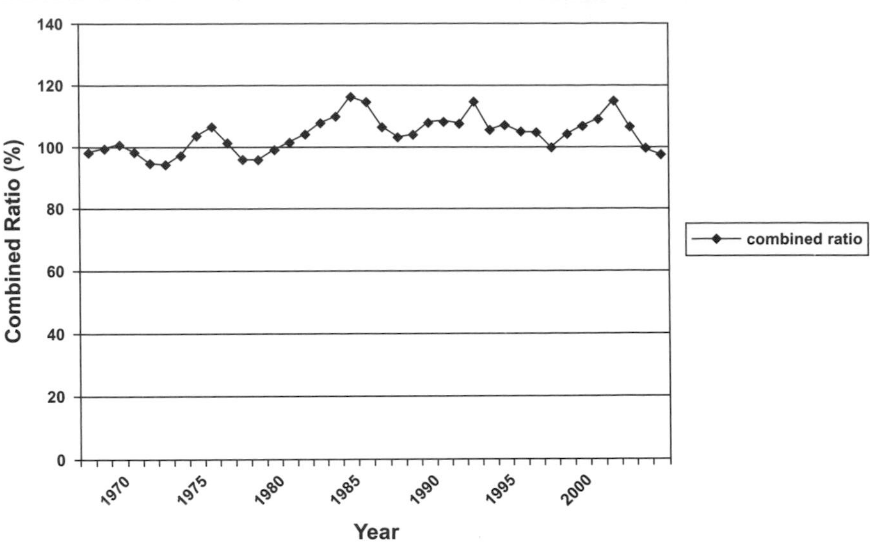

Source: A. M. Best, *Aggregates and Averages: Property-Casualty, United States and Canada,* 2005 ed. (Oldwick, NJ: A. M. Best, 2005).

in soft markets when premiums are low. These insurers also must avoid having a short memory about historical claim experience during periods when claim experience has been good.

Life Insurance

Underwriting Risk. In contrast to PC insurers, life insurers of sufficient size usually can estimate quite accurately the number of people who will die or become disabled or ill in a period. Of course, this assumes that pandemics, natural disasters, or terrorist acts causing the death or illness of large numbers of people do not occur.

Importance of Investments. Since life insurers' claim losses usually are predictable, they invest in higher-risk assets than do PC insurers to increase their investment income. In this regard, life insurance is an interest-rate-spread business, like banking. Accordingly, analysis of life insurers focuses on the quality of their investments. For example, in the late 1980s and early 1990s, many life insurers suffered losses on investments in junk bonds and real estate, with some of the largest life insurers holding such assets in amounts well in excess of their capital and surplus. Some very large life insurers failed or were seized by regulators, the most notable being Executive Life and Mutual Benefit Life, which were seized by regulators in 1991. Executive Life held junk bonds in an amount over 13 times its capital plus surplus. Mutual Benefit

Life's problem was illiquidity, with 27% of its assets in loans to policyholders and with an even larger portfolio of mortgages in a declining real estate market. When money managers moved their cash out of Mutual Benefit Life, it was forced to sell off its liquid assets and was unable to liquidate its other assets.

As in PC insurance, the amount of investment income that life insurers expect to generate from underwriting a policy increases with its float period. Unlike for PC insurance policies, however, the primary source of variation in the float period across life insurance policies is duration, which ranges from one year to the entire remaining life of the insured individual. Duration affects the float period for life insurance policies for two distinct reasons:

1. The probability that an insured event occurs in any year during the duration of these policies is small, even though this probability can be high or even certain over their duration. Life insurers can reinvest the cumulative premiums received on these policies until an insured event occurs.
2. The underwriting risks associated with these policies generally rise over time while periodic insurance premiums often do not, and so premiums paid early in the policy duration effectively subsidize insurance coverage later on.

In contrast, the first two sources of tail for PC insurance policies listed in the "Underwriting Income versus Investment Income" section usually do not apply to a significant extent to life insurance policies, because the occurrence of an insured party's death, disability, or illness generally is known almost immediately and claims usually are paid quickly unless fraud is suspected. The third source of tail can apply to life insurance policies, however, because they may be or pay out as fixed annuities. The term "tail" generally is not used in life insurance, however, probably because of the insignificance of the first two sources of tail.

Because of the tax advantages of life insurance policies relative to other investment vehicles, such as bank accounts and mutual funds, the desirability of these policies is affected by changes in personal income tax rates.

Recent Developments Affecting Both Types of Insurers

Operating Costs. Cost efficiency in obtaining business is a very important driver of the profitability and growth of insurers. The most efficient distribution channel varies across lines of business, reflecting differences in business volumes, customer preferences, and other factors.

Until recently, there were only two primary kinds of insurer, which relied on quite different distribution channels: (1) direct writers that sold their own insurance, such as State Farm and Allstate, and (2) the rest, who used independent agents to sell their insurance. The cost structures of the two kinds of insurer differ in much the same way as the cost structures of retail and wholesale banks. Insurance agents for direct writers are paid salaries (fixed costs), while independent agents are paid commissions (variable costs). This difference implies that direct writers have higher operating leverage and risk, which is justified if direct writers have sufficiently lower costs than other insurers. This cost advantage is most likely to exist in high-volume personal lines of business, such as automobile and homeowners' insurance.

Recently, insurers have increasingly used the mail, telephone, Internet, and other financial institutions such as banks and broker-dealers as distribution channels to decrease the cost and increase the volume of the insurance they sell. Traditional direct writers are considerably less cost effective than these alternative distribution channels in some lines of business. For example, GEICO, a direct writer that primarily uses the telephone to sell automobile insurance policies, has estimated that it has a 15% cost advantage over traditional direct writers. Banks and broker-dealers now sell about 40% of individual annuities (but only 10% of life insurance policies), reflecting their access to investment-oriented customers and the substitutability of annuities with the other forms of investment offered by these financial institutions.[14] Due to the decreasing relative efficiency of direct writers in its primary lines of business, Allstate decided in 1999 to convert its in-house agents to independent contractors.

Self-Insurance. Corporations, groups of corporations, and trade associations have increasingly self-insured (an oxymoron if taken literally) both PC (especially casualty) and life insurance to reduce costs. This is most likely to occur in hard markets, such as 2001 to 2004, when premiums are high given the underwriting risk involved. Captive insurers may be created to perform certain insurance functions. Captive insurers often are located in countries such as Bermuda that provide tax advantages to insurers, as discussed in the "Tax Accounting" section. Captive insurers often purchase reinsurance, thus insuring their owners but bypassing primary insurers. This trend works to increase competition and reduce premiums in primary insurance markets.

Demutualizations. As with thrifts, insurers can be organized either as mutual or stock companies, with mutuals being policyholder-focused cooperatives and stock companies being shareholder-focused corporations. The first insurers were mutuals, and many insurers in the United States (including State Farm, the largest PC insurer, and New York Life, the ninth-largest life insurer) remain mutuals. Recently, however, a number of the largest life insurers demutualized, including John Hancock and MetLife in 2000 and Prudential in 2001, and there have been many demutualizations of PC insurers as well. The primary reason for demutualization usually is to provide greater access to capital markets, which is increasingly important in the deregulated financial services environment created by GLBA.

There are two types of demutualization:

1. The primary type converts the mutual insurer into a stock corporation. This type normally is paired with an initial public offering.
2. Some states allow for the simultaneous formation of a mutual holding company that initially owns all of the stock of the corporation. This type

sometimes is paired with an initial public offering, but more commonly it is chosen to provide the insurer with the option of offering stock in the future (e.g., Liberty Mutual did this in 2001).

Under either type of demutualization, in most states insurers must identify the closed block of policies and associated investments for which preexisting participating policyholders are the residual claimants and account for the interests of the closed block separately from the interests of the shareholders going forward. If investments are insufficient to pay claims to the closed block, then the insurer will have to contribute assets. At the time of its demutualization, MetLife estimated that policies would remain in its closed block for over 100 years.

Financial Services Deregulation. GLBA poses risks and opportunities for insurers, allowing them to compete, cooperate, or combine with other types of financial institution through the creation of financial holding companies. Perhaps the most notable effect of GLBA thus far is that most types of insurance products are now more actively sold through banks and other financial institutions, a natural activity for institutions with access to individuals through retail networks and to commercial customers through long-standing relationships. For example, banks sold insurance generating $80 billion of premiums in 2005—with the two main sources being annuities ($42 billion) and commercial PC insurance ($24 billion)—compared to $45 billion of premiums in 2000.[15] Banks' sales of annuities and individual life policies are made primarily by their own employees, while their sales of commercial PC and group life insurance have resulted primarily from their numerous acquisitions of insurance agencies. Banks appear to be less interested in underwriting insurance than in selling it, however. Illustrating this point, banks earned total fee income from insurance of $4.6 billion in 2005, of which $3.9 billion (85%) is from selling and $.7 billion (15%) is from underwriting insurance.[16]

In part for this reason, the most celebrated combination of a U.S. bank and insurer, the 1998 merger of Citibank and Travelers that created Citigroup, was unwound when Citigroup spun off its PC insurance businesses in 2002 and sold its life insurance businesses to Metlife in 2005. Citigroup found it difficult to sell insurance to its commercial customers and was disenchanted with the lower and more variable rates of return earned by insurance underwriters than by banks. Although no longer underwriting insurance, Citigroup still actively sells annuities and other insurance products underwritten by others, however.

Unitary thrift holding companies have long been able to own insurers, as discussed in Chapter 3, but MetLife and a few other insurers have acquired commercial banks since the passage of GLBA.

REGULATION

Under the McCarran-Ferguson Act of 1945, insurers are regulated at the state level. Generally, an insurance holding company has legally separate subsidiaries in each state in which it operates, and the regulator in an insurer's state of domicile serves as its primary regulator. Regulators in an insurer's nondomicile states have the right to examine the holding company or its out-of-state subsidiaries insofar as they interact with or otherwise affect the solvency of the subsidiary in their state. There have been recent attempts to develop a federal insurance charter or, alternatively, to standardize state regulation, but no apparent political progress has yet been made along either of these fronts.

An insurer must be licensed by the regulator in its state of domicile. Licensing is rarely denied to a healthy insurance company, and relatively small total capital is required to sell insurance in a state. An insurer may or may not be licensed in other states in which it operates, however. If an insurer is licensed in a state, it is referred to as "admitted" in that state; otherwise it is referred to as a "surplus lines" insurer. It generally is necessary for purchasers of surplus lines insurance to demonstrate that the insurance cannot be obtained from admitted insurers in the state on reasonable terms. Admitted insurers are more highly regulated regarding insurance policies and premiums than are surplus lines insurers.

As with banking regulators, insurance regulators' main concern is insurer solvency, that is, the ability of the insurer to pay off claims as they arise. Accordingly, both admitted and surplus lines insurers must meet capital requirements and are subject to dividend restrictions. These requirements are based on SAP. As discussed in detail in the "Statutory Accounting Principles" section, SAP is more conservative than generally accepted accounting principles (GAAP) in most respects, which reduces the insurer's capital and can restrict its ability to grow.

In most states, PC insurers cannot underwrite premiums more than three times statutory capital plus surplus, although the multiple may depend on the type of insurance written. Most PC insurers currently hold far more capital than required, however; for example, the average ratio of net premiums written to statutory capital plus surplus for the PC insurance industry in the United States at the end of 2004 was slightly less than one.[17] Both PC and life insurers are subject to risk-based capital requirements set by the National Association of Insurance Commissioners (NAIC). Due to life insurers' lower risk, they hold a level of capital closer to that of banks than PC insurers; for example, the ratio of owners' equity to assets before separate accounts for the life insurance industry in the United States at the end of 2004 was 8.5%.[18] Dividend payments typically are capped at 10% of statutory surplus or at statutory net income excluding capital gains.

The regulatory climate varies across states, with some state regulators squeezing insurers more in response to political pressures. Insurers sometimes "redomesticate" (i.e., change their state of domicile) seeking a more favorable regulatory climate. The regulatory climate also varies across types of insurance policy, with PC policies covering automobiles, property highly subject to natural disasters, workers' compensation, and medical malpractice being particularly subject to political pressures. All states have shared and involuntary residual markets for some or all of these types of policies in which the insurers underwriting a particular type of insurance in the state are required to jointly underwrite high risk parties that find it difficult to obtain insurance voluntarily from insurers. It can be difficult for insurers to exit a state, especially if they underwrite politically sensitive lines of business.

Unlike Federal Deposit Insurance Corporation (FDIC) insurance of banks, and thrifts' deposits, there are no permanent insurance funds to pay off the policyholders of failed insurers. Guaranty associations in each state levy assessments on the healthy insurers in that state when an insurer fails. These assessments usually are capped at a maximum amount each year, so it can take a long time for policyholders to be paid back from these funds. These funds generally would be inadequate if one or at most a few large failures occurred at the same time in any state. Moreover, they often do not apply to certain types of insurance. Assessments can be a significant, persistent drag on an insurer's profitability.

PRIMARY INSURANCE ACCOUNTING STANDARDS

Like the accounting for credit losses discussed in Chapter 5, the overarching standard governing the accounting for insurance is SFAS No. 5, *Accounting for Contingencies* (1975). This standard requires that, for a liability to be recognized for a loss contingency, the loss must be probable and the amount of the loss must be capable of reasonable estimation based on current information. These requirements imply that a liability for unpaid claims will be recognized at the inception of homogeneous policies accounted for at a portfolio level, since losses at that level are assured and reasonably estimable at inception, but will not be recognized at the inception of heterogeneous policies with low probabilities of paying claims. An interpretation of SFAS No. 5 (1975), FASB Interpretation (FIN) No. 14, *Reasonable Estimation of the Amount of a Loss* (1976), states that if there is a range of possible losses and no point in the range is more likely than any other, then the liability should reflect the low end of the range. This requirement implies that the liability for unpaid claims tends to be revised upward over time as the range of possible losses contracts, more so for riskier insurance policies.

Unlike the accounting for credit losses, however, the accounting for insurance is subject to highly detailed rules in SFAS Nos. 60 (1982) and 97 (1987), whose primary features are described next.

SFAS No. 60: Property-Casualty and Traditional Life Insurance Policies

Terminology. Insurance accounting employs a considerable amount of specialized terminology. This section summarizes the terms used in SFAS No. 60 (1982). These terms reflect the fact that the effects of insurance underwriting are reported gross of qualifying reinsurance on the balance sheet and net of that reinsurance on the income statement under SFAS No. 113,

Accounting and Reporting for Reinsurance of Short-Duration and Long-Duration Contracts (1992), which is discussed in detail in Chapter 16.

These terms pertain to premiums received from policyholders and paid to reinsurers, the initial deferral of those premiums on the balance sheet, and the subsequent recognition of premium revenue:

- *Gross premiums written* are premiums received from policyholders during the period.
- *Net premiums written* are gross premiums written minus the cash premiums paid for reinsurance during the period.
- *Unearned premiums* are the deferred revenue liability for gross premiums written for future insurance coverage.
- *Prepaid reinsurance* is the deferred contra revenue asset for the premiums paid for future reinsurance coverage.
- *Net premiums earned* are the revenue for insurance coverage provided and not reinsured during the current period. Net premiums earned equal net premiums written minus the change in unearned premiums plus the change in prepaid reinsurance premiums.

These terms pertain to the accrual of liabilities and recognition of expense for claims on insurance coverage provided or reinsured, with some differences in terminology for PC insurers and life insurers indicated:

- *Incurred but not reported (IBNR) events* are insured events that are believed to have occurred but have not yet been reported to the insurer.
- *Loss reserves (PC insurance) or the liability for future policy benefits (life insurance)* are the estimated liability for unpaid claims on insurance coverage provided, including estimates for IBNR events. This liability is net of the realizable amounts from salvage (the value of damaged property) and subrogation (claims against third parties, including other insurers), but gross of claims against reinsurers.
- *Loss adjustment reserves* are the estimated liability for unpaid costs of settling claims on insurance coverage provided (e.g., claim adjustment, appraisals, and legal fees), including estimates for IBNR events. This liability is net of the realizable amount of subrogation but gross of the claims against reinsurers.
- *Reinsurance recoverables* are the asset for the cash expected to be received in the future from reinsurers on reinsurance coverage purchased. This asset usually is subdivided into recoverables for claims not yet paid by the insurer, for which a liability for unpaid claims remains on the insurer's books, and recoverables for claims already paid by the insurer, for which no such liability remains.
- *Loss expense (PC insurance) or benefits expense (life insurance)* is the recognized expense for claims costs, including estimates for IBNR events. This expense includes the initial estimate for current-period insurance

coverage and revisions of estimates for prior periods' insurance coverage. It is net of the amount expected to be recouped from reinsurance.

- *Claim adjustment expense (often called loss adjustment expense in PC insurance)* is the recognized expense for the costs of settling claims. This expense includes the initial estimate for current-period insurance coverage and revisions of prior estimates for prior periods' insurance coverage. It is net of the amount expected to be recouped from reinsurance.

These terms pertain to the costs of acquiring insurance policies:

- *Policy acquisition costs* are the costs incurred primarily to acquire or renew policies, such as agent commissions, medical evaluations, and administration. These costs must vary with the acquisition of policies.
- *Deferred policy acquisition costs (DPAC)* are the asset for the unamortized amount of policy acquisition costs.

Short- and Long-Duration Policies. SFAS No. 60 (1982) mandates different accounting for short- and long-duration insurance policies. Short-duration policies provide coverage on fixed terms for a period of short duration. The standard does not indicate the length of the period that separates short and long duration, but a one-year term is short duration. Short-duration policies may be renewable, but if so the insurer generally must be able to revise the policy terms at each renewal. Short-duration policies include essentially all PC, accident, and health insurance, and one-year term life insurance that is not guaranteed renewable on fixed terms.

Long-duration policies provide coverage on fixed terms for a long or indefinite period. Term life insurance with a sufficiently long term or that is guaranteed renewable on terms that do not vary with the health of the policyholder and whole life insurance and its variants are long-duration policies.

Accounting for Short-Duration Policies. For short-duration policies, SFAS No. 60 (1982) requires that insurers initially record premiums written in the unearned premiums liability and then gradually amortize this liability into premiums earned as insured events occur over the coverage period. If underwriting risk is evenly distributed over the period, then premiums earned should be recorded evenly over the period. Under SFAS No. 113 (1992), premiums paid for qualifying reinsurance are treated in mirror-image fashion to premiums received. Reinsurance premiums paid initially are capitalized in the prepaid reinsurance asset and then gradually reduce premiums earned over the period of reinsurance coverage. Exhibits 14.2 and 14.3 depict the accounts for unearned premiums and prepaid reinsurance, respectively, for short-duration policies.

SFAS No. 60 (1982) requires that liabilities for unpaid claims and claim adjustment be accrued and claim and claim adjustment expenses be recognized for short-duration policies as insured events occur over the policy term. Although these expenses fluctuate with actual claims, on average they are recognized in proportion to net premiums earned, and so on average insurers recognize income evenly over the policy term.

EXHIBIT 14.2 Unearned Premiums T Account

Unearned Premiums (Liability)	
	beginning balance
− amortization (increase in net premiums earned)	+ gross premiums written
	= ending balance

SFAS No. 60 (1982) does not require (or prohibit) discounting of the liabilities for unpaid claims and claim adjustment for short-duration policies. In practice, PC insurers generally do not discount their loss and loss adjustment reserves, regardless of the tail of the policy, except for settled workers' compensation and some other claims that pay out as annuities. This lack of discounting yields three related economically nondescriptive effects on PC insurers' financial statements:

1. Loss and loss adjustment reserves on the balance sheet and loss and loss adjustment expense in the period of coverage on the income statement are overstated.
2. Economic interest expense that would have been recorded had loss and loss adjustment reserves been discounted is misclassified as loss and loss adjustment expense on the income statement.
3. Underwriting and investment income are poorly matched in time, because loss and loss adjustment expense is recorded primarily in the period of coverage, while investment income is earned over the tail of the policies. This implies that the net income on a policy is mismeasured in each period over its tail.

Each of these effects is greater the longer the tail of the policy involved.

To illustrate these effects, assume a PC insurance policy is expected to pay a claim of $1 in four years (i.e., its tail), that the insurer expects to earn a 10% rate of return on investments each year, and that it sets the premium to yield zero cumulative net income over the tail (i.e., at the present value

EXHIBIT 14.3 Prepaid Reinsurance Premiums T Account

Prepaid Reinsurance Premiums (Asset)	
beginning balance	
+ premiums paid for reinsurance	− amortization (reduction of net premiums earned)
= ending balance	

of the claim payment of $\$1/1.1^4 = .\$68$). Assume also that the insurer records loss reserves for this policy at the undiscounted \$1 value of the claim payment, as is usually the case. This policy yields an underwriting loss of \$.32 (premiums earned of \$.68 minus loss expense of \$1) in the first year that is perfectly offset by investment income of the same amount (the interest from investing the \$.68 premium) spread over the four-year tail of the policy. Hence, the insurer reports a large underwriting loss and negative net income in the first year, but positive investment income and net income in the following three years. Economically, however, the insurer has zero underwriting loss in the first year, because the policy is actuarially fair, and zero investment income net of interest expense in all four years, because the interest revenue from reinvesting the premium is exactly offset by the economic interest expense on the discounted loss reserves.

Property-casualty insurers underwrite policies each period, of course, and the mismeasurement of net income for an insurer just identified will reflect the sum of the effects across the insurer's policies. The total amount of net income in a period will on average be correct for an insurer that underwrites the same types and amounts of insurance coverage each period, because the overstatement of loss and loss adjustment expenses on the current period's coverage will on average be offset by the nonrecognition of economic interest expense on the undiscounted loss and loss adjustment reserves for prior periods' coverage. However, for a growing (declining) PC insurer, the overstatement of loss and loss adjustment expense will be greater (less) than the nonrecognition of economic interest expense, and so net income will be too low (high) on average.

Accounting for Long-Duration Policies. The accounting for long-duration life insurance policies reflects the fact that premium payments are fixed even though insurance benefits typically increase over time, so these policies include an investment element, as depicted in Exhibit 14.4. For these policies, SFAS No. 60 (1982) requires that premiums be recorded as revenue when due from policyholders, usually the effective date of the policy. Thus, there is no unearned premiums liability unless the policyholder pays premiums before they are due. Similar to reinsurance of short-duration policies, premiums paid for qualifying reinsurance generally are treated in mirror-image fashion to premiums received, although the specific treatment required under SFAS No. 113 (1992) depends on whether the reinsurance is short- or long-duration, as discussed in Chapter 16.

A liability for future policy benefits is accrued and benefits expense is recognized as premiums earned are recognized. This liability and expense equal the amounts that would be accrued for a short-duration policy with the same premiums and payoffs in the current period plus incremental amounts that capture the investment element of long-duration policies. The incremental liability accrued equals the present value of benefits to be paid for insured events that have not yet occurred less the present value of future net premiums to be received over the current and expected renewal periods

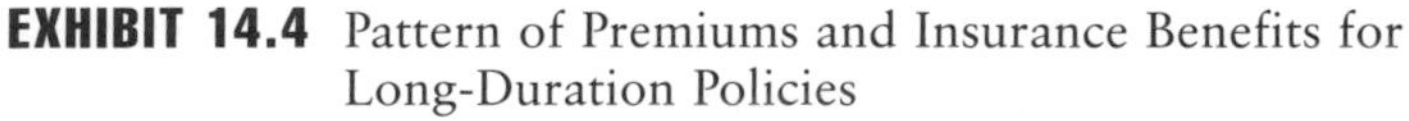

EXHIBIT 14.4 Pattern of Premiums and Insurance Benefits for Long-Duration Policies

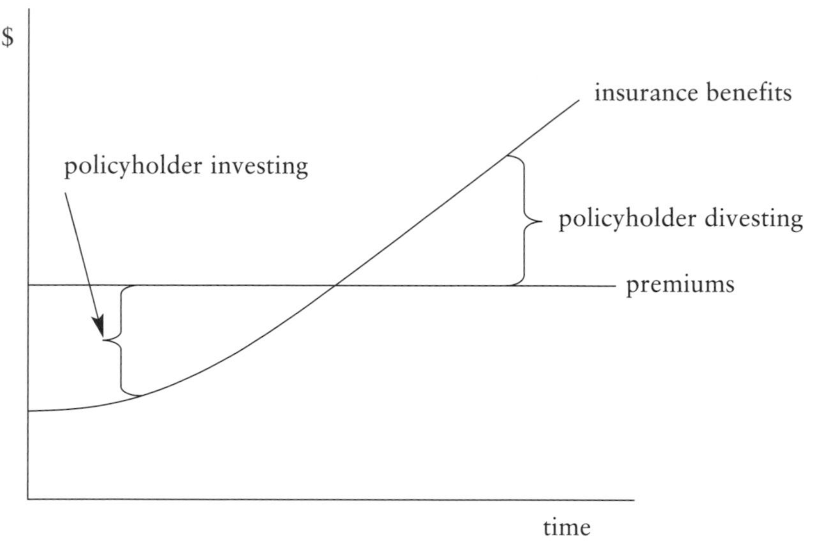

of the policy. Net premiums are defined as gross premiums less a normal profit margin, so this additional liability and expense are not reduced by the insurer's expectation of a future profit. The calculation of the incremental liability is rather complicated actuarially, requiring estimates of mortality, morbidity, renewal probabilities, investment yields, and expenses, taking into account the risk of adverse deviations in these estimates (a manifestation of conservatism). These estimates are made at the inception of a policy and used to account for it throughout its life, unless a premium deficiency (discussed later) is determined to exist.

Despite the fact that the liability for future policy benefits for long-duration policies is discounted under SFAS No. 60 (1982), the economic interest on that liability over time is incorrectly classified as benefits expense. Specifically, economic interest is treated as a deficiency in the liability for future policy benefits, as discussed later.

Although SFAS No. 60 (1982) does not include any requirements regarding cash flow statement classification, in practice all the cash flows on PC and traditional life insurance policies are classified as operating. This reflects the mistaken view that traditional insurance policies are operating, not financial, in nature.

Example. This example illustrates the distinct nature of and accounting for short- and long-duration policies under SFAS No. 60 (1982), using economically similar life insurance policies. Assume an individual has a 1% chance of dying this year and a 2% chance of dying next year conditional on living this year, so the individual's unconditional probability of dying next year is 2% × (1 − 1%) = 1.98%. The individual either engages in a succession of two one-year term life policies with rising premiums or one two-year term life policy with level premiums. For the purposes of this example, assume the two one-year term policies are accounted for as short-duration policies and the two-year term policy is accounted for as a long-duration policy. (In fact, one-year policies that are guaranteed renewable are long duration under SFAS No. 60 [1982], and a two-year policy that is not guaranteed renewable probably would not be deemed long duration in practice.) The premiums are paid at the beginning of each year, and any benefits are paid at the end of each year. The benefit payment in the event of death is 100. The insurer can earn investment income at a rate of 10% per year on its float, and 10% is also the rate at which the liability for future policy benefits for long-duration policies is discounted. The premiums are determined in an actuarially fair manner, assuming that the policies provide no profit to the insurer, taking into account both underwriting income and investment income on the float. For the one-year term life policies, the premium is .909 = .01 × 100/1.1 in year 1 and the expected premium is 1.800 = .0198 × 100/1.1 in year 2, taking into account the probability of death in year 1. The premium is higher in year 2 because the conditional probability of death is twice as high in that year. For the two-year term life policy, the premium each year that the individual is alive is 1.34 = 100 × (.01 + .0198/1.1)/(1.1 + .99), which yields an expected premium of 1.326 = 1.34 × .99 in year 2, taking into account the probability of death in year 1. The premium in year 1 subsidizes the insurance in year 2, providing an investment value to the policy. There are no acquisition costs or adjustment costs.

For simplicity, the accounting for the *expected* outcomes from these policies taking into account the probabilities of the individual dying each year is described next. If the insurer held large enough portfolios of these policies, these expectations would be realized. Exhibit 14.5 provides the expected income statements for the insurer in both years for both types of policy, taking into account the probabilities of dying each year. For the one-year term life policies, the expected net premiums earned during each year equal the expected premium received at the beginning of that year, .909 in year 1 and 1.800 in year 2. Expected benefits expense each year is the expected undiscounted benefit payment that year, 1 in year 1 and 1.980 in year 2. Expected underwriting income is negative both years, −.091 = .909 − 1 in year 1 and −.180 = 1.800 − 1.980 in year 2, because the expected benefits expense is overstated due to the lack of discounting. Economically, a portion of benefits expense should be classified as interest expense. By construction, this negative expected underwriting income is exactly made up by expected investment income on the float.

For the two-year term life policy, the expected net premiums earned in a year equal the expected premiums received at the beginning of the year, 1.340 in year 1 and 1.326 in year 2. The expected benefits expense in year 1 is 1.474, which equals the benefits expense in year 1 for the one-year term life policy plus an additional amount of .474 = (1.980/1.1) − 1.326, which

EXHIBIT 14.5 Example of the Expected Income Statements for Short- and Long-Duration Policies under SFAS No. 60

	Year 1	Year 2
Two short-duration one-year term life policies with rising premiums:		
Net premiums earned	.909	1.800
− Benefits expense	(1.000)	(1.980)
= Underwriting income	(.091)	(.180)
+ Investment income	.091	.180
= Net income	0	0
One long-duration two-year term life policy with level premiums:		
Net premiums earned	1.340	1.326
− Benefits expense	(1.474)	(1.506)
= Underwriting income	(.134)	(.180)
+ Investment income	.134	.180
= Net income	0	0

is the discounted value of the expected benefits payment in year 2 less the expected premium at the beginning of year 2. The benefits expense in year 2 is 1.506, which equals the benefits expense of 1.980 in year 2 for the one-year term life policy less the .474 additional accrual of expense in year 1. These calculations illustrate the subsidization of insurance coverage in the second year by premiums in the first year. There is again negative expected underwriting income in both years, $-.134 = 1.340 - 1.474$ in year 1 and $-.180 = 1.326 - 1.506$ in year 2, because economic interest expense on the liability for future policy benefits is classified as benefits expense. By construction, this negative underwriting income is again exactly made up by investment income on the float.

To illustrate the bookkeeping involved, here are the expected journal entries for the policies in the example (ignoring the straightforward accounting for the investment of float and thus investment income):

For the two short-duration one-year term life policies with rising premiums:		
beginning year 1:		
cash (+ asset)	.909	
unearned premiums (+ liability)		.909
during year 1:		
unearned premiums (− liability)	.909	
net premiums earned (+ income)		.909
benefits expense (− income)	1.000	
liability for future policy benefits (+ liability)		1.000

end year 1:		
liability for future policy benefits (− liability)	1	
cash (− asset)		1
beginning year 2:		
cash (+ asset)	1.800	
unearned premiums (+ liability)		1.800
during year 2:		
unearned premiums (− liability)	1.800	
net premiums earned (+ income)		1.800
benefits expense (− income)	1.980	
liability for future policy benefits (+ liability)		1.980
end year 2:		
liability for future policy benefits (− liability)	1.980	
cash (− asset)		1.980

For the long-duration two-year term life policy with level premiums:

beginning year 1:		
cash (+ asset)	1.340	
net premiums earned (+ income)		1.340
benefits expense (− income)	1.474	
liability for future policy benefits (+ liability)		1.474
end year 1:		
liability for future policy benefits (− liability)	1.000	
cash (− asset)		1.000
beginning year 2:		
cash (+ asset)	1.326	
net premiums earned (+ income)		1.326
benefits expense (− income)	1.506	
liability for future policy benefits (+ liability)		1.506
end year 2:		
liability for future policy benefits (− liability)	1.980	
cash (− asset)		1.980

Reserve Redundancies and Deficiencies. Because claims and claim adjustment costs are uncertain, the liabilities for unpaid claims and claim adjustment initially recorded by an insurer usually turn out to be either too high (redundant) or too low (deficient) given its actual or revised expected costs. These *ex post* misestimations are more likely to occur and be significant for PC insurers' loss and loss adjustment reserves than for life insurers' liability for future policy benefits, and so they are generally referred to as reserve redundancies and deficiencies, terms that are rarely if ever used in life insurance. PC insurers' individually riskier, more correlated, and longer-tailed policies are more likely to yield reserve redundancies and deficiencies.

PC insurers must eliminate reserve redundancies (deficiencies) by decreasing (increasing) loss and loss adjustment reserves and loss and loss adjustment expense. Recognition of prior reserve redundancies is called reserve releases, while recognition of prior reserve deficiencies is called reserve strengthening. The total loss and loss adjustment expense in a period is the loss and loss adjustment expense for the current year's insurance coverage plus reserve deficiencies and minus reserve redundancies for prior years' coverage.

Although the terms "redundancies" and "deficiencies" generally are not used in life insurance, the economic interest expense on life insurers' discounted liability for future policy benefits for long-duration policies is effectively recognized thorough deficiencies in that liability.

Exhibit 14.6 presents the structure of the T account for loss and loss adjustment reserves for PC insurers and the liability for future policy benefits for life insurers under SFAS No. 60 (1982). For PC insurers, Securities and Exchange Commission (SEC) Securities Act Industry Guide 6 requires that the increases and decreases to the loss and loss adjustment reserve T account for each of the past three years be disclosed in the footnotes in Form 10-K filings. These and other disclosures regarding PC insurers' loss and loss adjustment reserves are discussed in detail in Chapter 15.

Policy Acquisition Costs. Policy acquisition costs are initially capitalized in the DPAC asset. This asset is then amortized over the expected life of the policy in proportion to the present value of expected net premiums.

DPAC invariably is much smaller relative to annual policy acquisition costs for PC insurers underwriting short-duration policies than for life insurers underwriting long-duration policies. For short-duration PC policies, DPAC typically is amortized on a straight-line basis over the policies' one-year term,

EXHIBIT 14.6 Insurance Liability T Account under SFAS No. 60

Loss and Loss Adjustment Reserves (PC Insurance) or Liability for Future Policy Benefits (Life Insurance)

	beginning balance
− claim payments (for current and prior years' coverage)	+ loss or benefits expense for current years' coverage
− reserve redundancy for prior years' coverage	+ reserve deficiency for prior years' coverage
	= ending balance

so DPAC amortization tends to be about twice DPAC. For long-duration life-insurance policies, DPAC can be amortized over decades, so DPAC amortization is a small fraction of DPAC. For example, for The Hartford in 2005, DPAC is $8.6 billion for life insurance and $1.1 billion for PC insurance, while DPAC amortization is $1.2 billion (14% of DPAC) for life insurance and $2.0 billion (176% of DPAC) for PC insurance.

Premium Deficiencies. A premium deficiency is distinct from a reserve deficiency. A premium deficiency exists when the insurer expects a net loss on the insurance policy going forward (i.e., the policy is impaired). The definition of a premium deficiency varies somewhat for short- and long-duration policies. For a short-duration policy, a premium deficiency exists if all the expected future costs associated with the policy (the expected loss and loss adjustment costs plus future amortization of DPAC plus expected policyholder dividends) exceed the balance of unearned premiums (the future revenue on the policy). For a long-duration policy, a premium deficiency exists if the present value of the expected future costs (other than policy acquisition costs) plus the balance of DPAC exceeds the present value of expected future gross premiums plus the balance of the liability for future policy benefits. Premium deficiencies may result from claims being larger or coming sooner than expected, from policies being terminated earlier than expected, and, for long-duration policies, from policy renewals or investment returns being lower then expected.

When premium deficiencies occur, insurers may under SFAS No. 60 (1982) and in practice usually do, unlock the estimates underlying the accounting for long-duration policies. Premium deficiencies must be eliminated by first reducing the DPAC asset by the amount of the deficiency; if the DPAC asset is not big enough, then an additional liability must be created. Summarizing this discussion, the structure of the T account for the DPAC asset under SFAS No. 60 (1982) is depicted in Exhibit 14.7.

Premium deficiencies and DPAC write-downs are more likely to occur for long-duration policies, all else being equal. The most common DPAC

EXHIBIT 14.7 Deferred Policy Acquisition Costs T Account

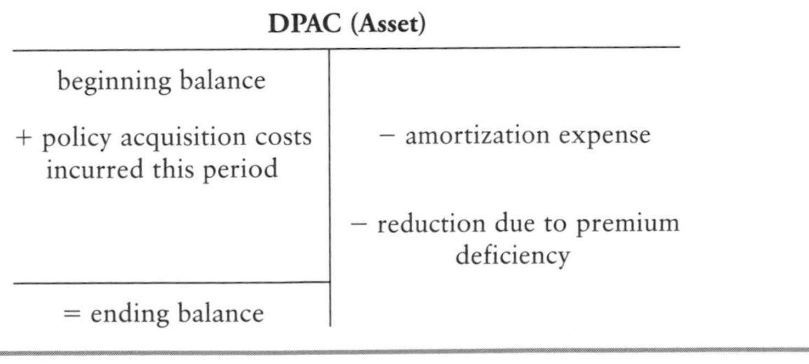

write-downs recently have been for variable annuities and other primarily investment-oriented life insurance policies due to either poor investment performance in the 2000 to 2002 period (e.g., Nationwide Financial recorded a $347 million DPAC write-down in the third quarter of 2002) or the recognition of costs for minimum guarantees and other contract features in 2004 discussed in the "Accounting Standards Governing Embedded Derivatives and Other Life Insurance Policy Features" section.

Disclosures. SFAS No. 60 (1982) requires various disclosures. Most important, insurers must describe the approach and assumptions underlying most of their accrual estimates. For example, they must disclose if and when they discount the liability for unpaid claims for short-duration policies and the range of discount rates they use to discount the liability for unpaid claims for short-duration policies.

SFAS No. 97: Primarily Investment-Oriented Life Insurance Policies

Accounting. In the 1980s, primarily investment-oriented insurance policies such as universal life policies and annuities became very popular. SFAS No. 60 (1982) did not yield descriptive accounting for these policies for reasons discussed in the prior section, and so SFAS No. 97 (1987) was developed to address these limitations. The standard requires that pure investment contracts that do not impose insurance risk on the insurer be accounted for like bank deposits, in which the policyholder is the depositor, the insurer is the bank, and premiums are the deposits. It requires that universal life–type policies that are primarily investment-oriented but that place some insurance risk on the insurer be accounted for using the "retrospective" deposit method (a poorly chosen term as there is nothing retrospective about the method). This method accounts for universal life–type policies in the same way as investment contracts but adjusts for the insurance aspects of the policies using the same accounting as required for short-duration policies under SFAS No. 60 (1982).

Under both the deposit and retrospective deposit methods, premiums add to a financial liability, referred to as policyholder account balances, rather than unearned premiums or premiums earned under SFAS No. 60 (1982). Policyholder account balances are increased by interest expense over time. Policyholder account balances are reduced by the portion of cash payments to the policyholder that constitute withdrawals from the investment balance, as opposed to insurance claim payments.

To capture the insurance aspects of universal life–type policies, under the retrospective deposit method, policyholder account balances are reduced by any assessments for insurance coverage and account administration. These assessments are treated as premiums for short-duration insurance under SFAS No. 60 (1982). Similarly, a liability for future policy benefits is accrued and benefits expense is recognized in the same way as these items for short-duration policies under SFAS No. 60 (1982). The portion of cash payments to policyholders that reflect the insurance aspects of universal life–type policies reduces the liability for future policy benefits, not policyholder account balances. Summarizing this discussion, the policyholder account balances T account for universal life–type policies and investment contracts are depicted in Exhibits 14.8 and 14.9, respectively.

SFAS No. 97 (1987) requires that interest accrues on DPAC (the T account in Exhibit 14.7 must be generalized accordingly), so it is treated like a financial asset rather than a deferred expense. Although this may seem odd, it effectively works to back-load amortization expense in a fashion similar to the accrual of interest expense on policyholder account balances. In addition, DPAC is amortized in proportion to the net present value of gross profit (a complicated variable that reflects all sources of benefit and cost for the insurer) rather than net premiums as under SFAS No. 60 (1982). If gross profit is a constant percentage of net premiums, then the use of gross profits rather than net premiums does not affect the amortization schedule of DPAC.

SFAS No. 97 (1987) does not include any requirements regarding cash flow statement classification, but in practice the cash flows that affect policyholder account balances are classified as financing.

SFAS No. 97 (1987) also changed the classification of realized gains and losses on the income statement. Realized gains and losses must reported pretax as part of other income, not as part of investment income or after tax.

Example. Consider this universal life–type policy that embeds the two-year term life policy with level premiums from the example in the "SFAS No. 60: Property-Casualty and Traditional Life Insurance Policies" section but also includes premium payments that represent pure investments. If the policyholder dies during the policy term, then an amount equal to the insurance benefit of 100 plus these additional premiums with accrued interest is paid to the policyholder. If the policyholder does not die during the policy term,

EXHIBIT 14.8 Policyholder Account Balances T Account for a Universal Life Policy under SFAS No. 97

Policyholder Account Balances (Liability)	
	beginning balance
− insurance revenue	+ cash premiums received
− cash payments (that reduce policyholder account balances)	+ interest expense
	= ending balance

EXHIBIT 14.9 Policyholder Account Balances T Account for Investment Contracts under SFAS No. 97

Policyholder Account Balances (Liability)	
	beginning balance
− cash payments	+ cash premiums received
	+ interest expense
	= ending balance

then only the additional premiums with accrued interest are paid at the end of the policy term. Additional premiums of 10 are paid at the beginning of each year that the policyholder lives, so that the premium payment at the beginning of year 1 is 11.34 = 10 + 1.34, and the expected premium payment at the beginning of year 2 is 11.226 = .99 × 10 + 1.326. The policyholder account balances earn interest at a 10% rate, the same rate earned on float by the insurer, so that the policies remain zero profit to the insurer. As is usually the case for the liability for unpaid claims for short-duration policies, no interest expense is accrued on the amount removed from policyholder account balances for the insurance assessment during the year. The value of the additional payments with accrued interest is 11 = 10 × 1.1 at the end of year 1, of which .11 = .01 × 11 is expected to be paid out that year, and is expected to be 22.869 = .99 × (10 × 1.1 + 10 × 1.1^2) at the end of year 2. Interest expense is 1.043 = (11.34 − .909) × .1 in year 1. The balance in the policyholder account balances at the end of year 1 is 11.364 = 11.34 + 1.043 − .909 − .11. Interest expense is expected to be 2.079 = (11.364 + 11.226 − 1.80) × .1 in year 2. At the end of year 2, the balance of policyholder account balances is paid to the policyholder, leaving a balance of zero in that account. The expected income statements for this policy are provided in Exhibit 14.10 and discussed in the next section.

These calculations are summarized in the expected journal entries for this universal life–type policy (ignoring the straightforward accounting for the reinvestment of float and thus investment income):

beginning year 1:

cash (+ asset)	11.34	
policyholder account balances (+ liability)		11.34
policyholder account balances (− liability)	.909	
unearned premiums (+ liability)		.909

during year 1:

unearned premiums (− liability)	.909	
net premiums earned (+ income)		.909

EXHIBIT 14.10 Example of the Difference between Expected Income Statements for a Universal Life–Type Policy under SFAS No. 97 and, for Comparison, SFAS No. 60

	Year 1	Year 2
Two-year universal life-type policy with level premiums:		
SFAS No. 97 (required method):		
Net premiums earned	.909	1.800
− Benefits expense	(1)	(1.980)
= Underwriting income	(.091)	(.180)
+ Interest revenue	1.134	2.259
− Interest expense	(1.043)	(2.079)
= Interest income	.091	.180
= Net income	0	0
SFAS No. 60 (for comparison):		
Net premiums earned	11.34	11.226
− Benefits expense	(12.474)	(13.485)
= Underwriting income	(1.134)	(2.259)
+ Investment income	1.134	2.259
= Net income	0	0

benefits expense (− income)	1	
liability for future policy benefits (+ liability)		1
interest expense (− income)	1.043	
policyholder account balances (+ liability)		1.043
end year 1:		
liability for future policy benefits (− liability)	1	
policyholder account balances (− liability)	.11	
cash (− asset)		1.11
beginning year 2:		
cash (+ asset)	11.226	
policyholder account balances (+ liability)		11.226
policyholder account balances (− liability)	1.800	
unearned premiums (+ liability)		1.800
during year 2:		
unearned premiums (− liability)	1.800	
net premiums earned (+ income)		1.800
benefits expense (− income)	1.980	
liability for future policy benefits (+ liability)		1.980

interest expense (− income)	2.079	
policyholder account balances (+ liability)		2.079
end year 2:		
liability for future policy benefits (− liability)	1.980	
policyholder account balances (− liability)	22.869	
cash (− asset)		24.849

Comparison of SFAS Nos. 60 and 97

SFAS Nos. 60 (1982) and 97 (1987) are fundamentally inconsistent standards in this respect. The spectrum from pure insurance policies to pure investment products runs: PC insurance and one-year term life that is not guaranteed renewable (close to pure insurance), guaranteed renewable or multiyear term life (mostly insurance, some investment), whole life and its variants (partly insurance, partly investment), universal life (mostly investment, some insurance), and investment contracts (close to or pure investment). However, the relative magnitude of loss or benefits expense does not monotonically decline as we move along this spectrum. In particular, benefits expense is smaller for both nonguaranteed renewable one-year term and universal life than for whole life and its variants. The inconsistency results from the fact that benefits expense calculated under SFAS No. 60 (1982) for whole life and its variants includes economic interest expense, whereas SFAS No. 97 (1987) properly classifies interest expense on universal life policies and annuities. Relatedly, in practice cash flows on whole life policies are classified as operating, while most cash flows on universal life–type policies and investment contracts are classified as financing. SFAS No. 97 (1987) is clearly a more descriptive standard for investment-oriented policies, including whole life and its variants, than is SFAS No. 60 (1982).

This inconsistency is illustrated by accounting for the example of a universal life policy in the "SFAS No. 97: Primarily Investment-Oriented Life Insurance Policies" section using the accounting required under SFAS No. 60 (1982). Exhibit 14.10 provides the expected income statements for this policy under the two accounting treatments. Although expected income is zero by construction under both treatments, the classification of this income is very different.

Accounting by Mutual Life Insurers

As originally written, SFAS Nos. 60 (1982) and 97 (1987) excluded mutual life insurers from their scope. SFAS No. 120, *Accounting and Reporting by Mutual Life Insurance Enterprises for Certain Long-Duration Participating Contracts* (1995), mandates that mutual life insurers follow these standards listed earlier as well as all the rest of GAAP, unless stringent conditions regarding dividend payout are met. These conditions basically require the policyholders to be the true residual claimants. Prior to SFAS No. 120 (1995), most mutual life insurers used SAP in their financial reports, and they often referred to SAP as GAAP.

ACCOUNTING STANDARDS GOVERNING EMBEDDED DERIVATIVES AND OTHER LIFE INSURANCE POLICY FEATURES

Minimum Benefits

Variable annuities and other primarily investment-oriented insurance policies may include minimum death or living (withdrawal, income, or accumulation) benefits and other contract features such as no-lapse guarantees that are accounted for under American Institute of Certified Public Accountants Statement of Position (SOP) No. 03-1, *Accounting and Reporting by Insurance Enterprises for Certain Nontraditional Long-Duration Contracts and for Separate Accounts*. This standard requires an assessment of the extent of the mortality and morbidity risks resulting from these features at the inception of policies. If these risks are nominal, then these policies should be accounted for as investment contracts under SFAS No. 97 (1987). Otherwise, the policies should be accounted for as universal life–type contracts under SFAS No. 97 (1987), with a liability for future policy benefits accrued and benefits expense recognized for these risks. SOP No. 03-1 also requires disclosures about the nature and extent of minimum guarantees, including the reported liabilities.

Insurers were required to adopt SOP No. 03-1 at the beginning of the 2004 fiscal year. The effect of adopting the standard depended on the types of contract features offered by the insurer and how the insurer had accounted for those features prior to SOP No. 03-1. For example, The Hartford disclosed in its 2003 Form 10-K filing that it accrued an additional gross liability of $199 million for its $92 billion of variable annuities with guaranteed minimum death benefits and other contract features. The Hartford disclosed it had not previously accrued any liability for these contract features. Nationwide Financial provided a more detailed disclosure of the additional liabilities it recorded for the contract features in its policies in its 2003 Form 10-K filing: $12.3 million for ratchet interest crediting, $2.4 million for secondary guarantees, $1.8 million for guaranteed minimum death benefits, and $1.0 million for guaranteed minimum income benefits.

Embedded Derivatives

Variable annuities and other insurance policies often include embedded options or other derivatives that may need to be unembedded from the host insurance contract and accounted for separately under SFAS No. 133, *Accounting for Derivative Instruments and Hedging Activities* (1998). As discussed in Chapter 11, embedded derivatives must be unembedded under this standard if all of these three criteria are met:

1. The host contract is not fair valued on the balance sheet and income statement under GAAP.
2. The embedded derivative is not "clearly and closely related" to the host contract.
3. The embedded derivative meets SFAS No. 133's (1998) criteria to be a derivative.

A number of Derivatives Implementation Group (DIG) issues consider examples of derivatives embedded in investment-oriented life insurance contracts and provide guidance regarding whether they should be unembedded. The embedded derivatives considered and conclusions are:

- DIG B8 (2000) states that contract features that cause policyholders and insurers to share investment risks in nontraditional annuities should be unembedded if they are not clearly and closely related to the host traditional annuities.
- DIGs B10 (2006), B29 (2006), and B30 (2006) state that annuities with equity-linked investment returns contain embedded derivatives that generally should be unembedded because they are not clearly and closely related to the host annuity.
- DIG B9 (2000) states that market value adjusted prepayment options should not be unembedded because they are clearly and closely related to the host contract.
- DIG B25 (2001) states that alternative payment options in the accumulation phase of a deferred annuity that benefit the policyholder only if she chooses to annuitize are not unembedded because these options do not settle net (i.e., the policyholder must invest the proceeds of the deferred annuity in an annuity).
- DIG B25 (2001) states that guaranteed minimum payments during the payout phase of an annuity must be unembedded because they are not clearly and closely related to the host annuity.

Separate Accounts

Primarily investment-oriented insurance policies often pay variable returns based on a separate pool of assets. For these assets to be treated as separate accounts under SOP No. 03-1:

- The assets must be legally separate from the insurer.
- Policyholders must receive all the upside from the assets but may be protected on the downside by minimum guarantees.

For separate accounts, SOP No. 03-1 requires that policyholders' interests in the assets and the associated liabilities be accounted for at fair value on separate lines on the balance sheet, with an additional liability for future policy benefits accrued for minimum benefits guarantees. In contrast, the insurer's interests in the assets are accounted for as general account assets.

In its 2003 Form 10-K filing, The Hartford disclosed that $17 billion of its separate account assets did not meet SOP No. 03-1's requirement for legal separation from the insurer and so could no longer be accounted for as separate accounts. Subsequently, the assets were accounted for primarily as investment securities and the liabilities were accounted for under SFAS No. 97 (1987).

Proposals to Change Insurance Accounting

A number of proposals have been made to change insurance accounting. The International Accounting Standards Board (IASB) has an ongoing project on this topic that will become a joint project with the FASB after the IASB issues an initial discussion document, which is currently scheduled for the first quarter of 2007. These proposals and project reflect the limitations and inconsistencies of insurance accounting, the intertwined nature of the underwriting and insurance aspects of insurance policies, and the accounting issues raised by the presence of embedded derivatives and other contract features discussed earlier. These proposals are summarized in detail the final section of Chapter 16.

FINANCIAL STATEMENTS

The Hartford's financial statements reported in its 2005 Form 10-K filing are described in this section, indicating how SFAS Nos. 60 (1982) and 97 (1987) differently affect those statements.

Balance Sheet

Exhibit 14.11 presents The Hartford's 2005 balance sheet. The Hartford holds $286 billion of assets, of which $151 billion are in separate accounts for variable annuities and other investment products. Its remaining $135 billion of assets include $107 billion of investments, $9.7 billion of DPAC and present value of future profits (an intangible asset resulting from acquisitions of other insurers), and $6.4 billion of reinsurance recoverables, reflecting the gross balance sheet presentation of reinsurance under SFAS No. 113 (1992). Thus, standard financial assets constitute most of The Hartford's assets, as is true of insurers generally.

The Hartford holds $270 billion of liabilities, of which $151 billion are again separate accounts. The remaining $119 billion of its liabilities include $22.3 billion of reserves for unpaid claims and claim adjustment expenses for short-duration PC insurance policies accounted for under SFAS No. 60 (1982), $13.0 billion of reserves for future policy benefits for traditional

EXHIBIT 14.11 The Hartford Financial Services Group, Inc., Consolidated Balance Sheets

	As of December 31,	
(in millions, except for share data)	**2005**	**2004**
Assets		
Investments		
Fixed maturities, available-for-sale, at fair value (amortized cost of $74,766 and $71,359)	$ 76,440	$ 75,100
Equity securities, held for trading, at fair value (cost of $19,570 and $12,514)	24,034	13,634
Equity securities, available-for-sale, at fair value (cost of $1,330 and $742)	1,461	832
Policy loans, at outstanding balance	2,016	2,662
Mortgage loans on real estate	1,731	1,174
Other investments	1,253	1,006
Total investments	106,935	94,408
Cash	1,273	1,148
Premiums receivable and agents' balances	3,734	3,235
Reinsurance recoverables	6,360	6,178
Deferred policy acquisition costs and present value of future profits	9,702	8,509
Deferred income taxes	675	419
Goodwill	1,720	1,720
Property and equipment, net	683	643
Other assets	3,600	3,452
Separate account assets	150,875	140,023
Total assets	**$ 285,557**	**$ 259,735**
Liabilities		
Reserve for future policy benefits and unpaid claims and claim adjustment expenses		
Property and casualty	$ 22,266	$ 21,329
Life	12,987	12,246
Other policyholder funds and benefits payable	64,452	52,833
Unearned premiums	5,566	4,807
Short-term debt	719	621
Long-term debt	4,048	4,308
Other liabilities	9,319	9,330
Separate account liabilities	150,875	140,023
Total liabilities	**270,232**	**245,497**
Stockholders' Equity		
Common stock, par value	3	3
Additional paid-in capital	5,067	4,567

EXHIBIT 14.11 *(Continued)*

(in millions, except for share data)	As of December 31, 2005	2004
Retained earnings	10,207	8,283
Treasury stock, at cost	(42)	(40)
Accumulated other comprehensive income	90	1,425
Total stockholders' equity	**15,325**	**14,238**
Total liabilities and stockholders' equity	**$ 285,557**	**$ 259,735**

life insurance policies accounted for under SFAS No. 60, and $64.5 billion of other policyholder funds and benefits payable for primarily investment-oriented insurance accounted for under SFAS No. 97 (1987). About 96% of its PC loss and loss adjustment reserves are undiscounted and thus overstated. The amount of this overstatement can be determined, as discussed in the "Tax Accounting" section. The Hartford also has $5.6 billion of unearned premiums.

The Hartford is highly leveraged, with $15.3 billion of owners' equity. Since its separate accounts are largely separate from its general account assets and liabilities (aside from some return guarantees), The Hartford effectively has a capital ratio of 11.4% = $15.3 billion owners' equity/$135 billion general account assets, which is not far from that of a bank. This statistic reflects the fact that The Hartford underwrites considerably more life insurance than PC insurance, and so is similar to a bank.

Income Statement

Exhibit 14.12 reports The Hartford's 2005 income statement. Revenues include earned premiums of $14.4 billion on both PC and traditional life insurance accounted for under SFAS No. 60 (1982). Revenues also include fee income of $4.0 billion, the majority of which is asset management fees on separate accounts. Net investment income of $8.2 billion reflects The Hartford's return on its investments. Expenses include benefits, claims, and claim adjustment expenses of $16.8 billion for policies accounted for under SFAS No. 60 (1982), $3.2 billion of amortization of DPAC and present value of future profits, and $3.2 billion of insurance operating costs and expenses, which must include interest expense on other policyholder funds and benefits payable accounted for under SFAS No. 97 (1987) since this expense appears nowhere else. The Hartford's earned premiums ($14.4 billion) are considerably less than the sum of its underwriting expenses ($16.8 billion for benefits, claims, and claim adjustment expenses plus $3.2 billion amortization of DPAC and present value of future profits plus $3.2 billion of insurance operating costs and expenses), but it makes up for this underwriting loss with investment income and asset management fees.

EXHIBIT 14.12 The Hartford Financial Services Group, Inc., Consolidated Statements of Operations

	For the Years Ended December 31,		
(in millions, except for per share data)	**2005**	**2004**	**2003**
Revenues			
Earned premiums	$14,359	$13,566	$11,891
Fee income	4,012	3,471	2,760
Net investment income			
Securities available-for-sale and other	4,384	4,144	3,233
Equity securities held for trading	3,847	799	—
Total net investment income	8,231	4,943	3,233
Other revenue	464	437	556
Net realized capital gains	17	291	279
Total revenues	**27,083**	**22,708**	**18,719**
Benefits, claims, and expenses			
Benefits, claims, and claim adjustment expenses	16,776	13,640	13,548
Amortization of deferred policy acquisition costs and present value of future profits	3,169	2,843	2,397
Insurance operating costs and expenses	3,227	2,776	2,314
Interest expense	252	251	271
Other expenses	674	675	739
Total benefits, claims, and expenses	**24,098**	**20,185**	**19,269**
Income tax expense (benefit)	711	385	(459)
Cumulative effect of accounting change, net of tax	—	(23)	—
Net income (loss)	**$ 2,274**	**$ 2,115**	**$ (91)**

Cash Flow Statement

Exhibit 14.13 presents The Hartford's 2005 cash flow statement. The changes in all the accounts associated with its traditional insurance products (reserve for future policy benefits, unpaid claims, and claim adjustment expenses and unearned premiums; reinsurance recoverables; and DPAC and present value of future profits) accounted for under SFAS Nos. 60 (1982) and 113 (1992) appear in the operating section. In contrast, net receipts from investment and universal life–type contracts accounted for under SFAS No. 97 (1987)

EXHIBIT 14.13 The Hartford Financial Services Group, Inc., Consolidated Statements of Cash Flow

	For the Years Ended December 31,		
(in millions)	**2005**	**2004**	**2003**
Operating Activities			
Net income (loss)	$ 2,274	$ 2,115	$ (91)
Adjustments to reconcile net income (loss) to net cash provided by operating activities			
Amortization of deferred policy acquisition costs and present value of future profits	3,169	2,843	2,397
Additions to deferred policy acquisition costs and present value of future profits	(4,131)	(3,914)	(3,313)
Change in:			
Reserve for future policy benefits, unpaid claims and claim adjustment expenses, and unearned premiums	2,163	877	5,597
Reinsurance recoverables	(361)	128	(1,105)
Receivables	(682)	(395)	(47)
Payables and accruals	(267)	(11)	576
Accrued and deferred income taxes	168	529	(327)
Net realized capital gains	(17)	(291)	(279)
Net increase in equity securities, held for trading	(12,872)	(7,409)	—
Net receipts from investment contracts credited to policyholder accounts associated with equity securities, held for trading	13,087	7,909	—
Depreciation and amortization	561	274	219
Cumulative effect of accounting change, net of tax	—	23	—
Other, net	640	(44)	269
Net cash provided by operating activities	**3,732**	**2,634**	**3,896**
Investing Activities			
Purchase of investments	(34,984)	(27,950)	(28,918)
Sale of investments	26,589	21,592	17,320
Maturity of investments	3,738	4,195	3,731
Purchase of business/affiliate, net of cash acquired	8	(58)	(464)
Sale of affiliates	—	—	33
Additions to property and equipment, net	(211)	(180)	(89)
Net cash used for investing activities	**(4,860)**	**(2,401)**	**(8,387)**

(continues)

EXHIBIT 14.13 *(Continued)*

	For the Years Ended December 31,		
(in millions)	**2005**	**2004**	**2003**
Financing Activities			
Issuance (repayment) of short-term debt, net	100	(477)	535
Issuance of long-term debt	—	197	1,235
Repayment of long-term debt	(250)	(450)	(500)
Issuance of common stock in underwritten offering	—	411	1,161
Net receipts from investment and universal life–type contracts	1,387	962	2,409
Dividends paid	(345)	(325)	(291)
Return of shares to treasury under incentive and stock compensation plans	(2)	(2)	(1)
Proceeds from issuances of shares under incentive and stock compensation plans	390	161	60
Net cash provided by financing activities	**1,280**	**477**	**4,608**
Foreign exchange rate effect on cash	(27)	(24)	(32)
Net increase in cash	125	686	85
Cash—beginning of year	**1,148**	**462**	**377**
Cash— end of year	**$ 1,273**	**$ 1,148**	**$ 462**
Supplemental Disclosure of Cash Flow Information:			
Net Cash Paid (Received) During the Year for:			
Income taxes	$ 447	$ 32	$ (107)
Interest	$ 248	$ 246	$ 233

appear in the financing section. In principle, the investment-oriented aspect of any insurance policy is financing from the insurer's point of view.

LINE OF BUSINESS DISCLOSURES

It is important for users of financial reports to analyze insurers by line of business to the extent possible given the insurer's disclosures, in order to adjust for the limitations of insurance accounting explained in the "Primary Insurance Accounting Standards" section. Fortunately, this analysis is often quite feasible, in large part because Regulation S-X requires these disclosures of the most important financial statement numbers for each segment as defined under SFAS No. 131, *Disclosures about Segments of an Enterprise and Related Information* (1997):

- Premiums written and earned
- Unearned premiums
- Investment income
- Loss and loss adjustment reserves, liability for future policy benefits, and policyholder account balances
- Loss and loss adjustment expense and benefits expense
- DPAC and DPAC amortization
- Other operating expense

Although some insurers provide this information only for very aggregated segments (e.g., PC versus life insurance), many provide it for segments defined as fairly homogeneous lines of business. For example, The Hartford provides disclosures for seven life insurance segments and four PC insurance segments that are reported in Exhibit 14.14. Moreover, in its management discussion and analysis, The Hartford provides considerable information about the types of policies written by each of these segments. This information is summarized in the "Products" section.

Detailed disclosures by type of policy are also provided in statutory filings described in the next section.

OTHER INSURANCE ACCOUNTING SYSTEMS

Statutory Accounting Principles

Insurance regulation is based on SAP, not GAAP. The two accounting systems overlap in many respects; for example, SFAS No. 60 (1982) was based substantially on SAP, while SAP reinsurance accounting was based substantially on SFAS No. 113 (1992). Where they differ, SAP generally is more conservative than GAAP, yielding lower capital for all insurers and lower income for growing insurers. This conservatism reflects insurance regulators' focus on solvency and their view that high growth is a threat to solvency. In addition, similar to certain adjustments to banks' regulatory capital ratios discussed in Chapter 2, some aspects of SAP yield lower capital and income volatility than GAAP.

There are four main reasons why SAP is more conservative than GAAP:

1. Policy acquisition costs are expensed immediately under SAP but capitalized and amortized under GAAP.
2. Insurance liabilities are calculated using statutory assumptions under SAP that generally are conservative.
3. An asset valuation reserve (akin to the allowance for loan losses) is recorded under SAP based on statutory assumptions that generally are conservative.

EXHIBIT 14.14 The Hartford Financial Services Group, Inc., Supplementary Insurance Information ($ in millions)

	As of December 31, 2005			
Segment [1]	**Deferred Policy Acquisition Costs** [2]	**Future Policy Benefits Unpaid Claims and Claim Adjustment Expenses**	**Unearned Premiums**	**Other Policyholder Funds and Benefits Payable**
Life				
Retail Products Group	$4,714	$ 747	$	$16,410
Retirement Plans	405	366		5,194
Institutional Solutions Group	81	5,315		9,233
Individual Life	1,975	586		4,990
Group Benefits	95	5,828		535
International	1,281	51		26,102
Other	16	94		1,988
Total Life	**8,567**	**12,987**	**69**	**64,452**
Property & Casualty				
Ongoing Operations				
Business Insurance	531	7,066	2,566	—
Personal Lines	468	2,152	1,809	—
Specialty Commercial	135	6,202	1,076	—
Total Ongoing Operations	1,134	15,420	5,451	—
Other Operations	—	6,846	51	—
Total Property & Casualty	**1,134**	**22,266**	**5,502**	—

EXHIBIT 14.14 *(Continued)*

Segment [1]	Earned Premiums, Fee Income and Other	Net Investment Income	Benefits, Claims, and Claim Adjustment Expenses	Amortization of Deferred Policy Acquisition Costs	Other Expenses [3]	Net Written Premiums
	For the Year Ended December 31, 2005					
Life						
Retail Products Group	$ 2,273	$ 933	$ 895	$ 744	$ 869	$
Retirement Plans	162	311	231	26	115	
Institutional Solutions Group	623	802	1,212	32	56	
Individual Life	769	305	469	205	167	
Group Benefits	3,810	398	2,794	31	1,022	
International	483	75	42	133	188	
Other	83	4,021	4,166	1	105	
Total Life	**8,203**	**6,345**	**9,809**	**1,172**	**2,522**	**N/A**
Property & Casualty						
Ongoing Operations						
Business Insurance	4,785		2,971	1,138		5,001
Personal Lines	3,731		2,294	581		3,676
Specialty Commercial	2,099		1,486	281		1,806
Total Ongoing Operations	10,615	1,082	6,751	2,000	1,326	10,483
Other Operations	4	283	212	(3)	22	4
Total Property & Casualty	**10,619**	**1,365**	**6,963**	**1,997**	**1,348**	**10,487**

[1] Segment information is presented in a manner by which The Hartford's chief operating decision maker views and manages the business.
[2] Also includes present value of future profits.
[3] Includes insurance operating costs, interest, and other expenses.
Note: Certain reclassifications have been made to prior-year financial information to conform to current year presentation.
N/A—Not applicable to life insurance pursuant to Regulation S-X.

4. Various illiquid assets (e.g., furniture and leasehold improvements) are not admitted as assets under SAP.

There are two main reasons why SAP yields lower capital and income volatility than GAAP:

1. Unrealized gains and losses on available-for-sale securities are not included in SAP capital.
2. Realized gains and losses arising from changes in the level of interest rates are recorded in an interest maintenance reserve and amortized into interest income over time under SAP.

Statutory accounting principles generally are consistent from state to state, because the NAIC worked to codify them in its *Accounting Practices and Procedures Manual*.[19] This manual first became effective in January 1, 2001, and is reissued annually. Although all states have accepted the manual for implementation, it does not override state laws and regulations, so differences in the implementation of SAP across states remain. The biggest change in SAP brought about by the NAIC's codification project was to allow deferred taxes. As discussed in the "Tax Accounting" section, most insurers have deferred tax assets, so this change worked to increase their capital.

Each insurance subsidiary must file SAP-based convention statements for each state in which it operates. These convention statements have a common form and are public information, and insurance industry analysts often find these detailed statements more useful than the much more highly aggregated annual reports. For example, these statements include every investment held and reinsurance contract engaged in by insurers.

SFAS No. 60 (1982) requires the reconciliation of SAP and GAAP net income and owners' equity in a footnote. This footnote is useful for assessing an insurer's capacity for growth.

Tax Accounting

Tax accounting differs from both SAP and GAAP. Like SAP but not GAAP, acquisition costs are immediately expensed for tax purposes, which reduces tax payments relative to tax expense and so yields deferred tax liabilities. In most other respects, tax accounting is relatively unfavorable for insurers, and so yields deferred tax assets. Unlike both SAP and GAAP, a portion of unearned premiums is taxable, and loss and loss adjustment reserves must be discounted for all policies, regardless of their type or duration.

The fact that loss and loss adjustment reserves are discounted for tax purposes allows the user of financial reports to calculate discounted reserves by using information in the tax footnote. This calculation is particularly important economically for PC insurers that underwrite long-tailed policies for which loss and loss adjustment reserves are most overstated. Divide a PC insurer's deferred tax asset associated with discounted loss and loss adjustment reserves for tax purposes by the insurer's tax rate to determine the difference of GAAP and tax (discounted) loss and loss adjustment reserves. Subtract this difference from the GAAP reserves to get the discounted reserves. For example, The Hartford discloses that it has a deferred tax asset of $730 million for discounted loss and loss adjustment reserves in 2005. Assuming a 35% tax rate, this implies that its discounted reserves for tax purposes are $2.1 billion = $730 million/.35 less than its GAAP reserves of $22.2 billion (i.e., $20.1 billion).

A strategy many U.S. insurers have used to avoid taxes is to relocate their corporate headquarters to Bermuda or be acquired by an insurer headquartered in Bermuda, referred to as corporate inversion. This tax scheme exploits the largely arbitrary division of insurers' income into investment income and underwriting income. Since underwriting income typically is negative, as long as the insurer's investment income can be located in a country with no corporate income tax, such as Bermuda, the insurer will pay no income taxes. Large, old insurers (that would have to pay capital gains taxes to relocate to Bermuda) have lobbied Congress to eliminate this tax scheme to maintain their competitive position, so far unsuccessfully.

Most states impose excise taxes on insurance premiums.

NOTES

1. A.M. Best, Best's *Aggregates & Averages: Property-Casualty, United States and Canada,* 2005 ed. (Oldwick, NJ: A.M. Best, 2005).
2. Ibid.
3. A.M. Best, *Best's Aggregates & Averages: Life/Health, United States and Canada,* 2005 ed. (Oldwick, NJ: A.M. Best, 2005).
4. Ibid.
5. Ibid.
6. Ibid.
7. Ibid.
8. Ibid.
9. Ibid.
10. Insurance Information Institute, "9/11 and Insurance: The Five Year Anniversary," September 2006.
11. Insurance Information Institute, Press Release, August 22, 2006.
12. Insurance Information Institute, Presentation by R. Hartwig, "Personal Lines Insurance: Overview & Outlook," March 2006.
13. "By the Numbers," *Best's Review* (January 2006).
14. M. Purushotham, "The Impact of Distribution on the Individual Life and Annuity Industry," *Actuary Magazine* (June 2006).
15. Insurance Information Institute and The Financial Services Roundtable, *Financial Services Fact Book 2006,* online version, www.financialservicesfacts.org/financial/.

16. Ibid.
17. A.M. Best, *Property-Casualty, United States and Canada.*
18. A.M. Best, *Life/Health, United States and Canada.*
19. National Association of Insurance Commissioners, Kansas City, MO.

CHAPTER 15

Property-Casualty Insurers' Loss Reserve Disclosures

This chapter illustrates the analysis of property-casualty (PC) insurers' loss and loss adjustment reserves using their mandated disclosures about those reserves. It also defines the expense ratios used in the analysis of the underwriting and total profitability of PC insurers and explains how these ratios should be evaluated in the context of the insurer's loss reserve development and lines of business. For convenience, net of reinsurance loss and loss adjustment reserves (expense) are referred to as loss reserves (expense) except when necessary to indicate the effects of reinsurance or to distinguish loss expense from loss adjustment expense.

The assessment of the adequacy, accuracy, and management of loss reserves is central to the financial analysis of PC insurers, for three reasons:

1. PC insurers that underestimate (overestimate) loss reserves tend to underprice (overprice) insurance, potentially leading to insolvency (difficulty obtaining business).
2. Insurers that estimate loss reserves inaccurately, compared to other insurers underwriting similar policies, are likely to have poor risk management expertise and thus difficulty maintaining underwriting discipline through the PC underwriting cycle.
3. Insurers exercise discretion over loss reserves. This behavior is more feasible for longer-tailed policies, because claim payments are made farther in the future and so provide less discipline on accrual estimates for these policies.

Empirical research provides considerable evidence that PC insurers exercise discretion over loss reserves. This research finds that financially weak insurers understate loss reserves to appear solvent, that high-tax insurers overstate loss reserves to defer taxes, and that insurers operating in lines of business or states with stricter rate regulation in the soft market of 1989 to 1993 underestimated loss reserves in order to offer more competitive rates.[1] It finds that insurers underestimate loss reserves to avoid reporting losses, implying that this management is a nonmonotonic function of insurer profitability. Specifically, although less profitable insurers usually understate loss reserves compared to more profitable insurers, insurers reporting a small profit understate loss reserves compared to those reporting a small loss.[2] It finds that loss reserve revisions are strongly positively serially correlated, implying that errors in estimating loss reserves are corrected gradually; this could reflect the anticonservative accounting for loss contingencies under Statement of Financial Accounting Standards (SFAS) No. 5, *Accounting for Contingencies* (1975) and FASB Interpretation (FIN) No. 14, *Reasonable Estimation of the Amount of a Loss* (1976) discussed in Chapter 14 rather than discretion, however.[3] Finally, research finds that upward revisions of loss reserves tend to be made by PC insurers with lower future profitability and higher risk, so these revisions are leading indicators of poor performance by these insurers.[4]

PC insurers must provide two disclosures about their loss reserves in their Form 10-K filings under Securities and Exchange Commission (SEC) Securities Act Industry Guide 6. The first is a footnote reporting the revisions in net of reinsurance loss reserves for each of the current and past two years. A useful feature of this disclosure is that loss expense and claim payments in each year are broken into the portions associated with the coverage provided in that year and in prior years. This feature is important because underwriting results for the current year's coverage are usually most representative of the ongoing operations of and conditions affecting PC insurers and so have direct relevance to forecasting their future performance. In contrast, revisions of loss reserves for prior years' coverage reflect insurers' luck, misestimation, or exercise of discretion regarding those reserves, which, while very useful for understanding insurers' past performance, have more complex implications for their future performance.

The second disclosure provides highly detailed information about revisions of loss reserves over time. For the net of reinsurance loss reserves reported on the balance sheet in each of the past 10 years, this disclosure reports the revised loss reserve estimates and claim payments made in each subsequent year up to the current year. To illustrate, for the reported loss reserves in 2000, the loss reserve development disclosure in 2005 reports the revised loss reserve estimates and claim payments made in 2001, 2002, 2003, 2004, and 2005. By tying a PC insurer's reported loss reserves to its revised estimates and realized claim payments, this disclosure provides users of financial reports with a rich data set to evaluate the adequacy, accuracy, and management of the insurer's loss reserves.

The insurance coverage provided in a given year is called an accident year, an important concept in the analysis of PC insurers. Results for individual accident years are aggregated and thus not clearly reflected in the amounts reported on the financial statements in these three respects:

1. Loss reserves reported on the balance sheet are the estimate of unpaid claims summed across all accident years up to and including the current year.

2. Loss expense reported on the income statement is the estimate of current and future claims for the current accident year plus the revisions during the year of loss reserves for prior accident years.
3. Claim payments (indirectly) reported on the cash flow statement are the sum of the claim payments for the current and all prior accident years.

This chapter demonstrates spreadsheet-based techniques using the information provided in loss reserve disclosures that allow users of financial reports to calculate PC insurers' loss reserves, loss reserve revisions, and claim payments for the current and nine prior accident years in each year up to the current year.

For most purposes, users should analyze accident year data rather than the aggregated data reported in the financial statements, because individual accident years (especially if far removed in time) are often subject to time-period-specific phenomena that have little or no effect on a PC insurer's ongoing ability to underwrite profitable coverage. For example, asbestos and environmental policies underwritten prior to 1986 were subject to broader court interpretations than PC insurers expected at the time. Although PC insurers have written these policies more carefully since then, they continue to experience sizable reserve deficiencies for accident years prior to 1986. Thus, it is important for users of financial reports to distinguish accident years prior to 1986 from subsequent accident years for insurers that underwrote these policies prior to 1986. In addition, farther removed accident years generally reflect longer-tailed policies, which tend to be riskier and otherwise different from the representative policy underwritten by an insurer.

Most important, users should attempt to determine the reasons for revisions of accident year loss reserves. Are these revisions attributable to discretionary understatement or overstatement of loss reserves? If so, what is the PC insurer's incentive to manage loss reserves? Is there evidence of income smoothing, with loss reserves being underestimated when additional income is desired, leading to reserve deficiencies, and vice versa? Relatedly, do revisions of loss reserves tend to reverse over time? Alternatively, are loss reserve revisions attributable to unintentional loss reserve inaccuracy? If so, is this inaccuracy due to the PC insurer's lack of risk management expertise or its good or bad luck on risky coverage?

The chapter also demonstrates how to calculate the tail of PC insurers' policies. As discussed in Chapter 14, tail is a primary determinant of the amount of investment income PC insurers can earn from underwriting insurance. Tail also is associated with PC insurers' ability to exercise discretion over loss reserves.

Chapter 14 briefly discusses PC insurers' combined ratio in the context of the underwriting cycle and tail. The combined ratio is the most inclusive and important of the expense ratios used in the analysis of PC insurers. This chapter defines the combined and other expense ratios in detail and explains how those ratios should be interpreted in the context of the PC insurer's loss reserve revisions and lines of business. Expense ratios vary across lines of business because different lines often are at different stages of the underwriting cycle or have different tails or cost structures.

The PC insurance operations of The Hartford Financial Services Group (The Hartford) in 2005 are used to illustrate the information contained in the loss reserve disclosures and the techniques for analyzing this information developed in this chapter. The first section of the chapter describes The Hartford's loss reserve footnote. The second section describes The Hartford's loss reserve development disclosure. Using these disclosures, the third through fifth sections calculate loss reserves, revisions of loss reserves, and claim payments by accident year for the Hartford. The fifth section also calculates tail for The Hartford. The sixth section constructs The Hartford's loss reserve T account for a representative accident year. The final section defines PC insurers' expense ratios and explains the use of these ratios in the analysis of these insurers.

LOSS RESERVE FOOTNOTE

Exhibit 15.1 presents excerpts from The Hartford's 2005 loss reserve footnote. As required, this footnote includes a table that has the same basic structure as the loss reserve T account depicted in Exhibit 14.6. This table reports the balances of and the increases and decreases in The Hartford's net of reinsurance loss reserves for each of the three years from 2003 to 2005. In each year, the amounts of both loss expense and claim payments for the current accident year and for the sum of all prior accident years are reported separately. The footnote also includes a brief discussion of reserve deficiencies for the three years reported in the table.

For example, the table reports that at the beginning of 2005, The Hartford's net of reinsurance loss reserves were $16,191 million, which equal gross loss reserves of $21,329 million minus reinsurance recoverables of $5,138 million. Loss reserves increased during 2005 by loss expense of $6,715 million for the current accident year and by a reserve strengthening to eliminate a deficiency of $248 million for prior accident years. Loss reserves decreased during the year by claim payments of $3,593 million for the current accident year and $2,698 million for prior accident years. These increases and decreases yield net loss reserves at the end of 2005 of $16,863 million, which equal gross loss reserves of $22,266 million minus reinsurance recoverables of $5,403 million. The ratio of reinsurance recoverables to gross loss reserves is consistently about 25% for The Hartford, indicating the extent of its use of reinsurance.

Although most or all of the information can be compiled from information in the financial statements and loss reserve development disclosure, the table conveniently summarizes some of the most important information users of financial reports need to evaluate PC insurers' loss reserves and loss expense. For example, it indicates that The Hartford recorded reserve strengthenings eliminating deficiencies of $2,824 million in 2003, $414 million in

EXHIBIT 15.1 The Hartford Financial Services Group, Inc., Excerpts from Loss Reserve Footnote in 2005 ($ in millions)

	For the Years Ended December 31,		
	2005	**2004**	**2003**
Beginning liabilities for property and casualty unpaid claims and claim adjustment expenses — gross	$21,329	$21,715	$17,091
Reinsurance and other recoverables	5,138	5,497	3,950
Beginning liabilities for property and casualty unpaid claims and claim adjustment expenses — net	16,191	16,218	13,141
Add provision for property and casualty unpaid claims and claim adjustment expenses			
Current year	6,715	6,590	6,102
Prior years	248	414	2,824
Total provision for property and casualty unpaid claims and claim adjustment expenses	6,963	7,004	8,926
Less payments			
Current year	3,593	2,616	2,369
Prior years	2,698	4,415	3,480
Total payments	6,291	7,031	5,849
Ending liabilities for property and casualty unpaid claims and claim adjustment expenses — net	16,863	16,191	16,218
Reinsurance and other recoverables	5,403	5,138	5,497
Ending liabilities for property and casualty unpaid claims and claim adjustment expenses — gross	$22,266	$21,329	$21,715

The prior year provision of $248 in 2005 includes reserve strengthening for workers' compensation claim payments expected to emerge after 20 years of development, assumed casualty reinsurance, adverse development in environmental reserves, the 2004 hurricanes, and general liability reserves for accident years 2000 to 2003. This strengthening was partially offset by reserve releases for allocated loss adjustment expenses and workers' compensation reserves for accident years 2003 and 2004. The prior year provision of $414 in 2004 includes reserve strengthening for construction defects claims, assumed casualty reinsurance and environmental claims as well as a reduction in the reinsurance recoverable asset associated with older, long-term casualty liabilities. The 2004 reserve strengthening was partially offset by a reduction in September 11 reserves. The prior year provision in 2003 is primarily due to reserve strengthening of $2.6 billion based on a ground-up study of asbestos reserves. The ground-up study confirmed the Company's view of the existence of a substantial long-term deterioration in the asbestos litigation environment.

2004, and $248 million in 2005, or 21.5%, 2.6%, and 1.5% of beginning-of-year loss reserves in those years, respectively.

The loss reserve footnote contains a brief discussion of these reasons, and more detail is provided elsewhere in The Hartford's 2005 Form 10-K filing. For example, The Hartford states in the footnote that $2.6 billion (92%) of the very large reserve deficiency in 2003 is primarily attributable to "a ground-up study of asbestos reserves" which "confirmed the Company's view of the existence of a substantial long-term deterioration in the asbestos litigation environment." Since it is known that class action lawyers have targeted unexpected defendants in asbestos lawsuits and most PC insurers that underwrote asbestos policies prior to 1986 recorded similarly large reserve strengthenings around this time, this reserve deficiency does not appear to be discretionary or otherwise suggest that The Hartford inappropriately estimated loss reserves for these policies. This reserve deficiency is the primary reason why The Hartford recorded negative income before taxes of $(.6) billion in 2003, a loss that could be expected to be nonrecurring.

In addition, the table's breakdown of claim payments into the amounts for the current and prior accident years is useful, because it is necessary to know the payment for the current accident year to estimate the tail of PC insurers' policies accurately, as discussed in the "Calculating Claim Payments by Accident Year and Tail" section. The Hartford paid claims for the current accident year of $2,369 million in 2003, $2,616 million in 2004, and $3,593 million in 2005. These payments are 38.8% of the $6,101 million loss expense for the 2003 accident year, 39.7% of the $6,590 million loss expense for the 2004 accident year, and 53.5% of the $6,715 million loss expense for the 2005 accident year, respectively. On average across the three accident years, 44% of the loss expense for the current accident year is paid in that year, implying that 56% is paid in subsequent accident years. Curiously, the percentage of loss expense for the current accident year paid in 2005 is much higher than the percentage in the prior two years; this could be due either to The Hartford underwriting a higher percentage of short-tailed policies or accruing less (underaccruing?) loss expense for its longer-tailed policies in 2005 compared to prior years. It does not appear to be attributable to high claims payments on the 2005 hurricanes, in part because The Hartford recorded less expense for these catastrophes than it did for the 2004 hurricanes and in part because a large portion of the claims for Hurricane Katrina were not paid in 2005 due to the extended periods of time that elapsed before many policyholders could return to their properties.

LOSS RESERVE DEVELOPMENT DISCLOSURES

Exhibit 15.2 reports The Hartford's 2005 loss reserve development disclosure. All amounts are net of reinsurance. The amounts in this loss reserve development disclosure correspond almost perfectly with those in The Hartford's financial statements and loss reserve footnote. For other insurers, these amounts may not correspond for reasons such as the insurer treating business combinations, insurance pooling arrangements, or other transactions involving loss reserves differently in the financial statements and loss reserve development disclosure. In these cases, the insurer usually provides sufficient information to allow users of financial reports to reconcile the amounts.

Each column of the loss reserve disclosure pertains to the loss reserves initially reported on the balance sheet (reported loss reserves) in a specific year from 10 years ago to the current year, yielding 11 columns. The top row of the disclosure presents the reported loss reserves for each of these years. Reported loss reserves reflect expected claims for any accident year up to and including the reporting year which have not been paid as of the end of that year. For example, the reported loss reserves of $12,316 million in 2000 equal the sum of the loss reserves for all accident years up to and including 2000 that have not been paid by the end of 2000. Since a primary purpose of this chapter is to illustrate spreadsheet-based analyses of loss reserve development disclosures, notation is introduced for the various pieces of information provided in these disclosures. The reported loss reserves in year t are denoted LR(t), for example, LR(2000) = $12,316 million.

The body of the loss reserve development disclosure contains the cumulative claims paid and loss reserve development "triangles," so called because each contains data pertaining to reported loss reserves in each of the past 10 years for each year from the reporting year to the current year, a triangular array of numbers. The cumulative claims paid triangle reports the cumulative claim payments on reported loss reserves. For example, for reported loss reserves in 2000, cumulative claims paid from 2001 through 2003 (three years later) are $6,972 million. Cumulative claims paid from year t + 1 through year t + s on reported loss reserves in year t is denoted CP(t,t + s), for example, CP(2000, 2003) = $6,972 million. The lowest diagonal of the cumulative claims paid triangle reflects cumulative claim payments as of the current year, 2005. In particular, CP(2004, 2005) = $3,594 million corresponds to the $3,593 claim payments in 2005 for prior accident years reported in The Hartford's loss reserve footnote in Exhibit 15.1; the $1 million difference appears to be a rounding error.

The loss reserve development triangle contains revised (developed) estimates of reported loss reserves. For example, the revised estimate in 2003 of the reported loss reserves in 2000 is $15,760 million. These revised loss reserves do not reflect claim payments after the reporting year, so each of the revised loss reserves in a given column reflects the same coverage as the reported loss reserves. Upward revisions of loss reserves indicate reserve strengthenings to eliminate reserve deficiencies and downward revisions indicate reserve releases to eliminate reserve redundancies. The revised estimate in year t + s of the reported loss reserves in year t is denoted LR(t,t + s), for example, LR(2000, 2003) = $15,760 million. The lowest diagonal of the triangle reports revised loss reserves as of the current year.

The deficiency (redundancy) row at the bottom of the loss reserve development disclosure reports the revised loss reserves as of the current year, 2005, minus the corresponding reported loss reserves, with reserve redundancies

EXHIBIT 15.2 The Hartford Financial Services Group, Inc., Excerpts from Loss Reserve Development Disclosure in 2005 ($ in millions)

	Property and Casualty Claim and Claim Adjustment Expense Liability Development—Net of Reinsurance for the Years Ended December 31, (*a*)										
	1995	**1996**	**1997**	**1998**	**1999**	**2000**	**2001**	**2002**	**2003**	**2004**	**2005**
Liabilities for unpaid claims and claim adjustment expenses, net of reinsurance	$11,574	$12,702	$12,770	$12,902	$12,476	$12,316	$12,860	$13,141	$16,218	$16,191	$16,863
Cumulative paid claims and claim expenses											
One year later	2,467	2,625	2,472	2,939	2,994	3,272	3,339	3,480	4,415	3,594	—
Two years later	4,126	4,188	4,300	4,733	5,019	5,315	5,621	6,781	6,779	—	—
Three years later	5,212	5,540	5,494	6,153	6,437	6,972	8,324	8,591	—	—	—
Four years later	6,274	6,418	6,508	7,141	7,652	9,195	9,710	—	—	—	—
Five years later	6,970	7,201	7,249	8,080	9,567	10,227	—	—	—	—	—
Six years later	7,630	7,800	8,036	9,818	10,376	—	—	—	—	—	—
Seven years later	8,147	8,499	9,655	10,501	—	—	—	—	—	—	—
Eight years later	8,786	10,044	10,239	—	—	—	—	—	—	—	—
Nine years later	10,290	10,576	—	—	—	—	—	—	—	—	—
Ten years later	10,780	—	—	—	—	—	—	—	—	—	—

EXHIBIT 15.2 *(Continued)*

	Property and Casualty Claim and Claim Adjustment Expense Liability Development—Net of Reinsurance for the Years Ended December 31, *(a)*										
	1995	**1996**	**1997**	**1998**	**1999**	**2000**	**2001**	**2002**	**2003**	**2004**	**2005**
Liabilities re-estimated											
One year later	12,529	12,752	12,615	12,662	12,472	12,459	13,153	15,965	16,632	16,439	—
Two years later	12,598	12,653	12,318	12,569	12,527	12,776	16,176	16,501	17,232	—	—
Three years later	12,545	12,460	12,183	12,584	12,698	15,760	16,768	17,338	—	—	—
Four years later	12,399	12,380	12,138	12,663	15,609	16,584	17,425	—	—	—	—
Five years later	12,414	12,317	12,179	15,542	16,256	17,048	—	—	—	—	—
Six years later	12,390	12,322	15,047	16,076	16,568	—	—	—	—	—	—
Seven years later	12,380	15,188	15,499	16,290	—	—	—	—	—	—	—
Eight years later	15,253	15,594	15,641	—	—	—	—	—	—	—	—
Nine years later	15,629	15,713	—	—	—	—	—	—	—	—	—
Ten years later	15,727	—	—	—	—	—	—	—	—	—	—
Deficiency (redundancy), net of reinsurance	**$ 4,153**	**$ 3,011**	**$ 2,871**	**$ 3,388**	**$ 4,092**	**$ 4,732**	**$ 4,565**	**$ 4,197**	**$ 1,014**	**$ 248**	**$ —**

(a) The table excludes Hartford Insurance, Singapore as a result of its sale in September 2001, Hartford Seguros as a result of its sale in February 2001, Zwolsche as a result of its sale in December 2000, and London and Edinburgh as a result of its sale in November 1998.

represented as negative reserve deficiencies. Using the notation above, the cumulative deficiency through 2005 for the 2000 loss reserves is LR(2000, 2005) − LR(2000) = $17,048 − 12,316 million = $4,732 million. The $248 million reserve strengthening recorded in 2005 for reported loss reserves in 2004 increases loss expense in 2005. This number corresponds to the deficiency in 2005 reported in The Hartford's loss reserve footnote disclosure in Exhibit 15.1.

The cumulative claims paid triangle is a necessary adjunct to the loss reserve development triangle, because the latter does not reflect claim payments made after the reporting year. The portions of reported loss reserves that remain in subsequent years (remaining loss reserves) are calculated by subtracting the cash payment triangle cell by cell from the loss reserve development triangle. The portion of reported loss reserves in year t that remains in year t + s is denoted RLR(t,t + s) = LR(t,t + s) − CP(t,t + s). Exhibit 15.3 presents calculated remaining loss reserves for The Hartford. For example, RLR(2000, 2003) = $15,760 − 6,972 million = $8,788 million. The bottom diagonal of this exhibit reports The Hartford's remaining loss reserves in 2005 for the current and prior 10 years. The remaining loss reserves of $4,947 million in 2005 for the 1995 reporting year are a sizable 29% of The Hartford's total loss reserves of $16,863 million in 2005. This fact implies that The Hartford underwrites a significant amount of long-tailed policies, a point illustrated in more detail in the "Calculating Claim Payments by Accident Year and Tail" section.

Some PC insurers voluntarily provide loss reserve development disclosures by line of business in their financial reports, which facilitates analysis at that (preferred) level. In the absence of such voluntary disclosures, PC insurers must report loss reserve development disclosures in an accident year format by line of business in convention statements filed with state regulators. Insurance industry analysts often collect this public information from regulators in each state in which the insurer operates and aggregate this information across states (or purchase the aggregated information from information intermediaries) in order to assess the insurer's loss reserve development by line of business.

CALCULATING LOSS RESERVES BY ACCIDENT YEAR

This section demonstrates the calculation of accident year loss reserves at the end of the accident year (accident year loss reserves) and in subsequent years (remaining accident year loss reserves).

Loss reserves for accident year t are reported loss reserves for year t, LR(t), minus remaining loss reserves in year t for coverage through year t − 1, RLR(t − 1,t). Loss reserves for accident year t are denoted LRAY(t) = LR(t) − RLR(t − 1,t). The first row of Exhibit 15.4 presents accident year loss reserves for The Hartford for the current and nine prior accident years. For example, LRAY(2000) = $12,316 − 9,478 million = $2,838 million.

EXHIBIT 15.3 The Hartford Financial Services Group, Inc., Calculated Remaining Loss Reserves ($ in millions)

Year	1995	1996	1997	1998	1999	2000	2001	2002	2003	2004
1 year later	10062	10127	10143	9723	9478	9187	9814	12485	12217	12845
2 years later	8472	8465	8018	7836	7508	7461	10555	9720	10453	
3 years later	7333	6920	6689	6431	6261	8788	8444	8747		
4 years later	6125	5962	5630	5522	7957	7389	7715			
5 years later	5444	5116	4930	7462	6689	6821				
6 years later	4760	4522	7011	6258	6192					
7 years later	4233	6689	5844	5789						
8 years later	6467	5550	5402							
9 years later	5339	5137								
10 years later	4947									

EXHIBIT 15.4 The Hartford Financial Services Group, Inc., Calculated Initial and Remaining Accident Year Loss Reserve ($ in millions)

Year	1996	1997	1998	1999	2000	2001	2002	2003	2004	2005
Initial loss reserves	2640	2643	2759	2753	2838	3673	3327	3733	3974	4018
1 year later	1655	1678	1705	1642	1679	2353	1930	2497	2392	
2 years later	1132	1098	1147	1077	1200	1767	1276	1706		
3 years later	795	727	801	739	831	1055	1032			
4 years later	518	514	592	495	700	894				
5 years later	356	408	451	431	629					
6 years later	289	322	414	403						
7 years later	222	294	387							
8 years later	211	265								
9 years later	190									

Remaining loss reserves in year t + s for accident year t are remaining loss reserves in year t + s for coverage through year t, RLR(t,t + s), minus remaining loss reserves in year t + s for coverage through year t − 1, RLR(t − 1,t + s). Remaining loss reserves in year t + s for accident year t are denoted RLRAY(t,t + s) = RLR(t,t + s) − RLR(t − 1,t + s). The second through last rows of Exhibit 15.4 report The Hartford's remaining loss reserves for each of the current and prior nine accident years in each year up to the current year. For example, RLRAY(2000, 2003) = $8,788 − 7,957 million = $831 million. The bottom diagonal of this exhibit reports The Hartford's remaining loss reserves in 2005 for the current and nine prior accident years. Remaining accident year loss reserves decline as accident years are farther removed, since more of the tail of these accident years has expired. Even the farthest removed accident year for which remaining loss reserves can be calculated, 1996, has a nontrivial $190 million of remaining loss reserves for The Hartford, however.

CALCULATING LOSS RESERVE REVISIONS BY ACCIDENT YEAR

This section demonstrates the calculation of revisions of accident year loss reserves (accident year reserve deficiencies and redundancies) for each of the nine prior accident years for each year up to the current year.

Accident year reserve deficiencies (redundancies if negative) are calculated in three steps.

1. Subtract reported loss reserves in year t, LR(t), from the corresponding revised loss reserves in year t + s, LR(t, t + s), to obtain the cumulative deficiency through year t + s for reported loss reserves in year t, denoted CD(t,t + s)=LR(t,t + s) − LR(t). Exhibit 15.5 presents these cumulative deficiencies for the current and prior 10 years in each year up to the current year for The Hartford. For example, CD(2000,2003) = $15,760 − 12,316 million = $3,444 million. The bottom diagonal of the exhibit contains the cumulative deficiencies through 2005, which equal the amounts reported in the bottom row of The Hartford's loss reserve development disclosure in Exhibit 15.2.
2. Subtract the portion of CD(t,t + s) that is due to accident years prior to year t from CD(t,t + s) to obtain the cumulative deficiency through year t + s for accident year t. The portion of CD(t,t + s) that is due to accident years prior to year t is the deficiency for accident years up to and including year t − 1 measured over the period from year t to year t + s, which is CD(t − 1,t + s) − CD(t − 1,t). The cumulative deficiency through year t + s for accident year t is denoted CDAY(t,t + s)=CD(t,t + s) − [CD(t − 1,t + s) − CD(t − 1,t)]. Exhibit 15.6 presents The Hartford's cumulative loss reserve deficiencies by accident year. For example, CDAY(2000 ,2003) = $3,444 − [3,133 − (−4)] million = $307 million.

EXHIBIT 15.5 The Hartford Financial Services Group, Inc., Calculated Cumulative Loss Reserve Deficiencies ($ in millions)

Year	1995	1996	1997	1998	1999	2000	2001	2002	2003	2004
1 year later	955	50	−155	−240	−4	143	293	2824	414	248
2 years later	1024	−49	−452	−333	51	460	3316	3360	1014	
3 years later	971	−242	−587	−318	222	3444	3908	4197		
4 years later	825	−322	−632	−239	3133	4268	4565			
5 years later	840	−385	−591	2640	3780	4732				
6 years later	816	−380	2277	3174	4092					
7 years later	806	2486	2729	3388						
8 years later	3679	2892	2871							
9 years later	4055	3011								
10 years later	4153									

EXHIBIT 15.6 The Hartford Financial Services Group, Inc., Calculated Cumulative Loss Reserve Deficiencies by Accident Year ($ in millions)

Accident Year	1996	1997	1998	1999	2000	2001	2002	2003	2004
1 year later	−19	−56	57	89	88	−24	−199	−122	−352
2 years later	−65	−160	99	129	234	15	−255	−359	
3 years later	−112	−215	159	221	307	−217	−75		
4 years later	−207	−197	197	253	484	−24			
5 years later	−246	−161	203	366	636				
6 years later	−231	−159	290	464					
7 years later	−238	−113	362						
8 years later	−208	−90							
9 years later	−187								

The bottom diagonal of the exhibit is the cumulative deficiency through 2005 for each of the nine prior accident years. For example, there is a cumulative redundancy of $636 million through 2005 for the 2000 accident year.

Comparison of Exhibits 15.5 and 15.6 illustrates the importance of time period–specific phenomena on loss reserve revisions. Specifically, Exhibit 15.5 reports that The Hartford has cumulative reserve *deficiencies* through 2005 for reported loss reserves in all nine prior years, while Exhibit 15.6 reports that it has cumulative reserve *redundancies* through 2005 for the 1996, 1997, and 2001 to 2004 accident years (i.e., six out of the nine accident years for which calculations can be made). The Hartford's cumulative deficiencies through 2005 for the reported loss reserves in these six years result from its very large $3,198 million cumulative deficiency through 2005 for the accident years prior to 1996 and, for the later years, also from its large $1,462 cumulative deficiency through 2005 for the accident years 1998 to 2000.

3. Subtract the portion of CDAY(t,t + s) that occurs in years up to t + s − 1, CDAY(t,t + s-1), from CDAY(t,t + s) to obtain the incremental deficiency recognized in year t + s for accident year t, denoted IDAY(t,t + s) = CDAY(t,t + s)-CDAY(t,t + s − 1), where CDAY(t,t) = 0. Exhibit 15.7 presents The Hartford's incremental loss reserve deficiencies by accident year. For example, IDAY(2000, 2003)=$73 million for The Hartford.

To assess the relative magnitude of cumulative or incremental accident year loss reserve revisions, it is useful to scale them by either initial or beginning-of-year remaining accident year loss reserves. Exhibit 15.8 reports accident year loss reserve revisions divided by accident year loss reserves, that is, IDAY(t,t+s)/LRAY(t), for The Hartford. Notice that there are some sizable deficiencies and redundancies in various cells. For example, a reserve release of 8.9% of accident year loss reserves was recorded in 2005 for the 2004 accident year.

CALCULATING CLAIM PAYMENTS BY ACCIDENT YEAR AND TAIL

This section demonstrates the calculation of accident year claim payments for each of the nine prior accident years for each year up to the current year. It also shows how to calculate the tail of PC insurers' policies using these accident year claim payments. Accident year data, not the aggregated data reported on the financial statements, should be used to assess tail because the reported data reflect prior accident years for which some portion of the tail has already elapsed. It is also important to incorporate the percentage of accident year loss expense that is paid during that year, which can be determined from information in the loss reserve footnote.

EXHIBIT 15.7 The Hartford Financial Services Group, Inc., Calculated Incremental Loss Reserve Deficiencies by Accident Year ($ in millions)

Accident Year	1996	1997	1998	1999	2000	2001	2002	2003	2004
1 year later	−19	−56	57	89	88	−24	−199	−122	−352
2 years later	−46	−104	42	40	146	39	−56	−237	
3 years later	−47	−55	60	92	73	−232	180		
4 years later	−95	18	38	32	177	193			
5 years later	−39	36	11	113	152				
6 years later	15	2	82	98					
7 years later	−7	46	72						
8 years later	30	23							
9 years later	21								

EXHIBIT 15.8 The Hartford Financial Services Group, Inc., Calculated Incremental Loss Reserve Deficiencies by Accident Year as a Percentage of Accident Year Loss Reserves

Accident Year	1996	1997	1998	1999	2000	2001	2002	2003	2004
1 year later	−0.72%	−2.12%	2.07%	3.23%	3.10%	−0.65%	−5.98%	−3.27%	−8.86%
2 years later	−1.74%	−3.93%	1.52%	1.45%	5.14%	1.06%	−1.68%	−6.35%	
3 years later	−1.78%	−2.08%	2.17%	3.34%	2.57%	−6.32%	5.41%		
4 years later	−3.60%	0.68%	1.38%	1.16%	6.24%	5.25%			
5 years later	−1.48%	1.36%	0.40%	4.10%	5.35%				
6 years later	0.57%	0.08%	2.97%	3.56%					
7 years later	−0.27%	1.74%	2.61%						
8 years later	1.14%	0.87%							
9 years later	0.80%								

As discussed in Chapter 14, tail is important because it determines the period over which the insurer can earn investment income on premiums it receives. Specifically, one dollar of premiums should generate $(1 + r)^{tail} - 1$ dollars of investment income over the tail, where *r* denotes the expected rate of return on investment. Accordingly, users of financial reports should interpret PC insurers' combined ratio and other expense ratios in conjunction with tail.

Tail is calculated in five steps.

1. Subtract the claim payments from year t + 1 to year t + s for coverage up to year t – 1, CP(t – 1,t + s) – CP(t – 1,t), from the claim payments from year t + 1 to year t + s for coverage up to year t, CP(t,t + s), to obtain the cumulative claim payment from year t + 1 through year t + s for accident year t, denoted CPAY(t,t + s)=CP(t,t + s) – [CP(t – 1,t + s) – CP(t – 1,t)]. Exhibit 15.9 presents calculated cumulative claim payments by accident year for The Hartford. For example, CPAY(2000, 2003) = $6,972 – [$7,652 – 2,994] million = $2,314 million.
2. Subtract the cumulative claim payment from year t + 1 through year t + s – 1 for accident year t, CPAY(t, t + s – 1) from the cumulative claim payment from year t + 1 through year t + s for accident year t, CPAY(t,t + s), to obtain the incremental claim payment in year t + s for accident year t, denoted IPAY(t,t + s) = CPAY(t,t + s) – CPAY(t,t + s – 1).
3. Divide these incremental claim payments, IPAY(t,t + s), for each of the nine prior accident years and each year up to the current year by the corresponding accident year loss reserves, LRAY(t), to obtain the percentage of accident year t loss reserves paid in the sth year subsequent to the year of estimation. Exhibit 15.10 presents The Hartford's percentages. The far right column of this exhibit reports simple averages of these percentages across the accident years from 1996 to 2004. These average percentages sum to 94.5%, implying that 5.5% of accident year loss reserves are paid more than nine years after the end of the accident year. (These calculations may need to be modified if loss reserves are discounted or otherwise biased away from the sum of the expected claim payments, but this is usually a minor concern.)
4. Estimate the percentage of loss expense for the current accident year that is paid in the same year using information provided in the loss reserve footnote. As discussed in the "Loss Reserve Footnote" section, on average across the 2003 to 2005 accident years, 44% of The Hartford's loss expense for the current accident year is paid during that year.
5. Tail is calculated as the weighted-average duration of claim payments using the percentages of accident year loss reserves paid in subsequent years reported in Exhibit 15.10 and the percentage of accident year loss expense paid in that year determined using information in the loss reserve footnote. Users of financial reports should exercise judgment in deciding

EXHIBIT 15.9 The Hartford Financial Services Group, Inc., Calculated Cumulative Cash Payments by Accident Year (CPAY, $ in millions)

Accident Year	1996	1997	1998	1999	2000	2001	2002	2003	2004
1 year later	966	909	1111	1200	1247	1296	1198	1114	1230
2 years later	1443	1385	1711	1805	1372	1921	1796	1668	
3 years later	1733	1701	2117	2235	2314	2401	2220		
4 years later	1915	1932	2364	2511	2522	2755			
5 years later	2038	2074	2516	2688	2345				
6 years later	2120	2162	2635	2814					
7 years later	2180	2236	2734						
8 years later	2221	2288							
9 years later	2263								

EXHIBIT 15.10 The Hartford Financial Services Group, Inc., Calculated Incremental Cash Payments by Accident Year as a Percentage of Accident Year Loss Reserves

Accident Year	1996	1997	1998	1999	2000	2001	2002	2003	2004	Average
1 year later	36.59%	34.39%	40.27%	43.59%	43.94%	35.28%	36.01%	29.84%	30.95%	36.76%
2 years later	18.07%	18.01%	21.75%	21.98%	22.02%	17.02%	17.97%	14.84%		18.96%
3 years later	10.98%	11.96%	14.72%	15.62%	15.57%	13.07%	12.74%			13.52%
4 years later	6.89%	8.74%	8.95%	10.03%	10.85%	9.64%				9.18%
5 years later	4.66%	5.37%	5.51%	6.43%	7.86%					5.97%
6 years later	3.11%	3.33%	4.31%	4.58%						3.83%
7 years later	2.27%	2.80%	3.59%							2.89%
8 years later	1.55%	1.97%								1.76%
9 years later	1.59%									1.59%
										94.46%

how much weight to put on more and less recent accident years' percentages, recognizing this trade-off: Percentages for more recent accident years generally reflect the insurer's current types of coverage and economic conditions better than percentages for less recent accident years, suggesting that more weight should be placed on more recent accident years. However, any accident year's claim payments will reflect time period specific effects, suggesting that accident years should be weighted evenly to provide maximum diversification of these effects across accident years. Regardless, users must rely on further lagged accident years for the portion of claim payments that occur farther from the year of estimate, as these data are not available for more recent accident years.

To illustrate the calculation of tail using The Hartford's average percentages just discussed, assume that 44% of loss expense for an accident year is paid in that year and 56% is paid thereafter. For payments that occur thereafter, assume the average percentages reported in the far-right column of Exhibit 15.10 apply. Assume reasonably that the average duration of claim payments occurring in the *n*th year after the end of the accident year is $n + .5$ years; this assumption is consistent with premiums being paid at the beginning of the accident year and claims being evenly distributed within each year. Assume purely for convenience that claim payments made more than nine years after the end of an accident year occur on average 15 years later; users might employ a more refined approach incorporating the pattern of decay in the percentages over the nine years after the end of the accident year. Under these assumptions, the estimated weighted-average tail of The Hartford's policies is:

$$\begin{aligned} \text{tail} = (.44 \times .5 \text{ years}) + (.57) \times [(.37 \times 1.5 \text{ years}) + \\ (.19 \times 2.5 \text{ years}) + (.14 \times 3.5 \text{ years}) + (.09 \times 4.5 \text{ years}) + \\ (.06 \times 5.5 \text{ years}) + (.04 \times 6.5 \text{ years}) + (.03 \times 7.5 \text{ years}) + \\ (.02 \times 8.5 \text{ years}) + (.02 \times 9.5 \text{ years}) + (.06 \times 15 \text{ years})] = 2.46 \text{ years} \end{aligned}$$

Thus, The Hartford can earn interest on premiums over an average tail of 2.46 years.

CONSTRUCTING ACCIDENT YEAR LOSS RESERVE T ACCOUNTS

The loss reserve footnote and loss reserve development disclosure together enable users of financial reports to construct the T account for each accident year's loss reserves and thus to explain fully the evolution of those reserves over time. Exhibits 15.1, 15.4, 15.7, and 15.9 report the balance of accident year loss reserves in each year from that year to the current year, increases in accident year loss reserves (reserve deficiencies), and decreases in accident year loss reserves (claim payments and reserve redundancies) for The Hartford. As an illustration, the 2003 accident year loss reserve T account for The Hartford is reported in Exhibit 15.11. (This year is chosen because that is the farthest removed year in the loss reserve footnote in The Hartford's 2005 filing; to fully construct the loss reserve T account for prior accident years, it is necessary to obtain the loss reserve footnotes from prior financial reports.) Note that the $554 million cash payment in 2005 for the 2003 accident year is calculated as the cumulative cash payment through 2005 of $1,668 million minus the cumulative cash payment through 2004 of $1,114 million for that accident year, as reported in Exhibit 15.9.

The ability to construct T accounts for accident year loss reserves illustrates how PC insurers' loss reserve disclosures link accrual estimates with subsequent revisions of those estimates and cash flows. These disclosures are close to unique; for almost all other major accruals, such as banks' allowances for loan losses, revisions of estimates for prior years' business are combined with estimates for new business, thereby obscuring management's ability to estimate and manipulation of those accruals. In contrast, users of financial reports have substantial ability to assess PC insurers' loss reserve estimation adequacy, accuracy, and manipulation. In this regard, PC insurers' loss reserve disclosures are a good model for disclosures of major accruals by other firms.

PROPERTY-CASUALTY EXPENSE RATIOS

The financial analysis of PC insurers focuses on these expense ratios to assess these insurers' loss rates and their efficiency in processing claims and obtaining insurance business:

- Loss ratio = loss expense/net premiums earned
- Loss adjustment expense ratio = loss adjustment expense/net premiums earned
- Underwriting expense ratio = underwriting expenses/net premiums written (SAP) or net premiums earned (GAAP)
- Combined ratio = loss ratio + loss adjustment expense ratio + underwriting expense ratio
- Dividends to policyholders ratio = dividends to policyholders/net premiums earned
- Combined ratio after dividends to policyholders = combined ratio + dividends to policyholders ratio

These ratios can be calculated using accounting numbers reported under either generally accepted accounting principles (GAAP) or statutory accounting principles (SAP). Underwriting expenses equal policy acquisition costs incurred during the period for SAP purposes and equal deferred policy acquisition costs (DPAC) amortization plus any noncapitalized underwriting expenses incurred during the period for GAAP purposes. This difference between SAP and GAAP underwriting expenses explains why the denominator of the underwriting expense ratio is net premiums written for SAP and net premiums

EXHIBIT 15.11 The Hartford Financial Services Group Accident Year 2003 Loss Reserve T Account

Accident Year 2003 Loss Reserves			
cash payment 2003 (Exhibit 15.1)	2,369	6,102	+ loss expense 2003 (Exhibit 15.1)
		3,733	= ending balance 2003 (Exhibit 15.4)
cash payment 2004 (Exhibit 15.9)	1,114		
redundancy 2004 (Exhibit 15.7)			
		2,497	= ending balance 2004 (Exhibit 15.4)
cash payment 2005 (Exhibit 15.9)	554		
redundancy 2005 (Exhibit 15.7)	237		
		1,706	= ending balance 2005 (Exhibit 15.4)

earned for GAAP. Catastrophe losses and revisions of loss reserves for prior years are often removed from the numerators of the loss ratio and the loss adjustment expense ratio so that they better predict the insurer's (persistent) future performance.

As discussed in Chapter 14, the PC underwriting cycle usually is depicted through the path of the combined ratio, but each of these ratios is affected by the underwriting cycle. In fact, the loss expense and loss adjustment expense ratios are more sensitive to the underwriting cycle than is the underwriting expense ratio.

Each of these ratios should be interpreted in the context of the types of policies the insurer underwrites, since different lines of business often are at different stages of the underwriting cycle or have different tails or cost structures. A longer tail provides the insurer with the ability to generate higher investment income that can offset insurance losses. To illustrate, assume (unreasonably) that all insurance costs are incurred at the end of the tail of a PC insurance policy. Then the total profit earned by the PC insurer over the tail of the policy on one dollar of premiums invested at rate r is $(1 + r)^{\text{tail}}$ – combined ratio. More generally, to interpret the combined ratio, users of financial reports should estimate the timing of the various insurance costs included in the combined ratio, and thus the amount of premiums left to be invested over the tail. In general, underwriting costs are incurred around the initiation of the policy, loss adjustment costs are incurred prior to the end of the tail of the policy (possibly over a long period for policies subject to significant negotiation or litigation, such as medical malpractice), and claims are paid at the end of the tail of the policy (possibly as an annuity, as for most workers' compensation).

Ignoring the multiplicative effects of compound interest, if The Hartford earns interest at an annual pretax rate of 5% (a typical rate given the low-risk investments PC insurers hold), then in total over the average 2.46 year tail calculated in the "Calculating Claim Payment by Accident Year and Tail" section it earns pretax interest income of $.123 on each dollar of premiums. Thus, The Hartford can have a combined ratio of up to 112.3% before it makes a net operating loss. Long-tailed policies can have much higher combined ratios. For example, product liability insurance had a combined ratio of 180% for the PC insurance industry in 2004.[5]

As illustrations of the effect of line of business on cost structure, product liability insurance has very large loss adjustment expenses (52.6% of net premiums earned for the PC insurance industry in 2004) due to the litigation involved with these claims, while boiler and machinery insurance has very high underwriting expenses (40.0% of net premiums written for the industry in 2004) due to the need for skilled inspectors to assess these exposures.[6] In this regard, detailed disclosures of the components of costs by segment must be provided in PC insurers' Form 10-K filings under SEC Regulation S-X, as discussed in Chapter 14.

NOTES

1. K. Petroni, "Optimistic Reporting in the Property-Casualty Insurance Industry," *Journal of Accounting and Economics* (December 1992); F. Penalva, "Loss Reserves and Accounting Discretion in the Property-Casualty Insurance Industry," University of California at Berkeley Working Paper, January 1998; K. Nelson, "Rate Regulation, Competition, and Loss Reserve Discounting by Property-Casualty Insurers," *Accounting Review* (January 2000).
2. W. Beaver, M. McNichols, and K. Nelson, "Management of the Loss Reserve Accrual and the Distribution of Earnings in the Property-Casualty Insurance Industry," *Journal of Accounting and Economics* (August 2003).
3. W. Beaver and M. McNichols, "The Characteristics and Valuation of Loss Reserves of Property-Casualty Insurers," *Review of Accounting Studies* (March 1998).
4. K. Petroni, S. Ryan, and J. Wahlen, "Discretionary and Non-Discretionary Revisions of Loss Reserves by Property-Casualty Insurers: Differential Implications for Future Profitability, Risk and Market Value," *Review of Accounting Studies* (June 2000).
5. A. M. Best, *Aggregates & Averages: Property-Casualty, United States and Canada,* 2005 ed. (Oldwick, NJ: A. M. Best, 2005).
6. Ibid.

CHAPTER 16

Reinsurance Accounting and Disclosure

Reinsurance transfers insurance risks from the ceding insurer to the assuming insurer (reinsurer). Except in the rare case of assumption reinsurance, it does not extinguish the ceding insurer's legal responsibility to pay claims on the underlying insurance, however. Like all insurance, reinsurance also involves financing, because the payment of premiums by the ceding insurer precedes recoveries from the reinsurer. Moreover, features commonly present in multiple-year reinsurance contracts, such as experience accounts, often enhance and make explicit this financing aspect by incorporating the time value of money in the contractual terms. This chapter explains the specialized accounting and disclosure rules for ceded reinsurance under generally accepted accounting principles (GAAP) and statutory accounting principles (SAP), specifically Statement of Financial Accounting Standards (SFAS) No. 113, *Accounting and Reporting for Reinsurance of Short-Duration and Long-Duration Contracts* (1992), and Statement of Statutory Accounting Principles (SSAP) No. 62, *Property and Casualty Reinsurance* (2000). It also discusses the implications of these rules for the analysis of ceding insurers' financial and statutory reports. Accounting and disclosure rules for assumed reinsurance are in most respects identical to those for written insurance discussed in Chapter 14 and so are not discussed in this chapter. To appreciate this chapter fully, the reader must understand the insurance terminology and the accounting for short-duration insurance under SFAS No. 60, *Accounting and Reporting by Insurance Enterprises* (1982), covered in Chapter 14.

This chapter focuses on reinsurance that is "finite" rather than "traditional." Finite reinsurance transfers a bounded and generally small portion of the underwriting risk (i.e., variability in the amount of claims) of the underlying insurance from the ceding insurer to the reinsurer, although it often transfers more of the timing risk (i.e., variability in the timing of claims). By deemphasizing risk transfer and sometimes by adding explicit financing elements to the transaction, finite reinsurance puts relative emphasis on financing/the time value of money. Reflecting this emphasis, the up-front net consideration paid by the ceding insurer (the reinsurance premium less any ceding commission paid by the reinsurer) usually is close to the present value of the subsequent actual recoveries from the reinsurer. The distinction between finite and traditional reinsurance pertains to a primary issue in accounting for reinsurance: When does reinsurance transfer sufficient risk to be accounted for as reinsurance (i.e., the purchase of insurance or the sale of the underlying insurance) instead of as financing (i.e., a deposit)?

Under SFAS No. 113 (1992) and SSAP No. 62 (2000), very general and highly judgmental criteria are used to determine whether the reinsurer has assumed sufficient risk for a reinsurance contract to qualify for reinsurance accounting. In practice, however, these criteria often have been replaced by the rule of thumb that the reinsurer assume at least a 10% probability of a loss of 10% of the present value of the reinsurance premiums it expects to receive (the "10-10 rule"). As a result of the recent scrutiny of finite reinsurance discussed below, the insurance industry and accounting standard setters are evaluating the appropriateness of the 10-10 rule.[1]

This chapter also focuses on reinsurance that is "retroactive" rather than "prospective." Retroactive reinsurance covers insured events that have occurred before the inception of the reinsurance contract but for which claims have not yet been paid. Prospective reinsurance covers insured events that occur after the inception of the contract. At the inception of retroactive reinsurance, the ceding insurer has a recorded liability for unpaid claims on the underlying insurance, whereas no such liability exists at the inception of prospective reinsurance. Retroactive reinsurance that qualifies for reinsurance accounting raises two related questions:

1. Should the liability for unpaid claims on the underlying insurance be derecognized at the inception of the reinsurance contract?
2. If so, should the difference between this liability and the reinsurance premium paid be recorded immediately as a gain (if positive) or loss (if negative), or should this implied gain or loss be deferred and amortized into income over some period?

The second question arises in large part because SFAS No. 60 (1982) and SAP require that liabilities for unpaid claims for most short-duration policies (settled workers' compensation claims are an exception) be recorded at the *undiscounted* sum of the future claim payments. As a result, ceding insurers usually can obtain retroactive reinsurance of short-duration but long-tailed underlying insurance at a cost significantly less than their recorded liabilities for unpaid claims on that insurance, yielding a sizable implied gain at the inception of the reinsurance contract. In this regard, retroactive reinsurance is often said to "unlock the discount" in the undiscounted liability for unpaid claims on the underlying insurance.

In part because the implied gain on retroactive reinsurance tends to be largest when the underlying insurance is short duration and long-tailed, this chapter focuses on property-casualty (PC) reinsurance (which almost always is short-duration and sometimes is long-tailed) and refers to the liability for unpaid claims on the underlying insurance as loss reserves. Most of the discussion in the chapter also applies to life reinsurance, however.

Finite reinsurance is likely to be motivated in part or whole by ceding insurers' desire to manage their financial and statutory report numbers. In many cases this management occurs in compliance with GAAP and SAP, but in some cases it does not. Reflecting the latter possibility, the Office of the New York State Attorney General, the Securities and Exchange Commission (SEC), state insurance regulators, and class action lawyers have scrutinized ceding insurers' use of finite reinsurance to manage their financial and/or statutory report numbers as well as reinsurers' role in these transactions.

The first section of this chapter summarizes the accounting effects of reinsurance on financial and statutory report numbers and introduces the analysis issues raised by reinsurance. The second section describes the economic purposes of reinsurance, the role of reinsurers, the main types of reinsurance, and the features that tend to make reinsurance contracts finite. The third section explains, illustrates, and compares GAAP and SAP accounting for reinsurance contracts. The fourth section describes GAAP and SAP disclosures for reinsurance and discusses the analysis issues involved with reinsurance. The final section briefly surveys recent and likely future developments in financial reporting for reinsurance.

ACCOUNTING AND ANALYSIS ISSUES

Immediate Enhancement of Accounting Numbers

Reinsurance that qualifies for reinsurance accounting usually immediately enhances ceding insurers' statutory report numbers (e.g., it usually increases statutory income and statutory surplus). This occurs primarily because of the extreme conservatism of SAP for the underlying insurance discussed in Chapter 14, in particular, the nondiscounting of loss reserves for most short-duration policies and the immediate expensing of policy acquisition costs. SSAP No. 62 (2000) reinsurance accounting allows ceding insurers to undo the effects of this conservatism at the inception of the reinsurance contract. It does so by reversing the expensing of policy acquisition costs (both retroactive and prospective reinsurance) and by effectively discounting the undiscounted loss reserves for the underlying insurance and recognizing the implied gain (retroactive reinsurance only). The magnitude of the enhancement tends to be larger for retroactive reinsurance due to the recognition of the implied gain.

In contrast, qualifying reinsurance does not immediately enhance ceding insurers' financial report income or owners' equity as long as GAAP is applied properly for both the underlying insurance and the reinsurance. This is primarily because of two differences between GAAP and SAP reinsurance accounting. First, GAAP reinsurance accounting requires that the implied gain at the inception of retroactive reinsurance be deferred and amortized over the expected settlement period of the reinsurance. Hence, the implied gain is recognized in income in ceding insurers' financial reports with a potentially long delay relative to their statutory reports. Second, GAAP reinsurance accounting requires that ceding commissions reduce deferred policy acquisition costs (DPAC) and thus subsequent DPAC amortization. Hence, ceding commissions also are recognized in income in ceding insurers' financial reports with a delay relative to their statutory reports.

Immediate enhancement of ceding insurers' financial report numbers can occur, however, if either the underlying insurance or reinsurance is accounted for improperly. For example, this would occur if ceding insurers have underreserved for the underlying insurance and shortly after the inception of reinsurance record reinsurance recoveries that offset the necessary increase in reserves for the underlying insurance.

Reflecting the immediate enhancing effect of reinsurance on statutory report numbers, reinsurance often is motivated in whole or part by ceding insurers' desire to enhance their statutory report numbers and the ratios of these numbers used in insurance regulation and analysis. For example, research shows that PC insurers enter into retroactive reinsurance to avoid violating the ratio-based phase of the Insurance Regulatory Information System (IRIS).[2] Similarly, the primary purpose of prospective "surplus relief" agreements is to raise the ceding insurer's statutory surplus and lower its net premiums written, generally so that the insurer can continue to write insurance while still meeting regulatory limits on the ratio of net premiums written to statutory surplus.

Income Smoothing

Qualifying reinsurance smoothes ceding insurers' GAAP and SAP accounting income over the settlement period (i.e., tail) of the reinsurance for three distinct reasons. First, reinsurance absorbs insurance losses economically, and this is captured for accounting purposes by reinsurance recoveries reducing loss expense. Second, reinsurance accounting mitigates the temporal mismatching of insurance losses and investment income for short-duration but long-tailed underlying insurance under SFAS No. 60 (1982) and SAP that is discussed in Chapter 14, reducing both the expected losses recognized as insured events occur over the duration of underlying insurance and the investment income earned over the tail of the underlying insurance. Last, for multiyear reinsurance contracts, reinsurance accounting effectively spreads ceding insurers' insurance losses occurring in a given year across the fiscal years of the contract. Reinsurance that involves less risk transfer (i.e., is more finite) smoothes accounting income in a less economically descriptive fashion.

Gross versus Net Presentation

On the balance sheet, GAAP requires prepaid reinsurance and reinsurance recoverables to be presented as assets gross of the liabilities for underlying insurance. In contrast, SAP requires these items to be presented net of the liabilities for the underlying insurance or as contra-liabilities. GAAP's gross balance sheet presentation reflects the fact that almost all reinsurance does not extinguish the ceding insurer's legal obligation to pay claims. Both GAAP and SAP present premiums earned and insurance expenses net of reinsurance on the income statement, however, reducing those items. Disclosures of gross premiums and loss expense are required, however.

Analysis Issues

For financial analysis purposes, it is critical for users of financial reports to understand the effects of reinsurance on ceding insurers' financial and statutory report numbers in order to evaluate the insurers' current and future economic profitability, solvency, and risk. The GAAP and SAP ratios used in PC insurance analysis discussed in Chapter 15 are significantly and differently affected by reinsurance. For finite and/or retroactive reinsurance, it will usually be appropriate to adjust those ratios using one of various available strategies.

In addition, finite and/or retroactive reinsurance transactions typically are highly structured, large, and infrequent compared to traditional reinsurance, and they raise many of the same issues as the accounting for tranched securitizations discussed in Chapter 8. Finite transactions usually transfer less of the risk than the value of the underlying insurance (although sometimes not much value is transferred either), and they can transform the risk as well. For example, insurance risk may be subdivided in "layers" that are economically similar to the sequenced classes of securities in a tranched securitization, with some of the layers being retained by the ceding insurer and others reinsured. How much risk is transferred to the reinsurer depends on which layers are reinsured and the variability of the claims in those layers. Although finite reinsurance deemphasizes risk transfer, it usually has some insurance aspects along with its financing aspects, and if so accounting for finite reinsurance as pure financing does not fully capture its economics.

As with tranched securitizations, accounting is not a substitute for clear disclosure of finite and/or retrospective reinsurance transactions. Statutory reports include fairly detailed disclosures of retroactive reinsurance. Although historically disclosures of finite reinsurance have been limited in both financial and statutory reports, in November 2005 the National Association of Insurance Commissioners (NAIC) required detailed disclosures about certain types of finite reinsurance that should be of significant use.

Because reinsurance does not extinguish the ceding insurer's legal responsibility to pay claims on the underlying insurance, analysis of the creditworthiness of the reinsurer and any mitigation of credit risk (e.g., by the ceding insurer withholding funds or the reinsurer posting letters of credit) is very important. Detailed disclosures about the credit risk of reinsurance recoverables is provided in statutory reports.

REINSURANCE CONTRACTS

Economic Purposes and the Role of Reinsurers

Traditionally, insurers cede reinsurance in order to underwrite more or larger insurance risks while being protected against losses bigger than their risk management guidelines allow. Such losses occur either because insurance claims are higher than expected (underwriting risk) or because insurance claims come sooner than expected and so have higher present value (timing risk). The smaller an insurer relative to the risks it insures and the less diversifiable its portfolio of risks insured, the more likely it will cede reinsurance. Small PC insurers underwriting high-risk (e.g., catastrophe) insurance should cede the most reinsurance.

Insurers generally cannot reinsure all of their risks. For example, to mitigate adverse selection problems, reinsurers often require ceding insurers to retain some risk. Like all insurance, reinsurance payments invariably are capped at some maximum amount. Reinsurers limit their coverage of risks that are difficult to understand and thus to diversify, such as terrorism.

At the inception of reinsurance contracts, the ceding insurer typically pays the reinsurer a premium for assuming the transferred insurance risk. The up-front nature of the premium implies that net financing is provided by ceding insurers to reinsurers, not vice versa. It also implies that insurers have to be sufficiently liquid in order to be able to purchase reinsurance.

The up-front premium is often offset in part by a ceding commission from the reinsurer to the ceding insurer. Ceding commissions usually are described as reimbursing a portion of the ceding insurer's acquisition costs, although in fact these commissions are just one type of contractual cash flow that is substitutable with other contractual cash flows. Both a ceding insurer and its reinsurer may be economically indifferent about changing both the premium and ceding commission by identical amounts. Because premiums and ceding commissions are accounted for differently, either the ceding insurer or reinsurer may care about the accounting effects of this change, however. Reflecting these issues, it usually makes more sense for users of financial reports to focus on the net consideration paid by the ceding insurer rather than the components of that consideration.

Reinsurers can themselves reinsure, ad infinitum, a process known as retrocession. Doing this allows the industry to spread large risks fairly evenly, so that a given insurance policy has the backing of a chain of insurance companies. Reinsurance serves many of the same functions that loan sales and securitizations do for banks, although it does not provide the ceding insurer with funds at inception.

Most reinsurance is assumed by a relatively small set of very large global reinsurers capable of absorbing large risks. More than one reinsurer can be involved in large reinsurance transactions, which can be syndicated in ways similar to large loans as discussed in Chapter 8. In multireinsurer transactions, different reinsurers may accept different layers of risk and/or they may share given layers of risk in proportion.

Primary insurance companies may also assume reinsurance. They can do this either by seeking out such business or by participating in pools that spread risks across companies in the pool. Such pools diversify risks for insurers in much the same way as correspondent banking relationships do for banks.

"Fronting" insurers write insurance that they cede immediately to reinsurers. The purpose of fronting insurers usually is to enable reinsurers to participate in insurance that they would not otherwise be able to write (e.g., due to state licensing requirements or required financial strength ratings) or would somehow be detrimentally affected by writing (e.g., due to capital adequacy constraints, tax inefficiencies, or branding concerns).

SAP distinguishes authorized and unauthorized reinsurers. Reinsurance with unauthorized reinsurers that is not secured by letters of credit or other collateral does not qualify for reinsurance accounting and any regulatory benefits it provides.

Traditional Types

Traditional reinsurance contracts may exhibit these contractual features. Reinsurance may be "indemnity" or "assumption." In indemnity reinsurance, by far the more common type, the legal responsibilities of the ceding insurer to the policyholder of the underlying insurance are not removed by reinsurance, and so the ceding insurer must make claim payments to the policyholder if the reinsurer defaults. Thus, the ceding insurer is exposed to the credit risk of the reinsurer. In assumption reinsurance, the ceding insurer is no longer legally responsible to the policyholder, and so the policyholder assumes the credit risk of the reinsurer.

Reinsurance may be "facultative" or "treaty." In facultative reinsurance, each policy reinsured is separately negotiated. This is feasible only for large policies. In treaty reinsurance, all or a proportion of policies in a specific line of business or meeting specified underwriting criteria that are written by the ceding insurer during a specified interval are reinsured. The distinction between facultative and treaty reinsurance blurs as more specific underwriting criteria are used to determine what policies fall under a treaty.

Reinsurance may be "proportional" or "nonproportional." In proportional reinsurance, depicted in Exhibit 16.1, the ceding insurer and reinsurer bear losses on the underlying risks in some proportion. The proportion can be a fixed percentage ("quota share" reinsurance) or the variable percentage that yields the value of the reinsurance equal to a constant dollar amount ("surplus share" reinsurance). Specific types of proportional reinsurance can be structured as either quota or surplus share. For example, these types of proportional life reinsurance that can be structured in either fashion: "yearly renewable term," which transfers mortality risk only; "coinsurance," which transfers mortality and investment risk; and "modified coinsurance," which

EXHIBIT 16.1 Proportional Reinsurance

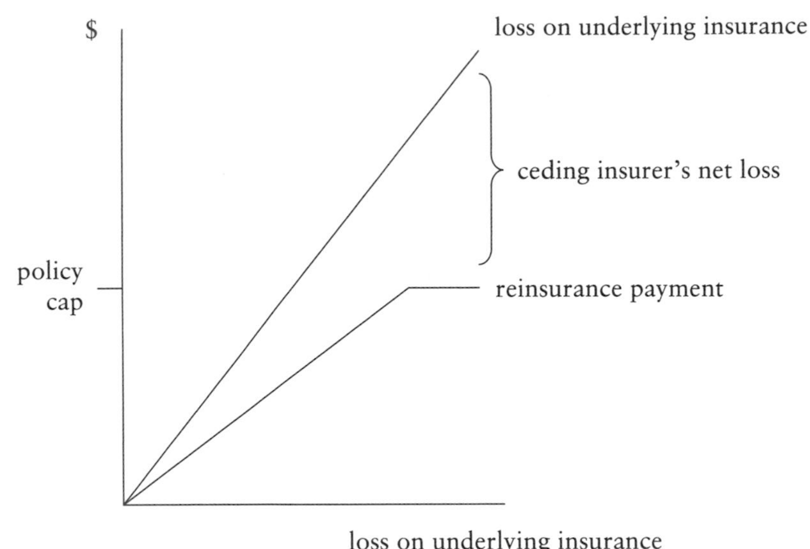

is like coinsurance but involves the ceding insurer retaining the assets and reserves for the reinsured coverage.

In nonproportional reinsurance, depicted in Exhibit 16.2, the ceding insurer and reinsurer bear losses on the underlying risks in sequence, with the reinsurer covering losses on the underlying policies beyond a predetermined limit called the "retention." For this reason, the reinsurer's claim payments tend to have a longer tail than the ceding insurer's claim payments, because the ceding insurer must bear losses up to the retention before the reinsurer pays anything. Of course, the ceding insurer also bears losses beyond any loss cap on the reinsurance.

The retention can pertain to losses summed across one or both of two dimensions:

1. Individual insurance policies ("excess-of-loss" reinsurance) versus portfolios of policies such as lines of business ("stop-loss" reinsurance)
2. Individual events ("per occurrence" reinsurance) versus periods of time ("aggregate" reinsurance)

Collectively, these dimensions yield four general types of nonproportional reinsurance. Holding the risk of the underlying policies and the total retention constant, the reinsurer bears less risk when summing occurs across a given dimension, due to greater diversification of losses.

The most common form of nonproportional PC reinsurance is per-occurrence excess-of-loss "catastrophe" reinsurance, which typically transfers

EXHIBIT 16.2 Nonproportional Reinsurance

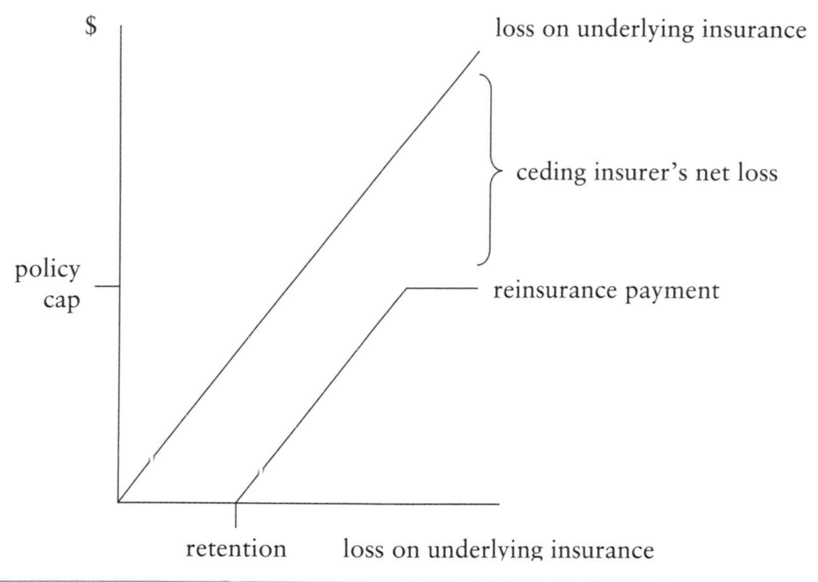

considerable risk to the reinsurer. Reflecting this fact, it is also descriptively referred to as "sleep" reinsurance, because the PC insurer's chief executive can go to bed at night knowing the insurer is unlikely to go bankrupt tomorrow. In contrast, aggregate stop-loss reinsurance is likely to be finite, and it is often used by ceding insurers more to smooth their income rather than to transfer risk.

A numerical example illustrating the distinct natures of proportional and nonproportional reinsurance is developed in the "Numerical Example" section.

Finite Features

Finite reinsurance involves less risk transfer and thus *relatively* more emphasis on financing/the time value of money than traditional reinsurance. For this reason, finite reinsurance is often referred to as financial reinsurance. This alternative terminology is somewhat misleading, however, because finite reinsurance does not necessarily involve different *absolute* financing than traditional reinsurance, and in practice it often involves less. A reinsurance contract calls for less (more) absolute financing to be provided by the ceding insurer to the reinsurer only if, holding the expected claims on the underlying insurance constant, the ceding insurer pays less (more) net consideration upfront and expects correspondingly less (more) recoveries from the reinsurer.

"Funds withheld" provisions—which allow the ceding insurer to retain and invest the reinsurance premium—are the contractual feature that most directly affects the level of financing in reinsurance contracts. These provisions reduce or even eliminate the financing provided by the ceding insurer to the reinsurer but they do not by themselves make the reinsurance more finite. In practice, however, large finite reinsurance transactions often involve withholding of funds as well. In this regard, reinsurance transactions that involve both minimal risk transfer (i.e., very finite) and minimal financing (i.e., funds largely withheld) are unlikely to have a significant business purpose unrelated to GAAP, SAP, or tax accounting and so are more likely to be subject to regulatory and legal scrutiny.

The financing provided by the ceding insurer to the reinsurer can be increased by the ceding insurer paying premiums that are too large given the risk transferred early in the term of a contract and then recouping those premiums through lower premiums, higher coverage, or higher ceding commissions late in the term of the contract. This is most likely to occur in multiple-year contracts called "funding covers." Funding covers are often retrospectively rated, as discussed below.

These aspects of reinsurance contracts affect the risk transferred by the policies. Any of these features may be present in either traditional or finite reinsurance; how these features are structured and combined determines whether and to what extent a transaction is traditional versus finite.

First, as discussed, reinsurance may be retroactive or prospective. Retroactive reinsurance is more likely to be finite because the risk of the underlying insurance is better known at the inception of the reinsurance contract than if the reinsurance were prospective.

There are two main types of retroactive reinsurance. "Loss portfolio transfers" cover previously accrued losses for well-defined portfolios of past insured events. This type of reinsurance is often used by insurers to exit lines of business or to deemphasize prior insurance coverage. "Adverse development" reinsurance covers currently unaccrued losses for well-defined portfolios of past insured events. By its nature, this type of reinsurance is nonproportional. Critics often allege that adverse development reinsurance is used by insurers who have not reserved adequately for the underlying insurance, although it can certainly be used to protect insurers against losses that currently are nonprobable or not capable of reliable estimation for which no liability should yet be accrued under SFAS No. 5, *Accounting for Contingencies* (1975).

Second, reinsurance may be multiple year and retrospectively rated, meaning that the ceding insurer participates in the reinsurer's past profit on the reinsurance contract. (In insurance terminology, reinsurance is either "retroactive" or "prospective," while "retrospective" refers to contractual features that look backward in time, such as retrospective rating.) The reinsurer's cumulative profit over the contract term to date is tracked in an "experience account," the balance of which typically equals reinsurance premiums received minus ceding commissions paid minus losses on the reinsured portion of the underlying insurance plus interest earned at a contractual rate minus a contractual profit margin. The reinsurer's cumulative profit is higher if fewer losses occur on the underlying insurance or if those losses occur later. The ceding insurer may participate in the reinsurer's profits through contingent (sliding-scale) ceding commissions, refunds of premiums or additional premiums for prior coverage, changes in prior or future interest rates, and changes in future premiums or reinsurance coverage. To the extent that the ceding insurer participates more in the reinsurer's profit, the reinsurer bears less risk. As discussed later, under both GAAP and SAP, assets and liabilities are recorded for the rights and obligations created by retrospective-rating provisions.

The interest earned in experience accounts is the most explicit way that finite reinsurance takes into account the time value of money.

Third, reinsurance can include "commutation" (i.e., termination and settlement) provisions. Commutation of a reinsurance contract usually causes the ceding insurer to participate in the reinsurer's profits, as described above. Finite reinsurance contracts typically are expected to commute as soon as contractually allowed after the ceding insurer has received the intended accounting benefits (e.g., surplus relief), which usually occurs when the experience account begins to show a cumulative profit. Commutation provisions often protect the reinsurer by prohibiting the commutation of a contract when the reinsurer is in a cumulative loss position.

Fourth, as discussed earlier, nonproportional reinsurance can involve retentions by the ceding insurer that are summed across portfolios of policies and/or time thereby reducing the variability of losses for the reinsurer.

Fifth, reinsurance can involve loss (ratio) caps or corridors that limit the maximum risk transferred to the reinsurer. The numerical example developed in the next section illustrates how loss caps can render reinsurance finite.

Sixth, reinsurance can involve a multiyear term that allows the ceding insurer to smooth its income by spreading losses across years, as reflected in the term "spread-loss" reinsurance. Although a multiyear term does not by itself make a contract finite, when it is combined with a low cumulative loss cap that is likely to bind, the reinsurance likely will not have much effect on the ceding insurer's total losses over the term of the reinsurance. Spread-loss reinsurance most commonly is used to reinsure relatively low frequency events that yield large losses when they occur. The term of the reinsurance typically is chosen to be long enough so that there is a high probability of at least one loss on the underlying insurance. Each year during the term of the reinsurance, the ceding insurer pays and expenses a premium approximately equal to the average discounted loss on the underlying insurance. In a year an insured event occurs that is covered by the reinsurance, the ceding insurer offsets the loss expense on the underlying insurance with the reinsurance recovery.

This example illustrates how spread-loss reinsurance smoothes the ceding insurer's income. A ceding insurer writes underlying insurance that experiences losses of $100 with 25% probability each year. The ceding insurer engages in an eight-year spread-loss reinsurance contract that bears all losses on the underlying insurance up to a cumulative loss cap of $100 (i.e., half of the expected losses of $200 on the underlying insurance over this term). This loss cap is reached if and when the ceding insurer experiences the first loss on the underlying insurance. The probability that no loss occurs during the term of the reinsurance is fairly low at $(.75)^8 = 10.01\%$. In the year if any that the first loss occurs on the underlying insurance, that loss is fully offset by the reinsurance recovery.

In this example, the cumulative loss cap on the reinsurance is reached as soon as the first loss occurs on the underlying insurance, and so the reinsurance does not transfer any risk for the remainder of the contract term. In principle, the ceding insurer should immediately expense the remaining contractually required reinsurance premiums, although it is unclear that this occurs in practice. (This is an extreme case of the general problem that, for any insurance that involves a cumulative loss cap, the amount of insurance coverage declines on average and in an uncertain fashion based on losses to date over the term of the contract. This implies that premiums on such insurance should be expensed on a faster than straight-line basis on average even if insured events occur evenly through time.)

Lengthening the term of a reinsurance contract also facilitates retrospective rating and the use of commutation provisions to mitigate risk transfer.

Seventh, reinsurance can involve multiple triggers that reduce the probability that reinsurance recoveries occur, provisions that delay timely payments by the reinsurer, blends of retroactive or less risky and prospective or riskier reinsurance, specific loss (ratio) caps for the prospective or riskier portions of the blends, and various other features that render the claim payments to be made and thus profit to be earned by the reinsurer each period during the policy term less variable.

Eighth, reinsurance contracts may be associated with side letters or oral agreements that limit the risk borne by the reinsurer on the contracts or that adjust the terms of future reinsurance contracts for the reinsurer's unexpectedly high or low profits on the contracts in a fashion similar to retrospective rating. As will be discussed, both GAAP and SAP are clear that any legally binding contract or agreement, written or oral, that affects the risk transferred by a given reinsurance contract should be considered in accounting for the reinsurance contract. (There is some debate as to whether other contracts or agreements that are not legally binding might affect the accounting for reinsurance contracts, but this is inconsistent with almost all GAAP and accounting practice, most notably, the GAAP standard governing retrospectively rated reinsurance contracts discussed in the section "Accounting for Retrospectively Rated Reinsurance Contracts.")

Last, reinsurance contracts often arise in the context of long-standing relationships between the ceding insurer and reinsurer and understandings that the reinsurer will earn a target rate of return over the duration of the relationship. Unlike legally binding contracts or agreements, such understandings do not yield accounting effects.

As discussed in the "Reinsurance Disclosures and Analysis" section, insurers are required to discuss significant retroactive and other significant reinsurance transactions in their description of the business in financial reports. In these disclosures, insurers rarely explicitly state that their reinsurance contracts are finite, but this usually can be inferred with some confidence from the contractual features disclosed. For example, consider this description of a reinsurance contract in CNA Financial's 2004 Form 10-K filing:

> The Company has an aggregate reinsurance treaty related to the 1999 through 2001 accident years that covers substantially all of the Company's property and casualty lines of business (the Aggregate Cover). The Aggregate Cover provides for two sections of coverage. These coverages attach at defined loss ratios for each accident year. Coverage under the first section of the Aggregate Cover, which is available for all accident years covered by the treaty, has a $500 million limit per accident year of ceded losses and an aggregate limit of $1 billion of ceded losses for the three accident years. The ceded premiums associated with the first section are a percentage of ceded losses and for each $500 million of limit the ceded premium is $230 million. The second section of the Aggregate Cover, which only relates to accident year 2001, provides additional coverage of up to $510 million of ceded losses for a maximum ceded premium of $310 million. Under the Aggregate Cover, interest charges on the funds withheld liability accrue at 8% per annum. The aggregate loss ratio for the three-year period has exceeded certain thresholds which requires additional premiums to be paid and an increase in the rate at which interest charges are accrued. This rate will increase to 8.25% per annum commencing in 2006. Also, if an additional aggregate loss ratio threshold is exceeded, additional premiums of 10% of amounts in excess of the aggregate loss ratio threshold are to be paid retroactively with interest. Any such premiums would be recorded in the period in which the loss ratio threshold is met.
>
> During 2003, as a result of the unfavorable net prior year development recorded related to accident years 2000 and 2001, the $500 million limit related to the 2000 and 2001 accident years under the first section was fully utilized and losses of $500 million were ceded under the first section of the Aggregate Cover. In 2001, as a result of reserve additions including those related to accident year 1999, the $500 million limit related to the 1999 accident year under the first section was fully utilized and losses of $510 million were ceded under the second section as a result of losses related to the WTC event. The aggregate limits for the Aggregate Cover have been fully utilized.

At least four aspects of CNA's Aggregate Cover suggest that this contract is finite:

1. Aggregate stop loss coverage of substantially all of CNA's PC lines of business

2. Coverage for three accident years under the first section, with the aggregate loss cap for the three years ($1 billion) being considerably lower than the sum of the loss caps for the individual years ($1.5 billion)
3. The full utilization of coverage for each the of three accident years covered, which suggests that the coverage limits are low relative to the distributions of possible losses
4. Retrospective rating in the form of additional premiums with interest and a higher interest rate on the funds-withheld liability (which operates like an experience account) if the aggregate loss ratio exceeds certain thresholds

The Aggregate Cover is also a partly funds-withheld contract, which reduces the financing provided by the ceding insurer to the reinsurer and enables CNA to control the investment of the reinsurance premiums.

Numerical Example

This section contains a numerical example that illustrates the distinction between proportional and nonproportional reinsurance and how loss caps can render reinsurance finite. This example is used later to demonstrate the distinct workings of GAAP and SAP accounting for both retroactive and prospective reinsurance. For ease of comparison, the risk, pricing, and acquisition costs of the underlying insurance are assumed to be identical regardless of whether the reinsurance is retroactive or prospective, even though the period of coverage for the underlying insurance and timing of the premium payment are one year earlier when the reinsurance is retroactive. For the same reason, loss reserves and loss expense on the underlying insurance are assumed to be identical for GAAP and SAP purposes.

The reinsurance contract is initiated at the beginning of the current year. The underlying insurance is a short-duration PC insurance policy that either was initiated at the beginning of the prior year and for which the insured events occurred in that year (yielding retroactive reinsurance) or that is initiated at the beginning of the current year and for which insured events occur evenly over the current year (yielding prospective reinsurance). Any claims on the underlying insurance will be paid exactly five years after the inception of the reinsurance. The total claim payment equals $50 with 10% probability, $100 with 80% probability, and $150 with 10% probability. This implies that the expected claim payment is $100 and the standard deviation of the claim payment is $22.36. The present value of the expected claim payment using a 10% interest rate is $62.09.

At the inception of the underlying insurance, the ceding insurer receives a premium of $82.09 and incurs acquisition costs of $20. Reflecting SFAS No. 60 (1982) and SAP accounting for short-duration insurance discussed in Chapter 14, the ceding insurer earns premium revenue of $82.09 and accrues loss reserves and loss expense of $100 as insured events occur. For GAAP purposes, the insurer capitalizes policy acquisition costs of \$20 and amortizes the DPAC asset over the coverage period, while for SAP purposes the ceding insurer expenses these costs when they are incurred.

These reinsurance contracts yield expected reinsurance recoveries of \$50 (i.e., half the expected total claims):

- A 50% quota share (proportional) policy
- An excess-of-loss (nonproportional) policy with a retention of \$(50-x) and a cap of \$(150-10x), where x can be any number from zero to five.

As x rises in the excess-of-loss policy, the retention falls by \$$x$ and the loss cap falls by \$10x, so the ceding insurer bears a smaller retention layer and a larger layer above the cap, and the reinsurer bears a single layer that begins at a lower level of claims and has a lower cap. For example, when $x = 3$, the policy specifies a retention of \$47 and a cap of \$120, so the ceding insurer bears losses on the underlying insurance from \$0 to \$47 and from \$120 to \$150, and the reinsurer bears losses from \$47 to \$120. Exhibit 16.3 summarizes reinsurance recoveries for each possible value of claim payments on the quota-share policy and on the excess-of-loss policy for each possible value of x.

Both the quota-share policy and the excess-of-loss policy with $x = 0$ (i.e., a retention of \$50 and a cap of \$150) transfer all of the risk of reinsured portions of the underlying insurance to the reinsurer. The risk transferred is considerably greater in the excess-of-loss policy, however, because this policy fully transfers the downside risk that the claim is above its minimum of \$50, while the quota share policy transfers both the certain and uncertain portions of the claim in proportion. Reflecting this fact, the quota-share policy reduces the standard deviation of the ceding insurer's net of reinsurance claim payment by half to \$11.18, while the excess-of-loss policy with $x = 0$ reduces this standard deviation to zero.

As x rises, the risk transferred by the excess-of-loss policy diminishes as the reinsurer's maximum payment becomes closer to its expected payment and, when $x = 5$, 90% probable to be \$55. In fact, when $x = 5$ the reinsurer bears all the variation in the claim below the expected \$100, while

EXHIBIT 16.3 Reinsurance Recoveries in Numerical Example

			Excess of Loss Policy					
		Quota Share Policy	$x=0$	$x=1$	$x=2$	$x=3$	$x=4$	$x=5$
Claim payments on underlying insurance	50	25	0	1	2	3	4	5
	100	50	50	51	52	53	54	55
	150	75	100	91	82	73	64	55

the ceding insurer bears all the variation in the claim above the expected \$100. Reflecting its finite nature, the excess-of-loss policy with $x = 5$ reduces the standard deviation of the PC insurer's net of reinsurance claim payment by less than the quota share policy, to \$15.

Reflecting their equal expected claims, all of the reinsurance contracts are assumed to require the ceding insurer to pay the reinsurer net consideration of \$31.05, the present value of \$50 based on a interest rate of 10%, at inception. This net consideration takes the form of a \$41.05 premium minus a \$10 ceding commission.

ACCOUNTING FOR REINSURANCE CONTRACTS

This section describes the risk-transfer criteria that must be met for reinsurance accounting to be required under GAAP and SAP. It describes the main aspects of GAAP and SAP reinsurance accounting and, using the numerical example, illustrates and compares the effects of the two approaches on financial and statutory reports. This section also describes the accounting for reinsurance contracts that are retrospectively rated, involve withholding of funds, or do not qualify for reinsurance accounting and so must be accounted for as deposits.

Risk-Transfer Criteria for Reinsurance Accounting

The risk-transfer criteria that must be met for reinsurance accounting to be required are substantially the same under SFAS No. 113 (1992) and SSAP No. 62 (2000). The reinsurer must assume either

- Significant insurance (i.e., underwriting and timing) risk and be exposed to a reasonable possibility of a significant loss on the reinsurance contract or
- Substantially all of the insurance risk on the reinsured portions of the underlying insurance.

Judgment is required in determining what is a reasonable possibility and what is a significant loss. Neither SFAS No. 113 (1992) nor SSAP No. 62 (2000) explicitly states whether the required probability is inversely related to the significance of the possible loss, although this makes sense economically and in practice appears to be the case for reinsurance involving low frequency but large losses such as catastrophe reinsurance. These criteria are to be evaluated at the level of individual reinsurance contracts, not at the level of all the ceding insurer's contracts with one or all of its reinsurers collectively. However, as discussed, if other legally binding contracts or agreements affect the risk transferred by a given reinsurance contract, then they should be treated as part of the reinsurance contract under GAAP and prohibit reinsurance accounting under SAP.

The reinsurer's loss reflects only the amount and timing of cash flows between the ceding insurer and reinsurer arising from the reinsurance contract, not investment or other losses arising outside the reinsurance contract. The significance of a potential loss is to be assessed relative to the net present value of gross premiums expected to be received by the reinsurer. Gross premiums are used even if the reinsurance contract allows for netting of premiums to be received by the reinsurer against ceding commissions made by the reinsurer or for the ceding insurer to withhold funds.

As discussed, for many types of insurance the 10-10 rule often is used to apply these judgmental criteria. This rule is conceptually problematic because it does not recognize that different types of underlying insurance vary in both the probability and magnitude of the loss that can be transferred to the reinsurer. For example, catastrophe insurance often exhibits a below-10% probability of a very large loss; for this reason, the rule is generally not used for catastrophe reinsurance. Similarly, less risky and more diversifiable automobile property insurance is unlikely to yield losses greater than 10%.

To illustrate how the criteria and rules of thumb work in practice, consider the excess-of-loss policy with $x = 5$ in the previous numerical example. The reinsurer experiences a loss on that policy only when it must make a claim payment of $55 (present value $34.15), which occurs the 90% of the time that claims on the underlying insurance are either $100 or $150. This payment yields a present-valued loss for the reinsurer of $3.10 (premium of $41.05 minus ceding commission of $10 minus present value of claim payment of $34.15), which is less than 10% of the gross premium of $41.05, and so the 10-10 rule is not met. This loss is almost exactly 10% of the premium net of the ceding commission, however, and so by eliminating the ceding commission and reducing the premium by the same amount, this policy would just about meet this rule of thumb.

In contrast, the quota-share policy and the excess-of-loss policies with x from 0 to 4 meet this rule of thumb even using gross premiums of $41.05. These policies experience a greater-than-10% loss the 10% of the time that claims on the underlying insurance are $150.

For the ceding insurer to obtain reinsurance accounting, the reinsurer must bear both underwriting and timing risk, not just one of these. For the reinsurer to be deemed to bear timing risk, the reinsurance contract should not include provisions that allow the reinsurer to delay payment to the ceding insurer. In the previous numerical example, there is no timing risk on the underlying insurance since it is known that claims will be paid in five years, and so the reinsurance also has no timing risk. SFAS No. 113 (1992) and SSAP No. 62 (2000) do not explicitly consider the (unusual) case where the underlying insurance has no timing risk. In the illustrations based on the numerical example to follow, it is assumed that these standards allow reinsurance accounting as long as the reinsurance transfers sufficient of the underwriting risk of the underlying insurance.

In addition to these risk-transfer criteria, SSAP No. 62 (2000) includes several requirements regarding the specification of the reinsurance contract that address regulatory concerns. For example, the contract must contain an acceptable clause specifying the reinsurer's responsibilities in the event of the ceding insurer's bankruptcy, and it must specify that claim reports will be made to the reinsurer on a quarterly basis and recoveries must occur without delay.

GAAP Accounting for Reinsurance Premiums and Recoveries

The specific type of reinsurance accounting required under SFAS No. 113 (1992) depends on whether the reinsurance is retroactive or prospective, whether the underlying insurance is short or long duration, and, if the underlying insurance is long duration, whether the reinsurance is short or long duration. Reinsurance accounting differs for retroactive and prospective reinsurance for three main reasons:

1. At inception, the ceding insurer records a reinsurance recoverable asset for retroactive reinsurance but a prepaid reinsurance asset for prospective reinsurance on the balance sheet.
2. Retroactive insurance raises the possibility that the reinsurance recoverable differs from the loss reserves for the underlying insurance, yielding an implied gain or loss for the ceding insurer that must be either deferred or recognized immediately.
3. There is no netting of retroactive reinsurance premiums against premium revenue for the underlying insurance on the ceding insurer's income statement because the insured events have already occurred and so the ceding insurer has already earned premium revenue.

Reinsurance accounting differs based on the durations of the underlying insurance and the reinsurance because these durations affect the period over which the prepaid reinsurance asset and any deferred gain or loss should be amortized.

SFAS No. 113 (1992) provides guidance for four cases:

1. The underlying insurance is short duration and the reinsurance is retroactive.
2. The underlying insurance is short duration and the reinsurance is prospective.
3. The underlying insurance is long duration and the reinsurance is short duration.
4. The underlying insurance is long duration and the reinsurance is long duration.

Because an implied gain often results from retroactive insurance, the first case is of the most concern and so receives the most detailed guidance. Since PC insurance almost always is short duration, the third and fourth cases generally involve life reinsurance. Reflecting this chapter's focus on PC reinsurance, the accounting is described in detail for the first two cases and briefly for the other two cases.

The excess-of-loss policy with $x = 0$ in the numerical example is used to illustrate reinsurance accounting. As discussed, this policy clearly meets the risk-transfer criteria for reinsurance accounting and so should be accounted for as reinsurance of a short-duration policy. In these illustrations, income is calculated for the first half the current year (rather than the entire year) in order to illustrate differences in GAAP and SAP accounting for policy acquisition costs and/or ceding commissions. Most of these differences disappear by the end of the current year, because these costs and/or commissions are fully reflected in income by that time.

Underlying Insurance Is Short Duration and the Reinsurance Is Retroactive. In this case, the ceding insurer records the reinsurance premium paid as a reinsurance recoverable, making certain adjustments either to that account or to loss reserves for any difference between the reinsurance premium and loss reserves for the reinsured portion of the underlying insurance. If the reinsurance premium paid is less than the loss reserves for the reinsured portion of the underlying insurance, as is usually the case when the underlying insurance is long-tailed, then an additional reinsurance recoverable and deferred gain are recorded for the difference. The deferred gain is amortized into loss expense (reducing it) over the period that reinsurance settlements are expected to settle. The deferred gain should be amortized using the effective interest method if the amount and timing of recoveries can be reasonably estimated and in proportion to actual recoveries otherwise. Larger implied gains tend to be amortized over longer settlement periods, because the reinsurance premium falls with the time until settlement due to the time value of money, all else being equal.

If instead the premium paid is greater than the loss reserves for the reinsured portion of the underlying insurance, then either the reinsurance recoverable should be reduced or additional loss reserves recorded for the difference and loss expense recorded immediately. Implied losses are recognized immediately because they suggest the ceding insurer has inadequately reserved for the underlying insurance.

To illustrate this accounting, assume the insured events occur in the prior year, so that the excess-of-loss policy with $x = 0$ is retroactive. The ceding insurer's journal entry for its premium payment at the inception of the reinsurance contract at the beginning of the current year is:

Reinsurance recoverable (+ asset)	50	
Cash (− asset)		41.05
Deferred gain (+ liability)		8.95

Applying effective interest amortization on an annual basis, the amortization of the deferred gain in the first half of the current year is $\$8.95 \times (1/1.1^5)/(1/1.1 + 1/1.1^2 + \ldots + 1/1.1^5)/2 = \$.73$, which yields a balance for the deferred gain of \$8.22. The journal entry to record the amortization of the deferred gain for the first half of the current year is:

Deferred gain (− liability)	.73	
Loss expense (+ income)		.73

When the ceding insurer learns at the end of the third year that the claim payment will be \$150 and so the reinsurer will pay \$100, not \$50, reinsurance recoverables increase and loss expense is reduced by \$50:

Reinsurance recoverable (+ asset)	50	
Loss expense (+ income)		50

Underlying Insurance Is Short Duration and the Reinsurance Is Prospective. In this case, the ceding insurer records the premium paid as prepaid reinsurance and amortizes this asset over the period covered by the reinsurance contract in proportion to the insurance protection provided. As insured events occur, the ceding insurer records an undiscounted reinsurance recoverable for the expected recoveries from the reinsurer.

To illustrate this accounting, assume the insured events occur in the current year, so that the excess-of-loss policy with $x = 0$ is prospective. The journal entry for the reinsurance premium at inception of the reinsurance contract at the beginning of the current year is:

Prepaid reinsurance (+ asset)	41.05	
Cash (− asset)		41.05

Since the insured events occur evenly over the current year, in the first half of the current year half of prepaid reinsurance is amortized into premium revenue (reducing it) and an undiscounted reinsurance recoverable for half the expected claim payment and a reduction of loss expense are recorded:

Premium revenue (− income)	20.52	
Prepaid reinsurance (− asset)		20.52
Reinsurance recoverable (+ asset)	25	
Loss expense (+ income)		25

The journal entry when the ceding insurer learns at the end of the third year that the claim payment will be \$150 and so the reinsurer will pay \$100, not \$50, is the same as in the prior case of retroactive reinsurance.

Underlying Insurance Is Long Duration. In both of these cases, the ceding insurer records a prepaid reinsurance asset for the estimated costs of the reinsurance. Reflecting the long duration of the underlying insurance, these estimated costs include the premium paid at inception plus any difference between the recorded liability for the underlying insurance and the premium paid. The ceding insurer amortizes this cost into premium revenue over the period covered by the reinsurance contract if the reinsurance is short duration and over the period covered by the underlying insurance if the reinsurance is long duration. SFAS No. 113 (1992) does not distinguish prospective and retroactive reinsurance of long-duration insurance, presumably because this reinsurance generally is primarily prospective. It does state that if practicable retroactive and prospective provisions within a single reinsurance contract should be accounted for separately, however.

GAAP Accounting for Ceding Commissions

Under SFAS No. 113 (1992), the accounting for ceding commissions that represent recovery of acquisition costs is the same regardless of the natures of the underlying insurance and the reinsurance as long as the reinsurance qualifies for reinsurance accounting. Specifically, the ceding insurer reduces DPAC by the amount of the ceding commission and amortizes the remaining net DPAC in proportion to "net revenue" recognized. For prospective reinsurance, net revenue is net premiums earned and net DPAC is amortized over the coverage period of the underlying insurance. For retroactive reinsurance, however, the ceding insurer has fully recorded the net premiums earned on the underlying insurance before the inception of the reinsurance. Hence, it is not clear what net revenue includes; the most likely suspect is plus the amortization of the deferred gain or minus the loss assuming one of these amounts is nonzero. For retroactive reinsurance, the ceding insurer also has fully amortized the DPAC for the underlying insurance before the inception of the reinsurance, and so the net DPAC to be amortized equals minus the ceding commission.

Again using the excess-of-loss policy with $x = 0$ in the numerical example to illustrate the accounting, the journal entry for the ceding commission at the inception of the policy is:

Cash (+ asset)	10	
DPAC (− asset)		10

When reinsurance is prospective, DPAC is amortized over the coverage period of the underlying insurance in proportion to net premiums earned, yielding this journal entry for the reduction of DPAC amortization in the first half of the current year:

DPAC (+ asset)	5	
DPAC amortization (+ income)		5

When the reinsurance is retroactive, the reduction of DPAC is assumed to be amortized over the settlement period of the reinsurance in proportion to the amortization of the deferred gain, which yields this journal entry in the first half of the of the current year:

DPAC (+ asset)	.82	
DPAC amortization (+ income)		.82

As demonstrated in the section "Comparing GAAP and SAP," a nice implication of amortizing the deferred gain from retroactive reinsurance using the effective interest method and amortizing the reduction in DPAC from the ceding commission in proportion to the deferred gain is that the sum of the amortizations of the deferred gain and DPAC approximate in amount and timing the amount of foregone interest income on cash balances attributable to the up-front payment of reinsurance premium less the ceding commission, so that retroactive reinsurance has approximately no effect on GAAP net income. In fact, this approximation is perfect if the interest rate used in the effective interest method is the same as the interest rate earned on cash balances.

SAP Reinsurance Accounting

SAP reinsurance accounting under SSAP No. 62 (2000) differs in five main respects from the GAAP reinsurance accounting just described:

1. On the balance sheet, SAP requires that the economic reinsurance recoverable asset associated with unpaid losses on the underlying insurance be netted against the loss reserves for the underlying insurance for prospective reinsurance and recorded as a contra-liability for retroactive reinsurance. Because retroactive reinsurance is potentially subject to abuse, this contra-liability is recorded in "aggregate write-ins for liabilities" rather than directly contra to loss reserves. (Relatedly, all disclosures pertaining to loss reserves in the statutory reports are gross of this contra-liability.)
2. On the balance sheet, SAP requires that prepaid prospective reinsurance premiums be netted against the unearned premiums liability for the underlying insurance.
3. On the income statement, SAP requires that both gains and losses on the inception of retroactive reinsurance be recorded immediately, although these items are classified separately from loss expense in "aggregate write-ins for miscellaneous income."
4. On the balance sheet, SAP requires that retroactive reinsurance gains be recorded in restricted special surplus (upon which the ceding insurer cannot pay dividends) until the claim payments paid by the reinsurer exceed the premium paid by ceding insurer.
5. On the income statement, SAP requires that ceding commissions immediately reduce acquisition cost expense.

In addition, SSAP No. 62 (2000) requires (with some exceptions) that reinsurance contracts not produced in written form with nine months of the inception of the contract be accounted for as retroactive reinsurance.

To illustrate this accounting, consider the excess-of-loss policy with $x = 0$. Assume the insured events occur in the prior year, so that the reinsurance is retroactive. At the inception of the reinsurance contract, the ceding insurer records:

Contra-liability for retroactive reinsurance (− liability)	50	
Cash (− asset)		41.05
Gain on retroactive reinsurance (+ income)		8.95

At the end of the accounting period, this gain is closed out to restricted special surplus where it remains until the ceding insurer recovers on the reinsurance in the fifth year:

Gain on retroactive reinsurance (close out income)	8.95	
Special surplus on retroactive reinsurance (+ restricted surplus)		8.95

Assume instead the insured events occur in the current year, so that the reinsurance is prospective. The reinsurance premium paid at the inception of the contract reduces the unearned premiums liability for the underlying insurance:

Unearned premiums (− liability)	41.05	
Cash (− asset)		41.05

As insured events occur, the ceding insurer records reductions of premium revenue and loss expense and adjusts the balance sheet accounts for the underlying insurance. In the first half of the current year, the journal entries are:

Premium revenue (− income)	20.52	
Unearned premiums (+ liability)		20.52
Loss reserves (− liabilities)	25	
Loss expense (+ income)		25

Regardless of whether the reinsurance is retroactive or prospective, when the ceding insurer receives the ceding commission at inception, SAP requires that this commission be recorded as a reduction of acquisition cost expense:

Cash (+ asset)	10	
Acquisition cost expense (+ income)		10

Comparing GAAP and SAP

GAAP and SAP accounting for the numerical example are summarized in Exhibit 16.4 for the retroactive-reinsurance case and Exhibit 16.5 for the prospective-reinsurance case. Both exhibits include the effects of the underlying insurance, the reinsurance, and interest on cash balances in the current year on financial and statutory reports. No interest is accrued on cash balances in the prior year for the retroactive-reinsurance case, however, in order to ease comparisons with the prospective-reinsurance case.

In Exhibit 16.4, the effects of the underlying insurance appear on the GAAP and SAP income statements for the prior year, while the effects of the retroactive reinsurance appear (along with interest on cash balances) on the income statements for the current year. In contrast, in Exhibit 16.5, the effects of the underlying insurance and the prospective reinsurance both appear on the income statements for the current year. To indicate clearly the effects of reinsurance, with- and without-reinsurance financial statements are provided in separate columns in each exhibit.

In the retroactive-reinsurance case summarized in Exhibit 16.4, the GAAP and SAP prior year income statements are identical, because acquisition costs for the underlying insurance are fully expensed prior to the inception of retroactive reinsurance and loss reserves for the underlying insurance are assumed to be identical for GAAP and SAP. In the first half of the current year, the ceding insurer's SAP income with reinsurance is $17.40 higher than its SAP income without reinsurance or its GAAP income with or without reinsurance, reflecting the enhancing effect of retroactive reinsurance on the ceding insurer's SAP financial statements. The difference between SAP and GAAP income with reinsurance is attributable in part to the entire $8.95 gain on retroactive reinsurance being recognized immediately in SAP income while only $.73 amortization of this gain is recognized in GAAP income during the period, and in part to the entire $10 ceding commission decreasing SAP policy acquisition costs immediately while only $.82 of this commission decreases GAAP DPAC amortization during this period. These differences carry over to the ceding insurer's ending balance sheet, with statutory surplus with reinsurance being $17.40 higher than statutory surplus without reinsurance or retained earnings with or without reinsurance, although $8.95 of this higher statutory surplus is restricted. In addition, the ceding insurer's liabilities are $58.22 higher on the GAAP with reinsurance ending balance sheet than on the SAP with reinsurance ending balance sheet, primarily because of the gross (net) presentation of reinsurance under GAAP (SAP), but also because of the deferred gain on retroactive reinsurance liability on the GAAP balance sheet. As mentioned earlier, retroactive reinsurance has no net effect on GAAP income in the first half of the current year or on ending retained earnings, because the amortization of the deferred gain and reduction of DPAC amortization from reinsurance exactly offset the foregone interest revenue on cash balances resulting from the net consideration paid for the reinsurance.

EXHIBIT 16.4 Comparison of GAAP and SAP Reinsurance Accounting for Example of Retroactive Excess-of-Loss Policy with $x = 0$

	GAAP		SAP	
	Without Reins.	**With Reins.**	**Without Reins.**	**With Reins.**
Income statement prior year (a):				
Net premiums earned	82.09	—	82.09	—
− Loss expense	(100)	—	(100)	—
− DPAC amortization (GAAP) or Acquisition cost expense (SAP)	(20)	—	(20)	—
Net income	(37.91)	—	(37.91)	—
Income statement first half of current year:				
Net premiums earned	0	0	0	0
+ Interest revenue on cash balances	3.10	1.55	3.10	1.55
+ Amortization of deferred gain (GAAP) or Gain (SAP) on retroactive reinsurance	—	.73	—	8.95
− DPAC amortization (GAAP) (*b*) or Acquisition cost expense (SAP)	0	.82	0	10
Net income	3.10	3.10	3.10	20.50
Balance sheet end of first half of current year:				
Cash	65.19	32.60	65.19	32.60
Reinsurance recoverable	0	50	—	—
DPAC (*b*)	0	(9.18)	—	—
Total assets	65.19	73.42	65.19	32.60
Loss reserves	100	100	100	100
Contra-liability for retroactive reinsurance	—	—	(0)	(50)
Deferred gain on retroactive reinsurance	0	8.22	—	—
Total liabilities	100	108.22	100	50
Retained earnings (GAAP) or statutory surplus (SAP)	(34.80)	(34.80)	(34.80)	(17.40)

(*a*) No interest revenue on cash balances is recorded in the prior year to make the retroactive and prospective-reinsurance cases as comparable as possible.

(*b*) DPAC is negative on the ending balance sheet because DPAC on the underlying insurance is fully amortized before the inception of the reinsurance. The reduction of DPAC amortization from the ceding commission is assumed to be in proportion to the amortization of the deferred gain.

EXHIBIT 16.5 Comparison of GAAP and SAP Reinsurance Accounting for Example of Prospective Excess-of-Loss Policy with $x = 0$

	GAAP		SAP	
	Without Reins.	With Reins.	Without Reins.	With Reins.
Income statement first half of current year:				
Net premiums earned	41.05	20.52	41.05	20.52
+ Interest revenue on cash balances	3.10	1.55	3.10	1.55
− Loss and LAE expense	(50)	(25)	(50)	(25)
− DPAC amortization (GAAP) or Acquisition cost expense (SAP)	(10)	(5)	(20)	(10)
Net income	(15.85)	(7.93)	(25.85)	(12.93)
Balance sheets end of first half of currernt year:				
Cash	65.19	32.60	65.19	32.60
Prepaid reinsurance	0	20.52	—	—
Reinsurance recoverable	0	25	—	—
DPAC	10	5	—	—
Total assets	75.19	83.12	65.19	32.60
Loss reserves	50	50	50	25
Unearned premiums	41.05	41.05	41.05	20.52
Total liabilities	91.05	91.05	91.05	45.52
Retained earnings or statutory surplus	(15.85)	(7.93)	(25.85)	(12.93)

In the prospective-reinsurance case summarized in Exhibit 16.5, the GAAP and SAP income statements for the first six months of the current year differ only in the amount of acquisition costs that are expensed. SAP expenses all of the net acquisition costs of $20 in the without-reinsurance case and of $10 in the with-reinsurance case, while in each case GAAP records only half as much DPAC amortization. As a result, net income is higher under GAAP than SAP by $10 in the without-reinsurance case and by $5 in the with-reinsurance case. Despite this, prospective reinsurance enhances SAP net income more than it does GAAP net income, by reversing $10 of SAP acquisition costs rather than $5 of GAAP DPAC amortization. These differences again carry over to the ceding insurer's ending balance sheet, with GAAP retained earnings being $10 ($5) higher than statutory surplus in the without- (with-) reinsurance cases. In addition, in the with-reinsurance case, on the ending balance sheets the ceding insurer's liabilities are twice as large for GAAP than SAP due to the gross (net) presentation of reinsurance under GAAP (SAP).

Comparison of the retroactive-reinsurance case in Exhibit 16.4 to the prospective-reinsurance case in Exhibit 16.5 shows that that the retroactive reinsurance has a much stronger enhancing effect on statutory statements in the period of the inception of the reinsurance than does the prospective reinsurance because of the immediate recognition of the gain required under SAP. The effect of prospective reinsurance on statutory statements is still nontrivially enhancing, however, because the extreme conservatism of SAP expensing of policy acquisition costs is reversed. Retroactive reinsurance does not have any effect on GAAP net income, while prospective reinsurance enhances GAAP net income only by reducing the size of the insurer and thus the size of the loss resulting from the temporal mismatching of insurance expense on the underlying insurance and investment income under SFAS No. 60 (1982) discussed in Chapter 14. Specifically, insurance expense on the underlying insurance is earned over the one-year coverage period of that insurance, while investment income is earned over the five-year tail of the underlying insurance.

Accounting for Retrospectively Rated Reinsurance Contracts

Retrospectively rated reinsurance contracts create rights or obligations for the ceding insurer as a result of the reinsurer's past profit on the contract. Emerging Issues Task Force (EITF) 93-6, *Accounting for Multiple-Year Retrospectively Rated Contracts by Ceding and Assuming Enterprises,* and SSAP No. 62 (2000) specify similar though not identical accounting for these rights and obligations. (EITF issues are first discussed in the year indicated by their first two digits.) EITF 93-6's requirements are described in this section, with the main way that SSAP No. 62's (2000) requirements differ indicated.

EITF 93-6 requires that, in addition to the risk-transfer criteria for reinsurance accounting described earlier, the amounts of premiums the ceding insurer is expected to pay under a retrospectively rated reinsurance contract must be reasonably estimable and allocable to the reinsurance coverage provided over the term of the contract. Otherwise, the contract is deemed substantively a financing, and deposit accounting is required.

If all the criteria for reinsurance accounting are met, then, in addition to the normal working of reinsurance accounting described, EITF 93-6 requires the ceding insurer to record assets (liabilities) to the extent that it expects to receive (pay) incremental cash or other consideration as a result of the contractual, obligatory, retrospectively rated features of the contract. Increases and decreases in future coverage should be treated the same way as the receipt or payment of cash or other consideration. The accrual of assets and liabilities under EITF 93-6 reduces the smoothing of the ceding insurer's income resulting from reinsurance accounting.

Under EITF 93-6, the ceding insurer may assume that the reinsurance will be terminated early, which tends to reduce the amounts of these assets and liabilities. This assumption may not be made under SSAP No. 62 (2000).

Accounting for Funds-Withheld Contracts

At the inception of a fully funds-withheld reinsurance contract, the only cash that changes hands between the ceding insurer and the reinsurer usually is some portion of the reinsurer's fee. If the contract is also finite, little cash usually changes hands after inception as well. Despite this, if the contract meets the risk-transfer criteria for reinsurance accounting, under both financial reporting practice (because SFAS No. 113 [1992] does not specify the accounting for funds-withheld contracts) and SAP, at inception the ceding insurer recognizes a funds-withheld liability for the amount it would contractually owe the reinsurer had funds not been withheld. Under financial reporting practice, the ceding insurer also records "prepaid" reinsurance (for prospective reinsurance) or a reinsurance recoverable (for retroactive reinsurance). Under SAP, the ceding insurer also records a reduction of loss reserves (for prospective reinsurance) or a contra-liability (for retroactive reinsurance). Given that the ceding insurer is not exposed to the reinsurer's credit risk on these reinsurance assets, the gross presentation of this asset under financial reporting practice is not necessarily preferable to the net or contra-liability presentation under SAP, especially when the reinsurance is also finite so that there is little insurance risk transfer as well.

After inception, the accounting for a funds-withheld liability follows the contractual specification of this liability, which usually is similar to an experience account. In particular, this liability typically increases by contractually specified reinsurance premiums and interest and decreases by payouts of claims. Retrospective-rating, commutation, and other contractual provisions may affect the funds-withheld liability.

An example of an actual funds-withheld reinsurance transaction and its effects of financial and statutory report numbers is provided in the "Sample Disclosure of a Significant Reinsurance Transaction" section and Exhibit 16.6.

Deposit Accounting

If reinsurance does not qualify for reinsurance accounting, then the ceding insurer accounts for it as a deposit. The ceding insurer's deposit balance initially equals the net consideration paid. Over time, this balance must incorporate any changes in expected recoveries from the reinsurer and the time value of money.

American Institute of Certified Public Accountants (AICPA) Statement of Position (SOP) No. 98-7, *Deposit Accounting: Accounting for Insurance and Reinsurance Contracts that Do Not Transfer Insurance Risk,* is the primary source of GAAP guidance on deposit accounting. (AICPA SOPs are issued in the year indicated by their first two digits.) SAP deposit accounting (SSAP No. 75, *Reinsurance Deposit Accounting* [2001]) is again similar but not identical. This section describes and illustrates using the numerical example SOP No. 98-7's deposit accounting, again indicating the main way that SSAP No. 75's (2001) requirements differ.

Depending on the risks borne by the reinsurer, SOP No. 98-7 requires one of two main types of deposit accounting by the ceding insurer. (A third type is required when the risk transferred is indeterminate.) The first and more common type is like bank deposit accounting modified to accommodate any risk transferred to the reinsurer. This type is used if the reinsurer does not bear significant underwriting risk, which could occur either because it does not bear any significant insurance risk or because it bears only significant timing risk. In this case, at inception the balance of the deposit asset equals the net consideration paid, and an effective yield is calculated that equates that balance to the expected recoveries from the reinsurer. As the ceding insurer's expectations of these recoveries change over time, the effective yield is recalculated as of the inception of the reinsurance contract so that the balance of the deposit asset at inception continues to equal the present value of the currently expected receipts. The balance of the deposit asset in any period after inception equals the present value of the expected future receipts using the most recently calculated effective yield. All changes in the balance of the deposit asset, whether due to the passage of time applying a given expected yield or to changes in the effective yield, are classified as interest revenue or expense on the income statement, reflecting the idea that such reinsurance is substantively financing.

To illustrate this type of deposit accounting, assume the excess-of-loss policy with $x = 5$ in the previous numerical example is determined not to transfer underwriting risk. At initiation the ceding insurer records the net consideration paid as a deposit asset:

Deposit (+ asset)	31.05	
Cash (− asset)		31.05

The initial effective yield is 10%. Using that interest rate, interest revenue in the current year equals \$3.10, and the ceding insurer records an increase in the deposit asset for that amount:

Deposit (+ asset)	3.10	
Interest revenue (+ income)		3.10

After accruing interest revenue at 10% for the three years, the balance of the deposit is \$41.32 = \$50/1.1^2. Assume that at that time the ceding insurer learns that the claim payment will be \$150 and so the reinsurer will pay \$55. The effective yield as of the time of inception of the reinsurance contract is recalculated to be 12.12%. At this yield, the balance of the deposit at the end of the third year should be \$43.75 = \$55/1.1212^2, \$2.44 higher, yielding the journal entry:

Deposit (+ asset)	2.44	
Interest revenue (+ income)		2.44

The second type of deposit accounting is like insurance accounting modified to take into account the time value of money. This type is used if the reinsurer bears significant underwriting risk but not significant timing risk, which could occur because there are contractual provisions that delay timely payments from the reinsurer to the ceding insurer. This type of accounting depends on whether an insured event covered under the reinsurance contract has not yet occurred (i.e., for prospective reinsurance before an insured event occurs) or has already occurred (i.e., for retroactive reinsurance throughout the contract term and for prospective reinsurance after an insured event occurs). If an insured event has not occurred at inception, then the balance of the ceding insurer's deposit asset at inception equals the net consideration paid, and this balance is amortized over the contract term like prepaid insurance. If insured events have occurred prior to inception or whenever changes in expected recoveries occur, the deposit asset is (re)measured as the present value of the expected net recoveries from the reinsurer using the current rate on U.S. government obligations with similar cash flow characteristics as those expected receipts plus any remaining unamortized prepaid insurance. Changes in the value of the deposit asset, whether due to the passage of time or to unexpected changes in net recoveries, are classified as adjustments to loss expense, like insurance, reflecting the transfer of underwriting risk by this reinsurance. Like accounting for insurance under SFAS No. 60 (1982) and SAP, this approach does not properly classify the nontrivial financing (e.g., interest) aspects of this reinsurance, however. In contrast, SSAP No. 75 (2001) requires changes in the deposit asset to be classified as interest.

To illustrate this type of deposit accounting, assume the excess-of-loss policy with $x = 5$ in the numerical example is deemed to transfer underwriting risk but not timing risk. The appropriate government bond rate equals 10%. Assume the insured event has already occurred at inception, so the prepaid reinsurance phase of deposit accounting does not occur. The ceding insurer records a deposit asset for the net consideration paid:

Deposit (+ asset)	31.05	
Cash (− asset)		31.05

This deposit accrues interest at 10% each year. For example, in the current year, the ceding insurer accrues interest of \$3.10 and records:

Deposit (+ asset)	3.10	
Loss expense (+ income)		3.10

The balance of the deposit at the end of the third year would be \$41.32 = \$50/1.1^2. Again assume that at that time the ceding insurer learns that the claim payment will be \$150 and so the reinsurer will pay \$55. The balance of the deposit at the end of year 3 should be \$45.45 = \$55/1.1^2, \$4.13 higher, yielding the journal entry:

Deposit (+ asset)	4.13	
Loss expense (+ income)		4.13

SOP No. 98-7 also requires distinct accounting for reinsurance contracts with indeterminate risk, meaning that the terms of contract are uncertain or there is insufficient information to reasonably estimate and allocate premiums over the (potentially unknown) coverage period. No income is recorded on these contracts until the sufficient information becomes available to reasonably estimate and allocate premiums, at which point the appropriate type of deposit accounting should be used.

REINSURANCE DISCLOSURES AND ANALYSIS

Disclosures in Financial Reports

Ceding insurers are required to make various disclosures about reinsurance in financial reports. SFAS No. 113 (1992) requires disclosures of the nature and purpose of reinsurance and encourages disclosures about the extent to which reinsurance contracts transfer insurance risk. SEC Securities Act Industry Guide 6 requires management to discuss these issues in its description of the business:

- Reinsurance transactions (including "swaps" of reserves, loss portfolio transfers, etc.) that have a material effect on earnings or loss reserves
- The nature of recent changes in the terms under which reinsurance is ceded to reinsurers
- Changes in payment patterns due to loss portfolio transfers, structured settlements, and other transactions and circumstances

These disclosures constitute the only significant mandated information about finite reinsurance in financial reports.

SFAS No. 113 (1992) requires disclosures of premiums written and earned from reinsurance ceded and assumed. It also requires disclosure of recoveries under reinsurance contracts, while SOP No. 94-5, *Disclosures of Certain Matters in the Financial Statements of Insurance Enterprises*, and Regulation S-X require disclosure of the amounts or reinsurance recoverable for unpaid losses and for paid losses, respectively. SFAS No. 113 (1992) requires disclosure of concentration of credit risk with particular reinsurers. The usefulness of these disclosures for evaluating insurers' reinsurance coverage is discussed later.

SOP No. 98-7 requires various disclosures about (re)insurance accounted for as a deposit, including descriptions of the contracts involved, the amounts of deposit assets and liabilities, and the changes in deposit balances due to (1) adjustment to loss expense, (2) interest revenue or expense, (3) amortization of coverage provided, and (4) changes in expected receipts and payments. Although these disclosures provide some indication of the use of finite reinsurance by the ceding insurer, the reinsurance described in these disclosures is not generally accounting-motivated because it is accounted for as a deposit.

Disclosures in Statutory Reports

Statutory reports contain various schedules and other information pertaining to reinsurance. Schedule F, Parts 1 to 3, provides information about the effects of ceded reinsurance on the main insurance assets, liabilities, revenues, and expenses that is similar to but somewhat more detailed than the information provided in financial reports.

Statutory reports provide considerable information about the credit risk of and credit losses on reinsurance recoverables, a significant regulatory concern in part because of the netting of recoverables for prospective reinsurance against loss reserves in statutory reports. Specifically, Schedule F, Parts 4 to 7, provides information about the aging of and provisions for losses on reinsurance recoverables. The reinsurance footnote reports reinsurance recoverables by reinsurer that are unsecured or in dispute if they meet certain materiality thresholds as well as all reinsurance recoverables by reinsurer that are deemed uncollectible.

Statutory reports provide considerable information about retroactive reinsurance in addition to the write-ins on statutory balance sheets and income statements discussed above. The reinsurance footnote reports these amounts for each of the beginning of the year, the changes during the year, and the end of the year: the amount of loss reserves transferred at the inception of retroactive reinsurance contracts still outstanding, the consideration paid for those contracts, the reinsurance recoveries on those contracts, and the special surplus on those contracts. This footnote also reports the reinsurers, lines of business, and accident years involved in these transactions.

Until recently, statutory reports contained only disjointed and at best suggestive bits of information about finite reinsurance. However, in November 2005, the NAIC approved significant required disclosures for finite reinsurance in the general interrogatories including:

- Whether the insurer has reinsured any risk under a quota share contract that includes a provision limiting the reinsurer's loss below the stated quota share percentage
- Whether the insurer has entered into any large ceded reinsurance contracts
  - With a noncancellable term longer than two years or the provision that cancellation requires entering into a new reinsurance contract
  - Involving aggregate stop-loss coverage
  - With an unconditional or unilateral right by either party to commute
  - With a provision designed to delay the timing of payments of reinsurance recoveries

- Whether the insurer has accounted for a contract as reinsurance under GAAP but a deposit under SAP or vice versa

If the insurer answers yes to any of these questions, then it must summarize the terms of the contracts, management's principal objectives in entering into the contracts, and the aggregate financial statement impact of the contracts.

Also in November 2005, the NAIC approved chief executive officer and chief financial officer attestation regarding the absence of written or oral side agreements and the required documentation of, proper accounting for, and internal control over finite reinsurance contracts. These enhanced disclosures first appeared in statutory reports filed in 2006.

Analysis

The user of financial reports should try to answer seven questions to assess a ceding PC insurer's use of reinsurance:

1. What are the risk and other economic characteristics of the underlying insurance?
   - Line of business?
   - Short- or long-tail?
   - Frequency, magnitude, and predictability of losses?
   - What is the need for reinsurance from a risk-management perspective?
2. What are the risk and other economic characteristics of the reinsurance?
   - What layers of risk are retained by the ceding insurer and transferred to the reinsurer?
   - Traditional or finite?
     - If finite, what contractual features make it so and how do they individually and collectively reduce the risk transfer involved?
   - Retrospective or prospective?
   - Funds withheld?
3. What are the purposes of the reinsurance?
   - Risk transfer?
     - If so, is the amount and nature of the risk transfer appropriate given the underlying insurance?
   - Statutory surplus enhancement?
     - Due to undiscounted loss reserves for long-tailed underlying insurance and resulting gain on retroactive reinsurance?
     - Due to ceding commissions reducing acquisition costs?
     - So that the ceding insurer can grow, avoid decline of written premiums, or avoid regulatory scrutiny?

- Reduction of statutory loss reserves and/or unearned premiums liabilities (solvency enhancement) due to net presentation of reinsurance?
- Financial report effects?
  - Earnings smoothing?
  - Offset loss reserve revisions from prior under-reserving for the underlying insurance?
- Other business purposes?
  - Allow managers to focus on new business?
  - Taxes?

4. Is the accounting for the underlying insurance and the reinsurance in accordance with GAAP and SAP?
   - If reinsurance accounting is used, are the risk-transfer criteria met?
   - Is reinsurance being used as an excuse to under-reserve for the underlying insurance?
5. Is the accounting for the underlying insurance and the reinsurance economically descriptive?
   - For the underlying insurance
     - Are loss reserves discounted?
     - Are acquisition costs expensed immediately while premiums are deferred?
   - For the reinsurance
     - Is the reinsurance so finite so that reinsurance accounting is not economically descriptive?
     - Is the accounting for the reinsurance consistent with the accounting for the underlying insurance?
6. What is the effect of the reinsurance on GAAP and SAP insurance ratios?
7. How credit risky are the reinsurance recoverables?
   - Are the reinsurers domestic or offshore?
   - Are the reinsurers authorized or unauthorized?
   - Are funds withheld by the ceding insurer?
   - Are letters of credit or other collateral posted by the reinsurer?

The effects of reinsurance on financial and statutory report numbers could be misleading either because the accounting is poor for either the underlying insurance or the reinsurance, or because the underlying insurance and reinsurance are accounted for inconsistently. The user of financial reports has various possible strategies to adjust financial and statutory statement numbers and the ratios that are based on these numbers for such misleading effects.

First, the user of financial reports could reverse the effects of reinsurance accounting and account for reinsurance as a deposit. This makes sense when the underlying insurance is accounted for well and the reinsurance does not transfer much insurance risk but still is accounted for using reinsurance accounting.

Second, the user could account better for the underlying insurance and make any adjustments to the accounting for the reinsurance that are necessary to maintain consistency. This makes sense whenever the accounting for the underlying insurance is poor, especially if the accounting for reinsurance is also poor as a result. For example, recording undiscounted loss reserves for short-duration but long-tailed underlying insurance does not capture the significant time-value-of-money considerations for this insurance. As shown in Chapter 14, users of financial reports can discount these loss reserves using the disclosed deferred tax asset resulting from discounting of loss reserves for tax purposes. If loss reserves for the underlying insurance were discounted, then retroactive reinsurance generally would yield smaller or no implied gains at inception, and so the user should also reverse any recognition of such gains. Ideally, the amounts and timing of the recognition of premium revenue, investment income, and the expensing of acquisition costs for both the underlying insurance and the reinsurance should all be determined in a consistent fashion taking into account the time value of money.

Third, in evaluating the significance of credit risk on reinsurance recoverables, the user usually should adopt GAAP's gross presentation of reinsurance recoverables because it reflects the fact that reinsurance does not eliminate the ceding insurer's obligation to pay claims. As discussed, the main exception to this rule occurs in the case of funds-withheld reinsurance.

Sample Disclosure of a Significant Reinsurance Transaction

Exhibit 16.6 contains Procentury Corp.'s disclosure in footnote 7 of its 2003 Form 10-K filing of a retroactive funds-withheld reinsurance transaction engaged in by its insurance subsidiary Century Surety (Century). This transaction was outstanding from 2001 to 2003, at which point it was commuted. Because this transaction is retroactive, similarly detailed disclosures can be found in the 2003 statutory reports of Century and two of its subsidiaries. The approximate total effect of the transaction on these statutory reports can easily be inferred from Procentury's financial report disclosure above, however. The effects of the transaction on Procentury's financial report numbers and Century and its subsidiaries's statutory report numbers for the years 2001 to 2003 are summarized in Exhibit 16.7.

As with the disclosure by CNA Financial discussed earlier, Procentury does not explicitly state that this transaction is finite, although it certainly appears to be so. Aside from being retroactive, after the fact the only involvement of the reinsurer during the term of the transaction is its receipt of initial consideration of $500,000 in 2001, an amount that appears to be its fee for providing Century with statutory surplus. Reflecting this fact, the total effect on Procentury's GAAP income and Century's SAP income over the term of the transaction is a reduction of $500,000.

EXHIBIT 16.6 Disclosure of Retroactive Funds-Withheld Reinsurance Transaction by Procentury Corp. in Its 2003 Form 10-K Filing, Footnote 7

Effective January 1, 2001, Century entered into a retroactive reinsurance treaty with a nonaffiliated reinsurer covering losses occurring on or before January 1, 2001, and unrecoverable reinsurance. The following activity occurred related to this reinsurance treaty:

	December 31		
	2003	**2002**	**2001**
Reserves transferred:			
Initial reserves	$ 20,000,000	$ 20,000,000	$ 20,000,000
Adjustments—prior years	(6,120,273)	4,400,000	—
Adjustments—current year	(13,879,727)	(10,520,273)	4,400,000
Reinsurance recoverables on retroactive reinsurance, end of year	$ —	$ 13,879,727	$ 24,400,000
Funds held:			
Consideration for reserves transferred	$ 20,000,000	$ 20,000,000	$ 20,000,000
Consideration paid in cash to reinsurer	(500,000)	(500,000)	(500,000)
Interest credited—prior years	2,108,908	877,500	—
Interest credited—current year	—	1,231,408	877,500
Paid losses recovered—prior years	(10,520,273)	—	—
Adjustments—current year	(11,088,635)	(10,520,273)	—
Funds held under retroactive reinsurance contract, end of year	$ —	$ 11,088,635	$ 20,377,500

Century paid initial consideration of $500,000, which was included as an offset to the funds held under retroactive reinsurance contract. Under the terms of the contract, the remaining consideration was maintained in a funds held account which accrued interest for the benefit of the reinsurer at a contracted annual rate of 6.0% and 4.5% during 2002 and 2001, respectively.

The $4,400,000 of additional transferred reserves during 2001 resulted in a deferred gain on retroactive reinsurance. The deferred gain is being amortized over the settlement period using the interest method. No additional reserves were transferred in 2002.

Interest on the funds held balance of $1,231,408 and $877,500 was recorded as other operating expenses during 2002 and 2001, respectively. This amount was substantially offset by amortization of the deferred retroactive reinsurance gain of $1,105,754 and $787,959 during 2002 and 2001, respectively, which was

EXHIBIT 16.6 *(Continued)*

included in other operating expenses in the accompanying consolidated statements of operations. Paid losses of $10,520,273 were reimbursed to Century under this contract in 2002 through a reduction of the funds held balance. No paid losses were reimbursed to Century under this contract in 2001.

Effective January 1, 2003, the retroactive reinsurance contract was commuted. The commutation resulted in a release of ceded reserves of $13,879,727, which was primarily offset by a release of the funds held account of $11,088,635 and the release of the remaining deferred retroactive reinsurance gain of $2,506,287. The net of these transactions resulted in a $284,805 pre-tax loss in 2003, which was recorded as an other operating expense in the accompanying 2003 statement of operations.

The main effect of the transaction on Procentury's financial report numbers is to gross up reinsurance recoverables and the funds-withheld liability in 2001 and 2002. This gross presentation is problematic to the extent that Century withholds funds and so is not exposed to the credit risk of the reinsurer. The other effects of the transaction on Procentury's financial report numbers summarized in Exhibit 16.6 are fairly minor and nonenhancing, because of the deferral of the $4.4 million implied gain on the inception of the reinsurance contract in 2001. In contrast, the transaction's effects on Century's statutory report numbers are far more enhancing in nature, due to the immediate recognition of the implied gain. In particular, the transaction provides Century with statutory surplus of $3.522 million in 2001 and $2.291 million in 2002.

Given that the transaction is funds withheld and apparently finite, it is not clear that it has any business purpose beyond raising Century's statutory capital. The natural approach for the user of financial reports is to eliminate the effects of the transaction on both its financial and statutory report except for the economic loss attributable to the $500,000 fee. For example, in 2001 reduce Century's statutory surplus by $4.022 million, that is, the $3.522 million statutory surplus enhancement plus the $500,000 fee.

EVOLUTION OF FINANCIAL REPORTING FOR REINSURANCE

Even before the recent scrutiny of finite reinsurance transactions, financial accounting standard setters were well aware of the significant limitations of current GAAP for insurance and reinsurance and had plans to revisit that accounting. The International Accounting Standards Board (IASB) has taken the lead in the development, recently issuing the preliminary and generally underwhelming standard IFRS No. 4, *Insurance Contracts* (2004), and currently being involved in a second-phase project that is intended to address the tough issues. This project will become a joint project with the FASB after

EXHIBIT 16.7 Summary of the Effects of Procentury Corp.'s Retroactive Funds-Withheld Reinsurance Transaction on Its Financial and Statutory Report Numbers

($ in thousands)	**2003**	**2002**	**2001**
Effects on Procentury's Financial Report Numbers:			
On income statement:			
Amortization of deferred gain on retroactive reinsurance	—	1,106	788
Loss on commutation	(285)		
Interest expense	—	(1,231)	(878)
Pretax income	(285)	(125)	(90)
On ending balance sheet:			
Cash	—	—	(500)
Reinsurance recoverables	—	13,880	24,400
Funds withheld liability	—	11,089	20,378
Deferred gain	—	2,506	3,612
Total liabilities	—	13,595	23,990
Retained earnings	(500)	(215)	(90)
Effects of Century's Statutory Report Numbers:			
On income statement:			
Gain on retroactive reinsurance	—	—	4,400
Loss on commutation	(2,791)	—	—
Interest expense	—	(1,231)	(878)
Pretax income	(2,791)	(1,231)	3,522
On ending balance sheet:			
Contra-liability for retroactive reinsurance	—	(13,880)	(24,400)
Funds withheld liability	—	11,098	20,378
Total liabilities	—	(2,782)	(4,022)
Statutory surplus	(500)	2,291	3,522

the IASB issues an initial discussion document, which is currently scheduled for the first quarter of 2007. In addition, the NAIC and state insurance regulators are working on outstanding proposals to change SAP. This section contains a brief summary of recent developments as well as likely future developments.

IFRS No. 4 (2004) introduced two interesting changes into insurance accounting. First, it prohibits netting of revenues and expenses for reinsurance and the underlying insurance on the income statement. Although this does not change the total information provided in financial reports, it makes the effects of reinsurance more apparent on the income statement. It seems likely that this change eventually will find its way into U.S. GAAP.

Second, IFRS No. 4 (2004) permits (and in certain settings that may not exist anywhere currently requires) unbundling of the insurance (risk transfer) and financing (deposit) components of insurance contracts if they can be measured separately. This change is possibly a precursor of more significant changes in GAAP and SAP. Specifically, despite the economic similarities between finite reinsurance and tranched securitizations, unlike sale accounting for securitizations described in Chapter 8, reinsurance accounting under SFAS No. 113 (1992) and SSAP No. 62 (2000) does not apply a financial components approach. As a result, the accounting for finite reinsurance is highly limited. Although finite reinsurance deemphasizes risk transfer, it usually has some insurance aspects along with its financing aspects, and if so, accounting for finite reinsurance as either pure insurance or pure financing does not fully capture its economics. The New York State Insurance Department recently has proposed that reinsurance contracts be unbundled (in its terminology "bifurcated") into their insurance and financing components, similar to the way that derivatives not clearly and closely related to their host instruments must be unembedded, as discussed in Chapter 11. Both the FASB and the NAIC currently are considering the possibility of such unbundling in their ongoing risk transfer projects. Due to the complexity and custom-tailored nature of finite reinsurance contracts, developing robust accounting rules governing the unbundling of reinsurance contracts likely will prove an even more difficult task than it was for derivatives, however.

In its second phase project, the IASB has tentatively concluded that it will require discounting of both loss reserves on underlying insurance and reinsurance recoverables. This will substantially eliminate the implied gain on retroactive reinsurance or short-duration but long-tailed underlying insurance and will lead to better insurance accounting generally.

Both the FASB and the NAIC are reassessing the judgmental risk-transfer criteria for reinsurance accounting in ongoing projects on risk transfer. It seems likely that these criteria will remain judgmental but the FASB and/or the NAIC will provide additional guidance as to how to assess risk transfer for different types of underlying insurance that vary in both the probability and magnitude of the loss that can be transferred to the reinsurer. If so, this would likely make these criteria more stringent than the 10-10 rule for some types of insurance and less stringent for others.

NOTES

1. American Academy of Actuaries, Committee on Property and Liability Financial Reporting, "Risk Transfer in P&C Reinsurance: Report to the Casualty Actuarial Task Force of the National Association of Insurance Commissioners," August 2005.
2. R. Adiel, "Reinsurance and the Management of Regulatory Ratios and Taxes in the Property-Casualty Insurance Industry," *Journal of Accounting and Economics* (August–December 1996).

Index

C

G

H

M

N